AFRICAN-AMERICAN LITERATURE

AFRICAN-AMERICAN LITERATURE

An Anthology

Second Edition

Demetrice A. Worley

Jesse Perry, Jr.

NTC Publishing Group

a division of NTC/CONTEMPORARY PUBLISHING COMPANY
Lincolnwood, Illinois USA

This anthology is dedicated to my parents, Ernestine R. Worley and Thomas D. Worley Jr., and my brothers, Timothy and Michael, who are my strength and foundation; to my friends, who have each given me love in a special way; and to the higher power that guides me in the light and the darkness.

D. A. W.

This volume is dedicated to my wife and best friend, Maxine Gray Perry, who supports me in every professional endeavor; to our sons, Desmond and Derrick, their wives and children; to our son, Brian, and to my sister, Mary J. Morris; to my brother, Willie, and to the memory of my late father and mother, Jesse and Caroline Perry, and to my late brother, Benny.

J. P. J.

Executive Editor: Marisa L. L'Heureux
Editor: Lisa A. De Mol
Cover and interior design: Kristy Sheldon
Cover illustration: Robert Earl Paige: "Chicago Fire"
Design Manager: Ophelia Chambliss
Production Manager: Margo Goia

Acknowledgments begin on page 489, which is to be considered an extension of this copyright page.

ISBN (student edition): 0-8442-5924-1
ISBN (instructor's edition): 0-8442-5926-8

Library of Congress Cataloging-in-Publication Data

African-American Literature / [compiled by] Demetrice A. Worley, Jesse
    Perry, Jr. — 2nd ed.
        p. cm.
    Includes index.
    ISBN 0-8442-5924-1
        1. American literature—Afro-American authors. I. Worley,
    Demetrice A. II. Perry, Jesse.
    PS508.N3A33   1997
    810.8´0896073—dc21   97-346
                                                       CIP
                                                       AC

7 8 9 0 1 VL 10 9 8 7 6 5 4 3 2 1

CONTENTS

CHAPTER ONE
THE FOLK TRADITION

CHAPTER TWO
LANGUAGE AND LITERACY

CHAPTER THREE

THE BLUES—
PAIN AND SURVIVAL

85

CHAPTER FOUR

SLAVERY—TIME OF TRIAL

147

CHAPTER FIVE
STANDING GROUND

CHAPTER EIGHT
WOMEN

CHAPTER NINE
MEN

PREFACE

This book was created to provide an anthology of fiction, poetry, drama, and nonfiction that would present you with an insight into the richness of African-American literature and African-American culture. This book was also created in the belief that the study of African-American literature provides you with an opportunity to better understand yourself as well as other cultures.

This book begins with an overview of the history and literary development of African Americans in the United States. This will acquaint you with the issues, struggles, and triumphs of African Americans and will help you better understand the literature itself.

The selections in this text are organized according to themes, although your instructor may choose to present them in a different order. The themes are: The Folk Tradition; Language and Literacy; The Blues—Pain and Survival; Slavery—Time of Trial; Standing Ground; Identity; Dreamers and Revolutionaries; Women; Men; Relationships; and Family and Ancestors. Each chapter opens with information about the social and historical framework of the theme. And each selection is preceded by biographical information about the writer. This background information will not only give you information about the themes and the authors, but will give you contextual information for the selections themselves.

Following each selection are questions to guide you as you think about the work. They will provide you with some direction as you reflect on the literary and cultural issues raised in the writings. There are discussion questions, which you may discuss with a classmate, in a small group, or with the entire class. The writing questions, on the other hand, are designed to help you respond to the selection on paper.

While reading this text, you may wish to keep a reading journal, which is the ideal place in which to keep your writings about what you have read. Your instructor may ask you to keep a reading journal for class as a place to respond to some of the questions in writing. Your reading journal can also be a place to write down questions, issues, and concerns as you read.

Through reading the selections and learning the history and culture of African Americans in the United States, you will better understand and appreciate the richness and variety of African-American literature.

SLAVERY (1700s–1865)

The beginnings of African-American literature go back to the seventeenth century. For nearly two hundred years, Africans from many different tribes were captured by slave traders. These diverse peoples endured unspeakable conditions on their voyage across the Atlantic Ocean. Those who survived the "middle passage" then had to survive lives as slaves. They were denied the right to retain their languages and religions. Instead, they were forced to learn a new language, English, and a new form of religion, Christianity.

It is remarkable that there is any evidence of African-American literature from before 1865, when the Civil War ended. In many areas, educating a slave was against the law and, therefore, most slaves were illiterate. Some slaves did learn to read, though, through a variety of ways. Some slaves were taught by their masters, who believed in educated slaves. Others tricked their owners' children into teaching them how to read and write. And some slaves were taught by other slaves who hid their knowledge from whites.

Illiteracy, however, should never be confused with a lack of culture or language. The slaves brought with them an oral tradition, not a written one. The customs, history, traditions, and values of the African Americans were passed along verbally. The earliest types of the African oral tradition were the work songs and field hollers that the slaves called to one another as they worked in the fields. Another spoken tradition was the folktale. Early African Americans shared folktales that expressed values, explained the unexplainable, and identified acceptable and unacceptable behavior. Folktales such as "How Buck Won His Freedom," "The Knee-High Man Tries to Get Sizable," and "People Who Could Fly" both entertained and gave hope to enslaved people.

A limited amount of African-American literature had been written or published by the late 1700s. Early African-American poetry, such as that of Lucy Terry, Jupiter Hammon, Phillis Wheatley, and Ann Plato, reflects the strong religious influences of the time. Writers such as the mathematician Benjamin Banneker and Olaudah Equiano (Gustavus Vassa) spoke out for the equality of all people, especially African Americans, during the Revolutionary War era.

By the early 1800s, African-American literature appeared in many forms. White abolitionists encouraged the writing and publication of slave narratives, such as *Incidents in the Life of a Slave Girl,* by Harriet Jacobs. Those African-American slaves who had not been educated were encouraged to tell their life stories to white writers, who then wrote them down. African-American abolitionists produced nonfiction, such as Nat Turner's pamphlet, "The Confession of Nat Turner" (1831), and drama, such as William Well Brown's *The Escape or a Leap for Freedom* (1858), the first African-American play. Harriet E. Wilson published *Our Nig; or, Sketches from the Life of a Free Black,* in 1859. This was the first novel published in the United States by an African American. The poet Frances Ellen Watkins Harper captured the horror of slavery. Other black writers, such as Frederick Douglass and David Walker, used both essays and speeches from the podium to promote freedom and equality for African Americans. Educated African Americans, such as Charlotte Forten Grimke, kept journals of their daily lives.

From the beginning of the tradition through the Civil War, many black texts, such as sermons, poems, fiction, nonfiction, and drama, contained the structures—call and response, repetition, double meaning of words—that were a part of the African and African-American oral traditions. Equally important is the fact that the African-American literary tradition was built and focused on the quest for freedom and equality. These oral tradition structures and this quest continue to serve as a foundation for many African-American literary efforts today.

POST-CIVIL WAR, RECONSTRUCTION AND REACTION (1865-1920)

After the Civil War, the Reconstruction Act of March 1867 provided federal protection to African Americans in the South. For the first time, education—although segregated—became a legal reality for all African Americans. However, because they needed to work for economic survival, many blacks still received little beyond a rudimentary education. By 1880, though, the economic and political gains made by African Americans after the Civil War were eroded by the Ku Klux Klan, lynchings, increased unemployment, and legalized segregation of public accommodations and facilities (Jim Crow Laws).

The African-American literature written between 1865 and 1920 reflects the disappointments, fears, and frustrations produced by America's failure to fulfill its promises of freedom and equality after the Civil War. Biographies and autobiographies, such as Frederick Douglass's *Narrative of the Life of Frederick Douglass, an American Slave* (1845) and Booker T. Washington's *Up from*

Slavery (1901) were created. Black women writers such as Anna Julia Cooper, Frances Ellen Watkins Harper, Josephine D. Henderson Heard, Lucy A. Delaney, and Angelina Weld Grimke wrote ex-slave narratives, novels, essays, poetry, and drama. Charles W. Chesnutt wrote well-crafted short stories and novels. Paul Laurence Dunbar wrote dialect poetry that was well received by whites, as well as novels, including *The Uncalled* (1898). Ida B. Wells, a journalist and essayist, crusaded against lynchings in newspaper articles and in pamphlets such as "Southern Horrors: Lynch Law in All Its Phases" (1892). Another excellent writer, James Weldon Johnson, author of *The Autobiography of an Ex-Coloured Man* (1912) published novels as well as sermons in verse. This literature, however, was often ignored by white literary critics.

As the numbers of educated African Americans grew, so did the number of African-American writers. At the beginning of the 1920s, this growing number of black writers were seeing their work published. More importantly, a growing number of educated African Americans were reading it.

HARLEM RENAISSANCE (EARLY 1920s–EARLY 1930s)

Between 1915 and 1918 two events occurred that contributed to the beginning of the Harlem Renaissance—the Great Migration and the end of World War I. Beginning in 1915, African Americans moved from the rural South to the urban North in search of jobs and a better life. Hundreds of thousands of African Americans migrated to large cities like Chicago, Detroit, New York, and Philadelphia, lured by the promise of better employment. After fighting in World War I to make the world safe for democracy, those African-American soldiers who survived returned home to racism, unemployment, and poverty. However, their participation in World War I had solidified their racial identity. Their experiences in Europe had made African Americans more aware of Americans' prejudices against them. After World War I, African Americans recognized even more that racism and poverty in the United States could not take their culture from them.

The Harlem Renaissance—a term credited to Alain Locke, a black philosopher and writer—was a celebration of African-American culture at a time in America's history when the restraints of the Victorian age were giving way to the boldness of the Roaring '20s. The word *renaissance* means, literally, rebirth. The Harlem Renaissance, though, was actually the first opportunity African Americans had to give birth to—and celebrate—the uniqueness of African-American culture. Both black and white readers were eager to experience a slice of African-American life, and the literature of the time provided that experience.

Young, educated African Americans of that time traveled to New York City and to Harlem in particular. Harlem was *the* cultural and artistic center of African Americans, the place to make a name for themselves in the literary scene. It was the gathering place for what black leader, sociologist, and historian W. E. B. Du Bois had labeled the talented tenth—that ten percent of gifted African-American intellectuals who would lead African Americans in the United States. In Harlem these intellectuals and artists argued about the future of African Americans. Some conservative African-American critics believed that the literature written by African Americans should "uplift" the race, that is, show African Americans in a positive light. Younger, more radical African Americans believed that a "realistic" view of African-American life had to be presented for the sake of art.

New York City provided a variety of publishing opportunities during the Harlem Renaissance. Major publishing companies solicited and published literary works by black writers. Several agencies had magazines that sponsored writing contests and published works by young black writers. Two such periodicals were *The Crisis,* published by the National Association for the Advancement of Colored People (NAACP) and edited by W. E. B. Du Bois, and *Opportunity,* published by the Urban League and edited by Charles S. Johnson. Independent magazines such as *The Messenger,* a militant socialist journal edited by A. Philip Randolph and Chandler Owen, published up-and-coming African-American writers. Some writers, such as Zora Neale Hurston, Wallace Thurman, Langston Hughes, John P. Davis, Aaron Douglas, Bruce Nugget, and Gwendolyn Bennet, even tried to start their own literary journal, *Fire! Fire!* lasted only one issue, which was published in November 1926.

Many young African-American writers came into prominence during the Harlem Renaissance. The five premier writers of the times were Claude McKay, Jean Toomer, Countee Cullen, Nella Larsen, and Langston Hughes. Many others, including James Weldon Johnson, Zora Neale Hurston, Dorothy West, Sterling Brown, Georgia Douglas Johnson, Jessie Faucet, and Rudolf Fisher, were recognized for their poetry, short stories, drama, and novels. W. E. B. Du Bois continued the work he had begun at the beginning of the century by producing books and essays on the position of African Americans in this country and on the necessary steps African Americans needed to take to achieve equality.

The Harlem Renaissance writers reflected both the "uplifting" theme of the conservative African-American critics and the "realistic" artist movement of the younger, more radical African-American critics. Each succeeded in showing both African Americans and the world that their culture was a worthy literary topic and that their culture was "beautiful"—a theme that would reemerge during the Black Panther movement of the mid-1960s and early 1970s.

SOCIAL CHANGES AND CIVIL RIGHTS (MID-1930s TO MID-1960s)

The Great Depression began with the stock market crash in 1929. African Americans were typically the last to be hired and the first to be fired and suffered extreme economic and political hardships during the 1930s.

Thousands of already poor African Americans joined the soup lines that formed across the country.

President Franklin D. Roosevelt was elected in 1932, promising the country a New Deal. The Federal Writer's Project, supervised by the Works Progress Administration, was one part of President Roosevelt's New Deal. Established African-American writers, such as Langston Hughes, Zora Neale Hurston, and Arna Bontemps, participated in the Federal Writer's Project, earning a living while they continued to write. New African-American literary voices emerged as well, including Richard Wright, Robert Hayden, Frank Yerby, and Margaret Walker.

Richard Wright was considered a major writer during the late 1930s and the 1940s. His novel *Native Son* (1940) protested the conditions under which African Americans lived in the urban North. Novelists Chester Himes, author of *If He Hollers, Let Him Go* (1945), and Ann Petry, author of *The Street* (1946), also wrote strong novels about the effect of environment on the individual.

After World War II, many African Americans were more disillusioned than ever with the state of equality in the United States. Black soldiers who had risked their lives fighting fascism in Europe were denied rights upon their return home. Many black soldiers had died to preserve the rights guaranteed to all citizens under the U. S. Constitution. Some African Americans saw the end of World War II as a sign that they could and should assimilate into the dominant culture. In the 1940s a number of African-American literary critics believed that black writers should merge into the mainstream of American literature and deny that the African-American experience in this country had any influence on their work. However, poets such as Naomi Long Madgett, Margaret Walker, and Gwendolyn Brooks continued to write poetry that reflected their knowledge of the African-American community.

In 1952 Ralph Ellison wrote *Invisible Man,* which won a National Book Award. *Invisible Man* established that black writers could write social protest literature about the conditions of African Americans in this country and, at the same time, write about the universal concerns of humanity. James Baldwin's first novel, *Go Tell It on the Mountain* (1953), further stressed black writers' abilities to present a uniquely African-American viewpoint and universal concern for personal identity. These works, and others by black writers such as dramatist Alice Childress, showed that works by African Americans did not have to fit within the literary mainstream to qualify as fine literature.

In 1955, the year-long bus boycott in Montgomery, Alabama, signaled the beginning of a new type of civil rights movement. Led by the Reverend Dr. Martin Luther King Jr., African Americans began to protest the denial of their rights as U. S. citizens. By the late 1950s and the early 1960s, black writers were responding to the African-American fight for civil rights. Such poets as Gwendolyn Brooks [who won a Pulitzer Prize in 1950 for *Annie Allen* (1949)], Robert Hayden, Melvin Tolson, Margaret Danner, Langston Hughes, Mary Elizabeth Vroman, and Sterling Brown registered their awareness of that fight in their poetry. Other writers, such as Lorraine Hansberry, Mari Evans, Paule Marshall, William Melvin Kelley, and Ernest Gaines, expressed their views in plays, short stories, and novels.

BLACK POWER MOVEMENT (EARLY 1960s TO THE MID-1970s)

During the 1960s, the African-American fight for civil rights was in full force. There were both peaceful demonstrations led by Dr. King and more militant calls for action in the early works of Malcolm X. Major battles were won in the middle and late 1960s. The Civil Rights Acts of 1964 and 1968 prohibited discrimination in public accommodations, schools, and employment. The Voting Rights Act of 1965 outlawed discrimination in voting because of color, religion, or national origin. A new African-American voice was heard across the country, chanting "Black is beautiful" and "Black power."

For the first time since the Harlem Renaissance, a movement emphasizing the beauty and uniqueness of African-American culture was underway. The Harlem Renaissance had taken place primarily in New York; the Black Power movement took place throughout the country. African Americans began to openly celebrate and incorporate into their lives the songs, stories, and customs of their African ancestors.

Many of the urban ghettos erupted into riots in the mid-1960s. During that time, African-American poetry became a political weapon. Such poets as Amiri Baraka (LeRoi Jones), Nikki Giovanni, Haki Madhubuti (Don L. Lee), Sonia Sanchez, June Jordan, Dudley Randle, Mari Evans, Lucille Clifton, and Etheridge Knight used their poetry not to speak for themselves as individuals, but to speak in a dramatic voice for all African Americans. The Black Power movement also made an impact on African-American novels, such as Margaret Walker's *Jubilee* (1966) and William Melvin Kelley's *dem* (1967). Powerful autobiographies and biographies appeared, including *The Autobiography of Malcolm X* (1964), by Malcolm X and Alex Haley, *Soul on Ice* (1968), by Eldridge Cleaver, and *I Know Why the Caged Bird Sings* (1970), by Maya Angelou. Playwrights dramatized the new awareness on the stage, in works such as Adrienne Kennedy's *Funnyhouse of a Negro* (1963), Amiri Baraka's *Dutchman* (1964), Douglas Turner Ward's *Day of Absence* (1965), Charles Gordon's *No Place to Be Somebody* (1967), and Alice Childress's *Wine in the Wilderness* (1969). Short stories by Paule Marshall and Ernest Gaines and books by Julius Lester expressed the feeling of black pride.

Amiri Baraka and Larry Neal published *Black Pride, An Anthology of Afro-American Writing* in 1968. In the foreword, the editors claimed that a new day had arrived for African-American art. This anthology served as the birth of the Black Arts movement. Larry Neal explained that this movement was opposed to any concept that separated African-American artists from their community, that African-American art was directly related to the quest of African Americans for self-determination. Many African-American writers and critics embraced the ideas of the Black Arts movement. Other more conservative African-American critics argued against it. Either way, the Black Arts movement focused attention on African-American literature, and more independent African-American and white publishers began to seek out and publish literature by black writers. The increased availability of African-American literature allowed the number of readers, both African-American and white, to grow.

BUILDING ON THE TRADITION (MID-1970S TO THE PRESENT)

In the early and mid-1970s, the civil rights protest movement began losing strength as attention shifted from gaining equal rights for African Americans as a whole to the quest for individual rights. Blacks had made some economic and political gains through the civil rights and Black Power movements, but unemployment, poverty, and discrimination still plagued African Americans across the United States.

The literary text of African-American writers in the middle and late 1970s reflected this shift in national focus. Writers like Nikki Giovanni and Haki Madhubuti moved from writing only black power poetry to writing poetry about the political and economic conditions of people of color throughout the world. Ishmael Reed's novels *Mumbo Jumbo* (1972) and *Flight to Canada* (1976) satirized America's culture. The theme running throughout these works is still prominent in African-American literature in the 1980s and 1990s: It is important for African Americans to know their history. August Wilson's dramas *Fences* (1987), which won a Pulitzer Prize, and *Piano Lesson* (1990) and Charles Johnson's National Book Award winner *Middle Passage* (1990), illustrate the power of historical knowledge.

The civil rights movement increased awareness of the inequality of women as well as of African Americans. The growing interest in women's issues helped African-American women writers gain prominence, both as African Americans and as women. Literature by black women often stresses the interconnectedness of family, home, and community, as well as black women's ability to survive in this country. In these works, characters name themselves and the world in which they live. This "specifying" of the African-American woman's experience can be seen in such works as Ntozake Shange's choreographed poem *for colored girls who have considered suicide/ when the rainbow is enuf* (1977), and in novels, such as *The Color Purple* (1982) and *Possessing the Secret of Joy* (1992) by Alice Walker; *The Women of Brewster Place* (1983) and *Bailey's Cafe* (1992) by Gloria Naylor; *Praisesong for the Widow* (1984) and *Daughters* (1992) by Paule Marshall; and *The Wedding* (1995) by legendary Harlem Renaissance writer Dorothy West. Rita Dove's Pulitzer Prize-winning book of poetry, *Thomas and Beulah*

(1986), and Toni Morrison's Pulitzer Prize-winning novel *Beloved* (1988) are powerful examples of women's literary voices. Three significant events in the 1990s gave recognition to the strength of black women writers' voices. First, in 1992, Maya Angelou became the first African American and first woman to read her poetry at a U. S. Presidential Inauguration. Second, in 1993 and 1995, Rita Dove became the first African American and first woman to be named Poet Laureate of the United States. And third, in 1993, Toni Morrison was the first African-American woman to receive the Nobel Prize for literature.

As we move into a new century, African-American writers such as J. California Cooper, James Alan McPherson, Angela Jackson, Toni McElroy Ansa, Walter Mosely, Bebe Moore Campbell, Ali, and Paula Childress White have established themselves in the black literary tradition. As the works of these and other black writers show, African-American literature continues to build on the foundation established in the eighteenth century: the structures of oral tradition and the quest for freedom and equality. This foundation has supported African Americans as they moved from the chains of slavery, through war and peace, to prosperity and poverty. African-American literature has recorded the defeats and the triumphs, the fears and the dreams. Its strength lies in its ability to present the truth, whether ugly or beautiful. African-American literature gives voice to the eternal spirit of African Americans.

CHAPTER ONE

THE FOLK TRADITION

Folklore, like other types of literature, serves as a mirror of what we like to call the human condition. Folklore helps explain human relationships, desires, and fears; it clarifies those doubts we have about life. Folktales and mythology have no cultural or ethnic boundaries. All people use them to tell of their culture, religion, and social customs.

Although both folklore and mythology are based on legend, they are different. Folklore consists of traditional tales handed down from one generation to the next by the common people. These tales may teach a lesson, impart history, or simply entertain. Myths, on the other hand, attempt to account for something that occurs in nature, something not easily explained. Myths may tell about a particular country or person.

Much of the early folk literature with black themes was written not by blacks but by whites, some of whom used this invented folklore to foster negative stereotypes of African Americans. In these folktales, African Americans were often portrayed as either comic or pathetic.

The use of folk material by African-American writers began with William Wells Brown, the first African American to publish a novel in the United States. He used folk anecdotes in *My Southern Home* (1880). Charles Waddell Chesnutt, the father of the African-American short story, also used folk material in *The Conjure Woman* (1899). Paul Laurence Dunbar used folk material in his poetry as he wrote about everyday events in the lives of common people.

Poet and scholar Sterling Brown, who taught for many years at Howard University in Washington, D.C., enlarged the use of folk characters by depicting them in a variety of situations, from trivial to tragic. Zora Neale Hurston, James Weldon Johnson, Langston Hughes, Jean Toomer, and Julius Lester were among those writers who utilized folk material in their literary works.

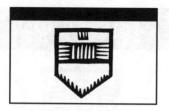

MOTHERLESS CHILD

Anonymous

This song is an African-American (Negro) spiritual. Songs such as these originated during slavery and are still sung today. W. E. B. Du Bois, a founder of the National Association for the Advancement of Colored People (NAACP) and the author of *The Souls of Black Folk*, called such spirituals "sorrow songs."

Sometimes I feel like a motherless child,
Sometimes I feel like a motherless child,
Sometimes I feel like a motherless child,
A long ways from home,
5   A long ways from home.

Sometimes I feel like I'm almost gone,
Sometimes I feel like I'm almost gone,
Sometimes I feel like I'm almost gone,
A long ways from home,
10   A long ways from home.

Sometimes I feel like a feather in the air,
Sometimes I feel like a feather in the air,
Sometimes I feel like a feather in the air,
And I spread my wings and I fly,

15   I spread my wings and I fly.

DISCUSSION QUESTIONS

1. How might a motherless child feel?
2. Do you think this song's writer actually lost his or her mother? Why?
3. What kind of person might sing this song?

WRITING TOPICS

1. W. E. B. Du Bois called spirituals such as this "sorrow songs." Write an essay explaining your interpretation of the term "sorrow songs." Use examples either from research you've done or by interviewing family members or other adults in your community.
2. The writer says in the second stanza, "Sometimes I feel like I'm almost gone / A long ways from home." Find other statements in the song that demonstrate figurative language. Then write an analytical essay about that particular figure of speech.

THE KNEE-HIGH MAN TRIES
TO GET SIZABLE

Retold by Carl Carmer

"The Knee-High Man Tries to Get Sizable" is an African-American folktale that has been told and retold by both African-American and white storytellers. During the 1930s and 1940s, many white folklorists recorded and published African-American folktales. Some of these white folklorists, such as Carl Carmer, presented the black folktales in the same form as they were told. However, other white folklorists presented their own interpretations. Today, many African-American storytellers, or *griots,* tell the story of "The Knee-High Man." Currently, the title is different from that of Carmer's version of the folktale in 1934, but it is the same story Diane Ferlattee tells in her travels as a modern-day African-American griot across the United States, Austria, New Zealand, and Australia.

1   The knee-high man who lived by the swamp wanted to be big instead of little. One day, he said to himself: "I am going to call on the biggest thing in the neighborhood and find out how I can get sizable." So he went to see Mr. Horse. He asked: "Mr. Horse, I come to get you to tell me how to grow as big as you are."

2   Mr. Horse said: "Eat a whole lot of corn and then run round and round and round until you have gone twenty miles. After a while you will be as big as me."

3   So the knee-high man, he did all Mr. Horse told him to do. And the corn made his stomach hurt, and running made his legs hurt, and the trying made his mind hurt. And he just got littler and littler. Then the knee-high man sat in his house and thought about how it was that Mr. Horse didn't help him at all. And he said to himself: "I'm going to go see Brer Bull."

4   So he went to see Brer Bull and he said: "Brer Bull, I come to ask you to tell me how to get as big as you are."

5   And Brer Bull, he told him: "Eat a whole lot of grass and then bellow and bellow, and first thing you know you will get as big as I am."

6   And the knee-high man did everything that Brer Bull told him to do. And the grass made his stomach hurt, and the bellowing made his neck hurt, and the thinking made his mind hurt. And he got littler and littler. The knee-high man sat in his house and he thought about how come Brer Bull didn't do him any better than Mr. Horse. After a while, he heard old Mr. Hoot Owl in the middle of the swamp preaching that bad people are going to have bad luck. The knee-high man said to himself: "I'm going to ask Mr. Hoot Owl how I can get to be sizable," and he went to see Mr. Hoot Owl.

7   And Mr. Hoot Owl said: "Why do you want to be big?" The knee-high man said: "I want to be big so that when I get into a fight I can win it." And Mr. Hoot Owl said: "Anybody ever try to pick a fight with you?" The knee-high man said no. So Mr. Hoot Owl said: "Well, if you don't have any cause to fight, then you don't have any reason to be any bigger than you are." The knee-high man thought about that and finally said: "But I want to be big so I can see a long way." Mr. Hoot Owl, he said: "When you climb a tree, can you see a long way from the top? You know, when it comes down to it you don't have any reason to be bigger in your body; but you sure have got a good reason to be bigger in the BRAIN."

DISCUSSION QUESTIONS

1. The knee-high man asks Mr. Horse and Brer Bull for help. When the knee-high man follows their advice, what happens to him? Why didn't Mr. Horse's and Brer Bull's suggestions work?
2. What is the meaning of Mr. Hoot Owl's statements: "'Well, if you don't have any cause to fight, you don't have any reason to be any bigger than you are"?
3. What type(s) of abilities does the knee-high man need in order to be "big"? Why?

WRITING TOPICS

1. In an essay, discuss the use of animal characters in African-American folktales. Explain why African-American slaves used animals in their retold stories.
2. Think about a lesson you learned as a child. In your journal, write a one-page story using at least two different animals to teach that lesson. Keep in mind that anyone who hears or reads your story should be able to figure out the moral from the actions of your animal characters.

HOW BUCK WON HIS FREEDOM

Anonymous

This folktale from the days of slavery tells how a slave outwits his master and wins his freedom.

1   Buck was the shrewdest slave on the big Washington plantation. He could steal things almost in front of his master's eyes without being detected. Finally, after having had his chickens and pigs stolen until he was sick, Master Henry Washington called Buck to him one day and said, "Buck, how do you manage to steal without getting caught?"

2   "Dat's easy, Massa," replied Buck, "dat's easy. Ah kin steal yo' clo'es right tonight, wid you aguardin' 'em."

3   "No, no," said the master, "you may be a slick thief, but you can't do that. I will make a proposition with you: If you steal my suit of clothes tonight, I will give you your freedom, and if you fail to steal them, then you will stop stealing my chickens."

4   "Aw right, Massa, aw right," Buck agreed. "Dat's uh go."

5   That night about nine o'clock the master called his wife into the bedroom, got his Sunday suit of clothes, laid it out on the table, and told his wife about the proposition he had made with Buck. He got on one side of the table and had his wife get on the other side, and they waited. Pretty soon, through a window that was open, the master heard the mules and the horses in the stable lot running as if someone were after them.

6   "Here wife," said he, "you take this gun and keep an eye on this suit. I am going to see what's the matter with those animals."

7   Buck, who had been out to the horse lot and started the stampede to attract the master's attention, now approached the open window. He was a good mimic, and in tones that sounded like his master's he called out, "Ol' lady, ol' lady, ol' lady, you better hand me that suit. That damn thief might steal it while I'm gone."

8   The master's wife, thinking it was her husband asking for his suit, took it from the table and handed it out the window to Buck. This is how Buck won his freedom.

DISCUSSION QUESTIONS

1. How does Buck outwit his slavemaster?
2. Buck was able to sound like his master. How was he able to do that, even though he usually spoke a nonstandard dialect of English?
3. How would you describe Master Henry Washington?

WRITING TOPICS

1. In your journal, imagine what Buck's feelings must have been after winning his freedom.
2. In an essay, describe the master's reaction to Buck's ability to get the suit from the master's wife.
3. Write a story about a slave winning his or her freedom by outsmarting the slavemaster.

FROM *THE EATONVILLE ANTHOLOGY*

Zora Neale Hurston

Zora Neale Hurston was born in Eatonville, Florida, in 1891. Educated at Morgan State College, Howard University, and Barnard College where she studied anthropology, Ms. Hurston became a significant folklorist. She was awarded a Guggenheim Fellowship in 1936–37 to study folklore in the Caribbean; she also studied voodoo in Haiti and Louisiana. Folk customs of African Americans throughout the South were also among her studies, especially those of her hometown of Eatonville, the first all-black township incorporated in the United States. She was a short story writer, novelist, and dramatist; her major publications are *Jonah's Gourd Vine* (1934), *Mules and Men* (1935), *Their Eyes Were Watching God* (1937), *Tell My Horse* (1938), *Moses, Man of the Mountain* (1939), *Dust Tracks on a Road* (1942), and *Seraph on the Suwanee* (1948). Hurston died in 1960. (For more biographical information, see page 432.)

1   Once 'way back yonder before the stars fell all the animals used to talk just like people. In them days dogs and rabbits was the best friends—even tho both of them was stuck on the same gal—which was Miss Nancy Coon. She had the sweetest smile and the prettiest striped and bushy tail to be found anywhere.

2   They both run their legs nigh off trying to win her for themselves—fetching nice ripe persimmons and such. But she never give one or the other no satisfaction.

3   Finally one night Mr. Dog popped the question right out. "Miss Coon," he says, "Ma'am, also Ma'am, which would you ruther be—a lark flyin' or a dove a settin'?"

4   Course Miss Nancy she blushed and laughed a little and hid her face behind her bushy tail for a spell. Then she said sorter shy like, "I does love yo' sweet voice, brother dawg—but—but I ain't jes' exactly set in my mind yit."

5   Her and Mr. Dog set on a spell, when up comes hopping Mr. Rabbit wid his tail fresh washed and his whiskers shining. He got right down to business and asked Miss Coon to marry him, too.

6 "Oh, Miss Nancy," he says, "Ma'am, also Ma'am, if you'd see me settin' straddle of a mud-cat leadin' a minnow, what would you think? Ma'am also Ma'am?" Which is a out and out proposal as everybody knows.

7 "Youse awful nice, Brother Rabbit, and a beautiful dancer, but you cannot sing like Brother Dog. Both you uns come back next week to gimme time for to decide."

8 They both left arm-in-arm. Finally, Mr. Rabbit says to Mr. Dog, "Taint no use in me going back—she ain't gwinter have me. So I mought as well give up. She loves singing, and I ain't got nothing but a squeak."

9 "Oh, don't talk that a' way," says Mr. Dog, tho' he is glad Mr. Rabbit can't sing none.

10 "Thass all right, Brer Dog. But if I had a sweet voice like you got, I'd have it worked on and make it sweeter."

11 "How! How! How!" Mr. Dog cried, jumping up and down.

12 "Lemme fix it for you, like I do for Sister Lark and Sister Mocking-bird."

13 "When? Where?" asked Mr. Dog, all excited. He was figuring that if he could sing just a little better Miss Coon would be bound to have him.

14 "Just you meet me t'morrer in de huckleberry patch," says the rabbit and off they both goes to bed.

15 The dog is there on time next day and after a while the rabbit comes loping up.

16 "Mawnin', Brer Dawg," he says kinder chippy like. "Ready to git yo' voice sweetened?"

17 "Sholy, Sholy, Brer Rabbit. Let's we all hurry about it. I wants tuh serenade Miss Nancy from de piney woods tuh night.

18 "Well, den, open yo' mouf and poke out yo' tongue," says the rabbit.

19 No sooner did Mr. Dog poke out his tongue than Mr. Rabbit split it with a knife and ran for all he was worth to a hollow stump and hid hisself.

20 The dog has been mad at the rabbit ever since.

21 Anybody who don't believe it happened, just look at the dog's tongue and he can see for himself where the rabbit slit it right up the middle.

22 Stepped on a tin, mah story ends.

DISCUSSION QUESTIONS

1. How does Mr. Rabbit outwit Mr. Dog?
2. How would you describe Mr. Rabbit?
3. Mr. Rabbit was able to convince Mr. Dog to meet him the next day. Why is Mr. Dog so gullible?

WRITING TOPICS

1. Write a paragraph or two describing the character of Mr. Rabbit.
2. In your journal, write how you feel about Miss Nancy. What kind of person is she?

PEOPLE WHO COULD FLY

Julius Lester

Julius Lester was born in 1939 and has been a newspaper columnist, folksinger, television and radio personality, and university professor. He has also written seventeen books—the most recent being *How Many Spots Does a Leopard Have?*, a retelling of twelve African and Jewish folktales. An early proponent of black pride, Lester spent his youth in the Midwest and South. He graduated from Fisk University and was an organizer of the Student Nonviolent Coordinating Committee (SNCC), a civil rights organization in the United States during the 1960s. Currently, Lester teaches at the University of Massachusetts, Amherst.

In much of his writing, such as *To Be a Slave* (1968)—a runner-up for the Newbery Medal—and *Black Folktales* (1969), Lester used African-American history and folklore to create literary works. "People Who Could Fly" is a retelling of a tale from slavery days.

1   It happened long, long ago, when black people were taken from their homes in Africa and forced to come here to work as slaves. They were put onto ships, and many died during the long voyage across the Atlantic Ocean. Those that survived stepped off the boats into a land they had never seen, a land they never knew existed, and they were put into the fields to work.

2   Many refused, and they were killed. Others would work, but when the white man's whip lashed their backs to make them work harder, they would turn and fight. And some of them killed the white men with the whips. Others were killed by the white men. Some would run away and try to go back home, back to Africa where there were no white people, where they worked their own land for the good of each other, not for the good of white men. Some of those who tried to go back to Africa would walk until they came to the ocean, and then they would walk into the water, and no one knows if they did walk to Africa through the water or if they drowned. It didn't matter. At least they were no longer slaves.

3   Now when the white man forced Africans onto the slave-ships, he did not know, nor did he care, if he took the village musicians, artists, or witch doctors. As long as they were black and looked strong, he wanted them—men, women, and children. Thus, he did not know that sometimes there would be a witch doctor among those he had captured. If he had known, and had also known that the witch doctor was the medium of the gods, he would have thought twice. But he did not care. These black men and black women were not people to him. He looked at them and counted each one as so much money for his pocket.

4   It was to a plantation in South Carolina that one boatload of Africans was brought. Among them was the son of a witch doctor who had not completed by many months studying the secrets of the gods from his father. This young man carried with him the secrets and powers of the generations of Africa.

5   One day, one hot day when the sun singed the very hair on the head, they were working in the fields. They had been in the fields since before the sun rose, and, as it made its journey to the highest part of the sky, the very air seemed to be on fire. A young woman, her body curved with the child that grew deep inside her, fainted.

6   Before her body struck the ground, the white man with the whip was riding toward her on his horse. He threw water in her face. "Get back to work, you lazy nigger! There ain't going to be no sitting down on the job as long as I'm here." He cracked the whip against her back and, screaming, she staggered to her feet.

7   All work had stopped as the Africans watched, saying nothing.

8   "If you niggers don't want a taste of the same, you'd better get to work!"

9   They lowered their heads and went back to work. The young witch doctor worked his way slowly toward the young mother-to-be, but before he could reach her, she collapsed again, and the white man with the whip was upon her, lashing her until her body was raised from the ground by the sheer violence of her sobs. The young witch doctor worked his way to her side and whispered something in her ear. She, in turn, whispered to the person beside her. He told the next person, and on around the field it went. They did it so quickly and quietly that the white man with the whip noticed nothing.

10   A few moments later, someone else in the field fainted, and, as the white man with the whip rode toward him, the young witch doctor shouted, "Now!" He uttered a strange word, and the person who had fainted rose from the ground and, moving his arms like wings, he flew into the sky and out of sight.

11   The man with the whip looked around at the Africans, but they only stared into the distance, tiny smiles softening their lips. "Who did that? Who was that who yelled out?" No one said anything. "Well, just let me get my hands on him."

12   Not too many minutes had passed before the young woman fainted once again. The man was almost upon her when the young witch doctor

shouted, "Now!" and uttered a strange word. She, too, rose from the ground and, waving her arms like wings, she flew into the distance and out of sight.

13   This time the man with the whip knew who was responsible, and as he pulled back his arm to lash the young witch doctor, the young man yelled, "Now! Now! Everyone!" He uttered the strange word, and all of the Africans dropped their hoes, stretched out their arms, and flew away, back to their home, back to Africa.

14   That was long ago, and no one now remembers what word it was that the young witch doctor knew that could make people fly. But who knows? Maybe one morning someone will awake with a strange word on his tongue and, uttering it, we will all stretch out our arms and take to the air, leaving these blood-drenched fields of our misery behind.

DISCUSSION QUESTIONS

1. What identifies this as an oral story in written form, or an oral signature? How many types of oral signatures can you find? What are they?
2. What do oral tradition signatures contribute to the oral nature of a story? What do they contribute to or detract from the written version of this oral story?
3. How were the Africans looked upon by the slave traders in "People Who Could Fly"?
4. What do you think the witch doctor whispered to the expectant mother?
5. Create a one-paragraph story and tell it to another person. Then have that person tell the story to someone else. Next, have the last person tell the story to one more person. Then have the last person tell you the story. How did the story change? Where did it stay the same? What did you learn about the oral nature of stories?

WRITING TOPICS

1. What is the role of the storyteller in the oral tradition? Using examples from the story, illustrate the role of the storyteller in the oral tradition.

2. What does the act of flying represent in this story? Is the act of flying a simile or a metaphor? Why? Write a paragraph or two explaining your answer.

3. Reread "How Buck Won His Freedom," the excerpt from *The Eatonville Anthology*, and "People Who Could Fly." Analyze the oral nature of these three stories. Develop a thesis about the oral structure of folktales and use specific examples from the three stories to support your thesis.

THE STEEL DRIVIN' MAN

A. Philip Randolph and Chandler Owen

A. Philip Randolph was born in 1889. He played a leading role in the struggle for black rights and was a key figure in the American labor movement. He and Chandler Owen edited and published the *Messenger,* a socialist journal. They published "The Steel Drivin' Man" in the *Messenger* in 1925. This folktale is based on the work-song "John Henry." The subject of many ballads and stories, the tale of John Henry was inspired by a real man with that name. Randolph died in 1979.

1   . . . John Henry was a "free man." . . . While a mere lad he had saved his master from a watery grave. For this heroic act he was given his liberty, and more, the former master became his best friend. He always called the old plantation his home.

2   Physically, John Henry was a mighty man. He was over six feet tall. He weighed more than two hundred and fifty pounds. He could muscle and toss a hundred pound anvil with one hand. He was a pure Negro . . .

3   What noble deed would John Henry not do? He would give his last crust of bread to a hungry child. He would sit up all night at the bedside of a sick slave and then work hard the following day, and the work was arduous indeed, but John Henry did not care. He was the best worker in the country.

4   John Henry was employed by Captain Walters, a railroad contractor. The Captain was a southerner of the old school. He loved his "niggahs" as he called them, and they loved him.

5   The Captain also employed many slaves, hiring them from their masters until he completed his contracts. He divided his army of workers into gangs, as best suited each individual's ability. There was the "plow gang" and the "wheeler gang," the "pick-and-shovel gang" and the "skinners," and last, but most important of all, the "blasting gang," which included the steel drivers.

6   John Henry was a steel driver. The Captain had never seen a man drive

steel as well as he did. No one on the job professed to be able to drive as well. Probably it was because he was a "free man," and was receiving into his own hand his three silver dollars per week, but . . . back on the old plantation a lassie, Lucy by name, was boss of the plantation kitchen, and John Henry was driving steel for her. John Henry loved her. He wanted her to be his wife but first he wanted her to be free, as he was. For years he had been saving his money to buy the girl, to pay for the home, and as he drove his steel into the solid rock to make the opening for the powder charge—often the echo of his hammer would speak to him his sweetheart's name—and his "buddies" had christened his hammer "Lucy" because John Henry repeated that name so often.

7   John Henry loved that servant of his, his hammer. It weighed ten pounds more than any other there. It occupied a special place in the tool shanty. No one touched it but him, for had they done so they would have touched John Henry's heart.

8   Well, one day, the Captain landed a contract for a few miles of road through the heart of the Virginia mountains. The work began in June and John Henry was happy. It was a rough country. There was much rock. This would make overtime work compulsory and that meant for him more money. They knew he was happy for he began to sing a new song to the echo of his hammer:—

>   "Ef ah makes-huh, June, July an' Augus'-huh,
>   Ise gwine home-huh, Ise gwine home-huh.
>   O ef ah makes-huh, June, July, an' Augus'-huh,
>   Ise a-comin' home, Lucy-huh, Ise a-com' home-huh!"

9   This would he sing as his drill went down, and he grinned much, despite the heat and the perspiration.

10   But one day there arrived at the camp an enemy to John Henry and to all good steel driving men. He came in the garb of a Yankee drummer, an agent for a so-called, "steam-drill." This new machine was guaranteed to drill a hole faster than any ten men could drill one in the old way with sledge hammer and steel.

11   That Yankee was determined to sell one to the Captain. He followed him around for days. But the old southerner was obdurate. He did not believe in the much advertised scientific improvements. It takes money to make improvements, despite their economical value in the end. Besides, he was working Negroes, and Negro labor cost him little. In those days a "nigger" was but a machine anyway—a tool to do the white man's work. Why pay for the use of brains when the use of muscle was so cheap? To rid himself of the Yankee the Captain told him:

12   "Suh, I have a niggah here who can take his hammah and steel and beat that three legged steam contraption of yours to a frazzle, suh. And ah'll bet yuh five hundred dollars on the spot that he can, suh."

13   "And I'll take your bet provided, that if I win you'll give me an order," said the wily Yankee. And thus it was settled.

14   The Captain was not at all afraid he would lose his money. . . . He made it his business the next day to visit the "blasting gang" just as John Henry was setting his drill. He noticed how fervently the swarthy driver gripped his sledge, and, with what apparent ease he forced the steel down into the solid rock. He saw the hot perspiration pouring from the seasoned muscles, and then the grin illuminating the ugly features, and the old Captain chuckled. He called the driver aside.

15   "John, John, come here John."

16   "John, I've bet that fool Yankee that you and your hammer can beat that steam contraption he's got. Think you can John?"

17   "Yassah Cap'n, yassah, yassah."

18   "Well, John, we'll have the race tomorrow and you do it. You beat him and I'll give you—ah—I'll give you fifty dollars."

19   John Henry had never been so happy before in all his life. Fifty dollars! Fifty dollars! Why to him it meant everything. It meant that Lucy would be free. It meant that Lucy would be his wife. It meant that Lucy and he would have a home of their own. Is it any wonder then, that when night had fallen, he rubbed from his hammer every speck of dirt, placed it reverently away, and as he lay there among the jutting rocks, gazing at the stars, the melody of his songs reverberated through those rugged mountains louder and sweeter than his "buddies,"—that night in the grading camp? . . .

20   The Yankee did not do right. . . for he never arrived the next day until the sun was hot, and it was a day in July. But John Henry did not care. He had been singing and grinning all the morning. They chose a spot favored by the Yankee, and, as all the hands crowded around, set their drills.

21   The race began! It was steam against muscle; brain against brawn; progress against retrogression; Yankee against Southerner; head against heart. John Henry kissed his hammer. The Yankee opened a valve.

22   John Henry did not sing as he usually did when driving steel. He could not spare the breath. But he drove, ah, how he did drive! With every stroke you could almost see the drill go down and, though the Yankee used much steam, the mark on the Negro's steel was approaching the surface of the stone faster than the mark of his own. And, as the mark on John Henry's steel entered the aperture, finally becoming invisible, he poised his sledge for one more mighty stroke—to clinch the argument, as it were—to make good. The sledge descended—it struck—but dropped from his hands. He staggered and fell full length upon the rocks. His face was ashen. His lips were pale. His buddies stooped over him, fanned him and some ran for water, but he only weakly beckoned for his hammer. Some one laid it in his arms. He touched it to his lips and his kiss and his blood mingled upon the iron head.

23   "Lucy—Lucy—O Lucy," he whispered.

24   The old Captain pushed through the crowd, bent over the stricken driver, and tenderly raised his head.

25   "John, John," he said. "You've beat that steam contraption. You've beat the Yankee."

26   "We've beat him, Cap'n?"

27   The steel driver opened his eyes and saw the glow of victory on the contractor's wrinkled face.

28   "Why Cap'n, we did beat him! We beat him shor," he said and died.

Discussion Questions

1. John Henry was a determined man; he promised to succeed by beating the "steam-drill" to the finish line. Identify passages in the story that demonstrate this determination.
2. Name other legendary African Americans who were determined to achieve their goals. In small groups, discuss some of these goals and how they were reached.
3. How would you describe the Captain's attitude toward John Henry?

Writing Topics

1. Write an essay describing the mood of John Henry's friends and co-workers on the day of the race.
2. What was uppermost in John Henry's mind as he drove the steel that day? In a paragraph or two, explain what John Henry was thinking about in the race.
3. John Henry, who was a free man, was driving steel to make enough money to free a slave woman named Lucy. He loved and wanted to marry her. Pretend you are John Henry and write Lucy a letter explaining why you have agreed to challenge the steam-drill.

SWING LOW, SWEET CHARIOT

Anonymous

To the slaves, "Swing Low, Sweet Chariot" had another, more important, meaning than that of being a spiritual or religious song.

Swing low, sweet chariot,
Coming for to carry me home,
Swing low, sweet chariot,
Coming for to carry me home.

5 I looked over Jordan and what did I see
Coming for to carry me home,
A band of angels, coming after me,
Coming for to carry me home.

If you get there before I do,
10 Coming for to carry me home,
Tell all my friends I'm coming too,
Coming for to carry me home.

Swing low, sweet chariot,
Coming for to carry me home,
15 Swing low, sweet chariot,
Coming for to carry me home.

DISCUSSION QUESTIONS

1. This, like many spirituals sung by the slaves, has a hidden meaning. What do you think is the hidden meaning of the first and last stanzas?
2. In the second stanza, the writer says: "I looked over Jordan and what did I see. . ." Jordan is a river in the Middle East. What do you think the metaphor "crossing over Jordan" means in the song?
3. Who is the "band of angels" referred to in the song?

WRITING TOPICS

1. Locate another African-American (Negro) spiritual and select one of its stanzas. Write an essay in which you interpret its underlying meaning.
2. In your journal, write your interpretation of the third stanza of "Swing Low, Sweet Chariot."
3. Write a hypothetical conversation between a singer of the third stanza and his or her friends once they have been reunited.

STAGOLEE

Julius Lester

Julius Lester has had a variety of careers, including writer, newspaper columnist, folksinger, and television and radio personality. Lester currently teaches at the University of Massachusetts, Amherst. (For more biographical information about Julius Lester, see page 11.)

"Stagolee" started out as a song about a real man. His story was likely told first in black neighborhoods in large, urban cities. This tale, as retold by Julius Lester, is of a man who grew up on a Georgia plantation. Early in his childhood Stagolee (sometimes referred to as Staggerlee) declared that he would not spend *his* life working on a plantation. He took mistreatment from no one—white or black. His legend and the retellings that grew out of it are the basis of "Stagolee," a story from Julius Lester's book *Black Folktales*, first published in 1969.

1   Stagolee was, undoubtedly and without question, the baddest nigger that ever lived. Stagolee was so bad that the flies wouldn't even fly around his head in the summertime, and snow wouldn't fall on his house in the winter. He was bad, jim.

2   Stagolee grew up on a plantation in Georgia, and by the time he was two, he'd decided that he wasn't going to spend his life picking cotton and working for white folks. Uh-uh. And when he was five, he left. Took off down the road, his guitar on his back, a deck of cards in one pocket and a .44 in the other. He figured that he didn't need nothing else. When the women heard him whup the blues on the guitar he could have

whichever one he laid his mind on. Whenever he needed money, he could play cards. And whenever somebody tried to mess with him, he had his .44. So he was ready. A man didn't need more than that to get along with in the world.

3   By the time Stack was grown, his reputation had spread around the country. It got started one night in one of them honky-tonks down there in Alabama, and Stagolee caught some dude trying to deal from the bottom of the deck. Ol' Stack pulled out his .44 and killed him dead, right there on the spot. Then he moved the dead guy over to the center of the room and used the body as a card table. Another time, something similar happened, and Stack pulled the body over next to him, so a buddy of his, who was kinda short, would have something to sit on. Didn't take long for the word to get around that this was one bad dude! Even white folks didn't mess with Stagolee.

4   Well, this one time, Stagolee was playing cards with a dude they called Billy Lyons. Billy Lyons was one of them folk who acted like they were a little better than anybody else. He'd had a little education, and that stuff can really mess your mind up. Billy Lyons had what he called a "scientific method" of cardplaying. Stagolee had the "nigger method." So they got to playing, and, naturally, Stagolee was just taking all of Billy Lyons's money, and Billy got mad. He got so mad that he reached over and knocked Stagolee's Stetson hat off his head and spit in it.

5   What'd he do that for? He could've done almost anything else in the world, but not that. Stack pulled his .44, and Billy started copping his plea. "Now, listen here, Mr. Stagolee. I didn't mean no harm. I just lost my head for a minute. I was wrong, and I apologize." He reached down on the ground, picked up Stack's Stetson, brushed it off, and put it back on his head. "I didn't mean no harm. See, the hat's all right. I put it back on your head." Billy was tomming[1] like a champ, but Stack wasn't smiling. "Don't shoot me. Please, Mr. Stagolee! I got two children and a wife to support. You understand?"

6   Stack said, "Well, that's all right. The Lawd'll take care of your children. I'll take care of your wife." And, with that, Stagolee blowed Billy Lyons away. Stagolee looked at the body for a minute and then went off to Billy Lyons's house and told Mrs. Billy that her husband was dead and he was moving in. And that's just what he did, too. Moved in.

7   Now there was this new sheriff in town, and he had gotten the word about Stagolee, but this sheriff was a sho' nuf' cracker. He just couldn't stand the idea of Stagolee walking around like he was free—not working, not buying war bonds, cussing out white folks. He just couldn't put up with it, so, when he heard that Stagolee had shot Billy Lyons, he figured that this was his chance.

---

[1] *tomming:* talking like "an Uncle Tom."

8   Sheriff told his deputies, said, "All right, men. Stagolee killed a man tonight. We got to get him."

9   The deputies looked at him. "Well, sheriff. Ain't nothing wrong with killing a man every now and then," said one.

10   "It's good for a man's health," added another.

11   "Well," said the sheriff, "that's all right for a white man, but this is a nigger."

12   "Now, sheriff, you got to watch how you talk about Stagolee. He's one of the leaders of the community here. You just can't come in here and start talking about one of our better citizens like that."

13   The sheriff looked at them. "I believe you men are afraid. Afraid of a nigger!"

14   Deputies thought it over for half a second. "Sheriff. Let's put it this way. We have a healthy respect for Stagolee. A long time ago, we struck a bargain with him. We promised him that if he let us alone, we'd let him alone. And everything has worked out just fine."

15   "Well, we're going to arrest Stagolee," the sheriff said. "Get your guns, and let's go."

16   The deputies stood up, took their guns, and laid 'em on the shelf. "Sheriff, if you want Stagolee, well, you can arrest him by yourself." And they went on out the door and over to the undertaker's parlor and told him to start making a coffin for the sheriff.

17   When all the other white folks heard what the sheriff was going to do, they ran over to talk to him. "Sheriff, you can't go around disturbing the peace." But couldn't nobody talk no sense into him.

18   Now Stagolee heard that the sheriff was looking for him, and, being a gentleman, Stagolee got out of bed, told Mrs. Billy he'd be back in a little while, and went on down to the bar. He'd barely gotten the first drink down when the sheriff came stepping through the door.

19   He walked over to the bartender. "Barkeep? Who's that man down at the other end of the bar? You know there's a law in this town against drinking after midnight. Who is that?"

20   Bartender leaned over the counter and whispered in his ear, "Don't talk so loud. That's Stagolee. He drinks when he gets thirsty and he's generally thirsty after midnight."

21   Sheriff walked over to Stagolee. Stagolee didn't even look around. Sheriff fired a couple of shots in the air. Stagolee poured himself another drink and threw it down. Finally, the sheriff said, "Stagolee, I'm the sheriff, and I'm white. Ain't you afraid?"

22   Stagolee turned around slowly. "You may be the sheriff, and you may be white, but you ain't Stagolee. Now deal with that."

23   The sheriff couldn't even begin to figure it out, no less deal with it, so he fell back in his familiar bag. "I'm placing you under arrest for the murder of Billy Lyons."

24   "You and what army? And it bet' not be the United States Army, 'cause I whupped them already."

25   "Me and this army," the sheriff growled, jabbing the pistol in Stack's ribs.

26   Before the sheriff could take another breath, Stagolee hit him upside the head and sent him flying across the room. Stagolee pulled out his gun, put three bullets in him, put his gun away, had another drink, and was on his way out the door before the body hit the floor.

27   The next day, Stagolee went to both of the funerals to pay his last respects to the sheriff and Billy Lyons, and then he settled down to living with Mrs. Billy. She really didn't mind too much. All the women knew how good-looking Stack was. And he was always respectful to women, always had plenty of money, and, generally, he made a good husband, as husbands go. Stagolee had one fault, though. Sometimes he drank too much. About once a month, Stagolee would buy up all the available liquor and moonshine in the county and proceed to get wasted, and when Stagolee got wasted, he got totally wasted.

28   The new sheriff waited until one of those nights when Stagolee was so drunk he was staggering in his sleep, and he was lying flat in the bed. If Judgment Day had come, the Lord would have had to postpone it until Stagolee had sobered up. Otherwise, the Lord might've ended up getting Gabriel shot and his trumpet wrapped around his head. When the sheriff saw Stagolee that drunk, he went and got together the Ku Klux Klan Alumni Association, which was every white man in four counties. After the sheriff had assured them that Stagolee was so drunk he couldn't wake up, they broke in the house just as bad as you please. They had the lynching rope all ready, and they dropped it around his neck. The minute that rope touched Stack's neck, he was wide awake and stone cold sober. When white folks saw that, they were falling over each other getting out of there. But Stack was cool. He should've been. He invented it.

29   "Y'all come to hang me?"

30   The sheriff said that that was so. Stagolee stood up, stretched, yawned, and scratched himself a couple of times. "Well, since I can't seem to get no sleep, let's go and get this thing over with so I can get on back to bed."

31   They took him on out behind the jail where the gallows was built. Stagolee got up on the scaffold, and the sheriff dropped the rope around his neck and tightened it. Then the hangman opened up on the trap door, and there was Stack, swinging ten feet in the air, laughing as loud as you ever heard anybody laugh. They let him hang there for a half-hour, and Stagolee was still laughing.

32   "Hey, man! This rope is ticklish."

33   The white folks looked at each other and realized that Stack's neck just wouldn't crack. So they cut him down, and Stagolee went back home and went back to bed.

34   After that, the new sheriff left Stagolee in peace, like he should've done to begin with.

35   Stagolee lived on and on, and that was his big mistake. 'Cause Stagolee lived so long, he started attracting attention up in Heaven. One day, St. Peter was looking down on the earth, and he happened to notice Stack sitting on the porch picking on the guitar. "Ain't that Stagolee?" St. Peter said to himself. He took a closer look. "That's him. That's him. Why, that nigger should've been dead a long time ago." So St. Peter went and looked it up in the record book, and sure enough, Stagolee was supposed to have died thirty years before.

36   St. Peter went to see the Lord.

37   "What's going on, St. Peter?"

38   "Oh, ain't nothing shaking, Lord. Well, that's not totally true. I was just checking out earth, and there's a nigger down there named Stagolee who is way overdue for a visit from Death."

39   "Is that so?"

40   "It's the truth, Lord."

41   "Well, we have to do something about that."

42   The Lord cleared his throat a couple of times and hollered out, "HEY DEATH! HEEEEY, DEATH!"

43   Now Death was laying up down in the barn catching up on some sleep, 'cause he was tired. Having to make so many trips to Vietnam was wearing him out, not to mention everywhere else in the world. He just couldn't understand why dying couldn't be systematized. He'd tried his best to convince God either to get a system to dying or get him some assistants. He'd proposed that, say, on Mondays, the only dying that would be done would be, say, in France, Germany, and a few other countries. Tuesday it'd be some other countries, and on like that. That way, he wouldn't have to be running all over the world twenty-four hours a day. But the Lord had vetoed the idea. Said it sounded to him like Death just wanted an excuse to eventually computerize the whole operation. Death had to admit that the thought had occurred to him. He didn't know when he was going to catch up on all the paperwork he had to do. A computer would solve everything. And now, just when he was getting to sleep, here come the Lord waking him up.

44   So Death got on his pale white horse. He was so tired of riding a horse he didn't know what to do. He'd talked to God a few months ago about letting him get a helicopter or something. But the Lord just didn't seem to understand. Death rode on off down through the streets of Heaven, and when folks heard him coming, they closed their doors, 'cause even in Heaven, folks were afraid of Death. And that was the other thing. Death was mighty lonely. Didn't nobody talk to him, and he was getting a little tired of it. He wished the Lord would at least let him wear a suit and tie and look respectable. Maybe then he could meet some nice young angel and raise a family. The Lord had vetoed that idea, too.

45   "What took you so long, Death?"

46   "Aw, Lord. I was trying to get some sleep. You just don't realize how fast folks are dying these days."

47   "Don't tell me you gon' start complaining again."

48   "I'm sorry, Lord, but I'd like to see you handle the job as well as I do with no help, no sleep, no wife, no nothing."

49   "Well, I got a special job for you today."

50   "Can't wait until tomorrow?"

51   "No, it can't wait, Death! Now hush up. There's a man in Fatback, Georgia, named Stagolee. You should've picked him up thirty years ago, and I want you to send me a memo on why you didn't."

52   "Well, I got such a backlog of work piled up."

53   "I don't want to have to be doing your job for you. You get the lists every day from the Record Bureau. How come you missed this one? If he's escaped for thirty years, who knows who else has been living way past their time. Speaking of folks living past their time, St. Peter, have the librarian bring me all the files on white folks. Seems to me that white folks sho' done outlived their time. Anyway, Death, go on down there and get Stagolee."

54   Death headed on down to earth. A long time ago, he used to enjoy the ride, but not anymore. There were so many satellites and other pieces of junk flying around through the air that it was like going through a junkyard barefooted. So he didn't waste any time getting on down to Fatback, Georgia.

55   Now on this particular day, Stagolee was sitting on the porch, picking the blues on the guitar, and drinking. All of a sudden, he looked up and saw this pale-looking white cat in this white sheet come riding up to his house on a white horse. "We ain't never had no Klan in the daytime before," Stagolee said.

56   Death got off his horse, pulled out his address book, and said, "I'm looking for Stagolee Booker T. Washington Nicodemus Shadrack Nat Turner Jones."

57   "Hey, baby! You got it down pat! I'd forgotten a couple of them names myself."

58   "Are you Stagolee Booker T. Wash—"

59   "You ain't got to go through the thing again. I'm the dude. What's going on?"

60   "I'm Death. Come with me."

61   Stagolee started laughing. "You who?"

62   "I'm Death. Come on, man. I ain't got all day."

63   "Be serious."

64   Death looked at Stagolee. No one had ever accused him of joking before. "I *am* serious. It's your time to die. Now come on here!"

65   "Man, you ain't bad enough to mess with me."

66   Death blinked his eyes. He'd never run up on a situation like this before. Sometimes folks struggled a little bit, but they didn't refuse. "Stagolee, let's go!" Death said in his baddest voice.

67   "Man, you must want to get shot."

68   Death thought that one over for a minute. Now he didn't know how to handle this situation, so he reached in his saddlebags and pulled out his

Death Manual. He looked up *resistance* and read what it said, but wasn't a thing in there about what to do when somebody threatens you. Then he looked up *guns* but that wasn't listed. He looked under everything he could think of, but nothing was of any help. So he went back to the porch. "You coming or not, Stagolee?"

69   Stagolee let one of them .44 bullets whistle past ol' Death's ear, and Death got hot. Death didn't waste no time getting away from there. Before he was sitting in the saddle good, he had made it back to Heaven.

70   "Lord! You must be trying to get me killed."

71   "Do what? Get you killed? Since when could you die?"

72   "Don't matter, but that man Stagolee you just sent me after took a shot at me. Now listen here, Lord, if you want that man dead, you got to get him yourself. I am not going back after him. I knew there was some reason I let him live thirty years too long. I'd heard about him on the grapevine and, for all I care, he can live three hundred more years. I am not going back—"

73   "O.K. O.K. You made your point. Go on back to sleep." After Death had gone, God turned to St. Peter and asked, "We haven't had any new applications for that job recently?"

74   "You must be joking."

75   "Well, I was just checking." The Lord lit a cigar. "Pete, looks like I'm going to have to use one of my giant death thunderbolts to get that Stagolee."

76   "Looks that way. You want me to tell the work crew?"

77   The Lord nodded, and St. Peter left. It took 3,412 angels 14 days, 11 hours, and 32 minutes to carry the giant death thunderbolt to the Lord, but he just reached down and picked it up like it was a toothpick.

78   "Uh, St. Peter? How you spell Stagolee?"

79   "Lord, you know everything. You're omnipotent, omnicient, omni—"

80   "You better shut up and tell me how to spell Stagolee."

81   St. Peter spelled it out for him, and the Lord wrote it on the thunderbolt. Then he blew away a few clouds and put his keen eye down on the earth. "Hey, St. Peter. Will you look at all that killing down there? I ain't never seen nothing like it."

82   "Lord, that ain't Georgia. That's Vietnam."

83   The Lord put his great eye across the world. "Tsk, tsk, tsk. Look at all that sin down there. Women wearing hardly no clothes at all. Check that one out with the black hair, St. Peter. Look at her! Disgraceful! Them legs!"

84   "LORD!"

85   And the Lord put his eye on the earth and went on across the United States—Nevada, Utah, Colorado, Kansas, Missouri—

86   "Turn right at the Mississippi, Lord!"

87   The Lord turned right and went on down into Tennessee.

88   "Make a left at Memphis, Lord!"

89   The Lord turned left at Memphis and went on up through Nashville and on down to Chattanooga into Georgia. Atlanta, Georgia. Valdosta. Rolling

Stone, Georgia, until he got way back out in the woods to Fatback. He let his eye go up and down the country roads until he saw Stagolee sitting on the porch.

90   "That's him, Lord! That's him!"

91   And the Great God Almighty, the God of Nat Turner and Rap Brown, the God of Muddy Waters and B. B. King, the God of Aretha Franklin and The Impressions, this great God Almighty Everlasting, *et in terra pax hominibus*,[2] and all them other good things, drew back his mighty arm—

92   "Watch your aim now, Lord."

93   And unloosed the giant thunderbolt. BOOM!

94   That was the end of Stagolee. You can't mess with the Lord.

95   Well, when the people found out Stagolee was dead, you ain't never heard such hollering and crying in all your life. The women were beside themselves with grief, 'cause Stagolee was nothing but a sweet man.

96   Come the day of the funeral, and Stagolee was laid out in a $10,000 casket. Had on a silk mohair suit and his Stetson hat was in his hand. In his right coat pocket was a brand new deck of cards. In his left coat pocket was a brand new .44 with some extra rounds of ammunition and a can of Mace. And by his side was his guitar. Folks came from all over the country to Stack's funeral, and all of 'em put little notes in Stagolee's other pockets, which were messages they wanted Stagolee to give to their kinfolk when he got to Hell.

97   The funeral lasted for three days and three nights. All the guitar pickers and blues singers had to come sing one last song for Stagolee. All the backsliders had to come backslide one more time for Stagolee. All the gamblers had to come touch Stack's casket for a little taste of good luck. And all the women had to come shed a tear as they looked at him for the last time. Those that had known him were crying about what they weren't going to have any more. And those that hadn't known him were crying over what they had missed. Even the little bitty ones was shedding tears.

98   After all the singing and crying and shouting was over, they took Stagolee on out and buried him. They didn't bury him in the cemetery. Uh-uh. Stagolee had to have a cemetery all his own. They dug his grave with a silver spade and lowered him down with a golden chain. And they went on back to their homes, not quite ready to believe that Stack was dead and gone.

99   But you know, it's mighty hard to keep a good man down, and long about the third day, Stagolee decided to get on up out of the grave and go check out Heaven. Stack just couldn't see himself waiting for Judgment Day. The thought of the white man blowing the trumpet on Judgment Day made him sick to his stomach, and Stagolee figured he was supposed to have his own Judgment Day, anyhow.

---

[2] *et in terra pax hominibus* (Latin): and on earth peace to mankind.

100   He started off for Heaven. Of course it took him a long time to get there, 'cause he had to stop on all the clouds and teach the little angels to play Pittat and Coon-Can and all like that, but, eventually, he got near to Heaven. Now as he got close, he started hearing all this harp music and hymn singing. Stagolee couldn't believe his ears. He listened some more, and then he shrugged his shoulders. "I'm approaching Heaven from the wrong side. This can't be the black part of Heaven, not with all that hymn singing and harp music I hear."

101   So Stack headed on around to the other side of Heaven, and when he got there, it was stone deserted. I mean, wasn't nobody there. Streets was as empty as the President's mind. So Stack cut on back around to the other side of Heaven. When he got there, St. Peter was playing bridge with Abraham, Jonah, and Mrs. God. When they looked up and saw who it was, though, they split, leaving St. Peter there by himself.

102   "You ain't getting in here!" St. Peter yelled.

103   "Don't want to either. Hey, man. Where all the colored folks at?"

104   "We had to send 'em all to Hell. We used to have quite a few, but they got to rocking the church service, you know. Just couldn't even sing a hymn without it coming out and sounding like the blues. So we had to get rid of 'em. We got a few nice colored folks left. And they nice, respectable people."

105   Stagolee laughed. "Hey, man. You messed up."

106   "Huh?"

107   "Yeah, man. This ain't Heaven. This is Hell. Bye."

108   And Stagolee took off straight for Hell. He was about 2,000 miles away, and he could smell the barbecue cooking and hear the jukeboxes playing, and he started running. He got there, and there was a big BLACK POWER sign on the gate. He rung on the bell, and the dude who come to answer it recognized him immediately. "Hey, everybody! Stagolee's here!"

109   And the folks came running from everywhere to greet him.

110   "Hey, baby!"

111   "What's going down!"

112   "What took you so long to get here?"

113   Stagolee walked in, and the brothers and sisters had put down wall-to-wall carpeting, indirect lighting, and best of all, they'd installed air-conditioning. Stagolee walked around, checking it all out. "Yeah. Y'all got it together. Got it uptight!"

114   After he'd finished checking it out, he asked "Any white folks down here?"

115   "Just the hip ones, and ain't too many of them. But they all right. They know where it's at."

116   "Solid." Stagolee noticed an old man sitting over in a corner with his hands over his ears. "What's his problem?"

117   "Aw, that's the Devil. He just can't get himself together. He ain't learned how to deal with niggers yet."

118   Stagolee walked over to him. "Hey, man. Get your pitchfork, and let's have some fun. I got my .44. C'mon. Let's go one round."

119   The Devil just looked at Stagolee real sadlike, but didn't say a word.
120   Stagolee took the pitchfork and laid it on the shelf. "Well, that's hip. I didn't want no stuff out of you nohow. I'm gon' rule Hell by myself!"
121   And that's just what he did, too.

DISCUSSION QUESTIONS

1. "Stagolee" is the story of a legendary African-American male. As with most folktales, the author uses exaggeration as a key literary device. What do you like or dislike about this tale?
2. What do you think makes Stagolee so tough?
3. What can you say about the language used in this folktale? What was happening in the United States at the time this version of Stagolee's story was written?

WRITING TOPICS

1. The storyteller of "Stagolee" says he was "one bad dude!" What is it in his character that makes him so? Write a short paper describing his character.
2. Stagolee seems to display his manhood primarily through acts of violence. Write an essay defending or condemning his actions. Support your point of view with evidence from your reading or personal experience.
3. It is said that "Stagolee" has heroic qualities. Write an essay describing at least one heroic quality the main character displays.

CHAPTER TWO

LANGUAGE AND LITERACY

Language, the way of using words and sounds so that one may be understood by a community, is necessary for the achievement of *literacy,* the ability to read and write. As our primary means of communication, language is crucial. To express ourselves, whether in joy, anger, or sorrow, or the myriad other emotions we feel, we use language. We also use language to communicate needs and wants, to talk about a movie or to buy shoes, and simply to connect with other human beings. Literacy, as the written extension of language, gives us the ability to communicate with a wider audience. We can write letters to senators about government policy, fill out job applications, or write poems. Language and literacy are also extremely important as the means for learning about and passing on our heritage.

Some of the selections in this chapter speak eloquently about the definition of language. Others demonstrate how a person with little or no formal education is able to convey profound thoughts to others. In some the writer uses a dialect of American English, while others use Standard American English. All convey the way finely crafted language enriches our lives.

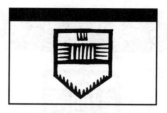

INTRODUCTION
FROM *BLACK TALK*

Geneva Smitherman

Geneva Smitherman obtained her B.A. and M.A. degrees from Wayne State University, Detroit, and her Ph.D. from the University of Michigan. Her interest in African-American English grew out of taking a speech class in order to obtain a Michigan teaching certificate. She is the author of several books, including *Talkin and Testifyin: The Language of Black America* (1977); *Black English and the Education of Black Children and Youth: Proceedings of the National Invitational Symposium on the King Decision* (1981); and *Black Talk: Words and Phrases from the Hood to the Amen Corner* (1994). Smitherman is University Distinguished Professor of English and director of the African-American Language and Literacy Program at Michigan State University. She also directs the My Brother's Keeper Program in Detroit.

In this "Introduction" from *Black Talk*, Smitherman presents the scientific linguistic analysis of African-American English (AAE).

1   . . . As far as historians, linguists, and other scholars go, during the first half of this century it was widely believed that enslavement had wiped out all traces of African languages and cultures, and that Black "differences" resulted from imperfect and inadequate imitations of EUROPEAN AMERICAN language and culture. George Philip Krapp, writing in the 1920s, is one linguist who held this view about the speech of Africans in America. In the 1960s these opinions came under close scrutiny and were soundly challenged by a number of experts, such as the historian John Blassingame and the linguist J. L. Dillard. Today scholars generally agree that the African heritage was not totally wiped out, and that both African American Language and African American Culture have roots in African patterns. (This view had also been advanced by anthropologist Melville Herskovits and linguist

Lorenzo Dow Turner in the 1930s and 1940s, but they were a distinct minority in those days.) Over time, and after prolonged contact with European Americans, Africans in America adopted some Eurocentric patterns, and their African patterns of language and culture were modified—but they were not erased. African American Language and Culture, then, reflects a dual heritage. As Dr. W. E. B. Du Bois put it nearly a century ago in *Souls of Black Folk,* "One ever feels his two-ness—an American, a Negro."

2   The uniqueness of AAE is evident in three areas: (1) patterns of grammar and pronunciation, many of which reflect the patterns that operate in West African languages (for example, many West African languages don't have the English "th" sounds, and in AAE "th" is rendered with the next closest sound, as a "d," a "t," or an "f"); (2) verbal rituals from the Oral Tradition and the continued importance of the Word, as in African cultures; and (3) lexicon, or vocabulary, usually developed by giving special meanings to regular English words, a practice that goes back to enslavement and the need for a system of communication that only those in the enslaved community could understand.

3   Although here we are concerned only with the words that make up the lexicon, there are correct ways of saying these words, of talking Black, that is, that depend on knowledge of the rules of AAE grammar and pronunciation. Like the popular DJ said to a DUDE who phoned in a request for D. J. Jazzy Jeff & The Fresh Prince's JAM "Summertime": "Okay, man, I'll play it for you, but see, it ain't summ*er*time, it's summ*ah*time."

4   A complete inventory and analysis of AAE grammar and pronunciation and its African language sources is beyond the scope of this introduction. This Africanized style of speaking the English language is a complicated system, made even more complex by the existence of Euro-American patterns of English within the Africanized English system. Interested readers may consult Lorenzo Dow Turner's *Africanisms in the Gullah Dialect;* Molefi Kete Asante's "African Elements in African American English" in Joseph Holloway's excellent collection, *Africanisms in American Culture;* J. L. Dillard's *Black English;* Mervyn Alleyne's *Comparative Afro-American;* my own *Talkin and Testifyin;* John Baugh's *Black Street Speech;* Walter Wolfram and Nona H. Clarke's *Black-White Speech Relationships;* Hanni U. Taylor's *Standard English, Black English and Bidialectalism,* and William Labov's *Language in the Inner City.*

5   Listed below are only a few of the patterns of AAE grammar and pronunciation; these patterns are found in some of the words and expressions in this dictionary:

1.   *Final and post-vocalic "r."* The "r" sound at the end of a word and after a vowel is not heard in AAE. Instead, use a vowel sound, as in "summ*ah*time," as that big-city DJ instructed his caller. The expression "Sure, you're right" becomes SHOW YOU RIGHT. "Torn up" would be

TOE UP. Use YO instead of "your."And RAP Music's popular, if controversial, word HO is the AAE pronunciation of "whore." (Not to be confused with "hoe," as the white teacher in the film *House Party* did when she asked her Black male student why he called another Black male student's mother a "garden tool.")

2. *Final and medial consonants.* Reduce to a vowel sound, or a single consonant sound. Thus, for example, "cold" is COAL in AAE. This can get a bit complicated if a word requires the operation of two rules simultaneously, as for example in the phrase "torn up," where the double consonant "rn" must be reduced, and at the same time, the "r" after the vowel sound deleted. Applying the rules correctly gives you *toe*, not "ton," as a beginning student of Black lingo produced.

3. *Stress on the first syllable.* For most words, put the stress, or emphasis, on the first syllable of the word. For example, AAE speakers say PO-leece, not po-LEECE, and DE-troit, not De-TROIT.

4. *The vowel sound in words that rhyme with "think" and "ring."* In AAE, this vowel is pronounced like the vowel in "thank" and "rang." Thus, "sing" is rendered as *sang*, "drink" is pronounced *drank*, etc. This pattern produced the *thang* of Dr. Dre's "Nuthin' But a 'G' Thang," from his 1992 album *The Chronic.*

5. *Indicate tense (time) by context, not with an "s" or "ed."* For example, "Mary do anythang she want to" and "They look for him everywhere but never did find him."

6. *"Be" and "Bees" to indicate continuous action or infrequently recurring activity.* For example, "Every time we see him, he be dressed like that." This is the rule that produced "It Bees dat way," which may be shortened to simply BEES.

7. *Final "th" sounds become "t" or "f."* This pattern gives us DEF, as in "Def Comedy Jam," from the 1970s expression *doin it to death*, with the final "th" in "death" pronounced as an "f." This is also where WIT, as in the HIP HOP phrase GIT WIT *you*, comes from, with the final "th" in "with" rendered as a "t" sound.

8. *Is* and *Are* in sentences. These words aren't necessary to make full statements; nor are the contracted forms of these words (that is, the "'s" for "is" and the "'re" for "are"). This is the rule that allows *What up?* for "What's up?"

DISCUSSION QUESTIONS

1. What are some unique features of African-American English (AAE)? Cite at least two examples.
2. Does the way one speaks affect communication with others? If so, how?
3. In a small group, discuss the roles of Standard English and dialects, such as AAE. Should Standard English be the official language of the United States? As you discuss this issue, consider particularly the use of language at school and in the workplace.

WRITING TOPICS

1. The author suggests that African Americans modified their speech patterns and adopted some speech patterns of European Americans. Dr. W. E. B. Du Bois in his classic book, *The Souls of Black Folk,* suggests: "On the one hand, Black people are the product of their African heritage and culture; on the other, they are shaped by the demands of a Euro-American culture." Write an essay in which you interpret what you believe Dr. Du Bois means by his statement. Support your opinion with examples from experience, history, or literature.
2. In your journal, list some slang or popular expressions used either by you or by others. As a class, compile a list of words and expressions and write definitions for each. The class may wish to appoint a committee to develop a Class Slang Dictionary.
3. The American language has adopted words from many countries. West African countries have contributed such words as *goobers* (peanuts) and *yams* (sweet potatoes). In your writing journal, list other African words that have been adopted by the American language. You may check with people in your community or conduct research in the library.

THE GOOPHERED GRAPEVINE

Charles W. Chesnutt

Charles W. Chesnutt, born in 1858, was a teacher, a school principal, a court reporter, an accountant, and, finally, a fiction writer.
Celebrated as the father of the African-American short story,
Chesnutt's fiction presents not only local color stories, typical of
southern regional writing of his time, but also intraracism stories (the
problems and prejudices of black people who are light enough to
pass for white). Chesnutt's first story for *Atlantic* magazine, "The
Goophered Grapevine" (August 1887), was unique in that it was
from an oral tale his father-in-law's gardener had told him. It presents
the lore of "conjuration" (black hoodoo beliefs and practices). Since
the reading audience for the *Atlantic* in the late 1880s was primarily
white, Chesnutt's story gave many white people their first information about black folk culture. Chesnutt died in 1932.

Some years ago my wife was in poor health, and our family doctor, in
whose skill and honesty I had implicit confidence, advised a change of climate. I shared, from an unprofessional standpoint, his opinion that the
raw winds, the chill rains, and violent changes of temperature that charac-
terized the winters in the region of the Great Lakes tended to aggravate
my wife's difficulty, and would undoubtedly shorten her life if she
remained exposed to them. The doctor's advice was that we seek, not a
temporary place of sojourn, but a permanent residence, in a warmer and
more equable climate. I was engaged at the time in grape-culture in northern Ohio, and as I liked the business and had given it much study, I
decided to look for some other locality suitable for carrying it on. I
thought of sunny France, of sleepy Spain, of Southern California, but
there were objections to them all. It occurred to me that I might find what
I wanted in some one of our own Southern States. It was a sufficient time
after the war for conditions in the South to have become somewhat settled; and I was enough of a pioneer to start a new industry, if I could not
find a place where grape-culture had been tried. I wrote to a cousin who

had gone into the turpentine business in central North Carolina. He assured me, in response to my inquiries, that no better place could be found in the South than the State and neighborhood where he lived; the climate was perfect for health, and in conjunction with the soil, ideal for grape-culture; labor was cheap, and land could be bought for a mere song. He gave us a cordial invitation to come and visit him while we looked into the matter. We accepted the invitation, and after several days of leisurely travel, the last hundred miles of which were up a river on a side-wheel steamer, we reached our destination, a quaint old town, which I shall call Patesville, because, for one reason, that is not its name. There was a red brick markethouse in the public square, with a tall tower, which held a four-faced clock that struck the hours, and from which there pealed out a curfew at nine o'clock. There were two or three hotels, a court-house, a jail, stores, offices, and all the appurtenances of a county seat and a commercial emporium; for while Patesville numbered only four or five thousand inhabitants, of all shades of complexion, it was one of the principal towns in North Carolina, and had a considerable trade in cotton and naval stores. This business activity was not immediately apparent to my unaccustomed eyes. Indeed, when I first saw the town, there brooded over it a calm that seemed almost sabbatic in its restfulness, though I learned later on that underneath its somnolent exterior the deeper currents of life—love and hatred, joy and despair, ambition and avarice, faith and friendship—flowed not less steadily than in livelier latitudes.

2   We found the weather delightful at that season, the end of summer, and were hospitably entertained. Our host was a man of means and evidently regarded our visit as a pleasure, and we were therefore correspondingly at our ease, and in a position to act with the coolness of judgment desirable in making so radical a change in our lives. My cousin placed a horse and buggy at our disposal, and himself acted as our guide until I became somewhat familiar with the country.

3   I found that grape-culture, while it had never been carried on to any great extent, was not entirely unknown in the neighborhood. Several planters thereabouts had attempted it on a commercial scale, in former years, with greater or less success; but like most Southern industries, it had felt the blight of war and had fallen into desuetude.

4   I went several times to look at a place that I thought might suit me. It was a plantation of considerable extent, that had formerly belonged to a wealthy man by the name of McAdoo. The estate had been for years involved in litigation between disputing heirs, during which period shiftless cultivation had well-nigh exhausted the soil. There had been a vineyard of some extent on the place, but it had not been attended to since the war, and had lapsed into utter neglect. The vines—here partly supported by decayed and broken-down trellises, there twining themselves among the branches of the slender saplings which had sprung up among them—grew in wild and unpruned luxuriance, and the few scattered grapes they bore were the

undisputed prey of the first comer. The site was admirably adapted to grape-raising; the soil, with a little attention, could not have been better; and with the native grape, the luscious scuppernong, as my main reliance in the beginning, I felt sure that I could introduce and cultivate successfully a number of other varieties.

5   One day I went over with my wife to show her the place. We drove out of the town over a long wooden bridge that spanned a spreading mill-pond, passed the long whitewashed fence surrounding the county fairground, and struck into a road so sandy that the horse's feet sank to the fetlocks. Our route lay partly up hill and partly down, for we were in the sand-hill county; we drove past cultivated farms, and then by abandoned fields grown up in scrub-oak and short-leaved pine, and once or twice through the solemn aisles of the virgin forest, where the tall pines, well-nigh meeting over the narrow road, shut out the sun, and wrapped us in cloistral solitude. Once, at a cross-roads, I was in doubt as to the turn to take, and we sat there waiting ten minutes—we had already caught some of the native infection of restfulness—for some human being to come along, who could direct us on our way. At length a little negro girl appeared, walking straight as an arrow, with a piggin full of water on her head. After a little patient investigation, necessary to overcome the child's shyness, we learned what we wished to know, and at the end of about five miles from the town reached our destination.

6   We drove between a pair of decayed gateposts—the gate itself had long since disappeared—and up a straight sandy lane, between two lines of rotting rail fence, concealed by jimson-weeds and briers, to the open space where a dwelling-house had once stood, evidently a spacious mansion, if we might judge from the ruined chimneys that were still standing, and the brick pillars on which the sills rested. The house itself, we had been informed, had fallen a victim to the fortunes of war.

7   We alighted from the buggy, walked about the yard for a while, and then wandered off into the adjoining vineyard. Upon Annie's complaining of weariness I led the way back to the yard, where a pine log, lying under spreading elm, afforded a shady though somewhat hard seat. One end of the log was already occupied by a venerable-looking colored man. He held on his knees a hat full of grapes, over which he was smacking his lips with great gusto, and a pile of grape-skins near him indicated that the performance was no new thing. We approached him at an angle from the rear, and were close to him before he perceived us. He respectfully rose as we drew near, and was moving away, when I begged him to keep his seat.

8   "Don't let us disturb you," I said. "There is plenty of room for us all."

9   He resumed his seat with somewhat of embarrassment. While he had been standing, I had observed that he was a tall man, and, though slightly bowed by the weight of years, apparently quite vigorous. He was not entirely black, and this fact, together with the quality of his hair, which was about six inches long and very bushy, except on the top of his head, where he was quite bald, suggested a slight strain of other than negro blood. There

was a shrewdness in his eyes, too, which was not altogether African, and which, as we afterwards learned from experience, was indicative of a corresponding shrewdness in his character. He went on eating the grapes, but did not seem to enjoy himself quite so well as he had apparently done before he became aware of our presence.

10   "Do you live around here?" I asked, anxious to put him at his ease.

11   "Yas, suh. I lives des ober yander, behine de, nex' san'-hill, on de Lumberton plank-road."

12   "Do you know anything about the time when this vineyard was cultivated?"

13   "Lawd bless you, suh, I knows all about it. Dey ain' na'er a man in dis settlement w'at won' tell you ole Julius McAdoo 'uz bawn en raise' on dis yer same plantation. Is you de Norv'n gemman w'at's gwine ter buy de ole vimya'd?"

14   "I am looking at it," I replied; "but I don't know that I shall care to buy unless I can be reasonably sure of making something out of it."

15   "Well, suh, you is a stranger ter me, en I is a stranger ter you, en we is bofe strangers ter one anudder, but 'f I 'uz in yo' place, I would n' buy dis vimya'd."

16   "Why not?" I asked.

17   "Well, I dunno whe'r you b'lieves in cunj'in' er not,—some er de w'ite folks don't, er says dey don't,—but de truf er de matter is dat dis yer ole vimya'd is goophered."

18   "Is what?" I asked, not grasping the meaning of this unfamiliar word.

19   "Is goophered,—conju'd, bewitch'."

20   He imparted this information with such solemn earnestness, and with such an air of confidential mystery, that I felt somewhat interested, while Annie was evidently much impressed, and drew closer to me.

21   "How do you know it is bewitched?" I asked.

22   "I would n' spec' fer you ter b'lieve me 'less you know all 'bout de fac's. But ef you en young miss dere doan' mine' lis'nin' ter a ole nigger run on a minute er two w'ile you er restin', I kin 'splain to you how it all happen'."

23   We assured him that we would be glad to hear how it all happened, and he began to tell us. At first the current of his memory—or imagination—seemed somewhat sluggish; but as his embarrassment wore off, his language flowed more freely, and the story acquired perspective and coherence. As he became more and more absorbed in the narrative, his eyes assumed a dreamy expression, and he seemed to lose sight of his auditors, and to be living over again in monologue his life on the old plantation.

24   "Ole Mars Dugal' McAdoo," he began, "bought dis place long many years befo' de wah, en I 'member well w'en he sot out all dis yer part er de plantation in scuppernon's. De vimes growed monst'us fas', en Mars Dugal' made a thousan' gallon er scuppernon' wine eve'y year.

25   "Now, ef dey's an'thing a nigger lub, nex' ter 'possum, en chick'n, en watermillyums, it's scuppernon's. Dey ain' nuffin dat kin stan' up side'n de scuppernon' for sweetness; sugar ain't a suckumstance ter scuppernon'.

W'en de season is nigh 'bout ober, en de grapes begin ter swivel up des a little wid de wrinkles er ole age,—w'en de skin git sof' en brown,—den de
scuppernon' make you smack yo' lip en roll yo' eye en wush fer mo'; so I
reckon it ain' very 'stonishin' dat niggers lub scuppernon'.

26   "Dey wuz a sight er niggers in de naberhood er de vimya'd. Dere wuz
Ole Mars Henry Brayboy's niggers, en Ole Mars Jeems McLean's niggers,
en Mars Dugal's own niggers; den dey wuz a settlement er free niggers en
po' buckrahs down by de Wim'l'ton Road, en Mars Dugal' had de only
vimya'd in de naberhood. I reckon it ain' so much so nowadays, but befo'
de wah, in slab'ry times, a nigger did n' mine goin' fi' er ten in a night, w'en
dey wuz sump'n good ter eat at de yuther een'.

27   "So atter a w'ile Mars Dugal' begin ter miss his scuppernon's. Co'se he
'cuse' de niggers er it, but dey all 'nied it ter de las'. Mars Dugal' sot spring
guns en steel traps, en he en de oberseah sot up nights once't er twice't, tel
one night Mars Dugal'—he 'uz a monst'us keerless man—got his leg shot
full er cow-peas. But somehow er nudder dey could n' nebber ketch none
er de niggers. I dunner how it happen, but it happen des like I tell you, en
de grapes kep' on agoin' des de same.

28   "But bimeby ole Mars Dugal' fix' up a plan ter stop it. Dey wuz a conjuh 'oman livin' down 'mongs' de free niggers on de Wim'l'ton Road, en all
de darkies from Rockfish ter Beaver Crick wuz feared er her. She could wuk
de mos' powerfulles' kin' er goopher,—could make people hab fits, er
rheumatiz, er make 'em des dwinel away en die; en dey say she went out
ridin' de niggers at night, fer she wuz a witch 'sides bein' a conjuh 'oman.
Mars Dugal' hearn 'bout Aun' Peggy's doin's, en begun ter 'flect whe'r er
no he could n' git her ter he'p him keep de niggers off'n de grapevimes.
One day in de spring er de year, ole miss pack' up a basket er chick'n en
poun'-cake, en a bottle er scuppernon' wine, en Mars Dugal' tuk it in his
buggy en driv ober to Aun' Peggy's cabin. He 'tuk de basket in, en had a
29 long talk wid Aun' Peggy.

"De nex' day Aun' Peggy come up ter de vimya'd. De niggers seed her
slippin' 'roun', en dey soon foun' out what she 'uz doin' dere. Mars Dugal'
had hi'ed her ter goopher de grapevimes. She sa'ntered 'roun' 'mongs' de
vimes, en tuk a leaf fum dis one, en a grape-hull fum dat one, en a grape-
seed fum anudder one; en den a little twig fum here, en a little pinch er dirt-
fum dere,—en put it all in a big black bottle, wid a snake's toof en a speckle'
hen's gall en some ha'rs fum a black cat's tail, en den fill' de bottle wid scuppernon' wine. W'en she got de goopher all ready en fix', she tuk'n went out
in de woods en buried it under de root uv a red oak tree, en den come back
en tole one er de niggers she done goopher de grapevimes, en a'er a nigger
30 w'at eat dem grapes 'ud be sho ter die inside'n twel' mont's.

"Atter dat de niggers let de scuppernon's 'lone, en Mars Dugal' did n'
hab no 'casion ter fine no mo' fault; en de season wuz mos' gone, w'en a
strange gemman stop at de plantation one night ter see Mars Dugal' on
some business; en his coachmen, seein' de scuppernon's growin' so nice en

sweet, slip 'roun' behine de smoke-house, en et all de scuppernon's he could hole. Nobody did n' notice it at de time, but dat night, on de way home, de gemman's hoss runned away en kill' de coachman. W'en we hearn de noos, Aun' Lucy, de cook, she up 'n say she seed de stranger nigger eat'n er de scuppernon's behine de smoke-house; en den we knowed de goopher had b'en er wukkin'. Den one er de nigger chilluns runned away fum de quarters one day, en got in de scuppernon's, en died de nex' week. W'ite folks say he die' er de fevuh, but de niggers knowed it wuz de goopher. So you k'n be sho de darkies did n' hab much ter do wid dem scuppenon' vimes.

31 "W'en de scuppernon' season 'uz ober fer dat year, Mars Dugal' foun' he had made fifteen hund'ed gallon er wine; en one er de niggers hearn him laffin' wid de oberseah fit ter kill, en sayin' dem fifteen hund'ed gallon er wine wuz monst'us good intrus' on de ten dollars he laid out on de vimya'd. So I 'low ez he paid Aun' Peggy ten dollars fer to goopher de grapevimes.

32 "De goopher did n' wuk no mo' tel de nex' summer, we'n 'long to'ds de middle er de season one er de fiel' han's died; en ez dat lef' Mars Dugal' sho't er han's, he went off ter town fer ter buy anudder. He fotch de noo nigger home wid 'im. He wuz er ole nigger, er de color er a gingy-cake, en ball ez a hoss-apple on de top er his head. He wuz a peart ole nigger, do', en could do a big day's wuk.

33 "Now it happen dat one er de niggers on de nex' plantation, one er ole Mars Henry Brayboy's niggers had runned away de day befo', en tuk ter de swamp, en ole Mars Dugal' en some er de yuther nabor w'ite folks had gone out wid dere guns en dere dogs fer ter he'p 'em hunt fer de nigger; en de han's on our own plantation wuz all so flusterated dat we fuhgot ter tell de noo han' 'bout de goopher on de scuppernon' vimes. Co'se he smell de grapes en see de vimes, an atter dahk de fus' thing he done wuz ter slip off ter de grapevimes 'dout sayin' nuffin to nobody. Nex' mawnin' he tole some er de niggers about de fine bait er scuppernon' he et de night befo'.

34 "W'en dey tole 'im 'bout de goopher on de grapevimes, he 'uz dat tarrified dat he turn pale, en look des like he gwine ter die right in his tracks. De oberseah come up en axed w'at 'uz de matter; en w'en dey tole 'im Henry be'n eatin' er de scuppernon's, en got de goopher on 'im, he gin Henry a big drink er w'iskey, en 'low day de nex' rainy day he take 'im ober ter Aun' Peggy's, en see ef she would n' take de goopher off'n him, seein' ez he did n' know nuffin erbout it tel he done et de grapes.

35 "Sho nuff, it rain de nex' day, en de oberseah went ober ter Aun' Peggy's wid Henry. En Aun' Peggy say dat bein' ez Henry did n' know 'bout de goopher, en et de grapes in ign'ance er de conseq'ences, she reckon she mought be able fer ter take de goopher off'n him. So she fotch out er bottle wid some conjuh medicine in it, en po'd some out in a go'd for Henry ter drink. He manage ter git it down; he say it tas'e like whiskey wid sump'n bitter in it. She 'lowed dat 'ud keep de goopher off'n him tel de spring; but w'en de sap begin ter rise in de grapevimes he ha'ter come en see her ag'in, en she tell him w'at e's ter do.

36   "Nex' spring, w'en de sap commence' ter rise in de scuppernon' vime, Henry tuk a ham one night. Whar 'd he git de ham? *I* doan know; dey wa'n't no hams on de plantation 'cep'n' w'at 'uz in de smoke-house, but I never see Henry 'bout de smoke-house. But ez I wuz a sayin', he tuk de ham ober ter Aun' Peggy's; en Aun' Peggy tole 'im dat w'en Mars Dugal' begin ter prune de grapevimes, he mus' go en take 'n scrape off de sap whar it ooze out'n de cut een's er de vimes, en 'n'int his ball head wid it; en ef he do dat once't a year de goopher would n' wuk agin 'im long ez he done it. En bein' ez he fotch her de ham, she fix' it so he kin eat all de scuppernon' he want.

37   "So Henry 'n'int his head wid de sap out'n de big grapevime des ha'f way 'twix' de quarters en de big house, en de goopher nebber wuk agin him dat summer. But de beatenes' thing you eber see happen ter Henry. Up ter dat time he wuz ez ball ez a sweeten' 'tater, but des ez soon ez de young leaves begun ter come out on de grapevimes, de ha'r begun ter grow out on Henry's head, en by de middle er de summer he had de bigges' head er ha'r on de plantation. Befo' dat, Henry had tol'able good ha'r 'round' de aidges, but soon ez de young grapes begun ter come, Henry's ha'r begun to quirl all up in little balls, des like dis yer reg'lar grapy ha'r, en by de time de grapes got ripe his head look des like a bunch er grapes. Combin' it did n' do no good; he wuk at it ha'f de night wid er Jim Crow, en think he git it straighten out, but in de mawnin' de grapes 'ud be dere des de same. So he gin it up, en tried ter keep de grapes down by havin' his ha'r cut sho't.

38   "But dat wa'n't de quares' thing 'bout de goopher. When Henry come ter de plantation, he wuz gittin' a little ole an stiff in de j'ints. But dat summer he got des ez spry en libely ez any young nigger on de plantation; fac', he got so biggity dat Mars Jackson, de oberseah, ha' ter th'eaten ter whip 'im if he did n' stop cuttin' up his didos en behave hisse'f. But de mos' cur'ouses' thing happen' in de fall, when de sap begin ter go down in de grapevimes. Fus', when de grapes 'uz gethered, de knots begun ter straighten out'n Henry's ha'r; en w'en de leaves begin ter fall, Henry's ha'r 'mence' ter drap out; en when de vimes 'uz bar', Henry's head wuz baller 'n it wuz in de spring, en he begin ter git ole en stiff in de j'ints ag'in, en paid no mo' 'tention ter de gals dyoin' er de whole winter. En nex' spring, w'en he rub de sap on ag'in, he got young ag'in, en so soopl en libely dat none er de young niggers on de plantation could n' jump, ner dance, ner hoe ez much cotton ez Henry. But in de fall er de year his grapes 'mence' ter straighten out, en his j'ints ter git stiff, en his ha'r drap off, en de rheumatiz begin ter wrastle wid'im.

39   "Now, ef you'd 'a' knowed ole Mars Dugal' McAdoo, you'd 'a' knowed dat it ha' ter be a mighty rainy day when he could n' fine sump'n fer his niggers to do, en it ha' ter be a mighty little hole he could n' crawl thoo, en ha' ter be a monst'us cloudy night when a dollar git by him in the darkness; en w'en he see how Henry git young in de spring en ole in de fall, he 'lowed ter hisse'f ez how he could make mo' money out'n Henry dan by wukkin' him in de cotton-fiel'. 'Long de nex' spring, atter de sap 'mence' ter rise, en

Henry 'n'int 'is head en sta'ted fer ter git young en soopl, Mars Dugal' up 'n tuk Henry ter town, en sole 'im fer fifteen hunder' dollars. Co'se de man w'at bought Henry did n' know nuffin 'bout de goopher, en Mars Dugal' did n' see no 'casion fer ter tell 'im. Long to'ds de fall, w'en de sap went down, Henry begin ter git ole ag'in same ez yu-zhal, en his noo marster begin to git skeered les'n he gwine ter lose his fifteen-hunder'-dollar nigger. He sent fer a mighty fine doctor, but de med'cine did n' 'pear ter do no good; de goopher had a good holt. Henry tole de doctor 'bout de goopher, but de doctor des laff at 'im.

40   "One day in de winter Mars Dugal' went ter town, en wuz santerin' 'long de Main Street, when who should he meet but Henry's noo marster. Dey said 'Hoddy,' en Mars Dugal' ax 'im ter hab a seegyar; en atter dey run on awhile 'bout de craps en de weather, Mars Dugal' ax 'im, sorter keerless, like ez ef he des thought of it,—

41   "'How you like de nigger I sole you las' spring?'

42   "Henry's master shuck his head en knock de ashes off'n his seegyar.

43   "'Spec' I made a bad bahgin when I bought dat nigger. Henry done good wuk all de summer, but sence de fall set in he 'pears ter be sorter pinin' away. Dey ain' nuffin pertickler de matter wid 'im—leastways de doctor say so—'cep'n' a tech er de rheumatiz; but his ha'r is all fell out, en ef he, don't pick up his strenk mighty soon, I spec' I'm gwine ter lose 'im.'

44   "Dey smoked on awhile, en bimeby ole mars say, 'Well, a bahgin's a bah-gin, but you en me is good fren's, en I doan wan 'ter see you lose all de money you paid fer dat nigger; en ef wa't you say is so, en I ain't 'sputin' it, he ain't wuf much now. I 'spec's you wukked him too ha'd dis summer, er e'se de swamps down here don't agree wid de san'-hill nigger. So you des lemme know, en ef he gits any wusser I 'll be willin' ter gib ye five hund'ed dollars fer 'im, en take my chances on his livin'.'

45   "Sho 'nuff, when Henry begun ter draw up wid de rheumatiz en it look like he gwine ter die fer sho, his noo marster sen' fer Mars Dugal', en Mars Dugal' gin him what he promus, en brung Henry home ag'in. He tuk good keer uv 'im dyoin' er de winter,—give 'im w'iskey ter rub his rheumatiz, en terbacker ter smoke, en all he want ter eat,—'caze a nigger w'at he could make a thousan' dollars a year off'n did n' grow on eve'y huckleberry bush.

46   "Nex' spring, w'en de sap ris en Henry's ha'r commence' ter sprout, Mars Dugal' sole 'im ag'in, down in Robeson County dis time; en he kep' dat sellin' business up fer five year er mo'. Henry nebber say nuffin 'bout de goopher ter his noo marsters, 'caze he know he gwine ter be tuk good keer uv de nex' winter, w'en Mars Dugal' buy him back. En Mars Dugal' made 'nuff money off'n Henry ter buy anudder plantation ober on Beaver Crick.

47   "But 'long 'bout de een' er dat five year dey come a stranger ter stop at de plantation. De fus' day he 'uz dere he went out wid Mars Dugal' en spent all de mawnin' lookin' ober de vimya'd, en atter dinner dey spent all de evenin' playin' kya'ds. De niggers soon 'skiver' dat he wuz a Yankee, en dat he come down ter Norf C'lina fer ter l'arn de w'ite folks how to raise grapes

en make wine. He promus Mars Dugal' he c'd make de grapevimes b'ar twice't ez many grapes, en dat de noo winepress he wuz a-sellin' would make mo' d'n twice't ez many gallons er wine. En ole Mars Dugal' des drunk it all in, des 'peared ter be bewitch' wid dat Yankee. W'en de darkies see dat Yankee runnin' 'roun' de vimya'd en diggin' under de grapevimes, dey shuk dere heads, en 'lowed dat dey feared Mars Dugal' losin' his min'. Mars Dugal' had all de dirt dug away fum under de roots er all de scuppernon' vimes, an' let 'em stan' dat away fer a week er mo'. Den dat Yankee made de niggers fix up a mixtry er lime en ashes en manyo, en po' it 'roun' de roots er de grapevimes. Den he 'vise Mars Dugal' fer ter trim de vimes close't, en Mars Dugal' tuck 'n done everything de Yankee tole him ter do. Dyoin' all er dis time, mind yer, dis yer Yankee wuz libbin' off'n de fat er de lan', at de big house, en playin' kya'ds wid Mars Dugal' eve'y night; en dey say Mars Dugal' los' mo'n a thousan' dollars dyoin' er de week dat Yankee wuz a-ruinin' de grapevimes.

48 "W'en de sap ris nex' spring, ole Henry 'n'inted his head ez yuzhal, en his ha'r 'mence' ter grow des de same ez it done eve'y year. De scuppernon' vimes growed monst's fas', en de leaves wuz greener en thicker dan dey eber be'n dyoin' my remem'ance; en Henry's ha'r growed out thicker dan eber, en he 'peared ter git younger 'n younger, en soopler 'n soopler; en seein' ez he wuz sho't ter han's dat spring, havin' tuk in consid'able noo groun', Mars Dugal' 'cluded he would n' sell Henry 'tel he git de crap in en de cotton chop'. So he kep' Henry on de plantation.

49 "But 'long 'bout time fer de grapes ter come on de scuppernon' vimes, dey 'peared ter come a change ober 'em; de leaves withered en swivel' up, en de young grapes turn' yaller, en bimeby eve'ybody on de plantation could see dat de whole vimeya'd wuz dyin'. Mars Dugal' tuk 'n water de vimes en done all he could, but 't wa'n' no use; dat Yankee had done bus' de water-millyum. One time de vimes picked up a bit, en Mars Dugal' 'lowed dey wuz gwine ter come out ag'in; but dat Yankee done dug too close under de roots, en prune de branches too close ter de vime, en all dat lime en ashes done burn' de life out'n de vimes, en dey kep' a-with'in en a-swivelin'.

50 "All dis time de goopher wuz a-wukkin.' When de vimes sta'ted ter wither, Henry 'mence' ter complain er his rheumatiz; en when de leaves begin ter dry up, his ha'r 'mence' ter drap out. When de vimes fresh' up a bit, Henry 'd git peart ag'in, en when de vimes wither' ag'in, Henry 'd git ole ag'in, en des kep' gittin' mo' en mo' fitten fer nuffin; he des pined away, en pined away, en fine'ly tuk ter his cabin; en when de big vime whar he got de sap ter 'n'int his head withered en turned yaller en died, Henry died too,—des went out sorter like a cannel. Dey did n't 'pear ter be nuffin de matter wid 'im, 'cep'n' de rheumatiz, but his strenk des dwinel' away 'tel he did n' hab ernuff lef' ter draw his bref. De goopher had got de under holt, en th'owed Henry dat time fer good en all.

51 "Mars Dugal' tuk on mightily 'bout losin' his vimes en his nigger in de same year; en he swo' dat ef he could git holt er dat Yankee he'd wear 'im

ter a frazzle, en den chaw up de frazzle; en he'd done it, too, for Mars Dugal' 'uz a monst'us brash man w'en he once git started. He sot de vimya'd out ober ag'in, but it wuz th'ee er fo' year befo' de vimes got ter b'arin' any scuppernon's.

52 "W'en de wah broke out, Mars Dugal' raise' a comp'ny, en went off ter fight de Yankees. He say he mighty glad dat wah come, en he des want ter kill a Yankee fer eve'y dollar he los' 'long er dat grape-raisin' Yankee. En I 'spec' he would 'a' done it, too, if de Yankees had n' s'picioned sump'n, en killed him fus'. Atter de s'render ole miss move' ter town, de niggers all scattered 'way fum de plantation, en de vimya'd ain' be'n cultervated sence."

53 "Is that story true?" asked Annie doubtfully, but seriously, as the old man concluded his narrative.

54 "It's des ez true ez I 'm a-settin' here, miss. Dey 's a easy way ter prove it: I kin lead de way right ter Henry's grave ober yander in de plantation buryin'-groun'. En I tell yer w'at, marster, I would n' vise you to buy dis yer ole vimya'd, 'case de goopher 's on it yit, en dey ain' no tellin' w'en it's gwine ter crap out."

55 "But I thought you said all the old vines died."

56 "Dey did 'pear ter die, but a few un 'em come out ag'in, en is mixed in 'mongs' de yuthers. I ain' skeered ter eat de grapes, 'caze I knows de old vimes fum de noo ones; but wid strangers dey ain' no tellin' w'at mought happen. I would n' 'vise yer ter buy dis vimya'd."

57 I bought the vineyard, nevertheless, and it has been for a long time in a thriving condition, and is often referred to by the local press as a striking illustration of the opportunities open to Northern capital in the develop-ment of Southern industries. The luscious scuppernong holds first rank among our grapes, though we cultivate a great many other varieties, and our income from grapes packed and shipped to the Northern markets is quite considerable. I have not noticed any developments of the goopher in the vineyard, although I have a mild suspicion that our colored assistants do not suffer from want of grapes during the season.

58 I found, when I bought the vineyard, that Uncle Julius had occupied a cabin on the place for many years, and derived a respectable revenue from the product of the neglected grapevines. This, doubtless, accounted for his advice to me not to buy the vineyard, though whether it inspired the goo-pher story I am unable to state. I believe, however, that the wages I paid him for his services as coachman, for I gave him employment in that capac-ity, were more than an equivalent for anything he lost by the sale of the vineyard.

DISCUSSION QUESTIONS

1. Uncle Julius displays his shrewdness and self-interest as he attempts to outwit the white buyer and keep his own economic advantage. Select specific passages from the story which support this view of Uncle Julius's actions.
2. "The Goophered Grapevine" is a framed story, or a story within a story. How does this framing add to the development of the story?
3. Dialect can sometimes be difficult to read. Nevertheless, it gives readers a sense of the language, style, and sounds of how a particular group of people, either in a specific region of the United States or from a specific time period, talked. Highlight some specific examples from Uncle Julius's dialect.

WRITING TOPICS

1. Using elements from Geneva Smitherman's "Introduction" from *Black Talk,* analyze a paragraph of dialect from the story. Identify as many African-American English (AAE) elements as possible. Write an essay showing the connection between AAE rules and dialect from the late 1880s.
2. In your journal define four nonstandard words or forms of words that you and your friends use when talking with each other. Include with each definition a sentence showing the word or the form of the word in context.

SEE HOW THEY RUN

Mary Elizabeth Vroman

Mary Elizabeth Vroman was born in Buffalo, New York, in 1923 and raised in the British West Indies. She graduated from Alabama State University. "See How They Run" and "And Have Not Charity," two of her short stories, were published in the *Ladies' Home Journal*. Her only adult novel, *Esther*, was published in 1963 and her young-adult novel, *Harlem Summer* in 1967. In 1953, her short story "See How They Run" was made into a film by MGM entitled *Bright Road*. Ms. Vroman was the first African-American woman granted membership in the Screen Writers Guild. She died in 1967 from complications of surgery.

1   A bell rang. Jane Richards squared the sheaf of records decisively in the large manila folder, placed it in the right-hand corner of her desk, and stood up. The chatter of young voices subsided, and forty-three small faces looked solemnly and curiously at the slight young figure before them. The bell stopped ringing.

2   I wonder if they're as scared of me as I am of them. She smiled brightly.

3   "Good morning, children, I am Miss Richards." As if they don't know—the door of the third-grade room had a neat new sign pasted above it with her name in bold black capitals; and anyway, a new teacher's name is the first thing that children find out about on the first day of school. Nevertheless she wrote it for their benefit in large white letters on the blackboard.

4   "I hope we will all be happy working and playing together this year." Now why does that sound so trite? "As I call the roll will you please stand, so that I may get to know you as soon as possible, and if you like to you may tell me something about yourselves, how old you are, where you live, what your parents do, and perhaps something about what you did during the summer."

5   Seated, she checked the names carefully. "Booker T. Adams."

6   Booker stood, gangling and stoop-shouldered: he began to recite tiredly. "My name is Booker T. Adams, I'se ten years old." Shades of Uncle Tom!

"I live on Painter's Path." He paused, the look he gave her was tinged with something very akin to contempt. "I didn't do nothing in the summer," he said deliberately.

7   "Thank you, Booker." Her voice was even. "George Allen." Must remember to correct that stoop. . . . Where is Painter's Path? . . . How to go about correcting those speech defects? . . . Go easy, Jane, don't antagonize them. . . . They're clean enough, but this is the first day. . . . How can one teacher do any kind of job with a load of forty-three? . . . Thank heaven the building is modern and well built even though it is overcrowded, not like some I've seen—no potbellied stove.

8   "Sarahlene Clover Babcock." Where do these names come from? . . . Up from slavery. . . . How high is up. Jane smothered a sudden desire to giggle. Outside she was calm and poised and smiling. Clearly she called the names, listening with interest, making a note here and there, making no corrections—not yet.

9   She experienced a moment of brief inward satisfaction: I'm doing very well, this is what is expected of me . . . Orientation to Teaching . . . Miss Murray's voice beat a distant tattoo in her memory. Miss Murray with the Junoesque figure and the moon face . . . "The ideal teacher personality is one which, combining in itself all the most desirable qualities, expresses itself with quiet assurance in its endeavor to mold the personalities of the students in the most desirable patterns." . . . Dear dull Miss Murray.

10   She made mental estimates of the class. What a cross section of my people they represent, she thought. Here and there signs of evident poverty, here and there children of obviously well-to-do parents.

11   "My name is Rachel Veronica Smith. I am nine years old. I live at Six-oh-seven Fairview Avenue. My father is a Methodist minister. My mother is a housewife. I have two sisters and one brother. Last summer Mother and Daddy took us all to New York to visit my Aunt Jen. We saw lots of wonderful things. There are millions and millions of people in New York. One day we went on a ferryboat all the way up the Hudson River—that's a great big river as wide across as this town, and—"

12   The children listened wide-eyed. Jane listened carefully. She speaks good English. Healthy, erect, and even perhaps a little smug. Immaculately well dressed from the smoothly braided hair, with two perky bows, to the shiny brown oxfords . . . Bless you, Rachel, I'm so glad to have you.

13   "—and the buildings are all very tall, some of them nearly reach the sky."

14   "Haw-haw"—this from Booker, cynically.

15   "Well, they are too." Rachel swung around, fire in her eyes and insistence in every line of her round, compact body.

16   "Ain't no building as tall as the sky, is dere, Miz Richards?"

17   Crisis No. 1. Jane chose her answer carefully. As high as the sky . . . mustn't turn this into a lesson in science . . . all in due time. "The sky is a long way out, Booker, but the buildings in New York are very tall indeed.

Rachel was only trying to show you how very tall they are. In fact, the tallest building in the whole world is in New York City."

18   "They call it the Empire State Building," interrupted Rachel, heady with her new knowledge and Jane's corroboration.

19   Booker wasn't through. "You been dere, Miz Richards?"

20   "Yes, Booker, many times. Someday I shall tell you more about it. Maybe Rachel will help me. Is there anything you'd like to add, Rachel?"

21   "I would like to say that we are glad you are our new teacher, Miss Richards." Carefully she sat down, spreading her skirt with her plump hands, her smile angelic.

22   Now I'll bet me a quarter her reverend father told her to say that. "Thank you, Rachel."

23   The roll call continued. . . . Tanya, slight and pinched, with the toes showing through the very white sneakers, the darned and faded but clean blue dress, the gentle voice like a tinkling bell, and the beautiful sensitive face. . . . Boyd and Lloyd, identical in their starched overalls, and the slightly vacant look. . . . Marjorie Lee, all of twelve years old, the well-developed body moving restlessly in the childish dress, the eyes too wise, the voice too high. . . . Joe Louis, the intelligence in the brilliant black eyes gleaming above the threadbare clothes. Lives of great men all remind us—Well, I have them all . . . Frederick Douglass, Franklin Delano, Abraham Lincoln, Booker T., Joe Louis, George Washington. . . . What a great burden you bear, little people, heirs to all your parents' stillborn dreams of greatness. I must not fail you. The last name on the list . . . C. T. Young. Jane paused, small lines creasing her forehead. She checked the list again.

24   "C. T., what is your name? I only have your initials on my list."

25   "Dat's all my name, C. T. Young."

26   "No, dear, I mean what does C. T. stand for? Is it Charles or Clarence?"

27   "No'm, jest C. T."

28   "But I can't put that in my register, dear."

29   Abruptly Jane rose and went to the next room. Rather timidly she waited to speak to Miss Nelson, the second-grade teacher, who had the formidable record of having taught all of sixteen years. Miss Nelson was large and smiling.

30   "May I help you, dear?"

31   "Yes, please. It's about C. T. Young. I believe you had him last year."

32   "Yes, and the year before that. You'll have him two years too."

33   "Oh? Well, I was wondering what name you registered him under. All the information I have is C. T. Young."

34   "That's all there is, honey. Lots of these children only have initials."

35   "You mean . . . can't something be done about it?"

36   "What?" Miss Nelson was still smiling, but clearly impatient.

37   "I . . . well . . . thank you." Jane left quickly.

38   Back in Room 3 the children were growing restless. Deftly Jane passed out the rating tests and gave instructions. Then she called C. T. to her. He

was as small as an eight-year-old, and hungry-looking, with enormous guile-less eyes and a beautifully shaped head.

39   "How many years did you stay in the second grade, C. T.?"

40   "Two."

41   "And in the first?"

42   "Two."

43   "How old are you?"

44   "'Leven."

45   "When will you be twelve?"

46   "Nex' month."

47   And they didn't care . . . nobody ever cared enough about one small boy to give him a name.

48   "You are a very lucky little boy, C. T. Most people have to take the name somebody gave them whether they like it or not, but you can choose your very own."

49   "Yeah?" The dark eyes were belligerent. "My father named me C. T. after hisself, Miz Richards, an dat's my name."

50   Jane felt unreasonably irritated. "How many children are there in your family, C. T.?"

51   "'Leven."

52   "How many are there younger than you?" she asked.

53   "Seven."

54   Very gently. "Did you have your breakfast this morning, dear?"

55   The small figure in the too-large trousers and the too-small shirt drew itself up to full height. "Yes'm, I had fried chicken, and rice, and coffee, and rolls, and oranges too."

56   Oh, you poor darling. You poor proud lying darling. Is that what you'd like for breakfast?

57   She asked, "Do you like school, C. T.?"

58   "Yes'm," he told her suspiciously.

59   She leafed through the pile of records. "Your record says you haven't been coming to school very regularly. Why?"

60   "I dunno."

61   "Did you ever bring a lunch?"

62   "No'm, I eats such a big breakfast, I doan git hungry at lunchtime."

63   "Children need to eat lunch to help them grow tall and strong, C. T. So from now on you'll eat lunch in the lunchroom"—an after-thought: Perhaps it's important to make him think I believe him—"and from now on maybe you'd better not eat such a big breakfast."

64   Decisively she wrote his name at the top of what she knew to be an already too large list. "Only those in absolute necessity," she had been told by Mr. Johnson, the kindly, harassed principal. "We'd like to feed them all, so many are underfed, but we just don't have the money." Well, this was absolute necessity if she ever saw it.

65   "What does your father do, C. T.?"

66   "He work at dat big factory cross-town, he make plenty money, Miz Richards." The record said "Unemployed."

67   "Would you like to be named Charles Thomas?"

68   The expressive eyes darkened, but the voice was quiet. "No'm."

69   "Very well." Thoughtfully Jane opened the register; she wrote firmly C. T. Young.

70   October is a witching month in the Southern United States. The richness of the golds and reds and browns of the trees forms an enchanted filigree through which the lilting voices of children at play seem to float, embodied like so many nymphs of Pan.

71   Jane had played a fast-and-furious game of tag with her class and now she sat quietly under the gnarled old oak, watching the tireless play, feeling the magic of the sun through the leaves warmly dappling her skin, the soft breeze on the nape of her neck like a lover's hands, and her own drowsy lethargy. Paul, Paul my darling . . . how long for us now? She had worshiped Paul Carlyle since they were freshmen together. On graduation day he had slipped the small circlet of diamonds on her finger. . . . "A teacher's salary is small, Jane. Maybe we'll be lucky enough to get work together, then in a year or so we can be married. Wait for me, darling, wait for me!"

72   But in a year or so Paul had gone to war, and Jane went out alone to teach. . . . Lansing Creek—one year . . . the leaky roof, the potbellied stove, the water from the well . . . Maryweather Point—two years . . . the tight-lipped spinster principal with the small, vicious soul. . . . Three hard lonely years and then she had been lucky.

73   The superintendent had praised her. "You have done good work, Miss—ah—Jane. This year you are to be placed at Centertown High—that is, of course, if you care to accept the position."

74   Jane had caught her breath. Centertown was the largest and best equipped of all the schools in the county, only ten miles from home and Paul—for Paul had come home, older, quieter, but still Paul. He was teaching now more than a hundred miles away, but they went home every other weekend to their families and each other. . . . "Next summer you'll be Mrs. Paul Carlyle, darling. It's hard for us to be apart so much. I guess we'll have to be for a long time till I can afford to support you. But, sweet, these little tykes need us so badly." He had held her close, rubbing the nape of the neck under the soft curls. "We have a big job, those of us who teach," he had told her, "a never-ending and often thankless job, Jane, to supply the needs of these kids who lack so much." Dear, warm, big, strong, gentle Paul.

75   They wrote each other long letters, sharing plans and problems. She wrote him about C. T. "I've adopted him, darling. He's so pathetic and so determined to prove that he's not. He learns nothing at all, but I can't let myself believe that he's stupid, so I keep trying."

76   "Miz Richards, please, ma'am." Tanya's beautiful amber eyes sought hers timidly. Her brown curls were tangled from playing, her cheeks a bright red under the tightly stretched olive skin. The elbows jutted awkwardly out of

the sleeves of the limp cotton dress, which could not conceal the finely chiseled bones in their pitiable fleshlessness. As always when she looked at her, Jane thought, What a beautiful child! So unlike the dark, gaunt, morose mother, and the dumpy, pasty-faced father who had visited her that first week. A fairy's changeling. You'll make a lovely angel to grace the throne of God, Tanya! Now what made me think of that?

77   "Please, ma'am, I'se sick."

78   Gently Jane drew her down beside her. She felt the parchment skin, noted the unnaturally bright eyes. Oh, dear God, she's burning up! "Do you hurt anywhere, Tanya?"

79   "My head, ma'am and I'se so tired." Without warning she began to cry.

80   "How far do you live, Tanya?"

81   "Two miles."

82   "You walk to school?"

83   "Yes'm."

84   "Do any of your brothers have a bicycle?"

85   "No'm."

86   "Rachel!" Bless you for always being there when I need you. "Hurry, dear, to the office and ask Mr. Johnson please to send a big boy with a bicycle to take Tanya home. She's sick."

87   Rachel ran.

88   "Hush now, dear, we'll get some cool water, and then you'll be home in a little while. Did you feel sick this morning?"

89   "Yes'm, but Mot Dear sent me to school anyway. She said I just wanted to play hooky." Keep smiling, Jane. Poor, ambitious, well-meaning parents, made bitter at the seeming futility of dreaming dreams for this lovely child . . . willing her to rise above the drabness of your own meager existence . . . too angry with life to see that what she needs most is your love and care and right now medical attention.

90   Jane bathed the child's forehead with cool water at the fountain. Do the white schools have a clinic? I must ask Paul. Do they have a lounge or a couch where they can lay one wee sick head? Is there anywhere in this town free medical service for one small child . . . born black?

91   The boy with the bicycle came. "Take care of her now, ride slowly and carefully, and take her straight home. . . . Keep the newspaper over your head, Tanya, to keep out the sun, and tell your parents to call the doctor." But she knew they wouldn't because they couldn't.

92   The next day Jane went to see Tanya.

93   "She's sho' nuff sick, Miz Richards," the mother said. "She's always been a puny child, but this time she's took real bad, throat's all raw, talk all out her haid las' night. I been using a poultice and some herb brew but she ain't got no better."

94   "Have you called a doctor, Mrs. Fulton?"

95   "No'm, we cain't afford it, an' Jake, he doan believe in doctors nohow."

96   Jane waited till the tide of high bright anger welling in her heart and

beating in her brain had subsided. When she spoke her voice was deceptively gentle. "Mrs. Fulton, Tanya is a very sick little girl. She is your only little girl. If you love her, I advise you to have a doctor for her, for if you don't . . . Tanya may die."

97   The wail that issued from the thin figure seemed to have no part in reality.

98   Jane spoke hurriedly. "Look, I'm going into town. I'll send a doctor out. Don't worry about paying him. We can see about that later." Impulsively she put her arms around the taut, motionless shoulders. "Don't you worry, honey, it's going to be all right."

99   There was a kindliness in the doctor's weather-beaten face that warmed Jane's heart, but his voice was brusque. "You sick, girl? Well?"

100   "No, sir. I'm not sick." What long sequence of events has caused even the best of you to look on even the best of us as menials? "I am a teacher at Centertown High. There's a little girl in my class who is very ill. Her parents are very poor. I came to see if you would please go to see her."

101   He looked at her, amused.

102   "Of course I'll pay the bill, Doctor," she added hastily.

103   "In that case . . . well . . . where does she live?"

104   Jane told him. "I think it's diphtheria, Doctor."

105   He raised his eyebrows. "Why?"

106   Jane sat erect. Don't be afraid, Jane! You're as good a teacher as he is a doctor, and you made an A in that course in childhood diseases. "High fever, restlessness, sore throat, headache, croupy cough, delirium. It could, of course, be tonsillitis or scarlet fever, but that cough—well, I'm only guessing, of course," she finished lamely.

107   "Humph." The doctor's face was expressionless. "Well, we'll see. Have your other children been inoculated?"

108   "Yes, sir, Doctor, if the parents ask, please tell them that the school is paying for your services."

109   This time he was wide-eyed.

110   The lie haunted her. She spoke to the other teachers about it the next day at recess.

111   "She's really very sick, maybe you'd like to help?"

112   Mary Winters, the sixth-grade teacher, was the first to speak. "Richards, I'd like to help, but I've got three kids of my own, and so you see how it is?"

113   Jane saw.

114   "Trouble with you, Richards, is you're too emotional." This from Nelson. "When you've taught as many years as I have, my dear, you'll learn not to bang your head against a stone wall. It may sound hardhearted to you, but one just can't worry about one child more or less when one has nearly fifty."

115   The pain in the back of her eyes grew more insistent. "I can," she said.

116   "I'll help, Jane, " said Marilyn Andrews, breathless, bouncy, newlywed Marilyn.

117   "Here's two bucks. It's all I've got, but nothing's plenty for me." Her laughter pealed echoing down the hall.

118   "I've got a dollar, Richards"—this from mousy, severe, little Miss Mitchell—"though I'm not sure I agree with you."

119   "Why don't you ask the high-school faculty?" said Marilyn. "Better still, take it up in teachers' meeting."

120   "Mr. Johnson has enough to worry about now," snapped Nelson. Why, she's mad, thought Jane, mad because I'm trying to give a helpless little tyke a chance to live, and because Marilyn and Mitchell helped.

121   The bell rang. Wordlessly Jane turned away. She watched the children troop in noisily, an ancient nursery rhyme running through her head:

> Three blind mice,
>   three blind mice,
> See how they run,
>   see how they run.
> They all ran after
>   the farmer's wife
> She cut off their tails
>   with a carving knife,
> Did you ever see
>   such a sight in your life
> As three blind mice?

122   Only this time it was forty-three mice. Jane giggled. Why, I'm hysterical, she thought in surprise. The mice thought the sweet-smelling farmer's wife might have bread and a wee bit of cheese to offer poor blind mice; but the farmer's wife didn't like poor, hungry, dirty blind mice. So she cut off their tails. Then they couldn't run any more, only wobble. What happened then? Maybe they starved, those that didn't bleed to death. Running round in circles. Running where, little mice?

123   She talked to the high-school faculty, and Mr. Johnson. All together, she got eight dollars.

124   The following week she received a letter from the doctor:

> Dear Miss Richards:
>   I am happy to inform you that Tanya is greatly improved, and with careful nursing will be well enough in about eight weeks to return to school. She is very frail, however, and will require special care. I have made three visits to her home. In view of the peculiar circumstances, I am donating my services. The cost of the medicines, however, amounts to the sum of fifteen dollars. I am referring this to you as you requested. What a beautiful child!
>   Yours sincerely,
>   Jonathan H. Sinclair, M.D.
>
> P.S. She had diphtheria.

125   Bless you forever and ever, Jonathan H. Sinclair, M.D. For all your long Southern heritage, "a man's a man for a' that . . . and a' that!"

126   Her heart was light that night when she wrote to Paul. Later she made plans in the darkness. You'll be well and fat by Christmas, Tanya, and you'll be a lovely angel in my pageant. . . . I must get the children to save pennies. . . . We'll send you milk and oranges and eggs, and we'll make funny little get-well cards to keep you happy.

127   But by Christmas Tanya was dead!

128   The voice from the dark figure was quiet, even monotonous. "Jake an' me, we always work so hard, Miz Richards. We didn't neither one have no schooling much when we was married—our folks never had much money, but we was happy. Jake, he tenant farm. I tuk in washing—we plan to save and buy a little house and farm of our own someday. Den the children come. Six boys, Miz Richards—all in a hurry. We both want the boys to finish school, mabbe go to college. We try not to keep them out to work the farm, but sometimes we have to. Then come Tanya. Just like a little yellow rose she was, Miz Richards, all pink and gold . . . and her voice like a silver bell. We think when she grow up an' finish school she take voice lessons—be like Marian Anderson. We think mabbe by then the boys would be old enough to help. I was kinda feared for her when she get sick, but then she start to get better. She was doing so well, Miz Richards. Den it get cold, an' the fire so hard to keep all night long, an' eben the newspapers in the cracks doan keep the win' out, an' I give her all my kivvers; but one night she jest tuk to shivering an' talking all out her haid—sat right up in bed, she did. She call your name onc't or twice, Miz Richards, then she say, 'Mot Dear, does Jesus love me like Miz Richards say in Sunday school?' I say, 'Yes, honey.' She say, 'Effen I die will I see Jesus?' I say, 'Yes, honey, but you ain't gwine die.' But she did, Miz Richards . . . jest smiled an' laid down—jest smiled an' laid down."

129   It is terrible to see such hopeless resignation in such tearless eyes. . . . One little mouse stopped running. . . . You'll make a lovely angel to grace the throne of God, Tanya!

130   Jane did not go to the funeral. Nelson and Rogers sat in the first pew. Everyone on the faculty contributed to a beautiful wreath. Jane preferred not to think about that.

131   C.T. brought a lovely potted rose to her the next day. "Miz Richards, ma'am, do you think this is pretty enough to go on Tanya's grave?"

132   "Where did you get it, C. T.?"

133   "I stole it out Miz Adams's front yard, right out of that li'l glass house she got there. The door was open, Miz Richards, she got plenty, she won't miss this li'l one."

134   You queer little bundle of truth and lies. What do I do now? Seeing the tears blinking back in the anxious eyes, she said gently, "Yes, C. T., the rose is nearly as beautiful as Tanya is now. She will like that very much."

135   "You mean she will know I put it there, Miz Richards? She ain't daid at all?"

136   "Maybe she'll know, C. T. You see, nothing that is beautiful ever dies as long as we remember it."

137   So you loved Tanya, a little mouse? The memory of her beauty is yours to keep now forever and always, my darling. Those things money can't buy. They've all been trying, but your tail isn't off yet, is it, brat? Not by a long shot. Suddenly she laughed aloud.

138   He looked at her wonderingly. "What you laughing at, Miz Richards?"

139   "I'm laughing because I'm happy, C. T.," and she hugged him.

140   Christmas with its pageantry and splendor came and went. Back from the holidays, Jane had an oral English lesson.

141   "We'll take this period to let you tell about your holidays, children."

142   On the weekend that Jane stayed in Centertown she visited different churches, and taught in the Sunday schools when she was asked. She had tried to impress on the children the reasons for giving at Christmastime. In class they had talked about things they could make for gifts, and ways they could save money to buy them. Now she stood by the window, listening attentively, reaping the fruits of her labors.

143   "I got a bicycle and a catcher's mitt."

144   "We all went to a party and had ice cream and cake."

145   "I got—"

146   "I got—"

147   "I got—"

148   Score one goose egg for Jane. She was suddenly very tired. "It's your turn, C. T." Dear God, please don't let him lie too much. He tears my heart. The children never laugh. It's funny how polite they are to C. T. even when they know he's lying. Even that day when Boyd and Lloyd told how they had seen him take food out of the garbage cans in front of the restaurant, and he said he was taking it to some poor hungry children, they didn't laugh. Sometimes children have a great deal more insight than grownups.

149   C. T. was talking. "I didn't get nothin' for Christmas, because Mamma was sick, but I worked all that week before for Mr. Bondel what owns the store on Main Street. I ran errands an' swep' up an' he give me three dollars, and so I bought Mamma a real pretty handkerchief an' a comb, an' I bought my father a tie pin, paid a big ole fifty cents for it too. . . an' I bought my sisters an' brothers some candy an' gum an' I bought me this whistle. Course I got what you give us, Miz Richards" (she had given each a small gift) "an' Mamma's white lady give us a whole crate of oranges, an' Miz Smith what live nex' door give me a pair of socks. Mamma she was so happy she made a cake with eggs an' butter an' everything; an' then we ate it an' had a good time."

150   Rachel spoke wonderingly, "Didn't Santa Claus bring you anything at all?"

151   C. T. was the epitome of scorn. "Ain't no Santa Claus," he said and sat down.

152   Jane quelled the age-old third-grade controversy absently, for her heart

was singing. C. T. . . . C. T., son of my own heart, you are the bright new hope of a doubtful world, and the gay new song of a race unconquered. Of them all—Sarahlene, sole heir to the charming stucco home on the hill, all fitted for gracious living; George, whose father is a contractor; Rachel, the minister's daughter; Angela, who has just inherited ten thousand dollars— of all of them who got, you, my dirty little vagabond, who have never owned a coat in your life, because you say you don't get cold; you, out of your nothing, found something to give, and in the dignity of giving found that it was not so important to receive. . . . Christ child, look down in blessing on one small child made in Your image and born black!

153   Jane had problems. Sometimes it was difficult to maintain discipline with forty-two children. Busy as she kept them, there were always some not busy enough. There was the conference with Mr. Johnson.

154   "Miss Richards, you are doing fine work here, but sometimes your room is a little . . . well—ah—well, to say the least, noisy. You are new here, but we have always maintained a record of having fine discipline here at this school. People have said that it used to be hard to tell whether or not there were children in the building. We have always been proud of that. Now take Miss Nelson. She is an excellent disciplinarian." He smiled. "Maybe if you ask her she will give you her secret. Do not be too proud to accept help from anyone who can give it, Miss Richards."

155   "No, sir, thank you, sir, I'll do my best to improve, sir." Ah, you dear, well-meaning, shortsighted, round, busy little man. Why are you not more concerned about how much the children have grown and learned in these past four months than you are about how much noise they make? I know Miss Nelson's secret. Spare not the rod and spoil not the child. Is that what you want me to do? Paralyze these kids with fear so that they will be afraid to move? afraid to question? afraid to grow? Why is it so fine for people not to know there are children in the building? Wasn't the building built for children? In her room Jane locked the door against the sound of the playing children, put her head on the desk, and cried.

156   Jane acceded to tradition and administered one whipping docilely enough, as though used to it; but the sneer in his eyes that had almost gone returned to haunt them. Jane's heart misgave her. From now on I positively refuse to impose my will on any of these poor children by reason of my greater strength. So she had abandoned the rod in favor of any other means she could find. They did not always work.

157   There was a never-ending drive for funds. Jane had a passion for perfection. Plays, dances, concerts, bazaars, suppers, parties, followed one on another in staggering succession.

158   "Look here, Richards," Nelson told her one day, "it's true that we need a new piano, and that science equipment, but, honey, these drives in a colored school are like the poor: with us always. It doesn't make too much difference if Suzy forgets her lines, or if the ice cream is a little lumpy. Cooperation is fine, but the way you tear into things you won't last long."

159 "For once in her life Nelson's right, Jane," Elise told her later. "I can understand how intense you are because I used to be like that; but, pet, Negro teachers have always had to work harder than any others and till recently have always got paid less, so for our own health's sake, we have to let up wherever possible. Believe me, honey, if you don't learn to take it easy, you're going to get sick."

160 Jane did. Measles!

161 "Oh, no," she wailed, "not in my old age!" But she was glad of the rest. Lying in her own bed at home, she realized how very tired she was.

162 Paul came to see her that weekend and sat by her bed, and read aloud to her the old classic poems they both loved so well. They listened to their favorite radio programs. Paul's presence was warm and comforting. Jane was reluctant to go back to work.

163 What to do about C. T. was a question that daily loomed larger in Jane's consciousness. Watching Joe Louis's brilliant development was a thing of joy, and Jane was hard pressed to find enough outlets for his amazing abilities. Jeanette Allen was running a close second, and even Booker, so long a problem, was beginning to grasp fundamentals, but C. T. remained static.

164 "I always stays two years in a grade, Miz Richards," he told her blandly. "I does better the second year.

165 "I don't keer." His voice had been cheerful. Maybe he really is slow, Jane thought. But one day something happened to make her change her mind.

166 C. T. was possessed of an unusually strong tendency to protect those he considered to be poor or weak. He took little Johnny Armstrong, who sat beside him in class, under his wing. Johnny was nearsighted and nondescript, his one outstanding feature being his hero-worship of C. T. Johnny was a plodder. Hard as he tried, he made slow progress at best.

167 The struggle with multiplication tables was a difficult one, in spite of all the little games Jane devised to make them easier for the children. On this particular day there was the uneven hum of little voices trying to memorize. Johnny and C. T. were having a whispered conversation about snakes.

168 Clearly Jane heard C. T.'s elaboration. "Man, my father caught a moccasin long as that blackboard, I guess, an' I held him while he was live right back of his ugly head—so."

169 Swiftly Jane crossed the room. "C. T. and Johnny, you are supposed to be learning your tables. The period is nearly up and you haven't even begun to study. Furthermore, in more than five months you haven't even learned the two-times table. Now you will both stay in at the first recess to learn it, and every day after this until you do."

170 Maybe I should make up some problems about snakes, Jane mused, but they'd be too ridiculous. . . . Two nests of four snakes—Oh, well, I'll see how they do at recess. Her heart smote her at the sight of the two little figures at their desks, listening wistfully to the sound of the children at play, but she busied herself and pretended not to notice them. Then she heard C. T.'s voice:

171 "Lissen, man, these tables is easy if you really want to learn them. Now see here. Two times one is two. Two times two is four. Two times three is six. If you forgit, all you got to do is add two like she said."

172 "Sho' nuff, man?"

173 "Sho'. Say them with me . . . two times one—" Obediently Johnny began to recite. Five minutes later they came to her. "We's ready, Miz Richards."

174 "Very well. Johnny, you may begin."

175 "Two times one is two. Two times two is four. Two times three is . . . Two times three is—"

176 "Six," prompted C. T.

177 In sweat and pain, Johnny managed to stumble through the two-times table with C. T.'s help.

178 "That's very poor, Johnny, but you may go for today. Tomorrow I shall expect you to have it letter perfect. Now it's your turn, C. T."

179 C. T.'s performance was a fair rival to Joe Louis's. Suspiciously she took him through in random order.

180 "Two times nine?"

181 "Eighteen."

182 "Two times four?"

183 "Eight."

184 "Two times seven?"

185 "Fourteen."

186 "C. T., you could have done this long ago. Why didn't you?"

187 "I dunno. . . . May I go to play now, Miz Richards?"

188 "Yes, C. T. Now learn your three-times table for me tomorrow."

189 But he didn't, not that day or the day after that or the day after that. . . . Why doesn't he? Is it that he doesn't want to? Maybe if I were as ragged and deprived as he I wouldn't want to learn either.

190 Jane took C. T. to town and bought him a shirt, a sweater, a pair of dungarees, some underwear, a pair of shoes and a pair of socks. Then she sent him to the barber to get his hair cut. She gave him the money so he could pay for the articles himself and figure up the change. She instructed him to take a bath before putting on his new clothes, and told him not to tell anyone but his parents that she had bought them.

191 The next morning the class was in a dither.

192 "You seen C. T.?"

193 "Oh, boy, ain't he sharp!"

194 "C. T., where'd you get them new clothes?"

195 "Oh, man, I can wear new clothes any time I feel like it, but I can't be bothered with being a fancypants all the time like you guys."

196 C. T. strutted in new confidence, but his work didn't improve.

197 Spring came in its virginal green gladness and the children chafed for the out-of-doors. Jane took them out as much as possible on nature studies and excursions.

198 C. T. was growing more and more mischievous, and his influence began to spread throughout the class. Daily his droll wit became more and more edged with impudence. Jane was at her wit's end.

199 "You let that child get away with too much, Richards," Nelson told her. "What he needs is a good hiding."

200 One day Jane kept certain of the class in at the first recess to do neglected homework, C. T. among them. She left the room briefly. When she returned C. T. was gone.

201 "Where is C. T.?" she asked.

202 "He went out to play, Miz Richards. He said couldn't no ole teacher keep him in when he didn't want to stay."

203 Out on the playground C. T. was standing in a swing gently swaying to and fro, surrounded by a group of admiring youngsters. He was holding forth.

204 "I gets tired of stayin' in all the time. She doan pick on nobody but me, an' today I put my foot down. From now on', I say, 'I ain't never goin' to stay in, Miz Richards.' Then I walks out." He was enjoying himself immensely. Then he saw her.

205 "You will come with me, C. T." She was quite calm except for the tell-tale veins throbbing in her forehead.

206 "I ain't comin'." The sudden fright in his eyes was veiled quickly by a nonchalant belligerence. He rocked the swing gently.

207 She repeated, "Come with me, C. T."

208 The children watched breathlessly.

209 "I done told you I ain't comin', Miz Richards." His voice was patient as though explaining to a child. "I ain't . . . comin' a . . . damn . . . tall!

210 Jane moved quickly, wrenching the small but surprisingly strong figure from the swing. Then she bore him bodily, kicking and screaming, to the building.

211 The children relaxed, and began to giggle. "Oh boy! Is he goin' to catch it!" they told one another.

212 Panting, she held him, still struggling, by the scruff of his collar before the group of teachers gathered in Marilyn's room. "All right, now you tell me what to do with him!" she demanded. "I've tried everything." The tears were close behind her eyes.

213 "What'd he do?" Nelson asked.

214 Briefly she told them.

215 "Have you talked to his parents?"

216 "Three times I've had conferences with them. They say to beat him."

217 "That, my friend, is what you ought to do. Now he never acted like that with me. If you'll let me handle him, I'll show you how to put a brat like that in his place."

218 "Go ahead," Jane said wearily.

219 Nelson left the room, and returned with a narrow but sturdy leather thong. "Now, C. T."—she was smiling, tapping the strap in her open left palm—"go to your room and do what Miss Richards told you to."

220   "I ain't gonna, an' you can't make me." He sat down with absurd dignity at a desk.

221   Still smiling, Miss Nelson stood over him. The strap descended without warning across the bony shoulders in the thin shirt. The whip became a dancing demon, a thing possessed, bearing no relation to the hand that held it. The shrieks grew louder. Jane closed her eyes against the blurred fury of a singing lash, a small boy's terror and a smiling face.

222   Miss Nelson was not tired. "Well, C. T.?"

223   "I won't, Yer can kill me but I won't!"

224   The sounds began again. Red welts began to show across the small arms and through the clinging sweat-drenched shirt.

225   "Now will you go to your room?"

226   Sobbing and conquered, C. T. went. The seated children stared curiously at the little procession. Jane dismissed them.

227   In his seat C. T. found pencil and paper.

228   What's he supposed to do, Richards?" Jane told her.

229   "All right, now write!"

230   C. T. stared at Nelson through swollen lids, a curious smile curving his lips. Jane knew suddenly that come hell or high water, C. T. would not write. I mustn't interfere. Please, God, don't let her hurt him too badly. Where have I failed so miserably? . . . Forgive us our trespasses. The singing whip and the shrieks became a symphony from hell. Suddenly Jane hated the smiling face with an almost unbearable hatred. She spoke, her voice like cold steel.

231   "That's enough, Nelson."

232   The noise stopped.

233   "He's in no condition to write now anyway."

234   C. T. stood up. "I hate you. I hate you all. You're mean and I hate you." Then he ran. No one followed him. Run, little mouse! They avoided each other's eyes.

235   "Well, there you are," Nelson said as she walked away. Jane never found out what she meant by that.

236   The next day C. T. did not come to school. The day after that he brought Jane the fatal homework, neatly and painstakingly done, and a bunch of wild flowers. Before the bell rang, the children surrounded him. He was beaming.

237   "Did you tell yer folks you got a whipping, C. T.?"

238   "Naw! I'd 'a' only got another."

239   "Where were you yesterday?"

240   "Went fishin'. Caught me six cats long as your haid, Sambo."

241   Jane buried her face in the sweet-smelling flowers. Oh, my brat, my wonderful resilient brat. They'll never get your tail, will they?

242   It was seven weeks till the end of term, when C. T. brought Jane a model wooden boat.

243   Jane stared at it. "Did you make this? It's beautiful, C. T."

244 "Oh, I make them all the time . . . an' airplanes an' houses too. I do 'em in my spare time," he finished airily.

245 "Where do you get the models, C. T.?" she asked.

246 "I copies them from pictures in the magazines."

247 Right under my nose . . . right there all the time, she thought wonderingly. "C. T., would you like to build things when you grow up? Real houses and ships and planes?"

248 "Reckon I could, Miz Richards," he said confidently.

249 The excitement was growing in her.

250 "Look, C. T. You aren't going to do any lessons at all for the rest of the year. You're going to build ships and houses and airplanes and anything else you want to."

251 "I am, huh?" He grinned. "Well, I guess I wasn't goin' to get promoted nohow."

252 "Of course if you want to build them the way they really are, you might have to do a little measuring, and maybe learn to spell the names of the parts you want to order. All the best contractors have to know things like that, you know."

253 "Say, I'm gonna have real fun, huh? I always said lessons wussent no good nohow. Pop say too much study eats out yer brains anyway."

254 The days went by. Jane ran a race with time. The instructions from the model companies arrived. Jane burned the midnight oil planning each day's work.

255 Learn to spell the following words: ship, sail, steamer—boat, anchor, airplane wing, fly.

256 Write a letter to the lumber company, ordering some lumber.

257 The floor of our model house is ten inches long. Multiply the length by the width and you'll find the area of the floor in square inches.

258 Read the story of Columbus and his voyages.

259 Our plane arrives in Paris in twenty-eight hours. Paris is the capital city of a country named France across the Atlantic Ocean.

260 Long ago sailors told time by the sun and the stars. Now, the earth goes around the sun—.

261 Work and pray, Jane, work and pray!

262 C. T. learned. Some things vicariously, some things directly. When he found that he needed multiplication to plan his models to scale, he learned to multiply. In three weeks he had mastered simple division.

263 Jane bought beautifully illustrated stories about ships and planes. He learned to read.

264 He wrote for and received his own materials.

265 Jane exulted.

266 The last day! Forty-two faces waiting anxiously for report cards. Jane spoke to them briefly, praising them collectively, and admonishing them to obey the safety rules during the holidays. Then she passed out the report cards.

267   As she smiled at each childish face, she thought, I've been wrong. The long arm of circumstance, environment and heredity is the farmer's wife that seeks to mow you down, and all of us who touch your lives are in some way responsible for how successful she is. But you aren't mice, my darlings. Mice are hated, hunted pests. You are normal, lovable children. The knife of the farmer's wife is double-edged for you, because you are Negro children, born mostly in poverty. But you are wonderful children, nevertheless, for you wear the bright protective cloak of laughter, the strong shield of courage, and the intelligence of children everywhere. Some few of you may indeed become as the mice—but most of you shall find your way to stand fine and tall in the annals of man. There's a bright new tomorrow ahead. For every one of us whose job it is to help you grow that is insensitive and unworthy, there are hundreds who daily work that you may grow straight and whole. If it were not so, our world could not long endure.

268   She handed C. T. his card.

269   "Thank you, ma'm."

270   "Aren't you going to open it?"

271   He opened it dutifully. When he looked up his eyes were wide with disbelief. "You didn't make no mistake?"

272   "No mistake, C. T. You're promoted. You've caught up enough to go to the fourth grade next year."

273   She dismissed the children. They were a swarm of bees released from a hive. "'By, Miss Richards." "Happy holidays, Miss Richards."

274   C. T. was the last to go.

275   "Well, C. T.?"

276   "Miz Richards, you remember what you said about a name being important?"

277   "Yes, C. T."

278   "Well, I talked to Mamma, and she said if I wanted a name it would be all right, and she'd go to the courthouse about it."

279   "What name have you chosen, C. T.?" she asked.

280   "Christopher Turner Young."

281   "That's a nice name, Christopher," she said gravely.

282   "Sho' nuff, Miz Richards?"

283   "Sure enough, C. T."

284   "Miz Richards, you know what?"

285   "What, dear?"

286   "I love you."

287   She kissed him swiftly before he ran to catch his classmates.

288   She stood at the window and watched the running, skipping figures, followed by the bold mimic shadows. I'm coming home, Paul. I'm leaving my forty-two children, and Tanya there on the hill. My work with them is finished now. The laughter bubbled up in her throat. But Paul, oh Paul. See how straight they run!

DISCUSSION QUESTIONS

1. Many of Miss Richards's students speak a nonstandard variety of English. A new teacher, she says to herself that she must "correct" Booker's speech defects. Do you think his speech is deficient? Why? How could the teacher help him with his nonstandard dialect? Discuss these issues with your classmates.
2. How would you describe Miss Richards? What kind of person do you think she is?
3. What is C. T.'s attitude about learning at the beginning of the story? At the end?
4. What kind of man was Dr. Sinclair? What was his attitude toward Miss Richards? Toward Tanya?

WRITING TOPICS

1. "What a burden you bear, little people, heirs to all your parents' still-born dreams of greatness." In your journal, paraphrase this statement made by Miss Richards and explain what you think she means.
2. Miss Richards says that sometimes children have a great deal more insight than grownups. Do you agree or disagree with this statement? Write a short essay supporting your belief; use examples from your reading, history, or personal experience.
3. In the last paragraph of the story, Miss Richards says, "My work with them is finished now. . . . See how straight they run!" Pretend you are Miss Richards and write a letter to Paul describing your feelings about the children and your accomplishments with them.

LIFT EVERY VOICE AND SING

James Weldon Johnson

James Weldon Johnson was born in Jacksonville, Florida, in 1871. Johnson grew up in a middle-class black family; he attended Atlanta and Columbia Universities. He wrote "Lift Every Voice and Sing" in 1900; this song is known as the "Negro national anthem." He wrote several volumes of poetry, namely *Sence You Went Away* (1900), *My City* (1923), and his best-known collection of poems, *God's Trombones* (1927). Johnson resigned as head of the National Association for the Advancement of Colored People (NAACP) in 1930 to accept the Spence Chair of Creative Literature at Fisk University in Tennessee. He held this position until his death as the result of a car accident in 1938.

Lift every voice and sing
Till earth and heaven ring,
Ring with the harmonies of Liberty;
Let our rejoicing rise
5   High as the listening skies,
Let it resound loud as the rolling sea.
Sing a song full of the faith that the dark past has taught us,
Sing a song full of the hope that the present has brought us,
Facing the rising sun of our new day begun
10   Let us march on till victory is won.

Stony the road we trod,
Bitter the chastening rod,
Felt in the days when hope unborn had died;
Yet with a steady beat,
15   Have not our weary feet
Come to the place for which our fathers sighed?
We have come over a way that with tears have been watered,
We have come, treading our path through the blood of the slaughtered,

Out from the gloomy past,
20   Till now we stand at last
Where the white gleam of our bright star is cast.

God of our weary years,
God of our silent tears,
Thou who has brought us thus far on the way;
25   Thou who has by Thy might
Led us into the light,
Keep us forever in the path, we pray.
Lest our feet stray from the places, Our God, where we met Thee,
Lest, our hearts drunk with the wine of the world, we forget Thee;
30   Shadowed beneath Thy hand,
May we forever stand.
True to our GOD,
True to our native land.

DISCUSSION QUESTIONS

1. Think about the United States of America's national anthem, "The Star-Spangled Banner." What does this song celebrate about the United States? What does "Lift Every Voice and Sing" celebrate about African Americans? What are the similarities between the two songs? Use specific examples from both songs to support your responses.

2. What period of time is being discussed in the first nine lines of the second stanza? Which star does the persona refer to in the last line of this stanza? What is the connection between the first nine lines of this stanza and the reference to the "bright star"?

WRITING TOPICS

1. In your journal, write a paragraph in which you support the position that the persona in the poem is referring to America in the last line of the third stanza. Write another paragraph in which you support the position that the persona in the poem is referring to Africa.

2. Look up the definition of "anthem" in a dictionary. In an essay, explain what an anthem is and discuss the various qualities about "Lift Every Voice and Sing" that help explain why this song became the "Negro national anthem."

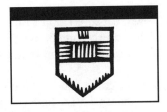

I DONE WORKED!

Lottie Jackson as told to Sherry Thomas

Sherry Thomas was born in Georgia in 1948. She attended Brown University and contributed to feminist publications. With Jeanne Tetrault, she started the magazine *Country Women.* In 1976, they published *Country Women: Handbook for the New Farmer.* She next worked gathering oral histories and photographs. These were published in 1981 in *We Didn't Have Much, But We Sure Had Plenty.*

1   I been out all day planting watermelon vines. Lord, if I didn' work I couldn't make it. No, if I didn' work, I'd jus die! I been workin ever day, *ever* day, in those big fields by myself. I *like* to work. I jus *want* to work, cause that keep me goin. I be jus settin round, I get so *stiff* you know. I walked through the fields, worked out there everyday, workin for Mr. John, you know. Yes suh, I been here ever since forty, right here on this place. Been here ever since forty! Been a *long* time. Came here young and done got old.

2   An I tole Mr. John, he better not throw me away! I done *raised* his chillun that's got grown and gone away. I said, "Now you better see bout me!"

3   An he say, "Lottie, I'm gonna see bout ya."

4   I said, "I knowed it cause if you don', I'm a-comin to your house! You ain't gettin rid of Lottie!"

5   An he jus laughed. "Lottie, we ain't gonna throw you away."

6   "You better not, cause I'm almos one of the family, I'm one *in* the family!" That what I tell him.

7   I hate movin so *bad!* But he say, "Lottie, I cain't help it, I had to do it."

8   It got confused in the family some way. I tole him he ought've looked out for us, though, he ought've leaved a space for us. I ain't goin to no town, not Dawson an not Americus, neither! An I cain't find me no house, cause they ain't no houses, ain't no house cause people is tearin 'em down soon's as people move out. I got to try to get me a trailer house or somethin. Somethin to live in. There ain't no houses.

9   Lord, I don' like no town, for sure I don'! I like to stay out where I can get *somptin* fer nothin! I kin go to somebody's house they give me some greens, peas, anything. If I go to town, I got to go to the market. Town ain't no place to live!

10   I fish a lot, I sure do. How come I goin to miss this place, we got a lot of fishin on this place. An I hate to leave here, on account of that fishin. I like to fish! There's a heap of dams down there where the beavers done dammed and jus left a little stream, made ponds out of it. I go from one pond to another, I catch 'em, I sure do! Trout, bass, catfish, all kinds!

11   Oooh, I had one of the purrrtiest gardens. But I don' have one now. See, I didn't know where I was gonna be. See, I'd've had this place cleaned up all the way around, but I let it growed up cause I didn' know *where* I was gonna be. My garden, I jus let it growed up. I grow beans, greens, peas, everthing like that. Oh, I have plenty of flowers in my yard, all kind of flowers in my yard.

12   Irene older than I am, I know that. I was born in Calhoun County but I don't know when I was born. Don't even know my mama because she died in chil'bed. Didn't never even see my mama. I had one brother, he die when I be a little thing like that; an one sister, she died year before last. Ain't nobody left but me. My aunt, one of my aunts, raised me. Didn't know my dad till I was bout grown! Sure didn't. Sure *didn't!*

13   Our aunt raised us. Not my brother, he died when us wasn't but little things. He was older than us. He had a *heap* of sense, you know. An he went over to fix the cane mill, they had a cane mill what had stopped, you know; and it caught him and it broke his neck.

14   My aunt had some more chilrun, you know, what their parents had died and she was raisin them with us. She didn't have none of her own. She had a husband that died; she were a widda. Her good. She was *good* to us. She was on her own place, she had hands workin for her, an a big old stove. She took care of us good. Dad, he'd come for us, but she'd tell us that wadn't our daddy, you know. Us'd run from him, us'd *run* from him! She did that to keep our daddy from gittin us, you know, and us didn' know no better, us'd jus *run* from him.

15   When I were at my aunt's, I jes worked in the field. Worked in the fields! Didn't get time to go to school fer in the fields! Yeah'm that what I did, work in the fields or in da house. Weren't nothin to do in the fields, then I were in the house. You go on in there, an they put you to work. I growed up workin, growed *up* workin! Sure did.

16   No'm they never tell me how old I was. Wouldn't tell you cause they think that make you grown! No, they sure wouldn't. Didn't do nothin but work ye, sure would work ye now. I'm *glad* they did it. I'm glad of it. Sure 'nough. Made me willin to do it right on.

17   Now my sista, she wasn't much of a worker, an I'd work hard, you know. I work hard enough fer her, where her wouldn't get a whuppin! She was older than I was, an I'd work *hard*. I'd show up right smart, you know, to

keep her from a-whuppin us. My sista cared that they whup her, but she jest a slow worker, couldn't work much. She scared of a whupping but she couldn't make work. I'd ruther be like I am.

18   Irene sure had a hard life. I didn't have it hard like she did. I have worked *hard* but she have done some things *I* didn' do.

19   When I were a little girl, I were choppin cotton, pickin cotton, all of that. Tha's right. First of the year, start plowin, pickin them old stalks, pilin them up. You didn' have no time for sittin around! Sure didn'. Ooooh girl, you better get up afore the sun rise, better get on out there afore the sun be up, or she be there with a strap. Yes ma'am! You better get up. Yes ma'am, you *better* get out of that bed! I'd wake up and wake the others up. She'd fix a breakfast for us, and she'd have that breakfast ready where we could hit the field. Soon's we was done, we had to git on. Sure did! They jes tell me what they want done. I never was hard to learn nothin. They tell me or show me *one* time, that be it, I'd do it.

20   We didn' have no birthdays, none of that, just "Go to the field!" No, we didn' know nothin bout birthdays! Christmas they bring us a little Santa Claus at night, give you an apple or orange, little candy, somptin like that. Bake a little cake, or somptin. Chillun gettin so much now, they don' want *this* an they don' want *that*, they kin get anything they want! Us was glad to git a biscuit on Sunday mornin!

21   An I done some of everthing in the field that could be done. I done plowed. Me an my huband, we worked that farm up there, just me an him. An I worked! I'd help him plow an he'd help me hoe. And come time together, we'd get our supper ourself. An then get out and help the other. Plowin with mules. We were sharecroppin. That where my huband died, up there. I think my huband died in . . . fifty-two . . . fifty-three! That right, he died in fifty-three. An I didn' have not nair a chile, not nair a one. Sure didn't.

22   I left my aunt's house after I married. I don' know how old I was. Round fifteen, sixteen year old, I think. I think I were that old cause they wouldn't let you marry along then fore you got old enough, you know. Chillun nowadays, they don' marry, they jus shack up together, they don' marry no more! Now an then, you find one that will marry, but mos they jest git together an say, "That my huband, that my wife." But you had to *marry* along in then. I think it better to get married.

23   You ask what'd I *do* when I got married!? Worked a farm! I moved to a place, jes me and my huband. An Lord, I jes work, work, work, work. I work harder here though, than I did then. I done some WORK on this place. An I wud be doin it now, if Mr. John be farmin it still! I'd be in the fields right now, sure I would. All over this place, I worked jus by myself. Nobody wif me. He'd come back and forth, see if nothin got at me. I'd be workin way out back and he'd come ever night an see if anything got me! He'd tell me what to do, but a heap a time, I'd tell him. "This place need to be worked, Mr. John."

24   "Well, Lottie, go ahead and do it," he'd say.

25   I never drove no tractor, I wished I'd've but if I did, I wudn't know how to turn it around! I tole him, "Mr. John, jus learn me how to turn it around, I'll drive it!" But he never did learn me. I hated fer the mules to go. I hated that. I like mules. I wanted to go *fast*. I wanted a fast mule, I didn't want no mule draggin. I wanted one gotta *go* when I went.

26   An I liked to shake peanuts an pick cotton. I liked-ed that. I put peanuts up, fast as my huband could plow them up. He'd get mad an take out the mule an go to the house! He wanted me to be slow where he could help shake some. He mad, he *mad!* Sure was!

27   I love to cook. I likes to cook, if I gots somethin to cook, I likes to do it. My huband cooked when I be workin sometimes. When we got through with our farmin, he wouldn't want me to go out nowhere an work. But I'd go out anyhow, an he'd stay home, look out for the cows and cook! I'd work and he'd fuss . . you know. I'd work my farm, then I'd go out an work, but he'd stay home and cook. He'd say when I done did my work, I ought to stay home an rest. But I'd go work an help other folks. Sometime he'd go, an most time he wudn't.

28   I worked, you *know* I worked. I'd plow an I'd plant. Get done plantin, it be hoein time. Yes sir, I done some work. And I still would be, followin them tractors, handin seed, *everthing*.

29   Them tractors put a lot of folks out of work. It were a bad time. Don't know what gonna happen to us now either, I just don' know! Lately now, I been figurin maybe they fixin to put us in *slavery times* agin!

30   You cain't get this an you cain't get that. No work, an no houses, no gas, *nothin*. Food up yonder so high you cain't buy it. I jus don't know what gonna happen. Ever year but this, I growed my food, but this year everthing done turned around. I don' have a garden cause I didn' know where I was gonna be. I just don' know what we goin to do! I ain't hear none of 'em talk bout slavery times lately, but I think on it.

31   It sure was worser in slavery times! In my times, we wudn't make much. But we'd get some, sure would! Maybe two hundred dollars fer the whole year. But fer us, that'd be—you know, when I first came here on this place, they weren't givin but fifty cent a day. An my huband were gittin sixty cent. He got sixty cause he was a man, I reckon, and I were a lady. An I worked harder than him, cause he couldn't work like me. That right! Sure did seem wrong to me, but I jus couldn't do no better. I hear some of 'em say they work for a quarter a day. I ain't never worked for no twenty-five cent a day, but I hear some of these folk round here say they *have* worked for twenty-five cents a day!

32   An I'm talkin bout you had to go to the field before sunup an work till the *bell* rang, an go back at one o'clock an work till dark. That right! For that money! Fifty cent! An come back an wash, an cook, an all that in the dark.

33   One time, my huband an me, we was with some white people wouldn't give us nothin. Was *worthless* folk, an wouldn't give us nothin. We couldn't

hardly git somptin to eat. So we moved over here. We stayed at that other place two years. Sure did. Cause we couldn't git nothin, we moved over here. I had knowed bout this place fore we came here. When we was down at them white folks, we'd visit some people, that stayed over here. So that how we knowed bout this place an we moved on over here. Been here ever since. I stayed here till my huband died, and I'm *still* here. Done pretty good on this place.

34 My huband had cancer. He was sick about two year. Sure was. Ooooh Lord, like to have bout worked me to *death!* I had to see bout him, an work that crop, an I had two mules, and four or five head of cows to see bout. You know, people'd come over there an help me wid him; Irene an them, they help me wid him. I had to keep a fire goin, you know, all day long, an I jus bout cleaned up them woods up there cuttin wood! To keep him warm. When some of them be there wif him, I'd go cut wood.

35 An he'd tell me, "Honey, I ain't gonna hurt right now, you kin go ahead an do what you gotta do. I ain't gonna hurt right now."

36 So, I'd get out an go do, an run back. I'd work out in the field an jus run back see bout him, sure would! When he went down, I worked, sure 'nough, cause I had *all* it to do! The cows an the mules, an seein bout him. His name Richard Jackson, but everbody called him Shorty. He bout a high as Irene. But he weren't little, he were stout!

37 My life didn' change much after he were gone. I got on just bout as good as when he was livin.

38 I couldn't do without my huband, you know, cause he was *good* to me. But I wouldn't have nair an un now! Uh uh, I'm doin *too* good!

39 You know, the Lord is removing the men, cause they ain't no good. More men die than the women, cause they ain't no good! Sure does! Why I coulda married the next week after my huband had died. The next *week,* they talkin bout marryin me! They knowed I was a hard worker an they thought I might take care of 'em! But I didn't want none of 'em! NOOOOOO! My huband been gone all that long, an I ain't married yet. An I'm doin all right. But my huband was good to me, sure was.

40 I never liked frolickin like Irene did. No, I *never* liked that. I always been *old* all of my days! Yeah, my sista was fast, like Rene. She'd get mad, you know, if I wudn't go out with her.

41 She'd tell me, "You'm too *slow!*"

42 "Yeah, I aim to be here a *long* time slow!"

43 I took care of myself, sure did. After my huband died, my sista and her fella'd come here trying to take me out. But I wudn't come out the door. I wudn't run my life out, uh uh! Got to take *care* of myself! I ain't missed a thing, not nothin. My sista's dead and *gone* now an I'm still right here.

44 Irene, she still here, but she ain't no *good* fer anything. She *here* all right. She can do her work round the house an everthing, she might could do a little work in the field maybe, but it wouldn't be much. Rene want to do, and she sure got the will. She sure do got the *will.* She ain't lazed up a bit.

But sometime she cain't, cause she be hurtin. I know she older than I am. An I is old, I'm pushin well on over seventy. I is *old*.

45   I seen some young people look older than I do! Young folk! Look older than I do! This day, OLD women look better than the chillun. Some of these old folk that got grown chillun look better than the chillun, that right! You know, I be *thankful* that I'm old an can be doin anything that I've been doin. I'm thankful! I do the *same* work I ever done. I thank the Lord for bein old an doin what I want to do!

46   Plenty old ones and plenty young ones cain't do nothin. Everthing I ever done, I still do now: cut wood, tote wood, work in the field, tote them big buckets ever day, time I put the buckets down, I got to hoe, hoe this big place, just me, that's right, fillin up them big tractors with peanuts an gettin them things. Big five-gallon buckets full of peanuts, one in each hand, and all them boys be turnin them big tractors, "All right, come on!" An I got to be right there with 'em.

47   I work ever day *now*. I work wif a man that go round an hire hands, you know. He hires hands an tell you what place to work. The man pay us eighteen dollar a day. Some works by the hour, different places, but he just pay so much a day. We go to the field at eight ever day and work till eleven, an then we go back at one-thirty an work till six after noon. Not bad pay, when I have worked for fifty cent a day!

48   But I cain't work much an get my Social Security. They don' like you to be workin. I kin make more money workin than I kin on Social Security. Sure! See, if I were on Social Security they don' pay but once a month an I can get money ever day workin!

49   Yeah, that Mr. John, he a good one. He look out for me. I said to his boy, I said to Mr. Dave, "If I get where I cain't do nothin, you better see bout me! I done set up wif you all day an all night when you was a little bitty thing, couldn't do nothin. An you better see bout me now!"

50   I bathed them chillun, bathed 'em an put 'em to bed! I set up there with 'em all night. Mr. John and them be gone, an I set up there *all* night till he come back, till *day* the next morning. An them chillun are bout grown now.

51   Yeah, the years don' stop now, they roll around. Sure do. One year roll round, an here come another one agin! An still here, thank the Lord! Yes sir, I been here with these people a *long* time!

DISCUSSION QUESTIONS

1. Lottie says that some of the old folks in her community look better than the young people. Do you think this is true? Why?
2. What is Lottie's attitude toward work? How does it differ from other people's attitudes about work? Explain.

3. Lottie says she earned fifty cents per day, while her husband earned sixty cents per day. What does she say is the reason for this disparity? Explain.

Writing Topics

1. "Lord, I don' like no town, for sure I don'! I like to stay out where I can get somptin' for nothin'! I kin go to somebody's house they give me some greens, peas, anything. If I go to town, I got to go to the market. Town ain't no place to live!" This is a thoughtful observation. Write an essay exploring the issues cited by Lottie. Present your point of view citing reasons from your experience, observations, or research.
2. In your journal, enter a particular dialect statement spoken by Lottie and convert that statement into standard American English. You may wish to share this with your small group.

FROM *THE AFRICAN GARDEN*

Alice Childress

Alice Childress was born in Charleston, South Carolina, in 1916. She grew up in Harlem and completed three years of high school. During the 1940s Childress performed in the American Negro Theater on Broadway and off-Broadway.

Best known for her adolescent novel, *A Hero Ain't Nothin' but a Sandwich* (1973), Childress's abilities as a screenplay writer and dramatist have often been ignored by critics. One of the reasons her work is not familiar to many readers could be because her straightforward language is often targeted by censors. Childress's first play *Florence* was produced in 1949. Her play *Trouble in Mind* (1955) won the first Obie Award in 1956 for best original, off-Broadway play. This play condemns racial stereotypes in the performing arts. *Wedding Band*, produced in 1966, focuses on interracial love. Childress liked to include music in her plays: *Just a Little Simple* (was adapted from Langston Hughes' collection *Simple Speaks His Mind*) (1950). *Gold Through the Trees* (1952) was the first play by a black woman to be professionally produced on the American stage. Other plays include *The African Garden* (1971) and *Gullah* (1984). In addition to adolescent novels, screenplays, and dramas, Childress wrote novels for adult audiences; *A Short Walk* (1979) was nominated for a Pulitzer Prize. Childress died in 1994.

TIME   One summer day . . . at the tail-end of a riot (mid-1960s)
PLACE   Harlem, U.S.A.
CHARACTERS
    SIMON, a boy about ten years old
    ASHLEY, a *man*, but definitely

SCENE   A kitchen—in an apartment.
(SIMON *enters, places a large paper bag on the table. The entrance to the apartment is through the kitchen. There is a knock on the door.*)

SIMON   Who is it?

ASHLEY   (*Off stage*) Mr. Ashley.

SIMON   (*Tries to place paper sack in the refrigerator, but the package is too large to fit inside. He frantically searches for a place to put it . . . finally puts it back on the table.*) Who? Whatcha say?

ASHLEY   (*Off stage*) You got a room for rent?

SIMON   Just a minute . . . a minute . . . (*He opens the door, but the safety chain is still fastened.*) Say what?

ASHLEY   Huh?

SIMON   I say . . . whatcha want?

ASHLEY   I understand you got a room for rent.

SIMON   Yessir. (*He opens the door.* ASHLEY *enters carrying a battered, much-traveled piece of luggage.* SIMON *clears one of the kitchen chairs of magazines and papers. The kitchen is clean but very mixed-up, things out of place, dishes from breakfast still in evidence on the table etc.*) Have a seat. My . . . my . . . mother, not home from work yet. She work downtown in a big hotel doin' what you call chambermaid. House was suppose to be straight fore anybody get here . . . but I was busy . . . just got here myself. Have a seat.

ASHLEY   The riot really hit this block hard.

SIMON   Oh, I don't know, the block jus' be lookin' like that anyway. (*Self-consciously studying the paper bag and wondering what to do with it.*) You can wait till Mama get here . . . or go and then come back . . . or whatever.

ASHLEY   (*Glancing at the bag and noticing the boy's confusion*) You been looting in the stores?

SIMON   No . . . no sir.

ASHLEY   Looks like it.

SIMON   A man give me this meat . . . but he wasn't lootin'. That's the kind of business he's in all the time.

ASHLEY   Hmmmmmmm, he's a butcher?

SIMON   No sir, he's a . . . he's a . . . I don't know.

ASHLEY   (*Resting his suitcase*) Look-a-here, boy, I don't carry no tales, so you can trust me. A man's word is his word, okay?

SIMON   Okay. (*The boy tears the bag open and displays a huge package of meat for Ashley's inspection.*)

ASHLEY   Great googa-mooga. Steaks, chops, chicken, and frankfooters.

SIMON   The man who give it to me is a cattle rustler. A cattle rustler is a man who cops meat outta the supermarket.

ASHLEY   Why did you say he wasn't lootin?

SIMON   I wasn't . . . and he wasn't either. He just be roundin' meat like that every day when they ain't even any riot. That's his regular business . . . and he sell it for half price and that way people can ford to eat steak and lamb chops and . . .

ASHLEY   Why did he give it to you?

SIMON   I don' know. He walk up to me an my friend, Carter, and he say . . . "You boys divide this govmint-branded cattle . . . and eat till you bust . . . someday you can maybe do somethin for me."

ASHLEY   That's the stuff you got to watch. Don' let nobody buy you or sell you.

SIMON   My mother not gonna believe anybody jus give me all-a this. But it sure be a terrible waste to throw it out.

ASHLEY   Sure would.

SIMON   I know. Why don't you tell her that you brought it for us.

ASHLEY   No, I can't do that for you. Put it away before it spoils. (ASHLEY *helps* SIMON *put the meat in the refrigerator as they continue talking.*) Tell her what you told me. She'll give you a good talkin too . . . then yall can eat the steak.

SIMON   You don't know her. She'd throw it away, I do believe. Maybe I could give it back to Old Soldier . . . but . . . but . . .

ASHLEY   Well, you didn't mean to tell his name. That comes from your mouth speakin before your mind thinks. Old Soldier, huh?

SIMON   He not so old, but he was in World War Two . . . and that's what he say alla time . . . "I'm a *old* soldier." He always hittin' on a new supermarket so nobody get to know his face too regular. He buy sugar and a sack-a potatoes . . . and maybe toilet paper . . . and pay for alla that. But underneath his coat he be rustlin steaks. Might be four or five at a haul . . .

ASHLEY   And you think that's smart, dontcha?

SIMON   No, sir.

ASHLEY   What's your name, boy?

SIMON   Simon. Simple Simon . . . they say that in school. Simon Brown . . . what's yours?

ASHLEY   M. D. Ashley. Everybody calls me Ashley . . . or Mr. Ashley. You know what the M. stands for? *Maytag* . . . how 'bout that? That's worse than Simon. Down home, in the back country . . . my folks couldn't read. Come time to make out a birth certificate . . . they look round maybe the kitchen . . . and copy any name they see off-a the calendar or the stove. My papa copied down *Maytag* off the washin' machine . . . and *Diamond* . . . from a box-a matches. Ashley was the name-a his grandpa's slave master . . . so there's my name—Maytag Diamond Ashley.

SIMON   It sound good though. Mister Maytag Diamond Ashley.

ASHLEY   They got to callin me "Doc" because-a the M. D. initials.

SIMON   I got a middle name too . . . but I leave it out most-a the time, Simon *T.* Brown. T stand for Turnbo, Simon Turnbo Brown. Turnbo is the name of my mother's stepfather . . . Turnbo Brown.

ASHLEY   Turnbo . . . sounds like a name you might find on a good farm tractor.

SIMON   Yessir.

ASHLEY   Turnbo Brown . . . Simon Turnbo Brown. You name is the same as your step-grandfather's?

SIMON   Yessir. He down in Mississippi. My mother say he was so kind to everybody. He treat my mama like she was his own child and not a step . . . she say he treat her better than some do their own. She put Simon on because her mother always had a wish for a son to name Simon . . . after a man name Simon-call-Peter . . . which is in the Bible.

ASHLEY   Boy, that is something to be proud of . . . you named by and for your grandparent.

SIMON   That right?

ASHLEY   Shows you come from a long line-a people. Course everybody did, when you come to think of it. But you're at least a third- or fourth-generation Brown. Simon Turnbo Brown . . . of the Browns of Mississippi and New York.

SIMON   And Grandpa Brown got a brother who lives in Detroit, Michigan.

ASHLEY   Oh, well, great googa-mooga, you're Simon Turnbo Brown of Mississippi, Michigan, *and* New York. Simon T. Brown, Esquire. A gentleman, a man of importance.

SIMON   (*Admiring the way his name is spoken.*) You kiddin.

ASHLEY   And when you're a man, you'll be a man of importance whether you use the Esquire or not. (**SIMON** *begins to straighten up the kitchen.*)

SIMON   A boy in my class is named Abdul. He's a Muslim . . . and his folks changed their name from Jackson, cause they say it was a slave name . . . and no African was ever name Jackson.

ASHLEY   That's very true. And I know a guy who named himself Chaka cause Chaka was the name of a great Zulu Warrior. This fella told me that no African had a Muslim name till they were converted and brought into the Nation of Islam by the Mohammedans of North Africa.

SIMON   That right? You just don't know what to think, huh?

ASHLEY   Yeah, there's a awful lotta bags out here to be jumped in when we ready to jump. But Simon, Abdul and Chaka gonna have to get together somehow and make everything all right. Fortunately, I get along with Africans, Afro-Americans, Colored people, Negroes, Blacks . . . and also even with some niggers, cause it's to my best interest. Boy, let me help you straighten up this kitchen. When your house is mixed up . . . it shows that your mind is confused.

SIMON   That right? I thought *your* name might be Abdul cause you don't gas your hair . . . and look like not even any grease on it.

ASHLEY   Right. That's just plain old, natural African bush. I used to gas it, but I put that down. Used to gas it and fingerwave it . . . Boy, so many waves it make you seasick. And shiny! Shiny and slick. When a fly light on it . . . he'd fall down and break his leg. Night and day, I was tyin it down, combin' it, lookin at it, gassed, with one big wave and a dip runnin straight cross the toppa my head. Fellas

I knew started goin' "natural" and naggin' me bout doing the same. But you can't talk a man into makin a change . . . He's gotta feel changed . . . gotta be your own change . . . otherwise you just jumpin cause they say jump. One day I got to feelin' this was me . . . "naturally me" . . . and then it was.

SIMON   Abdul say if you gas your hair it mean you don't like yourself.

ASHLEY   Ain't always so. Some folks don't like themselves gassed or ungassed. If you really don't like yourself . . . you can do what you want with your hair . . . and you still won't like yourself. Your mind has to go natural while you straighten your soul . . . the process got to be on the inside. Some-a my best buddies still gas and they like themselves and me too. I don't tell them how they should and oughta look cause that's not to my best interest. They might go from here to the grave with gassed heads . . . but we got other things in common.

SIMON   I know, you mean we all Black.

ASHLEY   No boy, I mean we all in trouble . . . terrible trouble, and we ain't in it in no bits, pieces, or sections. It's a common trouble, share and share alike, want to or not; the high and the low of us, the rich and the poor of us, the black and the yaller of us, the gas head and the natural bush, the Negro and the Black man, the dungarees and the African robe, the fat black lady with the blow-hair, and the long brown lady in the wig. You and me and your mama and your stepgrandpa . . . the Ph.D. and the high school dropout . . . we in some terrible deep trouble . . . and we in it together.

SIMON   You a fine speechmaker, but who's right? What's the right thing to do or not to do? Tell me who is right.

ASHLEY   Keep workin', work and talk. If there was just a plain, straight right and wrong to everything . . . a sort of ABC of life . . . all we'd have to do is write a rule book . . . and you could wake up in the mornin' and follow the rules in your little book all day long. But life keeps twistin' and turnin', what is so today ain't so tomorrow, nothin' stands still for you. Keep workin'. Boy, where's your dust-cloth? Life is like . . . well we can't stop you from growin', can we?

SIMON   No, that's somethin we can't help, also I *want* to grow. Mama say I might be small-built cause lotsa her folks was . . . but I wanta be tall.

ASHLEY   But a man is a man . . . be he flyweight or heavyweight, a man is a man. I don't wish to be tall, short, light, dark, keen-featured or heavy-featured . . . cause I am what I am . . . but I do wanta be free . . . and I'm gonna be . . . by any means possible . . . and you just better-black-believe-it.

SIMON   Oh, please rent the room. Maytag Diamond Ashley . . . I want you to live here. It's awful small but you can stay in the kitchen a lot . . . and the rent is only eight-fifty a week, eight if you don't cook. If I was grown and payin' the rent myself, I'd let you stay here for free. You the only grownup I ever met who just *talk* to me like I'm some other person. All grownups say . . . "How old are you? That's nice." What's so nice 'bout how old you are? You got nothin' to do with that at all. Then they say . . . "Study your lesson so you can be somebody." Everybody is somebody even if they just a wino. Then they say . . . "How is the school?" Ain't that a question? The school is fine . . . it just standin' there bein' a school. But how is Simon Turnbo Brown? Please take the room. This is it right in here. (*Opens door to room off kitchen*)

ASHLEY   (*Peeps in room, then sighs*) It is small. I'd have to back in to lay on the bed. But . . . I'll take it, my friend, if your mama wants me.

SIMON   She will, I know she will.

DISCUSSION QUESTIONS

1. Ashley gives Simon a lesson on the history of some African-American names. Why is this lesson an important one for Simon to learn?
2. Old Soldier says he is an "old soldier." Is he referring to his age or to something else? Why does Old Soldier steal meat and sell it for a low price to people in the neighborhood?
3. What type of relationship do Simon and Ashley have? Why is this relationship important not only for Simon, but also for Ashley?
4. Ashley tells Simon, "we are in some terrible deep trouble . . . and we in it together." Who are the "we"? What is the deep trouble? Why are the "we" in this trouble together?

WRITING TOPICS

1. During the 1960s a large number of riots occurred in the United States. Research one of the riots that occurred in a major city during the mid-1960s. Then write an essay in which you discuss the impact of one specific riot on that city. What actions led up to the riot? What was the aftermath of the riot? Photocopy pictures from newspapers, magazines, or books about the riot and use them to illustrate your essay.
2. Photocopy a picture from a newspaper, a magazine, or a book that discusses one of the riots in the U.S. during the mid-1960s. Attach the copy of the picture to your journal and write a short story about the people or the situation in the photograph. Who are the people? Why are they where they are? What is happening in the situation? How will it be resolved?

THE CREATION

James Weldon Johnson

James Weldon Johnson was born in Jacksonville, Florida, in 1871. Educated at Atlanta and Columbia universities, Johnson was a teacher, poet, novelist, and musician. He also served as a U.S. diplomat in Venezuela and Nicaragua. After a brief career as a teacher, he and his brother, John Rosamond, went to New York City to write music for the stage. From 1920 to 1930, Johnson served as executive secretary of the National Association for the Advancement of Colored People. The association awarded him the Spingarn Medal in 1925. He taught literature at Fisk University in Tennessee and was a visiting professor at New York University. His publications include *The Autobiography of an Ex-Coloured Man* (1912), *Fifty Years and Other Poems* (1917), *God's Trombones, or Seven Negro Sermons in Verse* (1927), *St. Peter Relates an Incident of the Resurrection Day* (1935), *The Book of American Negro Poetry* (1922; expanded, 1931), *Black Manhattan* (1930), and his autobiography, *Along This Way* (1933). He and his brother edited two collections of spirituals. Because of his many talents and careers, Johnson was considered a "true Renaissance man." He died in 1938.

A NEGRO SERMON

And God stepped out on space,
And He looked around and said,
"I'm lonely—
I'll make me a world."

5 And far as the eye of God could see
Darkness covered everything,
Blacker than a hundred midnights
Down in a cypress swamp.

Then God smiled,
10   And the light broke,
And the darkness rolled up on one side,
And the light stood shining on the other,
And God said, *"That's good!"*

Then God reached out and took the light in His hands,
15   And God rolled the light around in His hands,
Until He made the sun;
And He set that sun a-blazing in the heavens.
And the light that was left from making the sun
Got gathered up in a shining ball
20   And flung against the darkness,
Spangling the night with the moon and stars.
Then down between
The darkness and the light
He hurled the world;
25   And God said, *"That's good!"*

Then God himself stepped down—
And the sun was on His right hand,
And the moon was on His left;
The stars were clustered about His head,
30   And the earth was under His feet.
And God walked, and where He trod
His footsteps hollowed the valleys out
And bulged the mountains up.

Then He stopped and looked and saw
35   That the earth was hot and barren.
So God stepped over to the edge of the world
And He spat out the seven seas;
He batted His eyes, and the lightnings flashed;
He clapped His hands, and the thunders rolled;
40   And the waters above the earth came down,
The cooling waters came down.

Then the green grass sprouted,
And the little red flowers blossomed,
The pine-tree pointed his finger to the sky,
45   And the oak spread out his arms;
The lakes cuddled down in the hollows of the ground,
And the rivers ran down to the sea;
And God smiled again,
And the rainbow appeared,
50   And curled itself around His shoulder.

Then God raised His arm and He waved His hand
Over the sea and over the land,
And He said, *"Bring forth! Bring forth!"*
And quicker than God could drop His hand,
55   Fishes and fowls
And beast and birds
Swam the rivers and the seas,
Roamed the forests and the woods,
And split the air with their wings,
60   And God said, *"That's good!"*

Then God walked around
And God looked around
On all that He had made.
He looked at His sun,
65   And He looked at His moon,
And He looked at His little stars;
He looked on His world
With all its living things,
And God said, *"I'm lonely still."*

70   Then God sat down
On the side of a hill where He could think;
By a deep, wide river He sat down;
With His head in His hands,
God thought and thought,
75   Till He thought, *"I'll make me a man!"*

Up from the bed of the river
God scooped the clay;
And by the bank of the river
He kneeled Him down;
80   And there the great God Almighty,
Who lit the sun and fixed it in the sky,
Who flung the stars to the most far corner of the night,
Who rounded the earth in the middle of His hand—
This Great God,
85   Like a mammy bending over her baby,
Kneeled down in the dust
Toiling over a lump of clay
Till He shaped it in His own image;

Then into it He blew the breath of life,
90   And man became a living soul.
Amen. Amen.

DISCUSSION QUESTIONS

1. "The Creation" is taken from a collection of Johnson's poems entitled *God's Trombones*. His technique in writing this poem is similar to a sermon preached by an African-American minister. In a small group, discuss this technique.
2. What do you notice about Johnson's use of the English language? How would you classify this language?

WRITING TOPICS

1. How did this poem make you feel? In your journal, describe your feelings after you read it.
2. List the descriptive words and phrases Johnson uses to make the poem effective.

CHAPTER THREE

THE BLUES—PAIN AND SURVIVAL

The blues is a musical form that originated in the rural South among African Americans. Known as "folk poems," blues music consists of three-line stanzas. The second line repeats the first, sometimes in a slightly different form, and the third line states some answer to or commentary on the situation stated in the first two lines:

> I hate to see the evening sun go down.
> I hate to see the evening sun go down.
> 'Cause my baby, he done left this town.

Lyrics such as these from "St. Louis Blues" express the pain and despair of blues music. Ralph Ellison, author of *Invisible Man*, defines the blues as ". . . an impulse to keep the painful detail and episodes of a brutal existence alive in one's aching consciousness, to finger its jazzed grain, and to transcend it, not by the consolation of philosophy but by squeezing from it a near-tragic, near-comic lyricism. As a form, the blues is an autobiographical chronicle of personal catastrophe expressed lyrically."

"St. Louis Blues" was written by the legendary songwriter and bandleader W. C. Handy and performed by the even more legendary singer Bessie Smith. Another early proponent of this musical form was William "Big Bill" Broonzy, who was born in 1893 in Scott, Mississippi. He, like many African-American musicians, brought the blues to northern cities such as Chicago, where it still enjoys wide popularity.

Like jazz, blues music is based on improvisation. Early blues music was played on the harmonica. It has been played on many instruments since then, but it is most often heard on the electric guitar and piano, where it can be identified musically by its percussive beat and repetitive technique. Other singers and musicians known for their contributions to the blues idiom include Ma Rainey, B. B. King, and T-Bone Walker. Blues music and lyrics, filled with sorrow and longing, paved the way for jazz and other musical forms that started in the African-American community and spoke to the world.

MUSIC: BLACK, WHITE AND BLUE

Ishmael Reed

Ishmael Reed was born in Chattanooga, Tennessee, in 1938. He grew up in Brooklyn, New York and attended the State University of New York at Buffalo. Reed worked at various jobs before landing a position as manager of a Newark, New Jersey, newspaper and as an assistant at the *East Village Other* in New York City. Reed published his first novel, *The Free-Lance Pallbearers,* in 1967 and his second, *Yellow Back Radio Broke-Down,* in 1969. He also wrote *Shrovetide in Old New Orleans* (1978), *The Terrible Twos* (1982), and *Airing Dirty Laundry* (1993). He has taught at both Yale and Dartmouth, and he currently teaches at the University of California at Berkeley. He has published four volumes of poetry and two plays. He has been nominated once for the Pulitzer Prize in poetry, and twice for the National Book Award in poetry and in fiction. This selection comes from *Black World* and is a review of Ortiz Walton's book *Music: Black, White and Blue.*

1   The trouble with much criticism of Afro-American art is that politicians control it and usually approach music, painting, writing, sculpture, and dance with their minds already made up.

2   When Frantz Fanon (popular, presumably, because he was born, not in Detroit, but in Africa and spoke French) wrote, *"Without oppression and without racism you have no blues,"* the anti-exploiter was himself exploiting a great music by using it to promote one of his pet theories. Ortiz Walton, author of *Music: Black, White & Blue,* would ascribe such a generalization to ". . . a failure to include and conceptualize purely instrumental forms of Blues in traditional analyses, and a much too literal interpretation of the poetry of lyrics and vocal Blues."

3   Walton, a musician, composer, and sociologist is just the kind of super-scientist, super-artist an investigation of Afro-American music requires and so his book is the best work on Afro-American music to date. Cecil Taylor,

the pianist, recently commented: "Walton has raised points never before analyzed."

4   Walton sees important differences between what he calls "Classical European Music," and "Classical American Music," by which he means "African music transmuted by the American experience." These differences are stringently documented by surprising information (can you imagine Johannes Brahms humming a ragtime tune and yearning to use its rhythms?), marvelous graphs which complement points made in the text, and personal experience (Walton has performed with a "Major" American symphony orchestra, the Boston Symphony, as well as with leading Afro-American musicians).

5   The book is full of cogent, cool comments and saturated with precision. Take this line interpreting the Blues, for example: ". . . being neither wholly melancholy nor wholly joyous but rather, in most instances, a combination of polar opposites which results in a tension of mood. Juxtaposition of major upon minor tonality resulting in the production of what has become known as "blue notes," is a musicological correlate of psychological and physiological tensions . . ."

6   *Music: Black, White & Blue* traces the European and African traditions and offers original theories on how they got that way and how they were influenced by differences based upon religion, culture, ecology, and geography. For Walton, European classical music is "rigid, unalterable, predictable and a fixed phenomenon," while African music means collective participation, improvisation, richer scales and rhythms. European music wasn't always that way but changed when the Christian Church triumphed in the West, inaugurating ecclesiastical music, and repressing the ancient pagan music of interesting scales and rhythms produced by European tribes. "The culminating achievement toward complete rationalization of music was the development of the symphony orchestra," Walton argues. "Here specialization reached its peak, for every man had a specific sheet of music to play the same way each time. No melodic, harmonic or rhythmic deviations were to be allowed, and an assembly-line type operation was set in motion by a foreman, the conductor."

7   Afro-American music (American classical music), Walton says, can be enjoyed by anybody while European classical music is designed for the elite. "Imagine a symphony audience snapping its fingers or saying 'yeah, baby, swing'?"

8   Lest the reader think that *Music: Black, White & Blue* is a ponderous, abstract, cold, theoretical work, be assured that the writing is excellent, witty, and jammed with interesting insights.

9   To me, one of the most fascinating discussions in the book concerns unique contributions made to world music by Afro-Americans. Walton sees the need for people to realize their own cultural heritage and not hitchhike somebody else's.

10   The notion that no Afro-American culture exists and that history ends, for Afro-Americans, when they were, to put it in Mr. Walton's words, "captured, packed in ships, and thrown into America," was behind the bogus,

light "identity" discussions of the early 1950s and early 1960s carried on by Afro-Americans who ignorantly denied the existence of Afro-American contributions to writing, music, and the other arts and craved identification with other cultures. At that time it was Europe, still is for some. Their successors, equally contemptuous of the Afro-American mind and equally moony when it comes to tough thinking have adopted Africa (which they often speak of as one country). There's no denying that Afro-Americans have benefited from a rich African heritage; a continent which contains cultures going back two million years is bound to be very wise; but often the African heritage is used to undercut the considerable achievements in the arts made by Americans of African heritage. Charlie Parker was born in Kansas City, the town we homeboys call K.C., not Lagos, and Chicago's contribution to world writing and music equals or surpasses those of any number of European and African cities.

11   Thus when Ortiz Walton writes, "Although the social conditions peculiar to America have obviously been an economic disadvantage to Blacks, they have coalesced with African retentions to produce a new and highly influential cultural world view," he is departing from the current Fashion Show, and when he writes that Afro-Americans took African music and *recast* it into "forms having an independent character of their own," our team greets this as the tie-breaking run at the bottom of the ninth. That *recasting* has occurred in writing, painting, dance, and the other arts too and those who don't see this either don't want to see it (people who call themselves scientists but banish any information that might upset their wobbly hypotheses) or aren't looking hard enough. What Afro-Americans have done with what Walton calls those "essential qualities" derived from African art is one of the mightiest achievements in human history.

12   *Music: Black, White & Blue* contains interesting chapters on these home-grown forms like slave Music and blues, Ragtime, New Orleans Jazz, music of the twenties and thirties, and the strange career of that hermetic movement Be-bop, the music that was forced "underground."

13   Walton writes indignantly about the Public-Enemy-Number-One cast of characters who've wielded considerable control over Afro-American music in the past and present; the kind of rascals who drive around corners real fast and love machine guns.

14   Afro-Americans themselves do not escape the blame for the low esteem in which Afro-American music is often held. In a moving chapter, a tribute to Edward Kennedy Ellington ("The Duke"), Walton recounts how, after a symposium held at the University of California at Berkeley and devoted to Ellington (for which Walton wrote a handsome chapbook with graphics by Glenn Myles[1]) a black Californian wrote: "Ellington's music, on the other-hand, is for the white community. It always has been . . ." The anonymous

---

[1] *The Coronation of the King, Edward Kennedy Ellington's Contribution to Black Culture.*

symposium member and author of the remark, cited James Brown's music as being for the average black man and woman. Another example, to my mind, of a black critic leaning over backward to tell the black masses "you got it," instead of risking charges of elitism by challenging them into developing their senses—developing the most powerful equipment they have on the planet and then some. James Brown, to my ears, has merely learned the same lesson as the creators of *The Great Train Robbery:* that is, you can play the same scene over and over merely changing the titles and still get a gullible public to go for it.

15   *Music: Black, White & Blue* also includes a section concerning the suit waged against the New York Philharmonic by bassist Arthur Davis.

16   Walton appeals for more Afro-American musical training programs in a country in which Walton sees "too many symphonies." He criticizes funding policies of such institutions as the National Endowment for the Arts which he feels are geared to sustaining European culture instead of what he regards as the true American classical music.

17   Traditional "black" and "white" politics in America have been based upon catastrophe. Eagleton and McGovern were doomed from the outset because the public felt they weren't steady enough to commit what was an essentially insane act. Black politics have been based upon revolution, extermination, or exodus. (Objectives which are masses-oriented therefore sensationalistic [for the same reason the masses of people will continue to like loud and wrong films and music regardless of how often a handful of intellectuals sound off about "blaxploitation"].) Those who've tried to build a politics or culture based on the assumption that we're going to be here have been regarded as Uncle Toms. These "judgment day" assumptions have been enervating and wasteful but few intellectuals have dared to challenge them—Afro-American intellectuals meekly follow "the people" instead of asserting the many directions open to them—directions "the people" may not always be aware of. Therefore it took considerable courage for Ortiz Walton to write what amounts to a call for the transvaluation of Afro-American values: "The Afro-American has become heir to the myths that it is better to be poor than rich, lower-class rather than middle or upper, easygoing rather than industrious, extravagant rather than thrifty, and athletic rather than academic. Accordingly Afro-Americans, unlike other ethnic groups, are viewed, and often view themselves, as being better off not owning property, business and land. This capitalism is good only for Jews, Italians, Poles, Lithuanians, Irish, Germans, Wasps and other ethnic groups residing in America who are in the process of striving to better their lives." Walton's book ends with a proposal that Afro-American music is a huge industry and that Afro-Americans should be in charge of—not telling the artist how he should do his work, the traditional Communistic approach—but packaging, selling, distributing, and billing for that industry. Walton has done his HooDoo Work in *Music: Black, White & Blue;* a major event in Afro-American cultural history. A book that can't be recommended highly enough.

DISCUSSION QUESTIONS

1. According to the book, Walton writes that there are "too many symphonies." What do you think this statement means? Do you agree or disagree with it? Why?
2. Reed suggests: "The trouble with much criticism of Afro-(African) American art (music, dance, painting, literature) is that politicians control it . . . with their minds already made up." In a small group, discuss what you think the writer means by this statement.
3. Remembering that this review was written in 1972, whom do you think Walton is referring to when he talks about the "Public-Enemy-Number-One" cast of characters?

WRITING TOPICS

1. Frantz Fanon, referred to in the selection, is a French-speaking African and the author of the 1967 popular book *Black Skin, White Masks.* He wrote: "Without oppression and without racism you have no blues." Write an analytical essay in which you interpret the meaning of this statement. Or, you may wish to write an essay disagreeing with the statement. In either case, give specific examples from your experience or your research.
2. The writer suggests that African Americans, especially music critics, are also to blame for the low esteem in which the music (such as blues and jazz) originated by African Americans, is often held. One African-American critic wrote: "Duke Ellington's music, on the other hand, is for the white community." Write an essay in which you agree or disagree with this statement. Give specific examples from your reading, listening, or research.
3. If a particular statement in the selection struck a chord in you, freewrite about it in your journal. You might start with an emotional response that the passage evoked. You may wish to discuss your selected statement with members of your small group.

THE BLUES I'M PLAYING

Langston Hughes

Langston Hughes, born in 1902, was a key figure of the Harlem Renaissance and is considered by some critics to be the most significant African-American writer of the twentieth century. As a fiction writer and poet, Hughes presented realistic portrayals of African-American culture and values. Blues forms and themes are often the focus of his poetry and fiction. Hughes's work nobly celebrates the humblest voices of the black community, and his popularity has increased since his death. His works continue to be anthologized and collected: *Good Morning Revolution: Uncollected Social Protest Writings by Langston Hughes* (1973), *The Dream Keeper and Other Poems* (1986), *Mule Bone: A Comedy of Negro Life* (1991), and *The Collected Poems of Langston Hughes* (1994). Hughes died in 1967. (For further biographical information, see pages 133, 192, and 385.)

I

1 Oceola Jones, pianist, studied under Philippe in Paris. Mrs. Dora Ellsworth paid her bills. The bills included a little apartment on the Left Bank and a grand piano. Twice a year Mrs. Ellsworth came over from New York and spent part of her time with Oceola in the little apartment. The rest of her time abroad she usually spent at Biarritz or Juan les Pins, where she would see the new canvases of Antonio Bas, young Spanish painter who also enjoyed the patronage of Mrs. Ellsworth. Bas and Oceola, the woman thought, both had genius. And whether they had genius or not, she loved them, and took good care of them.

2 Poor dear lady, she had no children of her own. Her husband was dead. And she had no interest in life now save art, and the young people who created art. She was very rich, and it gave her pleasure to share her richness with beauty. Except that she was sometimes confused as to where beauty lay—in the youngsters or in what they made, in the creators or the creation. Mrs. Ellsworth had been known to help charming young people who wrote

terrible poems, blue-eyed young men who painted awful pictures. And she once turned down a garlic-smelling soprano-singing girl who, a few years later, had all the critics in New York at her feet. The girl was so sallow. And she really needed a bath, or at least a mouth wash, on the day when Mrs. Ellsworth went to hear her sing at an East Side settlement house. Mrs. Ellsworth had sent a small check and let it go at that—since, however, living to regret bitterly her lack of musical acumen in the face of garlic.

3   About Oceola, though, there had been no doubt. The Negro girl had been highly recommended to her by Ormond Hunter, the music critic, who often went to Harlem to hear the church concerts there, and had thus listened twice to Oceola's playing.

4   "A most amazing tone," he had told Mrs. Ellsworth, knowing her interest in the young and unusual. "A flare for the piano such as I have seldom encountered. All she needs is training—finish, polish, a repertoire."

5   "Where is she?" asked Mrs. Ellsworth at once. "I will hear her play."

6   By the hardest, Oceola was found. By the hardest, an appointment was made for her to come to East 63rd Street and play for Mrs. Ellsworth. Oceola had said she was busy every day. It seemed that she had pupils, rehearsed a church choir, and played almost nightly for colored house parties or dances. She made quite a good deal of money. She wasn't tremendously interested, it seemed, in going way downtown to play for some elderly lady she had never heard of, even if the request did come from the white critic, Ormond Hunter, via the pastor of the church whose choir she rehearsed, and to which Mr. Hunter's maid belonged.

7   It was finally arranged, however. And one afternoon, promptly on time, black Miss Oceola Jones rang the door bell of white Mrs. Dora Ellsworth's grey stone house just off Madison. A butler who actually wore brass buttons opened the door, and she was shown upstairs to the music room. (The butler had been warned of her coming.) Ormond Hunter was already there, and they shook hands. In a moment, Mrs. Ellsworth came in, a tall stately grey-haired lady in black with a scarf that sort of floated behind her. She was tremendously intrigued at meeting Oceola, never having had before amongst all her artists a black one. And she was greatly impressed that Ormond Hunter should have recommended the girl. She began right away, treating her as a protegee; that is, she began asking her a great many questions she would not dare ask anyone else at first meeting, except a protegee. She asked her how old she was and where her mother and father were and how she made her living and whose music she liked best to play and was she married and would she take one lump or two in her tea, with lemon or cream?

8   After tea, Oceola played. She played the Rachmaninoff *Prelude in C Sharp Minor.* She played from the Liszt *Études.* She played the *St. Louis Blues.* She played Ravel's *Pavanne pour une Enfante Défunte.* And then she said she had to go. She was playing that night for a dance in Brooklyn for the benefit of the Urban League.

9   Mrs. Ellsworth and Ormond Hunter breathed, "How lovely!"

10   Mrs. Ellsworth said, "I am quite overcome, my dear. You play so beautifully." She went on further to say, "You must let me help you. Who is your
teacher?"

11   "I have none now," Oceola replied. "I teach pupils myself. Don't have
time any more to study—nor money either."

12   "But you must have time," said Mrs. Ellsworth, "and money, also. Come
back to see me on Tuesday. We will arrange it, my dear."

13   And when the girl had gone, she turned to Ormond Hunter for advice
on piano teachers to instruct those who already had genius, and need only
to be developed.

II

14   Then began one of the most interesting periods in Mrs. Ellsworth's
whole experience in aiding the arts. The period of Oceola. For the Negro
girl, as time went on, began to occupy a greater and greater place in Mrs.
Ellsworth's interests, to take up more and more of her time, and to use up
more and more of her money. Not that Oceola ever asked for money, but
Mrs. Ellsworth herself seemed to keep thinking of so much more Oceola
needed.

15   At first it was hard to get Oceola to need anything. Mrs. Ellsworth had
the feeling that the girl mistrusted her generosity, and Oceola did—for she
had never met anybody interested in pure art before. Just to be given things
for *art's sake* seemed suspicious to Oceola.

16   That first Tuesday, when the colored girl came back at Mrs. Ellsworth's
request, she answered the white woman's questions with a why-look in her
eyes.

17   "Don't think I'm being personal, dear," said Mrs. Ellsworth, "but I must
know your background in order to help you. Now, tell me . . ."

18   Oceola wondered why on earth the woman wanted to help her.
However, since Mrs. Ellsworth seemed interested in her life's history, she
brought it forth so as not to hinder the progress of the afternoon, for she
wanted to get back to Harlem by six o'clock.

19   Born in Mobile in 1903. Yes, m'am, she was older than she looked. Papa
had a band, that is her step-father. Used to play for all the lodge turn-outs,
picnics, dances, barbecues. You could get the best roast pig in the world in
Mobile. Her mother used to play the organ in church, and when the dea-
cons bought a piano after the big revival, her mama played that, too. Oceola
played by ear for a long while until her mother taught her notes. Oceola
played an organ, also, and a cornet.

20   "My, my," said Mrs. Ellsworth.

21   "Yes, m'am," said Oceola. She had played and practiced on lots of instruments in the South before her step-father died. She always went to band
rehearsals with him.

22   "And where was your father, dear?" asked Mrs. Ellsworth.

23   "My step-father had the band," replied Oceola. Her mother left off play-ing in the church to go with him traveling in Billy Kersands' Minstrels. He had the biggest mouth in the world, Kersands did, and used to let Oceola put both her hands in it at a time and stretch it. Well, she and her mama and step-papa settled down in Houston. Sometimes her parents had jobs and sometimes they didn't. Often they were hungry, but Oceola went to school and had a regular piano-teacher, an old German woman, who gave her what technique she had today.

24   "A fine old teacher," said Oceola. "She used to teach me half the time for nothing. God bless her."

25   "Yes," said Mrs. Ellsworth. "She gave you an excellent foundation."

26   "Sure did. But my step-papa died, got cut, and after that Mama didn't have no more use for Houston so we moved to St. Louis. Mama got a job playing for the movies in a Market Street theater, and I played for a church choir, and saved some money and went to Wilberforce. Studied piano there, too. Played for all the college dances. Graduated. Came to New York and heard Rachmaninoff and was crazy about him. Then Mama died, so I'm keeping the little flat myself. One room is rented out."

27   "Is she nice?" asked Mrs. Ellsworth, "your roomer?"

28   "It's not a she," said Oceola. "He's a man. I hate women roomers."

29   "Oh!" said Mrs. Ellsworth. "I should think all roomers would be terrible."

30   "He's right nice," said Oceola. "Name's Pete Williams."

31   "What does he do?" asked Mrs. Ellsworth.

32   "A Pullman porter," replied Oceola, "but he's saving money to go to Med school. He's a smart fellow."

33   But it turned out later that he wasn't paying Oceola any rent.

34   That afternoon, when Mrs. Ellsworth announced that she had made her an appointment with one of the best piano teachers in New York, the black girl seemed pleased. She recognized the name. But how, she wondered, would she find time for study, with her pupils and her choir, and all. When Mrs. Ellsworth said that she would cover her entire living expenses, Oceola's eyes were full of that why-look, as though she didn't believe it.

35   "I have faith in your art, dear," said Mrs. Ellsworth, at parting. But to prove it quickly, she sat down that very evening and sent Oceola the first monthly check so that she would no longer have to take in pupils or drill choirs or play at house parties. And so Oceola would have faith in art, too.

36   That night Mrs. Ellsworth called up Ormond Hunter and told him what she had done. And she asked if Mr. Hunter's maid knew Oceola, and if she supposed that that man rooming with her were anything to her. Ormond Hunter said he would inquire.

37   Before going to bed, Mrs. Ellsworth told her housekeeper to order a book called "Nigger Heaven" on the morrow, and also anything else Brentano's had about Harlem. She made a mental note that she must go up there sometime, for she had never yet seen that dark section of New York;

and now that she had a Negro protegee, she really ought to know something about it. Mrs. Ellsworth couldn't recall ever having known a single Negro before in her whole life, so she found Oceola fascinating. And just as black as she herself was white.

38   Mrs. Ellsworth began to think in bed about what gowns would look best on Oceola. Her protegee would have to be well-dressed. She wondered, too, what sort of a place the girl lived in. And who that man was who lived with her. She began to think that really Oceola ought to have a place to herself. It didn't seem quite respectable. . . .

39   When she woke up in the morning, she called her car and went by her dressmaker's. She asked the good woman what kind of colors looked well with black; not black fabrics, but a black skin.

40   "I have a little friend to fit out," she said.

41   "A *black* friend?" said the dressmaker.

42   "A black friend," said Mrs. Ellsworth.

III

43   Some days later Ormond Hunter reported on what his maid knew about Oceola. It seemed that the two belonged to the same church, and although the maid did not know Oceola very well, she knew what everybody said about her in the church. Yes, indeedy! Oceola were a right nice girl, for sure, but it certainly were a shame she were giving all her money to that man what stayed with her and what she was practically putting through college so he could be a doctor.

44   "Why," gasped Mrs Ellsworth, "the poor child is being preyed upon."

45   "It seems to me so," said Ormond Hunter.

46   "I must get her out of Harlem," said Mrs. Ellsworth, "at once. I believe it's worse than Chinatown."

47   "She might be in a more artistic atmosphere," agreed Ormond Hunter. "And with her career launched, she probably won't want that man anyhow."

48   "She won't need him," said Mrs. Ellsworth. "She will have her art."

49   But Mrs. Ellsworth decided that in order to increase the rapprochement between art and Oceola, something should be done now, at once. She asked the girl to come down to see her the next day, and when it was time to go home, the white woman said, "I have a half-hour before dinner. I'll drive you up. You know I've never been to Harlem."

50   "All right," said Oceola. "That's nice of you."

51   But she didn't suggest the white lady's coming in, when they drew up before a rather sad-looking apartment house in 134th Street. Mrs. Ellsworth had to ask could she come in.

52   "I live on the fifth floor," said Oceola, "and there isn't any elevator."

53   "It doesn't matter, dear," said the white woman, for she meant to see the inside of this girl's life, elevator or no elevator.

54   The apartment was just as she thought it would be. After all, she had read

Thomas Burke on Limehouse. And here was just one more of those holes in the wall, even if it was five stories high. The windows looked down on slums. There were only four rooms, small as maids' rooms, all of them. An upright piano almost filled the parlor. Oceola slept in the dining-room. The roomer slept in the bed-chamber beyond the kitchen.

55 "Where is he, darling?"

56 "He runs on the road all summer," said the girl. "He's in and out."

57 "But how do you breathe in here?" asked Mrs. Ellsworth. "It's so small. You must have more space for your soul, dear. And for a grand piano. Now, in the Village . . ."

58 "I do right well here," said Oceola.

59 "But in the Village where so many nice artists live we can get . . ."

60 "But I don't want to move yet. I promised my roomer he could stay till fall."

61 "Why till fall?"

62 "He's going to Meharry then."

63 "To marry?"

64 "Meharry, yes m'am. That's a colored Medicine school in Nashville."

65 "Colored? Is it good?"

66 "Well, it's cheap," said Oceola. "After he goes, I don't mind moving."

67 "But I wanted to see you settled before I go away for the summer."

68 "When you come back is all right. I can do till then."

69 "Art is long," reminded Mrs. Ellsworth, "and time is fleeting, my dear."

70 "Yes, m'am," said Oceola, "but I gets nervous if I start worrying about time."

71 So Mrs. Ellsworth went off to Bar Harbor for the season, and left the man with Oceola.

IV

72 That was some years ago. Eventually art and Mrs. Ellsworth triumphed. Oceola moved out of Harlem. She lived in Gay Street west of Washington Square where she met Genevieve Taggard, and Ernestine Evans, and two or three sculptors, and a cat-painter who was also a protegee of Mrs. Ellsworth. She spent her days practicing, playing for friends of her patron, going to concerts, and reading books about music. She no longer had pupils or rehearsed the choir, but she still loved to play for Harlem house parties—for nothing—now that she no longer needed the money, out of sheer love of jazz. This rather disturbed Mrs. Ellsworth, who still believed in art of the old school, portraits that really and truly looked like people, poems about nature, music that had soul in it, not syncopation. And she felt the dignity of art. Was it in keeping with genius, she wondered, for Oceola to have a studio full of white and colored people every Saturday night (some of them actually drinking gin *from bottles*) and dancing to the most tomtom-like music she had ever heard coming out of a grand piano? She wished she could lift Oceola up bodily and take her away from all that, for art's sake.

73   So in the spring, Mrs. Ellsworth organized weekends in the upstate mountains where she had a little lodge and where Oceola could look from the high places at the stars, and fill her soul with the vastness of the eternal, and forget about jazz. Mrs. Ellsworth really began to hate jazz—especially on a grand piano.

74   If there were a lot of guests at the lodge, as there sometimes were, Mrs. Ellsworth might share the bed with Oceola. Then she would read aloud Tennyson or Browning before turning out the light, aware all the time of the electric strength of that brown-black body beside her, and of the deep drowsy voice asking what the poems were about. And then Mrs. Ellsworth would feel very motherly toward this dark girl whom she had taken under her wing on the wonderful road of art, to nurture and love until she became a great interpreter of the piano. At such times the elderly white woman was glad her late husband's money, so well invested, furnished her with a large surplus to devote to the needs of her protegees, especially to Oceola, the blackest—and most interesting of all.

75   Why the most interesting?

76   Mrs. Ellsworth didn't know, unless it was that Oceola really was talented, terribly alive, and that she looked like nothing Mrs. Ellsworth had ever been near before. Such a rich velvet black, and such a hard young body! The teacher of the piano raved about her strength.

77   "She can stand a great career," the teacher said. "She has everything for it."

78   "Yes," agreed Mrs. Ellsworth, thinking, however, of the Pullman porter at Meharry, "but she must learn to sublimate her soul."

79   So for two years then, Oceola lived abroad at Mrs. Ellsworth's expense. She studied with Philippe, had the little apartment on the Left Bank, and learned about Debussy's African background. She met many black Algerian and French West Indian students, too, and listened to their interminable arguments ranging from Garvey to Picasso to Spengler to Jean Cocteau, and thought they all must be crazy. Why did they or anybody argue so much about life or art? Oceola merely lived—and loved it. Only the Marxian students seemed sound to her for they, at least, wanted people to have enough to eat. That was important, Oceola thought, remembering, as she did, her own sometimes hungry years. But the rest of the controversies, as far as she could fathom, were based on air.

80   Oceola hated most artists, too, and the word *art* in French or English. If you wanted to play the piano or paint pictures or write books, go ahead! But why talk so much about it? Montparnasse was worse in that respect than the Village. And as for the cultured Negroes who were always saying art would break down color lines, art could save the race and prevent lynchings! "Bunk!" said Oceola. "My ma and pa were both artists when it came to making music, and the white folks ran them out of town for being dressed up in Alabama. And look at the Jews! Every other artist in the world's a Jew, and still folks hate them."

81   She thought of Mrs. Ellsworth (dear soul in New York), who never made uncomplimentary remarks about Negroes, but frequently did about Jews. Of little Menuhin she would say, for instance, "He's a *genius*—not a Jew," hating to admit his ancestry.

82   In Paris, Oceola especially loved the West Indian ball rooms where the black colonials danced the beguin. And she liked the entertainers at Bricktop's. Sometimes late at night there, Oceola would take the piano and beat out a blues for Brick and the assembled guests. In her playing of Negro folk music, Oceola never doctored it up, or filled it full of classical runs, or fancy falsities. In the blues she made the bass notes throb like tom-toms, the trebles cry like little flutes, so deep in the earth and so high in the sky that they understood everything. And when the night club crowd would get up and dance to her blues, and Bricktop would yell, "Hey! Hey!" Oceola felt as happy as if she were performing a Chopin étude for the nicely gloved Oh's and Ah-ers in a Crillon salon.

83   Music, to Oceola, demanded movement and expression, dancing and liv-ing to go with it. She liked to teach, when she had the choir, the singing of those rhythmical Negro spirituals that possessed the power to pull colored folks out of their seats in the amen corner and make them prance and shout in the aisles for Jesus. She never liked those fashionable colored churches where shouting and movement were discouraged and looked down upon, and where New England hymns instead of spirituals were sung. Oceola's background was too well-grounded in Mobile, and Billy Kersands' Minstrels, and the Sanctified churches where religion was a joy, to stare mys-tically over the top of a grand piano like white folks and imagine that Beethoven had nothing to do with life, or that Schubert's love songs were only sublimations.

84   Whenever Mrs. Ellsworth came to Paris, she and Oceola spent hours lis-tening to symphonies and string quartettes and pianists. Oceola enjoyed concerts, but seldom felt, like her patron, that she was floating on clouds of bliss. Mrs. Ellsworth insisted, however, that Oceola's spirit was too moved for words at such times—therefore she understood why the dear child kept quiet. Mrs. Ellsworth herself was often too moved for words, but never by pieces like Ravel's *Bolero* (which Oceola played on the phonograph as a dance record) or any of the compositions of *les Six*.

85   What Oceola really enjoyed most with Mrs. Ellsworth was not going to concerts, but going for trips on the little river boats in the Seine; or riding out to old chateaux in her patron's hired Renault; or to Versailles, and lis-tening to the aging white lady talk about the romantic history of France, the wars and uprising, the loves and intrigues of princes and kings and queens, about guillotines and lace handkerchiefs, snuff boxes and daggers. For Mrs. Ellsworth had loved France as a girl, and had made a study of its life and lore. Once she used to sing simple little French songs rather well, too. And she always regretted that her husband never understood the lovely words— or even tried to understand them.

86   Oceola learned the accompaniments for all the songs Mrs. Ellsworth knew and sometimes they tried them over together. The middle-aged white woman loved to sing when the colored girl played, and she even tried spirituals. Often, when she stayed at the little Paris apartment, Oceola would go into the kitchen and cook something good for late supper, maybe an oyster soup, or fried apples and bacon. And sometimes Oceola had pigs' feet.

87   "There's nothing quite so good as a pig's foot," said Oceola, "after playing all day."

88   "Then you must have pigs' feet," agreed Mrs. Ellsworth.

89   And all this while Oceola's development at the piano blossomed into perfection. Her tone became a singing wonder and her interpretations warm and individual. She gave a concert in Paris, one in Brussels, and another in Berlin. She got the press notices all pianists crave. She had her picture in lots of European papers. And she came home to New York a year after the stock market crashed and nobody had any money—except folks like Mrs. Ellsworth who had so much it would be hard to ever lose it all.

90   Oceola's one time Pullman porter, now a coming doctor, was graduating from Meharry that spring. Mrs. Ellsworth saw her dark protegee go South to attend his graduation with tears in her eyes. She thought that by now music would be enough, after all those years under the best teachers, but alas, Oceola was not yet sublimated, even by Philippe. She wanted to see Pete.

91   Oceola returned North to prepare for her New York concert in the fall. She wrote Mrs. Ellsworth at Bar Harbor that her doctor boyfriend was putting in one more summer on the railroad, then in the autumn he would intern at Atlanta. And Oceola said that he had asked her to marry him. Lord, she was happy!

92   It was a long time before she heard from Mrs. Ellsworth. When the letter came, it was full of long paragraphs about the beautiful music Oceola had within her power to give the world. Instead, she wanted to marry and be burdened with children! Oh, my dear, my dear!

93   Oceola, when she read it, thought she had done pretty well knowing Pete this long and not having children. But she wrote back that she didn't see why children and music couldn't go together. Anyway, during the present depression, it was pretty hard for a beginning artist like herself to book a concert tour—so she might just as well be married awhile. Pete, on his last run in from St. Louis, had suggested that they have the wedding Christmas in the South. "And he's impatient, at that. He needs me."

94   This time Mrs. Ellsworth didn't answer by letter at all. She was back in town in late September. In November, Oceola played at Town Hall. The critics were kind, but they didn't go wild. Mrs. Ellsworth swore it was because of Pete's influence on her protegee.

95   "But he was in Atlanta," Oceola said.

96   "His spirit was here," Mrs. Ellsworth insisted. "All the time you were playing on that stage, he was here, the monster! Taking you out of yourself, taking you away from the piano."

97   "Why, he wasn't," said Oceola. "He was watching an operation in Atlanta."

98   But from then on, things didn't go well between her and her patron. The white lady grew distinctly cold when she received Oceola in her beautiful drawing room among the jade vases and amber cups worth thousands of dollars. When Oceola would have to wait there for Mrs. Ellsworth, she was afraid to move for fear she might knock something over—that would take ten years of a Harlemite's wages to replace, if broken.

99   Over the tea cups, the aging Mrs. Ellsworth did not talk any longer about the concert tour she had once thought she might finance for Oceola, if no recognized bureau took it up. Instead, she spoke of that something she believed Oceola's fingers had lost since her return from Europe. And she wondered why any one insisted on living in Harlem.

100   "I've been away from my own people so long," said the girl, "I want to live right in the middle of them again."

101   Why, Mrs. Ellsworth wondered farther, did Oceola, at her last concert in a Harlem church, not stick to the classical items listed on the program. Why did she insert one of her own variations on the spirituals, a syncopated variation from the Sanctified Church, that made an old colored lady rise up and cry out from her pew, "Glory to God this evenin'! Yes! Hallelujah! Whooo-oo!" right at the concert? Which seemed most undignified to Mrs. Ellsworth, and unworthy of the teachings of Philippe. And furthermore, why was Pete coming up to New York for Thanksgiving? And who had sent him the money to come?

102   "Me," said Oceola. "He doesn't make anything interning."

103   "Well," said Mrs. Ellsworth, "I don't think much of him." But Oceola didn't seem to care what Mrs. Ellsworth thought, for she made no defense.

104   Thanksgiving evening, in bed, together in a Harlem apartment, Pete and Oceola talked about their wedding to come. They would have a big one in a church with lots of music. And Pete would give her a ring. And she would have on a white dress, light and fluffy, not silk. "I hate silk," she said. "I hate expensive things." (She thought of her mother being buried in a cotton dress, for they were all broke when she died. Mother would have been glad about her marriage.) "Pete," Oceola said, hugging him in the dark, "let's live in Atlanta, where there are lots of colored people, like us."

105   "What about Mrs. Ellsworth?" Pete asked. "She coming down to Atlanta for our wedding?"

106   "I don't know," said Oceola.

107   "I hope not, 'cause if she stops at one of them big hotels. I won't have you going to the back door to see her. That's one thing I hate about the South—where there're white people, you have to go to the back door."

108   "Maybe she can stay with us," said Oceola. "I wouldn't mind."

109   "I'll be damned," said Pete. "You want to get lynched?"

110   But it happened that Mrs. Ellsworth didn't care to attend the wedding, anyway. When she saw how love had triumphed over art, she decided she

could no longer influence Oceola's life. The period of Oceola was over. She would send checks, occasionally, if the girl needed them, besides, of course, something beautiful for the wedding, but that would be all. These things she told her the week after Thanksgiving.

111   "And Oceola, my dear, I've decided to spend the whole winter in Europe. I sail on December eighteenth, Christmas—while you are marrying—I shall be in Paris with my precious Antonio Bas. In January, he has an exhibition of oils in Madrid. And in the spring, a new young poet is coming over whom I want to visit Florence, to really know Florence. A charming white-haired boy from Omaha whose soul has been crushed in the West. I want to try to help him. He, my dear, is one of the few people who live for their art—and nothing else. . . . Ah, such a beautiful life! . . . You will come and play for me once before I sail?"

112   "Yes, Mrs. Ellsworth," said Oceola, genuinely sorry that the end had come. Why did white folks think you could live on nothing but art? Strange! Too strange! Too strange!

V

113   The Persian vases in the music room were filled with long-stemmed lilies that night when Oceola Jones came down from Harlem for the last time to play for Mrs. Dora Ellsworth. Mrs. Ellsworth had on a gown of black velvet, and a collar of pearls about her neck. She was very kind and gentle to Oceola, as one would be to a child who has done a great wrong but doesn't know any better. But to the black girl from Harlem, she looked very cold and white, and her grand piano seemed like the biggest and heaviest in the world—as Oceola sat down to play it with the technique for which Mrs. Ellsworth had paid.

114   As the rich and aging white woman listened to the great roll of Beethoven sonatas and to the sea and moonlight of the Chopin nocturnes, as she watched the swaying dark strong shoulders of Oceola Jones, she began to reproach the girl aloud for running away from art and music, for burying herself in Atlanta and love—love for a man unworthy of lacing up her boot straps, as Mrs. Ellsworth put it.

115   "You could shake the stars with your music, Oceola. Depression or no depression, I could make you great. And yet you propose to dig a grave for yourself. Art is bigger than love."

116   "I believe you, Mrs. Ellsworth," said Oceola, not turning away from the piano. "But being married won't keep me from making tours, or being an artist."

117   "Yes, it will," said Mrs. Ellsworth. "He'll take all the music out of you."

118   "No, he won't," said Oceola.

119   "You don't know, child," said Mrs. Ellsworth, "what men are like."

120   "Yes, I do," said Oceola simply. And her fingers began to wander slowly up and down the keyboard, flowing into the soft and lazy syncopation of a Negro blues, a blues that deepened and grew into rollicking jazz, then into

an earth-throbbing rhythm that shook the lilies in the Persian vases of Mrs. Ellsworth's music room. Louder than the voice of the white woman who cried that Oceola was deserting beauty, deserting her real self, deserting her hope in life, the flood of wild syncopation filled the house, then sank into the slow and singing blues with which it had begun.

121   The girl at the piano heard the white woman saying, "Is this what I spent thousands of dollars to teach you?"

122   "No," said Oceola simply. "This is mine. . . . Listen! . . . How sad and gay it is. Blue and happy—laughing and crying. . . . How white like you and black like me. . . . How much like a man. . . . And how like a woman. . . . Warm as Pete's mouth. . . . These are the blues. . . . I'm playing."

123   Mrs. Ellsworth sat very still in her chair looking at the lilies trembling delicately in the priceless Persian vases, while Oceola made the bass notes throb like tom-toms deep in the earth.

> O, if I could holler

sang the blues,

> Like a mountain jack,
> I'd go up on de mountain

sang the blues,

> And call my baby back.

124   "And I," said Mrs. Ellsworth rising from her chair, "would stand looking at the stars."

DISCUSSION QUESTIONS

1. In Part IV of the story, Dora Ellsworth holds a particular position concerning art. In this same section of the story, Oceola holds another position. What are these two positions? Use specific examples from the story to support your responses.

2. Discuss Hughes's use of irony when the narrator discusses Mrs. Ellsworth. Why is this tone effective for the story?

3. Describe Mrs. Ellsworth's characteristics at the beginning of the story and at the end of the story. Does she change? Why or why not?

4. What happens to Oceola when she plays jazz and blues music? Explain why she feels the way she does.
5. How does Oceola resolve the conflict between her beliefs and Mrs. Ellsworth's beliefs? Has she grown from resolving this conflict? Why or why not?

WRITING TOPICS

1. Write an essay in which you analyze the connections between jazz or blues music and classical music. What makes the two types of music similar? Dissimilar?
2. Think about a time in your life when you wanted to write, dance, sing, or whatever one particular way, and someone else wanted you to perform in another way. How did you resolve the situation? How do you now feel about the choice you made? Write a short essay about your choice.

IT'S THE LAW

A RAP POEM

Saundra Sharp

Saundra Sharp was born in Cleveland, Ohio. She is an actress, a screenwriter, poet, and independent filmmaker. She has written more than 100 segments on African-American history and a stage play, *The Sistuhs*. Her poetry collections include *From the Windows of My Mind* (1970), *In the Midst of Change* (1979), *Soft Song* (1978, reprinted by Harlem River Press, 1990), *Typing in the Dark* (1991), and *In the Midst of Change: On the Sharp Side*, a spoken-word recording. Her film credits include the shorts, *Picking Tribes* and *Back Inside Herself,* and a documentary, *Life is a Saxophone.*

You can learn about the state of the U.S.A.
By the laws we have on the books today.
The rules we break are the laws we make
The things that we fear, we legislate.

5 We got laws designed to keep folks in line
Laws for what happens when you lose your mind
Laws against stealing, laws against feeling,
The laws we have are a definite sign
That our vision of love is going blind.
10 (They probably got a law against this rhyme.)
Unh-hunh . . . . .

We got laws for cool cats & laws for dirty dogs
Laws about where you can park your hog
Laws against your mama and your papa, too
15 Even got a law to make the laws come true.

It's against the law to hurt an ol' lady,
It's against the law to steal a little baby,
The laws we make are what we do to each other
There is no law to make brother love brother
20 Hmmm . . . .

Now this respect thang is hard for some folks to do
They don't respect themselves
          so they can't respect you
This is the word we should get around—
25 These are the rules: we gonna run 'em on down.
Listen up!:

It ain't enough to be cute,
It ain't enough to be tough
You gotta walk tall
30 You gotta strut your stuff

You gotta learn to read, you gotta learn to write.
Get the tools you need to win this fight
Get your common sense down off the shelf
Start in the mirror . . . . Respect your Self!

35 When you respect yourself you keep your body clean
You walk tall, walk gentle, don't have to be mean
You keep your mind well fed, you keep a clear head
And you think 'bout who you let in your bed—
Unh-hunh . . . . . .

40 When you respect yourself you come to understand
That your body is a temple for a natural plan,
It's against that plan to use drugs or dope—
Use your heart and your mind when you need to cope . . .
It's the law!

45 We got laws that got started in '86
And laws made back when the Indians got kicked
If we want these laws to go out of favor
Then we've got to change our behavior

Change what!? you say, well let's take a look
50 How did the laws get on the books? Yeah.
I said it up front but let's get tougher
The laws we make are what we do to each other

If you never shoot at me then I don't need
A law to keep you from shooting at me, do you see?
55 There's a universal law that's tried and true
Says Don't do to me—
What you don't want done to you
Unh-hunh!
Don't do to me—
60 What you don't want done to you
It's the law!

DISCUSSION QUESTIONS

1. In stanzas six through nine, the speaker in the poem makes reference to "rules" we need to respect ourselves. To whom is the speaker addressing these rules? Why is the speaker addressing this particular audience? How are these rules different from the laws to which the speaker refers in stanzas one through four?
2. Analyze the difference between laws that the government enforces and the "laws" we impose on ourselves. Use specific laws from the poem to support your answer.
3. Which elements in this poem make it "a rap poem"? In what ways are these rap elements similar to blues elements? In what ways are they dissimilar?

WRITING TOPICS

1. In your journal, construct a set of laws "to make brother (or sister) love brother (or sister)." Why are these laws needed? Why are they good ones?
2. In your local library, research a law that had its beginning as accepted behavior in society. In an essay explain how this societal norm became a local, a state, or a national law. Is it still a law today?

SONNY'S BLUES

James Baldwin

James Baldwin was born in New York City in 1924. He attended Douglass High School in Harlem, where Countee Cullen was one of his teachers, and he served as editor of the student literary magazines at DeWitt Clinton High School in the Bronx. As a young man, Baldwin was a Pentecostal preacher for three years. He then lived in Greenwich Village until he left for France in 1948, the same year he was awarded a Rosenwald Fellowship. Although life in Paris was hard, he did complete his novel *Go Tell It on the Mountain.* His play, *The Amen Corner* was produced at Howard University during his visit to the states in 1954 to 1955. Baldwin was involved with the Civil Rights Movement during the late 1950s and the early 1960s. He wrote his major prose statements of Black protest in his *The Fire Next Time* (1963). Other works include *Going to Meet the Man* (1965), a collection of short stories, *Tell Me How Long the Train's Been Gone* (1968), a novel, and *Rap on Race* (1971), taped conversations with Margaret Mead, the anthropologist. Baldwin died in 1987.

1   I read about it in the paper, in the subway, on my way to work. I read it, and I couldn't believe it, and I read it again. Then perhaps I just stared at it, at the newsprint spelling out his name, spelling out the story. I stared at it in the swinging lights of the subway car, and in the faces and bodies of the people, and in my own face, trapped in the darkness which roared outside.

2   It was not to be believed and I kept telling myself that, as I walked from the subway station to the high school. And at the same time I couldn't doubt it. I was scared, scared for Sonny. He became real to me again. A great block of ice got settled in my belly and kept melting there slowly all day long, while I taught my classes algebra. It was a special kind of ice. It kept melting, sending trickles of ice water all up and down my veins, but it never got less. Sometimes it hardened and seemed to expand until I felt my guts were going to come spilling out or that I was going to choke or scream. This

would always be at a moment when I was remembering some specific thing Sonny had once said or done.

3   When he was about as old as the boys in my classes his face had been bright and open, there was a lot of copper in it; and he'd had wonderfully direct brown eyes, and great gentleness and privacy. I wondered what he looked like now. He had been picked up, the evening before, in a raid on an apartment downtown, for peddling and using heroin.

4   I couldn't believe it: but what I mean by that is that I couldn't find any room for it anywhere inside me. I had kept it outside me for a long time. I hadn't wanted to know. I had had suspicions, but I didn't name them, I kept putting them away. I told myself that Sonny was wild, but he wasn't crazy. And he'd always been a good boy, he hadn't ever turned hard or evil or disrespectful, the way kids can, so quick, so quick, especially in Harlem. I didn't want to believe that I'd ever see my brother going down, coming to nothing, all that light in his face gone out, in the condition I'd already seen so many others. Yet it had happened and here I was, talking about algebra to a lot of boys who might, every one of them for all I knew, be popping off needles every time they went to the head. Maybe it did more for them than algebra could.

5   I was sure that the first time Sonny had ever had horse, he couldn't have been much older than these boys were now. These boys, now, were living as we'd been living then, they were growing up with a rush and their heads bumped abruptly against the low ceiling of their actual possibilities. They were filled with rage. All they really knew were two darknesses, the darkness of their lives, which was now closing in on them, and the darkness of the movies, which had blinded them to that other darkness, and in which they now, vindictively, dreamed, at once more together than they were at any other time, and more alone.

6   When the last bell rang, the last class ended, I let out my breath. It seemed I'd been holding it for all that time. My clothes were wet—I may have looked as though I'd been sitting in a steam bath, all dressed up, all afternoon. I sat alone in the classroom a long time. I listened to the boys outside, downstairs, shouting and cursing and laughing. Their laughter struck me for perhaps the first time. It was not the joyous laughter which—God knows why—one associates with children. It was mocking and insular, its intent was to denigrate. It was disenchanted, and in this, also, lay the authority of their curses. Perhaps I was listening to them because I was thinking about my brother and in them I heard my brother. And myself.

7   One boy was whistling a tune, at once very complicated and very simple, it seemed to be pouring out of him as though he were a bird, and it sounded very cool and moving through all that harsh, bright air, only just holding its own through all those other sounds.

8   I stood up and walked over to the window and looked down into the courtyard. It was the beginning of the spring and the sap was rising in the boys. A teacher passed through them every now and again, quickly, as

though he or she couldn't wait to get out of the courtyard, to get those boys out of their sight and off their minds. I started collecting my stuff. I thought I'd better get home and talk to Isabel.

9   The courtyard was almost deserted by the time I got downstairs. I saw this boy standing in the shadow of a doorway, looking just like Sonny. I almost called his name. Then I saw that it wasn't Sonny, but somebody we used to know, a boy from around our block. He'd been Sonny's friend. He'd never been mine, having been too young for me, and, anyway, I'd never liked him. And now, even though he was a grown-up man, he still hung around that block, still spent hours on the street corners, was always high and raggy. I used to run into him from time to time and he'd often work around to asking me for a quarter or fifty cents. He always had some real good excuse, too, and I always gave it to him, I don't know why.

10   But now, abruptly, I hated him. I couldn't stand the way he looked at me, partly like a dog, partly like a cunning child. I wanted to ask him what the hell he was doing in the school courtyard.

11   He sort of shuffled over to me, and he said, "I see you got the papers. So you already know about it."

12   "You mean about Sonny? Yes, I already know about it. How come they didn't get you?"

13   He grinned. It made him repulsive and it also brought to mind what he'd looked like as a kid. "I wasn't there. I stay away from them people."

14   "Good for you." I offered him a cigarette and I watched him through the smoke. "You come all the way down here just to tell me about Sonny?"

15   "That's right." He was sort of shaking his head and his eyes looked strange, as though they were about to cross. The bright sun deadened his damp dark brown skin and it made his eyes look yellow and showed up the dirt in his kinked hair. He smelled funky. I moved a little away from him and I said, "Well, thanks. But I already know about it and I got to get home."

16   "I'll walk you a little ways," he said. We started walking. There were a couple of kids still loitering in the courtyard and one of them said goodnight to me and looked strangely at the boy beside me.

17   "What're you going to do?" he asked me. "I mean, about Sonny?"

18   "Look. I haven't seen Sonny for over a year, I'm not sure I'm going to do anything. Anyway, what the hell *can* I do?"

19   "That's right," he said quickly, "ain't nothing you can do. Can't much help old Sonny no more, I guess."

20   It was what I was thinking and so it seemed to me he had no right to say it.

21   "I'm surprised at Sonny, though," he went on—he had a funny way of talking, he looked straight ahead as though he were talking to himself—"I thought Sonny was a smart boy, I thought he was too smart to get hung."

22   "I guess he thought so too," I said sharply, "and that's how he got hung. And now about you? You're pretty damn smart, I bet."

23   Then he looked directly at me, just for a minute. "I ain't smart," he said. "If I was smart, I'd have reached for a pistol a long time ago."

24   "Look. Don't tell *me* your sad story, if it was up to me, I'd give you one." Then I felt guilty—guilty, probably, for never having supposed that the poor bastard *had* a story of his own, much less a sad one, and I asked, quickly. "What's going to happen to him now?"

25   He didn't answer this. He was off by himself some place. "Funny thing," he said, and from his tone we might have been discussing the quickest way to get to Brooklyn, "when I saw the papers this morning, the first thing I asked myself was if I had anything to do with it. I felt sort of responsible."

26   I began to listen more carefully. The subway station was on the corner, just before us, and I stopped. He stopped, too. We were in front of a bar and he ducked slightly, peering in, but whoever he was looking for didn't seem to be there. The juke box was blasting away with something black and bouncy and I half watched the barmaid as she danced her way from the juke box to her place behind the bar. And I watched her face as she laughingly responded to something someone said to her, still keeping time to the music. When she smiled one saw the little girl, one sensed the doomed, still-struggled woman beneath the battered face of the semi-whore.

27   "I never *give* Sonny nothing," the boy said finally, "but a long time ago I come to school high and Sonny asked me how it felt." He paused, I couldn't bear to watch him, I watched the barmaid, and I listened to the music which seemed to be causing the pavement to shake. "I told him it felt great." The music stopped, the barmaid paused and watched the juke box until the music began again. "It did."

28   All this was carrying me some place I didn't want to go. I certainly didn't want to know how it felt. It filled everything, the people, the houses, the music, the dark, quicksilver barmaid, with menace; and this menace was their reality.

29   "What's going to happen to him now?" I asked again.

30   "They'll send him away some place and they'll try to cure him." He shook his head. "Maybe he'll even think he's kicked the habit. Then they'll let him loose"—he gestured, throwing his cigarette into the gutter. "That's all."

31   "What do you mean, that's *all?*"

32   But I knew what he meant.

33   "I *mean* that's *all*." He turned his head and looked at me, pulling down the corners of his mouth. "Don't you know what I mean?" he asked, softly.

34   "How the hell *would* I know what you mean?" I almost whispered it, I don't know why.

35   "That's right," he said to the air, "how would *he* know what I mean?" He turned toward me again, patient and calm, and yet I somehow felt him shaking, shaking as though he were going to fall apart. I felt that ice in my guts again, the dread I'd felt all afternoon; and again I watched the barmaid, moving about the bar, washing glasses, and singing. "Listen. They'll let him out and then it'll just start all over again. That's what I mean."

36   "You mean—they'll let him out. And then he'll just start working his way back in again. You mean he'll never kick the habit. Is that what you mean?"

37   "That's right," he said, cheerfully. "*You* see what I mean."

38   "Tell me," I said it last, "why does he want to die? He must want to die, he's killing himself, why does he want to die?"

39   He looked at me in surprise. He licked his lips. "He don't want to die. He wants to live. Don't nobody want to die, ever."

40   Then I wanted to ask him—too many things. He could not have answered, or if he had, I could not have borne the answers. I started walking. "Well, I guess it's none of my business."

41   "It's going to be rough on old Sonny," he said. We reached the subway station. "This is your station?" he asked. I nodded. I took one step down. "Damn!" he said, suddenly. I looked up at him. He grinned again. "Damn it if I didn't leave all my money home. You ain't got a dollar on you, have you? Just for a couple of days, is all."

42   All at once something inside gave and threatened to come pouring out of me. I didn't hate him any more. I felt that in another moment I'd start crying like a child.

43   "Sure," I said. "Don't sweat." I looked in my wallet and didn't have a dollar, I only had a five. "Here," I said. "That hold you?"

44   He didn't look at it—he didn't want to look at it. A terrible, closed look came over his face, as though he were keeping the number on the bill a secret from him and me. "Thanks," he said, and now he was dying to see me go. "Don't worry about Sonny. Maybe I'll write him or something."

45   "Sure," I said. "You do that. So long."

46   "Be seeing you," he said. I went on down the steps.

47   And I didn't write Sonny or send him anything for a long time. When I finally did, it was just after my little girl died, he wrote me back a letter which made me feel like a bastard.

48   Here's what he said:

> Dear brother,
> You don't know how much I needed to hear from you. I wanted to write you many a time but I dug how much I must have hurt you and so I didn't write. But now I feel like a man who's been trying to climb up out of some deep, real deep and funky hole and just saw the sun up there, outside. I got to get outside.
> I can't tell you much about how I got here. I mean I don't know how to tell you. I guess I was afraid of something or I was trying to escape from something and you know I have never been very strong in the head (smile). I'm glad Mama and Daddy are dead and can't see what's happened to their son and I swear if I'd known what I was doing I would never have hurt you so, you and a lot of other fine people who were nice to me and who believed in me.
> I don't want you to think it had anything to do with me being

a musician. It's more than that. Or maybe less than that. I can't get anything straight in my head down here and I try not to think about what's going to happen to me when I get outside again. Sometime I think I'm going to flip and *never* get outside and sometime I think I'll come straight back. I tell you one thing, though, I'd rather blow my brains out than go through this again. But that's what they all say, so they tell me. If I tell you when I'm coming to New York and if you could meet me, I sure would appreciate it. Give my love to Isabel and the kids and I was sure sorry to hear about little Gracie. I wish I could be like Mama and say the Lord's will be done, but I don't know it seems to me that trouble is the one thing that never does get stopped and I don't know what good it does to blame it on the Lord. But maybe it does some good if you believe it.

Your brother,
Sonny

49   Then I kept in constant touch with him and I sent him whatever I could and I went to meet him when he came back to New York. When I saw him many things I thought I had forgotten came flooding back to me. This was because I had begun, finally, to wonder about Sonny, about the life that Sonny lived inside. This life, whatever it was, had made him older and thinner and it had deepened the distant stillness in which he had always moved. He looked very unlike my baby brother. Yet, when he smiled, when we shook hands, the baby brother I'd never known looked out from the depths of his private life, like an animal waiting to be coaxed into the light.

50   "How you been keeping?" he asked me.

51   "All right. And you?"

52   "Just fine." He was smiling all over his face. "It's good to see you again."

53   "It's good to see you."

54   The seven years' difference in our ages lay between us like a chasm: I wondered if these years would ever operate between us as a bridge. I was remembering, and it made it hard to catch my breath, that I had been there when he was born; and I had heard the first words he had ever spoken. When he started to walk, he walked from our mother straight to me. I caught him just before he fell when he took the first steps he ever took in this world.

55   "How's Isabel?"

56   "Just fine. She's dying to see you."

57   "And the boys?"

58   "They're fine, too. They're anxious to see their uncle."

59   "Oh, come on. You know they don't remember me."

60   "Are you kidding? Of course they remember you."

61   He grinned again. We got into a taxi. We had a lot to say to each other, far too much to know how to begin.

62 As the taxi began to move, I asked, "You still want to go to India?"

63 He laughed. "You still remember that. Hell, no. This place is Indian enough for me."

64 "It used to belong to them," I said.

65 And he laughed again. "They damn sure knew what they were doing when they got rid of it."

66 Years ago, when he was around fourteen, he'd been all hipped on the idea of going to India. He read books about people sitting on rocks, naked, in all kinds of weather, but mostly bad, naturally, and walking barefoot through hot coals and arriving at wisdom. I used to say that it sounded to me as though they were getting away from wisdom as fast as they could. I think he sort of looked down on me for that.

67 "Do you mind," he asked, "if we have the driver drive alongside the park? On the west side—I haven't seen the city in so long."

68 "Of course not," I said. I was afraid that I might sound as though I were humoring him, but I hoped he wouldn't take it that way.

69 So we drove along, between the green of the park and the stony, lifeless elegance of hotels and apartment buildings, toward the vivid, killing streets of our childhood. These streets hadn't changed, though housing projects jutted up out of them now like rocks in the middle of a boiling sea. Most of the houses in which we had grown up had vanished, as had the stores from which we had stolen, the basements in which we had first tried sex, the rooftops from which we had hurled tin cans and bricks. But houses exactly like the houses of our past yet dominated the landscape, boys exactly like the boys we once had been found themselves smothering in these houses, came down into the streets for light and air and found themselves encircled by disaster. Some escaped the trap, most didn't. Those who got out always left something of themselves behind, as some animals amputate a leg and leave it in the trap. It might be said, perhaps, that I had escaped, after all, I was a school teacher; or that Sonny had, he hadn't lived in Harlem for years. Yet, as the cab moved uptown through streets which seemed, with a rush, to darken with dark people, and as I covertly studied Sonny's face, it came to me that what we both were seeking through our separate cab windows was that part of ourselves which had been left behind. It's always at the hour of trouble and confrontation that the missing member aches.

70 We hit 110th Street and started rolling up Lenox Avenue. And I'd known this avenue all my life, but it seemed to me again, as it had seemed on the day I'd first heard about Sonny's trouble, filled with a hidden menace which was its very breath of life.

71 "We almost there," said Sonny.

72 "Almost." We were both too nervous to say anything more.

73 We live in a housing project. It hasn't been up long. A few days after it was up it seemed uninhabitably new, now, of course, it's already rundown. It looks like a parody of the good, clean, faceless life—God knows the people who live in it do their best to make it a parody. The best-looking grass

lying around isn't enough to make their lives green, the hedges will never hold out the streets, and they know it. The big windows fool no one, they aren't big enough to make space out of no space. They don't bother with the windows, they watch the TV screen instead. The playground is most popular with the children who don't play at jacks, or skip rope, or roller skate, or swing, and they can be found in it after dark. We moved in partly because it's not too far from where I teach, and partly for the kids; but it's really just like the houses in which Sonny and I grew up. The same things happen, they'll have the same things to remember. The moment Sonny and I started into the house I had the feeling that I was simply bringing him back into the danger he had almost died trying to escape.

74   Sonny has never been talkative. So I don't know why I was sure he'd be dying to talk to me when supper was over the first night. Everything went fine, the oldest boy remembered him, and the youngest boy liked him, and Sonny had remembered to bring something for each of them; and Isabel, who is really much nicer than I am, more open and giving, had gone to a lot of trouble about dinner and was genuinely glad to see him. And she's always been able to tease Sonny in a way that I haven't. It was nice to see her face so vivid again and to hear her laugh and watch her make Sonny laugh. She wasn't, or, anyway, she didn't seem to be, at all uneasy or embarrassed. She chatted as though there were no subject which had to be avoided and she got Sonny past his first, faint stiffness. And thank God she was there, for I was filled with that icy dread again. Everything I did seemed awkward to me, and everything I said sounded freighted with hidden meaning. I was trying to remember everything I'd heard about dope addiction and I couldn't help watching Sonny for signs. I wasn't doing it out of malice. I was trying to find out something about my brother. I was dying to hear him tell me he was safe.

75   "Safe!" my father grunted, whenever Mama suggested trying to move to a neighborhood which might be safer for children. "Safe, hell! Ain't no place safe for kids, nor nobody."

76   He always went on like this, but he wasn't, ever, really as bad as he sounded, not even on weekends, when he got drunk. As a matter of fact, he was always on the lookout for "something a little better," but he died before he found it. He died suddenly, during a drunken weekend in the middle of the war, when Sonny was fifteen. He and Sonny hadn't ever got on too well. And this was partly because Sonny was the apple of his father's eye. It was because he loved Sonny so much and was frightened for him, that he was always fighting with him. It doesn't do any good to fight with Sonny. Sonny just moves back, inside himself, where he can't be reached. But the principal reason that they never hit it off is that they were so much alike. Daddy was big, and rough and loud-talking, just the opposite of Sonny, but they both had—that same privacy.

77   Mama tried to tell me something about this, just after Daddy died. I was home on leave from the army.

78   This was the last time I ever saw my mother alive. Just the same, this picture gets all mixed up in my mind with pictures I had of her when she was younger. The way I always see her is the way she used to be on a Sunday afternoon, say, when the old folks were talking after the big Sunday dinner. I always see her wearing pale blue. She'd be sitting on the sofa. And my father would be sitting in the easy chair, not far from her. And the living room would be full of church folks and relatives. There they sit, in chairs all around the living room, and the night is creeping up outside, but nobody knows it yet. You can see the darkness growing against the windowpanes and you hear the street noises every now and again, or maybe the jangling beat of a tambourine from one of the churches close by, but it's real quiet in the room. For a moment nobody's talking, but every face looks darkening, like the sky outside. And my mother rocks a little from the waist, and my father's eyes are closed. Everyone is looking at something a child can't see. For a minute they've forgotten the children. Maybe a kid is lying on the rug, half asleep. Maybe somebody's got a kid in his lap and is absentmindedly stroking the kid's head. Maybe there's a kid, quiet and big-eyed, curled up in a big chair in the corner. The silence, the darkness coming, and the darkness in the faces frightens the child obscurely. He hopes that the hand which strokes his forehead will never stop—will never die. He hopes that there will never come a time when the old folks won't be sitting around the living room, talking about where they've come from, and what they've seen, and what's happened to them and their kinfolk.

79   But something deep and watchful in the child knows that this is bound to end, is already ending. In a moment someone will get up and turn on the light. Then the old folks will remember the children and they won't talk any more that day. And when light fills the room, the child is filled with darkness. He knows that every time this happens he's moved just a little closer to that darkness outside. The darkness outside is what the old folks have been talking about. It's what they've come from. It's what they endure. The child knows that they won't talk any more because if he knows too much about what's happened to *them*, he'll know too much too soon, about what's going to happen to *him*.

80   The last time I talked to my mother, I remember I was restless. I wanted to get out and see Isabel. We weren't married then and we had a lot to straighten out between us.

81   There Mama sat, in black, by the window. She was humming an old church song, *Lord, you brought me from a long ways off.* Sonny was out somewhere. Mama kept watching the streets.

82   "I don't know," she said, "if I'll ever see you again, after you go off from here. But I hope you'll remember the things I tried to teach you."

83   "Don't talk like that," I said, and smiled. "You'll be here a long time yet."

84   She smiled, too, but she said nothing. She was quiet for a long time. And I said, "Mama, don't you worry about nothing. I'll be writing all the time, and you be getting the checks. . . ."

85   "I want to talk to you about your brother," she said, suddenly. "If anything happens to me he ain't going to have nobody to look out for him."

86   "Mama," I said, "ain't nothing going to happen to you *or* Sonny. Sonny's all right. He's a good boy and he's got good sense."

87   "It ain't a question of his being a good boy," Mama said, "nor of his having good sense. It ain't only the bad ones, nor yet the dumb ones that gets sucked under." She stopped, looking at me. "Your Daddy once had a brother," she said, and she smiled in a way that made me feel she was in pain. "You didn't never know that, did you?"

88   "No," I said, "I never knew that," and I watched her face.

89   "Oh, yes," she said, "your Daddy had a brother." She looked out of the window again. "I know you never saw your Daddy cry. But *I* did—many a time, through all these years."

90   I asked her, "What happened to his brother? How come nobody's ever talked about him?"

91   This was the first time I ever saw my mother look old.

92   "His brother got killed," she said, "when he was just a little younger than you are now. I knew him. He was a fine boy. He was maybe a little full of the devil, but he didn't mean nobody no harm."

93   Then she stopped and the room was silent, exactly as it had sometimes been on those Sunday afternoons. Mama kept looking out into the streets.

94   "He used to have a job in the mill," she said, "and, like all young folks, he just liked to perform on Saturday nights. Saturday nights, him and your father would drift around to different place, go to dances and things like that, or just sit around with people they knew, and your father's brother would sing, he had a fine voice, and play along with himself on his guitar. Well, this particular Saturday night, him and your father was coming home from some place, and they were both a little drunk and there was a moon that night, it was bright like day. Your father's brother was feeling kind of good, and he was whistling to himself, and he had his guitar slung over his shoulder. They was coming down a hill and beneath them was a road that turned off from the highway. Well, your father's brother, being always kind of frisky, decided to run down this hill, and he did, with that guitar banging and clanging behind him, and he ran across the road, and he was making water behind a tree. And your father was sort of amused at him and he was still coming down the hill, kind of slow. Then he heard a car motor and that same minute his brother stepped from behind a tree, into the road, in the moonlight. And he started to cross the road. And your father started to run down the hill, he says he don't know why. This car was full of white men. They was all drunk, and when they seen your father's brother they let out a great whoop and holler and they aimed the car straight at him. They was having fun, they just wanted to scare him, the way they do sometimes, you know. But they was drunk. And I guess the boy, being drunk, too, and scared, kind of lost his head. By the time he jumped it was too late. Your father says he heard his brother scream when the car rolled over him, and he

heard the wood of that guitar when it give, and he heard them strings go flying, and he heard them white men shouting, and the car kept on a-going and it ain't stopped till this day. And, time your father got down the hill, his brother weren't nothing but blood and pulp."

95 Tears were gleaming on my mother's face. There wasn't anything I could say.

96 "He never mentioned it," she said, "because I never let him mention it before you children. Your Daddy was like a crazy man that night and for many a night thereafter. He says he never in his life seen anything as dark as that road after the lights of that car had gone away. Weren't nothing, weren't nobody on that road, just your Daddy and his brother and that busted guitar. Oh, yes. Your Daddy never did really get right again. Till the day he died he weren't sure but that every white man he saw was the man that killed his brother."

97 She stopped and took out her handkerchief and dried her eyes and looked at me.

98 "I ain't telling you all this," she said, "to make you scared or bitter or to make you hate nobody. I'm telling you this because you got a brother. And the world ain't changed."

99 I guess I didn't want to believe this. I guess she saw this in my face. She turned away from me, toward the window again, searching those streets.

100 "But I praise my Redeemer," she said at last, "that He called your Daddy home before me. I ain't saying it to throw no flowers at myself, but, I declare, it keeps me from feeling too cast down to know I helped your father get safely through this world. Your father always acted like he was the roughest, strongest man on earth. And everybody took him to be like that. But if he hadn't had *me* there—to see his tears!"

101 She was crying again. Still, I couldn't move. I said, "Lord, Lord, Mama, I didn't know it was like that."

102 "Oh, honey," she said, "there's a lot that you don't know. But you are going to find it out." She stood up from the window and came over to me. "You got to hold on to your brother," she said, "and don't let him fall, no matter what it looks like is happening to him and no matter how evil you gets with him. You going to be evil with him many a time. But don't you forget what I told you, you hear?"

103 "I won't forget," I said. "Don't you worry, I won't forget. I won't let nothing happen to Sonny."

104 My mother smiled as though she were amused at something she saw in my face. Then, "You may not be able to stop nothing from happening. But you got to let him know you's *there*."

105 Two days later I was married, and then I was gone. And I had a lot of things on my mind and I pretty well forgot my promise to Mama until I got shipped home on a special furlough for her funeral.

106 And, after the funeral, with just Sonny and me alone in the empty kitchen, I tried to find out something about him.

107   "What do you want to do?" I asked him.

108   "I'm going to be a musician," he said.

109   For he had graduated, in the time I had been away, from dancing to the juke box to finding out who was playing what, and what they were doing with it, and he had bought himself a set of drums.

110   "You mean, you want to be a drummer?" I somehow had the feeling that being a drummer might be all right for other people but not for my brother Sonny.

111   "I don't think," he said, looking at me very gravely, "that I'll ever be a good drummer. But I think I can play a piano."

112   I frowned. I'd never played the role of the older brother quite so seriously before, had scarcely ever, in fact, *asked* Sonny a damn thing. I sensed myself in the presence of something I didn't really know how to handle, didn't understand. So I made my frown a little deeper as I asked: "What kind of musician do you want to be?"

113   He grinned. "How many kinds do you think there are?"

114   "Be *serious*," I said.

115   He laughed, throwing his head back, and then looked at me. "I *am* serious."

116   "Well, then, for Christ's sake, stop kidding around and answer a serious question. I mean, do you want to be a concert pianist, you want to play classical music and all that, or—or what?" Long before I finished he was laughing again. "For Christ's *sake*, Sonny!"

117   He sobered, but with difficulty. "I'm sorry. But you sound so—*scared!*" and he was off again.

118   "Well, you may think it's funny now, baby, but it's not going to be so funny when you have to make your living at it, let me tell you *that*." I was furious because I knew he was laughing at me and I didn't know why.

119   "No," he said, very sober now, and afraid, perhaps, that he'd hurt me, "I don't want to be a classical pianist. That isn't what interests me. I mean"— he paused, looking hard at me, as though his eyes would help me to understand, and then gestured helplessly, as though perhaps his hand would help— "I mean, I'll have a lot of studying to do, and I'll have to study *everything*, but, I mean, I want to play *with*—jazz musicians." He stopped. "I want to play jazz," he said.

120   Well, the word had never before sounded as heavy, as real, as it sounded that afternoon in Sonny's mouth. I just looked at him and I was probably frowning a real frown by this time. I simply couldn't see why on earth he'd want to spend his time hanging around nightclubs, clowning around on bandstands, while people pushed each other around a dance floor. It seemed—beneath him, somehow. I had never thought about it before, had never been forced to, but I suppose I had always put jazz musicians in a class with what Daddy called "good-time people."

121   "Are you *serious?*"

122   "Hell, *yes*, I'm serious."

123   He looked more helpless than ever, and annoyed, and deeply hurt.

124   I suggested, helpfully: "You mean—like Louis Armstrong?"

125   His face closed as though I'd struck him. "No. I'm not talking about none of that old-time, down home crap."

126   "Well, look, Sonny, I'm sorry, don't get mad. I just don't altogether get it, that's all. Name somebody—you know, a jazz musician you admire."

127   "Bird."

128   "Who?"

129   "Bird! Charlie Parker! Don't they teach you nothing in the damn army?"

130   I lit a cigarette. I was surprised and then a little amused to discover that I was trembling. "I've been out of touch," I said. "You'll have to be patient with me. Now. Who's this Parker character?"

131   "He's just one of the greatest jazz musicians alive," said Sonny, sullenly, his hands in his pockets, his back to me. "Maybe *the* greatest," he added, bitterly, "that's probably why *you* never heard of him."

132   "All right," I said, "I'm ignorant. I'm sorry. I'll go out and buy all the cat's records right away, all right?"

133   "It don't," said Sonny, with dignity, "make any difference to me. I don't care what you listen to. Don't do me no favors."

134   I was beginning to realize that I'd never seen him so upset before. With another part of my mind I was thinking that this would probably turn out to be one of those things kids go through and that I shouldn't make it seem important by pushing it too hard. Still, I didn't think it would do any harm to ask: "Doesn't all this take a lot of time? Can you make a living at it?"

135   He turned back to me and half leaned, half sat, on the kitchen table. "Everything takes time," he said, "and—well, yes, sure. I can make a living at it. But what I don't seem to be able to make you understand is that it's the only thing I want to do—"

136   "Well, Sonny," I said, gently, "you know people can't always do exactly what they *want* to do."

137   "*No*, I don't know that," said Sonny, surprising me. "I think people *ought* to do what they want to do, what else are they alive for?"

138   "You getting to be a big boy," I said desperately, "it's time you started thinking about your future."

139   "I'm thinking about my future," said Sonny, grimly. "I think about it all the time."

140   I gave up. I decided, if he didn't change his mind, that we could always talk about it later. "In the meantime," I said, "you got to finish school." We had already decided that he'd have to move in with Isabel and her folks. I knew this wasn't the ideal arrangement because Isabel's folks are inclined to be dicey and they hadn't especially wanted Isabel to marry me. But I didn't know what else to do. "And we have to get you fixed up at Isabel's."

141   There was a long silence. He moved from the kitchen table to the window. "That's a terrible idea. You know it yourself."

142   "Do you have a *better* idea?"

143   He just walked up and down the kitchen for a minute. He was as tall as I was. He had started to shave. I suddenly had the feeling that I didn't know him at all.

144   He stopped at the kitchen table and picked up my cigarettes. Looking at me with a kind of mocking, amused defiance, he put one between his lips. "You mind?"

145   "You smoking already?"

146   He lit the cigarette and nodded, watching me through the smoke. "I just wanted to see if I'd have the courage to smoke in front of you." He grinned and blew a great cloud of smoke to the ceiling. "It was easy." He looked at my face. "Come on, now, I bet you was smoking at my age, tell the truth."

147   I didn't say anything but the truth was on my face, and he laughed. But now there was something very strained in his laugh. "Sure. And I bet that ain't all you was doing."

148   He was frightening me a little. "Cut the crap," I said. "We already decided that you was going to go and live at Isabel's. Now what's got into you all of a sudden?"

149   "You decided it," he pointed out. "I didn't decide nothing." He stopped in front of me, leaning against the stove, arms loosely folded. "Look, brother. I don't want to stay in Harlem no more, I really don't." He was very earnest. He looked at me, then over toward the kitchen window. There was something in his eyes I'd never seen before, some thoughtfulness, some worry all his own. He rubbed the muscle of one arm. "It's time I was getting out of here."

150   "Where do you want to *go*, Sonny?"

151   "I want to join the army. Or the navy, I don't care. If I say I'm old enough, they'll believe me."

152   Then I got mad. It was because I was so scared. "You must be crazy. You damn fool, what the hell do you want to go and join the *army* for?"

153   "I just told you. To get out of Harlem."

154   "Sonny, you haven't even finished *school*. And if you really want to be a musician, how do you expect to study if you're in the *army*?"

155   He looked at me, trapped, and in anguish. "There's ways. I might be able to work out some kind of deal. Anyway, I'll have the G.I. Bill when I come out."

156   "*If* you come out." We stared at each other. "Sonny, please. Be reasonable. I know the setup is far from perfect. But we got to do the best we can."

157   "I ain't learning nothing in school," he said. "Even when I go." He turned away from me and opened the window and threw his cigarette out into the narrow alley. I watched his back. "At least, I ain't learning nothing you'd want me to learn." He slammed the window so hard I thought the glass would fly out, and turned back to me. "And I'm sick of the stink of these garbage cans!"

158   "Sonny," I said, "I know how you feel. But if you don't finish school

now, you're going to be sorry later that you didn't." I grabbed him by the shoulders. "And you only got another year. It ain't so bad. And I'll come back and I swear I'll help you do *whatever* you want to do. Just try to put up with it till I come back. Will you please do that? For me?"

159   He didn't answer and he wouldn't look at me.

160   "Sonny. You hear me?"

161   He pulled away. "I hear you. But you never hear anything *I* say."

162   I didn't know what to say to that. He looked out of the window and then back at me. "OK," he said, and sighed. "I'll try."

163   Then I said, trying to cheer him up a little, "They got a piano at Isabel's. You can practice on it."

164   And as a matter of fact, it did cheer him up for a minute. "That's right," he said to himself. "I forgot that." His face relaxed a little. But the worry, the thoughtfulness, played on it still, the way shadows play on a face which is staring into the fire.

165   But I thought I'd never hear the end of that piano. At first, Isabel would write me, saying how nice it was that Sonny was so serious about his music and how, as soon as he came in from school, or wherever he had been when he was supposed to be at school, he went straight to that piano and stayed there until suppertime. And, after supper, he went back to that piano and stayed there until everybody went to bed. He was at the piano all day Saturday and all day Sunday. Then he bought a record player and started playing records. He'd play one record over and over again, all day long sometimes, and he'd improvise along with it on the piano. Or he'd play one section of the record, one chord, one change, one progression, then he'd do it on the piano. Then back to the record. Then back to the piano.

166   Well, I really don't know how they stood it. Isabel finally confessed that it wasn't like living with a person at all, it was like living with sound. And the sound didn't make any sense to her, didn't make any sense to any of them—naturally. They began, in a way, to be afflicted by this presence that was living in their home. It was as though Sonny were some sort of god, or monster. He moved in an atmosphere which wasn't like theirs at all. They fed him and he ate, he washed himself, he walked in and out of their door; he certainly wasn't nasty or unpleasant or rude, Sonny isn't any of those things; but it was as though he were all wrapped up in some cloud, some fire, some vision all his own; and there wasn't any way to reach him.

167   At the same time, he wasn't really a man yet, he was still a child, and they had to watch out for him in all kinds of ways. They certainly couldn't throw him out. Neither did they dare to make a great scene about that piano because even they dimly sensed, as I sensed, from so many thousands of miles away, that Sonny was at that piano playing for his life.

168   But he hadn't been going to school. One day a letter came from the school board and Isabel's mother got it—there had, apparently, been other letters but Sonny had torn them up. This day, when Sonny came in, Isabel's mother showed him the letter and asked where he'd been spending his time.

And she finally got it out of him that he'd been down in Greenwich Village, with musicians and other characters, in a white girl's apartment. And this scared her and she started to scream at him and what came up, once she began—though she denies it to this day—was what sacrifices they were making to give Sonny a decent home and how little he appreciated it.

169 Sonny didn't play the piano that day. By evening, Isabel's mother had calmed down but then there was the old man to deal with, and Isabel herself. Isabel says she did her best to be calm but she broke down and started crying. She says she just watched Sonny's face. She could tell, by watching him, what was happening with him. And what was happening was that they penetrated his cloud, they had reached him. Even if their fingers had been a thousand times more gentle than human fingers ever are, he could hardly help feeling that they had stripped him naked and were spitting on that nakedness. For he also had to see that his presence, that music, which was life or death to him, had been torture for them and that they had endured it, not at all for his sake, but only for mine. And Sonny couldn't take that. He can take it a little better today than he could then but he's still not very good at it and, frankly, I don't know anybody who is.

170 The silence of the next few days must have been louder than the sound of all the music ever played since time began. One morning, before she went to work, Isabel was in his room for something and she suddenly realized that all of his records were gone. And she knew for certain that he was gone. And he was. He went as far as the navy would carry him. He finally sent me a postcard from some place in Greece and that was the first I knew that Sonny was still alive. I didn't see him any more until we were both back in New York and the war had long been over.

171 He was a man by then, of course, but I wasn't willing to see it. He came by the house from time to time, but we fought almost every time we met. I didn't like the way he carried himself, loose and dreamlike all the time, and I didn't like his friends, and his music seemed to be merely an excuse for the life he led. It sounded just that weird and disordered.

172 Then we had a fight, a pretty awful fight, and I didn't see him for months. By and by I looked him up, where he was living, in a furnished room in the Village, and I tried to make it up. But there were lots of other people in the room and Sonny just lay on his bed, and he wouldn't come downstairs with me, and he treated these other people as though they were his family and I weren't. So I got mad and then he got mad, and then I told him that he might just as well be dead as live the way he was living. Then he stood up and he told me not to worry about him any more in life, that he *was* dead as far as I was concerned. Then he pushed me to the door and the other people looked on as though nothing were happening, and he slammed the door behind me. I stood in the hallway, staring at the door. I heard somebody laugh in the room and then the tears came to my eyes. I started down the steps, whistling to keep from crying, I kept whistling to myself, *You going to need me, baby, one of these cold, rainy days.*

173   I read about Sonny's trouble in the spring. Little Grace died in the fall. She was a beautiful little girl. But she only lived a little over two years. She died of polio and she suffered. She had a slight fever for a couple of days, but it didn't seem like anything and we just kept her in bed. And we would certainly have called the doctor, but the fever dropped, she seemed to be all right. So we thought it had just been a cold. Then, one day, she was up, playing, Isabel was in the kitchen fixing lunch for the two boys when they'd come in from school, and she heard Grace fall down in the living room. When you have a lot of children you don't always start running when one of them falls, unless they start screaming or something. And, this time, Grace was quiet. Yet, Isabel says that when she heard that *thump* and then that silence, something happened in her to make her afraid. And she ran to the living room and there was little Grace on the floor, all twisted up, and the reason she hadn't screamed was that she couldn't get her breath. And when she did scream, it was the worst sound, Isabel says, that she'd ever heard in all her life, and she still hears it sometimes in her dreams. Isabel will sometimes wake me up with a low moaning, strangled sound and I have to be quick to awaken her and hold her to me and where Isabel is weeping against me seems a mortal wound.

174   I think I may have written Sonny the very day that little Grace was buried. I was sitting in the living room in the dark, by myself, and I suddenly thought of Sonny. My trouble made his real.

175   One Saturday afternoon, when Sonny had been living with us, or, anyway, been in our house, for nearly two weeks, I found myself wandering aimlessly about the living room, drinking from a can of beer, and trying to work up the courage to search Sonny's room. He was out, he was usually out whenever I was home, and Isabel had taken the children to see their grandparents. Suddenly I was standing still in front of the living room window, watching Seventh Avenue. The idea of searching Sonny's room made me still. I scarcely dared to admit to myself what I'd be searching for. I didn't know what I'd do if I found it. Or if I didn't.

176   On the sidewalk across from me, near the entrance to a barbecue joint, some people were holding an old-fashioned revival meeting. The barbecue cook, wearing a dirty white apron, his conked hair reddish and metallic in the pale sun, and a cigarette between his lips, stood in the doorway, watching them. Kids and older people paused in their errands and stood there, along with some older men and a couple of very tough-looking women who watched everything that happened on the avenue, as though they owned it, or were maybe owned by it. Well, they were watching this, too. The revival was being carried on by three sisters in black, and a brother. All they had were their voices and their Bibles and a tambourine. The brother was testifying and while he testified two of the sisters stood together, seeming to say, amen, and the third sister walked around with the tambourine outstretched and a couple of people dropped coins into it. Then the brother's testimony ended and the sister who had been taking up the collection dumped the

coins into her palm and transferred them to the pocket of her long black robe. Then she raised both hands, striking the tambourine against the air, and then against one hand, and she started to sing. And the two other sisters and the brother joined in.

177   It was strange, suddenly, to watch, though I had been seeing these street meetings all my life. So, of course, had everybody else down there. Yet, they paused and watched and listened and I stood still at the window. *"Tis the old ship of Zion,"* they sang, and the sister with the tambourine kept a steady, jangling beat, *"it has rescued many a thousand!"* Not a soul under the sound of their voices was hearing this song for the first time, not one of them had been rescued. Nor had they seen much in the way of rescue work being done around them. Neither did they especially believe in the holiness of the three sisters and the brother, they knew too much about them, knew where they lived, and how. The woman with the tambourine, whose voice dominated the air, whose face was bright with joy, was divided by very little from the woman who stood watching her, a cigarette between her heavy, chapped lips, her hair a cuckoo's nest, her face scarred and swollen from many beatings, and her black eyes glittering like coal. Perhaps they both knew this, which was why, when, as rarely, they addressed each other, they addressed each other as Sister. As the singing filled the air the watching, listening faces underwent a change, the eyes focusing on something within; the music seemed to soothe a poison out of them; and time seemed, nearly, to fall away from the sullen, belligerent, battered faces, as though they were fleeing back to their first condition, while dreaming of their last. The barbecue cook half shook his head and smiled, and dropped his cigarette and disappeared into his joint. A man fumbled in his pockets for change and stood holding it in his hand impatiently, as though he had just remembered a pressing appointment further up the avenue. He looked furious. Then I saw Sonny, standing on the edge of the crowd. He was carrying a wide, flat notebook with a green cover, and it made him look, from where I was standing, almost like a schoolboy. The coppery sun brought out the copper in his skin, he was very faintly smiling, standing very still. Then the singing stopped, the tambourine turned into a collection plate again. The furious man dropped in his coins and vanished, so did a couple of the women, and Sonny dropped some change in the plate, looking directly at the woman with a little smile. He started across the avenue, toward the house. He has a slow, loping walk, something like the way Harlem hipsters walk, only he's imposed on this his own half-beat. I had never really noticed it before.

178   I stayed at the window, both relieved and apprehensive. As Sonny disappeared from my sight, they began singing again. And they were still singing when his key turned in the lock.

179   "Hey," he said.

180   "Hey, yourself. You want some beer?"

181   "No. Well, maybe." But he came up to the window and stood beside me, looking out. "What a warm voice," he said.

182   They were singing *If I could only hear my mother pray again!*

183   "Yes," I said, "and she can sure beat that tambourine."

184   "But what a terrible song," he said, and laughed. He dropped his notebook on the sofa and disappeared into the kitchen. "Where's Isabel and the kids?"

185   "I think they went to see their grandparents. You hungry?"

186   "No." He came back into the living room with his can of beer. "You want to come some place with me tonight?"

187   I sensed, I don't know how, that I couldn't possibly say no. "Sure. Where?"

188   He sat down on the sofa and picked up his notebook and started leafing through it. "I'm going to sit in with some fellows in a joint in the Village."

189   "You mean, you're going to play, tonight?"

190   "That's right." He took a swallow of his beer and moved back to the window. He gave me a sidelong look. "If you can stand it."

191   "I'll try," I said.

192   He smiled to himself and we both watched as the meeting across the way broke up. The three sisters and the brother, heads bowed, were singing *God be with you till we meet again.* The faces around them were very quiet. Then the song ended. The small crowd dispersed. We watched the three women and the lone man walk slowly up the avenue.

193   "When she was singing before," said Sonny, abruptly, "her voice reminded me for a minute of what heroin feels like sometimes—when it's in your veins. It makes you feel sort of warm and cool at the same time. And distant. And—and sure." He sipped his beer, very deliberately not looking at me. I watched his face. "It makes you feel—in control. Sometimes you've got to have that feeling."

194   "Do you?" I sat down slowly in the easy chair.

195   "Sometimes." He went to the sofa and picked up his notebook again. "Some people do."

196   "In order," I asked, "to play?" And my voice was very ugly, full of contempt and anger.

197   "Well"—he looked at me with great, troubled eyes, as though, in fact, he hoped his eyes would tell me things he could never otherwise say—"they *think* so. And *if* they think so—!"

198   "And what do *you* think?" I asked.

199   He sat on the sofa and put his can of beer on the floor. "I don't know," he said, and I couldn't be sure if he were answering my question or pursuing his thoughts. His face didn't tell me. "It's not so much to *play.* It's to *stand* it, to be able to make it at all. On any level." He frowned and smiled: "In order to keep from shaking to pieces."

200   "But these friends of yours," I said, "they seem to shake themselves to pieces pretty damn fast."

201   "Maybe." He played with the notebook. And something told me that I should curb my tongue, that Sonny was doing his best to talk, that I should

listen. "But of course you only know the ones that've gone to pieces. Some don't—or at least they haven't yet and that's just about all *any* of us can say." He paused. "And then there are some who just live, really, in hell, and they know it and they see what's happening and they go right on. I don't know." He sighed, dropped the notebook, folded his arms. "Some guys, you can tell from the way they play, they on something *all* the time. And you can see that, well, it makes something real for them. But of course," he picked up his beer from the floor and sipped it and put the can down again, "they *want* to, too, you've got to see that. Even some of them that say they don't—*some,* not all."

202 "And what about you?" I asked—I couldn't help it. "What about you? Do *you* want to?"

203 He stood up and walked to the window and remained silent for a long time. Then he sighed. "Me," he said. Then: "While I was downstairs before, on my way here, listening to that woman sing, it struck me all of a sudden how much suffering she must have had to go through—to sing like that. It's *repulsive* to think you have to suffer that much."

204 I said: "But there's no way not to suffer—is there, Sonny?"

205 "I believe not," he said and smiled, "but that's never stopped anyone from trying." He looked at me. "Has it?" I realized, with this mocking look, that there stood between us, forever, beyond the power of time or forgiveness, the fact that I had held silence—so long!—when he had needed human speech to help him. He turned back to the window. "No, there's no way not to suffer. But you try all kinds of ways to keep from drowning in it, to keep on top of it, and to make it seem—well, like *you.* Like you did something, all right, and now you're suffering for it. You know?" I said nothing. "Well you know," he said, impatiently, "why *do* people suffer? Maybe it's better to do something to give it a reason, *any* reason."

206 "But we just agreed," I said, "that there's no way not to suffer. Isn't it better, then, just to—take it?"

207 "But nobody just takes it," Sonny cried, "that's what I'm tellin you! *Everybody* tries not to. You're just hung up on the *way* some people try—it's not *your* way!"

208 The hair on my face began to itch, my face felt wet. "That's not true," I said, "that's not true. I don't give a damn what other people do, I don't even care how they suffer. I just care how *you* suffer." And he looked at me. "Please believe me," I said, "I don't want to see you—die—trying not to suffer."

209 "I won't," he said, flatly, "die trying not to suffer. At least, not any faster than anybody else."

210 "But there's no need," I said, trying to laugh, "is there? in killing yourself."

211 I wanted to say more, but I couldn't. I wanted to talk about will power and how life could be—well, beautiful. I wanted to say that it was all within; but was it? or, rather, wasn't that exactly the trouble? And I wanted to

promise that I would never fail him again. But it would all have sounded— empty words and lies.

212 So I made the promise to myself and prayed that I would keep it.

213 "It's terrible sometimes, inside," he said, "that's what's the trouble. You walk these streets, black and funky and cold, and there's not really a living ass to talk to, and there's nothing shaking, and there's no way of getting it out—that storm inside. You can't talk it and you can't make love with it, and when you finally try to get with it and play it, you realize *nobody's* listening. So *you've* got to listen. You got to find a way to listen."

214 And then he walked away from the window and sat on the sofa again, as though all the wind had suddenly been knocked out of him. "Sometimes you'll do *anything* to play, even cut your mother's throat." He laughed and looked at me. "Or your brother's." Then he sobered. "Or your own." Then: "Don't worry. I'm all right now and I think I'll *be* all right. But I can't for- get—where I've been. I don't mean just the physical place I've been, I mean where *I've* been. And *what* I've been."

215 "What have you been, Sonny?" I asked.

216 He smiled—but sat sideways on the sofa, his elbow resting on the back, his fingers playing with his mouth and chin, not looking at me. "I've been something I didn't recognize, didn't know I could be. Didn't know any- body could be." He stopped, looking inward, looking helplessly young, looking old. "I'm not talking about it now because I feel *guilty* or anything like that—maybe it would be better if I did, I don't know. Anyway, I can't really talk about it. Not to you, not to anybody," and now he turned and faced me. "Sometimes, you know, and it was actually when I was most *out* of the world, I felt that I was in it, that I was *with* it, really, and I could play or I didn't really have to *play*, it just came out of me, it was there. And I don't know how I played, thinking about it now, but I know I did awful things, those times, sometimes, to people. Or it wasn't that I *did* anything to them—it was that they weren't real." He picked up the beer can; it was empty; he rolled it between his palms: "And other times—well, I needed a fix, I needed to find a place to lean, I needed to clear a space to *listen*—and I couldn't find it, and I—went crazy, I did terrible things to *me*, I was terri- ble *for* me." He began pressing the beer can between his hands, I watched the metal begin to give. It glittered, as he played with it, like a knife, and I was afraid he would cut himself, but I said nothing. "Oh well, I can never tell you. I was all by myself at the bottom of something, stinking and sweat- ing and crying and shaking, and I smelled it, you know? *my* stink, and I thought I'd die if I couldn't get away from it and yet, all the same, I knew that everything I was doing was just locking me in with it. And I didn't know," he paused, still flattening the beer can, "I didn't know, I still *don't* know, something kept telling me that maybe it was good to smell your own stink, but I didn't think that *that* was what I'd been trying to do—and— who can stand it?" and he abruptly dropped the ruined beer can, looking at me with a small, still smile, and then rose, walking to the window as though

it were the lodestone rock. I watched his face, he watched the avenue. "I couldn't tell you when Mama died—but the reason I wanted to leave Harlem so bad was to get away from drugs. And then, when I ran away, that's what I was running from—really. When I came back, nothing had changed, *I* hadn't changed, I was just—older." And he stopped, drumming with his fingers on the windowpane. The sun had vanished, soon darkness would fall. I watched his face. "It can come again," he said, almost as though speaking to himself. Then he turned to me. "It can come again," he repeated. "I just want you to know that."

217   "All right," I said at last. "So it can come again. All right."

218   He smiled, but the smile was sorrowful. "I had to try to tell you," he said.

219   "Yes," I said. "I understand that."

220   "You're my brother," he said, looking straight at me, and not smiling at all.

221   "Yes," I repeated, "yes. I understand that."

222   He turned back to the window, looking out. "All that hatred down there," he said, "all that hatred and misery and love. It's a wonder it doesn't blow the avenue apart."

223   We went to the only nightclub on a short, dark street, downtown. We squeezed through the narrow, chattering, jampacked bar to the entrance of the big room, where the bandstand was. And we stood there for a moment, for the lights were very dim in this room and we couldn't see. Then, "Hello, boy," said a voice and an enormous black man, much older than Sonny or myself erupted out of all that atmospheric lighting and put an arm around Sonny's shoulder. "I been sitting right here," he said, "waiting for you."

224   He had a big voice, too, and heads in the darkness turned toward us.

225   Sonny grinned and pulled a little away, and said, "Creole, this is my brother. I told you about him."

226   Creole shook my hand. "I'm glad to meet you, son," he said, and it was clear that he was glad to meet me *there,* for Sonny's sake. And he smiled, "You got a real musician in *your* family," and he took his arm from Sonny's shoulder and slapped him, lightly, affectionately, with the back of his hand.

227   "Well. Now I've heard it all," said a voice behind us. This was another musician, and a friend of Sonny's, a coal-black, cheerful-looking man, built close to the ground. He immediately began confiding to me, at the top of his lungs, the most terrible things about Sonny, his teeth gleaming like a lighthouse and his laugh coming up out of him like the beginning of an earthquake. And it turned out that everyone at the bar knew Sonny, or almost everyone; some were musicians, working there, or nearby, or not working, some were simply hangers-on, and some were there to hear Sonny play. I was introduced to all of them and they were all very polite to me. Yet, it was clear that, for them, I was only Sonny's brother. Here, I was in Sonny's world. Or, rather: his kingdom. Here, it was not even a question that his veins bore royal blood.

228   They were going to play soon and Creole installed me, by myself, at a table in a dark corner. Then I watched them, Creole, and the little black man, and Sonny, and the others, while they horsed around, standing just below the bandstand. The light from the bandstand spilled just a little short of them and, watching them laughing and gesturing and moving about, I had the feeling that they, nevertheless, were being most careful not to step into that circle of light too suddenly: that if they moved into the light too suddenly, without thinking, they would perish in flame. Then, while I watched, one of them, the small, black man, moved into the light and crossed the bandstand and started fooling around with his drums. Then—being funny and being, also, extremely ceremonious—Creole took Sonny by the arm and led him to the piano. A woman's voice called Sonny's name and a few hands started clapping. And Sonny, also being funny and being ceremonious, and so touched, I think that he could have cried, but neither hiding it nor showing it, riding it like a man, grinned, and put both hands to his heart and bowed from the waist.

229   Creole then went to the bass fiddle and a lean, very bright-skinned brown man jumped up on the bandstand and picked up his horn. So there they were, and the atmosphere on the bandstand and in the room began to change and tighten. Someone stepped up to the microphone and announced them. Then there were all kinds of murmurs. Some people at the bar shushed others. The waitress ran around, frantically getting in the last orders, guys and chicks got closer to each other, and the lights on the bandstand, on the quartet, turned to a kind of indigo. Then they all looked different there. Creole looked about him for the last time, as though he were making certain that all his chickens were in the coop, and then he—jumped and struck the fiddle. And there they were.

230   All I know about music is that not many people ever really hear it. And even then, on the rare occasions when something opens within, and the music enters, what we mainly hear, or hear corroborated, are personal, private, vanishing evocations. But the man who creates the music is hearing something else, is dealing with the roar rising from the void and imposing order on it as it hits the air. What is evoked in him, then, is of another order, more terrible because it has no words, and triumphant, too, for that same reason. And his triumph, when he triumphs, is ours. I just watched Sonny's face. His face was troubled, he was working hard, but he wasn't with it. And I had the feeling that, in a way, everyone on the bandstand was waiting for him, both waiting for him and pushing him along. But as I began to watch Creole, I realized that it was Creole who held them all back. He had them on a short rein. Up there, keeping the beat with his whole body, wailing on the fiddle, with his eyes half closed, he was listening to everything, but he was listening to Sonny. He was having a dialogue with Sonny. He wanted Sonny to leave the shoreline and strike out for the deep water. He was Sonny's witness that deep water and drowning were not the same thing—he had been there, and he knew. And he wanted Sonny to know. He was

waiting for Sonny to do the things on the keys which would let Creole know that Sonny was in the water.

231   And, while Creole listened, Sonny moved, deep within, exactly like someone in torment. I had never before thought of how awful the relationship must be between the musician and his instrument. He has to fill it, this instrument, with the breath of life, his own. He has to make it do what he wants it to do. And a piano is just a piano. It's made out of so much wood and wires and little hammers and big ones, and ivory. While there's only so much you can do with it, the only way to find this out is to try; to try and make it do everything.

232   And Sonny hadn't been near a piano for over a year. And he wasn't on much better terms with his life, not the life that stretched before him now. He and the piano stammered, started one way, got scared, stopped; started another way, panicked, marked time, started again; then seemed to have found a direction, panicked again, got stuck. And the face I saw on Sonny I'd never seen before. Everything had been burned out of it, and, at the same time, things usually hidden were being burned in, by the fire and fury of the battle which was occurring in him up there.

233   Yet, watching Creole's face as they neared the end of the first set, I had the feeling that something had happened, something I hadn't heard. Then they finished, there was scattered applause, and then, without an instant's warning, Creole started into something else, it was almost sardonic, it was *Am I Blue*. And, as though he commanded, Sonny began to play. Something began to happen. And Creole let out the reins. The dry, low, black man said something awful on the drums, Creole answered, and the drums talked back. Then the horn insisted, sweet and high, slightly detached perhaps, and Creole listened, commenting now and then, dry, and driving, beautiful and calm and old. Then they all came together again, and Sonny was part of the family again. I could tell this from his face. He seemed to have found, right there beneath his fingers, a damn brand-new piano. It seemed that he couldn't get over it. Then, for awhile, just being happy with Sonny, they seemed to be agreeing with him that brand-new pianos certainly were a gas.

234   Then Creole stepped forward to remind them that what they were playing was the blues. He hit something in all of them, he hit something in me, myself, and the music tightened and deepened, apprehension began to beat the air. Creole began to tell us what the blues were all about. They were not about anything very new. He and his boys up there were keeping it new, at the risk of ruin, destruction, madness, and death, in order to find new ways to make us listen. For, while the tale of how we suffer, and how we are delighted, and how we may triumph is never new, it always must be heard. There isn't any other tale to tell, it's the only light we've got in all this darkness.

235   And this tale, according to that face, that body, those strong hands on those strings, has another aspect in every country, and a new depth in every generation. Listen, Creole seemed to be saying, listen. Now these are Sonny's blues. He made the little black man on the drums know it, and the bright,

brown man of the horn. Creole wasn't trying any longer to get Sonny in the water. He was wishing him Godspeed. Then he stepped back, very slowly, filling the air with the immense suggestion that Sonny speak for himself.

236   Then they all gathered around Sonny and Sonny played. Every now and again one of them seemed to say, amen. Sonny's fingers filled the air with life, his life. But that life contained so many others. And Sonny went all the way back, he really began with the spare, flat statement of the opening phrase of the song. Then he began to make it his. It was very beautiful because it wasn't hurried and it was no longer a lament. I seemed to hear with what burning he had made it his, with what burning we had yet to make it ours, how we could cease lamenting. Freedom lurked around us and I understood, at last, that he could help us to be free if we would listen, that he would never be free until we did. Yet, there was no battle in his face now. I heard what he had gone through, and would continue to go through until he came to rest in earth. He had made it his: that long line, of which we knew only Mama and Daddy. And he was giving it back, as everything must be given back, so that, passing through death, it can live forever. I saw my mother's face again, and felt, for the first time, how the stones of the road she had walked on must have bruised her feet. I saw the moonlit road where my father's brother died. And it brought something else back to me, and carried me past it, I saw my little girl again and felt Isabel's tears again, and I felt my own tears begin to rise. And I was yet aware that this was only a moment, that the world waited outside, as hungry as a tiger, and that trouble stretched above us, longer than the sky.

237   Then it was over. Creole and Sonny let out their breath, both soaking wet, and grinning. There was a lot of applause and some of it was real. In the dark, the girl came by and I asked her to take drinks to the bandstand. There was a long pause, while they talked up there in the indigo light and after awhile I saw the girl put a Scotch and milk on top of the piano for Sonny. He didn't seem to notice it, but just before they started playing again, he sipped from it and looked toward me, and nodded. Then he put it back on top of the piano. For me, then, as they began to play again, it glowed and shook above my brother's head like the very cup of trembling.

DISCUSSION QUESTIONS

1. What was Sonny's relationship with his father?
2. Sonny maintains that there is no one to talk to when one wishes to let go of the "storm inside." What do you think the "storm inside" is? Do you agree with the statement? Why?

3. What do you think the writer means when he says: ". . . how the stones of the road she had walked on must have bruised her feet"?

WRITING TOPICS

1. In your journal, pretend you are Sonny and write about your feelings when you play the blues.
2. Baldwin writes that there is nothing very new about the blues, which are expressed through suffering, delight, pain, and triumph over problems. Write an analytical essay in which you interpret what you think the blues really means.
3. Write an essay describing how the drug culture affected Sonny's life.

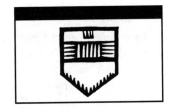

THE WEARY BLUES

Langston Hughes

Langston Hughes was born in Joplin, Missouri, in 1902 and spent most of his youth in the Midwest. Hughes went to Columbia University in 1921 for a year and eventually graduated from Lincoln University in Pennsylvania in 1929. His first volume of poetry, *The Weary Blues*, was published in 1926. Other poetry collections include *The Dream Keeper* (1932) and *Montage of a Dream Deferred* (1951). Hughes also published two full-length novels, *Not Without Laughter* (1930) and *Tambourines to Glory* (1958). He wrote two autobiographies, *The Big Sea* and *I Wonder as I Wander*, and several children's books. Some of the honors and awards he won include a Harmon Foundation Award, a Guggenheim Fellowship, a Rosenwald Fellowship, and the NAACP's Spingarn Medal. Hughes died in 1967. (For more information about Hughes, see pages 91, 192, and 385.)

> Droning a drowsy syncopated tune,
> Rocking back and forth to a mellow croon,
>   I heard a Negro play.
> Down on Lenox Avenue[1] the other night
> 5 By the pale dull pallor of an old gas light
>   He did a lazy sway . . .
>   He did a lazy sway . . .
> To the tune o' those Weary Blues.
> With his ebony hands on each ivory key
> 10 He made that poor piano moan with melody.
>   O Blues!
> Swaying to and fro on his rickety stool
> He played that sad raggy tune like a musical fool.
>   Sweet Blues!
> 15 Coming from a black man's soul.
>   O Blues!

---

[1] *Lenox Avenue* was a main street in Harlem.

In a deep song voice with a melancholy tone
I heard that Negro sing, that old piano moan—
  "Ain't got nobody in all this world,
20   Ain't got nobody but ma self.
  I's gwine[2] to quit ma frownin'
  And put ma troubles on the shelf."
Thump, thump, thump, went his foot on the floor.
He played a few chords then he sang some more—
25   I got the Weary Blues
  And I can't be satisfied.
  Got the Weary Blues
  And can't be satisfied—
  I ain't happy no mo'
30   And I wish that I had died."
And far into the night he crooned that tune.
The stars went out and so did the moon.
The singer stopped playing and went to bed
While the Weary Blues echoed through his head.
35   He slept like a rock or a man that's dead.

DISCUSSION QUESTIONS

1. What do you think Hughes means when he uses the term "weary blues"?
2. Are African Americans the only persons who can "have the blues"?
3. The author says the musician was "droning a drowsy syncopated tune." What do you think he means by this metaphor? Discuss with your small group.

WRITING TOPICS

1. In your journal, write a free verse blues poem on a subject of your own choosing. You may use "Weary Blues" as a model, or you may find another blues poem on which to model your poem.

---

2 "gwine" means "going."

2. The musician sang:

> "Ain't got nobody in all this world
> Ain't got nobody but ma self.
> I's gwine to quit ma frownin'
> And put ma troubles on the shelf."

Write an essay in which you explain the last two lines in the above stanza.

3. Pretend you are the speaker in the poem; write a letter to Hughes as that person, asking any questions you may have about certain lines in the poem. Or, write a paper in which you carry on a dialogue with Hughes. Ask the questions and give the answers as you think Hughes might.

DANCE BODIES #1

Eugene B. Redmond

Eugene B. Redmond was born in St. Louis, Missouri, in 1937 and raised in East St. Louis, Illinois. At the age of nine, Redmond went to live with his grandmother. He contributes his upbringing to his grandmother, neighborhood fathers, friends of his older brother, and members of the Seventh Day Adventist Church he attended. He received his B.A. in English literature from Southern Illinois University (1964) and a master's degree in English literature from Washington University. The late poet and fiction writer Henry Dumas was his close friend, and Redmond is the literary executor for the Dumas estate. He has also edited collections of Dumas' work. As a poet, critic, editor, journalist, playwright, and educator, Redmond is a significant African-American literary figure who helped shape the Black Arts Movement in the late 1960s. He has been poet-in-residence at Southern Illinois University, Southern University (Baton Rouge), and the University of Wisconsin. Currently, he is the editor of *Drumvoices*, a literary journal.

Redmond's poetry illustrates that music is an important part of the black cultural context. His poetry is filled with allusions to spirituals, blues, jazz, soul music, and black musicians. Throughout his poetry, Redmond makes connections between African culture and present-day African-American culture. His books of poetry include *Sentry of the Four Golden Pillars* (1970), *River of Bones and Flesh and Blood* (1971), *In a Time of Rain & Desire: New Love Poems* (1973), *Drumvoices: The Making of Afro-American Poetry, A Critical History* (1976), and, as editor, *Henry Dumas, Goodbye Sweetheart: New & Selected Stories* (1988), and *The Eye in the Ceiling: Poems* (1991).

Spitfire! from *BlackFleshMotors*
                /whirhums/
Under acrobatic howls:
Zig-grip! Zig-grip! Zig-grip!
5   *Zag-lore!* and bodies brush air;
Dip-twist! Down-bend! Dip-twist!
And kissing palms pancake/applaud air,
Chop smoke/humpsreams:
JamesBrowning the breakdown!
10   BrakeDowning the JamesBrown!
Washing air with sugarsweat/
With antiseptic potion and polish;
Caroling *fleshmotors* flinging/
Ringing from shirt or skirt:
15   *"Boogaloo on through!*
                 Breakdown the walls, brother!
                 Boogaloo on through!"
Footfire on floor of hot coals:
Split! Get up! Toe turn!
20   */Split!/Toe-turn!/*
Heel-tunes screeching:
                "Bank-here! Break-there!"
Kissing palms pancake/paralyze the air:
Sugarsweat sterilizing air
25   With gymnastic intelligence/
With braindance acrobatics/
With spitfire from *fleshmotors*—humming:
                "Boogaloo on through!
                 Breakdown the walls, brother!
30   *Boogaloo on through!"*

DISCUSSION QUESTIONS

1. In this poem Redmond uses italic type and regular type to convey the poem's message. What topic is covered in the italic print? What role does the italic print play within the poem?
2. The persona in the poem states *"Breakdown the walls, brother!"* What type of walls are being referred to in this line? Why is it important to break down these walls?

3. Which lines in the poem are similar to the blues song pattern? Which other blues elements does this poem contain? Theme? Language?

WRITING TOPICS

1. Dance, like music, can transport a person from one reality to another. What value does dance have for a society? In ancient times? In the 1900s? In the twentieth century?
2. In this poem the dance movements are described with an intensity. In an essay compare the description of the dance movements in "Dance Bodies #1" with the description of how Sonny plays the piano in "Sonny's Blues."

SOLO ON THE DRUMS

Ann Petry

Ann Petry was born Ann James in 1908 in Old Saybrook, Connecticut, and lived an economically comfortable life. Her father, a pharmacist, owned his own drugstore in Old Saybrook. Her mother graduated from the New York School of Chiropody and earned her license to practice in 1915. Petry graduated from Old Saybrook High School as the only African-American student in her class. In 1931 she graduated from the University of Connecticut School of Pharmacy and worked for the next seven years as a pharmacist in her family's drugstore. In 1938 she married George D. Petry and moved to New York City to pursue a career as a writer, taking a job as a reporter for the *People's Voice*. In the evenings she took creative writing classes at Columbia University. After receiving several rejections from magazine editors for her stories, she quit her job in order to pursue writing full time. In 1943 *Crisis* magazine published Petry's short story "On Saturday the Siren Sounds at Noon." Her short story "Like a Winding Sheet" brought her national attention. In 1945 she won a Houghton Mifflin Literary Fellowship for a portion of her first novel, *The Street.*

Petry's experiences growing up as one of only a few black families in her hometown, graduating from pharmacy school as the only African American in her class, and reporting on Harlem for the *People's Voice* provided her with a rich background for her stories. Her novels, which often focus on the effects of environment and bigotry on an individual, include *The Street* (1946), *Country Place* (1947), *The Narrows* (1954), and *The Common Ground* (1964). Her short stories are collected in *Miss Muriel and Other Stories* (1971). In addition to writing adult fiction, Petry has written fiction for children, publishing *The Drugstore Cat* (1949), *Tituba of Salem Village* (1964), and *Legends of the Saints* (1974).

1   The orchestra had a week's engagement at the Randlert Theater at Broadway and Forty-second Street. His name was picked out in lights on the marquee. The name of the orchestra and then his name underneath by itself.

2   There had been a time when he would have been excited by it. And stopped to let his mind and his eyes linger over it lovingly. Kid Jones. The name—his name—up there in lights that danced and winked in the brassy sunlight. And at night his name glittered up there on the marquee as though it had been sprinkled with diamonds. The people who pushed their way through the crowded street looked up at it and recognized it and smiled.

3   He used to eat it up. But not today. Not after what happened this morning. He just looked at the sign with his name on it. There it was. Then he noticed that the sun had come out, and he shrugged, and went on inside the theater to put on one of the cream-colored suits and get his music together.

4   After he finished changing his clothes, he glanced in the long mirror in his dressing room. He hadn't changed any. Same face. No fatter and no thinner. No gray hair. Nothing. He frowned. Because he felt that the things that were eating him up inside ought to show. But they didn't.

5   When it was time to go out on the stage, he took his place behind the drums, not talking, just sitting there. The orchestra started playing softly. He made a mental note of the fact that the boys were working together as smoothly as though each one had been oiled.

6   The long gray curtains parted. One moment they were closed. And then they were open. Silently. Almost like magic. The high-powered spots flooded the stage with light. He could see specks of dust gliding down the wide beams of light. Under the bands of light the great space out front was all shadow. Faces slowly emerged out of it—disembodied heads and shoulders that slanted up and back, almost to the roof.

7   He hit the drums lightly. Regularly. A soft, barely discernible rhythm. A background. A repeated emphasis for the horns and the piano and the violin. The man with the trumpet stood up, and the first notes came out sweet and clear and high.

8   Kid Jones kept up the drum accompaniment. Slow. Careful. Soft. And he felt his left eyebrow lift itself and start to twitch as the man played the trumpet. It happened whenever he heard the trumpet. The notes crept up, higher, higher, higher. So high that his stomach sucked in against itself. Then a little lower and stronger. A sound sustained. The rhythm of it beating against his ears until he was filled with it and sighing with it.

9   He wanted to cover his ears with his hands because he kept hearing a voice that whispered the same thing over and over again. The voice was trapped somewhere under the roof—caught and held there by the trumpet. "I'm leaving I'm leaving I'm leaving."

10   The sound took him straight back to the rain, the rain that had come with the morning. He could see the beginning of the day—raw and cold.

He was at home. But he was warm because he was close to her, holding her in his arms. The rain and the wind cried softly outside the window.

11   And now—well, he felt as though he were floating up and up and up on that long blue note of the trumpet. He half closed his eyes and rode up on it. It had stopped being music. It was that whispering voice, making him shiver. Hating it and not being able to do anything about it. "I'm leaving it's the guy who plays the piano I'm in love with him and I'm leaving now today." Rain in the streets. Heat gone. Food gone. Everything gone because a woman's gone. It's everything you ever wanted, he thought. It's everything you never got. Everything you ever had, everything you ever lost. It's all there in the trumpet—pain and hate and trouble and peace and quiet and love.

12   The last note stayed up in the ceiling. Hanging on and on. The man with the trumpet had stopped playing but Kid Jones could still hear that last note. In his ears. In his mind.

13   The spotlight shifted and landed on Kid Jones—the man behind the drums. The long beam of white light struck the top of his head and turned him into a pattern of light and shadow. Because of the cream-colored suit and shirt, his body seemed to be encased in light. But there was a shadow over his face, so that his features blended and disappeared. His hairline receding so far back that he looked like a man with a face that never ended. A man with a high, long face and dark, dark skin.

14   He caressed the drums with the brushes in his hands. They responded with a whisper of sound. The rhythm came over but it had to be listened for. It stayed that way for a long time. Low, insidious, repeated. Then he made the big bass drum growl and pick up the same rhythm.

15   The Marquis of Brund, pianist with the band, turned to the piano. The drums and the piano talked the same rhythm. The piano high. A little more insistent than the drums. The Marquis was turned sideway on the piano bench. His left foot tapped out the rhythm. His cream-color suit sharply outlined the bulkiness of his body against the dark gleam of the piano. The drummer and the pianist were silhouetted in two separate brilliant shafts of light. The drums slowly dominated the piano.

16   The rhythm changed. It was faster. Kid Jones looked out over the crowded theater as he hit the drums. He began to feel as though he were the drums and the drums were he.

17   The theater throbbed with the excitement of the drums. A man sitting near the front shivered, and his head jerked to the rhythm. A sailor put his arm around the girl sitting beside him, took his hand and held her face still and pressed his mouth close over hers. Close. Close. Close. Until their faces seemed to melt together. Her hat fell off and neither of them moved. His hand dug deep into her shoulder and still they didn't move.

18   A kid sneaked in through a side door and slid into an aisle seat. His mouth was wide open, and he clutched his cap with both hands, tight and hard against his chest as he listened.

19   The drummer forgot he was in the theater. There was only he and the drums and they were far away. Long gone. He was holding Lulu, Helen, Susie, Mamie close in his arms. And all of them—all those girls blended into that one girl who was his wife. The one who said, "I'm leaving." She had said it over and over again, this morning, while rain dripped down the window panes.

20   When he hit the drums again it was with the thought that he was fighting with the piano player. He was choking the Marquis of Brund. He was putting a knife in clean between his ribs. He was slitting his throat with a long straight blade. Take my woman. Take your life.

21   The drums leaped with the fury that was in him. The men in the band turned their heads toward him—a faint astonishment showed in their faces.

22   He ignored them. The drums took him away from them, took him back, and back, and back, in time and space. He built up an illusion. He was sending out the news. Grandma died. The foreigner in the litter has an old disease and will not recover. The man from across the big water is sleeping with the chief's daughter. Kill. Kill. Kill. The war goes well with the men with the bad smell and the loud laugh. It goes badly with the chiefs with the round heads and the peacock's walk.

23   It is cool in the deep track in the forest. Cool and quiet. The trees talk softly. They speak of the dance tonight. The young girl from across the lake will be there. Her waist is slender and her thighs are rounded. Then the words he wanted to forget were all around Kid Jones again. "I'm leaving I'm leaving I'm leaving."

24   He couldn't help himself. He stopped hitting the drums and stared at the Marquis of Brund—a long, malevolent look, filled with hate.

25   There was a restless, uneasy movement in the theater. He remembered where he was. He started playing again. The horn played a phrase. Soft and short. The drums answered. The horn said the same thing all over again. The drums repeated it. The next time it was more intricate. The phrase was turned around, it went back and forth and up and down. And the drums said it over, exactly the same.

26   He knew a moment of panic. This was where he had a solo again and he wasn't sure he could do it. He touched the drums lightly. They quivered and answered him.

27   And then it was almost as though the drums were talking about his own life. The woman in Chicago who hated him. The girl with the round, soft body who had been his wife and who had walked out on him, this morning, in the rain. The old woman who was his mother, the same woman who lived in Chicago, and who hated him because he looked like his father, his father who had seduced her and left her, years ago.

28   He forgot the theater, forgot everything but the drums. He was welded to the drums, sucked inside them. All of him. His pulse beat. His heart beat. He had become part of the drums. They had become part of him.

29   He made the big bass rumble and reverberate. He went a little mad on the big bass. Again and again he filled the theater with a sound like thunder.

The sound seemed to come not from the drums but from deep inside himself; it was a sound that was being wrenched out of him—a violent, raging, roaring sound. As it issued from him he thought, this is the story of my love, this is the story of my hate, this is all there is left of me. And the sound echoed and re-echoed far up under the roof of the theater.

30   When he finally stopped playing, he was trembling; his body was wet with sweat. He was surprised to see that the drums were sitting there in front of him. He hadn't become part of them. He was still himself. Kid Jones. Master of the drums. Greatest drummer in the world. Selling himself a little piece at a time. Every afternoon. Twice every evening. Only this time he had topped all his other performances. This time, playing like this after what had happened in the morning, he had sold all of himself—not just a little piece.

31   Someone kicked his foot. "Bow, you ape. Whassamatter with you?"

32   He bowed from the waist, and the spotlight slid away from him, down his pants legs. The light landed on the Marquis of Brund, the piano player. The Marquis' skin glistened like a piece of black seaweed. Then the light was back on Kid Jones.

33   He felt hot and he thought, I stink of sweat. The talcum he had dabbed on his face after he shaved felt like a constricting layer of cement. A thin layer but definitely cement. No air could get through to his skin. He reached for his handkerchief and felt the powder and the sweat mix as he mopped his face.

34   Then he bowed again. And again. Like a—like one of those things you pull the string and it jerks, goes through the motion of dancing. Pull it again and it kicks. Yeah, he thought, you were hot all right. The jitterbugs ate you up and you haven't any place to go. Since this morning you haven't had any place to go. "I'm leaving it's the guy who plays the piano I'm in love with the

35   Marquis of Brund he plays such sweet piano I'm leaving leaving leaving—"

36   He stared at the Marquis of Brund for a long moment.

37   Then he stood up and bowed again. And again.

DISCUSSION QUESTIONS

1. Describe Kid Jones's state of mind when he begins to play the drums. How does this description compare to his feelings when he finally stops playing the drums?
2. What does Kid Jones work out about his life while playing the drums?
3. Using specific evidence from the story, explain the audience's reaction to Kid Jones's first drum solo.
4. At the end of the story, why does Kid Jones compare himself to a puppet on a string? Is Kid Jones's view of himself distorted? If so, how?

WRITING TOPICS

1. In your journal, create a character sketch of Kid Jones. How old is he? What does he look like? What does he like to do? Not like to do? Use the relationships between him and the women in his life and the relationships between him and the men in his life to help describe Kid Jones.

2. Reread Langston Hughes's "The Blues I'm Playing." Analyze how Kid Jones feels when he plays the drums. Then analyze how Oceola feels when she plays jazz and blues. Write an essay in which you present an argument for the redeeming power of music.

CANARY

Rita Dove

Rita Dove was born in Akron, Ohio, in 1952. In 1973 she received her B.A. degree, summa cum laude, from the Miami University in Oxford, Ohio. During 1974 and 1975, she attended the University of Tübingen in West Germany on a Fulbright scholarship. Dove married Fred Viebahn, a writer in 1977. Dove had already received national acclaim for fiction and poetry in anthologies and magazines when her first book of poetry, *The Yellow House on the Corner* (1980), was published. In 1987 Dove received the Pulitzer Prize for *Thomas and Beulah* (1986), a collection of poems based on stories she knew about her grandfather and grandmother. President William Clinton named Dove U.S. Poet Laureate/Consultant in Poetry, Library of Congress in 1993 and in 1995. Dove has received numerous awards for her poetry, has received more than ten honorary doctorate degrees, and has served on numerous national panels and committees. She taught at Arizona State University and is now Commonwealth Professor at the University of Virginia.

Dove's poetry and fiction are lyrical, insightful, and poignant. Her books of poetry include *Museum* (1983), *Grace Notes* (1989), *Selected Poems* (1993), and *Mother Love* (1995). She has published fiction, *Fifth Sunday* (1985) and *Through the Ivory Gate* (1992), and nonfiction, *The Poet's World* (1995). In addition, she has published a full-length verse drama, *The Darker Face of Earth* (1993).

Billie Holiday's burned voice
had as many shadows as lights,
a mournful candelabra against a sleek piano,
the gardenia her signature under that ruined face.

5   (Now you're cooking, drummer to bass,
    magic spoon, magic needle.
    Take all day if you have to
    with your mirror and your bracelet of song.)

    Fact is, the invention of women under siege
10 has been to sharpen love in the service of myth.

    If you can't be free, be a mystery.

DISCUSSION QUESTIONS

1. The poem's persona describes Billie Holiday using such phrases as "burned voice" and "ruined face." What led to Billie Holiday having a "burned voice" and "ruined face"?
2. The second stanza is enclosed in a parenthesis. How would the poem change if the parentheses were removed?
3. Select words or phrases from the poem which support the idea that this poem has blueslike qualities.
4. The last line of the poem reads, "If you can't be free, be a mystery." What does the word "free" mean? How could being a mystery compensate for not being free?

WRITING TOPICS

1. Research Billie Holiday's life. Is there an illusion of mystery around her life? Write an essay in which you analyze how she was not "free."
2. The title of this poem is "Canary," but there are no references to a bird in the poem. What is the connection between the title of the poem and the subject of the poem?

CHAPTER FOUR

SLAVERY—TIME OF TRIAL

Slavery: a practice whereby one human being owns another human being. Slaves have no rights. They are the material property of their owner. Their lives depend on the whims of their owner. All that slaves possess and hold dear—even their children—is the property of their owner.

In today's society, the idea that one human being could be the property of another human being is unacceptable. But in the early 1600s, Africans bought or captured in sub-Saharan Africa were brought across the Middle Passage of the Atlantic to be sold in the American colonies. Many Africans died on the voyage, either by jumping overboard or from the unspeakable conditions in the hold of the ships. Those who survived were sold to the highest bidder. The practice of slavery continued in the colonies and eventually the United States for over 200 years. Slavery in the United States ended in 1863 with the signing of the Emancipation Proclamation by President Abraham Lincoln. All slaves were not free, however, until the end of the Civil War in 1865 and the passage of the 13th Amendment to the Constitution.

The original slaves and their slave descendants lived lives of hardship and degradation. Slavery influenced how white Americans viewed African Americans—as property to be managed and controlled. Many white Americans even regarded slaves as unintelligent and animal-like, fit only to work in fields or at menial tasks. This type of thinking caused many African Americans to be mistreated or killed.

Most of the time, African-American slaves could not marry in either civil or religious ceremonies. Families were not allowed to stay together—family members could be sold off at any time. Children were separated from their mothers and made to work in the fields at a young age. In many states before the Civil War, it was illegal for slaves to learn to read and write.

Survival under slavery took energy and dignity. Many African Americans did not survive, but those who did passed their strength and dignity on to others. Those slaves who learned to read and write and who were able to obtain their freedom told about the horrible conditions of slavery to both American and foreign audiences. During the time of slavery, and ever since its abolishment, African-American writers have told their stories about the effects of slavery on their very existence. The tradition continues today, with contemporary African Americans telling their own stories with a sense of connectedness with their ancestors.

THE SLAVE MOTHER

Frances Ellen Watkins Harper

Frances Ellen Watkins Harper was born in 1825, the only child of free black parents in Baltimore, Maryland. She attended a school owned by her uncle, William J. Watkins, a minister, craftsman, and abolitionist. Harper was trained in domestic arts and subsequently worked in a Baltimore bookstore. In 1850 she became an instructor of domestic science at a new school for free blacks, run by the African Methodist Episcopal Church. She later gave up her teaching career to become a lecturer. Harper was a writer and social reformer until her retirement at nearly eighty. She wrote and spoke against slavery until after the Civil War, when she turned to the causes of civil rights for blacks, temperance, and women's suffrage.

Harper, who also wrote under the name Effie Afton, was the major African-American woman poet of the nineteenth century. Her audiences called her the "Bronze Muse." She published numerous books of poetry, including *Poems on Miscellaneous Subjects* (1854); *Moses: A Story of the Nile* (1869); *Sketches of Southern Life* (1872); *The Sparrows Fall and Other Poems* (1890); and *Atlanta Offering, Poems* (1895). Harper also published a novel, *Iola Leroy; or Shadows Uplifted* (1872), and short stories. Her short story "The Two Offers" (1859) is credited with being the first short story published by an African-American woman in the United States. Three of Harper's serialized novels that originally appeared in the *Christian Recorder,* a black magazine, were recently rediscovered and published: *Minnie's Sacrifice, Sowing and Reaping,* and *Trial and Triumph.* Harper died in 1911.

Heard you that shriek? It rose
So wildly in the air,
It seemed as if a burdened heart
Was breaking in despair.

5   Saw you those hands so sadly clasped
        The bowed and feeble head
    The shuddering of that fragile form
        That look of grief and dread?

    Saw you the sad, imploring eye?
10   Its every glance was pain,
    As if a storm of agony
        Were sweeping through the brain.

    She is a mother, pale with fear,
        Her boy clings to her side,
15 And in her kirtle[1] vainly tries
        His trembling form to hide.

    He is not hers, although she bore
        For him a mother's pains;
    He is not hers, although her blood
20   Is coursing through his veins!

    He is not hers, for cruel hands
        May rudely tear apart
    The only wreath of household love
        That binds her breaking heart.

25 His love has been a joyous light
        That o'er her pathway smiled.
    A fountain gushing ever new,
        Amid life's desert wild.

    His lightest word has been a tone,
30   Of music round her heart,
    Their lives a streamlet blent in one–
        Oh, Father! must they part?

    They tear him from her circling arms,
        Her last and fond embrace.
35 Oh! never more may her sad eyes
        Gaze on his mournful face.

    No marvel, then, these bitter shrieks,
        Disturb the listening air:
    She is a mother, and her heart
40   Is breaking in despair.

---

1 *kirtle:* a woman's gown; a skirt or outer petticoat.

DISCUSSION QUESTIONS

1. Select words from the poem that evoke emotion. Discuss how Harper used these words in her writing on the antislavery movement.
2. This poem is written in four-line stanzas, with each quatrain expressing a complete idea. How do the quatrains work together to create a vivid description of this aspect of slavery?
3. Why was it an advantage for slave owners to separate mothers from their children?
4. In the sixth stanza, the persona states "The only wreath of household love." What is this figurative wreath? Why would a slave mother's home have a limited number of symbols of "household love"?

WRITING TOPICS

1. In your journal, describe a time when you felt as though you did not have control over your life. How did you feel? What did you do to help yourself through that difficult time?
2. Write a poem in which a five- or six-year-old describes being separated from his or her mother to work all day in a field. Use the same stanzaic form, the quatrain, and emotional language that Harper used in her poem.

ON BEING BROUGHT FROM AFRICA TO AMERICA

Phillis Wheatley

Phillis Wheatley was born about 1753 in West Africa, possibly in what is now Senegal, and brought to America on a slave ship in 1761. John Wheatley of Boston purchased her as a gift for his wife. Phillis Wheatley was given a classical education; she read the Bible, Alexander Pope, and Homer, and became proficient in grammar and in understanding style. Her favorite poet was John Milton, a seventeenth-century English poet. Wheatley's level of education was rare for young women in colonial society, but especially so for young black women. She was a devout Christian and a member of the Old South Meeting House. In 1772 Wheatley, accompanying the Wheatley's son Nathan, traveled to London, where a collection of her poems was published: *Poems on Various Subjects, Religious and Moral, By Phillis Wheatley, Negro Servant to Mr. John Wheatley of Boston.* The Wheatleys freed Phillis in 1773, and she married John Peters, a free black Bostonian, in 1778. She had three children, all of whom died in infancy.

During her lifetime, Wheatley wrote poetry for specific occasions, such as the poem "To His Excellency General Washington," which she sent to George Washington in honor of his being appointed commander of the American armies in 1775. Her use of heroic couplets, emotional detachment from the subject being discussed, the Biblical references all reflect the neoclassical literary style of the time. Wheatley's poetry has been criticized because it does not openly discuss slavery. However, evidence of her antislavery position is evident in a 1774 antislavery letter she wrote to a Presbyterian preacher. Wheatley died in 1784.

'Twas mercy brought me from my pagan land,
Taught my benighted[1] soul to understand
That there's a God, that there's a Savior too:
Once I redemption neither sought nor knew.
5 Some view that sable race with scornful eye:
"Their colour is a diabolic dye."[2]
Remember, Christians, Negroes black as Cain[3]
May be refined and join the angelic train.

DISCUSSION QUESTIONS

1. In lines 7 and 8, to what does the word "refined" refer? Why would this type of action be important during the religious time in which Wheatley lived?
2. Is the speaker in the poem sincere when he or she says, "'Twas mercy brought me from my pagan land"? Why is mercy important to the speaker?
3. In line 7 the speaker uses the phrase "Negroes black as Cain." Is the speaker referring to the color of Negroes or to something else? Explain your response.

WRITING TOPICS

1. Many slaves who spoke out against slavery were punished for expressing their opinions. After researching slavery in the United States, explain in an essay how slaves used songs, coded messages, and other forms of communication to express their feelings on slavery.
2. In your journal, discuss how you handle situations in which your words might upset others. Do you defend your unpopular opinions? Or do you keep silent so as not to cause "trouble"?

---

1 *benighted:* being in intellectual darkness
2 *diabolic dye:* color of or pertaining to the devil.
3 *Cain:* in the Bible, the first man to murder his brother, Abel.

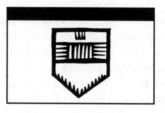

RUNAGATE RUNAGATE

Robert Hayden

Robert Hayden was born in Detroit, Michigan, in 1913. He received a bachelor's degree at Wayne State University and a master's degree at the University of Michigan. He taught at Fisk University, where he served as a Professor of English from 1946 to 1969 and then at the University of Michigan (1969–1980). Hayden researched African-American history for the Federal Writer's Project. In addition to poetry, he wrote criticism, radio scripts, and a play. His books of poetry include *Heart-Shape in the Dust* (1940), *The Lion and the Archer*, written in collaboration with Myron O'Higgins (1966), *A Ballad of Remembrance* (1962), and *Selected Poems* (1966). Hayden has received many honors, including the Hopwood Award from the University of Michigan, a Rosenwald Literary Fellowship, and a Ford Foundation grant for travel and writing in Mexico. In 1965 *A Ballad of Remembrance* received the Grand Prize for Poetry at the First World Festival of Negro Arts, held in Dakar, Senegal. Hayden died in 1980.

I.

Runs falls rises stumbles on from darkness into darkness
and the darkness thicketed with shapes of terror
and the hunters pursuing and the hounds pursuing
and the night cold and the night long and the river
5   to cross and the jack-muh-lanterns beckoning beckoning
and blackness ahead and when shall I reach that somewhere
morning and keep on going and never turn back and keep on going

    Runagate
      Runagate
10   Runagate

Many thousands rise and go
many thousands crossing over

O mythic North
O star-shaped yonder Bible city

15 Some go weeping and some rejoicing
some in coffins and some in carriages
some in silks and some in shackles

Rise and go or fare you well

No more auction block for me
20 no more driver's lash for me

If you see my Pompey, 30 yrs of age,
new breeches, plain stockings, negro shoes;
if you see my Anna, likely young mulatto
branded E on the right cheek, R on the left,
25 catch them if you can and notify subscriber.
Catch them if you can, but it won't be easy.

They'll dart underground when you try to catch them,
plunge into quicksand, whirlpools, mazes,
turn into scorpions when you try to catch them.

30 And before I'll be a slave
I'll be buried in my grave

North star and bonanza gold
I'm bound for the freedom, freedom-bound
and oh Susyanna don't you cry for me

35   Runagate

Runagate

II.

Rises from their anguish and their power,

Harriet Tubman,

woman of earth, whipscarred,
40 a summoning, a shining

Mean to be free

And this was the way of it, brethren brethren,
way we journeyed from Can't to Can.
Moon so bright and no place to hide,
45   the cry up and the patterollers riding,
hound dogs belling in bladed air.
And fear starts a-murbling, Never make it,
we'll never make it. *Hush that now,*
and she's turned upon us, levelled pistol
50   glinting in the moonlight:
Dead folks can't jaybird-talk, she says;
you keep on going now or die, she says.

Wanted   Harriet Tubman   alias The General
alias Moses   Stealer of Slaves
55   In league with Garrison   Alcott   Emerson
Garrett   Douglass   Thoreau   John Brown

Armed and known to be Dangerous

Wanted   Reward   Dead or Alive

Tell me, Ezekiel, oh tell me do you see
60   mailed Jehova coming to deliver me?

Hoot-owl calling in the ghosted air,
five times calling to the hants in the air.
Shadow of a face in the scary leaves,
shadow of a voice in the talking leaves:

65   Come ride-a my train

Oh that train, ghost-story train
through swamp and savanna movering movering,
over trestles of dew, through caves of the wish,
Midnight Special on a sabre track movering movering,
70   *first stop Mercy and the last Hallelujah.*

Come ride-a my train

Mean mean mean to be free.

DISCUSSION QUESTIONS

1. Discuss lines 15 to 17 in your small group. What do you think the poet means here?
2. Part I of the poem is written in free verse; the slaves' flight for freedom is shown by placing certain words in a specific arrangement on the page. Locate these words and discuss how they are visually displayed.
3. What role did Harriet Tubman play in the slaves' search for freedom?
4. Who is the person who is armed and known to be dangerous?

WRITING TOPICS

1. In your writing journal, explain what you think the phrase "Come ride-a my train" means.
2. Use your imagination and write a song or poem you think the slaves might have sung either during their flight to freedom or while they were still living on plantations.
3. Hayden writes: "And this was the way of it, . . . / way we journeyed from Can't to Can." In an analytical essay present your interpretation of what the phrase "journeyed from Can't to Can" means.

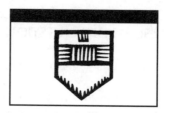

LETTER TO HIS MASTER

Frederick Douglass

Frederick Douglass was born in 1817 on a slave plantation in Talbot County, Maryland. Along with his parents, he escaped to freedom in New York and later moved to Massachusetts. A brilliant man with no formal education, Douglass taught himself how to read and write. He was a powerful speaker and dedicated fighter; his oratorical fame preceded him to London where he spoke out against slavery. In 1847, upon his return from England, he became the leading African-American spokesperson in the anti-slavery movement. He worked for the Underground Railroad (safe houses) in assisting slaves to find their way to Canada and freedom. Douglass wrote three autobiographies: his *Narrative of the Life of Frederick Douglass, an American Slave* (1845), *My Bondage and My Freedom* (1855), and *Life and Times of Frederick Douglass* (1881). Frederick Douglass died in Washington, D.C., in 1895.

Thomas Auld:

Sir—The long and intimate, though by no means friendly relation which unhappily subsisted between you and myself, leads me to hope that you will easily account for the great liberty which I now take in addressing you in this open and public manner. The same fact may possibly remove any disagreeable surprise which you may experience on again finding your name coupled with mine, in any other way than in an advertisement, accurately describing my person, and offering a large sum for my arrest. In thus dragging you again before the public, I am aware that I shall subject myself to no inconsiderable amount of censure. I shall probably be charged with an unwarrantable, if not a wanton and reckless disregard of the rights and proprieties of private life. There are those North as well as South who entertain a much higher respect for rights which are merely conventional, than they do for rights which are personal and essential. Not a few there are in our country, who, while they have no scruples against robbing the laborer of the hard earned results of his patient industry, will be shocked by the extremely indelicate manner of bringing your name before the public. . . .

2   I have selected this day on which to address you, because it is the anniversary of my emancipation; and knowing of no better way I am led to this as the best mode of celebrating that truly important event. Just ten years ago this beautiful September morning, yon bright sun beheld me a slave—a poor, degraded chattel—trembling at the sound of your voice, lamenting that I was a man, and wishing myself a brute. The hopes which I had treasured up for weeks of a safe and successful escape from your grasp, were powerfully confronted at this last hour by dark clouds of doubt and fear, making my person shake and my bosom to heave with the heavy contest between hope and fear. I have no words to describe to you the deep agony of soul which I experienced on that never to be forgotten morning—(for I left by daylight). I was making a leap in the dark. The probabilities, so far as I could by reason determine them, were stoutly against the undertaking. The preliminaries and precautions I had adopted previously, all worked badly. I was like one going to war without weapons—ten chances of defeat to one of victory. One in whom I had confided, and one who had promised me assistance, appalled by fear at the trial hour, deserted me, thus leaving the responsibility of success or failure solely with myself. You, sir, can never know my feelings. As I look back to them I can scarcely realize that I have passed through a scene so trying. Trying however as they were, and gloomy as was the prospect, thanks be to the Most High, who is ever the God of the oppressed, at the moment which was to determine my whole earthly career. His grace was sufficient, my mind was made up. I embraced the golden opportunity, took the morning tide at the flood, and a free man, young, active and strong, is the result. . . .

3   Since I left you, I have had a rich experience. I have occupied stations which I never dreamed of when a slave. Three out of the ten years since I left you, I spent as a common laborer on the wharves of New Bedford, Massachusetts. It was there I earned my first free dollar. It was mine. I could spend it as I pleased. I could buy hams or herring with it, without asking any odds of any body. That was a precious dollar to me. You remember when I used to make seven or eight, or even nine dollars a week in Baltimore, you would take every cent of it from me every Saturday night, saying that I belonged to you, and my earnings also. I never liked this conduct on your part—to say the best, I thought it a little mean. I would not have served you so. But let that pass. I was a little awkward about counting money in New England fashion when I first landed in New Bedford. I like to have betrayed myself several times. I caught myself saying phip, for fourpence; and at one time a man actually charged me with being a runaway, whereupon I was silly enough to become one by running away from him, for I was greatly afraid he might adopt measures to give me again into slavery, a condition I then dreaded more than death.

4   I soon, however, learned to count money, as well as to make it, and got

on swimmingly. I married soon after leaving you: in fact, I was engaged to be married before I left you; and instead of finding my companion a burden; she was truly a helpmeet. She went to live at service and I to work on the wharf, and though we toiled hard the first winter, we never lived more happily. After remaining in New Bedford for three years, I met with Wm. Lloyd Garrison, a person of whom you have *possibly* heard, as he is pretty generally known among slave-holders. He put it into my head that I might make myself serviceable to the cause of the slave by devoting a portion of my time to telling my own sorrows, and those of other slaves which had come under my observation. This was the commencement of a higher state of existence than any to which I had ever aspired. I was thrown into society the most pure, enlightened and benevolent that the country affords. Among these I have never forgotten you, but have invariably made you the topic of conversation—thus giving you all the notoriety I could do. I need not tell you that the opinion formed of you in these circles, is far from being favorable. They have little respect for your honesty, and less for your religion.

5   But I was going on to relate something of my interesting experience. I had not long enjoyed the excellent society to which I have referred, before the light of its excellence exerted a beneficial influence on my mind and heart. Much of my early dislike of white persons was removed, and their manners, habits and customs, so entirely unlike what I had been used to in the kitchen-quarters on the plantations of the South, fairly charmed me, and gave me a strong disrelish for the coarse and degrading customs of my former condition. I therefore made an effort so to improve my mind and deportment as to be somewhat fitted to the station to which I seemed almost providentially called. The transition from degradation to respectability was indeed great, and to get from one to the other without carrying some marks of one's former condition, is truly a difficult matter. I would not have you think that I am now entirely clear of all plantation peculiarities, but my friends here, while they entertain the strongest dislike to them, regard me with that charity to which my past life somewhat entitles me, so that my condition in this respect is exceedingly pleasant. So far as my domestic affairs are concerned, I can boast of as comfortable a dwelling as your own. I have an industrious and neat companion, and four dear children—the oldest a girl of nine years and three fine boys, the oldest eight, the next six, and the youngest four years old. The three oldest are now going regularly to school—two can read and write, and the other can spell with tolerable correctness words of two syllables. Dear fellows! they are all in comfortable beds, and are sound asleep, perfectly secure under my own roof. There are no slaveholders here to rend my heart by snatching them from my arms, or blast a mother's dearest hopes by tearing them from her bosom. These dear children are ours—not to work up into rice, sugar and tobacco, but to watch over, regard, and protect, and to rear them up in the nurture and admonition of the gospel—to train them up in the paths of wisdom and virtue, and, as far as we can to make them useful to the world and to themselves. Oh!

sir, a slaveholder never appears to me so completely an agent of hell, as when I think of and look upon my dear children. It is then that my feelings rise above my control. I meant to have said more with respect to my own prosperity and happiness, but thoughts and feelings which this recital has quickened unfit me to proceed further in that direction. The grim horrors of slavery rise in all their ghastly terror before me, the wails of millions pierce my heart, and chill my blood. I remember the chain, the gag, the bloody whip, the death-like gloom overshadowing the broken spirit of the fettered bondman, the appalling liability of his being torn away from wife and children, and sold like a beast in the market. Say not that this is a picture of fancy. You well know that I wear stripes on my back inflicted by your direction; and that you, while we were brothers in the same church caused this right hand, with which I am now penning this letter, to be closely tied to my left, and my person dragged at the pistol's mouth, fifteen miles, from the Bay side to Easton to be sold like a beast in the market for the alleged crime of intending to escape from your possession. All this and more you remember, and know to be perfectly true, not only of yourself, but of nearly all of the slaveholders around you.

6   At this moment, you are probably the guilty holder of at least three of my own dear sisters, and my only brother in bondage. These you regard as your property. They are recorded on your ledger, or perhaps have been sold to human flesh mongers, with a view to filling your own ever-hungry purse. Sir, I desire to know how and where these dear sisters are. Have you sold them? or are they still in your possession? What has become of them? are they living or dead? And my dear old grandmother, whom you turned out like an old horse, to die in the woods—is she still alive? Write and let me know all about them. If my grandmother be still alive, she is of no service to you, for by this time she must be nearly eighty years old—too old to be cared for by one to whom she has ceased to be of service, send her to me at Rochester, or bring her to Philadelphia, and it shall be the crowning happiness of my life to take care of her in her old age. Oh! she was to me a mother, and a father, so far as hard toil for my comfort could make her such. Send me my grandmother! that I may watch over and take care of her in her old age. And my sisters, let me know all about them. I would write to them, and learn all I want to know of them, without disturbing you in any way, but that, through your unrighteous conduct, they have been entirely deprived of the power to read and write. You have kept them in utter ignorance, and have therefore robbed them of the sweet enjoyments of writing or receiving letters from absent friends and relatives. Your wickedness and cruelty committed in this respect on your fellow-creatures, are greater than all the stripes you have laid upon my back, or theirs. It is an outrage upon the soul—a war upon the immortal spirit, and one for which you must give account at the bar of our common Father and Creator. . . .

7   I will now bring this letter to a close, you shall hear from me again unless you let me hear from you. I intend to make use of you as a weapon with

which to assail the system of slavery—as a means of concentrating public attention on the system, and deepening their horror of trafficking in the souls and bodies of men. I shall make use of you as a means of exposing the character of the American church and clergy—and as a means of bringing this guilty nation with yourself to repentance. In doing this I entertain no malice towards you personally. There is no roof under which you would be more safe than mine, and there is nothing in my house which you might need for your comfort, which I would not readily grant. Indeed, I should esteem it a privilege, to set you an example as to how mankind ought to treat each other.

8   I am your fellow man, but not your slave.

Frederick Douglass

DISCUSSION QUESTIONS

1. What do you think Douglass means by the statement at the end of paragraph 6: ". . . You must give account at the bar of our common Father and Creator . . ."?
2. What is the tone of Douglass's letter to his former slaveholder?
3. In paragraph 7 Douglass says: "I shall make use of you as a weapon with which to assail the system of slavery. . . ." What does he mean by the statement?

WRITING TOPICS

1. Douglass indicates that he holds no malice toward his former slaveholder. In your writing journal explore Douglass's behavior toward his former slaveholder. Is his attitude appropriate? Effective?
2. Assume that Douglass has received word that his former slaveholder still has his sisters and brother in bondage. Pretend you are Douglass and write a letter to your relatives telling them what freedom means to you.

AN ADDRESS TO THE SLAVES OF THE UNITED STATES OF AMERICA

Henry Highland Garnet

Henry Highland Garnet was born a slave in Maryland in 1815. In 1825 Garnet escaped with his mother and father to New York City. For a period of time, he was a student at the new African Free School in New York City. He then attended the Noyes Academy in New Hampshire. In 1843 he became a minister of a predominantly white congregation in Troy, New York. By 1865 he had become minister of New York City's Shiloh Presbyterian Church. Shiloh became the mecca for many African-American organizations; the Emancipation Proclamation was celebrated there in January 1863. He addressed the United States Congress on February 12, 1865, speaking about the demoralizing aspects of what he called the "peculiar institution." Garnet journeyed to Africa in 1881 and died there one year later in 1882.

1   Brethren and Fellow Citizens: Your brethren of the North, East, and West have been accustomed to meet together in National Conventions, to sympathize with each other, and to weep over your unhappy condition. In these meetings we have addressed all classes of the free, but we have never, until this time, sent a word of consolation and advice to you. We have been contented in sitting still and mourning over your sorrows, earnestly hoping that before this day your sacred liberties would have been restored. But, we have hoped in vain. Years have rolled on, and tens of thousands have been borne on streams of blood and tears to the shores of eternity. While you have been oppressed, we have also been partakers with you; nor can we be free while you are enslaved. We, therefore, write to you as being bound with you.

2   Many of you are bound to us, not only by the ties of a common humanity, but we are connected by the more tender relations of parents, wives, husbands, and sisters, and friends. As such we most affectionately address you.

3   Slavery has fixed a deep gulf between you and us, and while it shuts out from you the relief and consolation which your friends would willingly render, it afflicts and persecutes you with a fierceness which we might not expect to see in the fiends of hell. But still the Almighty Father of mercies has left to us a glimmering ray of hope, which shines out like a lone star in a cloudy sky. Mankind are becoming wiser, and better—the oppressor's power is fading, and you, every day, are becoming better informed, and more numerous. Your grievances, brethren, are many. We shall not attempt, in this short address, to present to the world all the dark catalogue of the nation's sins, which have been committed upon an innocent people. Nor is it indeed necessary, for you feel them from day to day, and all the civilized world looks upon them with amazement.

4   Two hundred and twenty-seven years ago the first of our injured race were brought to the shores of America. They came not with glad spirits to select their homes in the New World. They came not with their own consent, to find an unmolested enjoyment of the blessings of this fruitful soil. The first dealings they had with men calling themselves Christians exhibited to them the worst features of corrupt and sordid hearts: and convinced them that no cruelty is too great, no villainy and no robbery too abhorrent for even enlightened men to perform, when influenced by avarice and lust. Neither did they come flying upon the wings of liberty to a land of freedom. But they came with broken hearts, from their beloved native land, and were doomed to unrequited toil and deep degradation. Nor did the evil of their bondage end at their emancipation by death. Succeeding generations inherited their chains, and millions have come from eternity into time, and have returned again to the world of spirits, cursed and ruined by American slavery.

5   The propagators of the system, or their immediate successors, very soon discovered its growing evil, and its tremendous wickedness, and secret promises were made to destroy it. The gross inconsistency of a people holding slaves, who had themselves "ferried o'er the wave" for freedom's sake, was too apparent to be entirely overlooked. The voice of Freedom cried, "Emancipate your slaves." Humanity supplicated with tears for the deliverance of the children of Africa. Wisdom urged her solemn plea. The bleeding captive plead his innocence, and pointed to Christianity who stood weeping at the cross. Jehovah frowned upon the nefarious institution, and thunderbolts, red with vengeance, struggled to leap forth to blast the guilty wretches who maintained it. But all was vain. Slavery had stretched its dark wings of death over the land, the Church stood silently by—the priests prophesied falsely, and the people loved to have it so. Its throne is established, and now it reigns triumphant.

6   Nearly three millions of your fellow-citizens are prohibited by law and public opinion (which in this country is stronger than law) from reading the Book of Life. Your intellect has been destroyed as much as possible, and every ray of light they have attempted to shut out from your minds. The oppressors themselves have become involved in the ruin. They have become

weak, sensual, and rapacious—they have cursed you—they have cursed themselves—they have cursed the earth which they have trod.

7   The colonies threw the blame upon England. They said that the mother country entailed the evil upon them, and they would rid themselves of it if they could. The world thought they were sincere, and the philanthropic pitied them. But time soon tested their sincerity. In a few years the colonists grew strong, and severed themselves from the British Government. Their independence was declared, and they took their station among the sovereign powers of the earth. The declaration was a glorious document. Sages admired it, and the patriotic of every nation reverenced the God-like sentiments which it contained. When the power of Government returned to their hands, did they emancipate the slaves? No; they rather added new links to our chains. Were they ignorant of the principles of Liberty? Certainly they were not. The sentiments of their revolutionary orators fell in burning eloquence upon their hearts, and with one voice they cried, LIBERTY OR DEATH. Oh, what a sentence was that! It ran from soul to soul like electric fire, and nerved the arms of thousands to fight in the holy cause of Freedom. Among the diversity of opinions that are entertained in regard to physical resistance, there are but a few found to gainsay the stern declaration. We are among those who do not.

8   SLAVERY! How much misery is comprehended in that single word. What mind is there that does not shrink from its direful effects? Unless the image of God be obliterated from the soul, all men cherish the love of liberty. The nice discerning political economist does not regard the sacred right more than the untutored African who roams in the wilds of Congo. Nor has the one more right to the full enjoyment of his freedom than the other. In every man's mind the good seeds of liberty are planted, and he who brings his fellow down so low, as to make him contented with a condition of slavery, commits the highest crime against God and man. Brethren, your oppressors aim to do this. They endeavor to make you as much like brutes as possible. When they have blinded the eyes of your mind—when they have embittered the sweet waters of life—when they have shut out the light which shines from the word of God—then, and not till then, has American slavery done its perfect work.

9   TO SUCH DEGRADATION IT IS SINFUL IN THE EXTREME FOR YOU TO MAKE VOLUNTARY SUBMISSION. The divine commandments you are in duty bound to reverence and obey. If you do not obey them, you will surely meet with the displeasure of the Almighty. He requires you to love Him supremely, and your neighbor as yourself—to keep the Sabbath day holy—to search the Scriptures—and bring up your children with respect for His laws, and to worship no other God but Him. But slavery sets all these at nought, and hurls defiance in the face of Jehovah. The forlorn condition in which you are placed does not destroy your obligation to God. You are not certain of heaven, because you allow yourselves to remain in a state of slavery, where you cannot obey the commandments of the Sovereign of the universe. If the

ignorance of slavery is a passport to heaven, then it is a blessing, and no curse, and you should rather desire its perpetuity than its abolition. God will not receive slavery, nor ignorance, nor any other state of mind, for love and obedience to Him. Your condition does not absolve you from your moral obligation. The diabolical injustice by which your liberties are cloven down, NEITHER GOD NOR ANGELS, OR JUST MEN, COMMAND YOU TO SUFFER FOR A SINGLE MOMENT. THEREFORE IT IS YOUR SOLEMN AND IMPERATIVE DUTY TO USE EVERY MEANS, BOTH MORAL, INTELLECTUAL, AND PHYSICAL, THAT PROMISES SUCCESS. If a band of heathen men should attempt to enslave a race of Christians, and to place their children under the influence of some false religion, surely Heaven would frown upon the men who would not resist such aggression, even to death. If, on the other hand, a band of Christians should attempt to enslave a race of heathen men, and to entail slavery upon them, and to keep them in heathenism in the midst of Christianity, the God of heaven would smile upon every effort which the injured might make to disenthral themselves.

10   Brethren, it is as wrong for your lordly oppressors to keep you in slavery as it was for the man thief to steal our ancestors from the coast of Africa. You should therefore now use the same manner of resistance as would have been just in our ancestors when the bloody foot-prints of the first remorseless soul-thief was placed upon the shores of our fatherland. The humblest peasant is as free in the sight of God as the proudest monarch that ever swayed a sceptre. Liberty is a spirit sent out from God, and like its great Author, is no respecter of persons.

11   Brethren, the time has come when you must act for yourselves. It is an old and true saying that, "if hereditary bondmen would be free, they must themselves strike the blow." You can plead your own cause, and do the work of emancipation better than any others. The nations of the Old World are moving in the great cause of universal freedom, and some of them at least will, ere long, do you justice. The combined powers of Europe have placed their broad seal of disapprobation upon the African slave-trade. But in the slaveholding parts of the United States the trade is as brisk as ever. They buy and sell you as though you were brute beasts. The North has done much—her opinion of slavery in the abstract is known. But in regard to the South, we adopt the opinion of the *New York Evangelist*—"We have advanced so far, that the cause apparently waits for a more effectual door to be thrown open than has been yet." We are about to point you to that more effectual door. Look around you, and behold the bosoms of your loving wives heaving with untold agonies! Here the cries of your poor children! Remember the stripes your fathers bore. Think of the torture and disgrace of your noble mothers. Think of your wretched sisters, loving virtue and purity, as they are driven into concubinage and are exposed to the unbridled lusts of incarnate devils. Think of the undying glory that hangs around the ancient name of Africa—and forget not that you are native-born American citizens, and as such you are justly entitled to all the rights that are granted to the freest.

Think how many tears you have poured out upon the soil which you have cultivated with unrequited toil and enriched with your blood; and then go to your lordly enslavers and tell them plainly, that you are *determined to be free*. Appeal to their sense of justice, and tell them that they have no more right to oppress you than you have to enslave them. Entreat them to remove the grievous burdens which they have imposed upon you, and to remunerate you for your labor. Promise them renewed diligence in the cultivation of the soil, if they will render to you an equivalent for your services. Point them to the increase of happiness and prosperity in the British West Indies since the Act of Emancipation. Tell them in language which they cannot misunderstand of the exceeding sinfulness of slavery, and of a future judgment, and of the righteous retributions of an indignant God. Inform them that all you desire is FREEDOM, and that nothing else will suffice. Do this, and forever after cease to toil for the heartless tyrants, who give you no other reward but stripes and abuse. If they then commence work of death, they, and not you, will be responsible for the consequences. You had far better all die—die *immediately,* than live slaves, and entail your wretchedness upon your posterity. If you would be free in this generation, here is your only hope. However much you and all of us may desire it, there is not much hope of redemption without the shedding of blood. If you must bleed, let it all come at once—rather *die freemen than live to be the slaves*. It is impossible, like the children of Israel, to make a grand exodus from the land of bondage. The Pharaohs are on both sides of the blood-red waters! You cannot move *en masse* to the dominions of the British Queen—nor can you pass through Florida and overrun Texas, and at last find peace in Mexico. The propagators of American slavery are spending their blood and treasure that they may plant the black flag in the heart of Mexico and riot in the halls of the Montezumas. In language of the Reverend Robert Hall, when addressing the volunteers of Bristol, who were rushing forth to repel the invasion of Napoleon, who threatened to lay waste the fair homes of England, "Religion is too much interested in your behalf not to shed over you her most gracious influences."

12   You will not be compelled to spend much time in order to become inured to hardships. From the first movement that you breathed the air of heaven, you have been accustomed to nothing else but hardships. The heroes of the American Revolution were never put upon harder fare than a peck of corn and few herrings per week. You have not become enervated by the luxuries of life. Your sternest energies have been beaten out upon the anvil of severe trial. Slavery has done this to make you subservient to its own purposes; but it has done more than this, it has prepared you for any emergency. If you receive good treatment, it is what you can hardly expect; if you meet with pain, sorrow, and even death, these are the common lot of the slaves.

13   Fellowmen! patient sufferers! behold your dearest rights crushed to the earth! See your sons murdered, and your wives, mothers and sisters doomed to prostitution. In the name of the merciful God, and by all that life is

worth, let it no longer be a debatable question, whether it is better to choose *liberty* or *death.*

14   In 1822, Denmark Veazie, of South Carolina, formed a plan for the liberation of his fellowmen. In the whole history of human efforts to overthrow slavery, a more complicated and tremendous plan was never formed. He was betrayed by the treachery of his own people, and died a martyr to freedom. Many a brave hero fell, but history, faithful to her high trust, will transcribe his name on the same monument with Moses, Hampden, Tell, Bruce, and Wallace, Toussaint L'Ouverture, Lafayette, and Washington. That tremendous movement shook the whole empire of slavery. The guilty soul-thieves were overwhelmed with fear. It is a matter of fact that at this time, and in consequence of the threatened revolution, the slave States talked strongly of emancipation. But they blew but one blast of the trumpet of freedom, and then laid it aside. As these men became quiet, the slaveholders ceased to talk about emancipation: and now behold your condition to-day! Angels sigh over it, and humanity has long since exhausted her tears in weeping on your account!

15   The patriotic Nathaniel Turner followed Denmark Veazie. He was goaded to desperation by wrong and injustice. By despotism, his name has been recorded on the list of infamy, and future generations will remember him among the noble and brave.

16   Next arose the immortal Joseph Cinque, the hero of the Amistad. He was a native African, and by the help of God he emancipated a whole shipload of his fellowman on the high seas. And he now sings of liberty on the sunny hills of Africa and beneath his native palm-trees, where he hears the lion roar and feels himself as free as the king of the forest.

17   Next arose Madison Washington, that bright star of freedom, and took his station in the constellation of true heroism. He was a slave on board the brig *Creole,* of Richmond, bound to New Orleans, that great slave mart, with a hundred and four others. Nineteen struck for liberty or death. But one life was taken, and the whole were emancipated, and the vessel was carried into Nassau, New Providence.

18   Noble men! Those who have fallen in freedom's conflict, their memories will be cherished by the true-hearted and the God-fearing in all future generations; those who are living, their names are surrounded by a halo of glory.

19   Brethren, arise, arise! Strike for your lives and liberties. Now is the day and the hour. Let every slave throughout the land do this, and the days of slavery are numbered. You cannot be more oppressed than you have been— you cannot suffer greater cruelties than you have already. *Rather die freemen than live to be slaves.* Remember that you are FOUR MILLIONS!

20   It is in your power so to torment the God-cursed slaveholders that they will be glad to let you go free. If the scale was turned, and black men were the masters and white men the slaves, every destructive agent and element would be employed to lay the oppressor low. Danger and death would hang over their heads day and night. Yes, the tyrants would meet with plagues more terrible than those of Pharaoh. But you are a patient people. You act

as though you were made for the special use of these devils. You act as though your daughters were born to pamper the lusts of your masters and overseers. And worse than all, you tamely submit while your lords tear your wives from your embraces and defile them before your eyes. In the name of God, we ask, are you men? Where is the blood of your fathers? Has it all run out of your veins? Awake, awake; millions of voices are calling you! Your dead fathers speak to you from their graves. Heaven, as with a voice of thunder, calls on you to arise from the dust.

21   Let your motto be resistance! *resistance!* RESISTANCE! No oppressed people have ever secured their liberty without resistance. What kind of resistance you had better make you must decide by the circumstances that surround you, and according to the suggestion of expediency. Brethren, adieu! Trust in the living God. Labor for the peace of the human race, and remember that you are FOUR MILLIONS!

DISCUSSION QUESTIONS

1. Henry Highland Garnet is a minister of the gospel when he delivers this speech. How else would you describe him?
2. Garnet escapes from slavery in 1842 and finds his way to New York City and freedom. In paragraph 9 he says: "Your condition does not absolve you from your moral obligation." What does he believe is the moral obligation of the slaves?
3. Garnet lists several Africans and African Americans who have fought for the freedom of black people. In your small group, make a list of such people, either women or men. Be prepared to discuss their contributions with the class.

WRITING TOPICS

1. In paragraph 10, Garnet says, "The humblest peasant is as free in the sight of God. . . ." Write an analytical essay in which you interpret what you believe the writer is saying here. Give specific examples.
2. Garnet, like Frederick Douglass, was an abolitionist. Write a hypothetical conversation you think the two men might have had about slavery and freedom.
3. In your writing journal write a short biographical sketch of a fictional slave, highlighting that person's journey to freedom and the ways he or she then helped other slaves.

NAT TURNER'S CONFESSION

Nat Turner

Nat Turner was born a slave of Benjamin Turner of Southampton County, Virginia, on October 2, 1800. He was probably taught to read by his parents. His strong religious upbringing and his father's demonstrated dislike for slavery helped form his later thinking and actions. Turner ran away once from each of his two slave masters, Benjamin Turner and Putnam Moore. Nat Turner lead a rebellion composed of from sixty to eighty slaves, and approximately sixty whites were killed. The revolt was quickly suppressed and Turner was captured. He dictated the Confession in prison while he awaited death for having conducted the rebellion. Turner was hanged in Virginia in 1831.

1   You have asked me to give a history of the motives which induced me to undertake the late insurrection, as you call it. To do so I must go back to the day of my infancy, and even before I was born.

2   I was thirty-one years of age the 2nd of October last, and born the property of Benj. Turner, of this county. In my childhood a circumstance occurred which made an indelible impression on my mind, and laid the ground work of that enthusiasm, which has terminated so fatally to many, both white and black, and for which I am about to atone at the gallows. It is here necessary to relate this circumstance—trifling as it may seem, it was the commencement of that belief which has grown with time, and even now, sir, in this dungeon, helpless and forsaken as I am, I cannot divest myself of.

3   Being at play with other children, when three or four years old, I was telling them something, which my mother overhearing, said it had happened before I was born. I stuck to my story, however, and related some things which went, in her opinion, to confirm it. Others being called on were greatly astonished, knowing that these things had happened, and caused them to say in my hearing, I surely would be a prophet, as the Lord had shewn me things that had happened before my birth. And my father and

mother strengthened me in this my first impression, saying in my presence I was intended for some great purpose, which they had always thought from certain marks on my head and breast—My grandmother, who was very religious, and to whom I was much attached, my master, who belonged to the church, and other religious persons who visited the house, and whom I often saw at prayers, noticing the singularity of my manners, I suppose, and my uncommon intelligence for a child, remarked I had too much sense to be raised, and if I was, I would never be of any service to any one as a slave.

4   To a mind like mine, restless, inquisitive and observant of every thing that was passing, it is easy to suppose that religion was the subject to which it would be directed, and although this subject principally occupied my thoughts, there was nothing that I saw or heard of to which my attention was not directed. The manner in which I learned to read and write not only had great influence on my own mind, as I acquired it with the most perfect ease, so much so that I have no recollection whatever of learning the alphabet, but to the astonishment of the family, one day when a book was shewn to me to keep me from crying, I began spelling the names of different objects; this was a source of wonder to all in the neighborhood, particularly the blacks. And this learning was constantly improved at all opportunities.

5   When I got large enough to go to work, while employed, I was reflecting on many things that would present themselves to my imagination, and whenever an opportunity occurred of looking at a book, when the school children were getting their lessons, I would find many things that the fertility of my own imagination had depicted to me before; all my time, not devoted to my master's service, was spent either in prayer, or in making experiments in casting different things in moulds made of earth, in attempting to make paper, gun-powder, and many other experiments, that although I could not perfect, yet convinced me of its practicability if I had the means.

6   I was not addicted to stealing in my youth, nor have ever been. Yet such was the confidence of the negroes in the neighborhood, even at this early period of my life, in my superior judgment, that they would often carry me with them when they were going on any roguery, to plan for them. Growing up among them with this confidence in my superior judgment, and when this, in their opinions, was perfected by Divine inspiration, from the circumstances already alluded to in my infancy, and which belief was ever afterwards zealously inculcated by the austerity of my life and manners, which became the subject of remark by white and black. Having soon discovered to be great, I must appear so, and therefore studiously avoided mixing in society, and wrapped myself in mystery, devoting my time to fasting and prayer.

7   By this time, having arrived to man's estate, and hearing the scriptures commented on at meetings, I was struck with that particular passage which says: "Seek ye the kingdom of Heaven and all things shall be added unto you." I reflected much on this passage, and prayed daily for light on this subject. As I was praying one day at my plough, the spirit spoke to me,

saying "Seek ye the kingdom of Heaven and all things shall be added unto you." And I was greatly astonished, and for two years prayed continually, whenever my duty would permit. And then again I had the same revelation, which fully confirmed me in the impression that I was ordained for some great purpose in the hands of the Almighty. . . .

8   About this time I was placed under an overseer, from whom I ran away; and after remaining in the woods thirty days, I returned, to the astonishment of the negroes on the plantation, who thought I had made my escape to some other part of the country, as my father had done before. But the reason of my return was that the Spirit appeared to me and said I had my wishes directed to the things of this world, and not to the kingdom of Heaven and that I should return to the service of my earthly master. "For he who knoweth his Master's will, and doeth it not, shall be beaten with many stripes, and thus have I chastened you." And the negroes found fault, and murmured against me, saying that if they had my sense they would not serve any master in the world. And about this time I had a vision, and I saw white spirits and black spirits engaged in battle, and the sun was darkened, the thunder rolled in the Heavens, and blood flowed in streams, and I heard a voice saying, "Such is your luck, such you are called to see, and let it come rough or smooth, you must surely bare it." I now withdrew myself as much as my situation would permit, from the intercourse of my fellow servants, for the avowed purpose of serving the Spirit more fully. . . .

9   And on the 12th of May, 1828, I heard a loud noise in the heavens, and the Spirit instantly appeared to me and said the Serpent was loosened, and Christ had laid down the yoke he had borne for the sins of men, and that I should take it on and fight against the Serpent, for the time was fast approaching when the first should be last and the last should be first. And by signs in the heavens that it would make known to me when I should commence the great work; and until the first sign appeared, I should conceal it from the knowledge of men. And on the appearance of the sign, (the eclipse of the sun last February) I should arise and prepare myself, and slay my enemies with their own weapons. And immediately on the sign appearing in the heavens, the seal was removed from my lips, and I communicated the great work laid out for me to do, to four in whom I had the greatest confidence, (Henry, Hark, Nelson, and Sam). . . .

10   Since the commencement of 1830, I had been living with Mr. Joseph Travis, who was to me a kind master, and placed the greatest confidence in me; in fact, I had no cause to complain of his treatment to me. On Saturday evening, the 20th of August, it was agreed between Henry, Hark and myself, to prepare a dinner the next day for the men we expected, and then to concert a plan, as we had not yet determined on any. Hark, on the following morning, brought a pig, and Henry brandy, and being joined by Sam, Nelson, Will and Jack, they prepared in the woods a dinner, where, about three o'clock, I joined them.

11   I saluted them on coming up, and asked Will how came he there. He answered, his life was worth no more than others, and his liberty as dear to him. I asked him if he thought to obtain it. He said he would, or lose his life. This was enough to put him in full confidence. Jack, I knew, was only a tool in the hands of Hark. It was quickly agreed we should commence at home (Mr. J. Travis') on that night, and until we had armed and equipped ourselves, and gathered sufficient force, neither age nor sex was to be spared, (which was invariably adhered to).

12   We remained at the feast, until about two hours in the night, when we went to the house and found Austin; they all went to the cider press and drank, except myself. On returning to the house, Hark went to the door with an axe, for breaking it open, as we knew we were to murder the family, if they were awaked by the noise; but reflecting that it might create an alarm in the neighborhood, we determined to enter the house secretly, and murder them whilst sleeping. Hark got a ladder and set it against the chimney, on which I ascended, and hoisting a window, entered and came down stairs, unbarred the door, and removed the guns from their places. It was then observed that I must spill the first blood. On which, armed with a hatchet, and accompanied by Will, I entered my master's chamber. It being dark, I could not give a death blow; the hatchet glanced from his head, he sprank from the bed and called his wife. It was his last word. Will laid him dead, with a blow of his axe, and Mrs. Travis shared the same fate, as she lay in bed.

13   The murder of this family, five in number, was the work of a moment, not one of them awoke; there was a little infant sleeping in a cradle, that was forgotten, until we had left the house and gone some distance, when Henry and Will returned and killed it; we got here four guns that would shoot, and several old muskets, with a pound or two of powder. . . .

[Turner went on from house to house in the neighborhood, collecting weapons, horses and new slave recruits at each place. As his band increased to fifty or sixty, he sent out small groups to attack several households at once.]

14   I took my station in the rear, and as it was my object to carry terror and devastation wherever we went, I placed fifteen or twenty of the best armed and most relied on in front, who generally approached the houses as fast as their horses could run; this was for two purposes, to prevent escape and strike terror to the inhabitants. On this account I never got to the houses, after leaving Mrs. Whitehead's, until the murders were committed, except in one case. I sometimes got in sight in time to see the work of death completed, viewed the mangled bodies as they lay, in silent satisfaction and immediately started in quest of other victims.

[By midmorning, the whites had organized armed pursuit parties and during a day of bloody skirmishes, many of Turner's recruits deserted him. He decided to return to his own neighborhood for reinforcements.]

15   Pursuing our course back and coming in sight of Captain Harris',
where we had been the day before, we discovered a party of white men at
the house, on which all deserted me but two, (Jacob and Nat). We concealed ourselves in the woods until near night, when I sent them in search
of Henry, Sam, Nelson, and Hark, and directed them to rally all they
could, at the place we had had our dinner the Sunday before, where they
would find me. And I accordingly returned there as soon as it was dark and
remained until Wednesday evening, when discovering white men riding
around the place as though they were looking for some one, and none of
my men joining me, I concluded Jacob and Nat had been taken, and compelled to betray me. On this I gave up all hope for the present; and on
Thursday night, after having supplied myself with provisions from Mr.
Travis's, I scratched a hole under a pile of fence rails in a field, where I
concealed myself for six weeks, never leaving my hiding place but for a few
minutes in the dead of night to get water which was very near. Thinking
by this time I could venture out, I began to go about in the night and
eavesdrop the houses in the neighborhood; pursuing this course for about
a fortnight and gathering little or no intelligence, afraid of speaking to any
human being, and returning every morning to my cave before the dawn of
day.

16   I know not how long I might have led this life, if accident had not
betrayed me. A dog in the neighborhood, passing by my hiding place one
night while I was out, was attracted by some meat I had in my cave, and
crawled in and stole it, and was coming out just as I returned. A few nights
after, two negroes having started to go hunting with the same dog and
passed that way, the dog came again to the place, and having just gone out
to walk about, discovered me and barked, on which thinking myself discovered, I spoke to them to beg concealment. On making myself known they
fled from me.

17   Knowing then they would betray me, I immediately left my hiding place,
and pursued almost incessantly until I was taken a fortnight afterwards by
Mr. Benjamin Phipps, in a little hole I had dug out with my sword, for the
purpose of concealment, under the top of a fallen tree. On Mr. Phipps' discovering the place of my concealment, he cocked his gun and aimed at me.
I requested him not to shoot and I would give up, upon which he demanded my sword. I delivered it to him, and he brought me to prison. During
the time I was pursued, I had many hair breadth escapes, which your time
will not permit you to relate. I am here loaded with chains, and willing to
suffer the fate that awaits me.

DISCUSSION QUESTIONS

1. It is said that slaveholders used verses from the Bible to justify slavery. Did Nat Turner do the same thing to justify his fight for freedom? Discuss this question by giving specific examples taken from the selection.
2. How did Turner describe Joseph Travis, one of his slavemasters?
3. If all human life is sacred, was Nat Turner justified in doing what he did? Why or why not?

WRITING TOPICS

1. This being a confession, there must have been some specific questions asked of Nat Turner. Develop three or four questions you believe he might have been asked and list them in your writing journal. Choose from the selection the answers you believe Turner gave to the questions.
2. Turner concludes his confession: ". . . loaded with chains, and willing to suffer the fate that awaits me." Write an essay in which you characterize Turner's feelings about his impending punishment. Keep in mind the crimes he committed, the crimes committed against him, and his religious mysticism.

HARRIET TUBMAN IS IN MY BLOOD

Mariline J. Wilkins

Mariline J. Wilkins, the great-grandniece of Harriet Tubman, is a storyteller, oral historian, and lecturer. Her mother, Eva S. Northrup, told Wilkins stories about her "Aunt Harriet."

1   I am Mariline Wilkins, great-grandniece of Harriet Tubman. Most of the information that I have is information given to me by my mother when she would talk to people and answer questions about Harriet Tubman. My mother was raised by her, lived with her throughout her childhood and most of her young adult life. A lot of the things she told my mother were of her experiences during the Civil War, before the Civil War, and what went on prior to her wanting to free the slaves from bondage.

2   Harriet Tubman was the youngest of twelve children. She started out working when she was but five years old. She was small in stature. I always thought of her as big because of the things that she did; I just visualized her as being real tall and big, but this was not true. My mother was shorter than I am, and Harriet Tubman was about five feet one inch or five feet one and a half inches tall. She was small but she was strong physically.

3   Of course, you know that she did not read or write, but she had implicit confidence and trusted in God for everything that she did. She would pray to him for anything that she wanted to do, and she said He always answered her prayers. She conversed with Him on any item or anything that she wanted to do. Whatever she had in mind to do, she conversed with Him before she went through with it. She often had visions. This is the sort of thing that I think is most unusual. When you can't read or write, I think God gives you another group of senses to guide you. This is what happened with her.

4   The family had been bought by the Brodess family, which was considered one of the wealthiest slaveowners on the Eastern Shore, and Harriet Tubman worked for them from the time she was five until she left to work for Mr. Cook, another slaveowner. Mr. Cook's wife was pregnant, and he wanted someone to come to his place to look after the baby when it was

born and to help him with his muskrat trappings. So she was lent to Mr. Cook while still a child. Some of the stories say that she was sold to him, but she was not. She was lent to him, and Mr. Cook told Mr. Brodess that his wife would teach her how to weave cloth and this weaving would help clothe his family.

5   However, Harriet didn't like indoor work. She preferred to be outdoors. When the baby came, Harriet was so small that she would have to sit on the floor, and they would put the baby in her lap in order for her to take care of it. She also helped Mr. Cook with his muskrat trappings. While she was doing this, over two or three years, I think she caught cold. When her mother heard about it, she asked Mr. Brodess to get her child and bring her back to her so she could nurse her back to health. She heard that she had been sick for a long time. This was because of this trapping through the swamp in the wintertime. Mr. Brodess did go and get her and, after she got better, she went back to the Cook house.

6   Eventually Harriet left the Cook household and returned to the Brodesses again, working in the fields. It was at that time, while working in the fields at the Brodesses, that a worker in the field left the field and one of the field supervisors followed him. Harriet decided, after the field supervisor had gone, to follow the worker in the field who had left; she would see what was going on. When she did, she went to the little store, and there the field supervisor was after the field hand who had gone away. When she appeared at the door, the field supervisor told her to stop him. She refused to stop him. When she refused to stop him, he picked up a tool, iron weights, threw it and cut her. Some storybooks say she was hit in the back of the head but the scar is on her forehead. She carried that until death, and she developed sleeping seizures.

7   They thought she was a nitwit after that. They said she wasn't capable of work and all that sort of thing, so she let them believe that because it was to her advantage. She continued to work wherever she was available, but she preferred working out of doors. And it was when she was working at the Cook house again that she heard them discussing, at one of the evening meals, that they were going to sell some of her family, her sisters and brothers, to another slaveowner farther south. She decided then that this business of slavery was terrible, and she didn't like it. She said, "Dear God, help me get rid of this terrible thing and these terrible people." She listened some more and heard some more information, and she decided that that was what she was going to do, try to free them. The first time she tried to go free or leave, she wanted her brothers to go with her, but they didn't want to go. They started out but got scared, so she decided not to continue because, if they didn't go, she was sure they would come back and tell what she was trying to do. For a long time, she told my mother, they thought that this person who was freeing the slaves was a man.

8   She did not dress like a man. When she started freeing the slaves, she would put on old clothes and act decrepit like an old woman. Because she

was considered a nitwit, they never suspected her. They never suspected this little black woman, and it was to her advantage. She had many little tricks, and they never suspected this person who had gotten hit in the head and had these sleeping seizures.

9   She could be sitting here talking to you just like I am, and all of a sudden one of those spells would come over her, and she'd go to sleep. And when she woke up, she would start right where she left off. I don't think you could consider her a nitwit, not in any way, shape, or form. Several times she would get caught in one of those things, and people would say, "Oh, just wake her up, wake her up." You couldn't wake her up, Mama said. She just had to sleep it off. Once she was lying on a park bench with her face to the back of the park bench, and somebody put this poster up offering a reward for her, dead or alive. When the man finished, she woke up and saw the poster, and she just looked at it and went on. She knew who it was, she recognized her face.

10   Before Cicely Tyson played in that story they had on television, she went up to Auburn and stayed for a while and visited with my cousin Gladys, so she could get the feel and go out to the home and all of that. Gladys can remember Harriet Tubman because Gladys was seven years old when she died. Cicely Tyson played in that scene where they made Harriet Tubman take the place of a horse pulling a cart. She was strong mentally and physically, by all accounts, and even though she couldn't read or write, she could think and had common sense. Why she let them do that I'll never understand, and when Gladys and I saw the premiere, we objected to it. This woman was a living legend; she wasn't a fictitious person. If she had been white, she would have been all over the history books, but because this little black lady was not considered knowledgeable and couldn't read or write, people thought, Why should we recognize her?

11   She married Tubman because he was a free man and could read and write; she thought he could help her, but he was not sympathetic to her cause. When she went back to get slaves, to free them, she would sometimes run across him. The last time this happened she tried to see whether he would be interested in helping, and he was not. So she just gave him up. Mama said she had other things to do. She didn't bother him. Next thing she knew he had been killed. That ended that. But in that television story they had her making money and saving it and counting it while he was looking in the window. She was not braggadocious or showoffish like that; she was quiet and reserved.

12   She was always looking for ways to make money. She worked to get money in various places because she knew she needed to have money to clothe and feed some of the slaves on the route. If she didn't get help from some of her white friends or the Quakers who were helping her, then she would work for a short while and get a certain amount of money to help them along the way. She never dressed flashy. The story showed her coming into town to see William Grant, wearing a little brown poplin suit and a lit-

tle hat with fur around it. She never wore anything like that. She wore dark clothes, in the summertime white, navy blue, or black, and that was it. All during the time she was freeing the slaves and during her work in the Civil War, she wore navy blue and white. She would wear sunbonnets of different patterns. They might see her going down the street with a blue-and-white-checkered sunbonnet and then, when you looked again, she might have a plain blue one. And the bonnets covered part of her face so she wouldn't be visible. In the story they had her coming down the street with this little cocky hat on and her face was very visible. She would say she couldn't afford to be seen. Her face could not be viewed because she called herself the "ugly duckling." I thought all of that was wrong, to picture her in that vein.

13 When she was traveling, she wore several layers of clothing. She wore pantaloons on top of pantaloons and petticoats on top of petticoats. Why? She knew about the bloodhounds out for her, and if the bloodhounds got a taste of her blood, she would not be able to do the work any longer. So she had layers of clothing, and they would get the clothing instead of a taste of her blood. This was one reason why she kept layers and layers of clothing. What gave out, when she got older, were her limbs from all the water she had traveled through in the swamps and the cold winters and all of that. She did not get dressed up, and she didn't wear a man's hat while she was freeing the slaves during the Civil War. She wore bandannas or sunbonnets. I saw something where a family down in Maryland or Virginia had a reunion. One woman in the family was supposed to be dressed up like Harriet Tubman, and she wore this man's fedora. Mama used to say she wore bandannas and sunbonnets.

14 Harriet Tubman was born in Bucktown, Dorchester County, Maryland, near Cambridge. My mother, Eva S. Northrup, was born in Canada in St. Catherine. Her name was actually Evelyn Katherine Helena Harriet. The Harriet was from her father's side and the Helena was from her mother's side, but she cut the name in half. I was born in the States, in Auburn, New York, the same place as my cousin Gladys. Harriet Tubman raised most of her nieces and nephews, the children of her brothers and sisters who had passed on. My mother was the only one, I think, that lived with her for a long period of time. My mother's father, James Isaac, was Harriet Tubman's nephew. His father, James Henry, was her brother. There were William Henry's and James Henry's; they went down the line. Gladys's full name is Gladys Alidas Bryant, and William Henry was her grandfather.

15 Harriet Tubman had knowledge of many things, and this accounted for her success in bringing slaves to the North. For example, she knew about remedies, and this was how she helped the soldiers during the Civil War, knowing what herbs to pick and steep and how to help them with all the illnesses they had during the war. The family feels that she discovered penicillin. Whenever she did canning and air got into things that were canned, a mold formed on the top; she took that mold and didn't throw it away. She scooped the mold off and put it into another glass jar, and when that jar was

about half full (and Mama did this in my lifetime because I had some of it for colds), she filled the rest of it with fresh lemon juice, honey, and some brandy or whatever she had. If she didn't have brandy, she used bourbon or something like that. She shook it and then let it set, and anybody who had a cold got a teaspoon of it. It did not taste good, but it was good for colds. And what was the green stuff? It was nothing else but penicillin. She would say, "This is good for colds."

16   My mother cut her hand once while she was living on the farm with her, and her thumb was cut so badly that her thumb was loose from her hand. Now the family refers to Harriet Tubman as "Grandma" because she was the oldest person and the one they looked up to. Mama said that Grandma took her and said, "Come on, Kit. Let's go to the barn." She got some white cloths that she had folded up and kept in a drawer in the kitchen, just torn from old sheets and stuff. Whenever they cleaned up the barn, she never wanted to take the cobwebs down that were up at the top; they stayed there. So she went up on the ladder and got the cobwebs, brought them down, and slapped them on Mama's hand and tied it up. In three days she took it off and put some more on. You couldn't see where my mother's hand, her thumb, had been cut. Mama said anytime you had a severe cut, that's what would happen. But I could never see where the thumb had been severed from her hand. Also, anybody who had the gout used to make poultices out of poke salad and put them on the feet to take the swelling down. These are greens, just like dandelion greens. She made poultices out of them as well as out of onions, camphorated oil, and a piece of flannel cut in a circle to fit front and back. Cut the onions up fine and add the camphorated oil. Mix them and lay those onions on, and then sew it and put it on your chest and lungs. Pin it up at the top and put you in bed. In the morning, if those onions were brown and you had no temperature, it meant that your fever had broken. Mama used to do that often with me because I had severe colds.

17   There were other herbs that she used to use, but I do not have that knowledge. Maybe I didn't take enough time or didn't think much of it at the time, but Mama used to take milkweed. She used to go out in the field and get a piece of milkweed, break it, and put the milk from the weed on the part of the body that needed it, and then throw it away. You were not to look where you had thrown it. She did that two or three times for a wart which I had on my hand, and the warts went away. Mama said that Grandma, Harriet Tubman, used to do that too because she had several of them.

18   She used to make soap; she taught Mother how to make soap. But I don't do it. I take pieces of soap and melt them up, but Mama knew how to do it from scratch because she had taught her. I admit I don't know. And I wouldn't try to do it. It was as easy for Mama as mixing up biscuits.

19   I wish now that I had taken time to put down a lot of things that she taught me over the years. Now I realize just what they meant. I would catch cold often, and I had whooping cough for a long time. That old-fashioned

idea—they say that it's old-fashioned—of an asafetida bag. Mama once had one of those out—oh, that stuff smells! And there was something else, some nutmeg. I don't know what this nutmeg did, but she put a hole in the nutmeg and put a string around it and put it around my neck. Now I cannot tell you the significance of that nutmeg. Why I had to wear it I don't know because I don't think I ever remember asking my mother why.

20   I never heard my mother say that Harriet Tubman was superstitious. Maybe she believed in some things. If she did not have enough food (in the home that she lived in in Auburn) for the people staying with her, she would say, "Well, I have to get some more food in here," and she would take a basket and go out into the barn or near the barn and hold up the basket, and she'd start praying and ask the Lord to fill it. By nighttime, people would come out and bring her food so she would have enough to take care of all those people that were living with her. Her first thought was to have a home for the homeless and for orphan children and older people. She was always taking in somebody. That's why a lot of people who went to live with her claimed allegiance to her or claimed to be a relative of hers because everybody called her "Aunt Harriet" or "Grandma." They thought they were related to her, but many of them had no bloodline with her whatsoever because she never had a child.

21   In two marriages she never had any children. She never lived with John Tubman. She married Davis after the Civil War, and they never had any children. Her name was actually Harriet Tubman Davis, but the history books refer to her as Harriet Tubman; they don't add the Davis, and she herself held on to the name that was attached to her from the beginning.

22   She used to tell many stories of things that had happened to her and to other people. For example, there had been a man in Washington whose name was Eally, I think; she freed him. They were going to hang him up there in Albany. She heard about it and got the people in the community together, and she said, "When I give you the high sign, you holler 'Fire!'" They were having a meeting like a court, I guess, and she eased her way in like an old woman. By being small she was able to do a lot of this. That's why she wore dark clothes, so she wouldn't be conspicuous. She went in and stuck her head out of the window, and the people she had alerted started hollering "Fire!" When they brought Eally down the stairs, she wrestled him away from the guards. She had somebody waiting with a boat. She rushed him through the crowd and into the boat and pushed him off, and they were still trying to get him, but he went on to Canada. There is a school in Washington that is named after this man. They were going to kill him because he had escaped! They said he wasn't free, he was a slave and he had escaped.

23   As I said before, for years they thought this little black lady was a man. Before the Civil War, and after the Civil War had started, she had tried to get to Lincoln to tell him that in order for him to win the war, he was going to have to use the black soldiers. As you know they paid the white soldiers

more; I think it was $15 a month, and the black soldiers got $7. She said that unless he used the black man, he was not going to win the war.

24   She met Lincoln and talked, but he never listened. She would get to some of her friends who were influential, such as Mr. Alcott and John Greenleaf Whittier. She talked to them and they listened. Sometimes up in Massachusetts she went to Mr. Alcott's house, and other men would be there. She talked to them and sometimes entertained them by telling stories and ideas. She asked Lincoln about doing something in that manner, but he didn't listen. She thought that by talking with these other men it would eventually get to him. She told them that she wanted to do something, and she felt that she could do it. The battle that changed the Civil War was the one that she designed and engineered herself. They do not give her credit, but she engineered the Combahee River battle; she was the one who carried it out. She asked for three gunboats and for General Montgomery who, she knew, was a guerrilla warfare man. She knew him well; she had had contact with him and worked with him. She told them to go down the Combahee River into Charleston, where over sixty cannons were planted. She planned to dismantle them and take the slaves that were along that river. It ended up that she did. She got about eight hundred of them and dismantled all the torpedoes. She didn't lose anybody and nobody got hurt, but she set fire to some of the plantations and this was the turning point in the Civil War. When it was found out that this little woman had shaken the Southern forces so badly, this little black lady who couldn't read or write had done all this on her own, then Lincoln began to listen.

25   She used to talk often to Mrs. Lincoln when Lincoln did not have time. He told her once, "When I get a chance, Harriet, to hit this thing, I'll hit it hard." But she thought he was taking a long time to hit. She believed in women's rights and said then that it was important, and black men's rights were just as important as women's rights.

26   She met with William Grant Still many times. She came here to Philadelphia as a stop for him to help her move on when transporting slaves. He wrote letters for her and gave her information where she could get certain things. You see, many times when she brought slaves out of the South, she had to go a good distance on foot. Sometimes she picked up a horse and buggy, and then she had to hide slaves in somebody's secret barn or house. She did most of her traveling on weekends, from Friday night until Sunday night, because the slaveowners could not arrest or take any of the fugitive slaves on weekends. She brought them to New Jersey and Pennsylvania before the Fugitive Slave Law, but after the Fugitive Slave Law she had to take them on to Canada. If she had brought them here after the Fugitive Slave Law, if they got caught, they would have to be returned. She never lost any passengers on the eastern route of the Underground Railroad, but Levi Coffin, who was a Quaker, was bold on the western route and even had stationery printed with "Underground Railroad" on it, which was wrong. They could track people easier that way. He suffered. They lost him, he got killed.

Like John Brown, he was told and warned about what was going to happen. Harriet had a premonition, she said, but he was impatient. That's why he got killed. If he had just waited, he would not have gotten killed and massacred as he was. And, of course, she got help from Queen Victoria because she did not approve of slavery. That's why she went to Canada; she was safe there.

27   Mr. Brodess owned a lot of woodland in Maryland, and Harriet's father knew wood. Her father Benjamin had the right to supervise boat builders and lumber suppliers and teach them wood. Over the years he taught her. She had a good knowledge of which woods were for what use and could tell one kind from another. And she also followed tree signs. She tried to leave on moonlit nights, but the moon wasn't always bright, so she felt the trees for moss. The moss grew on the north side of trees, and she taught Mother that. People in the city don't have that advantage because there are no woods. At home, in the spring of the year and in the fall of the year, we would have trips through the woods.

28   You know these little black boys with the lanterns? They were used during the freeing of the slaves to let you know that his household was a place where you were welcome. That's what that was, a symbol to let you know that you were welcome. Harriet Tubman had boats that were taking slaves to Canada. They had two flags, a yellow and a blue. The blue one on top of the yellow one let you know that the boat had slaves on it. They used codes and symbols in their ranks, those she was freeing and those who were involved in the Underground Railroad. Her memory was keen, and when she went to someone's door and knocked and they asked who was there, she would say "a friend with friends." Sometimes the people said "a friend of a friend"; she knew then that she was welcome. Once or twice, maybe three or four times, she knocked on a person's door and was not given the right signal; she then knew she was not welcome or some changes had been made. One time in particular, she had some slaves with her and these slaves had infants. When she knocked, thinking that it had been a place they stopped before, someone stuck his head out the window, and then she knew this was not the same. They didn't know the code when she knocked on the door but responded with "What do you want?" She had to disperse everybody. They did not hide or keep on moving. She dispersed them. This particular time, she dispersed them and she took the children, the babies, and put them in a basket.

29   These are just some of the things that happened to her and other people when she was bringing the slaves out of bondage. The history books say that she was 93 years old when she died. She told Mama that she had been born somewhere between 1810 and 1815. That would have made her 103, not 93. No records were kept, so there was no way of finding out. She and her family, her mother and father, should have been freed before they went to the Brodesses because Mrs. Patterson, who had owned them before, said that when she died they were to be freed. Harriet's mother told her about

it. It wasn't until after the Civil War, when she went back to get a lawyer and dig it up, that she found out it was true. They should have been freed long before. This is what they did over the years, and they are still doing it. Mama said that Harriet used to say, "I feel that I have freed more than three hundred slaves," but no one kept records of the many slaves she helped escape.

DISCUSSION QUESTIONS

1. Chart the progress of Wilkins's story. Does it seem more like an essay or an oral folktale? Use specific examples from the text to support your response.
2. Which historical "legends" about Harriet Tubman does Wilkins clarify?
3. Why is Wilkins concerned about presenting the "true" picture of Harriet Tubman?
4. Should readers accept the credibility of Wilkins's remembrances of Tubman? Why or why not?

WRITING TOPICS

1. Compare the stanzas about Harriet Tubman in the Poem "Runagate Runagate" with Wilkins's discussion. Is Tubman's portrayal in the poem based on history or folklore?
2. Research the development of penicillin. In an essay, explain whether Harriet Tubman's "cold cure" had some of the medicinal properties of penicillin. If so, what were they?

SONG OF THE SON

Jean Toomer

Jean Toomer was born in Washington, D.C., in 1894, to Nathan and Nina Pinchback Toomer. His grandfather was the controversial P.B.S. Pinchback of post-Civil War Louisiana political fame who claimed that he was black although he had the physical appearance of a white man. Toomer had a difficult time deciding on a career and attended more than six colleges and universities in his quest. In 1921 he traveled to the South for the first time and taught at a rural black school in Georgia. This experience became the foundation for his highly acclaimed book *Cane,* a volume of prose narratives, poetry, and one dramatic piece.

Cane (1923) was well received by critics. No previous book on African-American culture had ever captured the beauty and the pain of blacks living in the South. Toomer was less pleased with the book than the critics. He was upset that he was called a "Negro" writer. He claimed that he was not a Negro, but an American with at least seven bloodlines running through his veins. Between 1926 and 1930 Toomer published four prose pieces and a few poems.

In 1940 Toomer became a Quaker and traveled and lectured for the society. His post-1936 writings addressed religious and universal issues, especially human kind's alienation in an industrial/technological world. Throughout the rest of his life, Toomer never called himself a Negro writer. In 1980 Darwin Turner edited a collection of Toomer's work: *The Wayward and the Seeking: A Collection of Writings by Jean Toomer.* Toomer died in 1936.

Pour O pour that parting soul in song,
O pour it in the sawdust glow of night,
Into the velvet pine-smoke air to-night,
And let the valley carry it along.
5   And let the valley carry it along.

O land and soil, red soil and sweet-gum tree,
So scant of grass, so profligate of pines,
Now just before an epoch's sun declines
Thy son, in time, I have returned to thee,
10 Thy son, I have in time returned to thee.

In time, for though the sun is setting on
A song-lit race of slaves, it has not set;
Though late, O soil, it is not too late yet
To catch thy plaintive soul, leaving, soon gone,
15 Leaving, to catch thy plaintive soul soon gone.

O Negro slaves, dark purple ripened plums,
Squeezed, and bursting in the pine-wood air,
Passing, before they stripped the old tree bare
One plum was saved for me, one seed becomes

20 An everlasting song, a singing tree
Caroling softly souls of slavery,
What they were, and what they are to me,
Caroling softly souls of slavery.

DISCUSSION QUESTIONS

1. The speaker in the poem refers to a "parting soul in song." What souls are parting from where in this poem?
2. In the second stanza, why does the speaker in the poem refer to himself as "Thy son"?
3. How does the speaker in the poem propose to save what is being lost? Why is this method an effective one?

WRITING TOPICS

1. Think about a place that you have visited that had a positive impact on you. Close your eyes and visualize how the place looked. On a white sheet of paper, use colored markers or crayons to create a picture of the place you visualized. Then write a poem about the place. Use your

drawing as a reference point. Try to capture the mood of the place with the words you use in the poem.

2. In an essay present an argument that "A region of a country can contain the cultural heritage of the people who live there." Use examples from Toomer's "Song of the Son" and other African-American writers' works to support your argument.

CHAPTER FIVE

STANDING GROUND

From the time that Africans were brought to America as slaves up through the present, African Americans have had to stand ground. To stand ground means to have a belief that you refuse to give up. No matter what conditions you are faced with, if you stand your ground, you will hold on to your convictions. Standing ground can be as simple as making a choice and holding firm to it or as complicated as believing in something when there is no evidence to support it. During slavery, those slaves who believed their servitude would one day end stood their ground when they held onto their dignity in the face of horror. Blacks who believed they could end lynching though protests stood their ground. Sharecroppers who worked other people's land, barely making enough money to survive until the next crop, stood their ground. African-American soldiers who volunteered to serve and die for their country during the World Wars stood their ground. African Americans have stood ground to end segregation, to obtain an education, to vote, to live in decent housing, and to work in jobs where they are paid in equal salary.

Standing ground does not always involve some type of physical action. African-American writers stand ground when they create stories and poems that celebrate the spirit of resistance. Their work records the ability of African Americans to stand ground by taking pride in their culture and celebrating their African *and* American heritages. It records their ability to stand ground by affirming that they are entitled to the same rights as other American citizens. Finally, their work records blacks' ability to stand ground by refusing to give in when conditions are inhumane. African-American writers illustrate how black people can take strength from within themselves and choose actions within their control.

IF WE MUST DIE

Claude McKay

Claude McKay was born in 1889 to peasant farmers Thomas Francis McKay and Ann Elizabeth Edwards McKay in Jamaica. When McKay was a child, his father, a descendant of the Ashanti tribe of West Africa, told him African folktales. In 1912 McKay received the Jamaican Medal of the Institute of Arts and Sciences for his first two volumes of poetry: *Songs of Jamaica* (1912) and *Constab Ballads* (1912). He used the prize money to move to the United States where he attended Tuskegee Institute in Alabama before transferring to Kansas State College. In 1914 he went to New York City, where he worked odd jobs and wrote poetry. By 1919 his poetry was appearing regularly in *Pearson's* and *The Liberator* magazines. McKay then left the United States and, from 1923 to 1934, lived in Europe and visited Russia. His novel *Home to Harlem* (1928), published while he was living abroad, was the first commercially successful novel by a black writer. In 1934 McKay returned to Harlem and continued his writing career. In 1944, after being baptized in the Roman Catholic church, McKay began writing poetry about his religion.

McKay's poetry fights against the idea that any group can confine another. McKay was one of the most radical African-American writers of the Harlem Renaissance, and some African-American magazines would not publish his poetry because they considered it too radical. McKay published two additional volumes of poetry: *Spring in New Hampshire* (1920) and *Harlem Shadows: The Poems of Claude McKay* (1922). He also published two other novels *Banjo—A Story Without a Plot* (1929) and *Banana Bottom* (1933) as well as a collection of short stories entitled *Gingertown* (1932). His autobiography, *A Long Way from Home,* was published in 1937. McKay died in 1948.

If we must die, let it not be like hogs
Hunted and penned in an inglorious spot,
While round us bark the mad and hungry dogs,
Making their mock at our accursed lot.
5 If we must die, O let us nobly die,
So that our precious blood may not be shed
In vain; then even the monsters we defy
Shall be constrained to honor us though dead!
O kinsmen! we must meet the common foe!
10 Though far outnumbered let us show us brave,
And for their thousand blows deal one deathblow!
What though before us lies the open grave?
Like men we'll face the murderous, cowardly pack,
Pressed to the wall, dying, but fighting back!

DISCUSSION QUESTIONS

1. McKay wrote this poem in the form of a Shakespearean sonnet. What problem or situation is presented in the three quatrains? What solution or resolution is presented in the couplet?
2. McKay uses similes and metaphors throughout the poem to describe the treatment of African Americans. What do you think the speaker means in lines 1 through 4?
3. What is the "one deathblow" discussed in line 11? How will it stop the "thousand blows"?
4. The speaker in the poem says, "If we must die, O let us nobly die, . . ." Who would consider their death noble? Why? What are the advantages of a noble death over a less than noble death?

WRITING TOPICS

1. Investigate the summer riots of 1919. McKay wrote "If We Must Die" in response to the many blacks who died in these riots. In an essay, analyze what conditions prompted the riots. Also discuss why McKay's poem is or is not an appropriate response.
2. In your journal, defend the position of standing one's ground with words instead of physical action. Why might words have a greater effect on changing a situation than physical action?
3. Compare this poem with the first stanza of James Weldon Johnson's "Lift Every Voice and Sing." In a brief essay, describe the similarities and differences between the two.

I, Too

Langston Hughes

Langston Hughes was born in Joplin, Missouri, in 1902 to Carrie Langston Hughes and James Nathaniel Hughes. In 1903 Hughes's mother and father separated and his father moved to Mexico. Hughes went to live with his maternal grandmother Mary Leary Langston, in Lawrence, Kansas. While in high school, Hughes ran track, made the honor roll, and edited the school yearbook, besides writing poetry. In 1925, while working as a busboy at the Wardman Park hotel, Hughes left some of his poems by noted poet Vachel Lindsay's dinner plate. The next day Hughes read in the paper that a Negro busboy poet had been discovered.

Hughes published a substantial amount of writing during his lifetime. He wrote books of poetry, short story collections, novels, plays, and essays. His poetry collections include *The Weary Blues* (1926), *The Negro Mother and Other Dramatic Recitations* (1931), *Lament for Dark Peoples, and Other Poems* (1944), and *Selected Poems by Langston Hughes* (1959). His short stories are collected in *The Ways of White Folks* (1934), *Language to Keep from Crying* (1952), *Something in Common* (1963) and five volumes of *Sketches* of his character Jesse B. Semple, or "Simple." He wrote about his life in *The Big Sea: An Autobiography* (1940) and *I Wonder as I Wander: An Autobiographical Journey* (1956). Hughes died in 1967. (For further biographical information, see pages 91, 133, and 385.)

I, too, sing America.

I am the darker brother.
They send me to eat in the kitchen
When company comes,
5 But I laugh,
And eat well,
And grow strong.

Tomorrow,
I'll be at the table
10   When company comes.
Nobody'll dare
Say to me,
"Eat in the kitchen,"
Then.

15   Besides,
They'll see how beautiful I am
And be ashamed—

I, too, am America.

DISCUSSION QUESTIONS

1. The poem beings with the line "I, too, sing America." It ends with the line "I, too, am America." What are the similarities and differences between these two statements?
2. The first line of the second stanza reads: "I am the darker brother." Whose "darker brother" is the speaker in the poem? Discuss the multiple meanings of the word "darker" and how those definitions affect the meaning of the line and the meaning of the poem.
3. Who or what are the "They" referred to in the second stanza? What role or roles do you think "They" have played in the poem's speaker's life?
4. In the third stanza, the speaker says: "Nobody'll dare / Say to me / 'Eat in the kitchen,' / Then." What is the tone of these lines? How is this tone different from the tone in the first and second stanzas?

WRITING TOPICS

1. Imagine someone from another country has asked you what it means to be an "American." Write an essay explaining what the term "American" means to you.
2. Write a free verse poem about being an American. You may want to write about what it means to be a part of American society today, with its many diverse voices.

A SUMMER TRAGEDY

Arna Bontemps

Arna (Arnaud) Wendell Bontemps was born in 1902 in Alexandria, Louisiana, to Paul Bismark and Marla Carolina Pembrole Bontemps. His parents were Creole, and Bontemps used Creole dialect in many of his early writings. Bontemps graduated with honors from Pacific Union College in 1923. At the age of twenty-one, Bontemps published his poem "Hope" in *Crisis* magazine and moved to New York City to begin teaching at the Harlem Academy. He won *Opportunity* magazine's Alexander Pushkin Poetry Prize in 1926 for "Golgotha Is a Mountain" and again in 1927 for "Nocturne at Bethesda."

Bontemps's teaching career took him from New York City to Alabama to Chicago, where he earned a master's degree in library science from the University of Chicago. From 1943 until his retirement, Bontemps was a librarian at Fisk University in Nashville, Tennessee. While at Fisk, Bontemps was responsible for the collection of works by African-American writers. He also compiled several anthologies used in schools. In 1958 Bontemps and Langston Hughes (a close friend) published *The Book of Negro Folklore*. Bontemps and Hughes also published *The Poetry of the Negro* (1949, 1970) together.

Bontemps was a poet, critic, novelist, playwright, anthologist, librarian, and author of children's books. He influenced, and was influenced by, many writers including Langston Hughes, Willa Cather, Countee Cullen, Katherine Porter, Ernest Hemingway, James Weldon Johnson, and Robert Lowell. The following is a brief list of some of Bontemps's published works: *God Sends Sunday* (1931), *You Can't Pet a Possum* (1934), *Black Thunder* (1936), *Drums at Dusk* (1939), *George Washington Carver* (1950), *Personals* (1963), and *Mr. Kelso's Lion* (1970). Bontemps died in 1973.

1 Old Jeff Patton, the black share farmer,[1] fumbled with his bow tie. His fingers trembled and the high, stiff collar pinched his throat. A fellow loses his hand for such vanities after thirty or forty years of simple life. Once a year, or maybe twice if there's a wedding among his kinfolks, he may spruce up; but generally fancy clothes do nothing but adorn the wall of the big room and feed the moths. That had been Jeff Patton's experience. He had not worn his stiff-bosomed shirt more than a dozen times in all his married life. His swallow-tailed coat lay on the bed beside him, freshly brushed and pressed, but it was as full of holes as the overalls in which he worked on weekdays. The moths had used it badly. Jeff twisted his mouth into a hideous toothless grimace as he contended with the obstinate bow. He stamped his good foot and decided to give up the struggle.

2 "Jennie," he called.

3 "What's that, Jeff?" His wife's shrunken voice came out of the adjoining room like an echo. It was hardly bigger than a whisper.

4 "I reckon you'll have to he'p me wid this heah bow tie, baby," he said meekly. "Dog if I can hitch it up."

5 Her answer was not strong enough to reach him, but presently the old woman came to the door, feeling her way with a stick. She had a wasted, dead-leaf appearance. Her body, as scrawny and gnarled as a string bean, seemed less than nothing in the ocean of frayed and faded petticoats that surrounded her. These hung an inch or two above the tops of her heavy unlaced shoes and showed little grotesque piles where the stocking had fallen down from her negligible legs.

6 "You oughta could do a heap mo' wid a thing like that'n me— beingst as you got yo' good sight."

7 "Looks like I oughta could," he admitted. "But my fingers is gone democrat[2] on me. I get all mixed up in the looking glass an' can't tell wicha way to twist the devilish thing."

8 Jennie sat on the side of the bed, and old Jeff Patton got down on one knee while she tied the bow knot. It was a slow and painful ordeal for each of them in this position. Jeff's bones cracked, his knee ached, and it was only after a half dozen attempts that Jennie worked a semblance of a bow into the tie.

9 "It got to dress maself now," the old woman whispered. "These is ma old shoes an' stockings, and I ain't so much as unwrapped ma dress."

10 "Well, don't worry 'bout me no mo', baby," Jeff said. "That 'bout finishes me. All I gotta do now is slip on that old coat 'n ves' an' I'll be fixed to leave."

---

1 *share farmer:* one who farms land as a tenant.

2 *gone democrat:* (here) being disorderly. Historically, at the time in which Bontemps's story is set, many African Americans were members of the Republican political party. Most members of the Democratic party were aligned with monied, Southern white interest groups at that time.

11	Jennie disappeared again through the dim passage into the shed room. Being blind was no handicap to her in that black hole. Jeff heard the cane placed against the wall beside the door and knew that his wife was on easy ground. He put on his coat, took a battered top hat from the bed post, and hobbled to the front door. He was ready to travel. As soon as Jennie could get on her Sunday shoes and her old black silk dress, they would start.

12	Outside the tiny log house, the day was warm and mellow with sunshine. A host of wasps were humming with busy excitement in the trunk of a dead sycamore. Gray squirrels were searching through the grass for hickory nuts, and blue jays were in the trees, hopping from branch to branch. Pine woods stretched away to the left like a black sea. Among them were scattered scores of log houses like Jeff's, houses of black share farmers. Cows and pigs wandered freely among the trees. There was no danger of loss. Each farmer knew his own stock and knew his neighbor's as well as he knew his neighbor's children.

13	Down the slope to the right were the cultivated acres on which the colored folks worked. They extended to the river, more than two miles away, and they were today green with the unmade cotton crop. A tiny thread of a road, which passed directly in front of Jeff's place, ran through these green fields like a pencil mark.

14	Jeff, standing outside the door, with his absurd hat in his left hand, surveyed the wide scene tenderly. He had been forty-five years on these acres. He loved them with the unexplained affection that others have for the countries to which they belong.

15	The sun was hot on his head, his collar still pinched his throat, and the Sunday clothes were intolerably hot. Jeff transferred the hat to his right hand and began fanning with it. Suddenly the whisper that was Jennie's voice came out of the shed room.

16	"You can bring the car round front whilst you's waitin'," it said feebly. There was a tired pause; then it added, "I'll soon be fixed to go."

17	"A'right, baby," Jeff answered. "I'll get it in a minute."

18	But he didn't move. A thought struck him that made his mouth fall open. The mention of the car brought to his mind, with new intensity, the trip he and Jennie were about to take. Fear came into his eyes; excitement took his breath. Lord Jesus!

19	"Jeff. . . . O Jeff," the old woman's whisper called.

20	He awakened with a jolt. "Hunh, baby?"

21	"What you doin'?"

22	"Nuthin. Jes studyin'. I jes been turnin' things round 'n round in ma mind."

23	"You could be gettin' the car," she said.

24	"Oh yes, right away, baby."

25	He started round to the shed, limping heavily on his bad leg. There were three frizzly chickens in the yard. All his other chickens had been killed or stolen recently. But the frizzly chickens had been saved somehow. That was fortunate indeed, for these curious creatures had a way of devouring "poison" from the yard and in that way protecting against conjure and black luck and spells. But even the frizzly chickens seemed now to be in a stupor. Jeff thought they had some ailment; he expected all three of them to die shortly.

26　　The shed in which the old T-model Ford stood was only a grass roof held up by four corner poles. It had been built by tremulous hands at a time when the little rattletrap car had been regarded as a peculiar treasure. And, miraculously, despite wind and downpour, it still stood.

27　　Jeff adjusted the crank and put his weight upon it. The engine came to life with a sputter and bang that rattled the old car from radiator to tail light. Jeff hopped into the seat and put his foot on the accelerator. The sputtering and banging increased. The rattling became more violent. That was good. It was good banging, good sputtering and rattling, and it meant that the aged car was still in running condition. She could be depended on for this trip.

28　　Again Jeff's thought halted as if paralyzed. The suggestion of the trip fell into the machinery of his mind like a wrench. He felt dazed and weak. He swung the car out into the yard, made a half turn, and drove around to the front door. When he took his hands off the wheel, he noticed that he was trembling violently. He cut off the motor and climbed to the ground to wait for Jennie.

29　　A few minutes later she was at the window, her voice rattling against the pane like a broken shutter.

30　　"I'm ready, Jeff."

31　　He did not answer, but limped into the house and took her by the arm. He led her slowly through the big room, down the step, and across the yard.

32　　"You reckon I'd oughta lock the do'?" he asked softly.

33　　They stopped and Jennie weighed the question. Finally she shook her head.

34　　"Ne' mind the do'," she said. "I don't see no cause to lock up things."

35　　"You right," Jeff agreed. "No cause to lock up."

36　　Jeff opened the door and helped his wife into the car. A quick shudder passed over him. Jesus! Again he trembled.

37　　"How come you shaking so?" Jennie whispered.

38　　"I don't know," he said.

39　　"You mus' be scairt, Jeff."

40　　"No, baby, I ain't scairt."

41　　He slammed the door after her and went around to crank up again. The motor started easily. Jeff wished that it had not been so responsive. He would have liked a few more minutes in which to turn things around in his head. As it was, with Jennie chiding him about being afraid, he had to keep going. He swung the car into the little pencil-mark road and started off toward the river, driving very slowly, very cautiously.

42　　Chugging across the green countryside, the small battered Ford seemed tiny indeed. Jeff felt a familiar excitement, a thrill, as they came down the first slope to the immense levels on which the cotton was growing. He could not help reflecting that the crops were good. He knew what that meant, too; he had made forty-five of them with his own hands. It was true that he had worn out nearly a dozen mules, but that was the fault of old man Stevenson, the owner of the land. Major Stevenson had the odd notion that one mule was all a share farmer needed to work a thirty-acre plot. It was an expensive notion, the way it killed mules from overwork, but the old man held to it. Jeff thought it killed a good many share farmers as well as mules, but he had no sympathy for them. He had always been strong, and he had been taught to have no patience with weakness in men. Women or children might be tolerated if they were puny, but a weak man was a curse. Of course, his own children—

43   Jeff's thought halted there. He and Jennie never mentioned their dead children any more. And naturally, he did not wish to dwell upon them in his mind. Before he knew it, some remark would slip out of his mouth and that would make Jennie feel blue. Perhaps she would cry. A woman like Jennie could not easily throw off the grief that comes from losing five grown children within two years. Even Jeff was still staggered by the blow. His memory had not been much good recently. He frequently talked to himself. And, although he had kept it a secret, he knew that his courage had left him. He was terrified by the least unfamiliar sound at night. He was reluctant to venture far from home in the daytime. And that habit of trembling when he felt fearful was now far beyond his control. Sometimes he became afraid and trembled without knowing what had frightened him. The feeling would just come over him like a chill.

44   The car rattled slowly over the dusty road. Jennie sat erect and silent with a little absurd hat pinned to her hair. Her useless eyes seemed very large, very white in their deep sockets. Suddenly Jeff heard her voice, and he inclined his head to catch the words.

45   "Is we passed Delia Moore's house yet?" she asked.

46   "Not yet," he said.

47   "You must be drivin' mighty slow, Jeff."

48   "We just as well take our time, baby."

49   There was a pause. A little puff of steam was coming out of the radiator of the car. Heat wavered above the hood. Delia Moore's house was nearly half a mile away. After a moment Jennie spoke again.

50   "You ain't really scairt, is you, Jeff?"

51   "Nah, baby, I ain't scairt."

52   "You know how we agreed—we gotta keep on goin'."

53   Jewels of perspiration appeared on Jeff's forehead. His eyes rounded, blinked, became fixed on the road.

54   "I don't know," he said with a shiver, "I reckon it's the only thing to do."

55   "Hm."

56   A flock of guinea fowls[3] pecking in the road, were scattered by the pass-

---

[3] *guinea fowls:* a common domestic fowl with slate-colored plumage and white spots.

ing car. Some of them took to their wings; others hid under bushes. A blue jay, swaying on a leafy twig, was annoying a roadside squirrel. Jeff held an even speed till he came near Delia's place. Then he slowed down noticeably.

57   Delia's house was really no house at all, but an abandoned store building converted into a dwelling. It sat near a crossroads, beneath a single black cedar tree. There Delia, a cattish old creature of Jennie's age, lived alone. She had been there more years than anybody could remember, and long ago had won the disfavor of such women as Jennie. For in her young days Delia had been gayer, yellower, and saucier than seemed proper in those parts. Her ways with menfolks had been dark and suspicious. And the fact that she had had as many husbands as children did not help her reputation.

58   "Yonder's old Delia," Jeff said as they passed.

59   "What she doin'?"

60   "Jes sittin' in the do'," he said.

61   "She see us?"

62   "Hm," Jeff said. "Musta did."

63   That relieved Jennie. It strengthened her to know that her old enemy had seen her pass in her best clothes. That would give the old she-devil something to chew her gums and fret about, Jennie thought. Wouldn't she have a fit if she didn't find out? Old evil Delia! This would be just the thing for her. It would pay her back for being so evil. It would also pay her, Jennie thought, for the way she used to grin at Jeff—long ago, when her teeth were good.

64   The road became smooth and red, and Jeff could tell by the smell of the air that they were nearing the river. He could see the rise where the road turned and ran along parallel to the stream. The car chugged on monotonously. After a long silent spell, Jennie leaned against Jeff and spoke.

65   "How many bale o' cotton you think we got standin'?" she said.

66   Jeff wrinkled his forehead as he calculated.

67   "'Bout twenty-five, I reckon."

68   "How many you make las' year?"

69   "Twenty-eight," he said. "How come you ask that?"

70   "I's jes thinkin'," Jennie said quietly.

71   "It don't make a speck o' difference though," Jeff reflected. "If we get much or if we get little, we still gonna be in debt to old man Stevenson when he gets through counting up agin us. It's took us a long time to learn that."

72   Jennie was not listening to these words. She had fallen into a trance-like meditation. Her lips twitched. She chewed her gums and rubbed her gnarled hands nervously. Suddenly, she leaned forward, buried her face in the nervous hands, and burst into tears. She cried aloud in a dry, cracked voice that suggested the rattle of fodder on dead stalks. She cried aloud like a child, for she had never learned to suppress a genuine sob. Her slight old frame shook heavily and seemed hardly able to sustain such violent grief.

73   "What's the matter, baby?" Jeff asked awkwardly. "Why you cryin' like all that?"

74   "I's jes thinkin'," she said.

75   "So you the one what's scairt now, hunh?"

76   "I ain't scairt, Jeff. I's jes thinkin' 'bout leavin' eve'thing like this— eve'thing we been used to. It's right sad-like."

77   Jeff did not answer, and presently Jennie buried her face again and cried.

78   The sun was almost overhead. It beat down furiously on the dusty wagon-path road, on the parched roadside grass and the tiny battered car. Jeff's hands, gripping the wheel, became wet with perspiration; his forehead sparkled. Jeff's lips parted. His mouth shaped a hideous grimace. His face suggested the face of a man being burned. But the torture passed and his expression softened again.

79   "You mustn't cry, baby," he said to his wife. "We gotta be strong. We can't break down."

80   Jennie waited a few seconds, then said, "You reckon we oughta do it, Jeff? You reckon we oughta go 'head an' do it, really?"

81   Jeff's voice choked; his eyes blurred. He was terrified to hear Jennie say the thing that had been in his mind all morning. She had egged him on when he had wanted more than anything in the world to wait, to reconsider, to think things over a little longer. Now she was getting cold feet. Actually, there was no need of thinking the question through again. It would only end in making the same painful decision once more. Jeff knew that. There was no need of fooling around longer.

82   "We jes as well to do like we planned," he said. "They ain't nothin' else for us now—it's the bes' thing."

83   Jeff thought of the handicaps, the near impossibility, of making another crop with his leg bothering him more and more each week. Then there was always the chance that he would have another stroke, like the one that had made him lame. Another one might kill him. The least it could do would be to leave him helpless. Jeff gasped—Lord Jesus! He could not bear to think of being helpless, like a baby, on Jennie's hands. Frail, blind Jennie.

84   The little pounding motor of the car worked harder and harder. The puff of steam from the cracked radiator became larger. Jeff realized that they were climbing a little rise. A moment later the road turned abruptly, and he looked down upon the face of the river.

85   "Jeff."

86   "Hunh?"

87   "Is that the water I hear?"

88   "Hm. Tha's it."

89   "Well, which way you goin' now?"

90   "Down this-a way," he said. "The road runs 'long 'side o' the water a lil piece."

91   She waited a while calmly. Then she said, "Drive faster."

92   "A'right baby," Jeff said.

93   The water roared in the bed of the river. It was fifty or sixty feet below

the level of the road. Between the road and the water there was a long smooth slope, sharply inclined. The slope was dry, the clay hardened by prolonged summer heat. The water below, roaring in a narrow channel, was noisy and wild.

94   "Jeff."

95   "Hunh?"

96   "How far you goin'?"

97   "Jes a lil piece down the road."

98   "You ain't scairt, is you, Jeff?"

99   "Nah, baby," he said trembling. "I ain't scairt."

100   "Remember how we planned it, Jeff. We gotta do it like we said. Brave-like."

101   "Hm."

102   Jeff's brain darkened. Things suddenly seemed unreal, like figures in a dream. Thoughts swam in his mind foolishly, hysterically, like little blind fish in a pool within a dense cave. They rushed again. Jeff soon became dizzy. He shuddered violently and turned to his wife.

103   "Jennie, I can't do it. I can't." His voice broke pitifully.

104   She did not appear to be listening. All the grief had gone from her face. She sat erect, her unseeing eyes wide open, strained and frightful. Her glossy black skin had become dull. She seemed as thin, as sharp and bony, as a starved bird. Now, having suffered and endured the sadness of tearing herself away from beloved things, she showed no anguish. She was absorbed with her own thoughts, and she didn't even hear Jeff's voice shouting in her ear.

105   Jeff said nothing more. For an instant there was light in his cavernous brain. The great chamber was, for less than a second, peopled by characters he knew and loved. They were simple, healthy creatures, and they behaved in a manner that he could understand. They had quality. But since he had already taken leave of them long ago, the remembrance did not break his heart again. Young Jeff Patton was among them, the Jeff Patton of fifty years ago who went down to New Orleans with a crowd of country boys to the Mardi Gras doings. The gay young crowd, boys with candy-striped shirts and rouged brown girls in noisy silks, was like a picture in his head. Yet it did not make him sad. On that very trip Slim Burns had killed Joe Beasley—the crowd had been broken up. Since then Jeff Patton's world had been the Greenbriar Plantation. If there had been other Mardi Gras carnivals, he had not heard of them. Since then there had been no time; the years had fallen on him like waves. Now he was old, worn out. Another paralytic stroke (like the one he had already suffered) would put him on his back for keeps. In that condition, with a frail blind woman to look after him, he would be worse off than if he were dead.

106   Suddenly Jeff's hand became steady. He actually felt brave. He slowed down the motor of the car and carefully pulled off the road. Below, the water of the stream boomed, a soft thunder in the deep channel. Jeff ran the

car onto the clay slope, pointed it directly toward the stream, and put his foot heavily on the accelerator. The little car leaped furiously down the steep incline toward the water. The movement was nearly as swift and direct as a fall. The two old black folks, sitting quietly side by side, showed no excitement. In another instant the car hit the water and dropped immediately out of sight.

107   A little later it lodged in the mud of a shallow place. One wheel of the crushed and upturned little Ford became visible above the rushing water.

DISCUSSION QUESTIONS

1. How do the time and place in which the story is set help shape the story?
2. What types of crops did Jeff and Jennie grow on their farm? Were they successful farmers? Why or why not?
3. How have the hardships that Jeff and Jennie have endured shaped them as individuals? As a married couple?
4. At the end of the story, as the car goes into the stream, what was your reaction? What do you assume happened? Support your response with specific information from the story.
5. Against whom or what do you think Jeff and Jennie take a stand? Do you think their choice of action was the best? Why or why not?

WRITING TOPICS

1. Between the mid-1860s and the late 1940s, thousands of African Americans were share croppers. In an essay, analyze the effect of share cropping on the lives of African Americans such as Jeff and Jennie.
2. In your journal, discuss in what ways Jeff and Jennie's story is a "summer tragedy."

WILLIE

Maya Angelou

Maya Angelou was born Marguerite Johnson in 1928, in St. Louis, Missouri, to Bailey and Vivian Baxter Johnson. She took the name Maya Angelou when she began her dancing career in San Francisco. When Angelou's parents divorced, she went to live with her maternal grandmother, Annie Henderson, in Stamps, Arkansas. After graduating at the top of her eighth-grade class, Angelou moved to San Francisco to live with her mother. After graduating from high school in 1945, Angelou worked at a variety of jobs—streetcar driver, cook, dancer, waitress. In the late 1950s and early 1960s, Angelou made a commitment to her writing career and became a member of the Harlem Writers Guild. With the support of the group, she began to treat her writing seriously. Dr. Martin Luther King Jr. named her the Northern Coordinator of the Southern Christian Leadership Conference. Angelou has received honorary degrees from many colleges and universities, including Smith College, Mills College, and Lawrence University.

Since 1970, Angelou has published five autobiographical volumes; *I Know Why the Caged Bird Sings* (1970) is the most critically acclaimed volume. The other volumes are *Gather Together in My Name* (1974), *Singin' and Swingin' and Gettin' Merry Like Christmas* (1976), *The Heart of a Woman* (1981), and *All God's Children Need Traveling Shoes* (1986). She has also published a book of meditations, *Won't Take Nothing for My Journey Now* (1993). Angelou's poetry collections include *Just Give Me a Cool Drink of Water 'fore I Die* (1971), *And Still I Rise* (1976), *Shaker, Why Don't You Sing* (1983), *I Shall Not Be Moved* (1990), *Life Doesn't Frighten Me: Poem* (1993), and *The Complete Collected Works of Maya Angelou* (1994). In January 1993, Angelou became the first African-American and the first woman poet to read her work, *On the Pulse of Morning* (1993), at a presidential inauguration.

Willie was a man without fame
Hardly anybody knew his name.
Crippled and limping, always walking lame,
He said, "I keep on movin'
5   Movin' just the same."

Solitude was the climate in his head
Emptiness was the partner in his bed,
Pain echoed in the steps of his tread,
He said, "I keep on followin'
10 Where the leaders led."

I may cry and I will die,
But my spirit is the soul of every spring.
Watch for me and you will see
That I'm present in the songs that children sing.

15 People called him "Uncle," "Boy" and "Hey,"
Said, "You can't live through this another day."
Then, they waited to hear what he would say.
He said, "I'm living
In the games that children play.

20 "You may enter my sleep, people my dreams,
Threaten my early morning's ease,
But I keep comin' followin' laughin' cryin',
Sure as a summer breeze.

"Wait for me, watch for me.
25 My spirit is the surge of open seas.
Look for me, ask for me.
I'm the rustle in the autumn leaves.

"When the sun rises
I am the time.
30 When the children sing
I am the Rhyme."

DISCUSSION QUESTIONS

1. The poem begins by the speaker saying, "Willie was a man without fame" and ends with a quotation from Willie, "I am the Rhyme." How does the first line prepare you for the rest of the poem? When you reach the last line of the poem, do you feel the same way about the poem? How did your thoughts change or stay the same?
2. Why do you think Willie describes himself using metaphors that refer to nature and children?
3. How does Willie stand his ground? What belief has he refused to give up? How is this belief supported by the last stanza of the poem?

WRITING TOPICS

1. In your journal, create a metaphor that shows how you stand your ground. Why is this metaphor the best one for you?
2. In an essay, compare the tone of the third stanza of "Willie" with the tone of the third stanza of Hughes's "I, Too." What type of stance does each persona take? Are these stances effective ones that could cause change?

AN ADDRESS DELIVERED AT THE OPENING OF THE COTTON STATES' EXPOSITION IN ATLANTA, GEORGIA, SEPTEMBER, 1895

Booker T. Washington

Booker T. Washington was born in 1856 on a plantation in Virginia. Born Booker Taliaferro, he later added the surname Washington. His mother was a cook and his father was white. After the Civil War, Washington and his mother moved to Malden, West Virginia, where his mother married Washington Ferguson. Washington taught himself the alphabet, studied at night, and worked at salt furnaces and coal mines during the day. In 1872 he began studying at Hampton Institute, a school established for blacks. He graduated with honors from Hampton in 1875.

After teaching for a while in Malden, he became an instructor at Hampton. In 1881, he was recommended for the position of principal for a normal school (a teacher's institution) for blacks in Tuskegee, Alabama, where he stayed for thirty-five years. Students who attended Tuskegee Institute (currently Tuskegee University) were trained in industrial skills and agriculture. Washington became an important social thinker. He believed blacks would achieve equality through economic strength and education, a position harshly criticized by several black intellectuals (especially W. E. B. Du Bois).

Washington was a well-known lecturer and his most famous speech was "An Address Delivered at the Opening of the Cotton States' Exposition in Atlanta, Georgia, September, 1895." Washington advised several U.S. presidents, including Theodore Roosevelt, on racial issues. His essays were published in book form: *The Future of the American Negro* (1899) and *The Negro in the South: His Economic Progress in Relation to His Moral and Religious Development* (1907, with W. E. B. Du Bois). Washington's life is presented in three autobiographies: *The Story of My Life* (1901), *Up from Slavery* (1901), and *Working with the Hands* (1904). Booker T. Washington died at Tuskegee in 1915.

1   Mr. President and Gentlemen of the Board of Directors and Citizens: One-third of the population of the South is of the Negro race. No enterprise seeking the material, civil, or moral welfare of this section can disregard this element of our population and reach the highest success. I but convey to you, Mr. President and Directors, the sentiment of the masses of my race when I say that in no way have the value and manhood of the American Negro been more fittingly and generously recognized than by the managers of this magnificent Exposition at every stage of its progress. It is a recognition that will do more to cement the friendship of the two races than any occurrence since the dawn of freedom.

2   Not only this, but the opportunity here afforded will awaken among us a new era of industrial progress. Ignorant and inexperienced, it is not strange that in the first years of our new life we began at the top instead of at the bottom; that a seat in Congress or the State Legislature was more sought than real estate or industrial skill; that the political convention or stump speaking had more attractions than starting a dairy farm or truck garden.

3   A ship lost at sea for many days suddenly sighted a friendly vessel. From the mast of the unfortunate vessel was seen a signal, "Water, water; we die of thirst!" The answer from the friendly vessel at once came back: "Cast down your bucket where you are." A second time the signal, "Water, water; send us water!" ran up from the distressed vessel, and was answered: "Cast down your bucket where you are." The captain of the distressed vessel, at last heeding the injunction, cast down his bucket, and it came up full of fresh, sparkling water from the mouth of the Amazon River. To those of my race who depend upon bettering their condition in a foreign land, or who underestimate the importance of cultivating friendly relations with the Southern white man, who is his next door neighbor, I would say: "Cast down your buck where you are"—cast it down in making friends in every manly way of the people of all races by whom we are surrounded.

4   Cast it down in agriculture, mechanics, in commerce, in domestic service, and in the professions. And in this connection it is well to bear in mind that whatever other sins the South may be called to bear, when it comes to business, pure and simple, it is in the South that the Negro is given a man's chance in the commercial world, and in nothing is this Exposition more eloquent than in emphasizing this chance. Our greatest danger is, that in the great leap from slavery to freedom we may overlook the fact that the masses of us are to live by the productions of our hands, and fail to keep in mind that we shall prosper in proportion as we learn to dignify and glorify common labor, and put brains and skill into the common occupation of life; shall prosper in proportion as we learn to draw the line between the superficial and the substantial, the ornamental gewgaws of life and the useful. No race can prosper till it learns that there is as much dignity in tilling a field as in writing a poem. It is at the bottom of life we must begin, and not at the top. Nor should we permit our grievances to overshadow our opportunities.

5   To those of the white race who look to the incoming of those of foreign birth and strange tongue and habits for the prosperity of the South,
were I permitted I would repeat what I say to my own race, "Cast down
your bucket where you are." Cast it down among the 8,000,000 Negroes
whose habits you know, whose fidelity and love you have tested in days
when to have proved treacherous meant the ruin of your firesides. Cast
down your bucket among these people who have, without strikes and
labor wars, tilled your fields, cleared your forests, builded your railroads
and cities, and brought forth treasures from the bowels of the earth, and
helped make possible this magnificent representation of the progress of
the South. Casting down your bucket among my people, helping and
encouraging them as you are doing on these grounds, and, with education
of head, hand and heart, you will find that they will buy your surplus land,
make blossom the waste places in your fields, and run your factories. While
doing this, you can be sure in the future, as in the past, that you and your
families will be surrounded by the most patient, faithful, law-abiding, and
unresentful people that the world has seen. As we have proved our loyalty
to you in the past, in nursing your children, watching by the sick bed of
your mothers and fathers, and often following them with tear-dimmed
eyes to their graves, so in the future, in our humble way, we shall stand by
you with a devotion that no foreigner can approach, ready to lay down our
lives, if need be, in defense of yours, interlacing our industrial, commercial, civil, and religious life with yours in a way that shall make the interests of both races one. In all things that are purely social we can be as separate as the fingers, yet one as the hand in all things essential to mutual
progress.

6   There is no defense to security for any of us except in the highest intelligence and development of all. If anywhere there are efforts tending to
curtail the fullest growth of the Negro, let these efforts be turned into stim-
ulating, encouraging, and making him the most useful and intelligent citizen. Effort or means so invested will pay a thousand per cent interest.
These efforts will be twice blessed—blessing him that gives and him that
takes.

7   There is no escape through the law of man or God from the inevitable:

The laws of changeless justice bind
   Oppressor with oppressed;
And close as sin and suffering joined
   We march to fate abreast.

8   Nearly sixteen millions of hands will aid you in pulling the load upwards
or they will pull against you the load downwards. We shall constitute one-
third and more of the ignorance and crime of the South, or one-third its
intelligence and progress; we shall contribute one-third to the business and
industrial prosperity of the South, or we shall prove a veritable body of

death, stagnating, depressing, retarding every effort to advance the body politic.

9   Gentlemen of the Exposition, as we present to you our humble effort at an exhibition of our progress, you must not expect overmuch. Starting thirty years ago with ownership here and there in a few quilts and pumpkins and chickens (gathered from miscellaneous sources), remember the path that has led from these to the invention and production of agricultural implements, buggies, steam engines, newspapers, books, statuary, carving, paintings, the management of drug stores and banks has not been trodden without contact with thorns and thistles. While we take pride in what we exhibit as a result of our independent efforts, we do not for a moment forget that our part in this exhibition would fall far short of your expectations but for the constant help that has come to our educational life, not only from the Southern States, but especially from Northern philanthropists, who have made their gifts a constant stream of blessing and encouragement.

10   The wisest among my race understand that the agitation of questions of social equality is the extremist folly, and that progress in the enjoyment of all the privileges that will come to us must be the result of severe and constant struggle rather than of artificial forcing. No race that has anything to contribute to the markets of the world is long in any degree ostracized. It is important and right that all privileges of the law be ours, but it is vastly more important that we be prepared for the exercise of those privileges. The opportunity to earn a dollar in a factory just now is worth infinitely more than the opportunity to spend a dollar in an opera house.

11   In conclusion, may I repeat that nothing in thirty years has given us more hope and encouragement, and drawn us so near to you of the white race, as this opportunity offered by the Exposition; and here bending, as it were, over the altar that represents the results of the struggles of your race and mine, both starting practically empty-handed three decades ago, I pledge that, in your effort to work out the great and intricate problem which God has laid at the doors of the South, you shall have at all times the patient, sympathetic help of my race; only let this be constantly in mind that, while from representations in these buildings of the products of field, of forest, of mine, of factory, letters, and art, much good will come, yet far above and beyond material benefits will be the higher good, that let us pray God will come, in a blotting out of sectional differences and racial animosities and suspicions, in a determination to administer absolute justice, in a willing obedience among all classes to the mandates of law. This, coupled with our material prosperity, will bring into our beloved South a new heaven and a new earth.

DISCUSSION QUESTIONS

1. Using specific evidence from the speech, explain the similarities and differences between the two ways (first, concerning black people; second, concerning white people) Washington uses his analogy of "Cast down your buckets where you are."

2. Washington states: "It is at the bottom of life we must begin, and not at the top. Nor should we permit our grievances to overshadow our opportunities." Do you agree or disagree with this statement? Why?

3. One of the most often quoted lines from this speech is: "In all things that are purely social we can be as separate as fingers, yet one as the hand in all things essential to mutual progress." Why would Washington want to assure the southern and northern industrialists that blacks and whites did not have to socialize together, but that they could work in businesses together?

4. Washington's critics often accused him of not being an aggressive fighter for the advancement of African Americans. Using specific examples from this speech, illustrate how Washington is working for the advancement of African Americans.

WRITING TOPICS

1. In your journal, discuss the possibility that black and white people could be socially separate from each other but work well together in businesses.

2. Research the immigration situation in the 1880s. Write an essay in which you use your research to support Washington's plea to southern and northern industrialists to "Cast it [their need for employees] among the 8,000,000 Negroes whose habits you know, . . ."

OF MR. BOOKER T. WASHINGTON AND OTHERS

W. E. B. Du Bois

W. E. B. (William Edward Burghardt) Du Bois, one of the most important leaders of black protest in the United States, was born in Great Barrington, Massachusetts, in 1868. Du Bois was raised by his mother, a New Englander of Dutch-African descent. She was an inspirational force in his life, encouraging him to excel in his studies. In 1888 Du Bois received a B.A. from Fisk University, where he began his writing and public speaking career. He received a second B.A. and an M.A. from Harvard University, and in 1896 Du Bois became the first African American to receive a Ph.D. from Harvard.

Du Bois believed that the problems of African Americans could not be understood without systematic investigation and intelligent understanding. In 1899 he published *The Philadelphia Negro: A Social Study,* the first systematic sociological study of a large number of African Americans in any major city of the United States. One of the founders of the National Association for the Advancement of Colored People (NAACP), Du Bois edited its journal, *The Crisis,* from 1910 to 1930. He left the NAACP in the early thirties, disagreeing on ideologies. From the 1930s until his death, Du Bois continued to speak out against discrimination against black people in the United States and in Africa.

The Souls of Black Folk (1904) is Du Bois's most recognized book, known around the world. The most important issues discussed in this book include "The problem of the twentieth century will be the problem of the color line," "the Talented Tenth," and Du Bois's challenge to Booker T. Washington's views (Washington accepted segregation and the disenfranchisement of black voters). Shortly after becoming a citizen of Ghana, Du Bois died there in 1963. (For more biographical information, see pages 260 and 297.)

From birth till death enslaved; in word, in deed, unmanned!
. . . .
Hereditary bondsmen! Know ye not
Who would be free themselves must strike the blow?

BYRON

1   Easily the most striking thing in the history of the American Negro since 1876 is the ascendancy of Mr. Booker T. Washington. It began at the time when war memories and ideals were rapidly passing; a day of astonishing commercial development was dawning; a sense of doubt and hesitation overtook the freedmen's sons,—then it was that his leading began. Mr. Washington came, with a single definite programme, at the psychological moment when the nation was a little ashamed of having bestowed so much sentiment on Negroes, and was concentrating its energies on Dollars. His programme of industrial education, conciliation of the South, and submission and silence as to civil and political rights, was not wholly original; the Free Negroes from 1830 up to war-time had striven to build industrial schools, and the American Missionary Association had from the first taught various trades; and Price and others had sought a way of honorable alliance with the best of the Southerners. But Mr. Washington first indissolubly linked these things; he put enthusiasm, unlimited energy, and perfect faith into his programme, and changed it from a by-path into a veritable Way of Life. And the tale of the methods by which he did this is a fascinating study of human life.

2   It startled the nation to hear a Negro advocating such a programme after many decades of bitter complaint; it startled and won the applause of the South, it interested and won the admiration of the North; and after a confused murmur of protest, it silenced if it did not convert the Negroes themselves.

3   To gain the sympathy and coöperation of the various elements comprising the white South was Mr. Washington's first task; and this, at the time Tuskegee was founded, seemed, for a black man, well-nigh impossible. And yet ten years later it was done in the word spoken at Atlanta: "In all things purely social we can be as separate as the five fingers, and yet one as the hand in all things essential to mutual progress." This "Atlanta Compromise" is by all odds the most notable thing in Mr. Washington's career. The South interpreted it in different ways: the radicals received it as a complete surrender of the demand for civil and political equality; the conservatives, as a generously conceived working basis for mutual understanding. So both approved it, and to-day its author is certainly the most distinguished Southerner since Jefferson Davis, and the one with the largest personal following.

4   Next to this achievement comes Mr. Washington's work in gaining place and consideration in the North. Others less shrewd and tactful had formerly essayed to sit on these two stools and had fallen between them; but as Mr. Washington knew the heart of the South from birth and training, so by singular insight he intuitively grasped the spirit of the age which was dominat-

ing the North. And so thoroughly did he learn the speech and thought of triumphant commercialism, and the ideals of material prosperity, that the picture of a lone black boy poring over a French grammar amid the weeds and dirt of a neglected home soon seemed to him the acme of absurdities. One wonders what Socrates and St. Frances of Assisi would say to this.

5   And yet this very singleness of vision and thorough oneness with his age is a mark of the successful man. It is as though Nature must needs make men narrow in order to give them force. So Mr. Washington's cult has gained unquestioning followers, his work has wonderfully prospered, his friends are legion, and his enemies are confounded. To-day he stands as the one recognized spokesman of his ten million fellows, and one of the most notable figures in a nation of seventy millions. One hesitates, therefore, to criticise a life which beginning with so little, has done so much. And yet the time is come when one may speak in all sincerity and utter courtesy of the mistakes and shortcomings of Mr. Washington's career, as well as of his triumphs, without being thought captious or envious, and without forgetting that it is easier to do ill than well in the world.

6   The criticism that has hitherto met Mr. Washington has not always been of this broad character. In the South especially has he had to walk warily to avoid the harshest judgments—and naturally so, for he is dealing with the one subject of deepest sensitiveness to that section. Twice—once when at the Chicago celebration of the Spanish-American War he alluded to the color-prejudice that is "eating away the vitals of the South," and once when he dined with President Roosevelt—has the resulting Southern criticism been violent enough to threaten seriously his popularity. In the North the feeling has several times forced itself into words, that Mr. Washington's counsels of submission overlooked certain elements of true manhood, and that his educational programme was unnecessarily narrow. Usually, however, such criticism has not found open expression, although, too, the spiritual sons of the Abolitionists have not been prepared to acknowledge that the schools founded before Tuskegee, by men of broad ideals and self-sacrificing spirit, were wholly failures or worthy of ridicule. While, then, criticism has not failed to follow Mr. Washington, yet the prevailing public opinion of the land has been but too willing to deliver the solution of a wearisome problem into his hands, and say, "If that is all you and your race ask, take it."

7   Among his own people, however, Mr. Washington has encountered the strongest and most lasting opposition, amounting at times to bitterness, and even to-day continuing strong and insistent even though largely silenced in outward expression by the public opinion of the nation. Some of this opposition is, of course, mere envy; the disappointment of displaced demagogues and the spite of narrow minds. But aside from this, there is among educated and thoughtful colored men in all parts of the land a feeling of deep regret, sorrow, and apprehension at the wide currency and ascendancy which some of Mr. Washington's theories have gained. These same men admire his sincerity of purpose, and are willing to forgive much to honest endeavor which

is doing something worth the doing. They coöperate with Mr. Washington as far as they conscientiously can; and, indeed, it is no ordinary tribute to this man's tact and power that, steering as he must between so many diverse interests and opinions, he so largely retains the respect of all.

8   But the hushing of the criticism of honest opponents is a dangerous thing. It leads some of the best of the critics to unfortunate silence and paralysis of effort, and others to burst into speech so passionately and intemperately as to lose listeners. Honest and earnest criticism from those whose interests are most nearly touched,—criticism of writers by readers, of government by those governed, of leaders by those led,—this is the soul of democracy and the safeguard of modern society. If the best of the American Negroes receive by outer pressure a leader whom they had not recognized before, manifestly there is here a certain palpable gain. Yet there is also irreparable loss,—a loss of that peculiarly valuable education which a group receives when by search and criticism it finds and commissions its own leaders. The way in which this is done is at once the most elementary and the nicest problem of social growth. History is but the record of such group-leadership; and yet how infinitely changeful is its type and character! And of all types and kinds, what can be more instructive than the leadership of a group within a group?—that curious double movement where real progress may be negative and actual advance be relative retrogression. All this is the social student's inspiration and despair.

9   Now in the past the American Negro has had instructive experience in the choosing of group leaders, founding thus a peculiar dynasty which in the light of present conditions is worth while studying. When sticks and stones and beasts form the sole environment of a people, their attitude is largely one of determined opposition to and conquest of natural forces. But when to earth and brute is added an environment of men and ideas, then the attitude of the imprisoned group may take three main forms—a feeling of revolt and revenge; an attempt to adjust all thought and action to the will of the greater group; or, finally, a determined effort at self-realization and self-development despite environing opinion. The influence of all of these attitudes at various times can be traced to the history of the American Negro, and in the evolution of his successive leaders.

10   Before 1750, while the fire of African freedom still burned in the veins of the slaves, there was in all leadership or attempted leadership but the one motive of revolt and revenge,—typified in the terrible Maroons, the Danish blacks, and Cato of Stono, and veiling all the Americans in fear of insurrection. The liberalizing tendencies of the latter half of the eighteenth century brought, along with kindlier relations between black and white, thoughts of ultimate adjustment and assimilation. Such aspiration was especially voiced in the earnest songs of Phyllis, in the martyrdom of Attucks, the fighting of Salem and Poor, the intellectual accomplishments of Banneker and Derham, and the political demands of the Cuffes.

11   Stern financial and social stress after the war cooled much of the previ-

ous humanitarian ardor. The disappointment and impatience of Negroes at the persistence of slavery and serfdom voiced itself in two movements. The slaves in the South, aroused undoubtedly by vague rumors of the Haytian revolt, made three fierce attempts at insurrection,—in 1800 under Gabriel in Virginia, in 1822 under Vesey in Carolina, and in 1831 again in Virginia under the terrible Nat Turner. In the Free States, on the other hand, a new and curious attempt at self-development was made. In Philadelphia and New York color-prescription led to a withdrawal of Negro communicants from white churches and the formation of a peculiar socio-religious institution among the Negroes known as the African Church,—an organization still living and controlling in its various branches over a million of men.

12   Walker's wild appeal against the trend of the times showed how the world was changing after the coming of the cotton-gin. By 1830 slavery seemed hopelessly fastened on the south and the slaves thoroughly cowed into submission. The free Negroes of the North, inspired by the mulatto immigrants from the West Indies, began to change the basis of their demands; they recognized the slavery of slaves, but insisted that they themselves were freemen, and sought assimilation and amalgamation with the nation on the same terms with other men. Thus, Forten and Purvis of Philadelphia, Shad of Wilmington, Du Bois of New Haven, Barbadoes of Boston, and others, strove singly and together as men, they said, not as slaves; as "people of color," not as "Negroes." The trend of the times, however, refused them recognition save in individual and exceptional cases, considered them as one with all the despised blacks, and they soon found themselves striving to keep even the rights they formerly had of voting and working and moving as freemen. Schemes of migration and colonization arose among them; but these they refused to entertain, and they eventually turned to the Abolition movement as a final refuge.

13   Here, led by Remond, Nell, Wells-Brown, and Douglass, a new period of self-assertion and self-development dawned. To be sure, ultimate freedom and assimilation was the ideal before the leaders, but the assertion of the manhood rights of the Negro by himself was the main reliance, and John Brown's raid was the extreme of its logic. After the war and emancipation, the great form of Frederick Douglass, the greatest of American Negro leaders, still led the host. Self-assertion, especially in political lines, was the main programme, and behind Douglass came Elliot, Bruce, and Langston, and the Reconstruction politicians, and, less conspicuous but of greater social significance, Alexander Crummell and Bishop Daniel Payne.

14   Then came the Revolution of 1876, the suppression of the Negro votes, the changing and shifting of ideals, and the seeking of new lights in the great night. Douglass, in his old age, still bravely stood for the ideals of his early manhood—ultimate assimilation *through* self-assertion, and on no other terms. For a time Price arose as a new leader, destined, it seemed, not to give up, but to re-state the old ideals in a form less repugnant to the white South. But he passed away in his prime. Then came the new leader. Nearly all the

former ones had become leaders by the silent suffrage of their fellows, had sought to lead their own people alone, and were usually, save Douglass, little known outside their race. But Booker T. Washington arose as essentially the leader not of one race but of two—a compromiser between the South, the North, and the Negro. Naturally the Negroes resented, at first bitterly, signs of compromise which surrendered their civil and political rights, even though this was to be exchanged for larger chances of economic development. The rich and dominating North, however, was not only weary of the race problem, but was investing largely in Southern enterprises, and welcomed any method of peaceful coöperation. Thus, by national opinion, the Negroes began to recognize Mr. Washington's leadership; and the voice of criticism was hushed.

15   Mr. Washington represents in Negro thought the old attitude of adjustment and submission; but adjustment at such a peculiar time as to make his programme unique. This is an age of unusual economic development, and Mr. Washington's programme naturally takes an economic cast, becoming a gospel of Work and Money to such an extent as apparently almost completely to overshadow the higher aims of life. Moreover, this is an age when the more advanced races are coming in closer contact with the less developed races, and the race-feeling is therefore intensified; and Mr. Washington's programme practically accepts the alleged inferiority of the Negro races. Again, in our own land, the reaction from the sentiment of war times has given impetus to race-prejudice against Negroes, and Mr. Washington withdraws many of the high demands of Negroes as men and American citizens. In other periods of intensified prejudice all the Negro's tendency to self-assertion has been called forth; at this period a policy of submission is advocated. In the history of nearly all other races and peoples the doctrine preached at such crises has been that manly self-respect is worth more than lands and houses, and that a people who voluntarily surrender such respect, or cease striving for it, are not worth civilizing.

16   In answer to this, it has been claimed that the Negro can survive only through submission. Mr. Washington distinctly asks that black people give up, at least for the present, three things,—

1. First, political power,
2. Second, insistence on civil rights,
3. Third, higher education of Negro youth,—

and concentrate all their energies on industrial education, and accumulation of wealth, and the conciliation of the South. This policy has been courageously and insistently advocated for over fifteen years, and has been triumphant for perhaps ten years. As a result of this tender of the palm-branch, what has been the return? In these years there have occurred:

The disfranchisement of the Negro.

The legal creation of a distinct status of civil inferiority for the Negro.

The steady withdrawal of aid from institutions for the higher training of the Negro.

17   These movements are not, to be sure, direct results of Mr. Washington's teachings; but his propaganda has, without a shadow of doubt, helped their speedier accomplishment. The question then comes: Is it possible, and probable, that nine millions of men can make effective progress in economic lines if they are deprived of political rights, made a servile caste, and allowed only the most meagre chance for developing their exceptional men? If history and reason give any distinct answer to these questions, it is an emphatic *No*. And Mr. Washington thus faces the triple paradox of his career:

1. He is striving nobly to make Negro artisans business men and property-owners; but it is utterly impossible, under modern competitive methods, for workingmen and property-owners to defend their rights and exist without the right of suffrage.

2. He insists on thrift and self-respect, but at the same time counsels a silent submission of civic inferiority such as is bound to sap the manhood of any race in the long run.

3. He advocates common-school and industrial training, and depreciates institutions of higher learning; but neither the Negro common-schools, nor Tuskegee itself, could remain open a day were it not for teachers training in Negro colleges, or trained by their graduates.

18   This triple paradox in Mr. Washington's position is the object of criticism by two classes of colored Americans. One class is spiritually descended from Toussaint the Savior, through Gabriel, Vesey, and Turner, and they represent the attitude of revolt and revenge; they hate the white South blindly and distrust the white race generally, and so far as they agree on definite action, think that the Negro's only hope lies in emigration beyond the borders of the United States. And yet, by the irony of fate, nothing has more effectually made this programme seem hopeless than the recent course of the United States toward weaker and darker peoples in the West Indies, Hawaii, and the Philippines,—for where in the world may we go and be safe from lying and brute force?

19   The other class of Negroes who cannot agree with Mr. Washington has hitherto said little aloud. They deprecate the sight of scattered counsels, of internal disagreement; and especially they dislike making their just criticism of a useful and earnest man an excuse for a general discharge of venom from small-minded opponents. Nevertheless, the questions involved are so fundamental and serious that it is difficult to see how men like the Grimkes, Kelly Miller, J. W. E. Bowen, and other representatives of this group, can much longer be silent. Such men feel in conscience bound to ask of this nation three things:

1. The right to vote.
2. Civic equality.
3. The education of youth according to ability.

They acknowledge Mr. Washington's invaluable service in counseling patience and courtesy in such demands; they do not ask that ignorant black men vote when ignorant whites are debarred, or that any reasonable restrictions in the suffrage should not be applied; they know that the low social level of the mass of the race is responsible for much discrimination against it, but they also know, and the nation knows, that relentless color-prejudice is more often a cause than a result of the Negro's degradation; they seek the abatement of this relic of barbarism, and not its systematic encouragement and pampering by all agencies of social power from the Associated Press to the Church of Christ. They advocate, with Mr. Washington, a broad system of Negro common schools supplemented by thorough industrial training; but they are surprised that a man of Mr. Washington's insight cannot see that no such educational system ever has rested or can rest on any other basis than that of the well-equipped college and university, and they insist that there is a demand for a few such institutions throughout the South to train the best of the Negro youth as teachers, professional men, and leaders.

20   This group of men honor Mr. Washington for his attitude of conciliation toward the white South; they accept the "Atlanta Compromise" in its broadest interpretation; they recognize, with him, many signs of promise, many men of high purpose and fair judgment, in this section; they know that no easy task has been laid upon a region already tottering under heavy burdens. But, nevertheless, they insist that the way to truth and right lies in straightforward honesty, not in indiscriminate flattery; in praising those of the South who do well and criticising uncompromisingly those who do ill; in taking advantage of the opportunities at hand and urging their fellows to do the same, but at the same time in remembering that only a firm adherence to their higher ideals and aspirations will ever keep those ideals within the realm of possibility. They do not expect that the free right to vote, to enjoy civic rights, and to be educated, will come in a moment; they do not expect to see the bias and prejudices of years disappear at the blast of a trumpet; but they are absolutely certain that the way for a people to gain their reasonable rights is not by voluntarily throwing them away and insisting that they do not want them; that the way for a people to gain respect is not by continually belittling and ridiculing themselves; that, on the contrary, Negroes must insist continually, in season and out of season, that voting is necessary to modern manhood, that color discrimination is barbarism, and that black boys need education as well as white boys.

21   In failing thus to state plainly and unequivocally the legitimate demands of their people, even at the cost of opposing an honored leader, the thinking classes of American Negroes would shirk a heavy responsibility,—a responsibility to themselves, a responsibility to the struggling masses, a responsibility to the darker races of men whose future depends so largely on this American experiment, but especially a responsibility to this nation,—this common Fatherland. It is wrong to encourage a man or a people in evildoing; it is wrong to aid and abet a national crime simply because it is unpopular not to do so. The growing spirit of kindliness and reconciliation between the North and South after the frightful differences of a generation

ago ought to be a source of deep congratulation to all, and especially to those whose mistreatment caused the war; but if that reconciliation is to be marked by the industrial slavery and civic death of those same black men, with permanent legislation into a position of inferiority, then those black men, if they are really men, are called upon by every consideration of patriotism and loyalty to oppose such a course by all civilized methods, even though such opposition involves disagreement with Mr. Booker T. Washington. We have no right to sit silently by while the inevitable seeds are sown for a harvest of disaster to our children, black and white.

22   First, it is the duty of black men to judge the South discriminatingly. The present generation of Southerners are not responsible for the past, and they should not be blindly hated or blamed for it. Furthermore, to no class is the indiscriminate endorsement of the recent course of the South toward Negroes more nauseating than to the best thought of the South. The South is not "solid"; it is a land in the ferment of social change, wherein forces of all kinds are fighting for supremacy; and to praise the ill the South is today perpetrating is just as wrong as to condemn the good. Discriminating and broad-minded criticism is what the South needs,—needs it for the sake of her own white sons and daughters, and for the insurance of robust, healthy mental and moral development.

23   To-day even the attitude of the Southern whites toward the blacks is not, as so many assume, in all cases the same; the ignorant Southerner hates the Negro, the workingmen fear his competition, the money-makers wish to use him as a laborer, some of the educated see a menace in his upward development, while others—usually the sons of the masters—wish to help him to rise. National opinion has enabled this last class to maintain the Negro common schools, and to protect the Negro partially in property, life, and limb. Through the pressure of money-makers, the Negro is in danger of being reduced to semi-slavery, especially in the country districts; the workingmen, and those of the educated who fear the Negro, have united to disfranchise him, and some have urged his deportation; while the passions of the ignorant are easily aroused to lynch and abuse any black man. To praise this intricate whirl of thought and prejudice is nonsense; to inveigh indiscriminately against "the South" is unjust; but to use the same breath in praising Governor Aycock, exposing Senator Morgan, arguing with Mr. Thomas Nelson Page, and denouncing Senator Ben Tillman, is not only sane, but the imperative duty of thinking black men.

24   It would be unjust to Mr. Washington not to acknowledge that in several instances he has opposed movements in the South which were unjust to the Negro; he sent memorials to the Louisiana and Alabama constitutional conventions, he has spoken against lynching, and in other ways has openly or silently set his influence against sinister schemes and unfortunate happenings. Notwithstanding this, it is equally true to assert that on the whole the distinct impression left by Mr. Washington's propaganda is first, that the South is justified in its present attitude toward the Negro because of the

Negro's degradation; secondly, that the prime cause of the Negro's failure to rise more quickly is his wrong education in the past; and, thirdly, that his future rise depends primarily on his own efforts. Each of these propositions is a dangerous half-truth. The supplementary truths must never be lost sight of: first, slavery and race-prejudice are potent if not sufficient causes of the Negro's position, second, industrial and common-school training were necessarily slow in planting because they had to await the black teachers trained by higher institutions,—it being extremely doubtful if any essentially different development was possible, and certainly a Tuskegee was unthinkable before 1880; and third, while it is a great truth to say that the Negro must strive and strive mightily to help himself it is equally true that unless his striving be not simply seconded, but rather aroused and encouraged, by the initiative of the richer and wiser environing group, he cannot hope for great success.

25   In his failure to realize and impress this last point, Mr. Washington is especially to be criticised. His doctrine has tended to make the whites, North and South, shift the burden of the Negro problem to the Negro's shoulders and stand aside as critical and rather pessimistic spectators; when in fact the burden belongs to the nation, and the hands of none of us are clean if we bend not our energies to righting these great wrongs.

26   The South ought to be led, by candid and honest criticism, to assert her better self and do her full duty to the race she has cruelly wronged and is still wronging. The North—her co-partner in guilt—cannot salve her conscience by plastering it with gold. We cannot settle this problem by diplomacy and suaveness, by "policy" alone. If worse comes to worst, can the moral fibre of this country survive the slow throttling and murder of nine millions of men?

27   The black men of America have a duty to perform, a duty stern and delicate,—a forward movement to oppose a part of the work of their greatest leader. So far as Mr. Washington preaches Thrift, Patience, and Industrial Training for the masses, we must hold up his hands and strive with him, rejoicing in his honors and glorying in the strength of this Joshua called of God and of man to lead the headless host. But so far as Mr. Washington apologizes for injustice, North or South, does not rightly value the privilege and duty of voting, belittles the emasculating effects of caste distinctions, and opposes the higher training and ambition of our brighter minds,—so far as he, the South, or the Nation, does this,—we must unceasingly and firmly oppose them. By every civilized and peaceful method we must strive for the rights which the world accords to men, clinging unwaveringly to those great words which the sons of the Fathers would fain forget: "We hold these truths to be self-evident: That all men are created equal; that they are endowed by their Creator with certain unalienable rights; that among these are life, liberty, and the pursuit of happiness."

DISCUSSION QUESTIONS

1. What does Du Bois identify as Booker T. Washington's "Atlanta Compromise"? Why does Du Bois consider it a compromise?
2. Why does Du Bois critique the identification of Negro leaders by groups outside of the black community?
3. According to Du Bois, Booker T. Washington asked black people to give up three things. What are these three things, and why does Du Bois consider the loss of them detrimental to black people as American citizens?

WRITING TOPICS

1. In your journal, write a letter to Booker T. Washington in which you describe what would have happened to the United States if African Americans had only received vocational training and only interacted with whites when they were working.
2. In an essay, analyze Du Bois's argument against Washington's "Atlanta Compromise." Does Du Bois present a balanced argument? What are the strengths of Du Bois's argument? What are the weaknesses?
3. Using Washington's speech, "An Address Delivered at the Opening of the Cotton States' Exposition in Atlanta, Georgia, September, 1895" and Du Bois's "Chapter 3: Of Mr. Booker T. Washington and Others" from *The Souls of Black Folk,* support an argument in which you explain how each text would have been beneficial for African Americans living during the time that each was written.

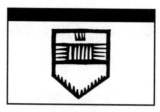

MISS ROSIE

Lucille Clifton

Lucille Clifton was born in DePew, New York, in 1936. She attended Howard University and graduated from Fredonia State Teachers College. Clifton's great-grandmother, Caroline Donald Sale, was born in the Dahomey tribe in Africa. She was captured as a small child and brought as a slave to America. When Sale was eight years old, she reportedly walked from New Orleans to Bedford County, Virginia. For Clifton, this accomplishment was both an indication of the power of African-American women and an inspiration for her poetry about the strength, love, and compassion of black women. Clifton has received a nomination for the Pulitzer Prize and two grants from the National Endowment for the Arts.

Clifton's poetry is powerful because of its realistic urban images and poetic devices. The combination of strong images and well-crafted poetic lines creates a complex message about the characters and locations in the poems. Clifton has published several volumes of poetry: *Good Times* (1969), *Good News About the Earth* (1972), *An Ordinary Woman* (1974), *Generations: A Memoir* (1976), *Two-Headed Woman* (1980), *Next: New Poems* (1987), *Quilting: Poems 1987–1990* (1991), *The Book of Light* (1993), and *The Terrible Stories: Poems* (1995). She has also published many children's books, including *The Black BC's* (1970), *The Boy Who Didn't Believe in Spring* (1973), *The Lucky Stone* (1979), *Sonora Beautiful* (1981), and *Everett Anderson's Goodbye* (1983).

When I watch you
wrapped up like garbage
sitting, surrounded by the smell
of too old potato peels
5   or
when I watch you

in your old man's shoes
with the little toe cut out
sitting, waiting for your mind
10 like next weeks grocery
I say
when I watch you
you wet brown bag of a woman
who used to be the best looking gal in Georgia
15 used to be called the Georgia Rose
I stand up
through your destruction
I stand up

DISCUSSION QUESTIONS

1. The poem names the homeless woman as Miss Rosie. What is the significance of the speaker's knowing Miss Rosie's name? Of the speaker knowing that the homeless woman was once called the "Georgia Rose"?
2. This poem does not have any punctuation except for one comma. How do the line breaks (where each line ends) help control the feeling of the poem?
3. The speaker watches Miss Rosie and sees the conditions in which Miss Rosie is living. These conditions, however, do not make the speaker lose respect for Miss Rosie. Why not?
4. The poem ends with the speaker saying "I stand up / through your destruction / I stand up." What do you think these statements mean? Why do you think the speaker feels this way about Miss Rosie's situation?

WRITING TOPICS

1. Write an entry in your journal in which you discuss your reactions to homeless people. How do they make you feel? What do you think about them?

2. Imagine Miss Rosie is a homeless woman you have befriended. Using information from the poem, write a letter to your city council in which you argue for a new shelter and a work program for the homeless.
3. In an essay, compare and contrast Clifton's use of the phrase "stand up" with Angelou's use of the phrases "I keep on movin'," "I keep on followin'," and "I keep comin'" in the poem "Willie." Do the phrases of Clifton's and Angelou's poems mean the same thing? Why or why not?

CHAPTER SIX

IDENTITY

Identity is not something given to us; it is something we develop as we live. Identity comes from knowledge of oneself. Knowledge of one's hopes and aspirations. Knowledge of one's capabilities and limitations. Identity is also shaped by our knowledge of the world in which we live.

Unlike people who chose to emigrate to this continent, from 1619 until 1808 (when the slave trade was abolished in the United States), black people were brought here against their will as slaves. They were identified by their skin color as less than human, and for more than two hundred years, they and their descendants were treated as property to be used. After the Civil War, no one could actually own another person, but this did not mean that blacks were automatically given the same rights or seen as equals by whites. It is impossible to comprehend fully the psychological impact on blacks. However, as can be seen in black folktales and African-American literature, blacks did not give up their humanity or their sense of self-worth. African-American literature often focuses on an individual black person who is learning to make his or her way in the world and coming to a sense of self.

In African-American communities, identity is often shaped by knowledge of one's ancestors and cultural practices. As a group of people, African Americans have survived slavery, injustice, and inequality by celebrating survival and the promise of tomorrow. Sometimes it hurts to see how outside forces have helped make them who they are. But instead of letting this pain overwhelm them, knowledge of their identity can make African Americans stronger and make them believe in what they can do as individuals.

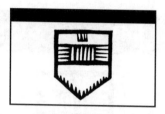

WE WEAR THE MASK

Paul Laurence Dunbar

Paul Laurence Dunbar was born in 1872 in Dayton, Ohio. He began writing verse as a youth and held several positions in high school—editor-in-chief of the school newspaper, president of the literary society, and class poet. Dunbar was the first African-American poet to win national recognition and acceptance by the larger American public. He sold his first book of poems, *Oak and Ivy*, in 1893. He published *Majors and Minors* in 1895 and in 1896, *Lyrics of Lowly Life*, which became an instant success. His poems and short stories appeared in many American magazines. He wrote poems in both standard American English (which he called *major*) and in dialect (which he called *minor*). He wrote the *minor* poems in dialect as a way to get his works published. Although these poems were well received by white Americans, they, in effect, confirmed many stereotypes about African Americans. Dunbar is best known today for his major poems written in standard English. He wrote numerous stories and four novels before he died at the age of thirty-four in 1906.

We wear the mask that grins and lies,
It hides our cheeks and shades our eyes,—
This debt we pay to human guile;
With torn and bleeding hearts we smile,
5   And mouth with myriad subtleties.

Why should the world be over-wise,
In counting all our tears and sighs?
Nay, let them only see us, while
  We wear the mask.

10 We smile, but, O great Christ, our cries
To thee from tortured souls arise.
We sing, but oh, the clay is vile
Beneath our feet, and long the mile;
But let the world dream otherwise,
15 We wear the mask.

DISCUSSION QUESTIONS

1. For whom is the poet speaking in "We Wear the Mask"?
2. How important is it for wearers of masks to "let the world dream otherwise" about their true feelings?
3. Do you know people who wear masks? What do these masks usually hide?

WRITING TOPICS

1. Can it be helpful to wear a mask? In your writing journal, write a short essay on the usefulness of masks, if any.
2. Dunbar wrote this poem after slavery was abolished in America. Write an essay describing how "wearing masks" by African Americans from the Reconstruction period through the 1950s might have saved many of them from humiliation and, in many cases, from violence.

FROM *THE AUTOBIOGRAPHY OF MALCOLM X*

Malcolm X with Alex Haley

Malcolm X was born Malcolm Little in Omaha, Nebraska, in 1925. His early years were filled with poverty, despair, and illness. When he was 21, he was imprisoned in a Massachusetts State Prison. While in prison, he studied the teaching of the Nation of Islam and eventually became a Black Muslim. Malcolm was an excellent speaker, especially in espousing the theories of the Nation of Islam. He became second in command to Elijah Muhammad, then leader of the Black Muslim organization and became the group's best-known spokesperson. After a pilgrimage to Mecca in 1964, Malcolm X withdrew from the separatist organization and began stressing a broader humanistic point of view. A number of his speeches have been collected and published in several volumes: *Malcolm X Speaks* (1965), edited by George Breitman, and *The Speeches of Malcolm X at Harvard* (1968), edited by Archie Epps. He was assassinated in 1965 while speaking at a rally in New York City's Harlem.

1   My father, the Reverend Earl Little, was a Baptist minister, a dedicated organizer for Marcus Aurelius Garvey's U.N.I.A. (Universal Negro Improvement Association). With the help of such disciples as my father, Garvey, from his headquarters in New York City's Harlem, was raising the banner of black-race purity and exhorting the Negro masses to return to their ancestral African homeland—a cause which had made Garvey the most controversial black man on earth.

2   Still shouting threats, the Klansmen finally spurred their horses and galloped around the house, shattering every window pane with their gun butts. Then they rode off into the night, their torches flaring, as suddenly as they had come.

3   My father was enraged when he returned. He decided to wait until I was

born—which would be soon—and then the family would move. I am not sure why he made this decision, for he was not a frightened Negro, as most then were, and many still are today. My father was a big, six-foot-four, very black man. He had only one eye. How he had lost the other one I have never known. He was from Reynolds, Georgia, where he had left school after the third or maybe fourth grade. He believed, as did Marcus Garvey, that freedom, independence and self-respect could never be achieved by the Negro in America, and that therefore the Negro should leave America to the white man and return to his African land of origin. Among the reasons my father had decided to risk and dedicate his life to help disseminate this philosophy among his people was that he had seen four of his six brothers die by violence, three of them killed by white men, including one by lynching. What my father could not know then was that of the remaining three, including himself, only one, my Uncle Jim, would die in bed, of natural causes. Northern white police were later to shoot my Uncle Oscar. And my father was finally himself to die by the white man's hands.

4   It has always been my belief that I, too, will die by violence. I have done all that I can to be prepared. . . .

5   One afternoon in 1931 when Wilfred, Hilda, Philbert, and I came home, my mother and father were having one of their arguments. There had lately been a lot of tension around the house because of Black Legion threats. Anyway, my father had taken one of the rabbits which we were raising, and ordered my mother to cook it. We raised rabbits, but sold them to whites. My father had taken a rabbit from the rabbit pen. He had pulled off the rabbit's head. He was so strong, he needed no knife to behead chickens or rabbits. With one twist of his big black hands he simply twisted off the head and threw the bleeding-necked thing back at my mother's feet.

6   My mother was crying. She started to skin the rabbit, preparatory to cooking it. But my father was so angry he slammed on out of the front door and started walking up the road toward town.

7   It was then that my mother had this vision. She had always been a strange woman in this sense, and had always had a strong intuition of things about to happen. And most of her children are the same way, I think. When something is about to happen, I can feel something, sense something. I never have known something to happen that has caught me completely off guard—except once. And that was when, years later, I discovered facts I couldn't believe about a man who, up until that discovery, I would gladly have given my life for.

8   My father was well up the road when my mother ran screaming out onto the porch. *"Early! Early!"* She screamed his name. She clutched up her apron in one hand, and ran down across the yard and into the road. My father turned around. He saw her. For some reason, considering how angry he had been when he left, he waved at her. But he kept on going.

9   She told me later, my mother did, that she had a vision of my father's

end. All the rest of the afternoon, she was not herself, crying and nervous and upset. She finished cooking the rabbit and put the whole thing in the warmer part of the black stove. When my father was not back home by our bedtime, my mother hugged and clutched us, and we felt strange, not knowing what to do, because she had never acted like that.

10   I remember waking up to the sound of my mother's screaming again. When I scrambled out, I saw the police in the living room; they were trying to calm her down. She had snatched on her clothes to go with them. And all of us children who were staring knew without anyone having to say it that something terrible had happened to our father.

11   My mother was taken by the police to the hospital, and to a room where a sheet was over my father in a bed, and she wouldn't look, she was afraid to look. Probably it was wise that she didn't. My father's skull, on one side, was crushed in, I was told later. Negroes in Lansing have always whispered that he was attacked, and then laid across some tracks for a streetcar to run over him. His body was cut almost in half.

12   He lived two and a half hours in that condition. Negroes then were stronger than they are now, especially Georgia Negroes. Negroes born in Georgia had to be strong simply to survive.

13   It was morning when we children at home got the word that he was dead. I was six, I can remember a vague commotion, the house filled up with people crying, saying bitterly that the white Black Legion had finally gotten him. My mother was hysterical. In the bedroom, women were holding smelling salts under her nose. She was still hysterical at the funeral.

14   I don't have a very clear memory of the funeral, either. Oddly, the main thing I remember is that it wasn't in a church, and that surprised me, since my father was a preacher, and I had been where he preached people's funerals in churches. But his was in a funeral home.

15   And I remember that during the service a big black fly came down and landed on my father's face, and Wilfred sprang up from his chair and he shooed the fly away, and he came groping back to his chair—there were folding chairs for us to sit on—and the tears were streaming down his face. When we went by the casket, I remember that I thought that it looked as if my father's strong black face had been dusted with flour, and I wished they hadn't put on such a lot of it.

16   Back in the big four-room house, there were many visitors for another week or so. They were good friends of the family, such as the Lyons from Mason, twelve miles away, and the Walkers, McGuires, Liscoes, the Greens, Randolphs, and the Turners, and others from Lansing, and a lot of people from other towns, whom I had seen at the Garvey meetings.

17   We children adjusted more easily than our mother did. We couldn't see, as clearly as she did, the trials that lay ahead. As the visitors tapered off, she became very concerned about collecting the two insurance policies that my father had always been proud he carried. He had always said that families should be protected in case of death. One policy apparently

paid off without any problem—the smaller one. I don't know the amount of it. I would imagine it was not more than a thousand dollars, and maybe half of that.

18   But after that money came, and my mother had paid out a lot of it for the funeral and expenses, she began going into town and returning very upset. The company that had issued the bigger policy was balking at paying off. They were claiming that my father had committed suicide. Visitors came again, and there was bitter talk about white people: how could my father bash himself in the head, then get down across the streetcar tracks to be run over?

19   So there we were. My mother was thirty-four years old now, with no husband, no provider or protector to take care of her eight children. But some kind of a family routine got going again. And for as long as the first insurance money lasted, we did all right.

20   Wilfred, who was a pretty stable fellow, began to act older than his age. I think he had the sense to see, when the rest of us didn't, what was in the wind for us. He quietly quit school and went to town in search of work. He took any kind of job he could find and he would come home, dog-tired, in the evenings, and give whatever he had made to my mother.

21   Hilda, who always had been quiet, too, attended to the babies. Philbert and I didn't contribute anything. We just fought all the time—each other at home, and then at school we would team up and fight white kids. Sometimes the fights would be racial in nature, but they might be about anything.

22   Reginald came under my wing. Since he had grown out of the toddling stage, he and I had become very close. I suppose I enjoyed the fact that he was the little one, under me, who looked up to me.

23   My mother began to buy on credit. My father had always been very strongly against credit. "Credit is the first step into debt and back into slavery," he had always said. And then she went to work herself. She would go into Lansing and find different jobs—in housework, or sewing—for white people. They didn't realize, usually, that she was a Negro. A lot of white people around there didn't want Negroes in their houses.

24   She would do fine until in some way or other it got to people who she was, whose widow she was. And then she would be let go. I remember how she used to come home crying, but trying to hide it, because she had lost a job that she needed so much.

25   Once when one of us—I cannot remember which—had to go for something to where she was working, and the people saw us, and realized she was actually a Negro, she was fired on the spot, and she came home crying, this time not hiding it.

26   When the state Welfare people began coming to our house, we would come from school sometimes and find them talking with our mother, asking a thousand questions. They acted and looked at her, and at us, and around in our house, in a way that had about it the feeling—at least for me—that we were not people. In their eyesight we were just *things*, that was all.

27   My mother began to receive two checks—a Welfare check and, I believe, a widow's pension. The checks helped. But they weren't enough, as many of us as there were. When they came, about the first of the month, one always was already owed in full, if not more, to the man at the grocery store. And, after that, the other one didn't last long.

28   We began to go swiftly downhill. The physical downhill wasn't as quick as the psychological. My mother was, above everything else, a proud woman, and it took its toll on her that she was accepting charity. And her feelings were communicated to us.

29   She would speak sharply to the man at the grocery store for padding the bill, telling him that she wasn't ignorant, and he didn't like that. She would talk back sharply to the state Welfare people, telling them that she was a grown woman, able to raise her children, that it wasn't necessary for them to keep coming around so much, meddling in our lives. And they didn't like that.

30   But the monthly Welfare check was their pass. They acted as if they owned us, as if we were their private property. As much as my mother would have liked to, she couldn't keep them out. She would get particularly incensed when they began insisting upon drawing us older children aside, one at a time, out on the porch or somewhere, and asking us questions, or telling us things—against our mother and against each other.

31   We couldn't understand why, if the state was willing to give us packages of meat, sacks of potatoes and fruit, and cans of all kinds of things, our mother obviously hated to accept. We really couldn't understand. What I later understood was that my mother was making a desperate effort to preserve her pride—and ours.

32   Pride was just about all we had to preserve, for by 1934, we really began to suffer. This was about the worst depression year, and no one we knew had enough to eat or live on. Some old family friends visited us now and then. At first they brought food. Though it was charity, my mother took it.

33   Wilfred was working to help. My mother was working, when she could find any kind of job. In Lansing, there was a bakery where, for a nickel, a couple of us children would buy a tall flour sack of day-old bread and cookies, and then walk the two miles back out into the country to our house. Our mother knew, I guess, dozens of ways to cook things with bread and out of bread. Stewed tomatoes with bread, maybe that would be a meal. Something like French toast, if we had any eggs. Bread pudding, sometimes with raisins in it. If we got hold of some hamburger, it came to the table more bread than meat. The cookies that were always in the sack with the bread, we just gobbled down straight.

34   But there were times when there wasn't even a nickel and we would be so hungry we would be dizzy. My mother would boil a big pot of dandelion greens, and we would eat that. I remember that some small-minded neighbor put it out, and children would tease us, that we ate "fried grass."

Sometimes, if we were lucky, we would have oatmeal or cornmeal mush three times a day. Or mush in the morning and cornbread at night.

35   Philbert and I were grown up enough to quit fighting long enough to take the .22 caliber rifle that had been our father's, and shoot rabbits that some white neighbors up or down the road would buy. I know now that they just did it to help us, because they, like everyone, shot their own rabbits. Sometimes, I remember, Philbert and I would take little Reginald along with us. He wasn't very strong, but he was always so proud to be along. We would trap muskrats out in the little creek in back of our house. And we would lie quiet until unsuspecting bullfrogs appeared, and we could spear them, cut off their legs, and sell them for a nickel a pair to people who lived up and down the road. The whites seemed less restricted in their dietary tastes.

36   Then, about in late 1934, I would guess, something began to happen. Some kind of psychological deterioration hit our family circle and began to eat away our pride. Perhaps it was the constant tangible evidence that we were destitute. We had known other families who had gone on relief. We had known without anyone in our home ever expressing it that we had felt prouder not to be at the depot where the free food was passed out. And, now, we were among them. At school, the "on relief" finger suddenly was pointed at us, too, and sometimes it was said aloud.

37   It seemed that everything to eat in our house was stamped Not To Be Sold. All Welfare food bore this stamp to keep the recipients from selling it. It's a wonder we didn't come to think of Not To Be Sold as a brand name.

38   Sometimes, instead of going home from school, I walked the two miles up the road into Lansing. I began drifting from store to store, hanging around outside where things like apples were displayed in boxes and barrels and baskets, and I would watch my chance and steal me a treat. You know what a treat was to me? Anything!

39   Or I began to drop in about dinnertime at the home of some family that we knew. I knew that they knew exactly why I was there, but they never embarrassed me by letting on. They would invite me to stay for supper, and I would stuff myself.

40   Especially, I liked to drop in and visit at the Gohannas' home. They were nice, older people, and great churchgoers. I had watched them lead the jumping and shouting when my father preached. They had, living with them—they were raising him—a nephew whom everyone called "Big Boy," and he and I got along fine. Also living with the Gohannas was old Mrs. Adcock, who went with them to church. She was always trying to help anybody she could, visiting anyone she heard was sick, carrying them something. She was the one who, years later, would tell me something that I remembered a long time: "Malcolm, there's one thing I like about you. You're no good, but you don't try to hide it. You are not a hypocrite."

41   The more I began to stay away from home and visit people and steal from the stores, the more aggressive I became in my inclinations. I never wanted to wait for anything.

42   I was growing up fast, physically more so than mentally. As I began to be recognized more around the town, I started to become aware of the peculiar attitude of white people toward me. I sensed that it had to do with my father. It was an adult version of what several white children had said at school, in hints, or sometimes in the open, which really expressed what their parents had said—that the Black Legion or the Klan had killed my father, and the insurance company had pulled a fast one in refusing to pay my mother the policy money.

43   When I began to get caught stealing now and then, the state Welfare people began to focus on me when they came to our house. I can't remember how I first became aware that they were talking of taking me away. What I first remember along that line was my mother raising a storm about being able to bring up her own children. She would whip me for stealing, and I would try to alarm the neighborhood with my yelling. One thing I have always been proud of is that I never raised my hand against my mother.

44   In the summertime, at night, in addition to all the other things we did, some of us boys would slip out down the road, or across the pastures, and go "cooning" watermelons. White people always associated watermelons with Negroes, and they sometimes called Negroes "coons" among all the other names, and so stealing watermelons became "cooning" them. If white boys were doing it, it implied that they were only acting like Negroes. Whites have always hidden or justified all of the guilts they could by ridiculing or blaming Negroes.

45   One Halloween night, I remember that a bunch of us were out tipping over those old country outhouses, and one old farmer—I guess he had tipped over enough in his day—had set a trap for us. Always, you sneak up from behind the outhouse, then you gang together and push it, to tip it over. This farmer had taken his outhouse off the hole, and set it just in *front* of the hole. Well, we came sneaking up in single file, in the darkness, and the two white boys in the lead fell down into the outhouse hole neck deep. They smelled so bad it was all we could stand to get them out, and that finished us all for that Halloween. I had just missed falling in myself. The whites were so used to taking the lead, this time it had really gotten them in the hole.

46   Thus, in various ways, I learned various things. I picked strawberries, and though I can't recall what I got per crate for picking, I remember that after working hard all one day, I wound up with about a dollar, which was a whole lot of money in those times. I was so hungry, I didn't know what to do. I was walking away toward town with visions of buying something good to eat, and this older white boy I knew, Richard Dixon, came up and asked me if I wanted to match nickels. He had plenty of change for my dollar. In about a half hour, he had all the change back, including my dollar, and instead of going to town to buy something, I went home with nothing, and I was bitter. But that was nothing compared to what I felt when I found out later that he had cheated. There is a way that you can catch and hold the nickel and make it come up, the way you want. This was my first lesson

about gambling: if you see somebody winning all the time, he isn't gambling, he's cheating. Later on in life, if I were continuously losing in any gambling situation, I would watch very closely. It's like the Negro in America seeing the white man win all the time. He's a professional gambler; he has all the cards and the odds stacked on his side, and he has always dealt to our people from the bottom of the deck.

47   About this time, my mother began to be visited by some Seventh Day Adventists who had moved into a house not too far down the road from us. They would talk to her for hours at a time, and leave booklets and leaflets and magazines for her to read. She read them, and Wilfred who had started back to school after we had begun to get the relief food supplies, also read a lot. His head was forever in some book.

48   Before long, my mother spent much time with the Adventists. It's my belief that what influenced her was that they had even more diet restrictions than she always had taught and practiced with us. Like us, they were against eating rabbit and pork; they followed the Mosaic dietary laws. They ate nothing of the flesh without a split hoof, or that didn't chew a cud. We began to go with my mother to the Adventist meetings that were held further out in the country. For us children, I know that the major attraction was the good food they served. But we listened, too. There were a handful of Negroes, from small towns in the area, but I would say that it was ninety-nine percent white people. The Adventists felt that we were living at the end of time, that the world soon was coming to an end. But they were the friendliest white people I had ever seen. In some ways, though, we children noticed, and, when we were back at home, discussed, that they were different from us—such as the lack of enough seasoning in their food, and the different way that white people smelled.

49   Meanwhile, the state Welfare people kept after my mother. By now, she didn't make it any secret that she hated them, and didn't want them in her house. But they exerted their right to come, and I have many, many times reflected upon how, talking to us children, they began to plant the seeds of division in our minds. They would ask such things as who was smarter than the other. And they would ask me why I was "so different."

50   I think they felt that getting children into foster homes was a legitimate part of their function, and the result would be less troublesome, however they went about it.

51   And when my mother fought them, they went after her—first, through me. I was the first target. I stole; that implied that I wasn't being taken care of by my mother.

52   All of us were mischievous at some time or another, I more so than any of the rest. Philbert and I kept a battle going. And this was just one of a dozen things that kept building up the pressure on my mother.

53   I'm not sure just how or when the idea was first dropped by the Welfare workers that our mother was losing her mind.

54   But I can distinctly remember hearing "crazy" applied to her by them when they learned that the Negro farmer who was in the next house down the road from us had offered to give us some butchered pork—a whole pig, maybe even two of them—and she had refused. We all heard them call my mother "crazy" to her face for refusing good meat. It meant nothing to them even when she explained that we had never eaten pork, that it was against her religion as a Seventh Day Adventist.

55   They were as vicious as vultures. They had no feelings, understanding, compassion, or respect for my mother. They told us, "She's crazy for refusing food." Right then was when our home, our unity, began to disintegrate. We were having a hard time, and I wasn't helping. But we could have made it, we could have stayed together. As bad as I was, as much trouble and worry as I caused my mother, I loved her.

56   The state people, we found out, had interviewed the Gohannas family, and the Gohannas' had said that they would take me into their home. My mother threw a fit, though, when she heard that—and the home wreckers took cover for a while.

57   It was about this time that the large, dark man from Lansing began visiting. I don't remember how or where he and my mother met. It may have been through some mutual friends. I don't remember what the man's profession was. In 1935, in Lansing, Negroes didn't have anything you could call a profession. But the man, big and black, looked something like my father. I can remember his name, but there's no need to mention it. He was a single man, and my mother was a widow only thirty-six years old. The man was independent; naturally she admired that. She was having a hard time disciplining us, and a big man's presence alone would help. And if she had a man to provide, it would send the state people away forever.

58   We all understood without ever saying much about it. Or at least we had no objection. We took it in stride, even with some amusement among us, that when the man came, our mother would be all dressed up in the best that she had—she still was a good-looking woman—and she would act differently, lighthearted and laughing, as we hadn't seen her act in years.

59   It went on for about a year, I guess. And then, about 1936, or 1937, the man from Lansing jilted my mother suddenly. He just stopped coming to see her. From what I later understood, he finally backed away from taking on the responsibility of those eight mouths to feed. He was afraid of so many of us. To this day, I can see the trap that Mother was in, saddled with all of us. And I can also understand why he would shun taking on such a tremendous responsibility.

60   But it was a terrible shock to her. It was the beginning of the end of reality for my mother. When she began to sit around and walk around talking to herself—almost as though she were unaware that we were there—it became increasingly terrifying.

61   The state people saw her weakening. That was when they began the definite steps to take me away from home. They began to tell me how nice it was going to be at the Gohannas' home where the Gohannas' and Big Boy

and Mrs. Adcock had all said how much they liked me, and would like to have me live with them.

62   I liked all of them, too. But I didn't want to leave Wilfred. I looked up to and admired my big brother. I didn't want to leave Hilda, who was like my second mother. Or Philbert; even in our fighting, there was a feeling of brotherly union. Or Reginald, especially, who was weak with his hernia condition, and who looked up to me as his big brother who looked out for him, as I looked up to Wilfred. And I had nothing, either, against the babies, Yvonne, Wesley, and Robert.

63   As my mother talked to herself more and more, she gradually became less responsive to us. And less responsible. The house became less tidy. We began to be more unkempt. And usually, now, Hilda cooked.

64   We children watched our anchor giving way. It was something terrible that you couldn't get your hands on, yet you couldn't get away from. It was a sensing that something bad was going to happen. We younger ones leaned more and more heavily on the relative strength of Wilfred and Hilda, who were the oldest.

65   When finally I was sent to the Gohannas' home, at least in a surface way I was glad. I remember that when I left home with the state man, my mother said one thing: "Don't let them feed him any pig."

66   It was better, in a lot of ways, at the Gohannas'. Big Boy and I shared his room together, and we hit it off nicely. He just wasn't the same as my blood brothers. The Gohannas' were very religious people. Big Boy and I attended church with them. They were sanctified Holy Rollers now. The preachers and congregations jumped even higher and shouted even louder than the Baptists I had known. They sang at the top of their lungs, and swayed back and forth and cried and moaned and beat on tambourines and chanted. It was spooky, with ghosts and spirituals and "ha'nts" seeming to be in the very atmosphere when finally we all came out of the church, going back home.

67   The Gohannas' and Mrs. Adcock loved to go fishing, and some Saturdays Big Boy and I would go along. I had changed schools now, to Lansing's West Junior High School. It was right in the heart of the Negro community, and a few white kids were there, but Big Boy didn't mix much with any of our schoolmates, and I didn't either. And when we went fishing, neither he nor I liked the idea of just sitting and waiting for the fish to jerk the cork under the water—or make the tight line quiver, when we fished that way. I figured there should be some smarter way to get the fish—though we never discovered what it might be.

68   Mr. Gohannas was close cronies with some other men who, some Saturdays, would take me and Big Boy with them hunting rabbits. I had my father's .22 caliber rifle; my mother had said it was all right for me to take it with me. The old men had a set rabbit-hunting strategy that they had always used. Usually when a dog jumps a rabbit, and the rabbit gets away, that rabbit will always somehow instinctively run in a circle and return sooner or later past the very spot where he originally was jumped. Well, the old men

would just sit and wait in hiding somewhere for the rabbit to come back, then get their shots at him. I got to thinking about it, and finally I thought of a plan. I would separate from them and Big Boy and I would go to a point where I figured that the rabbit, returning, would have to pass me first.

69   It worked like magic. I began to get three and four rabbits before they got one. The astonishing thing was that none of the old men ever figured out why. They outdid themselves exclaiming what a sure shot I was. I was about twelve, then. All I had done was to improve on their strategy, and it was the beginning of a very important lesson in life—that anytime you find someone more successful than you are, especially when you're both engaged in the same business—you know they're doing something that you aren't.

70   I would return home to visit fairly often. Sometimes Big Boy and one or another, or both, of the Gohannas' would go with me—sometimes not. I would be glad when some of them did go, because it made the ordeal easier.

71   Soon the state people were making plans to take over all of my mother's children. She talked to herself nearly all of the time now, and there was a crowd of new white people entering the picture—always asking questions. They would even visit me at the Gohannas'. They would ask me questions out on the porch, or sitting out in their cars.

72   Eventually my mother suffered a complete breakdown, and the court orders were finally signed. They took her to the State Mental Hospital at Kalamazoo.

73   It was seventy-some miles from Lansing, about an hour and a half on the bus. A Judge McClellan in Lansing had authority over me and all of my brothers and sisters. We were "state children," court wards; he had the full say-so over us. A white man in charge of a black man's children! Nothing but legal, modern slavery—however kindly intentioned.

74   My mother remained in the same hospital at Kalamazoo for about twenty-six years. Later, when I was still growing up in Michigan, I would go to visit her every so often. Nothing that I can imagine could have moved me as deeply as seeing her pitiful state. In 1963, we got my mother out of the hospital, and she now lives there in Lansing with Philbert and his family.

75   It was so much worse than if it had been a physical sickness, for which a cause might be known, medicine given, a cure effected. Every time I visited her, when finally they led her—a case, a number—back inside from where we had been sitting together, I felt worse.

76   My last visit, when I knew I would never come to see her again—there—was in 1952. I was twenty-seven. My brother Philbert had told me that on his last visit, she had recognized him somewhat. "In spots," he said.

77   But she didn't recognize me at all.

78   She stared at me. She didn't know who I was.

79   Her mind, when I tried to talk, to reach her, was somewhere else. I asked, "Mama, do you know what day it is?"

80 She said, staring, "All the people have gone."

81 I can't describe how I felt. The woman who had brought me into the world, and nursed me, and advised me, and chastised me, and loved me, didn't know me. It was as if I was trying to walk up the side of a hill of feathers. I looked at her. I listened to her "talk." But there was nothing I could do.

82 I truly believe that if ever a state social agency destroyed a family, it destroyed ours. We wanted and tried to stay together. Our home didn't have to be destroyed. But the Welfare, the courts, and their doctor, gave us the one-two-three punch. And ours was not the only case of this kind.

83 I knew I wouldn't be back to see my mother again because it could make me a very vicious and dangerous person—knowing how they had looked at us as numbers and as a case in their book, not as human beings. And knowing that my mother in there was a statistic that didn't have to be, that existed because of a society's failure, hypocrisy, greed, and lack of mercy and compassion. Hence I have no mercy or compassion in me for a society that will crush people, and then penalize them for not being able to stand up under the weight.

84 I have rarely talked to anyone about my mother, for I believe that I am capable of killing a person, without hesitation, who happened to make the wrong kind of remark about my mother. So I purposely don't make any opening for some fool to step into.

85 Back then when our family was destroyed, in 1937, Wilfred and Hilda were old enough so that the state let them stay on their own in the big four-room house that my father had built. Philbert was placed with another family in Lansing, a Mrs. Hackett, while Reginald and Wesley went to live with a family called Williams, who were friends of my mother's. And Yvonne and Robert went to live with a West Indian family named McGuire.

86 Separated though we were, all of us maintained fairly close touch around Lansing—in school and out—whenever we could get together. Despite the artificially created separation and distance between us, we still remained very close in our feelings toward each other.

DISCUSSION QUESTIONS

1. How would you describe Malcolm's father? Why do you think he was the kind of person he was?
2. After his father's death, Malcolm says of his mother, "We couldn't see, as clearly as she did, the trials that lay ahead." What do you think he meant by this statement? Cite some examples from the selection.
3. Malcolm X sensed that he would someday die a violent death, as his father did. Cite some specific examples from the reading that support his prognostication.

WRITING TOPICS

1. Consider the following quotation: "Credit is the first step into debt and back into slavery." This statement is attributed to Malcolm's father. Compare the Little's family life with credit with Jeff and Jennie's life as sharecroppers in Arna Bontemps' "A Summer Tragedy." In an essay, explore the similarities and differences between slavery and enforced indebtedness.

2. Malcolm X became a leader in the Black Muslim separatist religion. The Nation of Islam was founded in Detroit in 1930. Its members follow the Islamic religion and advocate economic cooperation and self-sufficiency. In your journal, list specific references from the reading showing how Malcolm X's childhood experiences helped forge his identity as a spokesperson for the original Nation of Islam.

HIDDEN NAME AND COMPLEX FATE

Ralph Ellison

Ralph Ellison was born in Oklahoma City, Oklahoma, in 1914. He won a scholarship and studied music for three years at the Tuskegee Institute in Alabama. He left before graduating and went to New York in 1936, intending to become a sculptor; however, his interests soon turned to literature. He met Richard Wright and Langston Hughes while working for the Federal Writers Project. Ellison and Wright became good friends and Wright encouraged him in his writing. He served briefly as editor of *Negro Quarterly* and received a Rosenwald Fellowship following his tour of duty with the Merchant Marines during World War II. He published *Invisible Man* in 1952. His first and only novel received wide acclaim, winning the National Book Award for fiction in 1953. A collection of his essays, *Shadow and Act*, was published in 1964. Ellison was a professor at New York University during the 1970s. He died in 1994.

1   In *Green Hills of Africa*, Ernest Hemingway reminds us that both Tolstoy and Stendhal had seen war, that Flaubert had seen a revolution and the Commune, that Dostoievsky had been sent to Siberia and that such experiences were important in shaping the art of these great masters. And he goes on to observe that "writers are forged in injustice as a sword is forged." He declined to describe the many personal forms which injustice may take in this chaotic world—who would be so mad as to try?—nor does he go into the personal wounds which each of these writers sustained. Now, however, thanks to his brother and sister, we do know something of the injustice in which he himself was forged, and his knowledge has been added to what we have long known of Hemingway's artistic temper.

2   In the end, however, it is the quality of his art which is primary. It is the art which allows the wars and revolutions which he knew, and the personal

and social injustice which he suffered, to lay claims upon our attention; for it was through his art that they achieved their most enduring meaning. It is a matter of outrageous irony, perhaps, but in literature the great social clashes of history no less than the painful experience of the individual are secondary to the meaning which they take on through the skill, the talent, the imagination and personal vision of the writer who transforms them into art. Here they are reduced to more manageable proportions; here they are imbued with humane values; here, injustice and catastrophe become less important in themselves than what the writer makes of them. This is *not* true, however, of the writer's struggle with that recalcitrant angel called Art; and it was through *this* specific struggle that Ernest Hemingway became *Hemingway* (now refined to a total body of transcendent work, after forty years of being endlessly dismembered and resurrected, as it continues to be, in the styles, and themes, the sense of life and literature of countless other writers). And it was through this struggle with form that he became the master, the culture hero, whom we have come to know and admire.

3   It was suggested that it might be of interest if I discussed here this evening some of my notions of the writer's experience in the United States, hence I have evoked the name of Hemingway, not by way of inviting far-fetched comparisons but in order to establish a perspective, a set of assumptions from which I may speak, and in an attempt to avoid boring you in emphasizing those details of racial hardship which for some forty years now have been evoked whenever writers of my own cultural background have essayed their experience in public.

4   I do this *not* by way of denying totally the validity of these by now stylized recitals, for I have shared and still share many of their detailed injustices—what Negro can escape them?—but by way of suggesting that they are, at least in a discussion of a writer's experience, as *writer*, as artist, somewhat beside the point.

5   For we select neither our parents, our race nor our nation; these occur to us out of the love, the hate, the circumstances, the fate, of others. But we *do* become writers out of an act of will, out of an act of choice; a dim, confused and ofttimes regrettable choice, perhaps, but choice nevertheless. And what happens thereafter causes all those experiences which occurred before we began to function as writers to take on a special quality of uniqueness. If this does not happen then as far as writing goes, the experiences have been misused. If we do not make of them a value, if we do not transform them into forms and images of meaning which they did not possess before, then we have failed as artists.

6   Thus for a writer to insist that his personal suffering is of special interest in itself, or simply because he belongs to a particular racial or religious group, is to advance a claim for special privileges which members of his group who are not writers would be ashamed to demand. The kindest judgment one can make of this point of view is that it reveals a sad misunderstanding of the relationship between suffering and art. Thomas Mann and André Gide have told us much of this and there are critics, like Edmund

Wilson, who have told of the connection between the wound and the bow.

7   As I see it, it is through the process of making artistic forms—plays, poems, novels—out of one's experience that one becomes a writer, and it is through this process, this struggle, that the writer helps give meaning to the experience of the group. And it is the process of mastering the discipline, the techniques, the fortitude, the culture, through which this is made possible that constitutes the writer's real experience as *writer*, as artist. If this sounds like an argument for the artist's withdrawal from social struggles, I would recall to you W. H. Auden's comment to the effect that:

> In our age, the mere making of a work of art is itself a politi-
> cal act. So long as artists exist, making what they please, and think
> they ought to make, even if it is not terribly good, even if it
> appeals to only a handful of people, they remind the Management
> of something managers need to be reminded of, namely, that the
> managed are people with faces, not anonymous members, that
> *Homo Laborans* is also *Homo Ludens*. . . .

8   Without doubt, even the most *engagé* writer—and I refer to true artists, not to artists *manqués*—begin their careers in play and puzzlement, in dreaming over the details of the world in which they become conscious of themselves.

9   Let Tar Baby, that enigmatic figure from Negro folklore, stand for the world. He leans, black and gleaming, against the wall of life utterly non-committal under our scrutiny, our questioning, starkly unmoving before our naive attempts at intimidation. Then we touch him playfully and before we can say *Sonny Liston!* we find ourselves stuck. Our playful investigations become a labor, a fearful struggle, an *agon*. Slowly we perceive that our task is to learn the proper way of freeing ourselves to develop, in other words, technique.

10   Sensing this, we give him our sharpest attention, we question him care-fully, we struggle with more subtlety; while he, in his silent way, holds on, demanding that we perceive the necessity of calling him by his true name as the price of our freedom. It is unfortunate that he has so many, many "true names"—all spelling chaos; and in order to discover even one of these we must first come into the possession of our own names. For it is through our names that we first place ourselves in the world. Our names, being the gift of others, must be made our own.

11   Once while listening to the play of a two-year-old girl who did not know she was under observation, I heard her saying over and over again, at first with questioning and then with sounds of growing satisfaction, "I am Mimi Livisay? . . . *I* am Mimi Livisay. I *am* Mimi Livisay . . . I am *Mimi* Li-vi-say! I am Mimi . . ."

12   And in deed and in fact she was—or became so soon thereafter, by work-ing playfully to establish the unity between herself and her name.

13   For many of us this is far from easy. We must learn to wear our names within all the noise and confusion of the environment in which we find ourselves; make them the center of all of our associations with the world, with man and with nature. We must charge them with all our emotions, our hopes, hates, loves, aspirations. They must become our masks and our shields and the containers of all those values and traditions which we learn and/or imagine as being the meaning of our familial past.

14   And when we are reminded so constantly that we bear, as Negroes, names originally possessed by those who owned our enslaved grandparents, we are apt, especially if we are potential writers, to be more than ordinarily concerned with the veiled and mysterious events, the fusions of blood, the furtive couplings, the business transactions, the violations of faith and loyalty, the assaults; yes, and the unrecognized and unrecognizable loves through which our names were handed down unto us.

15   So charged with emotion does this concern become for some of us, that we have, earlier, the example of the followers of Father Divine and, now, the Black Muslims, discarding their original names in rejection of the blood-stained, the brutal, the sinful images of the past. Thus they would declare new identities, would clarify a new program of intention and destroy the verbal evidence of a willed and ritualized discontinuity of blood and human intercourse.

16   Not all of us, actually only a few, seek to deal with our names in this manner. We take what we have and make of them what we can. And there are even those who know where the old broken connections lie, who recognize their relatives across the chasm of historical denial and the artificial barriers of society, and who see themselves as bearers of many of the qualities which were admirable in the original sources of their common line (Faulkner has made much of this); and I speak here not of mere forgiveness, nor of obsequious insensitivity to the outrages symbolized by the denial and the division, but of the conscious acceptance of the harsh realities of the human condition, of the ambiguities and hypocrisies of human history as they have played themselves out in the United States.

17   Perhaps, taken in aggregate, these European names which (sometimes with irony, sometimes with pride, but always with personal investment) represent a certain triumph of the spirit, speaking to us of those who rallied, reassembled and transformed themselves and who under dismembering pressures refused to die. "Brothers and sisters," I once heard a Negro preacher exhort, "let us make up our faces before the world, and our names shall sound throughout the land with honor! For we ourselves are our *true* names, not their epithets! So let us, I say, Make Up Our Faces and Our Minds!"

18   Perhaps my preacher had read T. S. Eliot, although I doubt it. And in actuality, it was unnecessary that he do so, for a concern with names and naming was very much a part of that special area of American culture from which I come, and it is precisely for this reason that this example should come to mind in a discussion of my own experience as a writer.

19   Undoubtedly, writers begin their *conditioning* as manipulators of words long before they become aware of literature—certain Freudians would say at the breast. Perhaps. But if so, that is far too early to be of use at this moment. Of this, though, I am certain: that despite the misconceptions of those educators who trace the reading difficulties experienced by large numbers of Negro children in Northern schools to their Southern background, these children are, in *their* familiar South, facile manipulators of words. I know, too, that the Negro community is deadly in its ability to create nicknames and to spot all that is ludicrous in an unlikely name or that which is incongruous in conduct. Names are not qualities; nor are words, in this particular sense, actions. To assume that they are could cost one his life many times a day. Language skills depend to a large extent upon a knowledge of the details, the manners, the objects, the folkways, the psychological patterns, of a given environment. Humor and wit depend upon much the same awareness, and so does the suggestive power of names.

20   "A small brown bowlegged Negro with the name 'Franklin D. Roosevelt Jones' might sound like a clown to someone who looks at him from the outside," said my friend Albert Murray, "but on the other hand he just might turn out to be a hell of a fireside operator. He might just lie back in all of that comic juxtaposition of names and manipulate you deaf, dumb and blind—and you not even suspecting it, because you're thrown out of stance by his name! There you are, so dazzled by the F.D.R. image—which you *know* you can't see—and so delighted with your own superior position that you don't realize that it's *Jones* who must be confronted."

21   Well, as you must suspect, all of this speculation on the matter of names has a purpose, and now, because it is tied up so ironically with my own experience as a writer, I must turn to my own name.

22   For in the dim beginnings, before I ever thought consciously of writing, there was, doubtless, a certain magic in it. From the start I was uncomfortable with it, and in my earliest years it caused me much puzzlement. Neither could I understand what a poet was, nor why, exactly, my father had chosen to name me after one. Perhaps I could have understood it perfectly well had he named me after his own father, but that name had been given to an older brother who died and thus was out of the question. But why hadn't he named me after a hero, such as Jack Johnson, or a soldier like Colonel Charles Young, or a great seaman like Admiral Dewey, or an educator like Booker T. Washington, or a great orator and abolitionist like Frederick Douglass? Or again, why hadn't he named me (as so many Negro parents had done) after President Teddy Roosevelt?

23   Instead, he named me after someone called Ralph Waldo Emerson, and then, when I was three, he died. It was too early for me to have understood his choice, although I'm sure he must have explained it many times, and it was also too soon for me to have made the connection between my name and my father's love for reading. Much later, after I began to write and work

with words, I came to suspect that he was aware of the suggestive powers of names and of the magic involved in naming.

24   I recall an odd conversation with my mother during my early teens in which she mentioned their interest in, of all things, prenatal culture! But for a long time I actually knew only that my father read a lot, and that he admired this remote Mr. Emerson, who was something called a "poet and philosopher" —so much so that he named his second son after him.

25   I knew, also, that whatever his motives, the combination of names he'd given me caused me no end of trouble from the moment when I could talk well enough to respond to the ritualized question which grownups put to very young children. Emerson's name was quite familiar to Negroes in Oklahoma during those days when World War I was brewing, and adults, eager to show off their knowledge of literary figures, and obviously amused by the joke implicit in such a small brown nubbin of a boy carrying around such a heavy moniker, would invariably repeat my first two names and then to my great annoyance, they'd add "Emerson."

26   And I, in my confusion, would reply, "No, *no, I'm* not Emerson; he's the little boy who lives next door." Which only made them laugh all the louder. "Oh no," they'd say, "*you're* Ralph Waldo Emerson," while I had fantasies of blue murder.

27   For a while the presence next door of my little friend, Emerson, made it unnecessary for me to puzzle too often over this peculiar adult confusion. And since there were other Negro boys named Ralph in the city, I came to suspect that there was something about the combination of names which produced their laughter. Even today, I know of only one other Ralph who had as much comedy made out of his name, a campus politician and deep-voiced orator whom I knew at Tuskegee, who was called in friendly ribbing, *Ralph Waldo Emerson Edgar Allan Poe*, spelled Powe. This must have been quite a trial for him, but I had been initiated much earlier.

28   During my early school years the name continued to puzzle me, for it constantly evoked in the faces of others some secret. It was as though I possessed some treasure or some defect, which was invisible to my own eyes and ears; something which I had but did not *possess,* like a piece of property in South Carolina, which was mine but which I could not have until some future time. I recall finding, about this time, while seeking adventure in back alleys—which possess for boys a superiority over playgrounds like that which kitchen utensils possess over toys designed for infants—a large photographic lens. I remember nothing of its optical qualities, of its speed or color correction, but it gleamed with crystal mystery and it was beautiful.

29   Mounted handsomely in a tube of shiny brass, it spoke to me of distant worlds of possibility. I played with it, looking through it with squinted eyes, holding it in shafts of sunlight, and tried to use it for a magic lantern. But most of this was as unrewarding as my attempts to make the music come from a phonograph record by holding the needle in my fingers.

30   I could burn holes through newspapers with it, or I could pretend that

it was a telescope, the barrel of a cannon, or the third eye of a monster—I being the monster—but I could do nothing at all about its proper function of making images; nothing to make it yield its secret. But I could not discard it.

31   Older boys sought to get it away from me by offering knives or tops, agate marbles or whole zoos of grass snakes and horned toads in trade, but I held on to it. No one, not even the white boys I knew, had such a lens, and it was my own good luck to have found it. Thus I would hold on to it until such time as I could acquire the part needed to make it function. Finally, I put it aside and it remained buried in my box of treasures, dusty and dull, to be lost and forgotten as I grew older and became interested in music.

32   I had reached by now the grades where it was necessary to learn something about Mr. Emerson and what he had written, such as the "Concord Hymn" and the essay "Self-Reliance," and in following his advice, I reduced the "Waldo" to a simple and, I hoped mysterious "W," and in my own reading I avoided his works like the plague. I could no more deal with my name—I shall never really master it—than I could find a creative use for my lens. Fortunately there were other problems to occupy my mind. Not that I forgot my fascination with names, but more about that later.

33   Negro Oklahoma City was starkly lacking in writers. In fact, there was only Roscoe Dungee, the editor of the local Negro newspaper and a very fine editorialist in that valuable tradition of personal journalism which is now rapidly disappearing; a writer who in his emphasis upon the possibilities for justice offered by the Constitution anticipated the anti-segregation struggle by decades. There were also a few reporters who drifted in and out, but these were about all. On the level of *conscious* culture the Negro community was biased in the direction of music.

34   These were the middle and late twenties, remember, and the state was still a new frontier state. The capital city was one of the great centers for southwestern jazz, along with Dallas and Kansas City. Orchestras which were to become famous within a few years were constantly coming and going. As were the blues singers—Ma Rainey and Ida Cox, and the old bands like that of King Oliver. But best of all, thanks to Mrs. Zelia N. Breaux, there was an active and enthusiastic school music program through which any child who had the interest and the talent could learn to play an instrument and take part in the band, the orchestra, the brass quartet. And there was a yearly operetta and a chorus and a glee club. Harmony was taught throughout the Negro school system, and we were also taught complicated patterns of military drill.

35   I tell you this to point out that although there were no incentives to write, there was ample opportunity to receive an artistic discipline. Indeed, once one picked up an instrument it was difficult to escape. If you chafed at the many rehearsals of the school band or orchestra and were drawn to the many small jazz groups, you were likely to discover that the jazzmen were

apt to rehearse far more than the school band; it was only that they seemed to enjoy themselves better and to possess a freedom of imagination which we were denied at school. And one soon learned that the wild, transcendent moments which occurred at dances or "battles of music," moments in which memorable improvisations were ignited, depended upon a dedication to a discipline which was observed even when rehearsals had to take place in the crowded quarters of Halley Richardson's shoeshine parlor. It was not the place which counted, although a large hall with good acoustics was preferred, but what one did to perfect one's performance.

36   If this talk of musical discipline gives the impression that there were no forces working to nourish one who would one day blunder, after many a twist and turn, into writing, I am misleading you. And here I might give you a longish lecture on the Ironies and Uses of Segregation. When I was a small child there was no library for Negroes in our city; and not until a Negro minister invaded the main library did we get one. For it was discovered that there was no law, only custom, which held that we could not use these public facilities. The results were the quick renting of two large rooms in a Negro office building (the recent site of a pool hall), the hiring of a young Negro librarian, the installation of shelves and a hurried stocking of the walls with any and every book possible. It was, in those first days, something of a literary chaos.

37   But how fortunate for a boy who loved to read! I started with the fairy tales and quickly went through the junior fiction; then through the Westerns and the detective novels, and very soon I was reading the classics—only I didn't know it. There were also the Haldeman Julius Blue Books, which seem to have floated on the air down from Girard, Kansas; the syndicated columns of O. O. McIntyre, and the copies of *Vanity Fair* and the *Literary Digest* which my mother brought home from work—how could I ever join uncritically in the heavy handed attacks on the so-called Big Media which have become so common today?

38   There were also the pulp magazines and, more important, that other library which I visited when I went to help my adopted grandfather, J. D. Randolph (my parents had been living in his rooming house when I was born), at his work as custodian of the law library of the Oklahoma State Capitol. Mr. Randolph had been one of the first teachers in what became Oklahoma city; and he'd also been one of the leaders of a group who walked from Gallatin, Tennessee, to the Oklahoma Territory. He was a tall man, as brown as smoked leather, who looked like the Indians with whom he'd herded horses in the early days.

39   And while his status was merely the custodian of the law library, I was to see the white legislators come down on many occasions to question him on points of law, and often I was to hear him answer without recourse to the uniform rows of books on the shelves. This was a thing to marvel at in itself, and the white lawmakers did so, but even more marvelous, ironic, intriguing, haunting—call it what you will—is the fact that the Negro who knew

the answers was named after Jefferson Davis. What Tennessee lost, Oklahoma was to gain, and after gaining it (a gift of courage, intelligence, fortitude and grace), used it only in concealment and, one hopes, with embarrassment.

So, let us, I say, make up our faces and our minds!

40   In the loosely structured community of that time, knowledge, news of other ways of living, ancient wisdom, the latest literary fads, hate literature—for years I kept a card warning Negroes away from the polls, which had been dropped by the thousands from a plane which circled over the Negro community—information of all kinds, found its level, catch-as-catch can, in the minds of those who were receptive to it. Not that there was no conscious structuring—I read my first Shaw and Maupassant, my first Harvard Classics in the home of a friend whose parents were products of that stream of New England education which had been brought to Negroes by the young and enthusiastic white teachers who staffed the schools set up for the freedmen after the Civil War. These parents were both teachers and there were others like them in our town.

41   But the places where a rich oral literature was truly functional were the churches, the schoolyards, the barbershops, the cotton-picking camps; places where folklore and gossip thrived. The drug store where I worked was such a place, where on days of bad weather the older men would sit with their pipes and tell tall tales, hunting yarns and homely versions of the classics. It was here that I heard stories of searching for buried treasure and of headless horsemen, which I was told were my own father's versions told long before. There were even recitals of popular verse, "The Shooting of Dan McGrew," and, along with these, stories of Jesse James, of Negro outlaws and black United States marshals, of slaves who became the chiefs of Indian tribes and of the exploits of Negro cowboys. There was both truth and fantasy in this, intermingled in the mysterious fashion of literature.

42   Writers, in their formative period, absorb into their consciousness much that has no special value until much later, and often much which is of no special value even then—perhaps, beyond the fact that it throbs with affect and mystery and in it "time and pain and royalty in the blood" are suspended in imagery. So, long before I thought of writing, I was claimed by weather, by speech rhythms, by Negro voices and their different idioms, by husky male voices, and by the high shrill singing voices of certain Negro women, by music; by tight spaces and by wide spaces in which the eyes could wander; by death, by newly born babies, by manners of various kinds, company manners and street manners; the manners of white society and those of our own high society; and by interracial manners; by street fights, circuses and minstrel shows; by vaudeville and moving pictures, by prize fights and foot races, baseball games and football matches. By spring floods and blizzards, catalpa worms and jack rabbits; honeysuckle and snapdragons (which

smelled like old cigar butts); by sunflowers and hollyhocks, raw sugar cane and baked yams; pigs' feet, chili and blue haw ice cream. By parades, public dances and jam sessions, Easter sunrise ceremonies and large funerals. By contests between fire-and-brimstone preachers and by presiding elders who got "laughing-happy" when moved by the spirit of God.

43   I was impressed by expert players of the "dozens" and certain notorious bootleggers of corn whiskey. By jazz musicians and fortunetellers and by men who did anything well, by strange sickness and by interesting brick or razor scars; by expert cursing vocabularies as well as by exalted praying and terrifying shouting, and by transcendent playing or singing of the blues. I was fascinated by old ladies, those who had seen slavery and those who were defiant of white folk and black alike; by the enticing walks of prostitutes and by the limping walks affected by Negro hustlers, especially those who wore Stetson hats, expensive shoes with well-starched overalls, usually with a diamond stickpin (when not in hock) in their tieless collars as their gambling uniforms.

44   And there were the blind men who preached on corners, and the blind men who sang the blues to the accompaniment of washboard and guitar; and the white junkmen who sang mountain music and the famous huckster of fruit and vegetables.

45   And there was the Indian-Negro confusion. There were Negroes who were part Indian and who lived on reservations, and Indians who had children who lived in towns as Negroes, and Negroes who were Indians and traveled back and forth between the groups with no trouble. And Indians who were as wild as wild Negroes and others who were as solid and as steady as bankers. There were the teachers, too, inspiring teachers and villainous teachers who chased after the girl students, and certain female teachers who one wished would chase after young male students. And a handsome old principal of military bearing who had been blemished by his classmates at West Point when they discovered on the eve of graduation that he was a Negro. There were certain Jews, Mexicans, Chinese cooks, a German orchestra conductor and an English grocer who owned a Franklin touring car. And certain Negro mechanics— "Cadillac Slim," "Sticks" Walker, Buddy Bunn and Oscar Pitman—who had so assimilated the automobile that they seemed to be behind a steering wheel even as they walked the streets or danced with girls. And there were the whites who despised us and the others who shared our hardships and our joys.

46   There is much more, but this is sufficient to indicate some of what was present even in a segregated community to form the background of my work, my sense of life.

47   And now comes the next step. I went to Tuskegee to study music, hoping to become a composer of symphonies and there, during my second year, I read *The Waste Land* and that, although I was then unaware of it, was the real transition to writing.

48   Mrs. I. C. McFarland had taught us much of Negro history in grade

school and from her I'd learned of the New Negro Movement of the twenties, of Langston Hughes, Countee Cullen, Claude McKay, James Weldon Johnson and the others. They had inspired pride and had given me a closer identification with poetry (by now, oddly enough, I seldom thought of my hidden name), but with music so much on my mind it never occurred to me to try to imitate them. Still I read their work and was excited by the glamour of the Harlem which emerged from their poems and it was good to know that there were Negro writers.—Then came *The Waste Land*.

49   I was much more under the spell of literature than I realized at the time. *Wuthering Heights* had caused me an agony of unexpressible emotion and the same was true of *Jude the Obscure*, but *The Waste Land* seized my mind. I was intrigued by its power to move me while eluding my understanding. Somehow its rhythms were often closer to those of jazz than were those of the Negro poets, and even though I could not understand then, its range of allusion was as mixed and as varied as that of Louis Armstrong. Yet there were its discontinuities, its changes of pace and its hidden system of organization which escaped me.

50   There was nothing to do but look up the references in the footnotes to the poem, and thus began my conscious education in literature.

51   For this, the library of Tuskegee was quite adequate and I used it. Soon I was reading a whole range of subjects drawn upon by the poet, and this led, in turn, to criticism and to Pound and Ford Madox Ford, Sherwood Anderson and Gertrude Stein, Hemingway and Fitzgerald and "round about 'til I was come" back to Melville and Twain the writers who are taught and doubtlessly overtaught today. Perhaps it was my good luck that they were not taught at Tuskegee, I wouldn't know. But at the time I was playing, having an intellectually interesting good time.

52   Having given so much attention to the techniques of music, the process of learning something of the craft and intention of modern poetry and fiction seemed quite familiar. Besides, it was absolutely painless because it involved no deadlines or credits. Even then, however, a process which I described earlier had begun to operate. The more I learned of literature in this conscious way, the more the details of my background became transformed. I heard undertones in remembered conversations which had escaped me before, local customs took on a more universal meaning, values which I hadn't understood were revealed; some of the people whom I had known were diminished while others were elevated in stature. More important, I began to see my own possibilities with more objective, and in some ways, more hopeful eyes.

53   The following summer I went to New York seeking work, which I did not find, and remained there, but the personal transformation continued. Reading had become a conscious process of growth and discovery, a method of reordering the world. And that world had widened considerably.

54   At Tuskegee I had handled manuscripts which Prokofiev had given to Hazel Harrison, a Negro concert pianist who taught there and who had

known him in Europe, and through Miss Harrison I had become aware of Prokofiev's symphonies. I had also become aware of the radical movement in politics and art, and in New York had begun reading the work of André Malraux, not only the fiction but chapters published from his *Psychology of Art*. And in my search for an expression of modern sensibility in the works of Negro writers I discovered Richard Wright. Shortly thereafter I was to meet Wright, and it was at his suggestion that I wrote both my first book review and my first short story. These were fatal suggestions.

55   For although I had tried my hand at poetry while at Tuskegee, it hadn't occurred to me that I might write fiction, but once he suggested it, it seemed the most natural thing to try. Fortunately for me, Wright, then on the verge of his first success, was eager to talk with a beginner and I was able to save valuable time in searching out those works in which writing was discussed as a craft. He guided me to Henry James' prefaces, to Conrad, to Joseph Warren Beach and to the letters of Dostoievsky. There were other advisers and other books involved, of course, but what is important here is that I was consciously concerned with the art of fiction, that almost from the beginning I was grappling quite consciously with the art through which I wished to realize myself. And this was not done in isolation; the Spanish Civil War was now in progress and the Depression was still on. The world was being shaken up, and through one of those odd instances which occur to young provincials in New York, I was to hear Malraux make an appeal for the Spanish Loyalists at the same party where I first heard the folk singer Leadbelly perform. Wright and I were there seeking money for the magazine which he had come to New York to edit.

56   Art and politics; a great French novelist and a Negro folk singer; a young writer who was soon to publish *Uncle Tom's Children;* and I who had barely begun to study his craft. It is such accidents, such fortuitous meetings, which count for so much in our lives. I had never dreamed that I would be in the presence of Malraux, of whose work I became aware on my second day in Harlem when Langston Hughes suggested that I read *Man's Fate* and *Days of Wrath* before returning them to a friend of his. And it is this fortuitous circumstance which led to my selecting Malraux as a literary "ancestor," whom, unlike a relative, the artist is permitted to choose. There was in progress at the time all the agitation over the Scottsboro boys and the Herndon Case, and I was aware of both. I had to be; I myself had been taken off a freight train at Decatur, Alabama, only three years before while on my way to Tuskegee. But while I joined in the agitation for their release, my main energies went into learning to write.

57   I began to publish enough, and not too slowly, to justify my hopes for success, and as I continued, I made a most perplexing discovery; namely that for all his conscious concern with technique, a writer did not so much create the novel as he was created *by* the novel. That is, one did not make an arbitrary gesture when one sought to write. And when I say that the novelist is created by the novel, I mean to remind you that fictional techniques

are not a mere set of objective tools, but something much more intimate: a way of feeling, of seeing and of expressing one's sense of life. And the process of *acquiring* technique is a process of modifying one's responses, of learning to see and feel, to hear and observe, to evoke and evaluate the images of memory and of summoning up and directing the imagination; of learning to conceive of human values in the ways which have been established by the great writers who have developed and extended the art. And perhaps the writer's greatest freedom, as artist, lies precisely in his possession of technique; for it is through technique that he comes to possess and express the meaning of his life.

58 Perhaps at this point it would be useful to recapitulate the route—perhaps as mazelike as that of *Finnegan's Wake*—which I have been trying to describe; that which leads from the writer's discovery of a sense of purpose, which is that of becoming a writer, and then the involvement in the passionate struggle required to master a bit of technique, and then, as this begins to take shape, the disconcerting discovery that it is *technique* which transforms the individual before he is able in turn to transform it. And in that personal transformation he discovers something else; he discovers that he has taken on certain obligations, that he must not embarrass his chosen form, and that in order to avoid this he must develop taste. He learns—and this is most discouraging—that he is involved with values which turn in their *own* way, and not in the ways of politics, upon the central issues affecting his nation and his time. He learns that the American novel, from its first consciousness of itself as a literary form, has grappled with the meaning of the American experience; that it has been aware and has sought to define the nature of the experience by addressing itself to the specific details, the moods, the landscapes, the cityscapes, the tempo of American change. And that it has borne, at its best, the full weight of that burden of conscience and consciousness which Americans inherit as one of the results of the revolutionary circumstances of our national beginnings.

59 We began as a nation not through the accidents of race or religion or geography (Robert Penn Warren has dwelled on these circumstances) but when a group of men, *some* of them political philosophers, put down, upon what we now recognize as being quite sacred papers, their conception of the nation which they intended to establish on these shores. They described, as we know, the obligations of the state to the citizen, of the citizen to the state; they committed themselves to certain ideas of justice, just as they committed us to a system which would guarantee all of its citizens equality of opportunity.

60 I need not describe the problems which have arisen from these beginnings. I need only remind you that the contradiction between these noble ideals and the actualities of our conduct generated a guilt, an unease of spirit, from the very beginning, and that the American novel at its best has always been concerned with this basic moral predicament. During Melville's time and Twain's, it was an implicit aspect of their major themes; by the

twentieth century and after the discouraging and traumatic effect of the Civil War and the Reconstruction it had gone underground, had become *understated*. Nevertheless it did not disappear completely and it is to be found operating in the work of Henry James as well as in that of Hemingway and Fitzgerald. And then (and as one who believes in the impelling moral function of the novel and who believes in the moral seriousness of the form) it pleases me no end that it comes into explicit statement again in the works of Richard Wright and William Faulkner, writers who lived close to moral and political problems which would not stay put underground.

61   I go into these details not to recapitulate the history of the American novel but to indicate the trend of thought which was set into motion when I began to discover the nature of that process with which I was actually involved. Whatever the opinions and decisions of critics, a novelist must arrive at his own conclusions as to the meaning and function of the form with which he is engaged, and these are, in all modesty, some of mine.

62   In order to orient myself I also began to learn that the American novel had long concerned itself with the puzzle of the one-and-the-many; the mystery of how each of us, despite his origin in diverse regions, with our-diverse racial, cultural, religious backgrounds, speaking his own diverse idiom of the American in his own accent, is, nevertheless, American. And with this concern with the implicit pluralism of the country and with the composite nature of the ideal character called "the American," there goes a concern with gauging the health of the American promise, with depicting the extent to which it was being achieved, being made manifest in our daily conduct.

63   And with all of this there still remained the specific concerns of literature. Among these is the need to keep literary standards high, the necessity of exploring new possibilities of language which would allow it to retain that flexibility and fidelity to the common speech which has been its glory since Mark Twain. For me this meant learning to add to it the wonderful resources of Negro American speech and idiom and to bring into range as fully and eloquently as possible the complex reality of the American experience as it shaped and was shaped by the lives of my own people.

64   Notice that I stress as "fully" as possible, because I would no more strive to write great novels by leaving out the complexity of circumstances which go to make up the Negro experience and which alone go to make the obvious injustice bearable, than I would think of preparing myself to become President of the United States simply by studying Negro American history or confining myself to studying those laws affecting civil rights.

65   For it seems to me that one of the obligations I took on when I committed myself to the art and form of the novel was that of striving for the broadest range, the discovery and articulation of the most exalted values. And I must squeeze these from the life which I know best. (A highly truncated impression of that life I attempted to convey to you earlier.)

66   If all this sounds a bit heady, remember that I did not destroy that troublesome middle name of mine, I only suppressed it. Sometimes it reminds me of my obligation to the man who named me.

67   It is our fate as human beings always to give up some good things for other good things, to throw off certain bad circumstances only to create others. Thus there is a value for the writer in trying to give as thorough a report of social reality as possible. Only by doing so may we grasp and convey the cost of change. Only by considering the broadest accumulation of data may we make choices that are based upon our own hard-earned sense of reality. Speaking from my own special area of American culture, I feel that to embrace uncritically values which are extended to us by others is to reject the validity, even the sacredness, of our own experience. It is also to forget that the small share of reality which each of our diverse groups is able to snatch from the whirling chaos of history belongs not to the group alone, but to all of us. It is a property and a witness which can be ignored only to the danger of the entire nation.

68   I could suppress the name of my namesake out of respect for the achievement of its original bearer but I cannot escape the obligation of attempting to achieve some of the things which he asked of the American writer. As Henry James suggested, being an American is an arduous task, and for most of us, I suspect, the difficulty begins with the name.

DISCUSSION QUESTIONS

1. What, according to Ellison, are the functions of a name?
2. How does Ellison view the personal experience of the writer in relationship to his art?
3. Does Ellison differentiate between his identity as an African-American male and his identity as a writer?
4. What is the main concern of the American novel, and what does a multicultural society contribute or require?

WRITING TOPICS

1. Ellison says: "Our names being the gifts of others, must be made our own." Write an essay in which you explain the meaning of this quotation. Support your position by using examples from your reading or from your own experience.

2. Write an analytical essay in which you interpret the meaning of the phrase "Unity of self and name."
3. One's name holds utmost importance in one's life; in many West African countries the naming ceremony for a newborn takes on great significance. For example, a newborn child's name is whispered to her or him first, before it is announced to other family members or friends. In your writing journal, list your given (first) name and explain its meaning or significance.

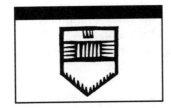

WHERE IS THE BLACK COMMUNITY?

Joyce Carol Thomas

Joyce Carol Thomas was born in Ponca, Oklahoma, in 1938, the fifth child in a family of nine. When she was eight years old, she could pick 100 pounds of cotton a day. By the age of ten, Thomas was an avid reader and storyteller. As an adult raising four children, Thomas worked during the day as a telephone operator and attended night classes, receiving a B.A. in Spanish from San Jose University. In 1967 she received a master's degree in education from Stanford University. Thomas has taught at various universities across the United States, including California State University and Purdue University. Currently, she teaches English at the University of Tennessee, Knoxville.

Thomas's creative work includes drama: *A Song in the Sky* (1976), *Look! What a Wonder!* (1976), *Magnolia* (1977), and *Ambrosia* (1978), and poetry: *Bittersweet* (1973), *Crystal Breezes* (1974), *Blessing* (1975), and *Inside the Rainbow* (1982). Since the early 1980s, Thomas has focused her writing on children's poetry and fiction: *Marked by Fire* (1982), *Water Girl* (1986), *The Golden Pasture* (1986), *Journey* (1988), *Brown Honey in Broomwheat Tea* (1993), *When the Nightingale Sings* (1994), and *Gingerbread Days* (1995).

Where is the Black community?
Holding down the corner where
Third Street meets B and

Sitting in the second pew
5   At Double Rock Baptist Church

Where is the Black community?
At Bob's Barber Shop
Busting jokes about the man

And at the Delta sisters
10 Fashioning J. Magnin and new hairdos

Where is the Black community?
Scrubbing chitlin grease
Off a kitchen stove eye

and hawking Muhammed Speaks
15 On a Stanford campus

Where is the Black community?
Transplanting kidneys
In a university hospital

And plowing cotton
20 In a Mississippi dawn

Where is the Black community?
Teaching English at Duke
And Purdue

And arranging four kids
25 In a twin sized bed

Where is the Black community?
Living in two story houses
On Poplar Drive

And swilling Old Crow
30 Out of a crystal flask

DISCUSSION QUESTIONS

1. Many people seem to think that African Americans live in one specific black community. Using specific information from the poem, explain why the black community cannot be in one place.
2. What types of images does each stanza evoke about African Americans? Choose two adjectives that summarize all of the images, and explain why these two adjectives best describe them.
3. The speaker describes images of African Americans that are not the ones often highlighted on the evening news. Identify these images and explain why they aren't seen in the news.

WRITING TOPICS

1. In an essay, discuss the characteristics of the African-American oral tradition. Include illustrations of how "Where Is the Black Community?" shares some characteristics of the African-American oral tradition.
2. Spend an hour walking around and observing your community. Then write a poem, similar in structure to Thomas's, in which you answer the question, "Where is the (your name) community?" Share your poem with others and discuss the similarities and differences between your communities.

OF OUR SPIRITUAL STRIVINGS

W. E. B. Du Bois

W. E. B. (William Edward Burghardt) Du Bois was born in 1868 in Great Barrington, Massachusetts. He earned a B.A. degree from Fisk University in Tennessee and B.A., M.A., and Ph.D. degrees from Harvard. He served as professor of Latin and Greek at Wilberforce University, Ohio, and professor of economics at Atlanta University in Georgia. Du Bois was an ardent speaker for the cause of black civil rights, and he co-founded the National Association for the Advancement of Colored People (NAACP) in 1909. His fiction includes *The Quest of the Silver Fleece* (1911) and *Dark Princess: A Romance* (1928). His nonfiction includes *The Suppression of the African Slave Trade to the United States of America (1638–1870)* (1896) and *The Souls of Black Folk* (1903). He also edited *The Crisis,* the journal of the NAACP, from 1910 to 1934. He died in Ghana, West Africa, in 1963; he is buried there. (For more biographical information, see pages 211 and 297.)

1   Between me and the other world there is ever an unasked question: unasked by some through feelings of delicacy; by others through the diffi-culty of rightly framing it. All, nevertheless, flutter round it. They approach me in a half-hesitant sort of way, eye me curiously or compassionately, and then, instead of saying directly, How does it feel to be a problem? they say, I know an excellent colored man in my town; or, I fought at Mechanicsville; or, Do not these Southern outrages make your blood boil? At these I smile, or am interested, or reduce the boiling to a simmer, as the occasion may require. To the real question, How does it feel to be a problem? I answer seldom a word.

2   And yet, being a problem is a strange experience,—peculiar even for one who has never been anything else, save perhaps in babyhood and in Europe. It is in the early days of rollicking boyhood that the revelation first bursts upon one, all in a day, as it were. I remember well when the shadow swept

across me. I was a little thing, away up in the hills of New England, where the dark Housatonic winds between Hoosac and Taghkanic to the sea. In a wee wooden schoolhouse, something put it into the boys' and girls' heads to buy gorgeous visiting-cards—ten cents a package—and exchange. The exchange was merry till one girl, a tall newcomer, refused my card,—refused it peremptorily, with a glance. Then it dawned upon me with a certain suddenness that I was different from the others; or like, mayhap, in heart and life and longing, but shut out from their world by a vast veil. I had thereafter no desire to tear down that veil, to creep through; I held beyond it in common contempt, and lived above it in a region of blue sky and great wandering shadows. That sky was bluest when I could beat my mates at examination-time, or beat them at a foot-race, or even beat their stringy heads. Alas, with the years all this fine contempt began to fade; for the worlds I longed for, and all their dazzling opportunities, were theirs, not mine. But they should not keep these prizes, I said; some, all, I would wrest from them. Just how I would do it I could never decide: by reading law, by healing the sick, by telling the wonderful tales that swim in my head,—some way. With other black boys the strife was not so fiercely sunny: their youth shrunk into tasteless sycophancy, or into silent hatred of the pale world about them and mocking distrust of everything white; or wasted itself in a bitter cry, Why did God make me an outcast and a stranger in mine own house? The shades of the prison-house closed round about us all: walls strait and stubborn to the whitest, but relentlessly narrow, tall and unscalable to sons of night who must plod darkly on in resignation, or beat unavailing palms against the stone, or steadily, half hopelessly, watch the streak of blue above.

3   After the Egyptian and Indian, the Greek and Roman, the Teuton and Mongolian, the Negro is a sort of seventh son, born with a veil, and gifted with second-sight in this American world,—a world which yields him no true self-consciousness, but only lets him see himself through the revelation of the other world. It is a peculiar sensation, this double-consciousness, this sense of always looking at one's self through the eyes of others, of measuring one's soul by the tape of a world that looks on in amused contempt and pity. One ever feels his twoness,—an American, a Negro; two souls, two thoughts, two unreconciled strivings; two warring ideals in one dark body, whose dogged strength alone keeps it from being torn asunder.

4   The history of the American Negro is the history of this strife,—this longing to attain self-conscious manhood, to merge his double self into a better and truer self. In this merging he wishes neither of the older selves to be lost. He would not Africanize America, for America has too much to teach the world and Africa. He would not bleach his Negro soul in a flood of white Americanism, for he knows that Negro blood has a message for the world. He simply wishes to make it possible for a man to be both a Negro and an American, without being cursed and spit upon by his fellows, without having the doors of Opportunity closed roughly in his face.

5   This then, is the end of his striving; to be a co-worker in the kingdom of culture, to escape both death and isolation, to husband and use his best powers and his latent genius. These powers of body and mind have in the past been strangely wasted, dispersed, or forgotten. The shadow of a mighty Negro past flits through the tale of Ethiopia the Shadowy and of Egypt the Sphinx. Throughout history, the powers of single black men flash here and there like falling stars, and die sometimes before the world has rightly gauged their brightness. Here in America, in the few days since Emancipation, the black man's turning hither and thither in hesitant and doubtful striving has often made his very strength to lose effectiveness, to seem like absence of power, like weakness. And yet it is not weakness,—it is the contradiction of double aims. The double-aimed struggle of the black artisan—on the one hand to escape white contempt for a nation of mere hewers of wood and drawers of water, and on the other hand to plough and nail and dig for a poverty-stricken horde—could only result in making him a poor craftsman, for he had but half a heart in either cause. By the poverty and ignorance of his people, the Negro minister or doctor was tempted toward quackery and demagogy; and by the criticism of the other world, toward ideals that made him ashamed of his lowly tasks. The would-be black *savant* was confronted by the paradox that the knowledge his people needed was a twice-told tale to his white neighbors, while the knowledge which would teach the white world was Greek to his own flesh and blood. The innate love of harmony and beauty that set the ruder souls of his people a-dancing and a-singing raised but confusion and doubt in the soul of the black artist; for the beauty revealed to him was the soul-beauty of a race which his larger audience despised, and he could not articulate the message of another people. This waste of double aims, this seeking to satisfy two unreconciled ideals, has wrought sad havoc with the courage and faith and deeds of ten thousand people—has sent them often wooing false gods and invoking false means of salvation, and at times has even seemed about to make them ashamed of themselves.

6   Away back in the days of bondage they thought to see in one divine event the end of all doubt and disappointment; few men ever worshiped Freedom with half such unquestioning faith as did the American Negro for two centuries. To him, so far as he thought and dreamed, slavery was indeed the sum of all villainies, the cause of all sorrow, the root of all prejudice; Emancipation was the key to a promised land of sweeter beauty than ever stretched before the eyes of wearied Israelites. In song and exhortation swelled one refrain—Liberty; in his tears and curses the God he implored had Freedom in his right hand. At last it came,—suddenly, fearfully, like a dream. With one wild carnival of blood and passion came the message in his own plaintive cadences:—

> "Shout, O children!
> Shout, you're free!
> For God has brought your liberty!"

7   Years have passed since then,—ten, twenty, forty; forty years of national life, forty years of renewal and development, and yet the swarthy spectre sits in its accustomed seat at the Nation's feast. In vain do we cry to this our vastest social problem:—

> "Take any shape but that, and my firm nerves
> Shall never tremble!"

The Nation has not yet found peace from its sins; the freedman has not yet found in freedom his promised land. Whatever of good may have come in these years of change, the shadow of a deep disappointment rests upon the Negro people,—a disappointment all the more bitter because the unattained ideal was unbounded save by the simple ignorance of a lowly people.

8   The first decade was merely a prolongation of the vain search for freedom, the boon that seemed ever barely to elude their grasp,—like a tantalizing will-o'-the-wisp, maddening and misleading the headless host. The holocaust of war, the terrors of the Ku-Klux Klan, the lies of carpet-baggers, the disorganization of industry, and the contradictory advice of friends and foes, left the bewildered serf with no new watchword beyond the old cry for freedom. As the time flew, however, he began to grasp a new idea. The ideal of liberty demanded for its attainment powerful means, and these the Fifteenth Amendment gave him. The ballot, which before he had looked upon as a visible sign of freedom, he now regarded as the chief means of gaining and perfecting the liberty with which war had partially endowed him. And why not? Had not votes made the war and emancipated millions? Had not votes enfranchised the freedmen? Was anything impossible to a power that had done all this? A million black men started with renewed zeal to vote themselves into the kingdom. So the decade flew away, the revolution of 1876 came, and left the half-free serf weary, wondering but still inspired. Slowly but steadily, in the following years, a new vision began gradually to replace the dream of political power,—a powerful movement, the rise of another ideal to guide the unguided, another pillar of fire by night after a clouded day. It was the ideal of "book-learning"; the curiosity, born to compulsory ignorance, to know and test the power of the cabalistic letters of the white man, the longing to know. Here at last seemed to have been discovered the mountain path to Canaan; longer than the highway of Emancipation and law, steep and rugged, but straight, leading to heights high enough to overlook life.

9   Up the new path the advance guard toiled, slowly, heavily, doggedly; only those who have watched and guided the faltering feet, the misty minds, the dull understandings, of the dark pupils of these schools know how faithfully, how piteously, this people strove to learn. It was weary work. The cold statistician wrote down the inches of progress here and there, noted also where here and there a foot had slipped or some one had fallen. To the tired climbers, the horizon was ever dark, the mists were often cold, the Canaan was always dim and far away. If, however, the vistas disclosed as yet no goal, no resting-place,

little but flattery and criticism, the journey at least gave leisure for reflection and self-examination; it changed the child of Emancipation to the youth with dawning self-consciousness, self-realization, self-respect. In those sombre forests of his striving his own soul rose before him, and he saw himself,—darkly as through a veil; and yet he saw in himself some faint revelation of his power, of his mission. He began to have a dim feeling that, to attain his place in the world, he must be himself, and not another. For the first time he sought to analyze the burden he bore upon his back,—before this there rises a sickening despair that would disarm and discourage any nation save that black host to whom "discouragement" is an unwritten word.

10   But the facing of so vast a prejudice could not but bring the inevitable self-questioning, self-disparagement, and lowering of ideals which ever accompany repression and breed in an atmosphere of contempt and hate. Whispering and portents came borne upon the four winds: Lo! we are diseased and dying, cried the dark hosts; we cannot write, our voting is vain; what need of education, since we must always cook and serve? And the Nation echoed and enforced this self-criticism, saying: Be content to be servants, and nothing more; what need of higher culture for half-men? Away with the black man's ballot, by force or fraud,—and behold the suicide of a race! Nevertheless, out of the evil came something of good,—the more careful adjustment of education to real life, the clearer perception of the Negroes' social responsibilities, and the sobering realization of the meaning of progress.

11   So dawned the time of *Sturm und Drang:* storm and stress to-day rocks our little boat on the mad waters of the world-sea; there is within and without the sound of conflict, the burning of body and rending of soul; inspiration strives with doubt, and faith with vain questionings. The bright ideals of the past,—physical freedom, political power, the training of brains and the training of hands,—all these in turn have waxed and waned, until even the last grows dim and overcast. Are they all wrong,—all false? No, not that, but each alone was over-simple and incomplete,—the dreams of a credulous race-childhood, or the fond imaginings of the other world which does not know and does not want to know our power. To be really true, all these ideals must be melted and welded into one. The training of the schools we need to-day more than ever,—the training of deft hands, quick eyes and ears, and above all the broader, deeper, higher culture of gifted minds and pure hearts. The power of the ballot we need in sheer self-defence,—else what shall save us from a second slavery? Freedom, too, the long-sought, we still seek—the freedom of life and limb, the freedom to work and think, the freedom to love and aspire. Work, culture, liberty,—all these we need, not singly but together, not successively but together, each growing and aiding each, and all striving toward that vaster ideal that swims before the Negro people, the ideal of human brotherhood, gained through the unifying ideal of Race; the ideal of fostering and developing the traits and talents of the

Negro, not in opposition to or contempt for other races, but rather in large conformity to the greater ideals of the American Republic, in order that some day on American soil two world-races may give each to each those characteristics both so sadly lack. We the darker ones come even now not altogether empty-handed: there are to-day no truer exponents of the pure human spirit of the Declaration of Independence than the American Negroes; there is no true American music but the wild sweet melodies of the Negro slave; the American fairy tales and folk-lore are Indian and African; and, all in all, we black men seem the sole oasis of simple faith and reverence in a dusty desert of dollars and smartness. Will America be poorer if she replace her brutal dyspeptic blundering with light-hearted but determined Negro humility? or her coarse and cruel wit with loving jovial good-humor? or her vulgar music with the soul of the Sorrow Songs?

12   Merely a concrete test of the underlying principles of the great republic is the Negro Problem, and the spiritual striving of the freedmen's sons is the travail of souls whose burden is almost beyond the measure of their strength, but who bear it in the name of an historic race, in the name of this the land of their fathers' fathers, and in the name of human opportunity.

DISCUSSION QUESTIONS

1. Du Bois published *The Souls of Black Folk* in 1903. He speaks to what many called the "Negro Problem." Is there still such a problem today? If not, why not?

2. At the end of paragraph 2, Du Bois says: ". . . walls strait [straight] and stubborn to the whitest but . . . unscalable to the sons of night." Who, in your opinion, are the sons of night?

3. In your small group, discuss what you believe to be the status of black people at the time Du Bois wrote this essay in 1903. Remember that only forty years had passed since the signing of the Emancipation Proclamation in 1863.

WRITING TOPICS

1. Du Bois speaks about the "twoness" experienced by African Americans, "an American, a Negro." In your journal, discuss what you think he means.

2. Write a letter to the author telling him what you like or dislike about the essay. Give specific examples, based upon your reading.

3. In paragraph 3, Du Bois writes about: ". . . this sense of looking at one's self through the eyes of others, of measuring one's soul by the tape of a world that looks on in amused contempt and pity." Write an analytical essay in which you interpret the quotation. Support your position with specific examples from your reading, history, or from your own experience.

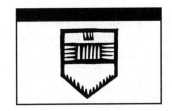

ALL ABOUT MY JOB

Alice Childress

Alice Childress, born in 1920, is a novelist, dramatist, actor, director, and lecturer. She has spoken out for accurate portrayals of black life and characters throughout her life. Early in Childress's career, she broke the more popular integration trends of the mid-1950s by writing *Trouble in Mind* (produced in 1955). In this play the main character, an older black woman actor, takes a stance by affirming blackness. *Trouble in Mind* won the first Obie Award in 1956 for best original, off-Broadway play.

Like Mildred, the main character in Childress's *Like One of the Family . . . Conversations from a Domestic's Life* (1956), the main character in "All about My Job" is a domestic worker. Childress based the character of Mildred on her Aunt Lorraine, who worked as a domestic for many years. According to Childress, her aunt, like the main character in her novel and story, had a strong sense of self and did not connect her worth as a person to the type of job she had.

1   Marge, I sure am glad that you are my friend. . . . No, I do not want to borrow anything or ask any favors and I wish you'd stop bein' suspicious everytime somebody pays you a compliment. It's a sure sign of a distrustful nature.

2   I'm glad that you are my friend because everybody needs a friend but I guess I need one more than most people. . . . Well, in the first place I'm colored and in the second place I do housework for a livin' and so you can see that I don't need a third place because the first two ought to be enough reason for anybody to need a friend.

3   You are not only a good friend but you are also a convenient friend and fill the bill in every other way. . . . Well, we are both thirty-two years old; both live in the same building; we each have a three-room apartment for which we pay too devilish much, but at the same time we got better sense than to try and live together. And there are other things, too. We both come from the South and we also do the same kinda work: *housework.*

4   Of course, you have been married, and I have not yet taken the vows, but I guess that's the only difference unless you want to count the fact that you are heavier than I am and wear a size eighteen while I wear a sixteen. . . . Marge, you know that you are larger, that's a fact! Oh, well, let's not get upset about it! The important thing is that I'm your friend, and you're mine and I'm glad about it.

5   Why, I do believe I'd lose my mind if I had to come home after a day of hard work, rasslin' 'round in other folks' kitchens, if I did not have a friend to talk to when I got here. . . . Girl, don't you move, 'cause it would be terrible if I couldn't run down a flight of steps and come in here to chew the fat in the evenin'. But if you ever get tired of me, always remember that all you have to do is say, "Mildred, go home," and I'll be on my way! . . . I did not get mad the last time you told me that! Girl, you ought to be ashamed of yourself! . . . No, I'm not callin' you a liar but I'm sayin' you just can't remember the truth.

6   Anyhow, I'm glad that we're friends! I got a story to tell you about what happened today. . . . No, not where I work although it was *about* where I work.

7   The church bazaar was open tonight and I went down to help out on one of the booths and, oh, my nerves! you never saw so many la de da fancy folks in all your life! And such introducin' that was goin' on. You shoulda *heard* 'em. "Do meet Mrs. So-and-so who has just returned from *Europe*," and "Do meet Miss This-and-that who has just finished her new *book*," and "Do meet Miss this-that-and-the-other who is on the Board of Directors of everything that is worthwhile!"

8   Honey, it was a dog! . . . Oh, yes, it was a real snazzy affair, and the booths was all fixed up so pretty, and they had these fine photographs pinned up on the wall. The photographs showed people doin' all manner of work. Yes, the idea of the pictures was to show how we are improvin' ourselves by leaps and bounds through the kinda work that we're doin'.

9   Well, that was a great old deal with me except that if they was talkin' 'bout people doin' work, it seemed to me that I was the only one around there that had took a lick at a snake in years! . . . No, it wasn't a drag at all because I was really enjoyin' the thing just like you'd go for a carnival or a penny-arcade once in a while.

10   My booth was the "Knick-Knack" corner and my counter was full of chipped china doo dads and ash trays and penny banks and stuff like that, and I was really sellin' it, too. There was a little quiet lady helpin' me out and for the life of me I couldn't figure why she was so scared-like and timid lookin'.

11   I was enjoyin' myself no end, and there was so many bigwigs floatin' around the joint 'til I didn't know what to expect next! . . . Yes, girl, any second I thought some sultan or king or somebody like that was gonna fall in the door! Honey, I was how-do-you-doin' left and right! Well, all the excitement keeps up 'til one group of grand folks stopped at our booth and

begun to chat with us and after the recitation 'bout what they all did, one lady turned to my timid friend and says, "What do *you* do?"

12 Marge, Miss Timid started sputterin' and stammerin' and finally she outs with, "Nothin' much." That was a new one on me 'cause I had never heard 'bout nobody who spent their time doin' "nothin' much." Then Miss Grand-lady turns to me and says, "And what do *you* do?" . . . Of course I told her! "I do housework," I said. "Oh," says she, "you are a housewife." "Oh, no," says I, "I do housework, and I do it every day because that is the way I make my livin' and if you look around at these pictures on the wall you will see that people do all kinds of work, I do housework."

13 Marge, they looked kinda funny for a minute but the next thing you know we were all laughin' and talkin' 'bout everything in general and nothin' in particular. I mean all of us was chattin' except Miss Timid.

14 When the folks drifted away, Miss Timid turns to me and says, "I do housework too but I don't always feel like tellin'. People look down on you so."

15 Well, I can tell you that I moved on in after that remark and straightened her out! . . . Now, wait a minute, Marge! I know people do make nasty cracks about houseworkers. Sure, they will say things like "pot-slingers" or "the Thursday-night-off" crowd, but nobody gets away with that stuff around me, and I will sound off in a second about how I feel about my work.

16 Marge, people who do this kinda work got a lot of different ideas about their jobs, I mean some folks are ashamed of it and some are proud of it, but I don't feel either way. You see, on accounta many reasons I find that I got to do it and while I don't think that housework is the grandest job I ever hope to get, it makes me *mad* for any fools to come lookin' down their nose at me!

17 If I had a child, I would want that child to do something that paid better and had some opportunity to it, but on the other hand it would distress me no end to see that child get some arrogant attitude toward me because I do domestic work. Domestic workers have done a awful lot of good things in this country besides clean up peoples' houses. We've taken care of our brothers and fathers and husbands when the factory gates and office desks and pretty near everything else was closed to them; we've helped many a neighbor, doin' everything from helpin' to clothe their children to buryin' the dead.

18 . . . Yes, man, and I'll help you to tell it! We built that church that the bazaar was held in! And it's a rare thing for anybody to find a colored family in this land that can't trace a domestic worker somewhere in their history. . . . How 'bout that, girl! . . . Yes, there's many a doctor, many a lawyer, many a teacher, many a minister that got where they are 'cause somebody worked in the kitchen to put 'em there, and there's also a lot of 'em that worked in kitchens themselves in order to climb up a little higher!

19 Of course, a lot of people think it's *smart* not to talk about *slavery*

anymore, but after freedom came, it was domestics that kept us from perishin' by the wayside. . . . Who you tellin'? I know it was our dollars and pennies that built many a school!

20   Yes, I know I said I wasn't particular proud about bein' a domestic worker, but I guess I am. What I really meant to say was that I had plans to be somethin' else, but time and trouble stopped me from doin' it. So I told this little Miss Meek, "Dear, throw back your shoulders and pop your fingers at the *world* because the way I see it there's nobody with common sense that can look down on the domestic worker!"

DISCUSSION QUESTIONS

1. What characteristics does the woman narrator display in this story? Use specific information to support your general statements. Are these characteristics connected to the type of work she does?
2. The protagonist states ". . . the idea of the pictures was to show how we are improvin' ourselves by leaps and bounds through the kinda work that we're doin'." What types of "improvements" have the black people attending the bazaar made in their lives? Have these improvements had an impact on how they treat people they consider beneath them in social standing? Why or why not?
3. The narrator in the story first tells her friend, Marge, that she is not proud of working as a domestic, but by the end of the story she tells Marge she is proud. Why does the protagonist change her mind?
4. What is the significance of the protagonist not having a name?

WRITING TOPICS

1. In your journal, discuss some stereotypical characteristics you associate with a specific job. Try to identify why you associate these types of behavior with this job.
2. Should we draw our identities from the type of work we do or how well we do our work? In a brief essay, discuss whether doing a good job is more important than the type of job performed. Use specific examples drawing from your own life or from the lives of people close to you.

STRANGER IN THE VILLAGE

James Baldwin

James Baldwin was born in 1924 in New York City. He was an avid reader as a child and began writing while a student at Public School 24 in Harlem. His stepfather was a minister, and Baldwin himself later became a minister. Some critics feel Baldwin always retained a preaching style in his writing.

During World War II, Baldwin moved to New Jersey and he worked in war-related industries. In 1948, he moved to Paris. There he completed his first novel, *Go Tell It on the Mountain* (1953). For the rest of his life he divided his time between the United States and France. His short stories and essays appeared in *Harper's, Esquire, Atlantic Monthly,* and *The Reporter* as well as in many other publications. Baldwin's other works include *Notes of a Native Son* (1955), from which this chapter is taken, *Giovanni's Room* (1956), *Nobody Knows My Name* (1961), *Another Country* (1962), *If Beale Street Could Talk* (1974), and *Just Above My Head* (1979). His plays, *Blues for Mr. Charlie* (1964) and *Amen Corner* (1965), were successfully produced. Many critics believe him to be one of the most outstanding essayists America has ever produced. Baldwin died in 1987.

1   From all available evidence no black man had ever set foot in this tiny Swiss village before I came. I was told before arriving that I would probably be a "sight" for the village; I took this to mean that people of my complexion were rarely seen in Switzerland, and also that city people are always something of a "sight" outside of the city. It did not occur to me—possibly because I am an American — that there could be people anywhere who had never seen a Negro.

2   It is a fact that cannot be explained on the basis of the inaccessibility of the village. The village is very high, but it is only four hours from Milan and three hours from Lausanne. It is true that it is virtually unknown. Few

people making plans for a holiday would elect to come here. On the other hand, the villagers are able, presumably to come and go as they please—which they do: to another town at the foot of the mountain, with a population of approximately five thousand, the nearest place to see a movie or go to the bank. In the village there is no movie house, no bank, no library, no theater; very few radios, one jeep, one station wagon; and, at the moment, one typewriter, mine, an invention which the woman next door to me here had never seen. There are about six hundred people living here, all Catholic—I conclude this from the fact that the Catholic church is open all year round, whereas the Protestant chapel, set off on a hill a little removed from the village, is open only in the summertime when the tourists arrive. There are four or five hotels, all closed now, and four or five *bistros,* of which, however, only two do any business during the winter. These two do not do a great deal, for life in the village seems to end around nine or ten o'clock. There are a few stores, butcher, baker, *épicerie,* a hardware store, and a money-changer—who cannot change travelers' checks, but must send them down to the bank, an operation which takes two or three days. There is something called the *Ballet Haus,* closed in the winter and used for God knows what, certainly not ballet, during the summer. There seems to be only one schoolhouse in the village, and this for the quite young children; I suppose this to mean that their older brothers and sisters at some point descend from these mountains in order to complete their education—possibly, again, to the town just below. The landscape is absolutely forbidding, mountains towering on all four sides, ice and snow as far as the eye can reach. In this white wilderness, men and women and children move all day, carrying washing, wood, buckets of milk or water, sometimes skiing on Sunday afternoons. All week long boys and young men are to be seen shoveling snow off the rooftops, or dragging wood down from the forest in sleds.

3   The village's only real attraction, which explains the tourist season, is the hot spring water. A disquietingly high proportion of these tourists are cripples, or semicripples, who come year after year—from other parts of Switzerland, usually—to take the waters. This lends the village, at the height of the season, a rather terrifying air of sanctity, as though it were a lesser Lourdes. There is often something beautiful, there is always something in the spectacle of a person who has lost one of his faculties, a faculty he never questioned until it was gone, and who struggles to recover it. Yet people remain people, on crutches or indeed on deathbeds; and wherever I passed, the first summer I was here, among the native villagers or among the lame, a wind passed with me—of astonishment, curiosity, amusement, and outrage. That first summer I stayed two weeks and never intended to return. But I did return in the winter, to work; the village offers, obviously, no distractions whatever and has the further advantage of being extremely cheap. Now it is winter again, a year later, and I am here again. Everyone in the village knows my name, though they scarcely ever use it, knows that I come from America—though, this, apparently, they will never really believe: black

men come from Africa—and everyone knows that I am the friend of the son of a woman who was born here, and that I am staying in their chalet. But I remain as much a stranger today as I was the first day I arrived, and the children shout *Neger! Neger!* as I walk along the streets.

4   It must be admitted that in the beginning I was far too shocked to have any real reaction. In so far as I reacted at all, I reacted by trying to be pleasant—it being a great part of the American Negro's education (long before he goes to school) that he must make people "like" him. This smile-and-the-world-smiles-with-you routine worked about as well in this situation as it had in the situation for which it was designed, which is to say that it did not work at all. No one, after all, can be liked whose human weight and complexity cannot be, or has not been, admitted. My smile was simply another unheard-of phenomenon which allowed them to see my teeth—they did not, really, see my smile and I began to think that, should I take to snarling, no one would notice any difference. All of the physical characteristics of the Negro which had caused me, in America, a very different and almost forgotten pain were nothing less than miraculous—or infernal—in the eyes of the village people. Some thought my hair was the color of tar, that it had the texture of wire, or the texture of cotton. It was jocularly suggested that I might let it all grow long and make myself a winter coat. If I sat in the sun for more than five minutes some daring creature was certain to come along and gingerly put his fingers on my hair, as though he were afraid of an electric shock, or put his hand on my hand, astonished that the color did not rub off. In all of this, in which it must be conceded there was the charm of genuine wonder and in which there was certainly no element of intentional unkindness, there was yet no suggestion that I was human: I was simply a living wonder.

5   I knew that they did not mean to be unkind, and I know it now; it is necessary, nevertheless, for me to repeat this to myself each time that I walk out of the chalet. The children who shout *Neger!* have no way of knowing the echoes this sound raises in me. They are brimming with good humor and the more daring swell with pride when I stop to speak with them. Just the same, there are days when I cannot pause and smile, when I have no heart to play with them; when, indeed, I mutter sourly to myself, exactly as I muttered on the streets of a city these children have never seen, when I was no bigger than these children are now: *Your* mother *was a nigger.* Joyce is right about history being a nightmare—but it may be the nightmare from which no one *can* awaken. People are trapped in history and history is trapped in them.

6   There is a custom in the village—I am told it is repeated in many villages—of "buying" African natives for the purpose of converting them to Christianity. There stands in the church all year round a small box with a slot for money, decorated with a black figurine, and into this box the villagers drop their francs. During the *carnaval* which precedes Lent, two village children have their faces blackened—out of which bloodless darkness their

blue eyes shine like ice—and fantastic horsehair wigs are placed on their blond heads; thus disguised, they solicit among the villagers for money for the missionaries in Africa. Between the box in the church and the blackened children, the village "bought" last year six or eight African natives. This was reported to me with pride by the wife of one of the *bistro* owners and I was careful to express astonishment and pleasure at the solicitude shown by the village for the souls of black folk. The *bistro* owner's wife beamed with a pleasure far more genuine than my own and seemed to feel that I might now breathe more easily concerning the souls of at least six of my kinsmen.

7   I tried not to think of these so lately baptized kinsmen, of the price paid for them, or the peculiar price they themselves would pay, and said nothing about my father, who having taken his own conversion too literally never, at bottom, forgave the white world (which he described as heathen) for having saddled him with a Christ in whom, to judge at least from their treatment of him, they themselves no longer believed. I thought of white men arriving for the first time in an African village, strangers there, as I am a stranger here, and tried to imagine the astounded populace touching their hair and marveling at the color of their skin. But there is a great difference between being the first white man to be seen by Africans and being the first black man to be seen by whites. The white man takes the astonishment as tribute, for he arrives to conquer and to convert the natives, whose inferiority in relation to himself is not even to be questioned; whereas I, without a thought of conquest, find myself among a people whose culture controls me, has even, in a sense, created me, people who have cost me more in anguish and rage than they will ever know, who yet do not even know of my existence. The astonishment with which I might have greeted them, should they have stumbled into my African village a few hundred years ago, might have rejoiced their hearts. But the astonishment with which they greet me today can only poison mine.

8   And this is so despite everything I may do to feel differently despite my friendly conversations with the *bistro* owner's wife, despite their three-year-old son who has at last become my friend, despite the *saluts* and *bonsoirs* which I exchange with people as I walk, despite the fact that I know that no individual can be taken to task for what history is doing, or has done. I say that the culture of these people controls me—but they can scarcely be held responsible for European culture. America comes out of Europe, but these people have never seen America, nor have most of them seen more of Europe than the hamlet at the foot of their mountain. Yet they move with an authority which I shall never have; and they regard me, quite rightly, not only as a stranger in their village but as a suspect latecomer, bearing no credentials, to everything they have—however unconsciously—inherited.

9   For this village, even were it incomparably more remote and incredibly more primitive, is the West, the West onto which I have been so strangely grafted. These people cannot be, from the point of view of power, strangers anywhere in the world; they have made the modern world, in effect, even if

they do not know it. The most illiterate among them is related, in a way that I am not, to Dante, Shakespeare, Michelangelo, Aeschylus, Da Vinci, Rembrandt, and Racine; the cathedral at Chartres says something to them which it cannot say to me, as indeed would New York's Empire State Building, should anyone here ever see it. Out of their hymns and dances come Beethoven and Bach. Go back a few centuries and they are in their full glory—but I am in Africa, watching the conquerors arrive.

10   The rage of the disesteemed is personally fruitless, but it is also absolutely inevitable; this rage, so generally discounted, so little understood even among the people whose daily bread it is, is one of the things that makes history. Rage can only with difficulty, and never entirely, be brought under the domination of the intelligence and is therefore not susceptible to any arguments whatever. This is a fact which ordinary representatives of the *Herrenvolk,* having never felt this rage and being unable to imagine it, quite fail to understand. Also, rage cannot be hidden, it can only be dissembled. This dissembling deludes the thoughtless, and strengthens rage and adds, to rage, contempt. There are, no doubt, as many ways of coping with the resulting complex of tensions as there are black men in the world, but no black man can hope ever to be entirely liberated from this internal warfare— rage, dissembling, and contempt having inevitably accompanied his first realization of the power of white men. What is crucial here is that, since white men represent in the black man's world so heavy a weight, white men have for black men a reality which is far from being reciprocal; and hence all black men have toward all white men an attitude which is designed really, either to rob the white man of the jewel of his naïveté, or else to make it cost him dear.

11   The black man insists, by whatever means he finds at his disposal, that the white man cease to regard him as an exotic rarity and recognize him as a human being. This is a very charged and difficult moment, for there is a great deal of will power involved in the white man's naïveté. Most people are not naturally reflective any more than they are naturally malicious, and the white man prefers to keep the black man at a certain human remove because it is easier for him thus to preserve his simplicity and avoid being called to account for crimes committed by his forefathers, or his neighbors. He is inescapably aware, nevertheless, that he is in a better position in the world than black men are, nor can he quite put to death the suspicion that he is hated by black men therefore. He does not wish to be hated, neither does he wish to change places, and at this point in his uneasiness he can scarcely avoid having recourse to those legends which white men have created about black men, the most usual effect of which is that the white man finds himself enmeshed, so to speak, in his own language which describes hell, as well as the attributes which lead one to hell, as being as black as night.

12   Every legend, moreover, contains its residuum of truth, and the root function of language is to control the universe by describing it. It is of quite

considerable significance that black men remain, in the imagination, and in overwhelming number in fact, beyond the disciplines of salvation; and this despite the fact that the West has been "buying" African natives for centuries. There is, I should hazard, an instantaneous necessity to be divorced from this so visibly unsaved stranger, in whose heart, moreover, one cannot guess what dreams of vengeance are being nourished; and, at the same time, there are few things on earth more attractive than the idea of the unspeakable liberty which is allowed the unredeemed. When, beneath the black mask, a human being begins to make himself felt one cannot escape a certain awful wonder as to what kind of human being it is. What one's imagination makes of other people is dictated, of course, by the laws of one's own personality and it is one of the ironies of black-white relations that, by means of what the white man imagines the black man to be, the black man is enabled to know who the white man is.

13   I have said, for example, that I am as much a stranger in this village today as I was the first summer I arrived, but this is not quite true. The villagers wonder less about the texture of my hair than they did then, and wonder rather more about me. And the fact that their wonder now exists on another level is reflected in their attitude and in their eyes. There are the children who make those delightful, hilarious, sometimes astonishingly grave overtures of friendship in the unpredictable fashion of children; other children, having been taught that the devil is a black man, scream in genuine anguish as I approach. Some of the older women never pass without a friendly greeting, never pass, indeed, if it seems that they will be able to engage me in conversation; other women look down or look away or rather contemptuously smirk. Some of the men drink with me and suggest that I learn how to ski—partly, I gather, because they cannot imagine what I would look like on skis—and want to know if I am married, and ask questions about my *métier.* But some of the men have accused *le sale nègre*—behind my back—of stealing wood and there is already in the eyes of some of them that peculiar, intent, paranoiac malevolence which one sometimes surprises in the eyes of American white men when, out walking with their Sunday girl, they see a Negro male approach.

14   There is a dreadful abyss between the streets of this village and the streets of the city in which I was born, between the children who shout *Neger!* today and those who shouted *Nigger!* yesterday—the abyss is experience, the American experience. The syllable hurled behind me today expresses, above all, wonder: I am a stranger here. But I am not a stranger in America and the same syllable riding on the American air expresses the war my presence has occasioned in the American soul.

15   For this village brings home to me this fact: that there was a day, and not really a very distant day, when Americans were scarcely Americans at all but discontented Europeans, facing a great unconquered continent and strolling, say, into a marketplace and seeing black men for the first time. The shock this spectacle afforded is suggested, surely, by the promptness with

which they decided that these black men were not really men but cattle. It is true that the necessity on the part of the settlers of the New World of reconciling their moral assumptions with the fact—and the necessity—of slavery enhanced immensely and charm of this idea, and it is also true that this idea expresses, with a truly American bluntness, the attitude which to varying extent all masters have had toward all slaves.

16 But between the former slaves and slave-owners and the drama which begins for Americans over three hundred years ago at Jamestown, there are at least two differences to be observed. The American Negro slave could not suppose, for one thing, as slaves in past epochs had supposed and often done, that he would ever be able to wrest the power from his master's hands. This was a supposition which the modern era, which was to bring about such vast changes in the aims and dimensions of power, put to death; it only begins, in unprecedented fashion, and with dreadful implications, to be resurrected today. But even had this supposition persisted with undiminished force, the American Negro slave could not have used it to lend his condition dignity, for the reason that this supposition rests on another: that the slave in exile yet remains related to his past, has some means—if only in memory—of revering and sustaining the forms of his former life, is able, in short, to maintain his identity.

17 This was not the case with the American Negro slave. He is unique among the black men of the world in that his past was taken from him, almost literally, at one blow. One wonders what on earth the first slave found to say to the first dark child he bore. I am told that there are Haitians able to trace their ancestry back to African kings, but any American Negro wishing to go back so far will find his journey through time abruptly arrested by the signature on the bill of sale which served as the entrance paper for his ancestor. At the time—to say nothing of the circumstances—of the enslavement of the captive black man who was to become the American Negro, there was not the remotest possibility that he would ever take power from his master's hands. There was no reason to suppose that his situation would ever change, nor was there, shortly, anything to indicate that his situation had ever been different. It was his necessity, in the words of E. Franklin Frazier, to find a "motive for living under American culture or die." The identity of the American Negro comes out of this extreme situation, and the evolution of this identity was a source of the most intolerable anxiety in the minds and the lives of his masters.

18 For the history of the American Negro is unique also in this: that the question of his humanity, and of his rights therefore as a human being, became a burning one for several generations of Americans, so burning a question that it ultimately became one of those used to divide the nation. It is out of this argument that the venom of the epithet *Nigger!* is derived. It is an argument which Europe has never had, and hence Europe quite sincerely fails to understand how or why the argument arose in the first place, why its effects are so frequently disastrous and always so unpredictable, why

it refuses until today to be entirely settled. Europe's black possessions remained—and do remain—in Europe's colonies, at which remove they represented no threat whatever to European identity. If they posed any problem at all for the European conscience, it was a problem which remained comfortingly abstract: in effect, the black man, *as a man,* did not exist in Europe. But in America, even as a slave, he was an inescapable part of the general social fabric and no American could escape having an attitude toward him. Americans attempt until today to make an abstraction of the Negro, but the very nature of these abstractions reveals the tremendous effects the presence of the Negro has had on the American character.

19   When one considers the history of the Negro in America it is of the greatest importance to recognize that the moral beliefs of a person, or a people, are never really as tenuous as life—which is not moral—very often causes them to appear; these create for them a frame of reference and a necessary hope, the hope being that when life has done its worst they will be enabled to rise above themselves and to triumph over life. Life would scarcely be bearable if this hope did not exist. Again, even when the worst has been said, to betray a belief is not by any means to have put oneself beyond its power; the betrayal of a belief is not the same thing as ceasing to believe. If this were not so there would be no moral standards in the world at all. Yet one must also recognize that morality is based on ideas and that all ideas are dangerous—dangerous because ideas can only lead to action and where the action leads no man can say. And dangerous in this respect: that confronted with the impossibility of remaining faithful to one's beliefs, and the equal impossibility of becoming free of them, one can be driven to the most inhuman excesses. The ideas on which American beliefs are based are not, though Americans often seem to think so, ideas which originated in America. They came out of Europe. And the establishment of democracy on the American continent was scarcely as radical a break with the past as was the necessity, which Americans faced, of broadening this concept to include black men.

20   This was, literally, a hard necessity. It was impossible, for one thing, for Americans to abandon their beliefs, not only because these beliefs alone seemed able to justify the sacrifices they had endured and the blood that they had spilled, but also because these beliefs afforded them their only bulwark against a moral chaos as absolute as the physical chaos of the continent it was their destiny to conquer. But in the situation in which Americans found themselves, these beliefs threatened an idea which, whether or not one likes to think so, is the very warp and woof of the heritage of the West, the idea of white supremacy.

21   Americans have made themselves notorious by the shrillness and the brutality with which they have insisted on this idea, but they did not invent it; and it has escaped the world's notice that those very excesses of which Americans have been guilty imply a certain, unprecedented uneasiness over the idea's life and power, if not, indeed, the idea's validity. The idea of white supremacy rests simply on the fact that white men are the creators of civi-

lization (the present civilization, which is the only one that matters; all previous civilizations are simply "contributions" to our own) and are therefore civilization's guardians and defenders. Thus it was impossible for Americans to accept the black man as one of themselves, for to do so was to jeopardize their status as white men. But not so to accept him was to deny his human reality, his human weight and complexity, and the strain of denying the overwhelmingly undeniable forced Americans into rationalizations so fantastic that they approached the pathological.

22   At the root of the American Negro problem is the necessity of the American white man to find a way of living with the Negro in order to be able to live with himself. And the history of this problem can be reduced to the means used by Americans—lynch law and law, segregation and legal acceptance, terrorization and concession—either to come to terms with this necessity, or to find a way around it, or (most usually) to find a way of doing both these things at once. The resulting spectacle, at once foolish and dreadful, led someone to make the quite accurate observation that "the Negro-in-America is a form of insanity which overtakes white men."

23   In this long battle, a battle by no means finished, the unforeseeable effects of which will be felt by many future generations, the white man's motive was the protection of his identity; the black man was motivated by the need to establish an identity. And despite the terrorization which the Negro in America endured and endures sporadically until today, despite the cruel and totally inescapable ambivalence of his status in his country, the battle for his identity has long ago been won. He is not a visitor to the West, but a citizen there, an American; as American as the Americans who despise him, the Americans who fear him, the Americans who love him—the Americans who became less than themselves, or rose to be greater than themselves by virtue of the fact that the challenge he represented was inescapable. He is perhaps the only black man in the world whose relationship to white men is more terrible, more subtle, and more meaningful than the relationship of bitter possessed to uncertain possessor. His survival depended, and his development depends, on his ability to turn his peculiar status in the Western world to his own advantage and, it may be, to the very great advantage of that world. It remains for him to fashion out of his experience that which will give him sustenance, and a voice.

24   The cathedral at Chartres, I have said, says something to the people of this village which it cannot say to me; but it is important to understand that this cathedral says something to me which it cannot say to them. Perhaps they are struck by the power of the spires, the glory of the windows; but they have known God after all, longer than I have known him, and in a different way, and I am terrified by the slippery bottomless well to be found in the crypt, down which heretics were hurled to death, and by the obscene, inescapable gargoyles jutting out of the stone and seeming to say that God and the devil can never be divorced. I doubt that the villagers think of the devil when they face a cathedral because they have never been identified with

the devil. But I must accept the status which myth, if nothing else, gives me in the West before I can hope to change the myth.

25   Yet, if the American Negro has arrived at his identity by virtue of the absoluteness of his estrangement from his past, American white men still nourish the illusion that there is some means of recovering the European innocence, of returning to a state in which black men do not exist. This is one of the greatest errors Americans can make. The identity they fought so hard to protect has, by virtue of that battle, undergone a change: Americans are as unlike any other white people in the world as it is possible to be. I do not think, for example, that it is too much to suggest that the American vision of the world—which allows so little reality, generally speaking, for any of the darker forces in human life, which tends until today to paint moral issues in glaring black and white—owes a great deal to the battle waged by Americans to maintain between themselves and black men a human separation which could not be bridged. It is only now beginning to be borne in on us—very faintly, it must be admitted, very slowly, and very much against our will—that this vision of the world is dangerously inaccurate, and perfectly useless. For it protects our moral high-mindedness at the terrible expense of weakening our grasp of reality. People who shut their eyes to reality simply invite their own destruction, and anyone who insists on remaining in a state of innocence long after that innocence is dead turns himself into a monster.

26   The time has come to realize that the interracial drama acted out on the American continent has not only created a new black man, it has created a new white man, too. No road whatever will lead Americans back to the simplicity of this European village where white men still have the luxury of looking on me as a stranger. I am not, really, a stranger any longer for any, American alive. One of the things that distinguishes Americans from other people is that no other people has ever been so deeply involved in the lives of black men, and vice versa. This fact faced, with all its implications, it can be seen that the history of the American Negro problem is not merely shameful, it is also something of an achievement. For even when the worst has been said, it must also be added that the perpetual challenge posed by this problem was always, somehow, perpetually met. It is precisely this black-white experience which may prove of indispensable value to us in the world we face today. This world is white no longer, and it will never be white again.

DISCUSSION QUESTIONS

1. What did the village people think about Baldwin and how did they react to him?

2. Baldwin says being called *Neger! Neger!* by the children caused him to react by trying to be pleasant. What experience did he have in America that caused him to react this way?
3. What do you think Baldwin means when he says that the most illiterate villagers, in a way, are related to Dante, Shakespeare, Michelangelo, and others, and that he is not?

WRITING TOPICS

1. Baldwin says: "People are trapped in history and history is trapped in them." Write a short essay in which you explain the quotation. Support your position with examples from history or from literature.
2. Baldwin claims that African Americans have arrived at their identities by being forcibly separated from their past. In your journal, list ways this new identity has strengthened all Americans. Use specific examples from the reading.

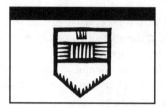

EPILOGUE FROM *INVISIBLE MAN*

Ralph Ellison

Ralph Ellison was born in 1914 and is considered one of the most influential American authors of the twentieth century. Best known for his novel *Invisible Man* (1952), Ellison demonstrated that an African-American writer could write about issues of concern to black Americans that were also of universal concern. Ellison was born in Oklahoma City. His father, who died when Ellison was three, named him after Ralph Waldo Emerson. Ellison was raised by his mother, a domestic worker who also worked at enlisting blacks into the Socialist Party. In the early 1930s, Ellison received a scholarship to the Tuskegee Institute where he studied music until 1936. Ellison traveled to New York to earn money for college. In New York he met Richard Wright and began writing essays for Wright's magazine, *New Challenge*. During World War II, Ellison served in the merchant marines where, instead of writing a war novel as he had envisioned himself doing, he began writing *Invisible Man*. Ellison taught at several universities and lectured widely throughout the United States.

Ellison's novel *Invisible Man*, unlike many other African-American writers' works, received a great deal of praise from white critics; it continues to generate scholarship among white scholars. Ellison's other publications include two essay collections: *Shadow and Act* (1964) and *Going to the Territory* (1986). His short stories appeared in *A New Southern Harvest* (1957), *The Angry Black* (1962), and *Southwest Fiction* (1980). Ellison died in 1994.

1   So there you have all of it that's important. Or at least you *almost* have it. I'm an invisible man and it placed me in a hole—or showed me the hole I was in, if you will—and I reluctantly accepted the fact. What else could I have done? Once you get used to it, reality is as irresistible as a club, and I was clubbed into the cellar before I caught the hint. Perhaps that's the way

it had to be; I don't know. Nor do I know whether accepting the lesson has placed me in the rear or in the *avant-garde*. *That*, perhaps, is a lesson for history, and I'll leave such decisions to Jack and his ilk while I try belatedly to study the lesson of my own life.

2   Let me be honest with you—a feat which, by the way, I find of the utmost difficulty. When one is invisible he finds such problems as good and evil, honesty and dishonesty, of such shifting shapes that he confuses one with the other, depending upon who happens to be looking through him at the time. Well, now I've been trying to look through myself, and there's a risk in it. I was never more hated than when I tried to be honest. Or when, even as just now I've tried to articulate exactly what I felt to be the truth. No one was satisfied—not even I. On the other hand, I've never been more loved and appreciated than when I tried to "justify" and affirm someone's mistaken beliefs; or when I've tried to give my friends the incorrect, absurd answers they wished to hear. In my presence they could talk and agree with themselves, the world was nailed down, and they loved it. They received a feeling of security. But here was the rub: Too often, in order to justify *them,* I had to take myself by the throat and choke myself until my eyes bulged and my tongue hung out and wagged like the door of an empty house in a high wind. Oh, yes, it made them happy and it made me sick. So I became ill of affirmation, of saying "yes" against the nay-saying of my stomach—not to mention my brain.

3   There is, by the way, an area in which a man's feelings are more rational than his mind, and it is precisely in that area that his will is pulled in several directions at the same time. You might sneer at this, but I know now. I was pulled this way and that for longer than I can remember. And my problem was that I always tried to go in everyone's way but my own. I have also been called one thing and then another while no one really wished to hear what I called myself. So after years of trying to adopt the opinions of others I finally rebelled. I am an *invisible* man. Thus I have come a long way and returned and boomeranged a long way from the point in society toward which I originally aspired.

4   So I took to the cellar; I hibernated. I got away from it all. But that wasn't enough. I couldn't be still even in hibernation. Because, damn it, there's the mind, the *mind*. It wouldn't let me rest. Gin, jazz and dreams were not enough. Books were not enough. My belated appreciation of the crude joke that had kept me running, was not enough. And my mind revolved again and again back to my grandfather. And, despite the farce that ended my attempt to say "yes" to Brotherhood, I'm still plagued by his deathbed advice . . . Perhaps he hid his meaning deeper than I thought, perhaps his anger threw me off—I can't decide. Could he have meant—hell, he *must* have meant the principle, that we were to affirm the principle on which the country was built and not the men, or at least not the men who did the violence. Did he mean say "yes" because he knew that the principle was greater than the men, greater than the numbers and the vicious power and

all the methods used to corrupt its name? Did he mean to affirm the principle, which they themselves had dreamed into being out of the chaos and
darkness of the feudal past, and which they had violated and compromised
to the point of absurdity even in their own corrupt minds? Or did he mean
that we had to take the responsibility for all of it, for the men as well as the
principle, because we were the heirs who must use the principle because no
other fitted our needs? Not for the power or for vindication, but because we,
with the given circumstance of our origin, could only thus find transcen-
dence? Was it that we of all, we, most of all, had to affirm the principle, the
plan in whose name we had been brutalized and sacrificed—not because we
would always be weak nor because we were afraid or opportunistic, but
because we were older than they, in the sense of what it took to live in the
world with others and because they had exhausted in us, some—not much,
but some—of the human greed and smallness, yes, and the fear and superstition that had kept them running. (Oh, yes, they're running too, running
all over themselves.) Or was it, did he mean that we should affirm the principle because we, through no fault of our own, were linked to all the others
in the loud, clamoring semi-visible world, that world seen only as a fertile
field for exploitation by Jack and his kind, and with condescension by
Norton and his, who were tired of being the mere pawns in the futile game
of "making history?" Had he seen that for these too we had to say "yes" to
the principle, lest they turn upon us to destroy both it and us?

5   "Agree 'em to death and destruction," grandfather had advised. Hell,
weren't they their own death and their own destruction except as the principle lived in them and in us? And here's the cream of the joke: Weren't we
part of them as well as apart from them and subject to die when they died?
I can't figure it out; it escapes me. But what do *I* really want, I've asked
myself. Certainly not the freedom of a Rinehart or the power of a Jack, nor
simply the freedom not to run. No, but the next step I couldn't make, so
I've remained in the hole.

6   I'm not blaming anyone for this state of affairs, mind you; nor merely
crying *mea culpa*. The fact is that you carry part of your sickness within you,
at least I do as an invisible man. I carried my sickness and though for a long
time I tried to place it in the outside world, the attempt to write it down
shows me that at least half of it lay within me. It came upon me slowly, like
that strange disease that affects those black men whom you see turning
slowly from black to albino, their pigment disappearing as under the radia-
tion of some cruel, invisible ray. You go along for years knowing something
is wrong, then suddenly you discover that you're as transparent as air. At first
you tell yourself that it's all a dirty joke, or that it's due to the "political situation." But deep down you come to suspect that you're yourself to blame,
and you stand naked and shivering before the millions of eyes who look
through you unseeingly. *That* is the real soul-sickness, the spear in the side,
the drag by the neck through the mob-angry town, the Grand Inquisition,
the embrace of the Maiden, the rip in the belly with the guts spilling out,

the trip to the chamber with the deadly gas that ends in the oven so hygienically clean—only it's worse because you continue stupidly to live. But live you must, and you can either make passive love to your sickness or burn it out and go on to the next conflicting phase.

7   Yes, but what *is* the next phase? How often have I tried to find it! Over and over again I've gone up above to seek it out. For, like almost everyone else in our country, I started out with my share of optimism. I believed in hard work and progress and action, but now, after first being "for" society and then "against" it, I assign myself no rank or any limit, and such an attitude is very much against the trend of the times. But my world has become one of infinite possibilities. What a phrase—still it's a good phrase and a good view of life, and a man shouldn't accept any other; that much I've learned underground. Until some gang succeeds in putting the world in a strait jacket, its definition is possibility. Step outside the narrow borders of what men call reality and you step into chaos—ask Rinehart, he's a master of it—or imagination. That too I've learned in the cellar, and not by deadening my sense of perception; I'm invisible, not blind.

8   No indeed, the world is just as concrete, ornery, vile and sublimely wonderful as before, only now I better understand my relation to it and it to me. I've come a long way from those days when, full of illusion, I lived a public life and attempted to function under the assumption that the world was solid and all the relationships therein. Now I know men are different and that all life is divided and that only in division is there true health. Hence again I have stayed in my hole, because up above there's an increasing passion to make men conform to a pattern. Just as in my nightmare, Jack, and the boys are waiting with their knives, looking for the slightest excuse to . . . well, to "ball the jack," and I do not refer to the old dance step, although what they're doing is making the old eagle rock dangerously.

9   Whence all this passion toward conformity anyway?—diversity is the word. Let man keep his many parts and you'll have no tyrant states. Why, if they follow this conformity business they'll end up by forcing me, an invisible man, to become white, which is not a color but the lack of one. Must I strive toward colorlessness? But seriously, and without snobbery, think of what the world would lose if that should happen. America is woven of many strands; I would recognize them and let it so remain. It's "winner take nothing" that is the great truth of our country or of any country. Life is to be lived, not controlled; and humanity is won by continuing to play in face of certain defeat. Our fate is to become one, and yet many—This is not prophecy, but description. Thus one of the greatest jokes in the world is the spectacle of the whites busy escaping blackness and becoming blacker every day, and the blacks striving toward whiteness, becoming quite dull and gray. None of us seems to know who he is or where he's going.

10   Which reminds me of something that occurred the other day in the subway. At first I saw only an old gentleman who for the moment was lost. I knew he was lost, for as I looked down the platform I saw him approach

several people and turn away without speaking. He's lost, I thought, and he'll keep coming until he sees me, then he'll ask his direction. Maybe there's an embarrassment in it if he admits he's lost to a strange white man. Perhaps to lose a sense of *where* you are implies the danger of losing a sense of *who* you are. That must be it, I thought—to lose your direction is to lose your face. So here he comes to ask his direction from the lost, the invisible. Very well, I've learned to live without direction. Let him ask.

11 But then he was only a few feet away and I recognized him; it was Mr. Norton. The old gentleman was thinner and wrinkled now but as dapper as ever. And seeing him made all the old life live in me for an instant, and I smiled with tear-stinging eyes. Then it was over, dead, and when he asked me how to get to Centre Street, I regarded him with mixed feelings.

12 "Don't you know me?" I said.

13 "Should I?" he said.

14 "You see me?" I said, watching him tensely.

15 "Why, of course—Sir, do you know the way to Centre Street?"

16 "So. Last time it was the Golden Day, now it's Centre Street. You've retrenched, sir. But don't you really know who I am?"

17 "Young man, I'm in a hurry," he said, cupping a hand to his ear. "Why should I know you?"

18 "Because I'm your destiny."

19 "My destiny, did you say?" He gave me a puzzled stare, backing away. "Young man, are you well? Which train did you say I should take?"

20 "I didn't say," I said, shaking my head. "Now, aren't you ashamed?"

21 "Ashamed? ASHAMED!" he said indignantly.

22 I laughed, suddenly taken by the idea. "Because, Mr. Norton, if you don't know *where* you are, you probably don't know who *you* are. So you came to me out of shame. You are ashamed, now aren't you?"

23 "Young man, I've lived too long in this world to be ashamed of anything. Are you light-headed from hunger? How do you know my name?"

24 "But I'm your destiny, I made you. Why shouldn't I know you?" I said, walking closer and seeing him back against a pillar. He looked around like a cornered animal. He thought I was mad.

25 "Don't be afraid, Mr. Norton," I said. "There's a guard down the platform there. You're safe. Take any train; they all go to the Golden D—"

26 But now an express had rolled up and the old man was disappearing quite spryly inside one of its doors. I stood there laughing hysterically. I laughed all the way back to my hole.

27 But after I had laughed I was thrown back on my thoughts—how had it all happened? And I asked myself if it were only a joke and I couldn't answer. Since then I've sometimes been overcome with a passion to return into that "heart of darkness" across the Mason-Dixon line, but then I remind myself that the true darkness lies within my own mind, and the idea loses itself in the gloom. Still the passion persists. Sometimes I feel the need to reaffirm all of it, the whole unhappy territory and all the things loved and unlovable

in it, for all of it is part of me. Till now, however, this is as far as I've ever gotten, for all life seen from the hole of invisibility is absurd.

28   So why do I write, torturing myself to put it down? Because in spite of myself I've learned some things. Without the possibility of action, all knowledge comes to one labeled "file and forget," and I can neither file nor forget. Nor will certain ideas forget me; they keep filing away at my lethargy, my complacency. Why should I be the one to dream this nightmare? Why should I be dedicated and set aside—yes, if not to at least *tell* a few people about it? There seems to be no escape. Here I've set out to throw my anger into the world's face, but now that I've tried to put it all down the old fascination with playing a role returns, and I'm drawn upward again. So that even before I finish I've failed (maybe my anger is too heavy; perhaps, being a talker, I've used too many words). But I've failed. The very act of trying to put it all down has confused me and negated some of the anger and some of the bitterness. So it is that now I denounce and defend, or feel prepared to defend. I condemn and affirm, say no and say yes, say yes and say no. I denounce because though implicated and partially responsible, I have been hurt to the point of abysmal pain, to the point of invisibility. And I defend because in spite of all I find that I love. In order to get some of it down I *have* to love. I sell you no phony forgiveness, I'm a desperate man—but too much of your life will be lost, its meaning lost, unless you approach it as much through love as through hate. So I approach it through division. So I denounce and I defend and I hate and I love.

29   Perhaps that makes me a little bit as human as my grandfather. Once I thought my grandfather incapable of thoughts about humanity, but I was wrong. Why should an old slave use such a phrase as, "This and this or this has made me more human," as I did in my arena speech? Hell, he never had any doubts about his humanity—that was left to his "free" offspring. He accepted his humanity just as he accepted the principle. It was his, and the principle lives on in all its human and absurd diversity. So now having tried to put it down I have disarmed myself in the process. You won't believe in my invisibility and you'll fail to see how any principle that applies to you could apply to me. You'll fail to see it even though death waits for both of us if you don't. Nevertheless, the very disarmament has brought me to a decision. The hibernation is over. I must shake off the old skin and come up for breath. There's a stench in the air, which, from this distance underground, might be the smell either of death or of spring—I hope of spring. But don't let me trick you, there *is* a death in the smell of spring and in the smell of thee as in the smell of me. And if nothing more, invisibility has taught my nose to classify the stenches of death.

30   In going underground, I whipped it all except the mind, the *mind*. And the mind that has conceived a plan of living must never lose sight of the chaos against which that pattern was conceived. That goes for societies as well as for individuals. Thus, having tried to give pattern to the chaos which lives within the pattern of your certainties, I must come out, I must emerge.

And there's still a conflict within me: With Louis Armstrong one half of me says, "Open the window and let the foul air out," while the other says, "It was good green corn before the harvest." Of course Louie was kidding, *he* wouldn't have thrown old Bad Air out, because it would have broken up the music and the dance, when it was the good music that came from the bell of old Bad Air's horn that counted. Old Bad Air is still around with his music and his dancing and his diversity, and I'll be up and around with mine. And, as I said before, a decision has been made. I'm shaking off the old skin and I'll leave it here in the hole. I'm coming out, no less invisible without it, but coming out nevertheless. And I suppose it's damn well time. Even hibernations can be overdone, come to think of it. Perhaps that's my greatest social crime, I've overstayed my hibernation, since there's a possibility that even an invisible man has a socially responsible role to play.

31   "Ah," I can hear you say, "so it was all a build-up to bore us with his buggy jiving. He only wanted us to listen to him rave!" But only partially true: Being invisible and without substance, a disembodied voice, as it were, what else could I do? What else but try to tell you what was really happening when your eyes were looking through? And it is this which frightens me:

32   Who know but that, on the lower frequencies, I speak for you?

DISCUSSION QUESTIONS

1. Is the unnamed protagonist figuratively or literally "invisible"? Use specific information from the reading to support your response.
2. Whom does the invisible man blame for his invisibility? Others? Himself? Both? Why?
3. By the end of the reading, does the protagonist come to a sense of self? Support your response with specific information from the reading.

WRITING TOPICS

1. In your journal, write about a time when you felt invisible. What was happening in your life? How did others treat you? How did you resolve your feelings of invisibility?
2. Write an essay comparing the unnamed African-American male protagonist in this selection with the unnamed African-American female protagonist in Alice Childress's "All about My Job." In what ways are the two characters similar? Dissimilar?

CHAPTER SEVEN

DREAMERS AND REVOLUTIONARIES

"Some people are not disposed to give us credit for having feelings, passions, ambitions and desires like other races; they are satisfied to relegate us to the back-heap of human aspirations; but this is a mistake."

—*Marcus Garvey*

The push for freedom and equality by African Americans has been going on ever since they first landed on American soil. They have risked and even lost their lives in the quest for justice. The first revolutionary to die was Crispus Attucks, a former slave. He was killed by British troops in the Boston Massacre in 1770. Harriet Tubman dreamed of freedom for her people. After escaping from slavery, she made 19 journeys back to the South to lead more than three hundred slaves—including her own parents—to their freedom. And Nat Turner sought freedom for himself and others by leading an insurrection against white slaveholders in 1831.

African Americans have always protested against unjust treatment, be it slavery, discrimination, or segregation. Their experiences in the United States have been chronicled by men and women who have used the pen, not the sword, to draw attention to the plight of African Americans and their quest for equality and respect.

The Civil Rights and Black Arts movements in the 1960s and beyond used the pen to foster confrontation and discussion of those burning issues that were being side-stepped by the majority community. An increased interest in their heritage has encouraged African-American writers to create literature reflecting their own identity. Revolutionary writers and poets such as Amiri Baraka, Malcolm X, Mari Evans, and Haki Madhubuti and dreamers such as Martin Luther King Jr., W. E. B. Du Bois, and Nikki Giovanni were at the vanguard in unleashing their thoughts and admonitions. The goal was to achieve change in all areas—social, political, and moral. The dreams and the quest for change continue today.

VIVE NOIR!

Mari Evans

Mari Evans was born in Toledo, Ohio, and attended public school there. Later, she studied fashion design at the University of Toledo. Evans credits her father and the poetry of Langston Hughes as having had strong influences on her writing career. From 1968 to 1973, Evans was a producer, writer, and director of *The Black Experience* at WTTV in Indianapolis. She has also served as a consultant with the National Endowment for the Arts (1969–70), a director of the Literary Advisory Panel for the Indiana Arts Commission (1976–77), and a member of the board of directors of the First World Foundation. In 1981 Evans received a National Endowment for the Arts Creative Writing Award. Evans has combined her writing career with an academic one, teaching at Indiana University, Purdue University, Washington University, Cornell University, Spelman College, and the State University of New York at Albany.

Evans's short fiction, essays, poetry, and dramatic literature present authentic voices from African-American communities. Her published works and play productions include *I Am a Black Woman*, (1970), *I Look at Me!* (1973), *River of My Song* (1977), *Eyes* (1979), *Nightstar: 1973–1978* (1981), and *A Dark and Splendid Mass* (1992). She also edited *Black Women Writers (1950–1980): A Critical Evaluation* (1984).

i

am going to rise
en masse
from Inner City

5   sick
           of newyork ghettos
           chicago tenements
           l a's slums

Vive Noir!: Long Live Black!

weary
10   of exhausted lands
        sagging privies
        saying yessuh yessah
        yesSIR
        in an assortment
15   of geographical dialects i
have seen my last
broken down plantation
even from a
distance
20   i
will load all my goods
in '50 Chevy pickups '53
Fords fly United and '66
caddys i
25   have packed in
        the old man and the old lady and
        wiped the children's noses
        I'm tired
          of hand me downs
30   shut me ups
            pin me ins
              keep me outs
                messing me over have
              just had it
35   baby
            from
              you . . .
i'm
gonna spread out
40 over America
                intrude
my proud blackness
all
      over the place
45   i have wrested wheat fields
                from the forests

                turned rivers
                from their courses

                leveled mountains
50   at a word
                festooned the land with
                bridges
                    gemlike

on filaments of steel
55   moved
glistening towersofBabel in place
like blocks
sweated a whole
civilization
60   . . . for you
now
        i'm
gonna breathe fire
through flaming nostrils BURN
65   a place for
        me
in the skyscrapers and the
schoolrooms on the green
lawns and the white
70 beaches
        i'm
gonna wear the robes and
sit on the benches
make the rules and make
75 the arrests say
who can and who
can't
        baby you don't stand
        a
80   chance
i'm
gonna put black angels
in all the books and a black
Christchild in Mary's arms i'm
85 gonna make black bunnies black
fairies black santas black
nursery rhymes and
        black
ice cream
90   i'm
gonna make it a
crime
to be anything BUT black
pass the coppertone

₉₅ gonna make white
a twentyfourhour
lifetime
J.O.B.
         an' when all the coppertone's gone . . . . ?

DISCUSSION QUESTIONS

1. Evans uses limited punctuation in this poem. There are no commas or periods and sentences start with lowercase letters. She uses ellipses three times and a question mark once. How does the placement of the words on the lines and the limited use of punctuation affect the overall feeling of the poem?
2. The speaker in the poem refers to himself or herself with a lowercase *i*. Who do you think the speaker is? How would you describe the speaker based on the description or images he or she presents in this poem?
3. Throughout the poem the speaker is talking to someone whom he or she calls "baby" and "you." To whom is the speaker addressing the poem? What is the speaker's attitude toward this person or group?
4. Is the speaker in the poem a dreamer or a revolutionary? Why? Use specific information from the poem to support your response.

WRITING TOPICS

1. In an essay discuss the similarities in voice and poetic style between "Vive Noir" and Lucille Clifton's "Miss Rosie." What conclusions do these similarities lead you to make about African-American women poets?
2. Reread the last five lines of the poem. What do you think the speaker is saying about a person being white? If you change the word *white* to *black,* would that change the meaning of the sentence? Write a paragraph explaining the shift in meaning.

NIKKI-ROASA

Nikki Giovanni

Nikki Giovanni was born Yolande Cornelia Giovanni Jr. in Knoxville, Tennessee, in 1943. Her father, Gus Giovanni, was a social worker, and her mother, Yolande, was a supervisor for the welfare department. Her maternal grandmother, Louvenia Terrell Watson, was a strong influence in Giovanni's life. Giovanni lived with her grandmother during her sophomore and junior years in high school, and her grandmother instilled in her a responsibility for other African Americans.

While attending Fisk University, Giovanni developed her writing skills and became politically active. In 1964 she founded a chapter of the Student Non-Violent Coordinating Committee (SNCC), a civil rights organization, on the Fisk campus. Giovanni graduated *magna cum laude* in history in 1967. For a short time, she attended graduate school at the University of Pennsylvania School of Social Work and the School of Fine Arts at Columbia University. During this time, Giovanni was active in many arts and culture programs in African-American communities. Her experiences became the inspiration for the poems in her first published works: *Black Feeling, Black Talk* (1967), *Black Judgment* (1968) and *Re: Creation* (1970). These three volumes of poetry brought Giovanni national attention. In 1968 she received a National Foundation for the Arts grant and began teaching. She has taught at Queen's Village, Rutgers University, and Livingston College; currently, she teaches at Virginia Polytechnic and State University.

Giovanni, along with Haki Madhubuti (Don L. Lee) and Sonia Sanchez, has been recognized as one of the three leading figures in black poetry between 1968 and 1971. Due in part to her international travels in the mid-1970s and 1980s, her work has moved from black nationalism toward a more humanistic world view. Giovanni has published poetry collections, dialogues, an autobiography, and essays, including *Spin a Soft Black Song: Poems for Children* (1971), *My House: Poems* (1972), *Ego-tripping and Other Poems for Young*

People (1973), *Cotton Candy on a Rainy Day* (1978), *My House* (1983), *Sacred Cows . . . and Other Edibles* (1988), *Racism 101* (1994), *The Selected Poems of Nikki Giovanni* (1996), and *Love Poems* (1997).

childhood remembrances are always a drag
if you're Black
you always remember things like living in Woodlawn
with no inside toilet
5   and if you become famous or something
they never talk about how happy you were to have your mother
all to yourself and
how good the water felt when you got your bath from one of those
big tubs that folk in chicago barbecue in
10   and somehow when you talk about home
it never gets across how much you
understood their feelings
as the whole family attended meetings about Hollydale
and even though you remember
15   your biographers never understand
your father's pain as he sells his stock
and another dream goes
and though you're poor it isn't poverty that
concerns you
20   and though they fought a lot
it isn't your father's drinking that makes any difference
but only that everybody is together and you
and your sister have happy birthdays and very good christ-
masses and I really hope no white person ever has cause to
25   write about me because they never understand Black love
is Black wealth and they'll probably talk about my hard
childhood and never understand that all the while I was
quite happy

Nikki-Roasa: also published under the title "Nikki-Rosa"; this poem was originally entitled "Nikki-Roasa" by the author, that name being a childhood nickname.

DISCUSSION QUESTIONS

1. In lines 24 through 26 the speaker says that a "white person" would not understand that "Black love is black wealth." Why or why not? Do you agree?

2. In lines 18 and 19, the speaker says "and though you're poor it isn't poverty that / concerns you." What things are important to the speaker? Why would these things be more important than poverty?

3. Examine the occasions the speaker describes. What conclusions can you draw about these occasions? Is there something special about the locations or the people who are involved?

4. The poem begins with the line "childhood remembrances are always a drag" and ends with ". . . all the while I was / quite happy." Are these two thoughts contradictory? Use words and phrases from the poem to support your answer.

WRITING TOPICS

1. When we view others' experiences, seeing them one way is easy for us while those who are living through those experiences will see them another way. Remember an occasion that made you happy. In your journal, write about that occasion, explaining why you consider it a happy occasion and why others may not.

2. List some family activities that represent love to you. Change the list into a "list poem." Share your poem with several other people. What types of activities are common among the group? Which activities are unique to a specific individual?

THE IMMEDIATE PROGRAM OF THE AMERICAN NEGRO

W. E. B. Du Bois

W. E. B. Du Bois was born in Great Barrington, Massachusetts, in 1868. He was a strong proponent of civil rights for African Americans and was dedicated to principle and truth. He was a prolific writer of books, essays, and speeches and was a major revolutionary African-American writer. As an intellectual and scholar, Du Bois traveled internationally, writing and speaking on the conditions of African Americans in the United States. During the McCarthy era, Du Bois was charged with subversion. In 1961, Du Bois—disappointed with the lack of progress in civil rights for blacks and the system of government in this country—moved to Ghana.

Du Bois was one of the founders of the National Association for the Advancement of Colored People (NAACP). He believed that the problems of African Americans could not be understood without systematic investigation and intelligent understanding. He published *The Philadelphia Negro: A Social Study* in 1899. It was the first systematic sociological study of a large number of African Americans in any major city in the United States.

His most famous work is *The Souls of Black Folk: Essays and Sketches,* which he published in 1905. Some of his other works include: *Dusk of Dawn: An Essay toward an Autobiography of a Race Concept* (1940), *In Battle for Peace: The Story of My 83rd Birthday* (1952), and *The Autobiography of W. E. B. Du Bois: A Soliloquy on Viewing My Life From the Last Decade of Its First Century*, edited by Herbert Aptheker (1968). Du Bois died in Accra, Ghana, in 1963. (For more biographical information, see pages 211 and 260.)

1   The immediate program of the American Negro means nothing unless it is mediate to his great ideal and the ultimate ends of his development. We need not waste time by seeking to deceive our enemies into thinking

that we are going to be content with a half loaf, or by being willing to lull our friends into a false sense of our indifference and present satisfaction.

2   The American Negro demands equality—political equality, industrial equality and social equality; and he is never going to rest satisfied with anything less. He demands this in no spirit of braggadocio and with no obsequious envy of others, but as an absolute measure of self-defense and the only one that will assure to the darker races their ultimate survival on earth.

3   Only in a demand and a persistent demand for essential equality in the modern realm of human culture can any people show a real pride of race and a decent self-respect. For any group, nation or race to admit for a moment the present monstrous demand of the white race to be the inheritors of the earth, the arbiters of mankind and the sole owners of a heritage of culture which they did not create, nor even improve to any greater extent than the other great division of men—to admit such pretense for a moment is for the race to write itself down immediately as indisputably inferior in judgment, knowledge and common sense.

4   The equality in political, industrial and social life which modern men must have in order to live, is not to be confounded with sameness. On the contrary, in our case, it is rather insistence upon the right of diversity—upon the right of a human being to be a man even if he does not wear the same cut of vest, the same curl of hair or the same color of skin. Human equality does not even entail, as is sometimes said, absolute equality of opportunity; for certainly the natural inequalities of inherent genius and varying gift make this a dubious phrase. But there is a more and more clearly recognized minimum of opportunity and maximum of freedom to be, to move and to think, which the modern world denies to no being which it recognizes as a real man.

5   These involve both negative and positive sides. They call for freedom on the one hand and power on the other. The Negro must have political freedom; taxation without representation is tyranny. American Negroes of today are ruled by tyrants who take what they please in taxes and give what they please in law and administration, in justice and in injustice; and the great mass of black people must stand helpless and voiceless before a condition which has time and time again caused other peoples to fight and die.

6   The Negro must have industrial freedom. Between the peonage of the rural South, the oppression of shrewd capitalists and the jealousy of certain trade unions, the Negro laborer is the most exploited class in the country, giving more hard toil for less money than any other Americans, and have less voice in the conditions of his labor.

7   In social intercourse every effort is being made today from the President of the United States and the so called Church of Christ down to saloons and boot-blacks to segregate, strangle and spiritually starve Negroes so as to give them the least possible chance to know and share civilization.

8   These shackles must go. But that is but the beginning. The Negro must have power; the power of men, the right to do, to know, to feel and to express that knowledge, action and spiritual gift. He must not simply be free

from the political tyranny of white folk, he must have the right to vote and to rule over the citizens, white and black, to the extent of his proven foresight and ability. He must have a voice in the new industrial democracy which is building and the power to see to it that his children are not in the next generation trained to be the mudsills of society. He must have the right to social intercourse with his fellows. There was a time in the atomic individualistic group when "social intercourse" meant merely calls and tea-parties; today social intercourse means theatres, lectures, organizations, churches, clubs, excursions, travel, hotels,—it means in short Life; to bar a group from such methods of thinking, living and doing is to bar them from the world and bid them create a new world;—a task to which no single group is to-day equal; it is to crucify them and taunt them with not being able to live.

9   What now are the practical steps which must be taken to accomplish these ends?

10   First of all before taking steps the wise man knows the object and end of his journey. There are those who would advise the black man to pay little or no attention to where he is going so long as he keeps moving. They assume that God or his vice-gerent the White Man will attend to the steering. This is arrant nonsense. The feet of those that aimlessly wander land as often in hell as in heaven. Conscious self-realization and self-direction is the watchword of modern man, and the first article in the program of any group that will survive must be the great aim, equality and power among men.

11   The practical steps to this are clear. First we must fight obstructions; by continual and increasing effort we must first make American courts either build up a body of decisions which will protect the plain legal rights of American citizens or else make them tear down the civil and political rights of all citizens in order to oppress a few. Either result will bring justice in the end. It is lots of fun and most ingenious just now for courts to twist law so as to say I shall not live here or vote there, or marry the woman who wishes to marry me. But when tomorrow these decisions throttle all freedom and overthrow the foundation of democracy and decency there is going to be some judicial house cleaning.

12   We must *secondly* seek in legislature and congress remedial legislation; national aid to public school education, the removal of all legal discriminations based simply on race and color, and those marriage laws passed to make the seduction of black girls easy and without legal penalty.

13   *Third,* the human contact of human beings must be increased; the policy which brings into sympathetic touch and understanding, men and women, rich and poor, capitalist and laborer, Asiatic and European, must bring into closer contact and mutual knowledge the white and black people of this land. It is the most frightful indictment of a country which dares to call itself civilized that it has allowed itself to drift into a state of ignorance where ten million people are coming to believe that all white people are liars and thieves, and the whites in turn to believe that the chief industry of Negroes is raping white women.

14   *Fourth,* only the publication of the truth repeatedly and incisively and uncompromisingly can secure that change in public opinion which will correct these awful lies. THE CRISIS, our record of the darker races, must have a circulation of 35,000 chiefly among colored folk but of at least 250,000 among all men who believe in men. It must not be a namby-pamby box of salve, but a voice that thunders fact and is more anxious to be true than pleasing. There should be a campaign of tract distribution—short well-written facts and arguments—rained over this land by millions of copies, particularly in the South, where the white people know less about the Negro than in any other part of the civilized world. The press should be utilized—the 400 Negro weeklies, the great dailies and eventually the magazines, when we get magazine editors who will lead public opinion instead of following afar with resonant brays. Lectures, lantern-slides and moving pictures, cooperating with a bureau of information and eventually becoming a Negro encyclopedia, all these are efforts along the line of making human beings realize that Negroes are human.

15   Such is the program of work against obstructions. Let us now turn to constructive effort. This may be summed up under (1) economic cooperation, (2) a revival of art and literature, (3) political action, (4) education, and (5) organization.

16   Under economic co-operation we must strive to spread the idea among colored people that the accumulation of wealth is for social rather than individual ends. We must avoid, in the advancement of the Negro race, the mistakes of ruthless exploitation which have marked modern economic history. To this end we must seek not simply home ownership, small landholding and saving accounts, but also all forms of co-operation, both in production and distribution, profit sharing, building and loan associations, systematic migration from mob rule and robbery, to freedom and enfranchisement, the emancipation of women and the abolition of child labor.

17   In art and literature we should try to loose the tremendous emotional wealth of the Negro and the dramatic strength of his problems through writing, the stage, pageantry and other forms of art. We should resurrect forgotten ancient Negro art and history, and we should set the black man before the world as both a creative artist and a strong subject for artistic treatment.

18   In political action we should organize the votes of Negroes in such congressional districts as have any number of Negro voters. We should systematically interrogate candidates on matters vital to Negro freedom and uplift. We should train colored voters to reject the bribe of office and to accept only decent legal enactments both for their own uplift and for the uplift of laboring classes of all races and both sexes.

19   In education we must seek to give colored children free public school training. We must watch with grave suspicion the attempt of those who, under the guise of vocational training, would fasten ignorance and menial service on the Negro for another generation. Our children must not in large

numbers, be forced into the servant class; for menial service is still, in the main, little more than an antiquated survival of impossible conditions. It has always been as statistics show, a main cause of bastardy and prostitution and despite its many marvelous exceptions it will never come to the light of decency and honour until the house servant becomes the Servant in the House. It is our duty then, not drastically but persistently, to seek out colored children of ability and genius, to open up to them broader, industrial opportunity and above all, to find that Talented Tenth[1] and encourage it by the best and most exhaustive training in order to supply the Negro race and the world with leaders, thinkers and artists.

20   For the accomplishment of all these ends we must organize. Organization among us already has gone far but it must go much further and higher. Organization is sacrifice. It is sacrifice of opinions, of time, of work and of money, but it is, after all, the cheapest way of buying the most priceless of gifts—freedom and efficiency. I thank God that most of the money that supports the National Association for the Advancement of Colored People comes from black hands; a still larger proportion must so come, and we must not only support but control this and similar organizations and hold them unwaveringly to our objects, our aims and our ideals.

DISCUSSION QUESTIONS

1. Du Bois opens his essay by stating that "The American Negro demands equality—political equality, industrial equality, and social equality." The essay was written in 1914. Why was it necessary for African Americans to insist on equality in each of these areas then?

2. Du Bois presents four practical stages to accomplish the goal of equality. Identify these steps and establish the connections between them and Du Bois's three aspects of equality.

3. Du Bois argues against giving African-American children only vocational training. He says that African Americans will not have "decency and honour until the house servant becomes the Servant in the House." What does Du Bois mean by this statement?

---

[1] *Talented Tenth*: A term Du Bois created to describe the intellectual top ten percent of African Americans who would be leaders, thinkers, and artists of the race.

WRITING TOPICS

1. In your journal, write a letter to Du Bois describing to what degree African Americans have obtained political, economic, and social equality in the United States. What has changed since Du Bois wrote this essay in 1914? What has stayed the same?

2. Du Bois supported additional development of the "Talented Tenth"—the intellectual top ten percent of African Americans. In an essay, contrast this view with Booker T. Washington's views of vocational training for all African Americans as a way to ensure African-American success. Be sure to include the strengths and weaknesses of each position.

3. Compare Du Bois's stand on African-American rights in "Chapter 3: Of Mr. Booker T. Washington and Others," written in 1904, and "The Immediate Program of the American Negro," written in 1914. Have his views changed? If so, how?

PREFACE TO A TWENTY VOLUME SUICIDE NOTE

Amiri Baraka

Amiri Baraka (Le Roi Jones) was born in 1934 in Newark, New Jersey. He left Howard University at the age of nineteen, and later studied at Columbia University. He served in the U.S. Air Force for three years (1954–57), during which time he traveled throughout the world. Following his service, he taught creative writing and theatre arts at Columbia. Baraka has produced three collections of poetry: *Preface to a Twenty Volume Suicide Note* (1961), *The Dead Lecturer* (1964), and *Black Art* (1966). His drama contributions include: *Dutchman*, which won the Obie Award as the best off-Broadway play of 1964, *The Slave* (1964), *Baptism* (1967), *The Toilet* (1967), and *Slave Ship* (1967), among others. He is a co-founder of the Black Arts Repertory Theatre in Harlem and Spirit House of Newark, New Jersey. Baraka was the recipient of the John Hay Whitney Fellowship (1961–62) and a Guggenheim grant (1964–65).

Lately, I've become accustomed to the way
The ground opens up and envelops me
Each time I go out to walk the dog.
Or the broad edged silly music the wind
5   Makes when I run for a bus . . .

Things have come to that.

And now, each night I count the stars,
And each night I get the same number.
And when they will not come to be counted,
10   I count the holes they leave.

Nobody sings anymore.

And then last night, I tiptoed up
To my daughter's room and heard her
Talking to someone, and when I opened
15   The door, there was no one there . . .
Only she on her knees, peeking into

Her own clasped hands.

DISCUSSION QUESTIONS

1. What is the poet's attitude about life as expressed in lines 1 and 2 of the first stanza?
2. What do you find ironic about the poem's title?
3. After having read the last stanza of the poem, what do you think the poet's attitude is about suicide?

WRITING TOPICS

1. In your writing journal, describe the poem's speaker after having read the second stanza.
2. "Nobody sings anymore" expresses the poet's feelings about the world. In an analytical essay, present your interpretation of the statement. You may use examples from your reading, from history, or from your background.
3. Write a letter to the poet, Amiri Baraka, and tell him how you feel about the poem. Cite specific passages from the poem to support your opinion.

ASSASSINATION

Haki R. Madhubuti

Haki R. Madhubuti was born in Arkansas in 1942. He grew up in Detroit and later moved to Chicago, where he established the Third World Press. Madhubuti was an early promoter of the Black Arts Movement—he started out by writing and publishing poems on single sheets and selling them in barbershops, beauty salons, and wherever African Americans gathered in Chicago. His writings include *Think Black* (1967), *Black Pride* (1968), and *Don't Cry, Scream* (1969). In 1971 he published a group of essays in a volume entitled *Dynamite Voices I*. Madhubuti has been poet-in-residence at Cornell, Howard, and Central State universities and at the University of Illinois at Chicago. He currently teaches at Chicago State University.

it was wild.
the
bullet hit high.
    (the throat-neck)
5 & from everywhere:
   the motel, from under bushes and cars,
   from around corners and across streets,
   out of the garbage cans and from rat holes
   in the earth
10 they came running.
with
guns
drawn
they came running
15 toward the King—
    all of them
    fast and sure—

as if
20 the King
was going to fire back.
they came running,
fast and sure,
in the
25 wrong
direction.

DISCUSSION QUESTIONS

1. Who is the "they" the speaker is referring to in the poem?
2. Lines 21 to 25 say: "they came running in the wrong direction." Discuss the irony of this statement.
3. What, in your opinion, is the right direction?
4. How does calling the victim "the King" make the poem more powerful than if the poet referred to Dr. King by name?

WRITING TOPICS

1. Pretend you are a friend of Dr. King and his family. Write a letter to Dr. King's wife, Mrs. Coretta Scott King, telling her how the death of her husband and your friend affected you.
2. Write an analytical essay interpreting what is meant by the statement: "You may kill the dreamer, but not the dream." Use examples from your reading, from history, or from your personal experience.
3. Dr. King was in Memphis organizing a Poor People's Campaign and supporting striking garbage collectors when he was assassinated. Pretend you are one of the motel maids or janitors present the day of the assassination and, in your journal, write an account of that day and your reactions.

WINTER IN AMERICA

Gil Scott-Heron

Gil Scott-Heron was born in Chicago in 1949, the son of a Jamaican professional soccer player and a librarian. By the time he was in fifth grade, he was writing detective stories. Scott-Heron attended Lincoln University, a small private black college for three years where he received the university's Langston Hughes Creative Writing Award in 1968. While at Lincoln University, Scott-Heron associated with Glyan Kain, Steve Cannon, Ishmael Reed, and Larry Neal and collaborated with Brian Jackson to formulate a jazz-supported oral style poetry. Scott-Heron earned a master's degree in creative writing from John Hopkins University. Besides his recording career as a singer and a poet, Scott-Heron has taught creative writing at the college level.

The oral poetry of street-raps and songs of Scott-Heron express a national and international concern for social issues. He has published several books: *The Vulture* (1970), *Small Talk at 125th & Lenox* (1970), *The Nigger Factory* (1972), and *So Far, So Good* (1990). However, Scott-Heron's decision to record as well as to write has established him within the African-American oral tradition. His recordings include *The Revolution Will Not Be Televised* (1972), *Winter in America* (1973), *From South Africa to South Carolina* (1975), *The Mind of Gil Scott-Heron* (1978), *Real Eyes* (1980), and *Reflections* (1981). "The Bottle" was his first hit on the popular charts. Other hits include "Winter in America" and "Johannesburg."

From the Indians who welcomed the pilgrims
to the buffalo who once ruled the plains;
like the vultures circling beneath the dark clouds
looking for the rain/looking for the rain.

5   From the cities that stagger on the coast lines
    in a nation that just can't take much more/
    like the forest buried beneath the highways
    never had a chance to grow/never had a chance to grow.
    It's winter; winter in america
10 and all of the healers have been killed or forced away.
    It's winter; winter in america
    and ain't nobody fighting 'cause nobody knows what to save.
    The con-stitution was a noble piece of paper;
    with Free Society they struggled but they died in vain/
15 and now Democracy is ragtime on the corner
    hoping that it rains/hoping that it rains.
    And I've seen the robins perched in barren treetops
    watching last ditch racists marching across the floor
    and like the peace signs that melted in our dreams
20 never had a chance to grow/never had a chance to grow.
    it's winter; winter in america
    and all of the healers done been killed or put in jail
    it's winter, winter in america
    and ain't nobody fighting 'cause nobody knows what to save.

DISCUSSION QUESTIONS

1. Scott-Heron uses the phrase "winter in america" as a metaphor through-out the song. What does this metaphor represent? Why is it an effective metaphor? Use specific information from the song to support your responses.

2. The speaker says "All of the healers done been killed or put in jail." Which African-American healers and leaders were killed or jailed? How did their deaths or imprisonment affect African-American communities?

3. The song ends with the speaker saying "ain't nobody fighting 'cause nobody knows what to save." Is the speaker giving up the hope that conditions in America can change? Why or why not?

WRITING TOPICS

1. Write a poem titled "Spring in America." This poem should contradict the "winter in america" metaphor. Compare and discuss your poem with other people's poems.
2. In an essay explain how a song or poem can be an instrument of action. Use "Winter in America" and two other poems or songs to support your position.

TO MISSISSIPPI YOUTH

Malcolm X

Malcolm X was born Malcolm Little in Omaha, Nebraska, in 1925. He moved to Boston when he was a teenager, and then to Harlem. In New York he was involved in a series of crimes that led to a ten-year prison term. While in prison, he became a Black Muslim, and after his release he became a spokesperson for the Nation of Islam. He rejected his given surname—his "slave-name"—and took the surname "X." After a pilgrimage to Mecca in 1964, Malcolm X broke with the Nation of Islam because he no longer accepted the doctrine that all white men were evil. He went on to form his own congregation, the Organization of Afro-American Unity, which concentrated on political rights for African Americans.

The story of his life, *The Autobiography of Malcolm X,* was completed with the assistance of Alex Haley, author of *Roots.* He also left a legacy of speeches, one of which is "To Mississippi Youth," given to a group of black teenagers from McComb, Mississippi. He was assassinated in New York on February 21, 1965.

1   One of the first things I think young people, especially nowadays, should learn is how to see for yourself and listen for yourself and think for yourself. Then you can come to an intelligent decision for yourself. If you form the habit of going by what you hear others say about someone, or going by what others think about someone, instead of searching that thing out for yourself and seeing for yourself, you will be walking west when you think you're going east, and you will be walking east when you think you're going west. This generation, especially of our people, has a burden, more so than any other time in history. The most important thing that we can learn to do today is think for ourselves.

2   It's good to keep wide-open ears and listen to what everybody else has to say, but when you come to make a decision, you have to weigh all of what

you've heard on its own, and place it where it belongs, and come to a decision for yourself; you'll never regret it. But if you form the habit of taking what someone else says about a thing without checking it out for yourself, you'll find that other people will have you hating your friends and loving your enemies. This is one of the things that our people are beginning to learn today— that it is very important to think out a situation for yourself. If you don't do it, you'll always be maneuvered into a situation where you are never fighting your actual enemies, where you will find yourself fighting your own self.

3   I think our people in this country are the best examples of that. Many of us want to be nonviolent and we talk very loudly, you know, about being nonviolent. Here in Harlem, where there are probably more black people concentrated than any place in the world, some talk about nonviolent talk too. But we find that they aren't nonviolent with each other. You can go out to Harlem Hospital, where there are more black patients than any hospital in the world, and see them going in there all cut up and shot up and busted up where they got violent with each other.

4   My experience has been that in many instances where you find Negroes talking about nonviolence, they are not nonviolent with each other, and they're not loving with each other, or forgiving with each other. Usually when they say they're nonviolent, they mean they're nonviolent with somebody else. I think you understand what I mean. They are nonviolent with the enemy. A person can come to your home, and if he's white and wants to heap some kind of brutality on you, you're nonviolent; or he can come to take your father and put a rope around his neck, and you're nonviolent. But if another Negro just stomps his foot, you'll rumble with him in a minute. Which shows you that there's an inconsistency there.

5   I myself would go for nonviolence if it was consistent, if everybody was going to be nonviolent all the time. I'd say, okay, let's get with it, we'll all be nonviolent. But I don't go along with any kind of nonviolence unless everybody's going to be nonviolent. If they make the Ku Klux Klan nonviolent, I'll be nonviolent. If they make the White Citizens Council nonviolent, I'll be nonviolent. But as long as you've got somebody else not being nonviolent, I don't want anybody coming to me talking any nonviolent talk. I don't think it is fair to tell our people to be nonviolent unless someone is out there making the Klan and the Citizens Council and these other groups also be nonviolent.

6   Now, I'm not criticizing those here who are nonviolent. I think everybody should do it the way they feel is best, and I congratulate anybody who can be nonviolent in the face of all that kind of action in that part of the world. I don't think that in 1965 you will find the upcoming generation of our people, especially those who have been doing some thinking, who will go along with any form of nonviolence unless nonviolence is going to be practiced all the way around.

7   If the leaders of the nonviolent movement can go into the white community and teach nonviolence, good. I'd go along with that. But as long as

I see them teaching nonviolence only in the black community, we can't go along with that. We believe in equality, and equality means that you have to put the same thing over here that you put over there. And if black people alone are going to be the ones who are nonviolent, then it's not fair. We throw ourselves off guard. In fact, we disarm ourselves and make ourselves defenseless. . . .

8   The Organization of Afro-American Unity is a nonreligious group of black people who believe that the problems confronting our people in this country need to be re-analyzed and a new approach devised toward trying to get a solution. Studying the problem, we recall that prior to 1939 all of our people, in the North, South, East, and West, no matter how much education we had, were segregated. We were segregated in the North just as much as we were segregated in the South. Even now there's as much segregation in the North as there is in the South. There's some worse segregation right here in New York City than there is in McComb, Mississippi; but up here they're subtle and tricky and deceitful, and they make you think you've got it made when you haven't even begun to make it yet.

9   Prior to 1939, our people were in a very menial position or condition. Most of us were waiters and porters and bellhops and janitors and waitresses and things of that sort. It was not until war was declared with Germany, and America became involved in a manpower shortage in regards to her factories plus her army, that the black man in this country was permitted to make a few strides forward. It was never out of some kind of moral enlightenment or moral awareness on the part of Uncle Sam. Uncle Sam only let the black man take a step forward when he himself had his back to the wall.

10   In Michigan, where I was brought up at that time, I recall that the best jobs in the city for blacks were waiters out at the country club. In those days if you had a job waiting tables in the country club, you had it made. Or if you had a job at the State House. Having a job at the State House didn't mean that you were a clerk or something of that sort; you had a shoeshine stand at the State House. Just by being there you could be around all those big-shot politicians—that made you a big-shot Negro. You were shining shoes, but you were a big-shot Negro because you were around big-shot white people and you could bend their ear and get up next to them. And ofttimes you were chosen by them to be the voice of the Negro community.

11   Around that time, 1939 or '40 or '41, they weren't drafting Negroes in the army or navy. A Negro couldn't join the navy in 1940 or '41. They wouldn't take a black man in the navy except to make him a cook. He couldn't just go and join the navy, and I don't think he could just go and join the army. They weren't drafting him when the war first started. This is what they thought of you and me in those days. For one thing, they didn't trust us; they feared that if they put us in the army and trained us in how to use rifles and other things, we might shoot at some targets that they hadn't picked out. And we would have. Any thinking man knows what target to shoot at.

If a man has to have someone else to choose his target, then he isn't think-ing for himself—they're doing the thinking for him.

12   The Negro leaders in those days were the same type we have today. When the Negro leaders saw all the white fellows being drafted and taken into the army and dying on the battlefield, and no Negroes were dying because they weren't being drafted, the Negro leaders came up and said, "We've got to die too. We want to be drafted too, and we demand that you take us in there and let us die for our country too." That was what the Negro leaders said back in 1940. I remember. A. Philip Randolph was one of the leading Negroes in those days who said it, and he's one of the Big Six right now; and this is why he's one of the Big Six.

13   So they started drafting Negro soldiers then, and started letting Negroes get into the navy. But not until Hitler and Tojo and the foreign powers were strong enough to put pressure on this country, so that it had its back to the wall and needed us, [did] they let us work in factories. Up until that time we couldn't work in the factories; I'm talking about the North as well as the South. And when they let us work in the factories, at first they let us in only as janitors. After a year or so passed by, they let us work on machines. We became machinists, got a little more skill. If we got a little more skill, we made a little more money, which enabled us to live in a little better neigh-borhood. When we lived in a little better neighborhood, we went to a little better school, got a little better education and could come out and get a lit-tle better job. So the cycle was broken somewhat.

14   But the cycle was not broken out of some kind of sense of moral respon-sibility on the part of the government. No, the only time that cycle was bro-ken even to a degree was when world pressure was brought to bear on the United States government. They didn't look at us as human beings—they just put us into their system and let us advance a little bit farther because it served their interests. They never let us advance a little bit farther because they were interested in us as human beings. Any of you who have a knowl-edge of history, sociology, or political science, or the economic development of this country and its race relations—go back and do some research on it and you'll have to admit that this is true.

15   It was during the time that Hitler and Tojo made war with this country and put pressure on it [that] Negroes in this country advanced a little bit. At the end of the war with Germany and Japan, then Joe Stalin and Communist Russia were a threat. During that period we made a little more headway. Now the point that I'm making is this: Never at any time in the history of our people in this country have we made advances or progress in any way based upon the internal good will of this country. We have made advancement in this country only when this country was under pressure from forces above and beyond its control. The internal moral consciousness of this country is bankrupt. It hasn't existed since they first brought us over here and made slaves out of us. They make it appear they have our good interests at heart, but when you study it, every time, no matter how many

steps they take us forward, it's like we're standing on a—what do you call that thing—a treadmill. The treadmill is moving backwards faster than we're able to go forward in this direction. We're not even standing still—we're going backwards.

16   In studying the process of this so-called progress during the past twenty years, we of the Organization of Afro-American Unity realized that the only time the black man in this country is given any kind of recognition, or even listened to, is when America is afraid of outside pressure, or when she's afraid of her image abroad. So we saw that it was necessary to expand the problem and the struggle of the black man in this country until it went above and beyond the jurisdiction of the United States. . . .

17   I was fortunate enough to be able to take a tour of the African continent during the summer. I went to Egypt, then to Arabia, Kuwait, Lebanon, Sudan, Ethiopia, Kenya, Tanganyika, Zanzibar, Nigeria, Ghana, Guinea, Liberia, and Algeria. I found, while I was traveling on the African continent, I had already detected it in May, that someone had very shrewdly planted the seed of division on this continent to make the Africans not show genuine concern with our problem, just as they plant seeds in your and my minds so that we won't show concern with the African problem. . . .

18   I also found that in many of these African countries the head of state is genuinely concerned with the problem of the black man in this country; but many of them thought if they opened their mouths and voiced their concern that they would be insulted by the American Negro leaders. Because one head of state in Asia voiced his support of the civil-rights struggle [in 1963] and a couple of the Big Six had the audacity to slap his face and say they weren't interested in that kind of help—which in my opinion is asinine. So the African leaders only had to be convinced that if they took an open stand at the governmental level and showed interest in the problem of black people in this country, they wouldn't be rebuffed.

19   And today you'll find in the United Nations, and it's not an accident, that every time the Congo question or anything on the African continent is being debated, they couple it with what is going on, or what is happening to you and me, in Mississippi and Alabama and these other places. In my opinion, the greatest accomplishment that was made in the struggle of the black man in America in 1964 toward some kind of real progress was the successful linking together of our problem with the African problem, or making our problem a world problem. Because now, whenever anything happens to you in Mississippi, it's not just a case of somebody in Alabama getting indignant, or somebody in New York getting indignant. The same repercussions that you see all over the world when an imperialist or foreign power interferes in some section of Africa—you see repercussions, you see the embassies being bombed and burned and overturned—nowadays, when something happens to black people in Mississippi, you'll see the same repercussions all over the world.

20   I wanted to point this out to you because it is important for you to know

that when you're in Mississippi, you're not alone. As long as you think you're alone, then you take a stand as if you're a minority or as if you're outnumbered, and that kind of stand will never enable you to win a battle. You've got to know that you've got as much power on your side as that Ku Klux Klan has on its side. And when you know that you've got as much power on your side as the Klan has on its side, you'll talk the same kind of language with that Klan as the Klan is talking with you. . . .

21   I think in 1965, whether you like it, or I like it, or they like it, or not, you will see that there is a generation of black people becoming mature to the point where they feel that they have no more business being asked to take a peaceful approach than anybody else takes, unless everybody's going to take a peaceful approach.

22   So we here in the Organization of Afro-American Unity are with the struggle in Mississippi one thousand percent. We're with the efforts to register our people in Mississippi to vote one thousand percent. But we do not go along with anybody telling us to help nonviolently. We think that if the government says that Negroes have a right to vote, and then some Negroes come out to vote, and some kind of Ku Klux Klan is going to put them in the river, and the government doesn't do anything about it, it's time for us to organize and band together and equip ourselves and qualify ourselves to protect ourselves. And once you can protect yourself, you don't have to worry about being hurt. . . .

23   I hope you don't think I'm trying to incite you. Just look here: Look at yourselves. Some of you are teenagers, students. How do you think I feel—and I belong to a generation ahead of you—how do you think I feel to have to tell you, "We, my generation, sat around like a knot on a wall while the whole world was fighting for its human rights—and you've got to be born into a society where you still have the same fight." What did we do, who preceded you? I'll tell you what we did: Nothing. And don't you make the same mistake we made. . . .

DISCUSSION QUESTIONS

1. Malcolm X says that young people should look, listen, and make their own decisions before taking any action. Do you agree with this advice? Why or why not?

2. At the time he made this speech, Malcolm X was opposed to nonviolence unless everyone was forced to behave nonviolently. How do you think he would react if he were alive today? Do you think his opinions might have changed?

3. Malcolm X maintains that he does not criticize those persons who advocate nonviolence in gaining freedom for African Americans. Name one or two people to whom he might be referring.

WRITING TOPICS

1. Malcolm X says: "We [African Americans] have made advancement in this country only when this country was under pressure from forces above and beyond its control." Write an analytical essay in which you interpret this statement. You may use examples from your reading, history, or personal experience.
2. Assume you are a member of the generation between Malcolm X's generation and yours. Write a speech telling both how the advice you received from Malcolm X affected your life, and what advice you would give to youth today.

I HAVE A DREAM

Martin Luther King Jr.

Martin Luther King Jr. was born in 1929 in Atlanta, Georgia. His now-famous "Letter from Birmingham (Alabama) Jail," written in 1963, is said to have been the spark that changed the thinking about the Civil Rights Movement in America. This letter to white clergymen in that city admonished them to act in defense of freedom rather than criticize him and the other leaders of the Movement. King was chosen to lead the bus boycott (which lead to desegregation of Montgomery, Alabama's public transportation system) shortly after he became the pastor of Dexter Avenue Baptist Church of that city. He later became president of the Southern Christian Leadership Council (SCLC).

It was at the 1963 March on Washington that he gave his now-famous "I Have a Dream" speech at the Lincoln Memorial. In 1964, King received the Nobel Peace Prize. He was assassinated in 1968 while standing on a motel balcony in Memphis, Tennessee; he had gone there to support the black garbagemen who were on strike against the city.

1   I am happy to join with you today in what will go down in history as the greatest demonstration for freedom in the history of our nation.

2   Five score years ago a great American in whose symbolic shadow we stand today signed the Emancipation Proclamation. This momentous decree is a great beacon light of hope to millions of Negro slaves who had been seared in the flames of withering injustice. It came as a joyous daybreak to end the long night of their captivity. But 100 years later the Negro still is not free. One hundred years later the life of the Negro is still badly crippled by the manacles of segregation and the chains of discrimination. One hundred years later the Negro lives on a lonely island of poverty in the midst of a vast ocean of material prosperity. One hundred years later the Negro is still languished in the corners of American society and finds

himself in exile in his own land. So we've come here today to dramatize a shameful condition.

3 In a sense we've come to our nation's capital to cash a check. When the architects of our Republic wrote the magnificent words of the Constitution and the Declaration of Independence, they were signing a promissory note to which every American was to fall heir. This note was a promise that all men—black men as well as white men—would be guaranteed the unalienable rights of life, liberty, and the pursuit of happiness. It is obvious today that America has defaulted on this promissory note insofar as her citizens of color are concerned. Instead of honoring this sacred obligation, America has given the Negro people a bad check which has come back marked "insufficient funds."

4 But we refuse to believe that the bank of justice is bankrupt. We refuse to believe that there are insufficient funds in the great vaults of opportunity of this nation. So we've come to cash this check, a check that will give us upon demand the riches of freedom and the security of justice.

5 We have also come to this hallowed spot to remind America of the fierce urgency of now. This is no time to engage in the luxury of cooling off or to take the tranquilizing drug of gradualism. Now is the time to make real the promises of democracy. Now is the time to rise from the dark and desolate valley of segregation to the sunlit path of racial justice. Now is the time to lift our nation from the quicksands of racial injustice to the solid rock of brotherhood.

6 Now is the time to make justice a reality for all of God's children. It would be fatal for the nation to overlook the urgency of the moment. This sweltering summer of the Negro's legitimate discontent will not pass until there is an invigorating autumn of freedom and equality—1963 is not an end but a beginning. Those who hope that the Negro needed to blow off steam and will now be content will have a rude awakening if the nation returns to business as usual.

7 There will be neither rest nor tranquility in America until the Negro is granted his citizenship rights. The whirlwinds of revolt will continue to shake the foundations of our nation until the bright day of justice emerges. And that is something that I must say to my people who stand on the worn threshold which leads into the palace of justice. In the process of gaining our rightful place we must not be guilty of wrongful deeds. Let us not seek to satisfy our thirst for freedom by drinking from the cup of bitterness and hatred.

8 We must forever conduct our struggle on the high plane of dignity and discipline. We must allow our creative protests to degenerate into physical violence. Again and again we must rise to the majestic heights of meeting physical force with soul force. The marvelous new militancy which has engulfed the Negro community must not lead us to distrust all white people, for many of our white brothers, as evidenced by their presence here today, have come to realize that their destiny is tied up with our destiny.

9   They have come to realize that their freedom is inextricably bound to our freedom. We cannot walk alone. And as we walk we must make the pledge that we shall always march ahead. We cannot turn back. There are those who are asking the devotees of civil rights, "When will you be satisfied?" We can never be satisfied as long as the Negro is the victim of the unspeakable horrors of police brutality.

10   We can never be satisfied as long as our bodies, heavy with the fatigue of travel, cannot gain lodging in the motels of the highways and the hotels of the cities.

11   We cannot be satisfied as long as the Negro's basic mobility is from a smaller ghetto to a larger one. We can never be satisfied as long as our children are stripped of their adulthood and robbed of their dignity by signs stating "For Whites Only."

12   We cannot be satisfied as long as the Negro in Mississippi cannot vote and the Negro in New York believes he has nothing for which to vote.

13   No, no, we are not satisfied and we will not be satisfied until justice rolls down like waters and righteousness like a mighty stream.

14   I am not unmindful that some of you have come here out of great trials and tribulation. Some of you have come fresh from narrow jail cells. Some of you have come from areas where your quest for freedom left you battered by the storms of persecution and staggered by the winds of police brutality. You have been the veterans of creative suffering.

15   Continue to work with the faith that unearned suffering is redemptive. Go back to Mississippi, go back to Alabama, go back to South Carolina, go back to Georgia, go back to Louisiana, go back to the slums and ghettos of our Northern cities, knowing that somehow this situation can and will be changed. Let us not wallow in the valley of despair.

16   I say to you today, my friends, though, even though we face the difficulties of today and tomorrow, I still have a dream. It is a dream deeply rooted in the American dream. I have a dream that one day this nation will rise up, live out the true meaning of its creed: "We hold these truths to be self-evident, that all men are created equal."

17   I have a dream that one day on the red hills of Georgia sons of former slaves and the sons of former slave-owners will be able to sit down together at the table of brotherhood. I have a dream that one day even the state of Mississippi, a state sweltering with the heat of injustice, sweltering with the heat of oppression, will be transformed into an oasis of freedom and justice.

18   I have a dream that my four little children will one day live in a nation where they will not be judged by the color of their skin but by the content of their character. I have a dream . . . I have a dream that one day in Alabama, with its vicious racists, with its governor having his lips dripping with the words of interposition and nullification, one day right there in Alabama little black boys and black girls will be able to join hands with little white boys and white girls as sisters and brothers.

19   I have a dream today . . . I have a dream that one day every valley shall

be exalted, every hill and mountain shall be made low. The rough places will be made plain, and the crooked places will be made straight. And the glory of the Lord shall be revealed, and all flesh shall see it together. This is our hope. This is the faith that I go back to the South with. With this faith we will be able to hew out of the mountain of despair a stone of hope. With this faith we will be able to transform the jangling discords of our nation into a beautiful symphony of brotherhood. With this faith we will be able to work together, to pray together, to struggle together, to go to jail together, to stand up for freedom together, knowing that we will be free one day.

20   This will be the day when all of God's children will be able to sing with new meaning, "My country, 'tis of thee, sweet land of liberty, of thee I sing. Land where my fathers died, land of the pilgrim's pride, from every mountain side, let freedom ring." And if America is to be a great nation, this must become true. So let freedom ring from the prodigious hilltops of New Hampshire. Let freedom ring from the mighty mountains of New York. Let freedom ring from the heightening Alleghenies of Pennsylvania. Let freedom ring from the snow-capped Rockies of Colorado. Let freedom ring from the curvaceous slopes of California.

21   But not only that. Let freedom ring from Stone Mountain of Georgia. Let freedom ring from Lookout Mountain of Tennessee. Let freedom ring from every hill and molehill of Mississippi, from every mountain side. Let freedom ring. . . .

22   When we allow freedom to ring—when we let it ring from every city and every hamlet, from every state and every city, we will be able to speed up that day when all of God's children, black men and white men, Jews and Gentiles, Protestants and Catholics, will be able to join hands and sing in the words of the old Negro spiritual, "Free at last, Free at last, Great God a-mighty, We are free at last."

DISCUSSION QUESTIONS

1. King says: "We must forever conduct our struggle on the high plane of dignity and discipline." Discuss in your small group what you think he means.
2. What is this "check" King mentions in his speech?
3. When King made this speech, there was blatant segregation and discrimination against African Americans. If he were alive today, what kind of speech would he make and what are some of the things he might say?

Writing Topics

1. King says: ". . . unearned suffering is redemptive." Write an essay in which you explain the meaning of this statement. Before beginning, you may wish to discuss the quotation in your small group.
2. In your writing journal, list some "dreams" you have for yourself. Use complete sentences to describe these dreams.

CHAPTER EIGHT

WOMEN

Since their arrival in the United States, African-American women have faced unique struggles as they sought their place in society. As slaves, they did strenuous labor in fields, gave birth to children who were often taken away from them, raised their slave owner's children, and cleaned and cooked for their slave owners. After slavery, and well into the twentieth century, women could find jobs (most often as housekeepers, cooks, and maids), which allowed the African-American family to survive financially. Those fortunate African-American women who could get an education returned to black communities to teach and work to uplift their communities.

Though confronted with negative stereotypes from both society as a whole and the African-American community itself, African-American women have not been defeated. They continue to rise and demand their rightful place in society. As individuals, mothers, daughters, sisters, aunts, and grandmothers, they have worked within their families, in their jobs, and in their communities to search for and to create a sense of themselves as African Americans and as women.

African-American women writers have created women characters who pass on their knowledge of life and survival through respect for their black culture and through the stories that pass from one generation to the next. These characters are neither perfect nor totally flawed. They are all trying to survive in an imperfect world that passes immediate judgement on them because of the color of their skin and their gender. Each generation of African-American women strives to rise beyond the conditions in which they live and to reach a new level of understanding about life and about what it means to be an African-American woman.

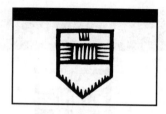

THE TREE OF LOVE

Linda Goss

Linda Goss was born in Alcoa, Tennessee. She currently lives in Philadelphia where she is recognized as Philadelphia's official *griot* (storyteller). She performs often at the National Association for the Preservation and Perpetuation of Storytelling in Jonesboro, Tennessee. She is the founder of Hola-Cumbaya and one of the founders of Patchwork, a storytelling guild in the Delaware Valley. Goss is also co-founder of the "In the Tradition . . ." National Festival of Black Storytelling and president of the Association of Black Storytellers.

Goss has edited anthologies and authored children's books, including *Talk That Talk: An Anthology of African-American Storytelling* (1989), edited with Clay Goss; *Jump Up and Say!: A Collection of Black Storytelling* (1995), co-authored with Clay Goss; *It's Kwanza Time* (1995); and *The Frog Who Wanted to Be a Singer* (1996).

1 Momma used to say, "Listen, Baby Dear, I can't be around with you always, but I want you to remember that no matter where you go or what you do, I want you to always be able to look out and see the trees."

2 At first I didn't know what she was talking about—some of her homespun folklore, I supposed. But I listened because, after all, this was Momma talking.

3 "I want you to go out and walk among the trees. Go to the park, the woods, wherever they are. I want you to find one that appeals to you and then I want you to give it a big hug. Now, I know what you're thinking, even though you ain't saying nothing. I raised you so you wouldn't talk back to me or sass me."

4 "But, Momma," I interrupted.

5 "Listen, Baby Dear, I know you worry about people seeing you hugging trees and thinking you're crazy or something. If they look at you strange, you go ahead and hug that tree anyway."

6   I was beginning to worry about Momma.

7   "I'm telling you that, no matter how far you climb to the top of the tallest building, you got to be able to come back down and plant your feet on the ground, on the grass, on the dirt. We are a part of nature. Trees are God's gift to us human beings. Sometimes we act foolish and forget how precious life is. A tree is a living thing."

8   "Momma, I love you," I said, and I kissed her gently on her cheeks. Momma was preaching now, so I listened all the more.

9   "Behold the beauty of a tree. Feel how firm and tough it is. Shake hands with the branches. Kiss the leaves. Don't be embarrassed. Trees have seen it all. They were here before we were. And if they ever disappear from the face of the earth, what hope or belief will humankind have then? The tree won't reject your love. My momma, your grandmother, used to say. 'The tree of love gives shade to all.'

10   "When I was a young child around nine or so, living down in Alabama, there was a great big old weeping willow in our backyard. The branches were so long and flowing that the children called them 'arms.' My oldest brother, Matthew, called the tree Old Willa.

11   "Now, that weeping willow had been standing in back of our farm before my great-great-uncle was born, which would have been your great-great-great-uncle. My momma and poppa were married under Old Willa. We would have family gatherings, picnics, and good-time parties near Old Willa. Some folks thought the tree had mystical powers. Miss Sally Mae, a root doctor, would come by every now and then and rub Old Willa's trunk. It was an interesting sight. Miss Sally Mae would talk to Old Willa and rub right in the middle of her trunk as if she were rubbing her stomach.

12   "Sometimes Poppa would gather me, my sisters and brothers around Old Willa. Poppa was a storyteller, you know. He would tell us about Uncle Love Joy, your great-great-great-uncle. One night Uncle Love Joy escaped from the plantation, which was a few miles away from the farm. He could hear the dogs and the slave catchers on the horses gaining up on him. He ran like the devil. He didn't know which direction to run but he could hear something or someone whispering. He ran and bumped his head right into the weeping willow tree, and he hid behind it. Those dogs took another trail. Uncle Love Joy thanked that tree. Twenty years later he came back with his wife and children and his brothers and sisters. They bought the land with the tree on it and built the farm.

13   "We'd have some fun times beneath Old Willa—but one day it all came to an end. The city developers came through and said that Old Willa had to be cut down because the tree was standing in the way of progress. Our farm and property were declared condemned by the city. The highways were coming through.

14   "The workers cut Old Willa down. They poured heaps of salt on her trunk so she wouldn't grow back. My momma was sad after that. You might say she never got over it.

15   "Poppa gathered the family around what was left of Old Willa. He said a prayer. We held hands and sang softly. Momma began weeping and she cried out, 'Old Willa was a love tree and the Tree of Love gives shade to all. No matter where you go, children, or what you do, you find a tree and give it a big hug. It doesn't matter what kind of tree it is. It can be a

Sycamore,

      Maple,

            Elm,

                  Oak,

                        Birch . . .

"My momma kept naming different kinds of trees. We were amazed. We didn't know she knew the names of so many trees.

'Pine,

      Cypress,

            Chestnut,

                  Walnut . . .'

"She named fruit trees, 'Lemon,

Apple,
      Peach,
            Plum,'

16   And then she said,
            'Weeping Willow.'
She clutched her heart as if she had a pain. She walked over to Poppa and collapsed in his arms.

17   "After Momma's funeral, Poppa was too sad to stay around the area, so he took me and my seven brothers and sisters up North to Tennessee. We didn't forget Momma but we eventually forgot Old Willa. At least, we never talked about the tree.

18   "Baby Dear, I tell you the story now because, when I saw you marching down the aisle getting your diploma, you stood tall and proud as a tree. Then I saw an image of Old Willa running through my mind."

19   I grabbed Momma and hugged her tightly. I felt like I was hugging Old

Willa. "Oh, Momma," I cried, "I thank you dearly for telling me this story. I promise you, Momma, that I will hug and kiss as many trees as I can."

20   The phone rings, interrupting my daydream. The administrative assistant informs me that the board meeting will begin in ten minutes. I thank her and go back to my dream. Every time I see Momma, she tells me about Old Willa. For ten years now, since my college graduation, she always has something new to say about the weeping willow. I sit in a swivel highback/lowback chair working in a gray color-coded office suite in one of the busiest cities in the world, the Big Apple. I haven't seen any apple trees. I do, however, go over to Central Park every now and then. I take my family with me. Sometimes I go alone. I have found an Old Willa in the park. I don't even call her Old Willa. I call her Nuba. I talk to her and she listens; she understands. Momma was right. The Tree of Love gives shade to all.

DISCUSSION QUESTIONS

1. What does the protagonist's grandmother mean when she says "Old Willa was a love tree and the Tree of Love gives shade to all?" Is her comment a metaphor? Explain your response.
2. In your small group, find and discuss some of the folkloric events in this story. How do these details add to the story's plot and theme?
3. What type of strength does the protagonist get from her mother's story? Why would the protagonist need this strength as an administrator working in a company in New York?

WRITING TOPICS

1. Name an object to complete this phrase: "The _____ of Love." Next, draw a picture of your object in which it becomes a reflection of your idea of love. In your writing journal, explain your phrase "The _____ of Love" and explain what your drawing represents.
2. What do you know about willow trees? Briefly research their sturdiness and how and where they grow. Then, in an essay, explore Old Willa as a metaphor for the lives of African-American women.

THE WOMAN'S MOURNING SONG

bell hooks

bell hooks is a feminist activist and social critic. Born as Gloria Watkins in 1955, hooks writes under the name of her great-grand-mother, Bell Hooks, to pay tribute to the unheard voices of black women past and present. She uses lowercase letters with her name to symbolize her skepticism of fame and ego. Currently, hooks teaches at Columbia University in New York.

As a lecturer, hooks has traveled across the United States and has published numerous works in which she presents her intellectual and personal ideas on African-American feminism, capitalism, the civil rights movement, critical theory, and contemporary society. hooks's first book, *Ain't I a Woman* (1981), examines the voice of black women within current mainstream feminism by looking at class, race, and gender; it launched her as a contemporary black intellectual. She has continued her intellectual and personal cri-tiques of society and the individual in such works as *Feminist Theory from Margin to Center* (1984), *Talking Back: Thinking Feminist, Thinking Black* (1988), *Yearning: Race, Gender, and Cultural Politics* (1990), *Breaking Bread: Insurgent Black Intellectual Life* (1991), *Black Looks: Race and Representation* (1992), *A Woman's Mourning Song* (1992), *Sisters of the Yam: Black Women and Self-Recovery* (1993), *Killing Rage: Ending Racism* (1995), and *Bone Black: Memories of Girlhood* (1996).

> i cry
> i cry high
> this mourning song
> my heart rises
> 5 sun in hand
> to make the bread
> i rise

my heavy work hand
needs
10 the voice of many singers
alone
the warmth of many ovens
comfort
the warrior in me returns
15 to slay sorrow
to make the bread
to sing the mourning song
i cry high
i cry high
20 i cry
the mourning song
go away death
go from love's house
go make your empty bed

DISCUSSION QUESTIONS

1. What is the woman mourning in this poem? Use specific lines and phrases from the poem to support your response.
2. Identify the blues qualities and/or structures in this poem. How do these elements contribute to the meaning of the poem?
3. In line 10, who are the singers to whom the speaker refers? What does the speaker mean when she says "the warmth of many ovens / comforts"? What are the connections between lines 8 through 10 and lines 11 through 13?

WRITING TOPICS

1. In your journal, compare the speaker's tone in lines 1 through 10 with the speaker's tone in lines 11 through 24. Specifically discuss the two different meanings of the phrases "I cry" and "I cry high."
2. In an essay, support either the position that "the woman's mourning song" is a poem about despair or a poem about hope. Use specific words, phrases, and lines from the poem to support your thesis.

GETTING THE FACTS OF LIFE

Paulette Childress White

Paulette Childress White was born in Hamtramck, Michigan, in 1948. She attended high school in Ecorse, Michigan, and married Bennie White Jr., a postal employee and artist. Since 1972 Childress has pursued a career as a writer.

White's work examines the lives of African-American women in the urban environment and celebrates everyday occurrences. She is the author of *Love Poem to a Black Junkie* (1975) and *The Watermelon Dress* (1983). Her work is represented in anthologies such as *Sturdy Black Bridges* (1979) and *Midnight Birds* (1980). Her works have also appeared in *Essence, Redbook*, and *Callaloo* magazines. White currently lives in Detroit.

1   The August morning was ripening into a day that promised to be a burner. By the time we'd walked three blocks, dark patches were showing beneath Momma's arms, and inside tennis shoes thick with white polish, my feet were wet against the cushions. I was beginning to regret how quickly I'd volunteered to go.

2   "Dog. My feet are getting mushy," I complained.

3   "You should've wore socks," Momma said, without looking my way or slowing down.

4   I frowned. In 1961, nobody wore socks with tennis shoes. It was bare legs, Bermuda shorts and a sleeveless blouse. Period.

5   Momma was chubby but she could really walk. She walked the same way she washed clothes—up-and-down, up-and-down until she was done. She didn't believe in taking breaks.

6   This was my first time going to the welfare office with Momma. After breakfast, before we'd had time to scatter, she corralled everyone old enough to consider and announced in her serious-business voice that someone was going to the welfare office with her this morning. Cries went up.

7   Junior had his papers to do. Stella was going swimming at the high

school. Dennis was already pulling the *Free Press* wagon across town every first Wednesday to get the surplus food—like that.

8   "You want clothes for school, don't you?" That landed. School opened in two weeks.

9   "I'll go," I said.

10   "Who's going to baby-sit if Minerva goes?" Momma asked.

11   Stella smiled and lifted her golden nose. "I will," she said. "I'd rather baby-sit than do *that*."

12   That should have warned me. Anything that would make Stella offer to baby-sit had to be bad.

13   A small cheer probably went up among my younger brothers in the back rooms where I was not too secretly known as "The Witch" because of the criminal licks I'd learned to give on my rise to power. I was twelve, third oldest under Junior and Stella, but I had long established myself as first in command among the kids. I was chief baby-sitter, biscuit-maker and broom-wielder. Unlike Stella, who'd begun her development at ten, I still had my girl's body and wasn't anxious to have that changed. What would it mean but a loss of power? I liked things just the way they were. My interest in bras was even less than my interest in boys, and that was limited to keeping my brothers—who seemed destined for wildness—from taking over completely.

14   Even before we left, Stella had Little Stevie Wonder turned up on the radio in the living room, and suspicious jumping-bumping sounds were beginning in the back. They'll tear the house down, I thought, following Momma out the door.

15   We turned at Salliotte, the street that would take us straight up to Jefferson Avenue where the welfare office was. Momma's face was pinking in the heat, and I was huffing to keep up. From here, it was seven more blocks on the colored side, the railroad tracks, five blocks on the white side and there you were. We'd be cooked.

16   "Is the welfare office near the Harbor Show?" I asked. I knew the answer, I just wanted some talk.

17   "Across the street."

18   "Umm. Glad it's not way down Jefferson somewhere."

19   Nothing. Momma didn't talk much when she was outside. I knew that the reason she wanted one of us along when she had far to go was not for company but so she wouldn't have to walk by herself. I could understand that. To me, walking alone was like being naked or deformed—everyone seemed to look at you harder and longer. With Momma, the feeling was probably worse because you knew people were wondering if she were white, Indian maybe or really colored. Having one of us along, brown and clearly hers, probably helped define that. Still, it was like being a little parade, with Momma's pale skin and straight brown hair turning heads like the clang of cymbals. Especially on the colored side.

20   "Well," I said, "here we come to the bad part."

21   Momma gave a tiny laugh.

22   Most of Salliotte was a business street, with Old West-looking storefronts and some office places that never seemed to open. Ecorse, hinged onto southwest Detroit like a clothes closet, didn't seem to take itself seriously. There were lots of empty fields, some of which folks down the residential streets turned into vegetable gardens every summer. And there was this block where the Moonflower Hotel raised itself to three stories over the poolroom and Beaman's drugstore. Here, bad boys and drunks made their noise and did an occasional stabbing. Except for the cars that lined both sides of the block, only one side was busy—the other bordered a field of weeds. We walked on the safe side.

23   If you were a woman or a girl over twelve, walking this block—even on the safe side—could be painful. They usually hollered at you and never mind what they said. Today, because it was hot and early, we made it by with only one weak *Hey baby* from a drunk sitting in the poolroom door.

24   "Hey baby yourself," I said but not too loudly, pushing my flat chest out and stabbing my eyes in his direction.

25   "Minerva girl, you better watch your mouth with grown men like that," Momma said, her eyes catching me up in real warning though I could see that she was holding down a smile.

26   "Well, he can't do nothing to me when I'm with you, can he?" I asked, striving to match the rise and fall of her black pumps.

27   She said nothing. She just walked on, churning away under a sun that clearly meant to melt us. From here to the tracks it was mostly gardens. It felt like the Dixie Peach[1] I'd used to help water-wave my hair was sliding down with the sweat on my face, and my throat was tight with thirst. Boy, did I want a pop. I looked at the last little store before we crossed the tracks without bothering to ask.

28   Across the tracks, there were no stores and no gardens. It was shady, and the grass was June green. Perfect-looking houses sat in unfenced spaces far back from the street. We walked these five blocks without a word. We just looked and hurried to get through it. I was beginning to worry about the welfare office in earnest. A fool could see that in this part of Ecorse, things got serious.

29   We had been on welfare for almost a year. I didn't have any strong feelings about it—my life went on pretty much the same. It just meant watching the mail for a check instead of Daddy getting paid, and occasional visits from a social worker that I'd always managed to miss. For Momma and whoever went with her, it meant this walk to the office and whatever went on there that made everyone hate to go. For Daddy, it seemed to bring the most change. For him, it meant staying away from home more than when he was working and a reason not to answer the phone.

30   At Jefferson, we turned left and there it was, halfway down the block. The Department of Social Services. I discovered some strong feelings. That

---

[1] *Dixie Peach:* a brand of hair oil.

fine name meant nothing. This was the welfare. The place for poor people. People who couldn't or wouldn't take care of themselves. Now I was going to face it, and suddenly I thought what I knew the others had thought, *What if I see someone I know?* I wanted to run back all those blocks to home.

31   I looked at Momma for comfort, but her face was closed and her mouth looked locked.

32   Inside, the place was gray. There were rows of long benches like church pews facing each other across a middle aisle that led to a central desk. Beyond the benches and the desk, four hallways led off to a maze of partitioned offices. In opposite corners, huge fans hung from the ceiling, humming from side to side, blowing the heavy air for a breeze.

33   Momma walked to the desk, answered some questions, was given a number and told to take a seat. I followed her through, trying not to see the waiting people—as though that would keep them from seeing me.

34   Gradually, as we waited, I took them all in. There was no one there that I knew, but somehow they all looked familiar. Or maybe I only thought they did, because when your eyes connected with someone's, they didn't quickly look away and they usually smiled. They were mostly women and children, and a few low-looking men. Some of them were white, which surprised me. I hadn't expected to see them in there.

35   Directly in front of the bench where we sat, a little girl with blond curls was trying to handle a bottle of Coke. Now and then, she'd manage to turn herself and the bottle around and watch me with big gray eyes that seemed to know quite well how badly I wanted a pop. I thought of asking Momma for fifteen cents so I could get one from the machine in the back but I was afraid she'd still say no so I just kept planning more and more convincing ways to ask. Besides, there was a water fountain near the door if I could make myself rise and walk to it.

36   We waited three hours. White ladies dressed like secretaries kept coming out to call numbers, and people on the benches would get up and follow down a hall. Then more people came in to replace them. I drank water from the fountain three times and was ready to put my feet up on the bench before us—the little girl with the Coke and her momma got called—by the time we heard Momma's number.

37   "You wait here," Momma said as I rose with her.

38   I sat down with a plop.

39   The lady with the number looked at me. Her face reminded me of the librarian's at Bunch school. Looked like she never cracked a smile. "Let her come," she said.

40   "She can wait here," Momma repeated, weakly.

41   "It's OK. She can come in. Come on," the lady insisted at me.

42   I hesitated, knowing that Momma's face was telling me to sit.

43   "Come on," the woman said.

44   Momma said nothing.

45   I got up and followed them into the maze. We came to a small room

where there was a desk and three chairs. The woman sat behind the desk and we before it.

46   For a while, no one spoke. The woman studied a folder open before her, brows drawn together. On the wall behind her there was a calendar with one heavy black line drawn slantwise through each day of August, up to the twenty-first. That was today.

47   "Mrs. Blue, I have a notation here that Mr. Blue has not reported to the department on his efforts to obtain employment since the sixteenth of June. Before that, it was the tenth of April. You understand that department regulations require that he report monthly to this office, do you not?" Eyes brown as a wren's belly came up at Momma.

48   "Yes," Momma answered, sounding as small as I felt.

49   "Can you explain his failure to do so?"

50   Pause. "He's been looking. He says he's been looking."

51   "That may be. However, his failure to report those efforts here is my only concern."

52   Silence.

53   "We cannot continue with your case as it now stands if Mr. Blue refuses to comply with departmental regulations. He is still residing with the family, is he not?"

54   "Yes, he is. I've been reminding him to come in . . . he said he would."

55   "Well, he hasn't. Regulations are that any able-bodied man, head-of-household and receiving assistance who neglects to report to this office any effort to obtain work for a period of sixty days or more is to be cut off for a minimum of three months, at which time he may reapply. As of this date, Mr. Blue is over sixty days delinquent, and officially, I am obliged to close the case and direct you to other sources of aid."

56   "What is that?"

57   "Aid to Dependent Children would be the only source available to you. Then, of course, you would not be eligible unless it was verified that Mr. Blue was no longer residing with the family."

58   Another silence. I stared into the gray steel front of the desk, everything stopped but my heart.

59   "Well, can you keep the case open until Monday? If he comes in by Monday?"

60   "According to my records, Mr. Blue failed to come in May and such an agreement was made then. In all, we allowed him a period of seventy days. You must understand that what happens in such cases as this is not wholly my decision." She sighed and watched Momma with hopeless eyes, tapping the soft end of her pencil on the papers before her. "Mrs. Blue, I will speak to my superiors on your behalf. I can allow you until Monday next . . . that's the"—she swung around to the calendar—"twenty-sixth of August, to get him in here."

61   "Thank you. He'll be in," Momma breathed. "Will I be able to get the clothing order today?"

62   Hands and eyes searched in the folder for an answer before she cleared her throat and tilted her face at Momma. "We'll see what we can do," she said, finally.

63   My back touched the chair. Without turning my head, I moved my eyes down to Momma's dusty feet and wondered if she could still feel them; my own were numb. I felt bodyless—there was only my face, which wouldn't disappear, and behind it, one word pinging against another in a buzz that made no sense. At home, we'd have the house cleaned by now, and I'd be waiting for the daily appearance of my best friend, Bernadine, so we could comb each other's hair or talk about stuck-up Evelyn and Brenda. Maybe Bernadine was already there, and Stella was teaching her to dance the bop.

64   Then I heard our names and ages—all eight of them—being called off like items in a grocery list.

65   "Clifford, Junior, age fourteen." She waited.

66   "Yes."

67   "Born? Give me the month and year."

68   "October 1946," Momma answered, and I could hear in her voice that she'd been through these questions before.

69   "Stella, age thirteen."

70   "Yes."

71   "Born?"

72   "November 1947."

73   "Minerva, age twelve." She looked at me. "This is Minerva?"

74   "Yes."

75   No. I thought, no, this is not Minerva. You can write it down if you want to, but Minerva is not here.

76   "Born?"

77   "December 1948."

78   The woman went on down the list, sounding more and more like Momma should be sorry or ashamed, and Momma's answers grew fainter and fainter. So this was welfare. I wondered how many times Momma had had to do this. Once before? Three times? Every time?

79   More questions. How many in school? Six. Who needs shoes? Everybody.

80   "Everybody needs shoes? The youngest two?"

81   "Well, they don't go to school . . . but they walk."

82   My head came up to look at Momma and the woman. The woman's mouth was left open. Momma didn't blink.

83   The brown eyes went down. "Our allowances are based on the median costs for moderately priced clothing at Sears, Roebuck." She figured on paper as she spoke. "That will mean thirty-four dollars for children over ten . . . thirty dollars for children under ten. It comes to one hundred ninety-eight dollars. I can allow eight dollars for two additional pairs of shoes."

84   "Thank you."

85   "You will present your clothing order to a salesperson at the store, who will be happy to assist you in your selections. Please be practical as further

clothing requests will not be considered for a period of six months. In cases of necessity, however, requests for winter outerwear will be considered beginning November first."

86   Momma said nothing.

87   The woman rose and left the room.

88   For the first time, I shifted in the chair. Momma was looking into the calendar as though she could see through the pages to November first. Everybody needed a coat.

89   I'm never coming here again, I thought. If I do, I'll stay out front. Not coming back in here. Ever again.

90   She came back and sat behind her desk. "Mrs. Blue, I must make it clear that, regardless of my feelings, I will be forced to close your case if your husband does not report to this office by Monday, the twenty-sixth. Do you understand?"

91   "Yes. Thank you. He'll come. I'll see to it."

92   "Very well." She held a paper out to Momma.

93   We stood. Momma reached over and took the slip of paper. I moved toward the door.

94   "Excuse me, Mrs. Blue, but are you pregnant?"

95   "What?"

96   "I asked if you were expecting another child."

97   "Oh. No, I'm not," Momma answered, biting down on her lips.

98   "Well, I'm sure you'll want to be careful about a thing like that in your present situation."

99   "Yes."

100   I looked quickly to Momma's loose white blouse. We'd never known when another baby was coming until it was almost there.

101   "I suppose that eight children are enough for anyone," the woman said, and for the first time her face broke into a smile.

102   Momma didn't answer that. Somehow, we left the room and found our way out onto the street. We stood for a moment as though lost. My eyes followed Momma's up to where the sun was burning high. It was still there blazing white against a cloudless blue. Slowly, Momma put the clothing order into her purse and snapped it shut. She looked around as if uncertain which way to go. I led the way to the corner. We turned. We walked the first five blocks.

103   I was thinking about how stupid I'd been a year ago, when Daddy lost his job. I'd been happy.

104   "You all better be thinking about moving to Indianapolis," he announced one day after work, looking like he didn't think much of it himself. He was a welder with the railroad company. He'd worked there for eleven years. But now, "Company's moving to Indianapolis," he said. "Gonna be gone by November. If I want to keep my job, we've got to move with it."

105   We didn't. Nobody wanted to move to Indianapolis—not even Daddy.

Here, we had uncles, aunts and cousins on both sides. Friends. Everybody and everything we knew. Daddy could get another job. First came unemployment compensation. Then came welfare. Thank goodness for welfare, we said, while we waited and waited for that job that hadn't yet come.

106 The problem was that Daddy couldn't take it. If something got repossessed or somebody took sick or something was broken or another kid was coming, he'd carry on terribly until things got better—by which time things were always worse. He'd always been that way. So when the railroad left, he began to do everything wrong. Stayed out all hours. Drank and drank some more. When he was home, he was so grouchy we were afraid to squeak. Now when we saw him coming, we got lost. Even our friends ran for cover.

107 At the railroad tracks, we sped up. The tracks were as far across as a block was long. Silently, I counted the rails by the heat of the steel bars through my thin soles. On the other side, I felt something heavy rise up in my chest and I knew that I wanted to cry. I wanted to cry or run or kiss the dusty ground. The little houses with their sun scorched lawns and backyard gardens were mansions in my eyes. "Ohh, Ma . . . look at those collards!"

108 "Umm-hummm," she agreed, and I knew that she saw it too.

109 "Wonder how they grew so big?"

110 "Cow dung, probably. Big Poppa used to put cow dung out to fertilize the vegetable plots, and everything just grew like crazy. We used to get tomatoes this big"—she circled with her hands—"and don't talk about squash or melons."

111 "I bet y'all ate like rich people. Bet y'all had everything you could want."

112 "We sure did," she said. "We never wanted for anything when it came to food. And when the cash crops were sold, we could get whatever else that was needed. We never wanted for a thing."

113 "What about the time you and cousin Emma threw out the supper peas?"

114 "Oh! Did I tell you about that?" she asked. Then she told it all over again. I didn't listen. I watched her face and guarded her smile with a smile of my own.

115 We walked together, step for step. The sun was still burning, but we forgot to mind it. We talked about an Alabama girlhood in a time and place I'd never know. We talked about the wringer washer and how it could be fixed, because washing every day on a scrub-board was something Alabama could keep. We talked about how to get Daddy to the Department of Social Services.

116 Then we talked about having babies. She began to tell me things I'd never known, and the idea of womanhood blossomed in my mind like some kind of suffocating rose.

117 "Momma," I said, "I don't think I can be a woman."

118 "You can," she laughed, "and if you live, you will be. You gotta be some kind of woman."

119 "But it's hard," I said, "sometimes it must be hard."

120 "Umm-humm," she said, "sometimes it is hard."

121 When we got to the bad block, we crossed to Beaman's drugstore for two orange crushes. Then we walked right through the groups of men standing in the shadows of the poolroom and the Moonflower Hotel. Not one of them said a word to us. I supposed they could see in the way we walked that we weren't afraid. We'd been to the welfare office and back again. And the facts of life, fixed in our minds like the sun in the sky, were no burning mysteries.

DISCUSSION QUESTIONS

1. Why hasn't Minerva thought about her family being on welfare even though the family has been on welfare for a year?
2. How do Minerva and her mother interact with each other when they are alone? When they are with others? Why are the two types of behavior important?
3. Minerva says she is: "chief baby-sitter, biscuit-maker and broom-wielder." Does being one of two sisters in a family of eight children have an influence on these descriptions?
4. At the beginning of the story, how does Minerva feel about moving from childhood into womanhood? How does she feel at the end of the story? Use specific evidence from the story to support your responses.
5. Discuss the "facts of life" that Minerva gets from being a sister and daughter, from the African-American community she lives in, and from the white case worker. How do they prepare her for life as a black woman?

WRITING TOPICS

1. Minerva feels that her body is invisible as a reaction to the conversation she hears between her mother and the case worker at the welfare office. In your journal, write about a time when you were embarrassed about a situation, but you were powerless to change the situation. How did you feel? Did you want to become invisible?
2. In an essay discuss the societal limitations Minerva might encounter as she becomes a young woman that she might not encounter if she were a boy becoming a young man.
3. "Getting the Facts of Life" is set in 1961. Write an essay in which you contrast the types of careers African-American women could participate in the early 1960s with the types of careers African-American women can participate in today.

RESTORATION: A MEMORIAL—9/18/91

Audre Lorde

Audre Lorde was born in New York City in 1934 to Frederic Byron Lorde and Linda Belmar Lorde. From her early childhood, Lorde enjoyed reading and writing. She wrote her first poem when she was in the eighth grade. In 1959 she received her B.A. from Hunter College, and in 1961 she received her M.A. in library science from Columbia University. Lorde worked as a public librarian until 1968, when she received a National Endowment for the Arts grant. In the spring of 1968, she became poet-in-residence at Tougaloo College in Mississippi. She also taught at John Jay College of Criminal Justice and Hunter College. Lorde's honors include the Manhattan Borough President's Award for Excellence in the Arts (1988) and designation as New York State Poet in 1991.

As an international poet, essayist, fiction writer, and activist, Lorde used her fifteen volumes of poetry and prose writings to protest racial, sexual, and gender injustice. Whereas her early work, *The First City* (1968), focused on introspection, her later books expressed a social anger. *From a Land where Other People Live* (1973) was nominated for a National Book Award. Lorde's critically received book of poetry, *The Black Unicorn* (1978), expresses the racial, political, and sexual liberation views that appear throughout the rest of her work. In 1980 Lorde published *Cancer Journals,* which chronicled her struggle with breast cancer. *A Burst of Light,* an essay collection, was awarded the American Book Award in 1989. Lorde wrote poetry collections, fiction, and nonfiction, including *Cables to Rage* (1970), *New York Head Shop and Museum* (1974), *Coal* (1976), *Zami, A New Spelling of My Name* (1982), *Sister Outsider: Essays and Speeches* (1984), *Our Dead Behind Us* (1986), *Cancer Journals,* second edition (1987), *Undersong: Chosen Poems Old and New* (1992), *Poetry Is Not a Luxury* (1993), and *The Marvelous Arithmetics of Distances: Poems 1987–1992* (1993). Lorde died in 1992.

Berlin again   after chemotherapy
I reach behind me once more
for days to come
sweeping around the edges of authenticity
5   two years after Hugo blew one life away
Death like a burnt star
perched on the rim of my teacup
flaming the honey drips from my spoon
sunlight flouncing off the gargoyles opposite.

10   Somewhere it is Tuesday
in the ordinary world
ravishment fades
into compelling tasks
our bodies learn to perform
15   quite a bit of the house is left
our bedroom spared
except for the ankle-deep water
and terrible stench.

Would I exchange this safety of exile
20   for the muddy hand-drawn water
wash buckets stashed
where our front porch had been
half-rotten vegetables
the antique grey settling over your face
25   that October?

I want you laughing again
After the stinking rugs are dragged away
the crystal chandelier dug
from the dining-room floor
30   refrigerator righted
broken cupboards stacked outside
to dry for our dinner fire.

A few trees still stand
in a brand-new landscape
35   but the sea road is impassable.
Your red shirt
hung out on a bush to dry
is the only flower for weeks.
No escape. No return.
40   No other life
half so sane.

In this alien and temporary haven
my poisoned fingers
slowly return to normal
45 I read your letter dreaming
the perspective of a bluefish
or a fugitive parrot
watch the chemicals leaving my nails
as my skin takes back its weaknesses.
50 Learning to laugh again.

DISCUSSION QUESTIONS

1. Mark the metaphors and similes in this poem. What makes each unique or stand out from the other words and descriptions in the poem?
2. The first two lines in the second stanza read: "Somewhere it is Tuesday / in the ordinary world." Why does the speaker make reference to "the ordinary world" as if she were not a part of it?
3. In the last line of the poem, the speaker says "Learning to laugh again." Is the speaker's ability to laugh again a sign of weakness or strength? Support your response with words, phrases, or lines from the poem.

WRITING TOPICS

1. The title of this poem is "Restoration: A Memorial—9/18/91." Explain in an essay what the speaker "rebuilds" and how it serves as a memorial.
2. Write a poem in which you create a memorial for a person from African-American history. Include personal information about the person in the poem.

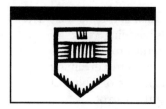

TO DA-DUH, IN MEMORIAM

Paule Marshall

Paule Marshall was born in Brooklyn, New York, in 1929. Her parents, Samuel and Ada Burke, had emigrated from Barbados after World War I. The mixture of Caribbean and American cultures gave her both a sense of ritual and a sense of the importance of history. This background highly influenced the issues covered in her fiction. In 1953 Marshall received her B.A., Phi Beta Kappa, from Brooklyn College. She wrote her first novel, *Brown Girl, Brownstones* in 1959. At that time she worked as a writer for *Our World,* a small magazine, which sent her to Brazil and the Caribbean. Marshall left the magazine in 1956, and since 1959 she has continued her career as a fiction writer. In addition, she is a lecturer in creative writing at Yale University.

Although Marshall's novels did not do well commercially in the 1960s, she has continued to write about topics most important to her, namely, African-American women and the cultures within which they live. Marshall was one of the first authors to focus her work on the psychological traits and concerns of African-American women.

Marshall's other works include *Soul Clap Hands and Sing* (1961), and *The Chosen Place, the Timeless People* (1969). Early in the 1980s, Marshall began to enjoy commercial success as well as critical acclaim with *Reena and Other Stories* (1983), *Praisesong for the Widow* (1983), and *Daughters* (1992).

"...Oh Nana! all of you is not involved in this evil business
Death,
Nor all of us in life."
—From "At My Grandmother's Grave," by Lebert Bethune

1   I did not see her at first I remember. For not only was it dark inside the crowded disembarkation shed in spite of the daylight flooding in from out-

side, but standing there waiting for her with my mother and sister I was still somewhat blinded from the sheen of tropical sunlight on the water of the bay which we had just crossed in the landing boat, leaving behind us the ship that had brought us from New York lying in the offing. Besides, being only nine years of age at the time and knowing nothing of islands I was busy attending to the alien sights and sounds of Barbados, the unfamiliar smells.

2   I did not see her, but I was alerted to her approach by my mother's hand which suddenly tightened around mine, and looking up I traced her gaze through the gloom in the shed until I finally made out the small, purposeful, painfully erect figure of the old woman headed our way.

3   Her face was drowned in the shadow of an ugly rolled-brim brown felt hat, but the details of her slight body and of the struggle taking place within it were clear enough—an intense, unrelenting struggle between her back which was beginning to bend ever so slightly under the weight of her eighty-odd years and the rest of her which sought to deny those years and hold that back straight, keep it in line. Moving swiftly toward us (so swiftly it seemed she did not intend stopping when she reached us but would sweep past us out the doorway which opened onto the sea and like Christ walk upon the water!), she was caught between the sunlight at her end of the building and the darkness inside—and for a moment she appeared to contain them both: the light in the long severe old-fashioned white dress she wore which brought the sense of a past that was still alive into our bustling present and in the snatch of white at her eye; the darkness in her black high-top shoes and in her face which was visible now that she was closer.

4   It was as stark and fleshless as a death mask, that face. The maggots might have already done their work, leaving only the framework of bone beneath the ruined skin and deep wells at the temple and jaw. But her eyes were alive, unnervingly so for one so old, with a sharp light that flicked out of the dim clouded depths like a lizard's tongue to snap up all in her view. Those eyes betrayed a child's curiosity about the world, and I wondered vaguely seeing them, and seeing the way the bodice of her ancient dress had collapsed in on her flat chest (what had happened to her breasts?), whether she might not be some kind of child at the same time that she was a woman, with fourteen children, my mother included to prove it. Perhaps she was both, both child and woman, darkness and light, past and present, life and death—all the opposites contained and reconciled in her.

5   "My Da-duh," my mother said formally and stepped forward. The name sounded like thunder fading softly in the distance.

6   "Child," Da-duh said, and her tone, her quick scrutiny of my mother, the brief embrace in which they appeared to shy from each other rather than touch, wiped out the fifteen years my mother had been away and restored the old relationship. My mother, who was such a formidable figure in my eyes, had suddenly with a word been reduced to my status.

7   "Yes, God is good," Da-duh said with a nod that was like a tic. "He has spared me to see my child again."

8   We were led forward then, apologetically because not only did Da-duh prefer boys but she also liked her grandchildren to be "white," that is, fair-skinned, and we had, I was to discover, a number of cousins, the outside children of white estate managers and the like, who qualified. We, though, were as black as she.

9   My sister being the oldest was presented first. "This one takes after the father," my mother said and waited to be reproved.

10   Frowning, Da-duh tilted my sister's face toward the light. But her frown soon gave way to a grudging smile, for my sister with her large mild eyes and little broad winged nose, with our father's high-cheeked Barbadian cast to her face, was pretty.

11   "She's goin' be lucky," Da-duh said and patted her once on the cheek. "Any girl child that takes after the father does be lucky."

12   She turned then to me. But oddly enough she did not touch me. Instead leaning close, she peered hard at me, and then quickly drew back. I thought I saw her hand start up as though to shield her eyes. It was almost as if she saw not only me, a thin truculent child who it was said took after no one but myself, but something in me which for some reason she found disturbing, even threatening. We looked silently at each other for a long time in the noisy shed, our gaze locked. She was the first to look away.

13   "But Adry," she said to my mother and her laugh was cracked, thin, apprehensive. "Where did you get this one here with this fierce look?"

14   "We don't know where she came out of, my Da-duh," my mother said, laughing also. Even I smiled to myself. After all I had won the encounter. Da-duh had recognized my small strength—and this was all I ever asked of the adults in my life then.

15   "Come, soul," Da-duh said and took my hand. "You must be one of those New York terrors you hear so much about."

16   She led us, me at her side and my sister and mother behind, out of the shed into the sunlight that was like a bright driving summer rain and over to a group of people clustered beside a decrepit lorry.[1] They were our relatives, most of them from St. Andrews although Da-duh herself lived in St. Thomas, the women wearing bright print dresses, the colors vivid against their darkness, the men rusty black suits that encased them like straightjackets. Da-duh, holding fast to my hand, became my anchor as they circled round us like a nervous sea, exclaiming, touching us with their calloused hands, embracing us shyly. They laughed in awed bursts, "But look Adry got big-big children!"/ "And see the nice things they wearing, wrist watch and all!" / "I tell you, Adry has done all right for sheself in New York. . . ."

17   Da-duh, ashamed at their wonder, embarrassed for them, admonished them the while. "But oh Christ," she said, "why you all got to get on like you never saw people from 'Away' before? You would think New York is the

---

[1] *lorry:* a large motor vehicle, a bus.

only place in the world to hear wunna. That's why I don't like to go anyplace with you St. Andrews people, you know. You all ain't been colonized."[2]

18   We were in the back of the lorry finally, packed in among the barrels of ham, flour, cornmeal, and rice and the trunks of clothes that my mother had brought as gifts. We made our way slowly through Bridgetown's clogged streets, part of a funeral procession of cars and open-sided buses, bicycles and donkey carts. The dim little limestone shops and offices along the way marched with us, at the same mournful pace, toward the same grave cere-mony—as did the people, the women balancing huge baskets on top their heads as if they were no more than hats they wore to shade them from the sun. Looking over the edge of the lorry I watched as their feet slurred the dust. I listened, and their voices, raw and loud and dissonant in the heat, seemed to be grappling with each other high overhead.

19   Da-duh sat on a trunk in our midst, a monarch amid her court. She still held my hand, but it was different now. I had suddenly become her anchor, for I felt her fear of the lorry with its asthmatic motor (a fear and distrust, I later learned, she held of all machines) beating like a pulse in her rough palm.

20   As soon as we left Bridgetown behind though, she relaxed, and while the others around us talked she gazed at the canes standing tall on either side of the winding marl road. "C'dear," she said softly to herself after a time. "The canes this side are pretty enough."

21   They were too much for me. I thought of them as giant weeds that had overrun the island, leaving scarcely any room for the small tottering houses of sunbleached pine we passed or the people, dark streaks as our lorry hur-tled by. I suddenly feared that we were journeying, unaware that we were, toward some dangerous place where the canes, grown as high and thick as a forest, would close in on us and run us through with their stiletto blades. I longed then for the familiar; for the street in Brooklyn where I lived, for my father who had refused to accompany us ("Blowing out good money on foolishness," he had said of the trip), for a game of tag with my friends under the chestnut tree outside our aging brownstone house.

22   "Yes, but wait till you see St. Thomas canes," Da-duh was saying to me. "They's canes father,[3] bo," she gave a proud arrogant nod. "Tomorrow, God willing, I goin' take you out in the ground and show them to you."

23   True to her word, Da-duh took me with her the following day out into the ground. It was a fairly large plot adjoining her weathered board and shingle house and consisting of a small orchard, a good-sized canepiece and behind the canes, where the land sloped abruptly down, a gully. She had purchased it with Panama money sent her by her eldest son, my uncle

---

2 *"You all ain't been colonized"*: a satirical comment referring to the British Empire's colonial influence in Barbados.

3 *"They's canes father"*: meaning the St. Thomas variety of sugar canes were larger.

Joseph, who had died working on the canal. We entered the ground along a trail no wider than her body and as devious and complex as her reasons for showing me her land. Da-duh strode briskly ahead, her slight form filled out this morning by the layers of sacking petticoats she wore under her working dress to protect her against the damp. A fresh white cloth, elaborately arranged around her head, added to her height, and lent her a vain, almost roguish air.

24   Her pace slowed once we reached the orchard, and glancing back at me occasionally over her shoulder, she pointed out the various trees.

25   "This here is a breadfruit," she said. "That one yonder is a papaw. Here's a guava. This is a mango. I know you don't have anything like these in New York. Here's a sugar apple." (The fruit looked more like artichokes than apples to me.) "This one bears limes. . . ." She went on for some time, intoning the names of the trees as though they were those of her gods. Finally turning to me, she said, "I know you don't have anything this nice where you come from." Then, as I hesitated: "I said I know you don't have anything this nice where you come from. . . ."

26   "No," I said and my world did seem suddenly lacking.

27   Da-duh nodded and passed on. The orchard ended and we were on the narrow cart road that led through the canepiece, the canes clashing like swords above my cowering head. Again she turned and her thin muscular arms spread wide, her dim gaze embracing the small field of canes, she said—and her voice almost broke under the weight of her pride, "Tell me, have you got anything like these in that place where you were born?"

28   "No."

29   "I din' think so. I bet you don't even know that these canes here and the sugar you eat is one and the same thing. That they does throw the canes into some damn machine at the factory and squeeze out all the little life in them to make sugar for you all so in New York to eat. I bet you don't know that."

30   "I've got two cavities and I'm not allowed to eat a lot of sugar."

31   But Da-duh didn't hear me. She had turned with an inexplicably angry motion and was making her way rapidly out of the canes and down the slope at the edge of the field which led to the gully below. Following her apprehensively down the incline amid a stand of banana plants whose leaves flapped like elephants ears in the wind, I found myself in the middle of a small tropical wood—a place dense and damp and gloomy and tremulous with the fitful play of light and shadow as the leaves high above moved against the sun that was almost hidden from view. It was a violent place, the tangled foliage fighting each other for a chance at the sunlight, the branches of the trees locked in what seemed an immemorial struggle, one both necessary and inevitable. But despite the violence, it was pleasant, almost peaceful in the gully, and beneath the thick undergrowth the earth smelled like spring.

32   This time Da-duh didn't even bother to ask her usual question, but simply turned and waited for me to speak.

33   "No," I said, my head bowed. "We don't have anything like this in New York."

34   "Ah," she cried, her triumph complete. "I din' think so. Why, I've heard that's a place where you can walk till you drop and never see a tree."

35   "We've got a chestnut tree in front of our house," I said.

36   "Does it bear?" She waited. "I ask you, does it bear?"

37   "Not anymore," I muttered. "It used to, but not anymore."

38   She gave the nod that was like a nervous twitch. "You see," she said. "Nothing can bear there." Then, secure behind her scorn, she added, "But tell me, what's this snow like that you hear so much about?"

39   Looking up, I studied her closely, sensing my chance, and then I told her, describing at length and with as much drama as I could summon not only what snow in the city was like, but what it would be like here, in her perennial summer kingdom.

40   ". . . And you see all these trees you got here," I said. "Well, they'd be bare. No leaves, no fruit, nothing. They'd be covered in snow. You see your canes. They'd be buried under tons of snow. The snow would be higher than your head, higher than your house, and you wouldn't be able to come down into this here gully because it would be snowed under. . . ."

41   She searched my face for the lie, still scornful but intrigued. "What a thing, huh?" she said finally, whispering it softly to herself.

42   "And when it snows you couldn't dress like you are now," I said. "Oh no, you'd freeze to death. You'd have to wear a hat and gloves and galoshes and ear muffs so your ears wouldn't freeze and drop off, and a heavy coat. I've got a Shirley Temple coat with fur on the collar. I can dance. You wanna see?"

43   Before she could answer I began, with a dance called the Truck which was popular back then in the 1930's. My right forefinger waving, I trucked around the nearby trees and around Da-duh's awed and rigid form. After the Truck I did the Suzy-Q, my lean hips swishing, my sneakers sidling zigzag over the ground "I can sing," I said and did so, starting with "I'm Gonna Sit Right Down and Write Myself a Letter," then without pausing, "Tea for Two," and ending with "I Found a Million Dollar Baby in a Five and Ten Cent Store."

44   For long moments afterwards Da-duh stared at me as if I were a creature from Mars, an emissary from some world she did not know but which intrigued her and whose power she both felt and feared. Yet something about my performance must have pleased her, because bending down she slowly lifted her long skirt and then, one by one, the layers of petticoats until she came to a drawstring purse dangling at the end of a long strip of cloth tied round her waist. Opening the purse she handed me a penny. "Here," she said half-smiling against her will. "Take this to buy yourself a sweet at the shop up the road. There's nothing to be done with you, soul."

45   From then on, whenever I wasn't taken to visit relatives, I accompanied Da-duh out into the ground, and alone with her amid the canes or down in

the gully I told her about New York. It always began with some slighting remark on her part: "I know they don't have anything this nice where you come from," or "Tell me, I hear those foolish people in New York does do such and such. . . ." But as I answered, recreating my towering world of steel and concrete and machines for her, building the city out of words, I would feel her give way. I came to know the signs of her surrender: the total stillness that would come over her little hard dry form, the probing gaze that like a surgeon's knife sought to cut through my skull to get at the images there, to see if I were lying, above all, her fear, a fear nameless and profound, the same one I had felt beating in the palm of her hand that day in the lorry.

46   Over the weeks I told her about refrigerators, radios, gas stoves, elevators, trolley cars, wringer washing machines, movies, airplanes, the cyclone at Coney Island, subways, toasters, electric lights: "At night, see, all you have to do is flip this little switch on the wall and all the lights in the house go on just like that. Like magic. It's like turning on the sun at night.

47   "But tell me," she said to me once with a faint mocking smile, "do the white people have all these things too or it's only the people looking like us?"

48   I laughed. "What d'ya mean," I said. "The white people have even better." Then: "I beat up a white girl in my class last term."

49   "Beating up white people!" Her tone was incredulous.

50   "How you mean!" I said, using an expression of hers. "She called me a name."

51   For some reason Da-duh could not quite get over this and repeated in the same hushed, shocked voice, "Beating up white people now! Oh, the lord, the world's changing up so I can scarce recognize it anymore."

52   One morning toward the end of our stay, Da-duh led me into a part of the gully that we had never visited before, an area darker and more thickly overgrown than the rest, almost impenetrable. There in a small clearing amid the dense bush, she stopped before an incredibly tall royal palm which rose cleanly out of the ground, and drawing the eye up with it, soared high above the trees around it into the sky. It appeared to be touching the blue dome of sky, to be flaunting its dark crown of fronds right in the blinding white face of the late morning sun.

53   Da-duh watched me a long time before she spoke, and then she said very quietly, "All right, now, tell me if you've got anything this tall in that place you're from."

54   I almost wished, seeing her face, that I could have said no. "Yes," I said. "We've got buildings hundreds of times this tall in New York. There's one called the Empire State Building that's the tallest in the world. My class visited it last year and I went all the way to the top. It's got over a hundred floors. I can't describe how tall it is. Wait a minute. What's the name of that hill I went to visit the other day, where they have the police station?"

55   "You mean Bissex?"

56   "Yes, Bissex. Well, the Empire State Building is way taller than that."

57   "You're lying now!" she shouted, trembling with rage. Her hand lifted to strike me.

58   "No, I'm not," I said. "It really is, if you don't believe me I'll send you a picture postcard of it as soon as I get back home so you can see for yourself. But it's way taller than Bissex."

59   All the fight went out of her at that. The hand poised to strike me fell limp to her side, and as she stared at me, seeing not me but the building that was taller than the highest hill she knew, the small stubborn light in her eyes (it was the same amber as the flame in the kerosene lamp she lit at dusk) began to fail. Finally, with a vague gesture that even in the midst of her defeat still tried to dismiss me and my world, she turned and started back through the gully, walking slowly, her steps groping and uncertain, as if she were suddenly no longer sure of the way, while I followed triumphant yet strangely saddened behind.

60   The next morning I found her dressed for our morning walk but stretched out on the Berbice[4] chair in the tiny drawing room where she sometimes napped during the afternoon heat, her face turned to the window beside her. She appeared thinner and suddenly indescribably old.

61   "My Da-duh," I said.

62   "Yes, nuh," she said. Her voice was listless and the face she slowly turned my way was, now that I think back on it, like a Benin[5] mask, the features drawn and almost distorted by an ancient abstract sorrow.

63   "Don't you feel well?" I asked.

64   "Girl, I don't know."

65   "My Da-duh, I goin' boil you some bush tea," my aunt, Da-duh's youngest child, who lived with her, called from the shed roof kitchen.

66   "Who tell you I need bush tea?" she cried, her voice assuming for a moment its old authority. "You can't even rest nowadays without some malicious person looking for you to be dead. Come girl," she motioned to me to a place beside her on the old-fashioned lounge chair, "give us a tune."

67   I sang for her until breakfast at eleven, all my brash irreverent Tin Pan Alley[6] songs, and then just before noon we went out into the ground. But it was a short, dispirited walk. Da-duh didn't even notice that the mangoes were beginning to ripen and would have to be picked before the village boys got to them. And when she paused occasionally and looked out across the canes or up at her trees it wasn't as if she were seeing them but something else. Some huge, monolithic shape had imposed itself, it seemed, between her and the land, obstructing her vision. Returning to the house she slept the entire afternoon on the Berbice chair.

---

4 *Berbice:* in reference to a type of lounge chair. (Berbice is the name of a river in South America.)

5 *Benin:* a West African country, famous for its fine metalwork.

6 *Tin Pan Alley:* a term that originated in New York City in the early 1900s, Tin Pan Alley refers to a district that is the center for composers and publishers of popular music.

68   She remained like this until we left, languishing away the mornings on the chair at the window gazing out at the land as if it were already doomed; then, at noon, taking the brief stroll with me through the ground during which she seldom spoke, and afterwards returning home to sleep till almost dusk sometimes.

69   On the day of our departure she put on the austere, ankle-length white dress, the black shoes and brown felt hat (her town clothes she called them), but she did not go with us to town. She saw us off on the road outside her house and in the midst of my mother's tearful protracted farewell, she leaned down and whispered in my ear, "Girl, you're not to forget now to send me the picture of that building, you hear."

70   By the time I mailed her the large colored picture postcard of the Empire State Building she was dead. She died during the famous '37 strike which began shortly after we left. On the day of her death England sent planes flying low over the island in a show of force—so low, according to my aunt's letter, that the downdraft from them shook the ripened mangoes from the trees in Da-duh's orchard. Frightened, everyone in the village fled into the canes. Except Da-duh. She remained in the house at the window so my aunt said, watching as the planes came swooping and screaming like monstrous birds down over the village, over her house, rattling her trees and flattening the young canes in her field. It must have seemed to her lying there that they did not intend pulling out of their dive, but like the hardback beetles which hurled themselves with suicidal force against the walls of the house at night, those menacing silver shapes would hurl themselves in an ecstasy of self-immolation on the land, destroying it utterly.

71   When the planes finally left and the villagers returned they found her dead on the Berbice chair at the window.

72   She died and I lived, but always, to this day even, within the shadow of her death. For a brief period after I was grown I went to live alone, like one doing penance, in a loft above a noisy factory in downtown New York and there painted seas of sugarcane and huge swirling Van Gogh suns and palm trees striding like brightly-plumed Tutsi[7] warriors across a tropical landscape, while the thunderous tread of the machines downstairs jarred the floor beneath my easel, mocking my efforts.

DISCUSSION QUESTIONS

1. Compare and contrast the personalities of Da-duh and the granddaughter. In what ways are they similar and dissimilar? What do these similarities and differences say about them?

---

[7] *Tutsi:* a tribe of Burundi, an east central African country; also known as the Watusi.

2. Da-duh becomes ill after hearing that the Empire State Building is taller than the tallest hill on the island. Why does this information disturb the grandmother?
3. Is the granddaughter responsible for Da-duh's death? Why does she consider painting tropical landscapes penance, or atonement for a sin?

WRITING TOPICS

1. Write an entry in your journal in which you discuss a time in your life when you paid attention to a story that an older relative told you. Since you heard that story, has anything about the story had an impact on the way you think or act?
2. Reread the last paragraph in Linda Goss's "The Tree of Love" and the last paragraph in "To Da-duh, In Memoriam." Write an essay in which you discuss the connections Paule Marshall and Linda Goss make between black women and the land.
3. Write a letter to a younger relative explaining the importance of listening to the stories of older relatives.

ONE THING I DONT NEED

Ntozake Shange

Ntozake Shange was born Paulette Williams in Trenton, New Jersey, in 1948. Her father, Paul, was a surgeon, and her mother, Eloise, a psychiatric social worker and educator. In 1973 she took the African name Ntozake (ĕn-tō-zä'ke) meaning "she who comes with her own things" and Shange (shän'gā) meaning "who walks like a lion." As a youth Shange met such notable African-American musicians and singers as Charlie Parker, Miles Davis, and Josephine Baker who were friends of her parents. Another friend, the African-American scholar and intellectual W. E. B. Du Bois, made a great impression on Shange. She received a B.A. with honors in American Studies from Barnard College in 1970 and her M.A. in American studies from the University of Southern California, Los Angeles in 1973. Shange became well known as a writer in 1976 with the Broadway production of *for colored girls who have considered suicide/when the rainbow is enuf*. The work was a *choreopoem*—a work combining poetry, music, dance, and drama. *for colored girls* won several awards, including an Obie in 1977. Shange has taught at such universities and colleges as Sonoma State College, Mills College, the University of California Extension, Yale, and Howard.

The differing facets of her experiences have influenced Shange's writing. She is an educator, dancer, writer, actress, and lecturer. Her poetry, fiction, and drama focus on the strengths of African-American women, and she often expresses this strength by using dance and music. Her works include the following: *Nappy Edges* (1978), *Sassafras, Cypress & Indigo* (1982), *A Daughter's Geography* (1983), *See No Evil: Prefaces, Essays & Accounts, 1976–1983* (1984), *From Okra to Greens: Poems* (1984), *Ridin' the Moon in Texas* (1987), *The Love Space Demands* (1992), *Betsey Brown* (1983), and *Liliane: Resurrection of the Daughter* (1994). The following poem is from *for colored girls;* it is spoken by the character "lady in blue." Shange is currently an associate professor of drama at the University of Houston.

one thing i dont need
is any more apologies
i got sorry greetin me at my front door
you can keep yrs
5 i dont know what to do wit em
they dont open doors
or bring the sun back
they dont make me happy
or get a mornin paper
10 didnt nobody stop usin my tears to wash cars
cuz a sorry

i am simply tired
of collectin
          i didnt know
15   i was so important toyou'
i'm gonna haveta throw some away
i cant get to the clothes in my closet
for alla the sorries
i'm gonna tack a sign to my door
20 leave a message by the phone
         'if you called
         to say yr sorry
         call somebody
         else
25   i dont use em anymore'
i let sorry/didnt meanta/& how cd i know abt that
take a walk down a dark & musty street in brooklyn
i'm gonna do exactly what i want to
& i wont be sorry for none of it
30 letta sorry soothe yr soul/i'm gonna soothe mine

you were always inconsistent
doin somethin & then bein sorry
beatin my heart to death
talkin bout you sorry
35 well
i will not call
i'm not goin to be nice
i will raise my voice
& scream & holler
40 & break things & race the engine
& tell all yr secrets bout yrself to yr face
& i will list in detail everyone of my wonderful lovers
& their ways

i will play oliver lake[1]
45 loud
& i wont be sorry for none of it

i loved you on purpose
i was open on purpose
i still crave vulnerability & close talk
50 & i'm not even sorry bout you bein sorry
you can carry all the guilt & grime ya wanna
just dont give it to me
i cant use another sorry
next time
55 you should admit
you're mean/low-down/triflin/& no count straight out
steda bein sorry alla the time
enjoy bein yrself

Discussion Questions

1. Using specific examples from the poem, show how "sorry" has filled the speaker's life.
2. Who is speaking in lines 14 and 15 and lines 21 through 25?
3. Reread the third stanza. How did the speaker in the poem modify her life to have a relationship with the other person? What impact did this modification have on her personality?
4. Compare the speaker's tone at the beginning of the poem and at the end of the poem. Are there similarities? Differences? What do these tones tell you about the speaker's attitude change?

Writing Topics

1. In the last line of the poem, the woman says "steda bein sorry alla the time / enjoy bein yrself." In your journal, explain what she means when she says "enjoy bein yrself."
2. Write an apology to a person you should have apologized to but never did. Do not use the word *sorry* in your apology. After you write, examine how you feel. How difficult was it to apologize without using the word *sorry?*
3. After analyzing Shange's lack of punctuation, line breaks, capitalization, and unique spelling in this poem, analyze Mari Evans's "Vive Noir," examining the same elements. In an essay, compare and contrast the two styles.

---

[1] *oliver lake:* a jazz saxophonist.

Magic

Rita Dove

Rita Dove was born in Akron, Ohio, in 1952, to Elvira and Ray Dove, a chemist. As one of the top high-school graduates in the country, Dove was invited to the White House as a Presidential Scholar in 1970. In 1973 she received her B.A., *summa cum laude,* from Miami University in Ohio. During 1974 and 1975 she won a Fulbright scholarship to attend the University of Tübingen in West Germany. She received her M.F.A. from University of Iowa in 1977. When her first poetry book, *Yellow House on the Corner*, was published in 1980, Dove had already received national attention for her work in anthologies and magazines. Dove received the Pulitzer Prize in 1987 for another book of poetry, *Thomas and Beulah* (1986), a collection of poetry based on stories she knew about her grandfather and grandmother. She has received many awards for her poetry and has served on numerous panels and committees. Dove taught at Arizona State University and is now a professor of English at the University of Virginia.

Dove's poetry and fiction are insightful and poignant. She has been heralded as one of the prominent poets of the late twentieth century. Her other books of poetry include *Museum* (1983), *Grace Notes* (1985), *Selected Poems* (1993), and *Mother Love: Poems* (1995). Though primarily known for her poetry, Dove has published fiction, including *Fifth Sunday* (1985), *Through the Ivory Gate* (1992), and a full-length verse drama, *The Darker Face of Earth* (1993). In 1993 President Clinton named Dove poet laureate of the United States, the first African American to hold that title. President Clinton renewed her position as poet laureate in 1995.

Practice makes perfect, the old folks said.
So she rehearsed deception
until ice cubes
dangled willingly
5   from a plain white string
and she could change
an egg into her last nickel.
Sent to the yard to sharpen,

she bent so long over
10 the wheel the knives
grew thin. When she stood up,
her brow shorn clean
as a wheatfield and
stippled with blood,
15 she felt nothing, even
when Mama screamed.

She fed sauerkraut to the apple tree;
the apples bloomed tarter
every year. Like all art
20 useless and beautiful,
like sailing in air,
things happened
to her. One night she awoke
and on the lawn blazed
25 a scaffolding strung in lights.
Next morning the Sunday paper
showed the Eiffel Tower
soaring through clouds.
It was a sign
30 she would make it to Paris one day.

DISCUSSION QUESTIONS

1. What is the emotional connection between the girl and the world in which she lives? How does the girl in the poem feel about her life? Support your description with words and phrases from the poem.
2. The poem states "So she rehearsed deception. . . ." Why is magic an important part of the girl's life?

3. Why is the picture of the Eiffel Tower in the Sunday paper a sign? Why is it important for her to "make it to Paris one day"?
4. Is the young girl's dream of going to Paris realistic? What might keep her from obtaining her dream?

WRITING TOPICS

1. In your writing journal, discuss a time you separated yourself from the world around you. How did you do it? How did you feel?
2. Are African-American women today able to achieve any dream that they have for themselves? Support your response with examples from texts you have read or from situations you have experienced in your life.

PLUMES

Georgia Douglas Johnson

Georgia Douglas Johnson was born in Atlanta, Georgia, in 1886 to George and Laura Jackson Camp. She attended public schools in Atlanta and briefly attended Atlanta University. She went on to Howard University in Washington, D. C., and Oberlin Conservatory of Music in Ohio. She married Henry Lincoln Johnson, a Washington lawyer and politician who died in 1925. Johnson's Washington, D.C., home was the meeting place of such Harlem Renaissance writers as Langston Hughes, Countee Cullen, Jessie Fauset, and Alain Locke. Throughout her career as a writer, Johnson was committed to the concerns of women and minorities.

Johnson was one of the first modern African-American female poets to gain recognition. More than two hundred of Johnson's poems were published in four volumes of poetry: *The Heart of a Woman and Other Poems* (1918), *Bronze: A Book of Verse* (1922), *An Autumn Love Cycle* (1928), and *Share My World* (1962). In the late 1920s, she began to write drama, including *Plumes: A Play in One Act* (1927). Two of her play productions appeared in New York, *Blue Blood* (1927) and *Plumes* (1928), and one appeared in Los Angeles, *Frederick Douglass Leaves for Freedom* (1940). Two plays Johnson wrote to protest lynchings, *Blue-Eyed Black Boy* (1935) and *Safe* (1936) were never performed during her lifetime because producers did not believe the stories she depicted would have actually led to white mobs lynching black people.

CHARACTERS

CHARITY BROWN,	the mother
EMMERLINE BROWN,	the daughter
TILDY,	the friend
DOCTOR SCOTT,	physician

Scene: A poor cottage in the South.
Time: Contemporary.

SCENE: *The kitchen of a two-room cottage. A window overlooking the street. A door leading to the street, one leading to the backyard and one to the inner room. A stove, a table with shelf over it, a washtub. A rocking-chair, a cane-bottom chair. Needle, thread, scissors, etc., on table.*

Scene opens with CHARITY BROWN *heating a poultice over the stove. A groaning is heard from the inner room.*

CHARITY.   Yes, honey, mamma is fixing somethin' to do you good. Yes, my baby, jus' you wait—I'm a-coming.
(*Knock is heard at door. It is gently pushed and* TILDY *comes in cautiously.*)

TILDY.   (*Whispering*) How is she?

CHARITY.   Poorly, poorly. Didn't rest last night none hardly. Move that dress and set in th' rocker. I been trying to snatch a minute to finish it but don't seem like I can. She won't have nothing to wear if she—she—

TILDY.   I understands. How near done is it?

CHARITY.   Ain't so much more to do.

TILDY.   (*Takes up dress from chair, looks at it*) I'll do some on it.

CHARITY.   Thank you, sister Tildy. Whip that torshon[1] on and turn down the hem in the skirt.

TILDY.   (*Measuring dress against herself*) How deep?

CHARITY.   Let me see, now (*Studies a minute with finger against lip*) I tell you—jus' baste it, 'cause you see—she wears 'em short, but—it might be—(*Stops.*)

TILDY.   (*Bowing her head comprehendingly*) Huh-uh, I see exzackly. (*Sighs*) You'd want it long—over her feet—then.

CHARITY.   That's it, sister Tildy. (*Listening*) She's some easy now! (*Stirring poultice*) Jest can't get this poltis' hot enough somehow this morning.

TILDY.   Put some red pepper in it. Got any?

CHARITY.   Yes. There ought to be some in one of them boxes on the shelf there. (*Points.*)

TILDY.   (*Goes to shelf, looks about and gets the pepper*) Here, put a-plenty of this in.

CHARITY.   (*Groans are heard from the next room*) Good Lord, them pains got her again. She suffers so, when she's 'wake.

TILDY.   Poor little thing. How old is she now, sister Charity?

CHARITY.   Turning fourteen this coming July.

TILDY.   (*Shaking her head dubiously*) I sho' hope she'll be mended by then.

CHARITY.   It don't look much like it, but I trusts so—(*Looking worried*) That doctor's mighty late this morning.

---

[1] *torshon:* decorative trim.

TILDY.
: I expects he'll be 'long in no time. Doctors is mighty oncon-cerned here lately.

CHARITY.
: (*Going toward inner room with poultice*) They surely is and I don't have too much confidence in none of 'em. (*You can hear her soothing the child.*)

TILDY.
: (*Listening*) Want me to help you put it on, sister Charity?

CHARITY.
: (*From inner room*) No, I can fix it. (*Coming back from sickroom shaking her head rather dejectedly.*)

TILDY.
: How is she, sister Charity?

CHARITY.
: Mighty feeble. Gone back to sleep now. My poor little baby. (*Bracing herself*) I'm going to put on some coffee now.

TILDY.
: I'm sho' glad. I feel kinder low-spirited.

CHARITY.
: It's me that low-sperited. The doctor said last time he was here he might have to oparate—said, she mought have a chance then. But I tell you the truth, I've got no faith a-tall in 'em. They takes all your money for nothing.

TILDY.
: They sho' do and don't leave a cent for putting you away decent.

CHARITY.
: That's jest it. They takes all you got and then you dies jest the same. It ain't like they was sure.

TILDY.
: No, they ain't sure. That's it exzackly. But they takes your money jest the same, and leaves you flat.

CHARITY.
: I been thinking 'bout Zeke these last few days—how he was put away—

TILDY.
: I wouldn't worry 'bout him now. He's out of his troubles.

CHARITY.
: I know. But it worries me when I think about how he was put away . . . that ugly pine coffin, jest one shabby old hack[2] and nothing else to show—to show—what we thought about him.

TILDY.
: Hush, sister! Don't you worry over him. He's happy now, anyhow.

CHARITY.
: I can't help it! Then little Bessie. We all jest scrooged in one hack and took her little coffin in our lap all the way out to the graveyard. (*Breaks out crying.*)

TILDY.
: Do hush, sister Charity. You done the best you could. Poor folks got to make the best of it. The Lord understands—

CHARITY.
: I know that—but I made up my mind the time Bessie went that the next one of us what died would have a shore nuff funeral, everything grand,—with plumes[3]!—I saved and saved and now—this yah doctor—

TILDY.
: All they think about is cuttin' and killing and taking your money. I got nothin' to put 'em doing.

CHARITY.
: (*Goes over to washtub and rubs on clothes*) Me neither. These clothes got to get out somehow, I needs every cent.

---

[2] *hack:* horse carriage for hire.
[3] *plumes:* ornate, fluffy feathers that decorate horses pulling a funeral hearse.

TILDY.   How much that washing bring you?

CHARITY.   Dollar and a half. It's worth a whole lot more. But what can you do?

TILDY.   You can't do nothing—Look there, sister Charity, ain't that coffee boiling?

CHARITY.   (*Wipes hands on apron and goes to stove*) Yes it's boiling good fashioned. Come on, drink some.

TILDY.   There ain't nothing I'd rather have than a good strong cup of coffee. (*Charity pours Tildy's cup.*) (*Sweetening and stirring hers*) Pour you some. (*Charity pours her own cup*) I'd been dead, too, long ago if it hadn't a been for my coffee.

CHARITY.   I love it, but it don't love me—gives me the shortness of breath.

TILDY.   (*Finishing her cup, taking up sugar with spoon*) Don't hurt me. I could drink a barrel.

CHARITY.   (*Drinking more slowly—reaching for coffeepot*) Here, drink another cup.

TILDY.   I shore will, that cup done me a lot of good.

CHARITY.   (*Looking into her empty cup thoughtfully*) I wish Dinah Morris would drop in now. I'd ask her what these grounds mean.

TILDY.   I can read em a little myself.

CHARITY.   You can? Well, for the Lord's sake, look here and tell me what this cup says! (*Offers cup to Tildy. Tildy wards it off.*)

TILDY.   You got to turn it 'round in your saucer three times first.

CHARITY.   Yes, that's right, I forgot. (*Turns cup 'round, counting*) One, two, three. (*Starts to pick it up.*)

TILDY.   Huhudh. (*Meaning no*) Let it set a minute. It might be watery. (*After a minute, while she finishes her own cup*) Now let me see. (*Takes cup and examines it very scrutinizingly.*)

CHARITY.   What you see?

TILDY.   (*Hesitatingly*) I ain't seen a cup like this one for many a year. Not since—not since—

CHARITY.   When?

TILDY.   Not since jest before ma died. I looked in the cup then and saw things and—I stopped looking . . .

CHARITY.   Tell me what you see, I want to know.

TILDY.   I don't like to tell no bad news—

CHARITY.   Go on. I can stan' anything after all I been thru'.

TILDY.   Since you're bound to know I'll tell you. (*Charity draws nearer*) I sees a big gethering!

CHARITY.   Gethering, you say?

TILDY.   Yes, a big gethering. People all crowded together. Then I see 'em going one by one and two by two. Long line stretching out and out and out!

CHARITY.   (*In a whisper*) What you think it is?

TILDY.   (*Awed like*) Looks like (*Hesitates*) a possession!

CHARITY.   (*Shouting*) You sure!

TILDY.   I know it is. (*Just then the toll of a church bell is heard and then the steady and slow tramp, tramp of horses' hoofs. Both women look at each other.*)

TILDY.   (*In a hushed voice.*) That must be Bell Gibson's funeral coming 'way from Mt. Zion. (*Gets up and goes to window*) Yes, it sho' is.

CHARITY.   (*Looking out of the window also*) Poor Bell suffered many a year; she's out of her pain now.

TILDY.   Look, here comes the hearse now!

CHARITY.   My Lord! ain't it grand! Look at them horses—look at their heads—plumes—how they shake 'em! Land o'mighty! It's a fine sight, sister Tildy.

TILDY.   That must be Jer'miah in that first carriage, bending over like; he shorely is putting her away grand.

CHARITY.   No mistake about it. That's Pickett's best funeral turnout he's got.

TILDY.   I'll bet it cost a lot.

CHARITY.   Fifty dollars, so Matilda Jenkins told me. She had it for Bud. The plumes is what cost.

TILDY.   Look at the hacks—(*Counts*) I believe to my soul there's eight.

CHARITY.   Got somebody in all of 'em too—and flowers—She shore got a lot of 'em. (*Both women's eyes follow the tail end of the procession, horses' hoofs die away as they turn away from window. The two women look at each other significantly.*)

TILDY.   (*Significantly*) Well!—(*They look at each other without speaking for a minute. Charity goes to the washtub*) Want these cups washed up?

CHARITY.   No don't mind 'em. I'd rather you get that dress done. I got to get these clothes out.

TILDY.   (*Picking up dress*) Shore, there ain't so much more to do on it now. (*Knock is heard on the door. Charity answers knock and admits* DR. SCOTT.)

DR. SCOTT.   Good morning. How's the patient today?

CHARITY.   Not so good, doctor. When she ain't 'sleep she suffers so; but she sleeps mostly.

DR. SCOTT.   Well, let's see, let's see. Just hand me a pan of warm water and I'll soon find out just what's what.

CHARITY.   All right, doctor. I'll bring it to you right away. (*Bustles about fixing water—looking toward dress Tildy is working on*) Poor little Emmerline's been wanting a white dress trimmed with torshon a long time—now she's got it and it looks like—well—(*Hesitates*) t'warn't made to wear.

TILDY.   Don't take on so, sister Charity—The Lord giveth and the Lord taketh.

CHARITY.   I know—but it's hard—hard—(*Goes into inner room with water.*

You can hear her talking with the doctor after a minute and the doctor expostulating with her—in a minute she appears at the door, being led from the room by the doctor.)

DR. SCOTT. No, my dear Mrs. Brown. It will be much better for you to remain outside.

CHARITY. But, doctor—

DR. SCOTT. NO. You stay outside and get your mind on something else. You can't possibly be of any service. Now be calm, will you?

CHARITY. I'll try, doctor.

TILDY. The doctor's right. You can't do no good in there.

CHARITY. I knows, but I thought I could hold the pan or somethin'. (*Lowering her voice*) Says he got to see if her heart is all right or somethin'. I tell you—nowadays—

TILDY. I know.

CHARITY. (*Softly to Tildy*) Hope he won't come out here saying he got to operate. (*Goes to washtub.*)

TILDY. I hope so, too. Won't it cost a lot?

CHARITY. That's jest it. It would take all I got saved up.

TILDY. Of course, if he's goin' to get her up—but I don't believe in 'em. I don't believe in 'em.

CHARITY. He didn't promise tho'—even if he did, he said maybe it wouldn't do no good.

TILDY. I'd think a long time before I'd let him operate on my chile. Taking all yuh money, promising nothing and ten to one killing her to boot.

CHARITY. This is a hard world.

TILDY. Don't you trus' him. Coffee grounds don't lie!

CHARITY. I don't trust him. I jest want to do what's right by her. I ought to put these clothes on the line while you're settlin' in here, but I jes hate to go outdoors while he's in there.

TILDY. (*Getting up*) I'll hang 'em out. You stay here. Where your clothespins at?

CHARITY. Hanging right there by the back door in the bag. They ought to dry before dark and then I can iron tonight.

TILDY. (*Picking up tub*) They ought to blow dry in no time. (*Goes toward back door.*)

CHARITY. Then I can shore rub 'em over tonight. Say, sister Tildy, hist 'em up with that long saplin' prop leaning in the fence corner.

TILDY. (*Going out*) All right.

CHARITY. (*Standing by the table beating nervously on it with her fingers — listens—and then starts to bustling about the kitchen*) (*Enter Doctor from inner room.*)

DR. SCOTT. Well, Mrs. Brown, I've decided I'll have to operate.

CHARITY. MY Lord! Doctor—don't say that!

DR. SCOTT. It's the only chance.

CHARITY.   You mean she'll get well if you do?

DR. SCOTT. No, I can't say that—It's just a chance—a last chance. And I'll do just what I said, cut the price of the operation down to fifty dollars. I'm willing to do that for you. (*Charity throws up her hands in dismay.*)

CHARITY.   Doctor, I was so in hopes you wouldn't operate—I—I—And yo' say you ain't a bit sure she'll get well—even then?

DR. SCOTT. No. I can't be sure. We'll just have to take the chance. But I'm sure you want to do everything—

CHARITY.   Sure, doctor, I do want to—do—everything I can do to—to— Doctor, look at this cup. (*Picks up fortune cup and shows the doctor*) My fortune's jes' been told this morning—look at these grounds—they says—(*Softly*) it ain't no use, no use a-tall.

DR. SCOTT. Why, my good woman, don't you believe in such senseless things! That cup of grounds can't show you anything. Wash them out and forget it.

CHARITY.   I can't forget it. I feel like it ain't no use; I'd just be spendin' the money that I needs—for nothing—nothing.

DR. SCOTT. But you won't though—You'll have a clear conscience. You'd know that you did everything you could.

CHARITY.   I know that, doctor. But there's things you don't know 'bout— there's other things I got to think about. If she goes—if she must go . . . I had plans—I been getting ready—now—Oh, doctor, I jest can't see how I can have this operation—you say you can't promise—nothing?

DR. SCOTT. I didn't think you'd hesitate about it—I imagined your love for your child—

CHARITY.   (*Breaking in*) I do love my child. My God, I do love my child. You don't understand . . . but . . . but—can't I have a little time to think about it, doctor? It means so much—to her—and—me!

DR. SCOTT. I tell you. I'll go on over to the office. I'd have to get my (*Hesitates*) my things, anyhow. And as soon as you make up your mind, get one of the neighbors to run over and tell me. I'll come right back. But don't waste any time now, Mrs. Brown, every minute counts.

CHARITY.   Thank you, doctor, thank you. I'll shore send you word as soon as I can. I'm so upset and worried I'm half crazy.

DR. SCOTT. I know you are . . . but don't take too long to make up your mind. . . . It ought to be done today. Remember—it may save her. (*Exits.*)

CHARITY.   (*Goes to door of sickroom—looks inside for a few minutes, then starts walking up and down the little kitchen, first holding a hand up to her head and then wringing them. Enter Tildy from yard with tub under her arm.*)

TILDY. Well, they're all out, sister Charity—(*Stops*) Why, what's the matter?

CHARITY. The doctor wants to operate.

TILDY. (*Softly*) Where he—gone?

CHARITY. Yes—he's gone, but he's coming back—if I send for him.

TILDY. You going to? (*Puts down tub and picks up white dress and begins sewing.*)

CHARITY. I dunno—I got to think.

TILDY. I can't see what's the use myself. He can't save her with no operation—Coffee grounds don't lie.

CHARITY. It would take all the money I got for the operation and then what about puttin' her away? He can't save her—don't even promise ter. I know he can't—I feel it . . . I feel it. . . .

TILDY. It's in the air. . . . (*Both women sit tense in the silence. Tildy has commenced sewing again. Just then a strange, strangling noise comes from the inner room.*)

TILDY. What's that?

CHARITY. (*Running toward and into inner room*) Oh, my God! (*From inside*) Sister Tildy—Come here—No,—Some water, quick. (*Tildy with dress in hand starts towards inner room. Stops at door, sighs and then goes hurriedly back for the water pitcher. Charity is heard moaning softly in the next room, then she appears at doorway and leans against jamb of door*) Rip the hem out, sister Tildy.

CURTAIN

DISCUSSION QUESTIONS

1. The play *Plumes* occurs in "a poor cottage in the South" in the 1920s. Explain how the setting of the play influences the action in the play. Use specific examples from the play to support your response.

2. In a play the character's name and the actor's facial expressions and body language convey as much information to the audience as the lines the actor speaks. Look up the definition of "charity" in a dictionary. Examine the stage directions for Charity. Describe Charity's characteristics using the definition of her name and specific examples from the stage directions to support your response.

3. Why is it so important to Charity that her daughter, Emmerline, have a nice "putting away"? What do the plumes represent to Charity?

4. Charity states that she loves Emmerline, but when the doctor offers to operate on Emmerline for fifty dollars, Charity hesitates because of what Tildy read in the coffee grounds. Why do you think Charity, as an African-American woman living in the South, would place more trust in the coffee grounds than in the white doctor saving her daughter's life?
5. Emmerline dies before her mother makes a decision about the operation. Is Charity responsible for her daughter's death? Why or why not?

WRITING TOPICS

1. In your journal discuss your opinion on the decision Charity has to make between believing the coffee grounds and medical science. Support your response with evidence from the play, and/or evidence from other readings.
2. In many rural communities, people cannot afford routine health care costs. Write an essay in which you argue for the establishment of community health care centers in rural communities.

CHAPTER NINE

MEN

Martin Luther King Jr. said, "A man who won't die for something is not fit to live." African-American men have struggled to demonstrate both their manhood and their identity ever since they arrived as slaves on the American shores. It has never been easy for an African-American male to be considered a man in the country of his birth—he must continually strive to be recognized and respected as a man. Nevertheless, African-American men have never given up on the ideal that, if given the opportunity, they can make a valuable contribution to the social and economic well-being of America.

In their writing, African-American male writers express their joy, sorrow, pain, love, and hate. The writers of the selections in this chapter are as varied in their renderings as any other set of writers, yet they sense the need to focus on those attributes that are inherent in being both a human being and a man.

STRONG MEN

Sterling Brown

Sterling Brown was born in Washington, D.C., in 1901. Educated in the public schools there, he graduated Phi Beta Kappa from Williams College and earned an M.A. at Harvard. He taught at Howard University, Lincoln University–Missouri, and New York University, among others. Brown was awarded a Guggenheim Fellowship in 1937, and he was a member of the American Folklore Society. His publications include a book of poetry, *Southern Road* (1932), and his two groundbreaking studies: *The Negro in American Fiction* (1937) and *Negro Poetry and Drama* (1937). Brown retired from Howard University in 1969 and died in 1989.

> The strong men keep coming on.
> —Sandburg

They dragged you from homeland,
They chained you in coffles,
They huddled you spoon-fashion in filthy hatches,
They sold you to give a few gentlemen ease.

5 They broke you in like oxen,
They scourged you,
They branded you,
They made your women breeders,
They swelled your numbers with bastards. . . .
10 They taught you the religion they disgraced.

You sang:
> Keep a-inchin' along
> Lak a po' inch worm. . . .

You sang:
15   Bye and bye
> I'm gonna lay dis heaby load. . . .

You sang:
> Walk togedder, chillen,
> Dontcha git weary. . . .
20   *The strong men keep a-comin' on*
> *The strong men git stronger.*

They point with pride to the roads you built
> for them,
They ride in comfort over the rails you laid
25   for them.
They put hammers in your hands
And said—Drive so much before sundown.

You sang:
> Ain't no hammah
30   In dis lan',
> Strikes lak mine, bebby,
> Strikes lak mine,

They cooped you in their kitchens,
They penned you in their factories,
35 They gave you the jobs that they were too good
> for,
They tried to guarantee happiness to themselves
By shunting dirt and misery to you.

You sang:
40   Me an' muh baby gonna shine, shine
> Me an' muh baby gonna shine.
>> *The strong men keep a-comin' on*
>> *The strong men git stronger. . . .*

They bought off some of your leaders
45 You stumbled, as blind men will. . .
They coaxed you, unwontedly soft-voiced. . . .
You followed a way.
Then laughed as usual.
They heard the laugh and wondered;
50 Uncomfortable;
Unadmitting a deeper terror. . . .
    The strong men keep a-comin' on
    Gittin' stronger. . . .

What, from the slums
55 Where they have hemmed you,
What, from the tiny huts
They could not keep from you—
What reaches them
Making them ill at ease, fearful?
60 Today they shout prohibition at you
"Thou shalt not this"
"Thou shalt not that"
"Reserved for whites only"
You laugh.

65 One thing they cannot prohibit —
    The strong men . . . coming on
    The strong men gittin' stronger.
    Strong men. . . .
    Stronger. . . .

DISCUSSION QUESTIONS

1. What does the poet mean when he says: "They taught you the religion they disgraced"?
2. Who are the "they" in the poem? Why do you think the poet used this pronoun rather a noun that is more specific?
3. Discuss the effect of dialect interspersed with standard English. What was the poet trying to convey? Do you think it was successful?

WRITING TOPICS

1. Note the last four lines of the poem:

   The strong men . . . coming on
   The strong men gittin' stronger.
   Strong men. . . .
   Stronger. . .

   In your writing journal, explain what these lines mean. How do they make you feel?
2. Try writing a poem, using the Brown poem as a model. Try to imply a buildup of tension.
3. Write a letter to a friend telling her or him about this poem. Be sure to include the title of the poem and its author's name. Tell your friend how you feel about the poem, including what you think the underlying meaning is.

MY SEARCH FOR ROOTS

Alex Haley

Alex Haley was born in Henning, Tennessee, in 1921. As he was growing up, his grandmother would tell him stories about their family. She frequently referred to a man whom she called "the African" who had lived across the ocean near a river he called the "Kamby Bolongo."

These stories led Haley to spend twelve years researching and writing his most famous novel, *Roots* (1974). Haley taught himself to write during a twenty-year stint with the U.S. Coast Guard. He eventually became a Chief Journalist and, after leaving the Coast Guard, a magazine writer and interviewer. Haley interviewed Malcolm X and published *The Autobiography of Malcolm X* in 1964. Haley died in 1992.

1   My earliest memory is of Grandma, Cousin Georgia, Aunt Plus, Aunt Liz, and Aunt Till talking on our front porch in Henning, Tennessee. At dusk, these wrinkled, graying old ladies would sit in rocking chairs and talk, about slaves and massas and plantations—pieces and patches of family history, passed down across the generations by word of mouth. "Old-timey stuff," Mama would exclaim. She wanted no part of it.

2   The furthest-back person Grandma and the others ever mentioned was "the African." They would tell how he was brought here on a ship to a place called "Naplis" and sold as a slave in Virginia. There he mated with another slave and had a little girl named Kizzy.

3   When Kizzy became four or five, the old ladies said, her father would point out to her various objects and name them in his native tongue. For example, he would point to a guitar and make a single-syllable sound, *ko*. Pointing to a river that ran near the plantation, he'd say "Kamby Bolongo." And when other slaves addressed him as Toby—the name given him by his massa—the African would strenuously reject it, insisting that his name was "Kin-tay."

4   Kin-tay often told Kizzy stories about himself. He said that he had been near his village in Africa, chopping wood to make a drum, when he had been set upon by four men, overwhelmed, and kidnapped into slavery. When Kizzy grew up and became a mother, she told her son these stories, and he in turn would tell *his* children. His granddaughter became my grandmother, and she pumped that saga into me as if it were plasma, until I knew by rote the story of the African, and the subsequent generational wending of our family through cotton and tobacco plantations into the Civil War and then freedom.

5   At 17, during World War II, I enlisted in the Coast Guard, and found myself a messboy on a ship in the Southwest Pacific. To fight boredom, I began to teach myself to become a writer. I stayed on in the service after the war, writing every single night, seven nights a week, for eight years before I sold a story to a magazine. My first story in the *Digest* was published in June 1954: "The Harlem Nobody Knows." At age 37, I retired from military service, determined to be a full-time writer. Working with the famous Black Muslim spokesman, I did the actual writing for the book *The Autobiography of Malcolm X*.

6   I remembered still the vivid highlights of my family's story. Could this account possibly be documented for a book? During 1962, between other assignments, I began following the story's trail. In plantation records, wills, census records, I documented bits here, shreds there. By now, Grandma was dead; repeatedly I visited other close sources, most notably our encyclopedic matriarch, "Cousin Georgia" Anderson in Kansas City, Kansas. I went as often as I could to the National Archives in Washington, and the Library of Congress, and the Daughters of the American Revolution Library.

7   By 1967, I felt I had the seven generations of the U.S. side documented. But the unknown quotient in the riddle of the past continued to be those strange, sharp, angular sounds spoken by the African himself. Since I lived in New York City, I began going to the United Nations lobby, stopping Africans and asking if they recognized the sounds. Every one of them listened to me, then quickly took off. I can well understand: me with a Tennessee accent, trying to imitate African sounds!

8   Finally, I sought out a linguistics expert who specialized in African languages. To him I repeated the phrases. The sound "Kintay," he said, was a Mandinka tribe surname. And "Kamby Bolongo" was probably the Gambia River in Mandinka dialect. Three days later, I was in Africa.

9   In Banjul, the capital of Gambia, I met with a group of Gambians. They told me how for centuries the history of Africa has been preserved. In the other villages of the back country there are old men, called *griots*, who are in effect living archives. Such men know, and, on special occasions, tell the cumulative histories of clans, or families, or villages, as those histories have long been told. Since my forefather had said his name was Kin-tay (properly spelled *Kinte*), and since the Kinte clan was known in Gambia, they would see what they could do to help me.

10   I was back in New York when a registered letter came from Gambia. Word had been passed in the back country, and a *griot* of the Kinte clan had,

indeed, been found. His name, the letter said, was Kebba Kanga Fofana. I returned to Gambia and organized a safari to locate him.

11   There is an expression called "the peak experience," a moment which, emotionally, can never again be equaled in your life. I had mine, that first day in the village of Juffure, in the back country in black West Africa.

12   When our 14-man safari arrived within sight of the village, the people came flocking out of their circular mud huts. From a distance I could see a small, old man with a pillbox hat, an off-white robe and an aura of "somebodiness" about him. The people quickly gathered around me in a kind of horseshoe pattern. The old man looked piercingly into my eyes, and he spoke in Mandinka. Translation came from the interpreters I had brought with me.

13   "Yes, we have been told by the forefathers that there are many of us from this place who are in exile in that place called America."

14   Then the old man, who was 73 rains of age—the Gambian way of saying 73 years old, based upon the one rainy season per year—began to tell me the lengthy ancestral history of the Kinte clan. It was clearly a formal occasion for the villagers. They had grown mouse-quiet, and stood rigidly.

15   Out of the *griot*'s head came spilling lineage details incredible to hear. He recited who married whom, two or even three centuries back. I was struck not only by the profusion of details, but also by the Biblical pattern of the way he was speaking. It was something like, "—and so-and-so took as a wife so-and-so, and begat so-and-so. . . ."

16   The *griot* had talked for some hours and had got to about 1750 in our calendar. Now he said, through an interpreter, "About the time the king's soldiers came, the eldest of Omoro's four sons, Kunta, went away from this village to chop wood—and he was never seen again. . . ."

17   Goose pimples came out on me the size of marbles. He just had no way in the world of knowing that what he told me meshed with what I'd heard from the old ladies on the front porch in Henning, Tennessee. I got out my notebook, which had in it what Grandma had said about the African. One of the interpreters showed it to the others, and they went to the *griot*, and they all got agitated. Then the *griot* went to the people, and *they* all got agitated.

18   I don't remember anyone giving an order, but those 70-odd people formed a ring around me, moving counterclockwise, chanting, their bodies close together. I can't begin to describe how I felt. A woman broke from the circle, a scowl on her jet-black face, and came charging toward me. She took her baby and almost roughly thrust it out at me. The gesture meant "Take it!" and I did, clasping the baby to me. Whereupon the woman all but snatched the baby away. Another woman did the same with her baby, then another, and another.

19   A year later, a famous professor at Harvard would tell me: "You were participating in one of the oldest ceremonies of humankind, called 'the laying on of hands.' In their way these tribespeople were saying to you, 'Through this flesh, which is us, we are you and you are us.'"

20   Later, as we drove out over the back-country road, I heard the staccato sound of drums. When we approached the next village, people were packed alongside the dusty road, waving, and the din from them welled louder as we came closer. As I stood up in the Land Rover, I finally realized what it was they were all shouting: "Meester Kinte! Meester Kinte!" In their eyes I was the symbol of all black people in the United States whose forefathers had been torn out of Africa while theirs remained.

21   Hands before my face, I began crying—crying as I have never cried in my life. Right at that time, crying was all I could do.

22   I went then to London. I searched and searched, and finally in the British Parliamentary records I found that the "king's soldiers" mentioned by the *griot* referred to a group called "Colonel O'Hare's forces," which had been sent up the Gambia River in 1767 to guard the then British-operated James Fort, a slave fort.

23   I next went to Lloyds of London, where doors were opened for me to research among all kinds of old maritime records. I pored through the records of slave ships that had sailed from Africa. Volumes upon volumes of these records exist. One afternoon about 2:30, during the seventh week of searching, I was going through my 1,023rd set of ship records. I picked up a sheet that had on it the reported movements of 30 slave ships, my eyes stopped at No. 18, and my glance swept across the column entries. This vessel had sailed directly from the Gambia River to America in 1767; her name was the *Lord Ligonier*, and she had arrived at Annapolis (Naplis) the morning of September 29, 1767.

24   Exactly 200 years later, on September 29, 1967, there was nowhere in the world for me to be except standing on a pier at Annapolis, staring seaward across those waters over which my great-great-great-great-grandfather had been brought. And there in Annapolis I inspected the microfilmed records of the *Maryland Gazette*. In the issue of October 1, 1767, on page 3, I found an advertisement informing readers that the *Lord Ligonier* had just arrived from the River Gambia, with "a cargo of choice, healthy SLAVES" to be sold at auction the following Wednesday.

25   In the years since, I have done extensive research in 50 or so libraries, archives, and repositories on three continents. I spent a year combing through countless documents to learn about the culture of Gambia's villages in the eighteenth and nineteenth centuries. Desiring to sail over the same waters navigated by the *Lord Ligonier*, I flew to Africa and boarded the freighter *African Star*. I forced myself to spend the ten nights of the crossing in the cold, dark cargo hold, stripped to my underwear, lying on my back on a rough, bare plank. But this was sheer luxury compared to the inhuman ordeal suffered by those millions who, chained and shackled, lay in terror and in their own filth in the stinking darkness through voyages averaging sixty to seventy days.

DISCUSSION QUESTIONS

1. Who told the writer about his ancestor?
2. How does the *Lord Ligonier* figure in Haley's story?
3. Who is Kinte and how was he captured?
4. Would Alex Haley have been able to research his family tree without being told the story by his grandmother? Why or why not?

WRITING TOPICS

1. Conduct interviews with some of your family members to gain information on as many generations as you can. Use your writing journal to record your questions and answers.
2. Like Kinte, pretend you have been stolen from your home and community. Write an essay in which you describe how you will let your descendants know where you came from and what your family traditions were. Give specific details to support your position.
3. Haley talks about having a "peak experience": that is, a moment in time that emotionally can never again be equaled. Some might call this an *epiphany,* a sudden realization of the meaning of something. Write an essay describing a peak experience in your life.

Speech Delivered at Madison Square Garden, March 1924

Marcus Garvey

Marcus Garvey was born in 1887 in Jamaica and was educated as a printer. He lived for a time in England, where he attended the University of London at night. He returned to Jamaica in 1914, where he founded the Universal Negro Improvement Association (UNIA). Garvey visited the United States in 1916 and toured thirty-eight states to learn about the plight of black Americans. He soon opened a branch of his organization in Harlem, where he founded his weekly newspaper, *Negro World.* Garvey eventually became Provisional President of the newly formed African Republic. He urged blacks to be proud of their race and started a movement to take blacks to Africa. This latter effort failed due to problems with the stock for the Black Star Line, a ship he planned to use in transporting blacks back to their forefathers' native land. He was deported in 1927 and lived for five years in London where he continued to conduct the business of his organization, UNIA. Garvey died in Jamaica in 1940.

In Honor of the Return to America of the
Delegation Sent to Europe and Africa by
the Universal Negro Improvement
Association to Negotiate for the
Repatriation of Negroes to a Homeland
of Their Own in Africa

Fellow Citizens:

1   The coming together, all over this country, of fully six million people of Negro blood, to work for the creation of a nation of their own in their motherland, Africa, is no joke.

2   There is now a world revival of thought and action, which is causing peoples everywhere to bestir themselves towards their own security, through

which we hear the cry of Ireland for the Irish, Palestine for the Jew, Egypt for the Egyptian, Asia for the Asiatic, and thus we Negroes raise the cry of Africa for the Africans, those at home and those abroad.

3   Some people are not disposed to give us credit for having feelings, passions, ambitions and desires like other races; they are satisfied to relegate us to the back-heap of human aspirations; but this is a mistake. The Almighty Creator made us men, not unlike others, but in his own image; hence, as a race, we feel that we, too, are entitled to the rights that are common to humanity.

4   The cry and desire for liberty is justifiable, and is made holy everywhere. It is sacred and holy to the Anglo-Saxon, Teuton and Latin; to the Anglo-American it precedes that of all religions, and now come the Irish, the Jew, the Egyptian, the Hindoo, and, last but not least, the Negro, clamoring for their share as well as their right to be free.

5   All men should be free—free to work out their own salvation. Free to create their own destinies. Free to nationally build up themsleves for the upbringing and rearing of a culture and civilization of their own. Jewish culture is different from Irish culture. Anglo-Saxon culture is unlike Teutonic culture. Asiatic culture differs greatly from European culture; and, in the same way, the world should be liberal enough to allow the Negro latitude to develop a culture of his own. Why should the Negro be lost among the other races and nations of the world and to himself? Did nature not make of him a son of the soil? Did the Creator not fashion him out of the dust of the earth?—out of that rich soil to which he bears such a wonderful resemblance?—a resemblance that changes not, even though the ages have flown? No, the Ethiopian cannot change his skin; and so we appeal to the conscience of the white world to yield us a place of national freedom among the creatures of present-day temporal materialism.

6   We Negroes are not asking the white man to turn Europe and America over to us. We are not asking the Asiatic to turn Asia over for the accommodation of the blacks. But we are asking a just and righteous world to restore Africa to her scattered and abused children.

7   We believe in justice and human love. If our rights are to be respected, then, we, too, must respect the rights of all mankind; hence, we are ever ready and willing to yield to the white man the things that are his, and we feel that he, too, when his conscience is touched, will yield to us the things that are ours.

8   We should like to see a peaceful, prosperous and progressive white race in America and Europe; a peaceful, prosperous and progressive yellow race in Asia, and, in like manner, we want, and we demand, a peaceful, prosperous and progressive black race in Africa. Is that asking too much? Surely not. Humanity, without any immediate human hope of racial oneness, has drifted apart, and is now divided into separate and distinct groups, each with its own ideals and aspirations. Thus, we cannot expect any one race to hold a monopoly of creation and be able to keep the rest satisfied.

DISTINCT RACIAL GROUP IDEALISM

9   From our distinct racial group idealism we feel that no black man is good enough to govern the white man, and no white man good enough to rule the black man; and so of all races and peoples. No one feels that the other, alien in race, is good enough to govern or rule to the exclusion of native racial rights. We may as well, therefore, face the question of superior and inferior races. In twentieth century civilization there are no inferior and superior races. There are backward peoples, but that does not make them inferior. As far as humanity goes, all men are equal, and especially where peoples are intelligent enough to know what they want. At this time all peoples know what they want—it is liberty. When a people have sense enough to know that they ought to be free, then they naturally become the equal of all, in the higher calling of man to know and direct himself. It is true that economically and scientifically certain races are more progressive than others; but that does not imply superiority. For the Anglo-Saxon to say that he is superior because he introduced submarines to destroy life, or the Teuton because he compounded liquid gas to outdo in the art of killing, and that the Negro is inferior because he is backward in that direction is to leave one's self open to the retort "Thou shalt not kill," as being the divine law that sets the moral standard of the real man. There is no superiority in the one race economically monopolizing and holding all that would tend to the sustenance of life, and thus cause unhappiness and distress to others; for our highest purpose should be to love and care for each other, and share with each other the things that our Heavenly Father has placed at our common disposal; and even in this, the African is unsurpassed, in that he feeds his brother and shares with him the product of the land. The idea of race superiority is questionable; nevertheless, we must admit that, from the white man's standard, he is far superior to the rest of us, but that kind of superiority is too inhuman and dangerous to be permanently helpful. Such a superiority was shared and indulged in by other races before, and even by our own, when we boasted of a wonderful civilization on the banks of the Nile, when others were still groping in darkness; but because of our unrighteousness it failed, as all such will. Civilization can only last when we have reached the point where we will be our brother's keeper. That is to say, when we feel it righteous to live and let live.

NO EXCLUSIVE RIGHT TO THE WORLD

10   Let no black man feel that he has the exclusive right to the world, and other men none, and let no white man feel that way, either. The world is the property of all mankind, and each and every group is entitled to a portion. The black man now wants his, and in terms uncompromising he is asking for it.

11   The Universal Negro Improvement Association represents the hopes and aspirations of the awakened Negro. Our desire is for a place in the world;

not to disturb the tranquility of other men, but to lay down our burden and rest our weary backs and feet by the banks of the Niger, and sing our songs and chant our hymns to the God of Ethiopia. Yes, we want rest from the toil of centuries, rest of political freedom, rest of economic and industrial liberty, rest to be socially free and unmolested, rest from lynching and burning, rest from discrimination of all kinds.

12   Out of slavery we have come with our tears and sorrows, and we now lay them at the feet of American white civilization. We cry to the considerate white people for help, because in their midst we can scarce help ourselves. We are strangers in a strange land. We cannot sing, we cannot play on our harps, for our hearts are sad. We are sad because of the tears of our mothers and the cry of our fathers. Have you not heard the plaintive wail? It is your father and my father burning at stake; but, thank God there is a larger humanity growing among the good and considerate white people of this country, and they are going to help. They will help us to recover our souls.

13   As children of captivity we look forward to a new day and a new, yet ever old, land of our fathers, the land of refuge, the land of the Prophets, the land of the Saints, and the land of God's crowning glory. We shall gather together our children, our treasures and our loved ones, and, as the children of Israel, by the command of God, faced the promised land, so in time we shall also stretch forth our hands and bless our country.

14   Good and dear America that has succored us for three hundred years knows our story. We have watered her vegetation with our tears for two hundred and fifty years. We have built her cities and laid the foundations of her imperialism with the mortar of our blood and bones for three centuries, and now we cry to her for help. Help us, America, as we helped you. We helped you in the Revolutionary War. We helped you in the Civil War, and, although Lincoln helped us, the price is not half paid. We helped you in the Spanish-American War. We died nobly and courageously in Mexico, and did we not leave behind us on the stained battlefields of France and Flanders our rich blood to make the poppies' bloom, and to bring back to you the glory of the flag that never touched the dust? We have no regrets in service to America for three hundred years, but we pray that America will help us for another fifty years until we have solved the troublesome problem that now confronts us. We know and realize that two ambitious and competitive races cannot live permanently side by side, without friction and trouble, and that is why the white race wants a white America and the black race wants and demands a black Africa.

15   Let white America help us for fifty years honestly, as we have helped her for three hundred years, and before the expiration of many decades there shall be no more race problem. Help us to gradually go home, America. Help us as you have helped the Jews. Help us as you have helped the Irish. Help us as you have helped the Poles, Russians, Germans and Armenians.

16   The Universal Negro Improvement Association proposes a friendly co-operation with all honest movements seeking intelligently to solve the race

problem. We are not seeking social equality; we do not seek intermarriage, nor do we hanker after the impossible. We want the right to have a country of our own, and there foster and reestablish a culture and civilization exclusively ours. Don't say it can't be done. The Pilgrims and colonists did it for America, and the new Negro, with sympathetic help, can do it for Africa.

BACK TO AFRICA

17   The thoughtful and industrious of our race want to go back to Africa, because we realize it will be our only hope of permanent existence. We cannot all go in a day or year, ten or twenty years. It will take time under the rule of modern economics, to entirely or largely depopulate a country of a people, who have been its residents for centuries, but we feel that, with proper help for fifty years, the problem can be solved. We do not want all the Negroes in Africa. Some are no good here, and naturally will be no good there. The no-good Negro will naturally die in fifty years. The Negro who is wrangling about and fighting for social equality will naturally pass away in fifty years, and yield his place to the progressive Negro who wants a society and country of his own.

18   Negroes are divided into two groups, the industrious and adventurous, and the lazy and dependent. The industrious and adventurous believe that whatsoever others have done it can do. The Universal Negro Improvement Association belongs to this group, and so you find us working, six million strong, to the goal of an independent nationality. Who will not help? Only the mean and despicable "who never to himself hath said, this is my own, my native land." Africa is the legitimate, moral and righteous home of all Negroes, and now, that the time is coming for all to assemble under their own vine and fig tree, we feel it our duty to arouse every Negro to a consciousness of himself.

19   White and black will learn to respect each other when they cease to be active competitors in the same countries for the same things in politics and society. Let them have countries of their own, wherein to aspire and climb without rancor. The races can be friendly and helpful to each other, but the laws of nature separate us to the extent of each and every one developing by itself.

20   We want an atmosphere all our own. We would like to govern and rule ourselves and not be encumbered and restrained. We feel now just as the white race would feel if they were governed and ruled by the Chinese. If we live in our own districts, let us rule and govern those districts. If we have a majority in our communities, let us run those communities. We form a majority in Africa and we should naturally govern ourselves there. No man can govern another's house as well as himself. Let us have fair play. Let us have justice. This is the appeal we make to white America.

DISCUSSION QUESTIONS

1. Garvey suggested that Africa should be the homeland for American blacks as well as for all blacks who were held as slaves by other countries. He thought all blacks should return to Africa. Keeping in mind when this speech was delivered (1924), what do you think of Garvey's proposal?
2. Do you think Garvey was practicing racism when he made his proposal? Why or why not?
3. In your small group, discuss Garvey's statement: "We are strangers in a strange land." What does he mean, and who are the strangers?
4. What do you think America would be like if every African American had returned to Africa?

WRITING TOPICS

1. Garvey says: "We are not seeking social equality. . . ." In your writing journal, explain what you think he means.
2. Early on in his role as a spokesperson for the Black Muslim movement, Malcolm X expressed the desire for a separate homeland for African Americans in the United States. Pretend that you are Malcolm X and write a letter to Garvey expressing how, after your visit to Mecca (the Holy Moslem shrine), your beliefs about setting up a separate homeland have been modified.

A BLACK MAN TALKS OF REAPING

Arna Bontemps

Arna (Arnaud) Bontemps was born in Alexandria, Louisiana, in 1902. Educated in California schools, he graduated with honors from Pacific Union College in 1923 and received an M.A. degree from the University of Chicago in 1942. He won the Alexander Pushkin Award for his "Golgotha Is a Mountain" in 1926 and in 1927 for his poem "Nocturne at Bethesda." From 1943 to 1965 he served as librarian at Fisk University in Tennessee and later as Director of University Relations. He published several children's books, including *You Can't Pet a Possum* (1934), *Lonesome Boy* (1955), and *Frederick Douglass* (1959). He also edited several anthologies, including *Golden Slippers* (1941), *American Negro Poetry* (1963), and, with Langston Hughes, the classic *The Poetry of the Negro* (1949, 1970). Bontemps died in 1973. (For more biographical information, see page 194.)

I have sown beside all waters in my day.
I planted deep, within my heart the fear
that wind or fowl would take the grain away.
I planted safe against this stark, lean year.

5   I scattered seed enough to plant the land
in rows from Canada to Mexico,
but for my reaping only what the hand
can hold at once is all that I can show.

Yet what I sowed and what the orchard yields
10 my brother's sons are gathering stalk and root;
small wonder then my children glean in fields
they have not sown, and feed on bitter fruit.

DISCUSSION QUESTIONS

1. What does Bontemps mean when he says "feed on bitter fruit"?
2. What does it mean *to glean,* and what type of person would more than likely engage in the act of gleaning?
3. The poet says: "I planted safe against this stark, lean year." What do you think he means by the statement?

WRITING TOPICS

1. Bontemps uses the metaphor of the harvest to illustrate problems of injustice. Write an analytical essay in which you interpret lines 9 and 10 of the poem.
2. In your writing journal, list at least two metaphors found in the poem and write an explanation for each of these literary forms.

FROM *THE BIG SEA*

Langston Hughes

Langston Hughes, born in 1902, was a prolific poet and writer who realistically depicted the life of African Americans. After attending Central High School in Cleveland, he attended Columbia University in New York for a year and then received his B.A. from Lincoln University in Pennsylvania in 1929. Throughout his life, Hughes traveled extensively, especially across the United States, Europe, and Russia.

Hughes felt a strong connection to the poor people he met, and they and their concerns became the material of much of his writing. Though Hughes was prominent in the Harlem Renaissance movement, some younger black poets of the 1960s did not consider Hughes's poetry to have a strong enough militant stance. Hughes, later poetry, *Ask Your Mama: 12 Moods for Jazz* (1961) and the posthumously published *The Panther and the Lash: Poems of Our Times* (1967) and *Black Misery* (1969) do respond to the racial, social, political and economic turbulence of the 1960s. Hughes died in 1967. (For more information about Hughes, see pages 91, 133, and 192.)

I'VE KNOWN RIVERS

1   That November the First World War ended. In Cleveland, everybody poured into the streets to celebrate the Armistice. Negroes, too, although Negroes were increasingly beginning to wonder where, for them, was that democracy they had fought to preserve. In Cleveland, a liberal city, the color line began to be drawn tighter and tighter. Theaters and restaurants in the downtown area began to refuse to accommodate colored people. Landlords doubled and tripled the rents at the approach of a dark tenant. And when the white soldiers came back from the war, Negroes were often discharged from their jobs and white men hired in their places.

2   The end of the war! But many of the students at Central kept talking, not about the end of the war, but about Russia, where Lenin had taken power in the name of the workers, who made everything, and who would now own everything they made. "No more pogroms," the Jews said, "no more race hatred, no more landlords." John Reed's *Ten Days That Shook the World* shook Central High School, too.

3   The daily papers pictured the Bolsheviki as the greatest devils on earth, but I didn't see how they could be that bad if they had done away with race hatred and landlords—two evils that I knew well at first hand.

4   My father raised my allowance that year, so I was able to help my mother with the expenses of our household. It was a pleasant year for me, for I was a senior. I was elected Class Poet and Editor of our Year Book. As an officer in the drill corps, I wore a khaki uniform and leather puttees, and gave orders. I went calling on a little brownskin girl, who was as old as I was— seventeen—but only in junior high school, because she had just come up from the poor schools of the South. I met her at a dance at the Longwood Gym. She had big eyes and skin like rich chocolate. Sometimes she wore a red dress that was very becoming to her, so I wrote a poem about her that declared:

> When Susanna Jones wears red
> Her face is like an ancient cameo
> Turned brown by the ages.
>
> Come with a blast of trumpets,
> Jesus!
>
> When Susanna Jones wears red
> A queen from some time-dead Egyptian night
> Walks once again.
>
> Blow trumpets, Jesus!
>
> And the beauty of Susanna Jones in red
> Burns in my heart a love-fire sharp like pain.
>
> Sweet silver trumpets,
> Jesus!

5   I had a whole notebook full of poems by now, and another one full of verses and jingles. I always tried to keep verses and poems apart, although I saw no harm in writing verses if you felt like it, and poetry if you could.

6   June came. And graduation. Like most graduations, it made you feel both sorry and glad: sorry to be leaving and glad to be going. Some students

were planning to enter college, but not many, because there was no money for college in most of Central's families.

7   My father had written me to come to Mexico again to discuss with him my future plans. He hinted that he would send me to college if I intended to go, and he thought I had better go.

8   I didn't want to return to Mexico, but I had a feeling I'd never get any further education if I didn't, since my mother wanted me to go to work and be, as she put it, "of some use to her." She demanded to know how I would look going off to college and she there working like a dog!

9   I said I thought I could be of more help to her once I got an education than I could if I went to work fresh out of high school, because nobody could do much on the salary of a porter or a bus boy. And such jobs offered no advancement for a Negro.

10   But about my going to join my father, my mother acted much as she had done the year before. I guess it is the old story of divorced parents who don't like each other, and take their grievances out on the offspring. I got the feeling then that I'd like to get away from home altogether, both homes, and that maybe if I went to Mexico one more time, I could go to college somewhere in some new place, and be on my own.

11   So I went back to Toluca.

12   My mother let me go to the station alone, and I felt pretty bad when I got on the train. I felt bad for the next three or four years, to tell the truth, and those were the years when I wrote most of my poetry. (For my best poems were all written when I felt the worst. When I was happy, I didn't write anything.)

13   The one of my poems that has perhaps been most often reprinted in anthologies, was written on the train during this trip to Mexico when I was feeling very bad. It's called "The Negro Speaks of Rivers" and was written just outside St. Louis, as the train rolled toward Texas.

14   It came about in this way. All day on the train I had been thinking about my father and his strange dislike of his own people. I didn't understand it, because I was a Negro, and I liked Negroes very much. One of the happiest jobs I had ever had was during my freshman year in high school, when I worked behind the soda fountain for a Mrs. Kitzmiller, who ran a refreshment parlor on Central Avenue in the heart of the colored neighborhood. People just up from the South used to come in for ice cream and sodas and watermelon. And I never tired of hearing them talk, listening to the thunderclaps of their laughter, to their troubles, to their discussions of the war and the men who had gone to Europe from the Jim Crow South, their complaints over the high rent and the long overtime hours that brought what seemed like big checks, until the weekly bills were paid. They seemed to me like the gayest and the bravest people possible—these Negroes from the Southern ghettos—facing tremendous odds, working and laughing and trying to get somewhere in the world.

15   I had been in to dinner early that afternoon on the train. Now it was just

sunset, and we crossed the Mississippi, slowly, over a long bridge. I looked out the window of the Pullman at the great muddy river flowing down toward the heart of the South, and I began to think what that river, the old Mississippi, had meant to Negroes in the past—how to be sold down the river was the worst fate that could overtake a slave in times of bondage. Then I remembered reading how Abraham Lincoln had made a trip down the Mississippi on a raft to New Orleans, and how he had seen slavery at its worst, and had decided within himself that it should be removed from American life. Then I began to think about other rivers in our past—the Congo, and the Niger, and the Nile in Africa—and the thought came to me: "I've known rivers," and I put it down on the back of an envelope I had in my pocket, and within the space of ten or fifteen minutes, as the train gathered speed in the dusk, I had written this poem, which I called "The Negro Speaks of Rivers":

> I've known rivers:
> I've known rivers ancient as the world and older than
> the flow of human blood in human veins.
>
> My soul has grown deep like the rivers.
>
> I bathed in the Euphrates when dawns were young.
> I built my hut near the Congo and it lulled me to sleep.
> I looked upon the Nile and raised the pyramids above it.
> I heard the singing of the Mississippi when Abe Lincoln
> went down to New Orleans, and I've seen its muddy
> bosom turn all golden in the sunset.
> I've known rivers:
> Ancient, dusky rivers.
>
> My soul has grown deep like the rivers.

16 No doubt I changed a few words the next day, or maybe crossed out a line or two. But there are seldom many changes in my poems, once they're down. Generally, the first two or three lines come to me from something I'm thinking about, or looking at, or doing, and the rest of the poem (if there is to be a poem) flows from those first few lines, usually right away. If there is a chance to put the poem down then, I write it down. If not, I try to remember it until I get to a pencil and paper; for poems are like rainbows: they escape you quickly. . . .

HARLEM LITERATI

17 The summer of 1926, I lived in a rooming house on 37th Street, where Wallace Thurman and Harcourt Tynes also lived. Thurman was then man-

aging editor of the *Messenger*, a Negro magazine that had a curious career. It began by being very radical, racial, and socialistic, just after the war. I believe it received a grant from the Garland Fund in its early days. Then it later became a kind of Negro society magazine and a plugger for Negro business, with photographs of prominent colored ladies and their nice homes in it. A. Phillip Randolph, now President of the Brotherhood of Sleeping Car Porters, Chandler Owen, and George S. Schuyler were connected with it. Schuyler's editorials, à la Mencken, were the most interesting things in the magazine, verbal brickbats that said sometimes one thing, sometimes another, but always vigorously. I asked Thurman what kind of magazine the *Messenger* was, and he said it reflected the policy of whoever paid off best at the time.

18   Anyway, the *Messenger* bought my first short stories. They paid me ten dollars a story. Wallace Thurman wrote me that they were very bad stories, but better than any others they could find, so he published them.

19   Thurman had recently come from California to New York. He was a strangely brilliant black boy, who had read everything, and whose critical mind could find something wrong with everything he read. I have no critical mind, so I usually either like a book or don't. But I am not capable of liking a book and then finding a million things wrong with it, too—as Thurman was capable of doing.

20   Thurman had read so many books because he could read eleven lines at a time. He would get from the library a great pile of volumes that would have taken me a year to read. But he would go through them in less than a week, and be able to discuss each one at great length with anybody. That was why, I suppose, he was later given a job as a reader at Macaulay's—the only Negro reader, so far as I know, to be employed by any of the larger publishing firms.

21   Later Thurman became a ghost writer for *True Story* and other publications, writing under all sorts of fantastic names, like Ethel Belle Mandrake or Patrick Casey. He did Irish and Jewish and Catholic "true confessions." He collaborated with William Jordan Rapp on plays and novels. Later he ghosted books. In fact, this quite dark young Negro is said to have written *Men, Women, and Checks*.

22   Wallace Thurman wanted to be a great writer, but none of his own work ever made him happy. *The Blacker the Berry*, his first book, was an important novel on a subject little dwelt upon in Negro fiction—the plight of the very dark Negro woman, who encounters in some communities a double wall of color prejudice within and without the race. His play, *Harlem*, considerably distorted for box office purposes, was, nevertheless, a compelling study—and the only one in the theater—of the impact of Harlem on a Negro family fresh from the South. And his *Infants of the Spring*, a superb and bitter study of the bohemian fringe of Harlem's literary and artistic life, is a compelling book.

23   But none of these things pleased Wallace Thurman. He wanted to be a *very* great writer, like Gorki or Thomas Mann, and he felt that he was merely

a journalistic writer. His critical mind, comparing his pages to the thousands of other pages he had read, by Proust, Melville, Tolstoy, Galsworthy, Dostoyevski, Henry James, Sainte-Beauve, Taine, Anatole France, found his own pages vastly wanting. So he contented himself by writing a great deal for money, laughing bitterly at his fabulously concocted "true stories," creating two bad motion pictures of the "Adults Only" type for Hollywood, drinking more and more gin, and then threatening to jump out of windows at people's parties and kill himself.

24   During the summer of 1926, Wallace Thurman, Zora Neale Hurston, Aaron Douglas, John P. Davis, Bruce Nugent, Gwendolyn Bennett, and I decided to publish "a Negro quarterly of the arts" to be called *Fire*—the idea being that it would burn up a lot of the old, dead conventional Negro-white ideas of the past, *épater le bourgeois* into a realization of the existence of the younger Negro writers and artists, and provide us with an outlet for publication not available in the limited pages of the small Negro magazines then existing, the *Crisis, Opportunity,* and the *Messenger*—the first two being house organs of inter-racial organizations, and the latter being God knows what.

25   Sweltering summer evenings we met to plan *Fire*. Each of the seven of us agreed to give fifty dollars to finance the first issue. Thurman was to edit it, John P. Davis to handle the business end, and Bruce Nugent to take charge of distribution. The rest of us were to serve as an editorial board to collect material, contribute our own work, and act in any useful way that we could. For artists and writers, we got along fine and there were no quarrels. But October came before we were ready to go to press. I had to return to Lincoln, John Davis to Law School at Harvard, Zora Hurston to her studies at Barnard, from whence she went about Harlem with an anthropologist's ruler, measuring heads for Franz Boas.

26   Only three of the seven had contributed their fifty dollars, but the others faithfully promised to send theirs out of tuition checks, wages, or begging. Thurman went on with the work of preparing the magazine. He got a printer. He planned the layout. It had to be on good paper, he said, worthy of the drawings of Aaron Douglas. It had to have beautiful type, worthy of the first Negro art quarterly. It had to be what we seven young Negroes dreamed our magazine would be—so in the end it cost almost a thousand dollars, and nobody could pay the bills.

27   I don't know how Thurman persuaded the printer to let us have all the copies to distribute but he did. I think Alain Locke, among others, signed notes guaranteeing payments. But since Thurman was the only one of the seven of us with a regular job, for the next three or four years his checks were constantly being attached and his income seized to pay for *Fire*. And whenever I sold a poem, mine went there, too—to *Fire*.

28   None of the older Negro intellectuals would have anything to do with *Fire*. Dr. DuBois in the *Crisis* roasted it. The Negro press called it all sorts of bad names, largely because of a green and purple story by Bruce Nugent,

in the Oscar Wilde tradition, which we had included. Rean Graves, the critic for the *Baltimore Afro-American,* began his review by saying: "I have just tossed the first issue of *Fire* into the fire." Commenting upon various of our contributors, he said: "Aaron Douglas who, in spite of himself and the meaningless grotesqueness of his creations, has gained a reputation as an artist, is permitted to spoil three perfectly good pages and a cover with his pen and ink hudge pudge. Countee Cullen has written a beautiful poem in his 'From a Dark Tower,' but tries his best to obscure the thought in superfluous sentences. Langston Hughes displays his usual ability to say nothing in many words."

29   So *Fire* had plenty of cold water thrown on it by the colored critics. The white critics (except for an excellent editorial in the *Bookman* for November, 1926) scarcely noticed it at all. We had no way of getting it distributed to bookstands or news stand. Bruce Nugent took it around New York on foot and some of the Greenwich Village bookshops put it on display, and sold it for us. But then Bruce, who had no job, would collect the money and, on account of salary, eat it up before he got back to Harlem.

30   Finally, irony of ironies, several hundred copies of *Fire* were stored in the basement of an apartment where an actual fire occurred and the bulk of the whole issue was burned up. Even after that Thurman had to go on paying the printer.

31   Now *Fire* is a collector's item, and very difficult to get, being mostly ashes.

32   That taught me a lesson about little magazines. But since white folks had them, we Negroes thought we could have one, too. But we didn't have the money.

33   Wallace Thurman laughed a long bitter laugh. He was a strange kind of fellow, who liked to drink gin, but *didn't* like to drink gin; who liked being a Negro, but felt it a great handicap; who adored bohemianism, but thought it wrong to be a bohemian. He liked to waste a lot of time, but he always felt guilty wasting time. He loathed crowds, yet he hated to be alone. He almost always felt bad, yet he didn't write poetry.

34   Once I told him if I could feel as bad as he did *all* the time, I would surely produce wonderful books. But he said you had to know how to *write,* as well as how to feel bad. I said I didn't have to know how to feel bad, because, every so often, the blues just naturally overtook me, like a blind beggar with an old guitar:

> You don't know,
> You don't know my mind—
> When you see me laughin',
> I'm laughin' to keep from cryin'.

35   About the future of Negro literature Thurman was very pessimistic. He thought the Negro vogue had made us all too conscious of ourselves, had flattered and spoiled us, and had provided too many easy opportunities for

some of us to drink gin and more gin, on which he thought we would always be drunk. With his bitter sense of humor, he called the Harlem literati, the "niggerati."

36   Of this "niggerati," Zora Neale Hurston was certainly the most amusing. Only to reach a wider audience, need she ever write books—because she is a perfect book of entertainment in herself. In her youth she was always getting scholarships and things from wealthy white people, some of whom simply paid her just to sit around and represent the Negro race for them, she did it in such a racy fashion. She was full of side-splitting anecdotes, humorous tales, and tragicomic stories, remembered out of her life in the south as a daughter of a travelling minister of God. She could make you laugh one minute and cry the next. To many of her white friends, no doubt, she was a perfect "darkie," in the nice meaning they give the term—that is a naive, childlike, sweet, humorous, and highly colored Negro.

37   But Miss Hurston was clever, too—a student who didn't let college give her a broad *a* and who had great scorn for all pretensions, academic or otherwise. That is why she was such a fine folklore collector, able to go among the people and never act as if she had been to school at all. Almost nobody else could stop the average Harlemite on Lenox Avenue and measure his head with a strange-looking, anthropological device and not get bawled out for the attempt, except Zora, who used to stop anyone whose head looked interesting, and measure it.

38   When Miss Hurston graduated from Barnard she took an apartment in West 66th Street near the park, in that row of Negro houses there. She moved in with no furniture at all and no money, but in a few days friends had given her everything from decorative silver birds, perched atop the linen cabinet, down to a footstool. And on Saturday night, to christen the place, she had a *hand*-chicken dinner, since she had forgotten to say she needed forks.

39   She seemed to know almost everybody in New York. She had been a secretary to Fannie Hurst, and had met dozens of celebrities whose friendship she retained. Yet she was always having terrific ups-and-downs about money. She tells this story on herself, about needing a nickel to go downtown one day and wondering where on earth she would get it. As she approached the subway, she was stopped by a blind beggar holding out his cup.

40   "Please help the blind! Help the blind! A nickel for the blind!"

41   "I need money worse than you today," said Miss Hurston, taking five cents out of his cup. "Lend me this! Next time, I'll give it back." And she went on downtown.

42   Harlem was like a great magnet for the Negro intellectual, pulling him from everywhere. Or perhaps the magnet was New York—but once in New York, he had to live in Harlem, for rooms were hardly to be found elsewhere unless one could pass for white or Mexican or Eurasian and perhaps live in the Village—which always seemed to me a very arty locale, in spite of the many real artists and writers who lived there. Only a few of the New Negoes lived in the Village, Harlem being their real stamping ground.

43   The wittiest of these New Negroes of Harlem, whose tongue was flavored with the sharpest and saltiest humor, was Rudolph Fisher, whose stories appeared in the *Atlantic Monthly*. His novel, *Walls of Jericho*, captures but slightly the raciness of his own conversation. He was a young medical doctor and X-ray specialist, who always frightened me a little, because he could think of the most incisively clever things to say—and I could never think of anything to answer. He and Alain Locke together were great for intellectual wisecracking. The two would fling big and witty words about with such swift and punning innuendo that an ordinary mortal just sat and looked wary for fear of being caught in a net of witticisms beyond his cultural ken. I used to wish I could talk like Rudolph Fisher. Besides being a good writer, he was an excellent singer, and had sung with Paul Robeson during their college days. But I guess Fisher was too brilliant and too talented to stay long on this earth. During the same week, in December, 1934, he and Wallace Thurman both died.

44   Thurman died of tuberculosis in the charity ward at Bellevue Hospital, having just flown back to New York from Hollywood.

DISCUSSION QUESTIONS

1. *The Big Sea* was Hughes's first autobiography. How did he come to write the poem "The Negro Speaks of Rivers"?
2. What was Hughes's relationship with his father? With his mother?
3. What is your opinion about Hughes's statement: "...the old story of divorced parents who don't like each other, and take their grievances out on the offspring"?
4. Who is the *I* in the poem "The Negro Speaks of Rivers"?

WRITING TOPICS

1. Hughes says his poems are written when he feels the worst. Other artists have also said they produce their best work when things seem darkest. How do you account for this? Write an essay in which you present your opinions; give specific examples.
2. In your writing journal, explain what you think the poet means by the statement: "My soul has grown deep like the rivers." You may wish to discuss this in your small group first.

THE ONLY MAN ON LIBERTY STREET

William Melvin Kelley

William Melvin Kelley was born in New York City in 1937 and graduated from Harvard University. His first novel, *A Different Drummer* (1962), deals with the exodus of blacks and whites from the South and the impact of this upon both groups who still remain in the South. He is very much interested in race relations and the African-American experience in America. Kelley is author of *Dancers on the Shore* (1964), a collection of short stories, and a *Drop of Patience* (1965), a novel about a blind musician. He has taught at the New School for Social Research and the State University of New York at Geneseo.

1   She was squatting in the front yard, digging with an old brass spoon in the dirt which was an ocean to the islands of short yellow grass. She wore a red and white checkered dress, which hung loosely from her shoulders, and obscured her legs. It was early spring and she was barefoot. Her toes stuck from under the skirt. She could not see the man yet, riding down Liberty Street, his shoulders square, the duster he wore spread back over the horse's rump, a carpetbag tied with a leather strap to his saddle horn and knocking against his leg. She could not see him until he had dismounted and tied his horse to a small, black, iron Negro jockey and unstrapped the bag. She watched now as he opened the wooden gate, came into the yard, and stood, looking down at her, his face stern, almost gray beneath the brim of his wide hat.

2   She knew him. Her mother called him Mister Herder and had told Jennie that he was Jennie's father. He was one of the men who came riding down Liberty Street in their fine black suits and starched shirts and large, dark ties. Each of these men had a house to go to, into which, in the evening usually, he would disappear. Only women and children lived on Liberty Street. All of them were Negroes. Some of the women were quite dark, but most were coffee-color. They were all very beautiful. Her mother was light. She was tall, had black eyes, and black hair so long she could sit on it.

3   The man standing over her was the one who came to her house once or twice a week. He was never there in the morning when Jennie got up. He was tall, and thin, and blond. He had a short beard that looked as coarse as the grass beneath her feet. His eyes were blue, like Jennie's. He did not speak English very well. Jennie's mother had told her he came from across the sea and Jennie often wondered if he went there between visits to their house.

4   "Jennie? Your mother tells me that you ask why I do not stay at night. Is so?"

5   She looked up at him. "Yes, Mister Herder." The hair under his jaw was darker than the hair on his cheeks.

6   He nodded. "I stay now. Go bring your mother."

7   She left the spoon in the dirt, and ran into the house, down the long hall, dark now because she had been sitting in the sun. She found her mother standing over the stove, a great black lid in her left hand, a wooden spoon in her right. There were beads of sweat on her forehead. She wore a full black skirt and a white blouse. Her one waist-length braid hung straight between her shoulder blades. She turned to Jennie's running steps.

8   "Mama? That man? My father? He in the yard. He brung a carpetbag."

9   First her mother smiled, then frowned, then looked puzzled. "A carpetbag, darling?"

10   "Yes, Mama."

11   She followed her mother through the house, pausing with her at the hall mirror where the woman ran her hand up the back of her neck to smooth stray black hair. Then they went onto the porch, where the man was now seated, surveying the tiny yard and the dark green hedge that enclosed it. The carpetbag rested beside his chair.

12   Her mother stood with her hands beneath her apron, staring at the bag. "Mister Herder?"

13   He turned to them. "I will not go back this time. No matter what. Why should I live in that house when I must come here to know what home is?" He nodded sharply as if in answer to a question. "So! I stay. I give her that house. I will send her money, but I stay here."

14   Her mother stood silently for an instant, then turned to the door. "Dinner'll be on the table in a half hour." She opened the screen door. The spring whined and cracked. "Oh." She let go the door, and picked up the carpetbag. "I'll take this on up." She went inside. As she passed, Jennie could see she was smiling again.

15   After that, Jennie's mother became a celebrity on Liberty Street. The other women would stop her to ask about the man. "And he staying for good, Josie?"

16   "Yes."

17   "You have any trouble yet?"

18   "Not yet."

19   "Well, child, you make him put that there house in your name. You don't want to be no Sissie Markham. That white woman come down the same day

he died and moved Sissie and her children right into the gutter. You get that house put in your name. You hear?"

20   "Yes."

21   "How is it? It different?"

22   Her mother would look dazed. "Yes, it different. He told me to call him Maynard."

23   The other women were always very surprised.

24   At first, Jennie too was surprised. The man was always there in the morning and sometimes even woke her up. Her mother no longer called him Mister Herder, and at odd times, though still quite seldom, said, No. She had never before heard her mother say No to anything the man ever said. It was not long before Jennie was convinced that he actually was her father. She began to call him Papa.

25   Daily now a white woman had been driving by their house. Jennie did not know who she was or what she wanted, but playing in the yard, would see the white woman's gray buggy turn the corner and come slowly down the block, pulled by a speckled horse that trudged in the dry dust. A Negro driver sat erect in his black uniform, a whip in his fist. The white woman would peer at the house as if looking for an address or something special. She would look at the curtained windows, looking for someone, and sometimes even at Jennie. The look was not kind or tender, but hard and angry as if she knew something bad about the child.

26   Then one day the buggy stopped, the Negro pulling gently on the reins. The white woman leaned forward spoke to the driver and handed him a small pink envelope. He jumped down, opened the gate, and without looking at Jennie, his face dark and shining, advanced on the porch, up the three steps, which knocked hollow beneath his boots, opened the screen door and twisted the polished brass bell key in the center of the open, winter door.

27   Her mother came drying her hands. The Negro reached out the envelope and her mother took it, looking beyond him for an instant at the buggy and the white woman who returned her look coldly. As the Negro turned, her mother opened the letter, and read it, moving her lips slightly. Then Jennie could see the twinkling at the corners of her eyes. Her mother stood framed in the black square of doorway, tall, fair, the black hair swept to hide her ears, her eyes glistening.

28   Jennie turned back to the white woman now and saw her lean deeper into her seat. Then she pulled forward. "Do you understand what I will have them do?" She was shouting shrilly and spoke like Jennie's father. "You tell him he has got one wife! You are something different!" She leaned back again, waved her gloved hand and the buggy lurched down the street, gained speed, and jangled out of sight around the corner.

29   Jennie was on her feet and pounding up the stairs. "Mama?"

30   "Go play, Jennie. Go on now, *play!*" Still her mother stared straight ahead, as if the buggy and the white woman remained in front of the

house. She still held the letter as if to read it. The corners of her eyes were wet. Then she turned and went into the house. The screen door clacked behind her.

31   At nights now Jennie waited by the gate in the yard for her father to turn the corner walking. In the beginning she had been waiting too for the one day he would not turn the corner. But each night he came, that day seemed less likely to come. Even so, she was always surprised to see him. When she did, she would wave, timidly, raising her hand only to her shoulder, wiggling only her fingers, as if to wave too wildly would somehow cause the entire picture of his advancing to collapse as only a slight wind would be enough to disarrange a design of feathers.

32   That night too she waved and saw him raise his hand high over his head, greeting her. She backed away when he reached the gate so he might open it, her head thrown way back, looking up at him.

33   "Well, my Jennie, what kind of day did you have?"

34   She only smiled, then remembered the white woman. "A woman come to visit Mama. She come in a buggy and give her a letter too. She made Mama cry."

35   His smile fled. He sucked his tongue, angry now. "We go see what is wrong. Come." He reached for her hand.

36   Her mother was in the kitchen. She looked as if she did not really care what she was doing or how, walking from pump to stove, stove to cupboard in a deep trance. The pink envelope was on the table.

37   She turned to them. Her eyes were red. Several strands of hair stuck to her temples. She cleared her nose and pointed to the letter. "She come today."

38   Her father let go Jennie's hand, picked up the letter and read it. When he was finished he took it to the stove and dropped it into the flame. There was a puff of smoke before he replaced the lid. He shook his head. "She cannot make me go back, Josephine."

39   Her mother fell heavily into a wooden chair, beginning to cry again. "But she's white, Maynard."

40   He raised his eyebrows like a priest or a displeased school teacher. "Your skin is whiter."

41   "My mother was a slave."

42   He threw up his hands, making fists. "Your mother did not ask to be a slave!" Then he went to her, crouched on his haunches before her, speaking quietly. "No one can make me go back."

43   "But she can get them to do what she say." She turned her gaze on Jennie, but looked away quickly. "You wasn't here after the war. But I seen things. I seen things happen to field niggers that . . . I was up in the house; they didn't bother me. My own father, General Dewey Willson, he stood on a platform in the center of town and promised to keep the niggers down. I was close by." She took his face in her hands. "Maynard, maybe you better go back, leastways—"

44   "I go back—dead! You hear! Dead. These children, these cowardly children in their masks will not move me! I go back dead. That is all. We do not discuss it." And he was gone. Jennie heard him thundering down the hall, knocking against the table near the stairs, going up to the second floor.

45   Her mother was looking at her now, her eyes even more red than before, her lips trembling, her hands active in her lap. "Jennie?"

46   "Yes, Mama." She took a step toward her, staring into the woman's eyes.

47   "Jennie, I want you to promise me something and not forget it."

48   "Yes, Mama." She was between her mother's knees, felt the woman's hands clutching her shoulders.

49   "Jennie, you'll be right pretty when you get grown. Did you know that? Promise me you'll go up North. Promise me if I'm not here when you get eighteen, you'll go north and get married. You understand?"

50   Jennie was not sure she did. She could not picture the North, except that she had heard once it was cold and white things fell from the sky. She could not picture being eighteen and her mother not being there. But she knew her mother wanted her to understand and she lied. "Yes, Mama."

51   "Repeat what I just said."

52   She did. Her mother kissed her mouth, the first time ever.

53   From the kitchen below came their voices. Her father's voice sound hard, cut short; Jennie knew he had made a decision and was sticking to it. Her mother was pleading, trying to change his mind. It was July the Fourth, the day of the shooting match.

54   She dressed in her Sunday clothes and coming downstairs, heard her mother: "Maynard, please don't take her." She was frantic now. "I'm begging you. Don't take that child with you today."

55   "I take her. We do not discuss it. I take her. Those sneaking cowards in their masks . . ." Jennie knew now what they were talking about. Her father had promised to take her to the shooting match. For some reason, her mother feared there would be trouble if Jennie went downtown. She did not know why her mother felt that way, except it might have something to do with the white woman, who continued to ride by their house each morning, after her father had left for the day. Perhaps her mother did not want to be alone in the house when the white woman drove by in her gray buggy, even though she had not stopped the buggy since the day two months ago, when the Negro had given her mother the pink envelope.

56   But other strange things had happened after that. In the beginning she and her mother, as always before, had gone downtown to the market, to stop amid the bright stalls brimming with green and yellow vegetables and brick-red meats, tended by dark, country Negroes in shabby clothes and large straw hats. It would get very quiet when they passed, and Jennie would see the Negroes look away, fear in their eyes, and knots of white men watching, sometimes giggling. But the white women in fine clothes were the most frightening; sitting on the verandas or passing in carriages, some even com-

ing to their windows, they would stare angrily as if her mother had done something terrible to each one personally, as if all these white women could be the one who drove by each morning. Her mother would walk through it all, her back straight, very like her father's, the bun into which she wove her waist-length braid on market days, gleaming dark.

57 In the beginning they had gone to the suddenly quiet market. But now her mother hardly set foot from the house, and the food was brought to them in a carton by a crippled Negro boy, who was coming just as Jennie and her father left the house that morning.

58 Balancing the carton on his left arm, he removed his ragged hat and smiled. "Morning, Mister Herder. Good luck at the shooting match, sir." His left leg was short and he seemed to tilt.

59 Her father nodded. "Thank you, Felix. I do my best."

60 "Then you a sure thing, Mister Herder." He replaced his hat and went on around the house.

61 Walking, her hand in her father's, Jennie could see some of the women of Liberty Street peering out at them through their curtains.

62 Downtown was not the same. Flags and banners draped the verandas; people wore their best clothes. The Square had been roped off, a platform set up to one side, and New Marsails Avenue, which ran into the Square, had been cleared for two blocks. Far away down the Avenue stood a row of cotton bales onto which had been pinned oilcloth targets. From where they stood, the bull's-eyes looked no bigger than red jawbreakers.

63 Many men slapped her father on the back, and furtively, looked at her with a kind of clinical interest. But mostly they ignored her. The celebrity of the day was her father, and unlike her mother, he was very popular. Everyone felt sure he would win the match; he was the best shot in the state.

64 After everyone shot, the judge came running down from the targets, waving his arms. "Maynard Herder. Six shots, and you can cover them all with a good gob of spit!" He grabbed her father's elbow and pulled him toward the platform, where an old man with white hair and beard, wearing a gray uniform trimmed with yellow, waited. She followed them to the platform steps, but was afraid to go any farther because now some women had begun to look at her as they had at her mother.

65 The old man made a short speech, his voice deep, but coarse, grainy-sounding, and gave her father a silver medal in a blue velvet box. Her father turned and smiled at her. She started up the steps toward him, but just then the old man put his hand on her father's shoulder.

66 People had begun to walk away down the streets leading out of the Square. There was less noise now but she could not hear the first words the old man said to her father.

67 Her father's face tightened into the same look she had seen the day the letter came, the same as this morning in the kitchen. She went halfway up the stairs, stopped.

68   The old man went on: "You know I'm no meddler. Everybody knows about Liberty Street. I had a woman down there myself . . . before the war."

69   "I know that." The words came out of her father's face, though his lips did not move.

70   The old man nodded. "But Maynard, what you're doing is different."

71   "She's your own daughter."

72   "Maybe that's why . . ." The old man looked down the street, toward the cotton bales and the targets. "But she's a nigger. And now the talking is taking an ugly turn and the folks talking are the ones I can't hold."

73   Her father spoke in an angry whisper. "You see what I do to that target? You tell those children in their masks I do that to the forehead of any man . . . or woman that comes near her or my house. You tell them."

74   "Maynard, that wouldn't do any real good *after* they'd done something to her." He stopped, looked at Jennie, and smiled. "That's my only grand-daughter, you know." His eyes clicked off her. "You're a man who knows firearms. You're a gunsmith. I know firearms too. Pistols and rifles can do lots of things, but they don't make very good doctors. Nobody's asking you to give her up. Just go back home. That's all. Go back to your wife."

75   Her father turned away, walking fast, came down the stairs and grabbed her hand. His face was red as blood between the white of his collar and the straw yellow of his hair.

76   They slowed after a block, paused in a small park with green trees shading several benches and a statue of a stern-faced young man in uniform, carrying pack and rifle. "We will sit."

77   She squirmed up onto the bench beside him. The warm wind smelled of salt from the Gulf of Mexico. The leaves were a dull, low tambourine. Her father was quiet for a long while.

78   Jennie watched birds bobbing for worms in the grass near them, then looked at the young, stone soldier. Far off, but from where she viewed it, just over the soldier's hat, gliding sea gull dived suddenly behind the rooftops. That was when she saw the white man, standing across the street from the park, smiling at her. There were other white men with him, some looking at her, others at the man, all laughing. He waved to her. She smiled at him though he was the kind of man her mother told her always to stay away from. He was dressed as poorly as any Negro. From behind his back, he produced a brown rag doll, looked at her again, then grabbed the doll by its legs, and tore it part way up the middle. . . . The other men laughed uproariously.

79   Jennie pulled her father's sleeve. "Papa? What he doing?"

80   "Who?" Her father turned. The man repeated the show and her father bolted to his feet, yelling: "I will kill you! You hear? I will kill you for that!"

81   The men only snickered and ambled away.

82   Her father was red again. He had clenched his fists; now his hands were white like the bottoms of fishes. He sighed, shook his head and sat down. "I cannot kill everybody." He shook his head again, then leaned forward to

get up. But first he thrust the blue velvet medal box into her hand. It was warm from his hand, wet and prickly. "When you grow up, you go to the North like your mother tells you. And you take this with you. It is yours. Always remember I gave it to you." He stood. "Now you must go home alone. Tell your mother I come later."

83   That night, Jennie tried to stay awake until he came home, until he was there to kiss her good night, his whiskers scratching her cheek. But all at once there was sun at her window and the sound of carts and wagons grating outside in the dirt street. Her mother was quiet while the two of them ate. After breakfast, Jennie went into the yard to wait for the gray buggy to turn the corner, but for the first morning in many months, the white woman did not jounce by, peering at the house, searching for someone or something special.

DISCUSSION QUESTIONS

1. Mister Herder says: "Why should I live in that house when I must come here to know what a home is?" What do you think he means by this statement?
2. How would you characterize Maynard Herder?
3. What irony, if any, do you see in the title "The Only Man on Liberty Street"?

WRITING TOPICS

1. Imagine you are Jennie's father. Write a letter to your wife telling her why you decided to stay, initially, with Jennie's mother on Liberty Street.
2. Write an essay about an interracial relationship that has worked well. The relationship may be true or ficticious, but use specific examples from your reading or personal experience.
3. In your journal, list those character traits that make for a strong, successful relationship regardless of ethnicity.

MINSTREL MAN

Langston Hughes

For biographical information on Langston Hughes, see pages 91, 133, 192, and 385.

> Because my mouth
> Is wide with laughter
> And my throat
> Is deep with song,
> 5 You do not think
> I suffer after
> I have held my pain
> So long.
>
> Because my mouth
> 10 Is wide with laughter
> You do not hear
> My inner cry;
> Because my feet
> Are gay with dancing
> 15 You do not know
> I die.

DISCUSSION QUESTIONS

1. Historically, the minstrel has been a happy-go-lucky stereotype of black men. Langston Hughes offers a different perspective on how the minstrel acts. In your small group, discuss what you think this new perspective is.

2. Is the person in this poem wearing a mask? If so, how can you tell?
3. What do you think the person is hiding behind his mask?
4. Compare this poem with "We Wear the Mask" by Paul Laurence Dunbar. How do these poems differ in their support of mask wearing?

WRITING TOPICS

1. Write an essay describing how you think the minstrel's mask affects him.
2. In your journal, list some ways in which masks are useful.
3. Write your own poem about mask wearing, using "Minstrel Man" as a model.

THE MAN WHO WAS ALMOST A MAN

Richard Wright

Richard Wright was born in 1908 on a plantation near Natchez, Mississippi. Wright migrated to Chicago in 1927; like other blacks, he left the South in search of a better life in the North. In 1936 he served as literary adviser and press agent for the Negro Federal Theatre of Chicago and became involved in dramatic productions. With Dorothy West, Wright coedited a magazine called *The New Challenge.* He distanced himself from the Harlem Renaissance, which he said only produced "humble novels, poems, and plays," written by "prim and decorous ambassadors who went a-begging to White America."

Wright wrote *Uncle Tom's Children* (1938), a collection of four novellas located in the segregated South. For this work, he won first prize in competition sponsored by the WPA Federal Writers' Project and a fellowship from the Guggenheim Foundation. Wright's next novel was *Native Son,* a monumental work that brought him national acclaim. *Native Son* was published in 1940 and Wright was awarded the Spingarn Medal by the NAACP for it. His autobiography, *Black Boy* (1945), was hailed as a literary masterpiece. Wright traveled throughout Europe and Africa in the 1950s from his home base in Paris. He died there in 1960.

1   Dave struck out across the fields, looking homeward through paling light. Whut's the usa talkin wid em niggers in the field? Anyhow, his mother was putting supper on the table. Them niggers can't understan nothing. One of these days he was going to get a gun and practice shooting, then they can't talk to him as though he were a little boy. He slowed, looking at the ground. Shucks, Ah ain scareda them even ef they are biggern me! Aw, Ah know whut Ahma do. . . . Ahm going by ol Joe's sto n git that Sears Roebuck catlog n look at them guns. Mabbe Ma will lemme buy one when she gits mah pay from ol man Hawkins. Ahma beg her t gimme some

money. Ahm ol ernough to hava gun. Ahm seventeen. Almos a man. He strode, feeling his long, loose-jointed limbs. Shucks, a man oughta hava little gun aftah he done worked hard all day. . . .

2   He came in sight of Joe's store. A yellow lantern glowed on the front porch. He mounted steps and went through the screen door, hearing it bang behind him. There was a strong smell of coal oil and mackerel fish. He felt very confident until he saw fat Joe walk in through the rear door, then his courage began to ooze.

3   "Howdy, Dave! Whutcha want?"

4   "How yuh, Mistah Joe? Aw, Ah don wanna buy nothing. Ah just wanted t see ef yuhd lemme look at tha ol catlog erwhile."

5   "Sure! You wanna see it here?"

6   "Nawsuh. Ah wans t take it home wid me. Ahll bring it back termorrow when Ah come in from the fiels."

7   "You plannin on buyin something?"

8   "Yessuh."

9   "Your ma letting you have yor own money now?"

10   "Shucks. Mistah Joe, Ahm gittin t be a man like anybody else!"

11   Joe laughed and wiped his greasy white face with a red bandanna.

12   "Whut you plannin on buyin?"

13   Dave looked at the floor, scratched his head, scratched his thigh, and smiled. Then he looked up shyly.

14   "Ahll tell yuh, Mistah Joe, ef yuh promise yuh won't tell."

15   "I promise."

16   "Waal, Ahma buy a gun."

17   "A gun? Whut you want with a gun?"

18   "Ah wanna keep it."

19   "You ain't nothing but a boy. You don't need a gun."

20   "Aw, lemme have the catlog, Mistah Joe. Ahll bring it back."

21   Joe walked through the rear door. Dave was elated. He looked around at barrels of sugar and flour. He heard Joe coming back. He craned his neck to see if he were bringing the book. Yeah, he's got it! Gawddog, he's got it!

22   "Here, but be sure you bring it back. It's the only one I got."

23   "Sho, Mistah Joe."

24   "Say, if you wanna buy a gun, why don't you buy one from me? I gotta gun to sell."

25   "Will it shoot?"

26   "Sure it'll shoot."

27   "Whut kind is it?"

28   "Oh, it's kinda old. . . . A lefthand Wheeler. A pistol. A big one."

29   "Is it got bullets in it?"

30   "It's loaded."

31   "Kin Ah see it?"

32   "Where's your money?"

33   "Whut yuh wan fer it?"

34   "I'll let you have it for two dollars."

35   "Just two dollahs? Shucks, Ah could buy tha when Ah git mah pay."

36   "I'll have it here when you want it."

37   "Awright, suh. Ah be in fer it."

38   He went through the door, hearing it slam again behind him. Ahma git some money from Ma n buy me a gun! Only two dollahs! He tucked the thick catalogue under his arm and hurried.

39   "Where yuh been, boy?" His mother held a steaming dish of black-eyed peas.

40   "Aw, Ma, Ah just stopped down the road t talk wid th boys."

41   "Yuh know bettah than t keep suppah waitin."

42   He sat down, resting the catalogue on the edge of the table.

43   "Yuh git up from there and git to the well n wash yosef! Ah ain feedin no hogs in mah house!"

44   She grabbed his shoulder and pushed him. He stumbled out of the room, then came back to get the catalogue.

45   "Whut this?"

46   "Aw, Ma, it's jusa catlog."

47   "Who yuh git it from?"

48   "From Joe, down at the sto."

49   "Waal, thas good. We kin use it around the house."

50   "Naw, Ma." He grabbed for it. "Gimme mah catlog, Ma."

51   She held onto it and glared at him.

52   "Quit hollerin at me! Whut's wrong wid yuh? Yuh crazy?"

53   "But Ma, please. It ain mine! It's Joe's! He tol me t bring it back t im termorrow."

54   She gave up the book. He stumbled down the back steps, hugging the thick book under his arm. When he had splashed water on his face and hands, he groped back to the kitchen and fumbled in a corner for the towel. He bumped into a chair; it clattered to the floor. The catalogue sprawled at his feet. When he had dried his eyes, he snatched up the book and held it again under his arm. His mother stood watching him.

55   "Now, ef yuh gonna acka fool over ol book, Ahll take it n burn it up."

56   "Naw, Ma, please."

57   "Waal, set down n be still!"

58   He sat down and drew the oil lamp close. He thumbed page after page, unaware of the food his mother set on the table. His father came in. Then his small brother.

59   "Whutcha got there, Dave?" his father asked.

60   "Jusa catlog," he answered, not looking up.

61   "Yawh, here they is!" His eyes glowed at blue and black revolvers. He glanced up, feeling sudden guilt. His father was watching him. He eased the book under the table and rested it on his knees. After the blessing was asked, he ate. He scooped up peas and swallowed fat meat without chewing. Buttermilk helped to wash it down. He did not want to mention money

before his father. he would do much better by cornering his mother when she was alone. He looked at his father uneasily out of the edge of his eye.

62 "Boy, how come yuh don quit foolin wid tha book n eat yo suppah."

63 "Yessuh."

64 "How yuh n ol man Hawkins gittin erlong?"

65 "Shuh?"

66 "Can't yuh hear. Why don yuh listen? Ah ast yuh how wuz yuh n ol man Hawkins gittin erlong?"

67 "Oh, swell, Pa. Ah plows mo lan than anybody over there."

68 "Waal, yuh oughta keep yo min on whut yuh doin."

69 "Yessuh."

70 He poured his plate full of molasses and sopped at it slowly with a dunk of cornbread. When all but his mother had left the kitchen he still sat and looked again at the guns in the catalogue. Lawd, ef Ah only had the pretty one! He could almost feel the slickness of the weapon with his fingers. If he had a gun like that he would polish it and keep it shining so it would never rust. N Ahd keep it loaded, by Gawd!

71 "Ma?"

72 "Hunh?"

73 "Ol man Hawkins give yuh mah money yit?"

74 "Yeah, but ain no usa yuh thinin bout thowin nona it erway. Ahm keepin tha money sos yuh kin have cloes t go to school this winter."

75 He rose and went to her side with the open catalogue in his palms. She was washing dishes, her head bent low over a pan. Shyly he raised the open book. When he spoke his voice was husky, faint.

76 "Ma, Gawd knows Ah wans one of these."

77 "One of whut?" she asked, not raising her eyes.

78 "One of these," he said again, not daring even to point. She glanced up at the page, then at him with wide eyes.

79 "Nigger, is yuh plum crazy?"

80 "Aw, Ma—"

81 "Git otta here! Don't yuh talk t me bout no gun! Yuh a fool!"

82 "Ma, Ah kin buy one fer two dollahs."

83 "Not ef Ah knows it yuh ain!"

84 "But yuh promised one more—"

85 "Ah don care whut Ah promised! Yuh ain nothing but a boy yit!"

86 "Ma, ef yuh lemme buy one Ahll never ast yuh fer nothing no mo."

87 "Ah tol yuh t git outta here! Yuh ain gonna toucha penny of tha money fer no gun! Thas how come Ah has Mistah Hawkins pay yo wages t me, cause Ah knows yuh ain got no sense."

88 "But Ma, we needa gun. Pa ain got no gun. We needa gun in the house. Yuh kin never tell whut might happen."

89 "Now don yuh try to maka fool outta me, boy! Ef we did hava gun yuh wouldn't have it!"

90 He laid the catalogue down and slipped his arm around her waist. "Aw,

Ma, Ah done worked hard alls summer n ain ast yuh fer nothing, is Ah, now?"

91   "Thas whut yuh spose t do!"

92   "But Ma. Ah wants a gun. Yuh kin lemme have two dollah outa mah money. Please Ma. I kin give it to Pa. . . . Please, Ma! Ah loves yuh, Ma."

93   When she spoke her voice came soft and low.

94   "What yuh wan wida gun, Dave? Yuh don need no gun. Yuhll git in trouble. N ef yo Pa just thought Ah letyuh have money t buy a gun he'd hava fit."

95   "Ahll hide it, ma. It ain but two dollahs."

96   "Lawd, chil, whuts wrong wid yuh?"

97   "Ain nothing wrong, Ma. Ahm almos a man now. Ah wants a gun."

98   "Who gonna sell yuh a gun?"

99   "Ol Joe at the sto."

100   "N it don cos but two dollahs?"

101   "Thas all, Ma. Just two dollahs. Please, Ma."

102   She was stacking the plates away; her hands moved slowly, reflectively. Dave kept an anxious silence. Finally she turned to him.

103   "Ahll let yuh git the gun ef yuh promise me one thing."

104   "Whuts tha, Ma?"

105   "Yuh bring it straight back t me, yuh hear? It'll be fer Pa."

106   "Yessum! Lemme go now, Ma."

107   She stooped, turned slightly to one side, raised the hem of her dress, rolled down the top of her stocking, and came up with a slender wad of bills.

108   "Here," she said. "Lawd knows yuh don need no gun. But yer Pa does. Yuh bring it right back t me, yuh hear. Ahma put it up. Now ef yuh don, Ahma have yuh pa lick yuh so hard yuh won ferget it."

109   "Yessum."

110   He took the money, ran down the steps, and across the yard.

111   "Dave! Yuuuuuuh Daaaaaave!"

112   He heard, but he was not going to stop now. "Naw, Lawd!"

113   The first movement he made the following morning was to reach under his pillow for the gun. In the gray light of dawn he held it loosely, feeling a sense of power. Could kill a man wida gun like this. Kill anybody, black or white. And if he were holding this gun in his hand nobody could run over him; they would have to respect him. It was a big gun, with a long barrel and a heavy handle. He raised and lowered it in his hand, marveling at its weight.

114   He had not come straight home with it as his mother had asked; instead he had stayed out in the fields, holding the weapon in his hand, aiming it now and then at some imaginary foe. But he had not fired it; he had been afraid that his father might hear. Also he was not sure he knew how to fire it.

115   To avoid surrendering the pistol he had not come into the house until he knew that all were asleep. When his mother had tiptoed to his bedside late

that night and demanded the gun, he had first played 'possum; then he had told her that the gun was hidden outdoors, that he would bring it to her in the morning. Now he lay turning it slowly in his hands. He broke it, took out the cartridges, felt them, and put them back.

116   He slid out of bed, got a long strip of flannel from a trunk, wrapped the gun in it, and tied it to his naked thigh while it was still loaded. He did not go into breakfast. Even though it was not yet daylight, he started for Jim Hawkins's plantation. Just as the sun was rising he reached the barns where the mules and plows were kept.

117   "Hey! That you, Dave?"

118   He turned. Jim Hawkins stood eyeing him suspiciously.

119   "What're yuh doing here so early?"

120   "Ah didn't know Ah wuz gittin up so early, Mistah Hawkins. Ah wuz fixing hitch up of Jenny n take her t the fiels."

121   "Good. Since you're here so early, how about plowing that stretch down by the woods?"

122   "Suits me, Mistah Hawkins."

123   "O.K. Go to it!"

124   He hitched Jenny to a plow and started across the fields. Hot dog! This was just what he wanted. If he could get down by the woods, he could shoot his gun and nobody would hear. He walked behind the plow, hearing the traces creaking, feeling the gun tied tight to his thigh.

125   When he reached the woods, he plowed two whole rows before he decided to take out the gun. Finally he stopped, looked in all directions, then untied the gun and held it his hand. He turned to the mule and smiled.

126   "Know whut this is, Jenny? Naw, yuh wouldn't know! Yuhs just ol mule! Anyhow, this is a gun, n it kin shoot, by Gawd!"

127   He held the gun at arm's length. Whut t hell, Ahma shoot this thing! He looked at Jenny again.

128   "Lissen here, Jenny! When Ah pull this ol triger Ah don wan yuh run n acka fool now."

129   Jenny stood with head down, her short ears pricked straight. Dave walked off about twenty feet, held the gun far out from him, at arm's length, and turned his head. Hell, he told himself, Ah ain afraid. The gun felt loose in his fingers; he waved it wildy for a moment. Then he shut his eyes and tightened his forefinger. Bloom! The report half-deafened him and he thought his right hand was torn from his arm. He heard Jenny whinnying and galloping over the field, and he found himself on his knees squeezing his fingers hard between his legs. His hand was numb; he jammed it into his mouth, trying to warm it, trying to stop the pain. The gun lay at his feet. He did not quite know what had happened. He stood up and stared at the gun as though it were a living thing. He gritted his teeth and kicked the gun. Yuh almos broke mah arm! He turned to look for Jenny; she was far over the fields, tossing her head and kicking wildly.

130   "Hol on there, ol mule!"

131   When he caught up with her she stood trembling, walling her big white eyes at him. The plow was far away; the traces had broken. Then Dave stopped short, looking, not believing. Jenny was bleeding. Her left side was red and wet with blood. He went closer. Lawd, have mercy! Wondah did Ah shoot this mule? He grabbed for Jenny's mane. She flinched, snorted, whirled, tossing her head.

132   "Hol on now! Hol on."

133   Then he saw the hole in Jenny's side, right between the ribs. It was round, wet, red. A crimson stream streaked down the front leg, flowing fast. Good Gawd! Ah wuzn't shootin at tha mule. He felt panic. He knew he had to stop that blood, or Jenny would bleed to death. He had never seen so much blood in all his life. He chased the mule for half a mile, trying to catch her. Finally she stopped, breathing hard, stumpy tail half arched. He caught her mane and led her back to where the plow and gun lay. Then he stooped and grabbed handfuls of damp black earth and tried to plug the bullet hole. Jenny shuddered, whinnied, and broke from him.

134   "Hol on! Hol on now!"

135   He tried to plug it again, but blood came anyhow. His fingers were hot and sticky. He rubbed dirt into his palms, trying to dry them. Then again he attempted to plug the bullet hole, but Jenny shied away, kicking her heels high. He stood helpless. He had to do something. He ran at Jenny; she dodged him. He watched a red stream of blood flow down Jenny's leg and form a bright pool at her feet.

136   "Jenny . . . Jenny . . ." he called weakly.

137   His lips trembled! She's bleeding t death! He looked in the direction of home, wanting to go back, wanting to get help. But he saw the pistol lying in the damp black clay. He had a queer feeling that if he only did something, this would not be; Jenny would not be there bleeding to death.

138   When he went to her this time, she did not move. She stood with sleepy, dreamy eyes; and when he touched her she gave a low-pitched whinny and knelt to the ground, her front knees slopping in blood.

139   "Jenny . . . Jenny . . ." he whispered.

140   For a long time she held her neck erect; then her head sank, slowly. Her ribs swelled with a mighty heave and she went over.

141   Dave's stomach felt empty. He picked up the gun and held it gingerly between his thumb and forefinger. He buried it at the foot of a tree. He took a stick and tried to cover the pool of blood with dirt but what was the use? There was Jenny lying with her mouth open and her eyes walled and glassy. He could not tell Jim Hawkins he had shot his mule. But he had to tell him something. Yeah, Ahll tell em Jenny started gittin wil n fell on the joint of the plow. . . . But that would hardly happen to a mule. He walked across the field slowly, head down.

142   It was sunset. Two of Jim Hawkins' men were over near the edge of the woods digging a hole in which to bury Jenny. Dave was surrounded by a knot of people; all of them were looking down at the dead mule.

143 "I don't see how in the world it happened," said Jim Hawkins for the tenth time.

144 The crowd parted and Dave's mother, father, and small brother pushed into the center.

145 "Where's Dave?" his mother called.

146 "There he is," said Jim Hawkins.

147 His mother grabbed him.

148 "Whut happened, Dave? Whut yuh done?"

149 "Nothing."

150 "C'mon, boy, talk," his father said.

151 Dave took a deep breath and told the story he knew nobody believed.

152 "Waal," he drawled. "Ah brung ol Jenny down here sos Ah could do mah plowin. Ah plowed bout two rows, just like yuh see." He stopped and pointed at the long rows of upturned earth. "Then something musta been wrong wid ol Jenny. She wouldn't ack right a-tall. She started sportin n kickin her heels. Ah tried to hol her, but she pulled erway, rearin n goin on. Then when the point of the plow was stickin up in the air, she swung erroun n twisted herself back on it. . . . She stuck herself n started t bleed. N fo Ah could do anything, she wuz dead."

153 "Did you ever hear of anything like that in all your life?" asked Jim Hawkins.

154 There were white and black standing in the crowd. They murmured. Dave's mother came close to him and looked hard into his face.

155 "Tell the truth, Dave," she said.

156 "Looks like a bullet hole ter me," said one man.

157 "Dave, whut yuh do wid tha gun?" his mother asked.

158 The crowd surged in, looking at him. He jammed his hands into his pockets, shook his head slowly from left to right, and backed away. His eyes were wide and painful.

159 "Did he hava gun?" asked Jim Hawkins.

160 "By Gawd, Ah tol yuh tha wuz a gunwound," said a man, slapping his thigh.

161 His father caught his shoulders and shook him till his teeth rattled.

162 "Tell whut happened, yuh rascal! Tell whut . . ."

163 Dave looked at Jenny's stiff legs and began to cry.

164 "Whut yuh do wid tha gun?" his mother asked.

165 "Come on and tell the truth," said Hawkins. "Ain't nobody going to hurt you. . . ."

166 His mother crowded close to him.

167 "Did yuh shoot tha mule, Dave?"

168 Dave cried, seeing blurred white and black faces.

169 "Ahh ddinnt gggo tt sshoooot hher. . . . Ah ssswear off Gawd Ahh ddint. . . . Ah wuz a-tryin t sssee ef the ol gggun would sshoot—"

170 "Where yuh git the gun from?" his father asked.

171 "Ah got it from Joe, at the sto."

172   "Where yuh git the money?"

173   "Ma give it t me."

174   "He kept worryin me, Bob. . . . Ah had t. . . . Ah tol im t bring the gun right back t me. . . . It was fer yuh, the gun."

175   "But how yuh happen to shoot that mule?" asked Jim Hawkins.

176   "Ah wuznt shootin at the mule, Mistah Hawkins. The gun jumped when Ah pulled the trigger. . . . N for Ah knowed anything Jenny wuz there a-bleedin."

177   Somebody in the crowd laughed. Jim Hawkins walked close to Dave and looked into his face.

178   "Well, looks like you have bought you a mule, Dave."

179   "Ah swear for Gawd, Ah didn't go t kill the mule, Mistah Hawkins!"

180   "But you killed her!"

181   All the crowd was laughing now. They stood on tiptoe and poked heads over one another's shoulders.

182   "Well, boy, looks like yuh done bought a dead mule! Hahaha!"

183   "Ain tha ershame."

184   "Hohohohoho."

185   Dave stood, head down, twisting his feet in the dirt.

186   "Well, you needn't worry about it, Bob," said Jim Hawkins to Dave's father. "Just let the boy keep on working and pay me two dollars a month."

187   "Whut yuh wan fer yo mule, Mistah Hawkins?"

188   Jim Hawkins screwed up his eyes.

189   "Fifty dollars."

190   "Whut yuh do wid tha gun?" Dave's father demanded.

191   Dave said nothing.

192   "Yuh wan me t take a tree lim n beat yuh till yuh talk!"

193   "Nawsuh!"

194   "Whut yuh do wid it?"

195   "Ah thowed it erway."

196   "Where?"

197   "Ah . . . Ah thowed it in the creek."

198   "Waal, c mon home. N firs thing in the mawnin git to tha creek n fin tha gun."

199   "Yessuh."

200   "Whut yuh pay fer it?"

201   "Two dollahs."

202   "Take tha gun n git yo money back n carry it t Mistah Hawkins, yuh hear? N don fergit Ahma lam you black bottom good fer this! Now march yosef on home, suh!"

203   Dave turned and walked slowly. He heard people laughing. Dave glared, his eyes welling with tears. Hot anger bubbled in him. Then he swallowed and stumbled on.

204   That night Dave did not sleep. He was glad that he had gotten out of killing the mule so easily, but he was hurt. Something hot seemed to turn

over inside him each time he remembered how they had laughed. He tossed on his bed, feeling his hard pillow. N Pa says he's gonna beat me. . . . He remembered other beatings, and his back quivered. Naw, naw, Ah sho don wan im t beat me tha way no mo. . . . Dam em all! Nobody ever gave him anything. All he did was work. They treat me lika mule. . . . N then they beat me. . . . He gritted his teeth. N Ma had t tell on me.

205   Well, if he had to, he would take old man Hawkins that two dollars. But that meant selling the gun. And he wanted to keep that gun. Fifty dollahs fer a dead mule.

206   He turned over, thinking how he had fired the gun. He had an itch to fire it again. Ef other men kin shoota gun, by Gawd, Ah kin! He was still listening. Mebbe they all sleepin now. . . . The house was still. He heard the soft breathing of his brother. Yes, now! He would go down an get that gun and see if he could fire it! He eased out of bed and slipped into overalls.

207   The moon was bright. He ran almost all the way to the edge of the woods. He stumbled over the ground, looking for the spot where he had buried the gun. Yeah, here it is. Like a hungry dog scratching for a bone he pawed it up. He puffed his black cheeks and blew dirt from the trigger and barrel. He broke it and found four cartridges unshot. He looked around; the fields were filled with silence and moonlight. He clutched the gun still and hard in his fingers But as soon as he wanted to pull the trigger, he shut his eyes and turned his head. Naw, Ah can't shoot wid mah eyes closed n mah head turned. With effort he held his eyes open; then he squeezed. Blooooom! He was stiff, not breathing. The gun was still in his hands. Dammit, he'd done it! He fired again. Blooooom! He smiled. Blooooom! Blooooom! Click, click. There! It was empty. If anybody could shoot a gun, he could. He put the gun into his hip pocket and started across the fields.

208   When he reached the top of a ridge he stood straight and proud in the moonlight, looking at Jim Hawkins' big white house, feeling the gun sagging in his pocket. Lawd, ef Ah had jus one mo bullet Ahd taka shot at tha house. Ahd like t scare ol man Hawkins jussa little. . . . Jussa enough t let im know Dave Sanders is a man.

209   To his left the road curved, running to the tracks of the Illinois Central. He jerked his head, listening. From far off came a faint hoooof-hoooof; hoooof-hoooof; hoooof-hoooof. . . . That's number eight. He took a swift look at Jim Hawkins' white house; he thought of Pa, of Ma, of his little brother, and the boys. He thought of the dead mule and heard hoooof-hoooof; hoooof-hoooof; hoooof-hoooof. . . . He stood rigid. Two dollahs a mont. Les see now. . . . Tha means itll take bout two years. Shucks! Ahll be dam! He started down the road, toward the tracks. Yeah, here she comes! He stood beside the track and held himself stiffly. Here she comes, erroun the ben. . . . C'mon, yuh slow poke! C mon! He had his hand on his gun; something quivered in his stomach. Then the train thundered past, the gray and brown boxcars rumbling and clinking. He gripped the gun tightly; then he jerked his hand out of his pocket. Ah betcha Bill wouldn't do it! Ah

betcha. . . . The cars slid past, steel grinding upon steel. Ahm riding yuh ternight so hep me Gawd! He was hot all over. He hesitated just a moment; then he grabbed, pulled atop of a car, and lay flat. He felt his pocket; the gun was still there. Ahead the long rails were glinting in moonlight, stretching away, away to somewhere, somewhere where he could be a man. . . .

DISCUSSION QUESTIONS

1. How did the accidental shooting of the mule change Dave's life?
2. Why did Dave's mother give him the money for the gun?
3. What is the relationship between Dave and his mother? Between Dave and his father? In your small group, discuss how his parents' actions did not teach him the maturity he so desperately wanted.

WRITING TOPICS

1. Assume you are Dave's father or mother. Write a letter to him in Chicago explaining what you believe defines a "man."
2. Have you, like Dave, ever thought of leaving home to declare your independence and adult status? In your journal, write about your feelings and what you did. Give specific examples.
3. Does owning a gun make a boy a man? Would staying home and paying off his debt for the mule's death make Dave a man? In a brief essay, contrast Dave's probable life in Chicago with the life he might have had if he had stayed home.

CHAPTER TEN

RELATIONSHIPS

External forces from society often influence relationships between men and women. During the times of slavery, for example, African-American men and women were not allowed to marry. Later, when they could legally marry, other external forces, such as racism and poverty, could tear apart a relationship that otherwise might have survived. If there is not enough money for the necessities of life (food, clothing, and shelter), people might separate from one another in order not to be a burden on those that they love. On the other hand, the same external forces that can tear apart a relationship can also act as a driving force to unite two people. For example, many slaves went against their owner's wishes and considered themselves married. Furthermore, many relationships have faced such negative forces as racism and poverty as common enemies that must be defeated through the survival of their relationship.

Besides external forces, internal forces, such as how men and women feel about themselves, can affect a relationship. If people do not have a strong sense of themsleves as individuals, the relationship can fall apart if one person is called upon to put the other person's welfare first. On the other hand, if the people in a relationship are confident about themselves as individuals, they can use this strength to help their relationships survive.

In the stories, poems, and letters in this chapter, the African-American writers illustrate the pain that racism, poverty, and ignorance can cause in a relationship. More important, they celebrate the joy and power that can come from that same relationship. These examples of strong, committed relationships serve as examples for younger generations as they try to find their way in our complex and sometimes alienating societies.

The Union of Two

Haki R. Madhubuti

Haki R. Madhubuti was born Don Luther Lee in Little Rock, Arkansas, in 1942. He was raised by his mother in Detroit, Michigan. She died when Madhubuti was sixteen, and he finished high school in Chicago. From 1960 to 1963, he served in the army. In the early 1960s, Madhubuti began writing poetry while working odd jobs. He founded the Third World Press in 1967 as a publication house for black writers. Now, Third World Press is the oldest black publishing house in the United States. Madhubuti's early books of poetry include *Black Pride* (1968), *Don't Cry, Scream* (1969), and *Book of Life* (1973). In 1973 he changed his name to Haki R. Madhubuti, which means "strong" and "precise" in Swahili. Madhubuti is currently an English professor and Director of the Gwendolyn Brooks Center at Chicago State University.

As a poet, essayist, and critic, Madhubuti uses his work to promote black culture, African-centered education, and the development of black institutions. His works include *Earthquakes and Sunrise Missions* (1984), *Killing Memories, Seeking Ancestors* (1987), *Black Men: Obsolete, Single, Dangerous?* (1990), *Why L.A. Happened: Implications of the '92 Los Angeles Rebellion* (1993), *Groundwork: New and Selected Poems of Don L. Lee/Haki R. Madhubuti, from 1966–1996* (1996), and *Million Man March/Day of Absence: A Commemorative Anthology* (1996).

For Ife and Jake

What matters is the renewing and long running kinship
seeking common mission, willing work, memory, melody, song.

marriage is an art,
created by the serious, enjoyed by the mature,
5   watered with morning and evening promises.

those who grow into love
remain anchored
like egyptian architecture and seasonal flowers.

it is afrikan that woman and man join in smile, tears, future.
it is traditional that men and women share expectations
10   celebrations, struggles.
it is legend that the nations start in the family.
it is afrikan that our circle expands.
it is wise that we believe in tomorrows, children, quality.
it is written that our vision will equal the promise.

15

so that your nation will live and tell your stories accurately,
you must be endless in your loving touch of each other,
your unification is the message,
continuance the answer.

DISCUSSION QUESTIONS

1. The speaker in the poem says "those who grow into love / remain anchored / like egyptian architecture and seasonal flowers." With a partner, analyze this simile and provide an interpretation of it.
2. To what other idea does the speaker in the poem connect the institution of marriage? Why is this connection important to African Americans?
3. What characteristics of this poem are similar to those found in folktales or stories from the oral tradition? What impact do these characteristics have on the message in the poem?

WRITING TOPICS

1. In your journal discuss how contemporary life often makes couples forget to include the positive things the speaker in the poem describes in their relationships.
2. Write a paragraph discussing what in the poem may be unique to African Americans. Contrast that with themes in the poem that are universal.

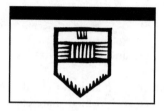

THE WIFE OF HIS YOUTH

Charles W. Chesnutt

Charles Waddell Chesnut was born in Cleveland, Ohio, in 1858 to parents of mixed race. Chesnutt and his family soon moved to Fayetteville, North Carolina, where he lived until he was twenty-five. In addition to his formal education, Chesnutt studied German, French, and Greek. He began teaching at the Howard School in Fayetteville at the age of fourteen and while still a student. Chesnutt later became the principal of the State Normal School in Fayetteville, mastered stenography, continued his literary studies on his own, and began writing short fiction. Chesnutt left the South in 1883 and became an interviewer and reporter for a Wall Street news agency. Six months later he took a position in the accounting department of a railroad company in Cleveland. Though Chesnutt had published short stories, poetry, and articles, he did not receive national attention until 1887 when the *Atlantic Monthly* published "The Goophered Grapevine." Chesnutt lived the rest of his life achieving literary fame, business success, and civic recognition. In 1928 Chesnutt was awarded the NAACP's Springarn Medal in recognition of his pioneering literary work.

As a short-story writer, novelist, and essayist, Chesnutt was one of the first African-American writers to create works that reflected a realistic and unsympathetic view of slavery and the Reconstruction. Much of his fiction focuses on the problems and prejudices of those blacks who were light enough to pass for white. Heralded as the pioneer of African-American fiction, Chesnutt did not publish any fiction after 1905. His published fiction includes *The Conjure Woman* (1899), *The Wife of His Youth* (1899), *The House behind the Cedars* (1900), *The Marrow of Tradition* (1901), and *The Colonel's Dream* (1905). Chesnutt died in 1932.

I

Mr. Ryder was going to give a ball. There were several reasons why this was an opportune time for such an event.

Mr. Ryder might aptly be called the dean of the Blue Veins. The original Blue Veins were a little society of colored persons organized in a certain Northern city shortly after the war. Its purpose was to establish and maintain correct social standards among a people whose social condition presented almost unlimited room for improvement. By accident, combined perhaps with some natural affinity, the society consisted of individuals who were, generally speaking, more white than black. Some envious outsider made the suggestion that no one was eligible for membership who was not white enough to show blue veins. The suggestion was readily adopted by those who were not of the favored few, and since that time the society, though possessing a longer and more pretentious name, had been known far and wide as the "Blue Vein Society," and its members as the "Blue Veins."

The Blue Veins did not allow that any such requirement existed for admission to their circle, but, on the contrary, declared that character and culture were the only things considered; and that if most of their members were light-colored, it was because such persons, as a rule, had had better opportunities to qualify themselves for membership. Opinions differed, too, as to the usefulness of the society. There were those who had been known to assail it violently as a glaring example of the very prejudice from which the colored race had suffered most; and later, when such critics had succeeded in getting on the inside, they had been heard to maintain with zeal and earnestness that the society was a lifeboat, an anchor, a bulwark and a shield—a pillar of cloud by day and of fire by night, to guide their people through the social wilderness. Another alleged prerequisite for Blue Vein membership was that of free birth; and while there was really no such requirement, it is doubtless true that very few of the members would have been unable to meet it if there had been. If there were one or two of the older members who had come up from the South and from slavery, their history presented enough romantic circumstances to rob their servile origin of its grosser aspects.

While there were no such tests of eligibility, it is true that the Blue Veins had their notions on these subjects, and that not all of them were equally liberal in regard to the things they collectively disclaimed. Mr. Ryder was one of the most conservative. Though he had not been among the founders of the society, but had come in some years later, his genius for social leadership was such that he had speedily become its recognized adviser and head, the custodian of its standards, and the preserver of its traditions. He shaped its social policy, was active in providing for its entertainment, and when the interest fell off, as it sometimes did, he fanned the embers until they burst again into a cheerful flame.

5   There were still other reasons for his popularity. While he was not as white as some of the Blue Veins, his appearance was such as to confer distinction upon them. His features were of a refined type, his hair was almost straight; he was always neatly dressed; his manners were irreproachable, and his morals above suspicion. He had come to Groveland a young man, and obtaining employment in the office of a railroad company as messenger had in time worked himself up to the position of stationery clerk, having charge of the distribution of the office supplies for the whole company. Although the lack of early training had hindered the orderly development of a naturally fine mind, it had not prevented him from doing a great deal of reading or from forming decidedly literary tastes. Poetry was his passion. He could repeat whole pages of the great English poets; and if his pronunciation was sometimes faulty, his eye, his voice, his gestures, would respond to the changing sentiment with a precision that revealed a poetic soul and disarmed criticism. He was economical, and had saved money; he owned and occupied a very comfortable house on a respectable street. His residence was handsomely furnished, containing among other things a good library, especially rich in poetry, a piano, and some choice engravings. He generally shared his house with some young couple, who looked after his wants and were company for him; for Mr. Ryder was a single man. In the early days of his connection with the Blue Veins he had been regarded as quite a catch, and young ladies and their mothers had manoeuvred with much ingenuity to capture him. Not, however, until Mrs. Molly Dixon visited Groveland had any woman ever made him wish to change his condition to that of a married man.

6   Mrs. Dixon had come to Groveland from Washington in the spring, and before the summer was over she had won Mr. Ryder's heart. She possessed many attractive qualities. She was much younger than he; he was old enough to have been her father, though no one knew exactly how old he was. She was whiter than he, and better educated. She had moved in the best colored society of the country, at Washington, and had taught in the schools of that city. Such a superior person had been eagerly welcomed to the Blue Vein Society, and had taken a leading part in its activities. Mr. Ryder had at first been attracted by her charms of person, for she was very good looking and not over twenty-five; then by her refined manners and the vivacity of her wit. Her husband had been a government clerk, and at his death had left a considerable life insurance. She was visiting friends in Groveland, and, finding the town and the people to her liking, had prolonged her stay indefinitely. She had not seemed displeased at Mr. Ryder's attentions, but on the contrary had given him every proper encouragement; indeed, a younger and less cautious man would long since have spoken. But he had made up his mind, and had only to determine the time when he would ask her to be his wife. He decided to give a ball in her honor, and at some time during the evening of the ball to offer her his heart and hand. He had no special fears about the outcome, but, with a little touch of romance, he wanted the surroundings to be in harmony with his own feelings when he should have received the answer he expected.

7 Mr. Ryder resolved that this ball should mark an epoch in the social history of Groveland. He knew, of course,—no one could know better,—the entertainments that had taken place in past years, and what must be done to surpass them. His ball must be worthy of the lady in which honor it was to be given, and must, by the quality of its guests, set an example for the future. He had observed of late a growing liberality, almost a laxity, in social matters, even among members of his own set, and had several times been forced to meet in a social way persons whose complexions and callings in life were hardly up to the standard which he considered proper for the society to maintain. He had a theory of his own.

8 "I have no race prejudice," he would say, "but we people of mixed blood are ground between the upper and the nether millstone. Our fate lies between absorption by the white race and extinction in the black. The one doesn't want us yet, but may take us in time. The other would welcome us, but it would be for us a backward step. 'With malice towards none, with charity for all,' we must do the best we can for ourselves and those who are to follow us. Self-presentation is the first law of nature."

9 His ball would serve by its exclusiveness to counteract leveling tendencies, and his marriage with Mrs. Dixon would help to further the upward process of absorption he had been wishing and waiting for.

II

10 The ball was to take place on Friday night. The house had been put in order, the carpets covered with canvas, the halls and stairs decorated with palms and potted plants; and in the afternoon Mr. Ryder sat on his front porch, which the shade of a vine running up over a wire netting made a cool and pleasant lounging place. He expected to respond to the toast "The Ladies" at the supper, and from a volume of Tennyson—his favorite poet— was fortifying himself with apt quotations. The volume was open at "A Dream of Fair Women." His eyes fell on these lines, and he read them aloud to judge better of their effect:—

At length I saw a lady within call,
   Stiller than chisell'd marble, standing there;
A daughter of the gods, divinely tall,
   And most divinely fair.

He marked the verse, and turning the page read the stanza beginning,—

O sweet pale Margaret,
   O rare pale Margaret.

He weighed the passage a moment, and decided that it would not do. Mrs. Dixon was the palest lady he expected at the ball, and she was of a rather ruddy complexion, and of lively disposition and buxom build. So he ran over the leaves until his eye rested on the description of Queen Guinevere:—

> She seem'd a part of joyous Spring:
> A gown of grass-green silk she wore,
> Buckled with golden clasps before;
> A light-green tuft of plumes she bore
> Closed in a golden ring.
>
> She look'd so lovely, as she sway'd
> The rein with dainty finger-tips,
> A man had given all other bliss,
> And all his worldly worth for this,
> To waste his whole heart in one kiss
> Upon her perfect lips.

11   As Mr. Ryder murmured these words audibly, with an appreciative thrill, he heard the latch of his gate click, and a light footfall sounding on the steps. He turned his head, and saw a woman standing before his door.

12   She was a little woman, not five feet tall, and proportioned to her height. Although she stood erect, and looked around her with very bright and restless eyes, she seemed quite old; for her face was crossed and recrossed with a hundred wrinkles, and around the edges of her bonnet could be seen protruding here and there a tuft of short gray wool. She wore a blue calico gown of ancient cut, a little red shawl fastened around her shoulders with an old-fashioned brass brooch, and a large bonnet profusely ornamented with faded red and yellow artificial flowers. And she was very black,—so black that her toothless gums, revealed when she opened her mouth to speak, were not red, but blue. She looked like a bit of the old plantation life, summoned up from the past by the wave of a magician's wand, as the poet's fancy had called into being the gracious shapes of which Mr. Ryder had just been reading.

13   He rose from his chair and came over to where she stood.

14   "Good-afternoon, madam," he said.

15   "Good-evenin', suh," she answered, ducking suddenly with a quaint curtsy. Her voice was shrill and piping, but softened somewhat by age. "Is dis yere whar Mistuh Ryduh lib, suh?" she asked, looking around her doubtfully, and glancing into the open windows, through which some of the preparations for the evening were visible.

16   "Yes," he replied, with an air of kindly patronage, unconsciously flattered by her manner, "I am Mr. Ryder. Did you want to see me?"

17   "Yas, suh, ef I ain't 'sturbin' of you too much."

18   "Not at all. Have a seat over here behind the vine, where it is cool. What can I do for you?"

19   "'Scuse me, suh," she continued, when she had sat down on the edge of

a chair, "'scuse me, suh, I's lookin' for my husban'. I heerd you wuz a big man an' had libbed heah a long time, an' I 'lowed you would n't min' ef I'd come roun' an' ax you ef you'd ever heer of a merlatter man by de name er Sam Taylor 'quirin' roun' in de chu'ches ermongs' de people fer his wife 'Liza Jane?"

20 Mr Ryder seemed to think for a moment.

21 "There used to be many such cases right after the war," he said, "but it has been so long that I have forgotten them. There are very few now. But tell me your story, and it may refresh my memory."

22 She sat back farther in her chair so as to be more comfortable, and folded her withered hands in her lap.

23 "My name's 'Liza," she began. "'Liza Jane. W'en I wuz young I us'ter b'long ter Marse Bob Smif, down in ole Missoura. I wuz bawn down dere. W'en I wuz a gal I wuz married ter a man named Jim. But Jim died, an' after dat I married a merlatter man named Sam Taylor. Sam wuz free-bawn, but his mammy and daddy died, an' de w' it folks 'prenticed him ter my marster fer ter work fer 'im 'tel he wuz growed up. Sam worked in de fiel', an' I wuz de cook. One day Ma'y Ann, ole miss's maid, came rushin' out ter de kitchen, an' says she, "'Liza Jane, ole marse gwine sell yo' Sam down de ribber.'

24 "'Go way f'm yere,' says I; 'my husban' 's free!'

25 "Don' make no diff'ence. I heerd ole marse tell ole miss he wuz gwine take yo' Sam 'way wid 'im ter-morrow, fer he needed money, an' he knowed whar he could git a t'ousan' dollars fer Sam an' no questions axed.'

26 "W'en Sam come home f'm de fiel' dat night, I tole him 'bout old marse gwine steal 'im, an' Sam run erway. His time wuz mos' up, an' he swo' dat w'en he wuz twenty-one he would come back an he'p me run erway, er else save up de money ter buy my freedom. An' I know he'd 'a' done it, fer he thought a heap er me, Sam did. But w'en eh come back he did n' fin' me, fer I wuz n' dere. Ole marse had heerd dat I warned Sam, so he had me whip' an' sol' down de ribber.

27 "Den de wah broke out, an' w'en it wuz ober de cullud folks wuz scattered. I went back ter de ole home; but Sam wuz n' dere, an' I could n' l'arn nuffin' 'bout 'im. But I knowed he'd be'n dere to look fer me an' had n' foun' me, an' had gone erway ter hunt fer me.

28 "I's be'n lookin' fer 'im eber sense," she added simply, as though twenty-five years were but a couple of weeks, "an' I knows he's be'n lookin' fer me. Fer he sot a heap er sto' by me, Sam did, an' I know he's be'n huntin' fer me all dese years,—'less'n he's be'n sick er sump'n, so he could n' work, er out'n his head, so he could n' 'member his promise. I went back down de ribber, fer I 'lowed he'd gone down dere lookin' fer me. I's be'n ter Noo Orleens, an 'Atlanty, an' Charleston, an' Richmon'; an' w'en I'd be'n all ober de Souf I come ter de Norf. Fer I knows I'll fin' 'im some er dese days," she added softly, "er he'll fin' me, an' den we'll bofe be as happy in freedom as we wuz in de ole days befo' de wah." A smile stole over her withered countenance as she paused a moment, and her bright eyes softened into a far-away look.

29 This was the substance of the old woman's story. She had wandered a little here and there. Mr Ryder was looking at her curiously when she finished.

30 "How have you lived all these years?" he asked.

31 "Cookin', suh. I's a good cook. Does you know anybody w'at needs a good cook, suh? I's stoppin' wid a cullud fam'ly roun' de corner yonder 'tel I kin git a place."

32 "Do you really expect to find your husband? He may be dead long ago."

33 She shook her head emphatically. "Oh no, he ain' dead. De signs an' de tokens tells me. I dremp three nights runnin' on'y dis las' week dat I foun' him."

34 "He may have married another woman. Your slave marriage would not have prevented him, for you never lived with him after the war, and without that your marriage doesn't count."

35 "Would n' make no diff'ence wid Sam. He would n' marry no yuther 'ooman 'tel he foun' out 'bout me. I knows it," she added. "Sump'n's be'n tellin' me all dese years dat I's gwine fin' Sam 'fo' I dies."

36 "Perhaps he's outgrown you, and climbed up in the world where he wouldn't care to have you find him."

37 "No, indeed, suh," she replied. "Sam ain' dat kin' er man. He wuz good ter me, Sam wuz, but he wuz n' much good ter nobody e'se, fer he wuz one er de triflin' es' han's on de plantation. I 'spec's ter haf ter suppo't 'im w'en I fin' 'im, fer he nebber would work 'less'n he had ter. But den he wuz free, an' he did n' git no pay fer his work, an' I don' blame 'im much. Mebbe he's done better sence he run erway, but I ain' 'spectin' much."

38 "You may have passed him on the street a hundred times during the twenty-five years, and not have known him; time works great changes."

39 She smiled incredulously. "I'd know 'im 'mongs' a hund'ed men. Fer dey wuz n' no yuther merlatter man like my man Sam, an' I could n' be mistook. I's toted his picture roun' wid me twenty-five years."

40 "May I see it?" asked Mr. Ryder. "It might help me to remember whether I have seen the original."

41 As she drew a small parcel from her bosom he saw that it was fastened to a string that went around her neck. Removing several wrappers, she brought to light an old-fashioned daguerreotype in a black case. He looked long and intently at the portrait. It was faded with time, but the features were still distinct, and it was easy to see what manner of man it had represented.

42 He closed the case, and with a slow movement handed it back to her.

43 "I don't know of any man in town who goes by that name," he said, "nor have I heard of any one making such inquiries. But if you will leave me your address, I will give the matter some attention, and if I find out anything I will let you know."

44 She gave him the number of a house in the neighborhood, and went away, after thanking him warmly.

45   He wrote the address on the fly-leaf of the volume of Tennyson, and, when she had gone, rose to his feet and stood looking after her curiously. As she walked down the street with mincing step, he saw several persons whom she passed turn and look back at her with a smile of kindly amusement. When she had turned the corner, he went upstairs to his bedroom, and stood for a long time before the mirror of his dressing-case, gazing thoughtfully at the reflection of his own face.

III

46   At eight o'clock the ballroom was a blaze of light and the guests had begun to assemble; for there was a literary programme and some routine business of the society to be gone through with before the dancing. A black servant in evening dress waited at the door and directed the guests to the dressing-rooms.

47   The occasion was long memorable among the colored people of the city; not alone for the dress and display, but for the high average of intelligence and culture that distinguished the gathering as a whole. There were a number of schoolteachers, several young doctors, three or four lawyers, some professional singers, an editor, a lieutenant in the United States army spending his furlough in the city, and others in various polite callings; these were colored, though most of them would not have attracted even a casual glance because of any marked difference from white people. Most of the ladies were in evening costume, and dress coats and dancing pumps were the rule among the men. A band of string music, stationed in an alcove behind a row of palms, played popular airs while the guests were gathering.

48   The dancing began at half past nine. At eleven o'clock supper was served. Mr. Ryder had left the ballroom some little time before the intermission, but reappeared at the supper-table. The spread was worthy of the occasion, and the guests did full justice to it. When the coffee had been served, the toast-master, Mr. Solomon Sadler, rapped for order. He made a brief introductory speech, complimenting host and guests, and then presented in their order the toasts of the evening. They were responded to with a very fair display of after-dinner wit.

49   "The last toast," said the toast-master, when he reached the end of the list, "is one which must appeal to us all. There is no one of us of the sterner sex who is not at some time dependent upon woman—in infancy for protection, in manhood for companionship, in old age for care and comforting. Our good host has been trying to live alone, but the fair faces I see around me to-night prove that he too is largely dependent upon the gentler sex for most that makes life worth living,—the society and love of friends,—and rumor is at fault if he does not soon yield entire subjection to one of them. Mr. Ryder will now respond to the toast,—The Ladies."

50   There was a pensive look in Mr. Ryder's eyes as he took the floor and adjusted his eyeglasses. He began by speaking of woman as the gift of

Heaven to man, and after some general observations on the relations of the sexes he said: "But perhaps the quality which most distinguishes woman is her fidelity and devotion to those she loves. History is full of examples, but has recorded none more striking than one which only today came under my notice."

51   He then related, simply but effectively, the story told by his visitor of the afternoon. He gave it in the same soft dialect, which came readily to his lips, while the company listened attentively and sympathetically. For the story had awakened a responsive thrill in many hearts. There were some present who had seen, and others who had heard their fathers and grandfathers tell, the wrongs and sufferings of this past generation, and all of them still felt, in their darker moments, the shadow hanging over them. Mr. Ryder went on:—

52   "Such devotion and confidence are rare even among women. There are many who would have searched a year, some who would have waited five years, a few who might have hoped ten years; but for twenty-five years this woman has retained her affection for and her faith in a man she has not seen or heard of in all that time.

53   "She came to me today in the hope that I might be able to help her find this long-lost husband. And when she was gone I gave my fancy rein, and imagined a case I will put to you.

54   "Suppose that this husband, soon after his escape, had learned that his wife had been sold away, and that such inquiries as he could make brought no information of her whereabouts. Suppose that he was young, and she much older than he; that he was light, and she was black; that their marriage was a slave marriage, and legally binding only if they chose to make it so after the war. Suppose, too, that he made his way to the North, as some of us have done, and there, where he had larger opportunities, had improved them, and had in the course of all these years grown to be as different from the ignorant boy who ran away from fear of slavery as the day is from the night. Suppose, even, that he had qualified himself, by industry, by thrift, and by study, to win the friendship and be considered worthy the society of such people as these I see around me tonight, gracing my board and filling my heart with gladness; for I am old enough to remember the day when such a gathering would not have been possible in this land. Suppose, too, that, as the years went by, this man's memory of the past grew more and more indistinct, until at last it was rarely, except in his dreams, that any image of this bygone period rose before his mind. And then suppose that accident should bring to his knowledge the fact that the wife of his youth, the wife he had left behind him,—not one who had walked by his side and kept pace with him in his upward struggle, but one upon whom advancing years and a laborious life had set their mark,—was alive and seeking him, but that he was absolutely safe from recognition or discovery, unless he chose to reveal himself. My friends, what would the man do? I will presume that he was one who loved honor, and tried to deal justly with all men. I will even carry the

case further, and suppose that perhaps he had set his heart upon another, whom he had hoped to call his own. What would he do, or rather what ought he to do, in such a crisis of a lifetime?

55   "It seemed to me that he might hesitate, and I imagined that I was an old friend, a near friend, and that he had come to me for advice; and I argued the case with him. I tried to discuss it impartially. After we had looked upon the matter from every point of view, I said to him, in words that we all know:—

> This above all: to thine own self be true,
> and it must follow, as the night the day,
> Thou canst not then be false to any man.

Then, finally, I put the question to him, 'Shall you acknowledge her?'

56   "And now, ladies and gentlemen, friends and companions, I ask you, what should he have done?"

57   There was something in Mr. Ryder's voice that stirred the hearts of those who sat around him. It suggested more than mere sympathy with an imaginary situation; it seemed rather in the nature of a personal appeal. It was observed, too, that his look rested more especially upon Mrs. Dixon, with a mingled expressed of renunciation and inquiry.

58   She had listened, with parted lips and streaming eyes. She was the first to speak: "He should have acknowledged her."

59   "Yes," they all echoed, "he should have acknowledged her."

60   "My friends and companions," responded Mr. Ryder, "I thank you, one and all. It is the answer I expected, for I knew your hearts."

61   He turned and walked toward the closed door of an adjoining room, while every eye followed him in wondering curiosity. He came back in a moment, leading by the hand his visitor of the afternoon, who stood startled and trembling at the sudden plunge into this scene of brilliant gayety. She was neatly dressed in gray, and wore the white cap of an elderly woman.

62   "Ladies and gentlemen," he said, "this is the woman, and I am the man, whose story I have told you. Permit me to introduce to you the wife of my youth."

DISCUSSION QUESTIONS

1. By the narrator's description, Mr. Ryder would not seem to fit exactly into the Blue Vein Society. Why has he been allowed to stay? What role does he play for the society?

2. 'Liza Jane tells Mr. Ryder that she has been searching for her husband, Sam, for more than twenty-five years. In your small group, discuss why you think 'Liza Jane has continued to search for Sam after all that time. Use specific information from the story to support your conclusions.

3. After talking with 'Liza Jane, Mr. Ryder went into his house: ". . . he went upstairs to his bedroom, and stood for a long time before the mirror of his dressing-case, gazing thoughtfully at the reflection of his own face." What were some of his thoughts as he stood in front of the mirror?

4. When Mr. Ryder introduces 'Liza Jane to the Blue Vein Society as "the wife of [his] youth," what does he lose? What does he gain?

WRITING TOPICS

1. Mr. Ryder asks the people at the party for their opinion on whether the man should acknowledge the wife of his youth. Rewrite the ending of this story so that the people at the party tell Mr. Ryder that the man should not acknowledge his wife. How do you think the story would have ended?

2. In your journal, write about a time when you knew the truth about something, but you did not tell the truth because you would have lost something you couldn't bear to lose. How did you feel afterwards? Do you still believe you made the right decision?

3. In an essay discuss the goals and purposes of the Blue Vein Society. Do these goals and purposes work toward unity within African-American society? Why or why not?

THE BEAN EATERS

Gwendolyn Brooks

Gwendolyn Brooks was born in 1917 in Topeka, Kansas. She was ridiculed in elementary school by other African-American children because of the darkness of her skin and her lack of athletic abilities. Brooks wrote poetry as an escape from intraracial prejudice. Both of her parents supported her writing, and in 1930 when she was thirteen, her poem, "Eventide" was published in *American Childhood.* During her high school years, her poetry was published in the *Chicago Defender* newspaper. Brooks corresponded with Harlem Renaissance poet James Weldon Johnson and shared some of her poetry with Langston Hughes, both of whom encouraged Brooks to continue her writing. By the time she graduated from Wilson Junior College in 1936, Brooks had written a large collection of poetry, including seventy-five poems that had been published in the *Chicago Defender.* Brooks's first poetry collection was *A Street in Bronzville,* published in 1945; it brought her national attention. In 1950, her collection *Annie Allen* won the Pulitzer Prize. Since then Brooks has continued to publish books of poetry, to conduct poetry workshops for young people, and to teach poetry at the university level. She currently teaches at Chicago State University where the Gwendolyn Brooks Center is located.

Brooks has been honored for her poetry at both national and international levels. In 1962, at the request of President John F. Kennedy, Brooks read at a Library of Congress poetry festival. In 1968 the Governor Otto Kerner of Illinois, appointed Brooks poet laureate of Illinois. In 1973 she was appointed an honorary consultant in American Letters to the Library of Congress. On January 3, 1980, she read her works at the White House with Robert Hayden and nineteen other distinguished poets. Brooks was named a poetry consultant to the Library of Congress in 1985.

Brooks's mastery of poetic techniques and themes of racial identity and equality have signaled her as one of the most distinguished American poets of the twentieth century. Her poetry forms a bridge between the academic poets of the 1940s and the black militant writers of the 1960s. She has produced a large body of works including poetry and essays. Her poetry collections include *The Bean Eaters* (1960), *In the Mecca* (1968), *Riot* (1969), *Beckoning* (1975), *Primer for Blacks* (1980), *The Near-Johannesburg Boy, and Other Poems* (1986), *Blacks* (1991), and *Report from Part Two* (1996).

They eat beans mostly, this old yellow pair.
Dinner is a casual affair.
Plain chipware on a plain and creaking wood,
Tin flatware.

5   Two who are Mostly Good.
Two who have lived their day,
But keep on putting on their clothes
And putting things away.

And remembering . . .
10 Remembering, with twinklings and twinges,
As they lean over the beans in their rented back room that
is full of beads and receipts and dolls and clothes,
tobacco crumbs, vases and fringes.

DISCUSSION QUESTIONS

1. What type of relationship does the couple have? Use specific information from the poem to support your opinion.
2. In your small group, discuss the economic situation of this couple. Refer to words and phrases from the poem.
3. What is unique about this couple? The couple's names are never given. How does this namelessness add to their uniqueness?
4. The couple's room is described as being ". . . full of beads and receipts and dolls and clothes, / tobacco crumbs, vases and fringes." What do these items tell you about the life that the couple has had together?

WRITING TOPICS

1. Reread Haki Madhubuti's "The Union of Two." In an essay, explain how the couple in "The Bean Eaters" answer the declaration about what couples must do in "The Union of Two."
2. Pretend you are elderly. In your journal, list the items you hope to have around you when you are older. Why are these items important to you? What would these items say about you to other people?

SWEAT

Zora Neale Hurston

Zora Neale Hurston was born in 1891 in Eatonville, Florida. Her father, John, was a carpenter and Baptist preacher, and her mother, Lucy, a former country school teacher. Zora Neale Hurston graduated from Morgan Academy and entered Howard University in 1918. There she studied under poet Georgia Douglas Johnson and philosophy professor Alain Locke. Hurston's first short story, "John Redding Goes to Sea" (1921), was published in *Stylus,* a Howard University literary magazine. The story brought her to the attention of sociologist Charles S. Johnson, who encouraged Hurston to move to New York City. Johnson published many of Hurston's stories in his magazine *Opportunity: A Journal of Negro Life.* Hurston was a part of the Harlem Renaissance, the black literary and cultural movement of the 1920s, along with such writers as W. E. B. Du Bois, Langston Hughes, Countee Cullen, and Claude McKay. She received a scholarship to Barnard College where she majored in anthropology, earning a B.A. degree in 1928. From 1927 to 1931, with the financial assistance of Charlotte Osgood Mason, Hurston traveled throughout the South collecting African-American folklore—stories, songs, lies, customs, superstitions, and jokes.

Hurston's first novel, *Jonah's Gourd Vine,* was published in 1934. In 1936 and 1938 Hurston received Guggenheim Fellowships to collect folklore. Throughout her life Hurston held a variety of jobs including teaching, writing for a newspaper, and housekeeping. Even with these jobs, a patron, and the publication of numerous short stories, musical reviews, and novels, Hurston was frequently without money. Hurston died in poverty and was buried in a segregated cemetery in Fort Pierce, Florida. In 1973, Alice Walker had a tombstone erected in the cemetery in honor of Hurston.

Hurston's works recorded a part of African-American culture that would have been lost had she not written them down. Her stories and novels capture the life and spirit of the common people. "Sweat" first appeared in the sole issue of *Fire!* (November 1926), a Harlem literary journal. Her other works include *Mules and Men* (1935),

Their Eyes Were Watching God (1937), *Tell My Horse* (1938), *Moses, Man of the Mountain* (1939), *Dust Tracks on the Road* (1942), *Seraph and the Suwanee* (1948), *I Love Myself When I Am Laughing . . . & Then Again When I Am Looking Mean & Impressive* (ed. Alice Walker, 1979), and *The Complete Stories by Zora Neale Hurston* (ed. Henry Louis Gates Jr. and Sieglinde Lemke, 1995). Hurston died in 1960.

I

1   It was eleven o'clock of a Spring night in Florida. It was Sunday. Any other night, Delia Jones would have been in bed for two hours by this time. But she was a washwoman, and Monday morning meant a great deal to her. So she collected the soiled clothes on Saturday when she returned the clean things. Sunday night after church, she sorted and put the white things to soak. It saved her almost a half-day's start. A great hamper in the bedroom held the clothes that she brought home. It was so much neater than a number of bundles lying around.

2   She squatted on the kitchen floor beside the great pile of clothes, sorting them into small heaps according to color, and humming a song in a mournful key, but wondering through it all where Sykes, her husband, had gone with her horse and buckboard.

3   Just then something long, round, limp and black fell upon her shoulders and slithered to the floor beside her. A great terror took hold of her. It softened her knees and dried her mouth so that it was a full minute before she could cry out or move. Then she saw that it was the big bull whip her husband like to carry when he drove.

4   She lifted her eyes to the door and saw him standing there bent over with laughter at her fright. She screamed at him.

5   "Sykes, what you throw dat whip on me like dat? You know it would skeer me—looks just like a snake, an' you knows how skeered Ah is of snakes."

6   "Course Ah knowed it! That's how come Ah done it." He slapped his leg with his hand and almost rolled on the ground in his mirth. "If you such a big fool dat you got to have a fit over a earth worm or a string, Ah don't keer how bad Ah skeer you."

7   "You ain't got no business doing it, Gawd knows it's a sin. Some day Ah'm gointuh drop dead from some of yo' foolishness. 'Nother thing, where you been wid mah rig? Ah feeds dat pony. He ain't fuh you to be drivin' wid no bull whip."

8   "You sho' is one aggravatin' nigger women!" he declared and stepped into the room. She resumed her work and did not answer him at once. "Ah

done tole you time and again to keep them white folks' clothes outa dis house."

9   He picked up the whip and glared at her. Delia went on with her work. She went out into the yard and returned with a galvanized tub and set it on the washbench. She saw that Sykes had kicked all of the clothes together again, and now stood in her way truculently, his whole manner hoping, *praying*, for an argument. But she walked calmly around him and commenced to re-sort the things.

10   "Next time, Ah'm gointer kick'em outdoors," he threatened as he struck a match along the leg of his corduroy breeches.

11   Delia never looked up from her work, and her thin, stooped shoulders sagged further.

12   "Ah ain't for no fuss t'night Sykes. Ah just come from taking sacrament at the church house."

13   He snorted scornfully. "Yeah, you just come from de church house on a Sunday night, but heah you is gone to work on them clothes. You ain't nothing but a hypocrite. One of them amen-corner Christians—sing, whoop and shout, then come home and wash white folks' clothes on the Sabbath."

14   He stepped roughly upon the whitest pile of things, kicking them helter-skelter as he crossed the room. His wife gave a little scream of dismay, and quickly gathered them together again.

15   "Sykes, you quit grindin' dirt into these clothes! How can Ah git through by Sat'day if Ah don't start on Sunday?"

16   "Ah don't keer if you never git through. Anyhow, Ah done promised Gawd and a couple of other men, Ah ain't gointer have it in mah house. Don't gimme no lip neither, else Ah'll throw'em out and put mah fist up side yo' head to boot."

17   Delia's habitual meekness seemed to slip from her shoulders like a blown scarf. She was on her feet; her poor little body, her bare knuckly hands bravely defying the strapping hulk before her.

18   "Looka heah, Sykes, you done gone too fur. Ah been married to you for fifteen years, and Ah been takin' in washin' fur fifteen years. Sweat, sweat, sweat! Work and sweat, cry and sweat, pray and sweat!"

19   "What's that got to do with me?" he asked brutally.

20   "What's it got to do with you, Sykes? Mah tub of suds is filled yo' belly with vittles more times than yo' hands is filled it. Mah sweat is done paid for this house and Ah reckon Ah kin keep on sweatin' in it."

21   She seized the iron skillet from the stove and struck a defensive pose, which act surprised him greatly, coming from her. It cowed him and he did not strike her as he usually did.

22   "Naw you won't" she panted, "that ole snaggle-toothed black woman you runnin' with ain't comin' heah to pile up on *mah* sweat and blood. You ain't paid for nothin' on this place, and Ah'm gointer stay right heah till Ah'm toted out foot foremost."

23   "Well, you better quit gittin' me riled up, else they'll be totin' you out sooner than you expect. Ah'm so tired of you Ah don't know whut to do. Gawd! How Ah hates skinny women!"

24   A little awed by this new Delia, he sidled out of the door and slammed the back gate after him. He did not say where he had gone, but she knew too well. She knew very well that he would not return until nearly daybreak also. Her work over, she went on to bed but not to sleep at once. Things had come to a pretty pass!

25   She lay awake, gazing upon the debris that cluttered their matrimonial trail. Not an image left standing along the way. Anything like flowers had long ago been drowned in the salty stream that had been pressed from her heart. Her tears, her sweat, her blood. She had brought love to the union and he had brought a longing after the flesh. Two months after the wedding, he had given her the first brutal beating. She had the memory of his numerous trips to Orlando with all of his wages when he had returned to her penniless, even before the first year had passed. She was young and soft then, but now she thought of her knotty, muscled limbs, her harsh knuckly hands, and drew herself up into an unhappy little ball in the middle of the big feather bed. Too late now to hope for love, even if it were not Bertha it would be someone else. This case different from the others only in that she was bolder than the others. Too late for everything except her little home. She had built it for her old days, and planted one by one the trees and flowers there. It was lovely to her, lovely.

26   Somehow, before sleep came, she found herself saying aloud: "Oh well, whatever goes over the Devil's back, is got to come under his belly. Sometime or ruther, Sykes, like everybody else, is gointer reap his sowing." After that she was able to build a spiritual earthworks against her husband. His shells could no longer reach her. AMEN. She went to sleep and slept until he announced his presence in bed by kicking her feet and rudely snatching the covers away.

27   "Gimme some kivah heah, an' git yo' damn foots over on yo' own side! Ah oughter mash you in you' mouf fuh drawing dat skillet on me."

28   Delia went clear to the rail without answering him. A triumphant indifference to all that he was or did.

II

29   The week was as full of work for Delia as all other weeks, and Saturday found her behind her little pony, collecting and delivering clothes.

30   It was a hot, hot day near the end of July. The village men on Joe Clarke's porch even chewed cane listlessly. They did not hurl the cane-knots as usual. They let them dribble over the edge of the porch. Even conversation had collapsed under the heat.

31   "Heah come Delia Jones," Jim Merchant said, as the shaggy pony came 'round the bend of the road toward them. The rusty buckboard was heaped with baskets of crisp, clean laundry.

32   "Yep," Joe Lindsay agreed. "Hot or col', rain or shine, jes'ez reg'lar ez de weeks roll roun' Delia carries 'em an' fetches 'em on Sat'day."

33   "She better if she wanter eat," said Moss. "Sykes Jones ain't wuth de shot an' powder hit would tek tuh kill 'em. Not to *huh* he ain't."

34   "He sho' ain't," Walter Thomas chimed in. "It's too bad, too, cause she wuz a right pretty li'l trick when he got huh. Ah'd uh mah'ied huh mahself if he hadnter beat me to it."

35   Delia nodded briefly at the men as she drove past.

36   "Too much knockin' will ruin *any*'oman. He done beat huh 'nough tuh kill three women, let 'lone change they looks," said Elijah Moseley. "How Syke kin stommuck dat big black greasy Mogul he's layin' roun' wid, gits me. Ah swear dat eight-rock couldn't kiss a sardine can Ah done thowed out de back do' 'way las' yeah."

37   "Aw, she's fat, thass how come. He's allus been crazy 'bout fat women," put in Merchant. "He'd a' been tied up wid one long time ago if he could a' found one tuh have him. Did Ah tell yuh 'bout him come sidlin' roun' mah wife—bringin' her a basket uh peecans outa his yard fuh a present? Yessir, mah wife! She tol' him tuh take 'em right straight back home, 'cause Delia works so hard ovah dat washtub she reckon everything on de place taste lak sweat an' soapsuds. Ah jus' wisht Ah's a' caught 'im 'roun' dere! Ah'd a' made his hips ketch on fiah down dat shell road."

38   "Ah know he done it, too. Ah sees 'im grinnin' at every 'oman dat passes," Walter Thomas said. "But even so, he useter eat some mighty big hunks uh humble pie tuh git dat li'l 'oman he got. She wuz ez pritty ez a speckled pup! Dat wuz fifteen years ago. He useter be so skeered uh losin' huh, she could make him do some parts of a husband's duty. Dey never wuz de same in de mind."

39   "There oughter be a law about him," said Lindsay. "He ai't fit tuh carry guts tuh a bear."

40   Clarke spoke for the first time. "Tain't no law on earth dat kin make a man be decent if it ain't in 'im. There's plenty men dat takes a wife lak dey do a joint uh sugar-cane. It's round, juicy an' sweet when dey gits it. But dey squeeze an' grind, squeeze an' grind an' wring tell dey wring every drop uh pleasure dat's in 'em out. When dey's satisfied dat dey is wrung dry, dey treats 'em jes' lak dey do a cane-chew. Dew thows 'em away. Dey knows whut dey is doin' while dey is at it, an' hates theirselves fuh it but they keeps on hangin' after huh tell she's empty. Den dey hates huh fuh bein' a cane-chew an' in de way."

41   "We oughter take Syke an' dat stray 'oman uh his'n down in Lake Howell swamp an' lay on de rawhide till they cain't say Lawd a' mussy. He allus wuz uh ovahbearin niggah, but since dat white 'oman from up north done teached 'im how to run a automobile, he done got too beggety to live—an' we oughter kill 'im," Old Man Anderson advised.

42   A grunt of approval went around the porch. But the heat was melting their civic virtue and Elijah Moseley began to bait Joe Clarke.

43　　"Come on, Joe, git a melon outa dere an' slice it up fo yo' customers. We'se all sufferin' wid de heat. De bear's done got *me!*"

44　　"Thass right, Joe, a watermelon is jes' whut Ah needs tuh cure de eppizudicks," Walter Thomas joined forces with Moseley. "Come on dere, Joe. We all is steady customers an' you ain't set us up in a long time. Ah chooses dat long, bowlegged Floridy favorite."

45　　"A god, an' be dough. You all gimme twenty cents and slice away," Clarke retorted. "Ah needs a col' slice m'self. Heah, everybody chip in. Ah'll lend y'all mah meat knife."

46　　The money was all quickly subscribed and the huge melon brought forth. At that moment, Sykes and Bertha arrived. A determined silence fell on the porch and the melon was put away again.

47　　Merchant snapped down the blade of his jacknife and moved toward the store door.

48　　"Come on in, Joe, an' gimme a slab uh sow belly an' uh pound uh coffee—almost fuhgot 'twas Sat'day. Got to git on home." Most of the men left also.

49　　Just then Delia drove past on her way home, as Sykes was ordering magnificently for Bertha. It pleased him for Delia to see.

50　　"Git whutsoever yo' heart desires, Honey. Wait a minute, Joe. Give huh two bottles uh strawberry soda-water, uh quart parched ground-peas, an' a block uh chewin' gum."

51　　With all this they left the store, with Sykes reminding Bertha that this was his town and she could have it if she wanted it.

52　　The men returned soon after they left, and held their watermelon feast.

53　　"Where did Sykes Jones git da 'oman from nohow?" Lindsay asked.

54　　"Ovah Apopka. Guess dey musta been cleanin' out de town when she lef'. She don't look lak a thing but a hunk uh liver wid hair on it."

55　　"Well, she sho' kin squall," Dave Carter contributed. "When she gits ready tuh laff, she jes' opens huh mouf an' latches it back tuh de las' notch. No ole grandpa alligator down in Lake Bell ain't got nothin' on huh."

III

56　　Bertha had been in town three months now. Sykes was still paying her roomrent at Della Lewis'—the only house in town that would have taken her in. Sykes took her frequently to Winter Park to "stomps."[1] He still assured her that he was the swellest man in the state.

57　　"Sho' you kin have dat l'l ole house soon's Ah git dat 'oman outa dere. Everythin b'longs tuh me an' you sho' kin have it. Ah sho' 'bominates uh skinny 'oman. Lawdy, you sho' is got one portly shape on you! You kin git *anything* you wants. Dis is *mah* town an' you sho' kin have it."

---

[1] *stomps:* parties.

58   Delia's work-worn knees crawled over the earth in Gethsemane and up the rocks of Calvary many, many times during these months. She avoided the villagers and meeting places in her efforts to be blind and deaf. But Bertha nullified this to a degree, by coming to Delia's house to call Sykes out to her at the gate.

59   Delia and Sykes fought all the time now with no peaceful interludes. They slept and ate in silence. Two or three times Delia had attempted a timid friendliness, but she was repulsed each time. It was plain that the breaches must remain agape.

60   The sun had burned July to August. The heat streamed down like a million hot arrows, smiting all things living upon the earth. Grass withered, leaves browned, snakes went blind in shedding and men and dogs went mad. Dog days!

61   Delia came home one day and found Sykes there before her. She wondered, but started to go on into the house without speaking, even though he was standing in the kitchen door and she must either stoop under his arm or ask him to move. He made no room for her. She noticed a soap box beside the steps, but paid no particular attention to it, knowing that he must have brought it there. As she was stooping to pass under his outstretched arm, he suddenly pushed her backward, laughingly.

62   "Look in de box dere Delia, Ah done brung yuh somethin'!"

63   She nearly fell upon the box in her stumbling, and when she saw what it held, she all but fainted outright.

64   "Syke! Syke, mah Gawd! You take dat rattlesnake 'way from heah! You *gottah*. Oh, Jesus, have mussy!"

65   "Ah ain't got tuh do nuthin' uh de kin'—fact is Ah ain't got tuh do nothin' but die. Tain't no use uh you puttin' on airs makin' out lak you skeered uh dat snake—he's gointer stay right heah tell he die. He wouldn't bite me cause Ah knows how tuh handle 'im. Nohow he wouldn't risk breakin' out his fangs 'gin *yo* skinny laigs."

66   "Naw, now Syke, don't keep dat thing 'round tryin' tuh skeer me tuh death. You knows Ah'm even feared uh earth worms. Thass de biggest snake Ah evah did see. Kill 'im Syke, please.'

67   "Doan ast me tuh do nothin' fuh yuh. Goin' 'round tryin' tuh be so damn asterperious. Naw, Ah ain't gonna kill it. Ah think uh damn sight mo' uh him dan you! Dat's a nice snake an' anybody doan lak 'im kin jes' hit de grit."

68   The village soon heard that Sykes had the snake, and came to see and ask questions.

69   "How de hen-fire did you ketch dat six-foot rattler, Syke?" Thomas asked.

70   "He's full uh frogs so he cain't hardly move, thass how Ah eased up on 'm. But Ah'm a snake charmer an' knows how tuh handle 'em. Shux, dat ain't nothin'. Ah could ketch one eve'y day if Ah so wanted tuh."

71   "Whut he needs is a heavy hick'ry club leaned real heavy on his head. Dat's de bes' way tuh charm a rattlesnake."

72   "Naw, Walt, y'all jes' don't understand dese diamon' backs lak Ah do," said Sykes in a superior tone of voice.

73   The village agreed with Walter, but the snake stayed on. His box remained by the kitchen door with its screen wire covering. Two or three days later it had digested its meal of frogs and literally came to life. It rattled at every movement in the kitchen or the yard. One day as Delia came down the kitchen steps she saw his chalky-white fangs curved like scimitars hung in the wire meshes. This time she did not run away with averted eyes as usual. She stood for a long time in the doorway in a red fury that grew bloodier for every second that she regarded the creature that was her torment.

74   That night she broached the subject as soon as Sykes sat down to the table.

75   "Syke, Ah wants you tuh take dat snake 'way fum heah. You done starved me an' Ah put up widcher, you done beat me an Ah took dat, but you done kilt all mah insides bringin' dat varmint heah."

76   Sykes poured out a saucer full of coffee and drank it deliberately before he answered her.

77   "A whole lot Ah keer 'bout how you feels inside uh out. Dat snake ain't goin' no damn wheah till Ah gits ready fuh 'im tuh go. So fur as beatin' is concerned, yuh ain't took near all dat you gointer take ef yuh stay 'round *me*."

78   Delia pushed back her plate and got up from the table. "Ah hates you, Sykes," she said calmly. "Ah hates you tuh de same degree dat Ah useter love yuh. Ah done took an' took till mah belly is full up tuh mah neck. Dat's de reason Ah got mah letter fum de church an' moved mah membership tuh Woodbridge—so Ah don't haftuh take no sacrament wid yuh. Ah don't wantuh see yuh 'round me atall. Lay 'round wid dat 'oman all yuh wants tuh, but gwan 'way fum me an' mah house. Ah hates yuh lak uh suck-egg dog."

79   Sykes almost let the huge wad of corn bread and collard greens he was chewing fall out of his mouth in amazement. He had a hard time whipping himself up to the proper fury to try to answer Delia.

80   "Well, Ah'm glad you does hate me. Ah'm sho' tiahed uh you hangin' ontuh me. Ah don't want yuh. Look at yuh stringey ole neck! Yo' rawbony laigs an' arms is enough tuh cut uh man tuh death. You looks jes' lak de devvul's doll-baby tuh *me*. You cain't hate me no worse dan Ah hates you. Ah been hatin' *you* fuh years."

81   "Yo' ole black hide don't look lak nothin' tuh me, but uh passle uh wrinkled up rubber, wid yo' big ole yeahs flappin' on each side lak uh paih uh buzzard wings. Don't think Ah'm gointuh be run 'way fum mah house neither. Ah'm goin' tuh de white folks 'bout *you,* mah young man, de very nex' time you lay yo' han's on me. Mah cup is done run ovah." Delia said this with no signs of fear and Sykes departed from the house, threatening her, but made not the slightest move to carry out any of them.

82   That night he did not return at all, and the next day being Sunday, Delia

was glad she did not have to quarrel before she hitched up her pony and drove the four miles to Woodbridge.

83 She stayed to the night service—"love feast"—which was very warm and full of spirit. In the emotional winds her domestic trials were borne far and wide so that she sang as she drove homeward,

> Jurden water, black an' col
> Chills de body, not de soul
> An' Ah wantah cross Jurden in uh calm time.

She came from the barn to the kitchen door and stopped.

84 "What's de mattah, ol' Satan, you ain't kickin' up yo' racket?" She addressed the snake's box. Complete silence. She went on into the house with new hope in its birth struggles. Perhaps her threat to go to the white folks had frightened Sykes! Perhaps he was sorry! Fifteen years of misery and suppression had brought Delia to the place where she would hope *anything* that looked towards a way over or through her wall of inhibitions.

85 She felt in the match-safe behind the stove at once for a match. There was only one there.

86 "Dat niggah wouldn't fetch nothin' heah tuh save his rotten neck, but he kin run thew whut Ah brings quick enough. Now he done toted off nigh on tuh haff uh box uh matches. He done had dat 'oman heah in mah house, too."

87 Nobody but a woman could tell how she knew this even before she struck the match. But she did and it put her into a new fury.

88 Presently she brought in the tubs to put the white things to soak. This time she decided she need not bring the hamper out of the bedroom; she would go in there and do the sorting. She picked up the pot-bellied lamp and went in. The room was small and the hamper stood hard by the foot of the white iron bed. She could sit and reach through the bedposts—resting as she worked.

89 "*Ah wantah cross Jurden in uh calm time.*" She was singing again. The mood of the "love feast" had returned. She threw back the lid of the basket almost gaily. Then, moved by both horror and terror, she sprang back toward the door. *There lay the snake in the basket!* He moved sluggishly at first, but even as she turned round and round, jumped up and down in an insanity of fear, he began to stir vigorously. She saw him pouring his awful beauty from the basket upon the bed, then she seized the lamp and ran as fast as she could to the kitchen. The wind from the open door blew out the light and the darkness added to her terror. She sped to the darkness of the yard, slamming the door after her before she thought to set down the lamp. She did not feel safe even on the ground, so she climbed up in the hay barn.

90 There for an hour or more she lay sprawled upon the hay a gibbering wreck.

91 Finally she grew quiet, and after that came coherent thought. With this stalked through her a cold, bloody rage. Hours of this. A period of intro-

spection, a space of retrospection, then a mixture of both. Out of this an awful calm.

92   "Well, Ah done de bes' Ah could. If things ain't right, Gawd knows tain't mah fault."

93   She went to sleep—a twitch sleep—and woke up to a faint gray sky. There was a loud hollow sound below. She peered out. Sykes was at the wood-pile, demolishing a wire-covered box.

94   He hurried to the kitchen door, but hung outside there some minutes before he entered, and stood some minutes more inside before he closed it after him.

95   The gray in the sky was spreading. Delia descended without fear now, and crouched beneath the low bedroom window. The drawn shade shut out the dawn, shut in the night. But the thin walls held back no sound.

96   "Dat ol' scratch is woke up now!" She mused at the tremendous whirr inside, which every woodman knows, is one of the sound illusions. The rattler is a ventriloquist. His whirr sounds to the right, to the left, straight ahead, behind, close under foot—everywhere but where it is. Woe to him who guesses wrong unless he is prepared to hold up his end of the argument! Sometimes he strikes without rattling at all.

97   Inside, Sykes heard nothing until he knocked a pot lid off the stove while trying to reach the match-safe in the dark. He had emptied his pockets at Bertha's.

98   The snake seemed to wake up under the stove and Sykes made a quick leap into the bedroom. In spite of the gin he had had, his head was clearing now.

99   "May Gawd!" he chattered, "ef Ah could on'y strack uh light!"

100   The rattling ceased for a moment as he stood paralyzed. He waited. It seemed that the snake waited also.

101   "Oh, fuh de light! Ah thought he'd be too sick"—Sykes was muttering to himself when the whirr began again, closer, right underfoot this time. Long before this, Sykes' ability to think had been flattened down to primitive instinct and he leaped—onto the bed.

102   Outside Delia heard a cry that might have come from a maddened chimpanzee, a stricken gorilla. All the terror, all the horror, all the rage that man possibly could express, without a recognizable human sound.

103   A tremendous stir inside there, another series of animal screams, the intermittent whirr of the reptile. The shade torn violently down from the window, letting in the red dawn, a huge brown hand seizing the window stick, great dull blows upon the wooden floor punctuating the gibberish of sound long after the rattle of the snake had abruptly subsided. All this Delia could see and hear from her place beneath the window, and it made her ill. She crept over to the four-o'clocks and stretched herself on the cool earth to recover.

104   She lay there. "Delia, Delia!" She could hear Sykes calling in a most despairing tone as one who expected no answer. The sun crept on up, and he called. Delia could not move—her legs had gone flabby. She never moved, he called, and the sun kept rising.

105   "Mah Gawd!" She heard him moan, "Mah Gawd fum Heben!" She heard him stumbling about and got up from her flower-bed. The sun was growing warm. As she approached the door she heard him call out hopefully, "Delia, is dat you Ah hear?"

106   She saw him on his hands and knees as soon as she reached the door. He crept an inch or two toward her—all that he was able, and she saw his horribly swollen neck and his one open eye shining with hope. A surge of pity too strong to support bore her away from that eye that must, could not, fail to see the tubs. He would see the lamp. Orlando with its doctors was too far. She could scarcely reach the chinaberry tree, where she waited in the growing heat while inside she knew the cold river was creeping up and up to extinguish that eye which must know by now that she knew.

Discussion Questions

1. Delia sweats while she earns a living washing clothes in hot water. Some townspeople say that they would not want to eat at Delia's house because the food would taste like sweat. How much "sweat" has Delia contributed to saving her marriage? What toll has this "sweat" taken on Delia's physical and mental health?

2. Delia often expresses herself through African-American folk proverbs or religious statements. Choose two of these expressions and explain how they foreshadow events in the story.

3. The townspeople all know that Sykes mistreats Delia. What unified action do they take to express their displeasure? Is this an effective action? Why or why not? What else could the townspeople have done?

4. After Sykes has been bitten by the snake, Delia hears him call her name. Why doesn't she respond to his calls for help? Since she does not respond, is Delia partly responsible for Sykes's death? Why or why not?

Writing Topics

1. Sykes scared Delia with the snake on purpose. In a journal entry, write about how that made you feel. What could Delia have done to cope both with her fears and her husband's actions?

2. Rewrite the ending of the story so that, instead of Sykes being bitten by the snake, Delia is bitten. Write a new ending to the story in which Sykes finds Delia dying in their bedroom. How would he feel? What would he say to Delia?

LETTER FROM CHARLES R. DREW

Charles R. Drew

Charles R. Drew was born in Washington, D.C., in 1904. Drew received his medical degree from McGill University in Montreal, Canada, and is best known for his pioneering work in developing the blood plasma method for preserving blood. Drew met his future wife, Lenore Robbins, in 1939; they were married the same year. He died in 1950 following an automobile accident; he was denied blood plasma by a hospital in the South because he was African American.

May 3, 1939

Dear Lenore,

1   What's the matter with your hand? Hope it's very minor. Don't write if it bothers you—but don't forget who I am.

2   Glad your soldier boy play went over so well, or is it that one?

3   I suppose I do write incoherently from time to time and fail to get the things over that I want to say but I didn't know that I had put anything into my last letter which would make you say "Frankly, I'm not sure a wife would help you." If I did I take it back.

4   May I attempt again? It's not just a wife for the sake of having a wife that's important to me Lenore. I've ducked, dodged and squirmed away from would-be wives for a long time, it's become almost an art. I don't need a wife just to have a woman,—the streets are full of them, the drawing rooms too, with feminine allure galore. Intellectual companionship may be had without marriage and there are those gentle souls who will gladly listen to the tales of trials and woe with relish, and even a rare spiritual bond may be firmly welded outside of the bounds of matrimony. Yet all of these things are a part of a harmonious wedded existance and I decry none of them. These are the things that one receives in some measure or degree.

5   When I think of you Lenore I think more largely in terms of the things I'd freely give what love there is in me unstintedly, my inner thoughts, my dearest dreams, my fondest hopes. My head strongness would listen to your council [*sic*], my fears I'd tell you, my weaknesses confess. This must sound silly but these are the things I don't do. I've walked alone it seems for so long that perhaps it's just loneliness, but it's a very specific kind of loneliness, the kind that only you, out of the many people I've met, seem capable of doing anything about. People have expected me to be strong and rather than disappoint them I've been strong, when I much rather would be weak. I'd not be ashamed to admit my weakness before you for there is no place for vanity in the presence of those we love and in the presence of those who love us, even weakness becomes strength. One must have faith in himself and go forward with a sure step but too much sureness may lead to arrogance—a word from one near and trustworthy may prevent this if the word is heeded. I feel that I could trust you always and heed you as the better part of my own conscience.

6   More than the things you'd bring to me and the small measure in which I'd be able to repay you in terms of care and devotion are the things we could do, build, dream together. Really I think I have possibilities if someone like you took the raw material in hand. A devil of a job I'll admit but if entered in the right frame of mind might keep you not too unhappily employed for years, and I'd love it.

7   When you were a little girl you must have thought of growing up some day and meeting some guy and marrying him, etc. (how many?) what was he like, what did you want to be, what did you want him to be, what would your house be like? I asked you before but you ignored me. Then you next said you didn't see how you could help. I almost dread your next letter but I'll await it with trembling knees.

Goodnight, loveliest of creatures,
Charlie

DISCUSSION QUESTIONS

1. How would you characterize Charles Drew's feelings toward Lenore?
2. What does Drew mean when he says: ". . . when I much rather would be weak"?
3. In your small group, discuss what you think Lenore's next letter might contain. What might she say about the type of prospective husband she would like?

WRITING TOPICS

1. In your journal, list those character traits you would like in a wife or husband. Then list those traits your husband or wife would like about you.
2. "One must have faith in himself and go forward with a sure step but too much sureness may lead to arrogance. . . ." Write an analytical essay in which you interpret what this statement means. Use examples from your reading, history, or from personal experience.
3. Write a letter to someone you admire. It may or may not be someone you know personally. Using Drew's letter as a model, tell that person what you admire about him or her.

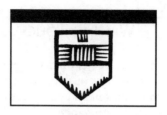

1927
FROM *SULA*

Toni Morrison

Toni Morrison was born Chole Anthony Wofford in Lorion, Ohio, in 1934. She attended Howard University, where she changed her name to Toni because Chole was hard to pronounce. She received her M.A. from Cornell University in 1955. Two years later she married Harold Morrison, a Jamaican architect. After their divorce six years later, Morrison worked as an editor for Random House. While working at Random House, she began her first novel, *The Bluest Eye* (1970). During the next seven years, two more of her novels, *Sula* (1973) and *Song of Solomon* (1977), were published. *Song of Solomon* won both the National Book Critic's Circle Award and the American Academy and Institute of Arts and Letters Award in 1977.

Morrison has served on numerous prestigious committees and won many national and international awards. In 1980, President Jimmy Carter appointed Morrison to the National Council on the Arts. She is a member of the American Academy and Institute of Arts and Letters. In 1993, Morrison became the first African-American woman to win the Nobel Prize for literature. She has taught at several universities, including Howard, Yale, Harvard, and Princeton.

Morrison's novels examine racial, gender, and identity conflicts. A poignant storytelling style and poetic language grace all of her novels, including *Tar Baby* (1981) and *Jazz* (1992). Her novel *Beloved* (1988) won the 1988 Pulitzer Prize. As a literary and social critic, Morrison has written texts that examine the creation of American literature, *Playing in the Dark: Whiteness and the Literary Imagination* (1992) and the impact of the Anita Hill/Clarence Thomas Senate hearings, *Race-ing Justice, En-gendering Power: Essays on Anita Hill, Clarence Thomas, and the Construction of Social Reality* (1992).

1   Old people were dancing with little children. Young boys with their sisters, and the church women who frowned on any bodily expression of joy (except when the hand of God commanded it) tapped their feet. Somebody (the groom's father, everybody said) had poured a whole pint jar of cane liquor into the punch, so even the men who did not sneak out the back door to have a shot, as well as the women who let nothing stronger than Black Draught enter their blood, were tipsy. A small boy stood at the Victrola turning its handle and smiling at the sound of Bert Williams' "Save a Little Dram for Me."

2   Even Helene Wright had mellowed with the cane, waving away apologies for drinks spilled on her rug and paying no attention whatever to the chocolate cake lying in the arm of her red-velvet sofa. The tea roses above her left breast had slipped from the brooch that fastened them and were hanging heads down. When her husband called her attention to the children wrapping themsleves into her curtains, she merely smiled and said, "Oh, let them be." She was not only a little drunk, she was weary and had been for weeks. Her only child's wedding—the culmination of all she had been, thought or done in this world—had dragged from her energy and stamina even she did not know she possessed. Her house had to be thoroughly cleaned, chickens had to be plucked, cakes and pies made, and for weeks she, her friends and her daughter had been sewing. Now it was all happening and it took only a little cane juice to snap the cords of fatigue and damn the white curtains that she had pinned on the stretcher only the morning before. Once this day was over she would have a lifetime to rattle around in that house and repair the damage.

3   A real wedding, in church, with a real reception afterward, was rare among the people of the Bottom. Expensive for one thing, and most newlyweds just went to the courthouse if they were not particular, or had the preacher come in and say a few words if they were. The rest just "took up" with one another. No invitations were sent. There was no need for that formality. Folks just came, bringing a gift if they had one, none if they didn't. Except for those who worked in valley houses, most of them had never been to a big wedding; they simply assumed it was rather like a funeral except afterward you didn't have to walk all the way out to Beechnut Cemetery.

4   This wedding offered a special attraction, for the bridegroom was a handsome, well-liked man—the tenor of Mount Zion's Men's Quartet, who had an enviable reputation among the girls and a comfortable one among men. His name was Jude Greene, and with the pick of some eight or ten girls who came regularly to services to hear him sing, he had chosen Nel Wright.

5   He wasn't really aiming to get married. He was twenty then, and although his job as a waiter at the Hotel Medallion was a blessing to his parents and their seven other children, it wasn't nearly enough to support a wife. He had brought the subject up first on the day the word got out that the town was building a new road, tarmac, that would wind through Medallion on down to the river, where a great new bridge was to be built to connect Medallion to Porter's Landing, the town on the other side. The war over, a fake prosperity was still around. In a state of euphoria, with a hunger

for more and more, the council of founders cast its eye toward a future that would certainly include trade from cross-river towns. Towns that needed-more than a house raft to get to the merchants of Medallion. Work had already begun on the New River Road (the city had always meant to name it something else, something wonderful, but ten years later when the bridge idea was dropped for a tunnel it was still called the New River Road).

6   Along with a few other young black men, Jude had gone down to the shack where they were hiring. Three old colored men had already been hired, but not for the road work, just to do the picking up, food bringing and other small errands. These old men were close to feeble, not good for much else, and everybody was pleased they were taken on; still it was a shame to see those white men laughing with the grandfathers but shying away from the young black men who could tear that road up. The men like Jude who could do real work. Jude himself longed more than anybody else to be taken. Not just for the good money, more for the work itself. He wanted to swing the pick or kneel down with the string or shovel the gravel. His arms ached for something heavier than trays, for something dirtier than peelings; his feet wanted the heavy work shoes, not the thin-soled black shoes that the hotel required. More than anything he wanted the camaraderie of the road men: the lunch buckets, the hollering, the body movement that in the end produced something real, something he could point to. "I built that road," he could say. How much better sundown would be than the end of a day in the restaurant, where a good day's work was marked by the number of dirty plates and the weight of the garbage bin. "I built that road." People would walk over his sweat for years. Perhaps a sledge hammer would come crashing down on his foot, and when people asked him how come he limped, he could say, "Got that building the New Road."

7   It was while he was full of such dreams, his body already feeling the rough work clothes, his hands already curved to the pick handle, that he spoke to Nel about getting married. She seemed receptive but hardly anxious. It was after he stood in lines for six days running and saw the gang boss pick out thin-armed white boys from the Virginia hills and the bull-necked Greeks and Italians and heard over and over, "Nothing else today. Come back tomorrow," that he got the message. So it was rage, rage and a determination to take on a man's role anyhow that made him press Nel about settling down. He needed some of his appetites filled, some posture of adulthood recognized, but mostly he wanted someone to care about his hurt, to care very deeply. Deep enough to hold him, deep enough to rock him, deep enough to ask, "How you feel? You all right? Want some coffee?" And if he were to be a man, that someone could no longer be his mother. He chose the girl who had always been kind, who had never seemed hell-bent to marry, who made the whole venture seem like his idea, his conquest.

8   The more he thought about marriage, the more attractive it became. Whatever his fortune, whatever the cut of his garment, there would always be the hem—the tuck and fold that hid his raveling edges; a someone sweet,

industrious and loyal to shore him up. And in return he would shelter her, love her, grow old with her. Without that someone he was a waiter hanging around a kitchen like a woman. With her he was head of a household pinned to an unsatisfactory job out of necessity. The two of them together would make one Jude.

9   His fears lest his burst dream of road building discourage her were never realized. Nel's indifference to his hints about marriage disappeared altogether when she discovered his pain. Jude could see himself taking shape in her eyes. She actually wanted to help, to soothe, and was it true what Ajax said in the Time and a Half Pool Hall? That "all they want, man, is they own misery. Ax em to die for you and they yours for life."

10   Whether he was accurate in general, Ajax was right about Nel. Except for an occasional leadership role with Sula, she had no aggression. Her parents had succeeded in rubbing down to a dull glow any sparkle or splutter she had. Only with Sula did that quality have free reign, but their friendship was so close, they themselves had difficulty distinguishing one's thoughts from the other's. During all of her girlhood the only respite Nel had had from her stern and undemonstrative parents was Sula. When Jude began to hover around, she was flattered—all the girls liked him—and Sula made the enjoyment of his attentions keener simply because she seemed always to want Nel to shine. They never quarreled, those two, the way some girlfriends did over boys, or competed against each other for them. In those days a compliment to one was a compliment to the other and cruelty to one was a challenge to the other.

11   Nel's response to Jude's shame and anger selected her away from Sula. And greater than her friendship was this new feeling of being needed by someone who saw her singly. She didn't even know she had a neck until Jude remarked on it, or that her smile was anything but the spreading of her lips until he saw it as a small miracle.

12   Sula was no less excited about the wedding. She thought it was the perfect thing to do following their graduation from general school. She wanted to be the bridesmaid. No others. And she encouraged Mrs. Wright to go all out, even to borrowing Eva's punch bowl. In fact, she handled most of the details very efficiently, capitalizing on the fact that most people were anxious to please her since she had lost her mamma only a few years back and they still remembered the agony in Hannah's face and the blood on Eva's.

13   So they danced up in the Bottom on the second Saturday in June, danced at the wedding where everybody realized for the first time that except for their magnificent teeth, the deweys would never grow. They had been forty-eight inches tall for years now, and while their size was unusual it was not unheard of. The realization was based on the fact that they remained boys in mind. Mischievous, cunning, private and completely unhousebroken, their games and interests had not changed since Hannah had them all put into the first grade together.

14   Nel and Jude, who had been the stars all during the wedding, were

forgotten finally as the reception melted into a dance, a feed, a gossip session, a playground and a love nest. For the first time that day they relaxed and looked at each other, and liked what they saw. They began to dance, pressed in among the others, and each one turned his thoughts to the night that was coming on fast. They had taken a housekeeping room with one of Jude's aunts (over the protest of Mrs. Wright, who had rooms to spare, but Nel didn't want to make love to her husband in her mother's house) and were getting restless to go there.

15   As if reading her thoughts, Jude leaned down and whispered, "Me too." Nel smiled and rested her cheek on his shoulder. The veil she wore was too heavy to allow her to feel the core of the kiss he pressed on her head. When she raised her eyes to him for one more look of reassurance, she saw through the open door a slim figure in blue, gliding, with just a hint of a strut, down the path toward the road. One hand was pressed to the head to hold down the large hat against the warm June breeze. Even from the rear Nel could tell that it was Sula and that she was smiling; that something deep down in that litheness was amused. It would be ten years before they saw each other again, and their meeting would be thick with birds.

DISCUSSION QUESTIONS

1. Describe Nel and Sula's relationship. Use specific examples from the chapter to support your responses.
2. Why was it important for Jude to marry? What would marriage give him?
3. Was Jude in love with Nel? What does this statement say about Jude's view of his relationship with Nel: "Whatever his fortune, whatever the cut of his garment, there would always be the hem—the tuck and fold that hid his raveling edges; a someone sweet, industrious and loyal to shore him up"?
4. What is the community's reaction to the marriage of Nel and Jude? By marrying, how have Nel and Jude fit the roles the community has established for men and women?

WRITING TOPICS

1. In your journal write a paragraph that describes what you think will happen in Nel and Jude's lives ten years after they are married.
2. Select two other stories or poems in this book that portray married couples. What qualities do Nel and Jude share or not share with the protagonists and/or personas in the other works?

VALENTINES

Henry Dumas

Henry Dumas was born in Sweet Home, Arkansas, in 1934 and migrated to Harlem when he was ten years old. He attended City College and Rutgers University. In 1953 he entered the Air Force and served four years. After his discharge in 1957, he became active in the civil rights movement. Dumas supported his wife and two children while writing poetry, short fiction, and an unfinished novel.

Dumas's work represents one of the original African-American voices of the 1960s. His posthumously published work was edited by Eugene B. Redmond and Hale Charfield. Dumas's works include *Ark of Bones and Other Stories* (1970), *Play Ebony: Play Ivory* (1974), and the unfinished novel *Jonah and the Green Stone* (1976), and *Goodbye Sweetwater: New and Selected Stories* (1988). He did not live to see any of his work published. In 1969 he was killed by a police officer on a subway platform in what was later determined to be a case of mistaken identity.

Forgive me if I have not sent you
a valentine
but I thought you knew
that you already have my heart
5 Here take the space where my
heart goes
I give that to you too

Discussion Questions

1. Select two lines from the poem that could be interpreted as an apology. Discuss how these two lines are an effective way to apologize without using the word "sorry."
2. Discuss the words, phrases, and lines that make this a love poem.

Writing Topics

1. In an essay compare the method and sincerity of the apology in "Valentines" with Ntozake Shange's "one thing i dont need."
2. Creating a love poem that is only seven lines long can be difficult. In your journal, try creating a love poem for a special person, place, or pet using only seven lines.

THANK YOU, M'AM

Langston Hughes

Biographical information about Langston Hughes can be found on pages 91, 133, 192, and 385.

1   She was a large woman with a large purse that had everything in it but a hammer and nails. It had a long strap, and she carried it slung across her shoulder. It was about eleven o'clock at night, dark, and she was walking alone, when a boy ran up behind her and tried to snatch her purse. The strap broke with the sudden single tug the boy gave it from behind. But the boy's weight and the weight of the purse combined caused him to lose his balance. Instead of taking off full blast as he had hoped, the boy fell on his back on the sidewalk and his legs flew up. The large woman simply turned around and kicked him right square in his blue-jeaned sitter. Then she reached down, picked the boy up by his shirt front, and shook him until his teeth rattled.

2   After that the woman said, "Pick up my pocketbook, boy, and give it here."

3   She still held him tightly. But she bent down enough to permit him to stoop and pick up her purse. Then she said, "Now ain't you ashamed of yourself?"

4   Firmly gripped by his shirt front, the boy said, "Yes'm."

5   The woman said, "What did you want to do it for?"

6   The boy said, "I didn't aim to."

7   She said, "You a lie!"

8   By that time two or three people passed, stopped, turned to look, and some stood watching.

9   "If I turn you loose, will you run?" asked the woman.

10   "Yes'm," said the boy.

11   "Then I won't turn you loose," said the woman. She did not release him.

12   "Lady, I'm sorry," whispered the boy.

13   "Um-hum! Your face is dirty. I got a great mind to wash your face for you. Ain't you got nobody home to tell you to wash your face?"

14 "No'm," said the boy.

15 "Then it will get washed this evening," said the large woman, starting up the street, dragging the frightened boy behind her.

16 He looked as if he were fourteen or fifteen, frail and willow-wild, in tennis shoes and blue jeans.

17 The woman said, "You ought to be my son. I would teach you right from wrong. Least I can do right now is to wash your face. Are you hungry?"

18 "No'm," said the being-dragged boy. "I just want you to turn me loose."

19 "Was I bothering you when I turned that corner?" asked the woman.

20 "No'm."

21 "But you put yourself in contact with *me*," said the woman. "If you think that that contact is not going to last awhile you got another thought coming. When I get through with you, sir, you are going to remember Mrs. Luella Bates Washington Jones."

22 Sweat popped out on the boy's face and he began to struggle. Mrs. Jones stopped, jerked him around in front of her, put a half nelson about his neck, and continued to drag him up the street. When she got to her door, she dragged the boy inside, down a hall, and into a large kitchenette-furnished room at the rear of the house. She switched on the light and left the door open. The boy could hear other roomers laughing and talking in the large house. Some of their doors were open, too, so he knew he and the woman were not alone. The woman still had him by the neck in the middle of her room.

23 She said, "What is your name?"

24 "Roger," answered the boy.

25 "Then, Roger, you go to that sink and wash your face," said the woman, whereupon she turned him loose—at last. Roger looked at the door— looked at the woman—looked at the door—*and went to the sink.*

26 "Let the water run till it gets warm," she said. "Here's a clean towel."

27 "You gonna take me to jail?" asked the boy, bending over the sink.

28 "Not with that face, I would not take you nowhere," said the woman. "Here I am trying to get home to cook me a bite to eat, and you snatch my pocketbook! Maybe you ain't been to your supper either, late as it be. Have you?"

29 "There's nobody home at my house," said the boy.

30 "Then we'll eat," said the woman. "I believe you're hungry—or been hungry—to try to snatch my pocketbook!"

31 "I want a pair of blue suede shoes," said the boy.

32 "Well, you didn't have to snatch *my* pocketbook to get some suede shoes," said Mrs. Luella Bates Washington Jones. "You could of asked me."

33 "Ma'am?"

34 The water dripping from his face, the boy looked at her. There was a long pause. A very long pause. After he had dried his face, and not knowing what else to do, dried it again, the boy turned around, wondering what next. The door was open. He could make a dash for it down the hall. He could run, run, run, *run!*

35   The woman was sitting on the daybed. After a while she said, "I were young once and I wanted things I could not get."

36   There was another long pause. The boy's mouth opened. Then he frowned, not knowing he frowned.

37   The woman said, "Um-humm! You thought I was going to say *but,* didn't you? You thought I was going to say, *but I didn't snatch people's pocketbooks.* Well, I wasn't going to say that." Pause. Silence. "I have done things, too, which I would not tell you, son—neither tell God, if He didn't already know. Everybody's got something in common. So you set down while I fix us something to eat. You might run that comb through your hair so you will look presentable."

38   In another corner of the room behind a screen was a gas plate and an icebox. Mrs. Jones got up and went behind the screen. The woman did not watch the boy to see if he was going to run now, nor did she watch her purse, which she left behind her on the daybed. But the boy took care to sit on the far side of the room, away from the purse, where he thought she could easily see him out of the corner of her eye if she wanted to. He did not trust the woman *not* to trust him. And he did not want to be mistrusted now.

39   "Do you need somebody to go to the store," asked the boy, "maybe to get some milk or something?"

40   "Don't believe I do," said the woman, "unless you just want sweet milk yourself. I was going to make cocoa out of this canned milk I got here."

41   "That will be fine," said the boy.

42   She heated some lima beans and ham she had in the icebox, made the cocoa, and set the table. The woman did not ask the boy anything about where he lived, or his folks, or anything else that would embarrass him. Instead, as they ate, she told him about her job in a hotel beauty shop that stayed open late, what the work was like, and how all kinds of women came in and out, blondes, redheads, and Spanish. Then she cut him a half of her ten-cent cake.

43   "Eat some more, son," she said.

44   When they were finished eating, she got up and said, "Now here, take this ten dollars and buy yourself some blue suede shoes. And next time, do not make the mistake of latching onto *my* pocketbook *nor nobody else's*—because shoes got by devilish ways will burn your feet. I got to get my rest now. But from here on in, son, I hope you will behave yourself."

45   She led him down the hall to the front door and opened it. "Goodnight! Behave yourself, boy!" she said, looking out into the street as he went down the steps.

46   The boy wanted to say something other than, "Thank you, m'am," to Mrs. Luella Bates Washington Jones, but although his lips moved, he couldn't even say that as he turned at the foot of the barren stoop and looked up at the large woman in the door. Then she shut the door.

DISCUSSION QUESTIONS

1. What kind of person was Mrs. Washington Jones? In your small group, describe her personality and her physical presence.
2. Mrs. Washington Jones said she had done things that she would not tell anyone else. Do you think some of the things she would not tell helped her relate to Roger? Why or why not?
3. Roger wanted to say something else other than, "Thank you, m'am." What else do you think he might have said to Mrs. Washington Jones?

WRITING TOPICS

1. For many years, it was not uncommon for African-American children in small and large communities to be disciplined by adults other than their parents. These "other" adults were called extended family members. Write a short essay in which you describe how you or someone whom you know was disciplined by someone other than their parents.
2. ". . . shoes got by devilish ways will burn your feet," says Mrs. Washington Jones. Write an analytical essay in which you interpret what she means by this statement.
3. Could this story have ended differently? Could it have had a happier ending? Sadder? Choose one or the other and write a different ending to the story.

CHAPTER ELEVEN

FAMILY AND ANCESTORS

When people know the history of their ancestors and culture, it allows them to celebrate the positive aspects, and it keeps them from repeating the negative. Many of the African cultures placed emphasis on their ancestors and their families. When Africans were brought to this country as slaves, they passed down names of ancestors, traditions in their cultures, and the songs and stories that captured the soul of their cultures to their children and their children's children. Remnants of these precious pieces of history are still being passed on in African-American families.

Most African Americans do not currently celebrate their ancestors or culture in the same way they were celebrated in Africa. Still, African Americans do recognize the importance of their ancestors—the people (family and others) who made it possible for them to live the lives they enjoy today. Many African-American families include several generations living in the same house; others include siblings or cousins or other various combinations of family and friends living together. Similarly, African Americans recognize not only the importance of their African culture (through African names and clothing), but also their African-American culture. For example, in the mid-1960s Kwanzaa originated as a cultural idea and as a unique American holiday to recognize and to strengthen the bonds of family, community, and African tradition.

In this chapter, African-American writers illustrate in stories and poems that, as we live our lives in a fragmented and impersonal world, we can draw inspiration and learn lessons from the hardships and successes of our ancestors and families. These writers also prove that our connections to those around us and to our ancestors is one major factor in the survival of African Americans and their culture.

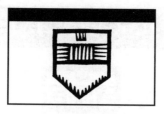

FOR MY PEOPLE

Margaret Walker

Margaret Walker was born in Birmingham, Alabama, to the Reverend Sigismund C. Walker and Marion Dozier Walker in 1915. She was graduated from Northwestern University. Early in her life, she was introduced to classic literature, both English and American, and she was profoundly influenced by Langston Hughes.

Her first book of poetry, *For My People*, published in 1942, began her career. She published two other volumes of poetry, *Prophets for a New Day* (1970) and *October Journey* (1973), as well as a historical novel, *Jubilee* (1966), and a collection of essays, *How I Wrote Jubilee and Other Essays on Life and Literature*. She also assisted her friend, Richard Wright, with the research for *Native Son*.

1   For my people everywhere singing their slave songs repeatedly: their dirges and their ditties and their blues and jubilees, praying their prayers nightly to an unknown god, bending their knees humbly to an unseen power;

2   For my people lending their strength to the years, to the gone years and the now years and the maybe years, washing ironing cooking scrubbing sewing mending hoeing plowing digging planting pruning patching dragging along never gaining never reaping never knowing and never understanding;

3   For my playmates in the clay and dust and sand of Alabama backyards playing baptizing and preaching and doctor and jail and soldier and school and mama and cooking and playhouse and concert and store and hair and Miss Choomby and company;

4   For the cramped bewildered years we went to school to learn to know the reasons why and the answers to and the people who and the places where and the days when, in memory of the bitter hours when we discovered

we were black and poor and small and different and nobody cared and nobody wondered and nobody understood;

5 For the boys and girls who grew in spite of these things to be man and woman, to laugh and dance and sing and play and drink their wine and religion and success, to marry their playmates and bear children and then die of consumption and anemia and lynching;

6 For my people thronging 47th Street in Chicago and Lenox Avenue in New York and Rampart Street in New Orleans, lost disinherited dispossessed and happy people filling the cabarets and taverns and other people's pockets needing bread and shoes and milk and land and money and something—something all our own;

7 For my people walking blindly spreading joy, losing time being lazy, sleeping when hungry, shouting when burdened, drinking when hopeless, tied and shackled and tangled among ourselves by the unseen creatures who tower over us omnisciently and laugh;

8 For my people blundering and groping and floundering in the dark of churches and schools and clubs and societies, associations and councils and committees and conventions, distressed and disturbed and deceived and devoured by money-hungry glory-craving leeches, preyed on by facile force of state and fad and novelty, by false prophet and holy believer;

9 For my people standing staring trying to fashion a better way from confusion, from hypocrisy and misunderstanding, trying to fashion a world that will hold all the people, all the faces, all the adams and eves and their countless generations;

10 Let a new earth rise. Let another world be born. Let a bloody peace be written in the sky. Let a second generation full of courage issue forth; let a people loving freedom come to growth. Let a beauty full of healing and a strength of final clenching be the pulsing in our spirits and our blood. Let the martial songs be written, let the dirges disappear. Let a race of men now rise and take control.

Discussion Questions

1. In the sixth stanza, Walker talks about the dispossessed, lost, and disinherited. About whom is she speaking? Do you agree with her description of these people?

2. How would you describe stanza nine? What is the poet's attitude toward her people?
3. In your small group, discuss what you think this poem means.

WRITING TOPICS

1. Walker says: "Let a second generation full of courage issue forth; let a people loving freedom come to growth." Write an essay in which you explain the meaning of this quotation.
2. ". . . standing staring trying to fashion a better way from confusion." In your journal, write a short explanation of what you think the poet is saying.
3. In a journal entry, list some descriptive adjectives that characterize the poem.

A DAY LOST IS A DAY GONE FOREVER

Dorothy West

Dorothy West was born in Boston, Massachusetts, in 1907, the only child of Rachel Pease Benson and Isaac Christopher West. She graduated from the prestigious Girls' Latin School in 1923 and attended Boston University and Columbia University School of Journalism. In the late 1920s she moved to New York and became a part of the great African-American literary movement known as the Harlem Renaissance. West became editor of the literary magazine *Challenge,* and later *New Challenge* magazine. She also worked as a welfare investigator and with the Federal Writers Project of the Works Progress Administration (WPA). West's family was among the first African Americans to purchase a summer vacation home on Martha's Vineyard, a location that plays a large part in her writings. She became a year-round resident in 1945.

1   There came a day in these later years of my life when I entered the hospital as an inpatient for the first time, with an operation scheduled for the next morning. Once various forms were signed, I was separated from my free will, led down the corridors into a room which was now to be the boundary of my existence, told to surrender my clothes, handed that comic invention, the hospital gown, and sent to bed in broad daylight like a child being stripped of her privileges.

2   In this unflattering way so ended my charmed existence of never having anything wrong with me that required a surgeon's knife. I trusted the surgeon's skills. His reputation confirmed his excellence. When we met in his office for the first time, there was a mutual liking. When his examination corroborated my doctor's opinion that surgery was advisable, I accepted the wisdom of that. The operation was said to be routine. There was no foreseeable reason for anything to go wrong.

3   Nevertheless there was an undercurrent of fear in me that I did not let show. It was not the surgery that I dreaded. It was the anesthesia, the settling

into a long sleep with no fixed limitation. Suppose I couldn't wake up. Suppose my vital signs diminished. There, like my mother before me, I would lie between two worlds, the one I knew and fiercely treasured, and one in whose ranks I had no wish to be included.

4   It seemed to me that I was awake all night, remembering my mother and the hours of her dying, and knowing that, in my state of surrender, I too would have no strength to break death's hold. And for me there would be no unseen force to reach out in resurrection.

5   I must have slept a little, for the nurse had to wake me to prepare me for the stretcher, which was presently rolling me along the busy corridors to the operating area. It felt very strange to be exposed to so many disinterested eyes.

6   On my arrival a doctor appeared and introduced himself to me as my anesthetist. Both of us made graceful small talk to ease this sudden intimacy of strangers. Then he was ready to put me under. I closed my eyes and tried to blot out of my mind the recurring image of my mother that had so unsettled my night. Then suddenly I was enveloped in nothingness and the remembering stopped.

7   My operation was a success from start to suture. I wakened in due time, back in my room, not even remembering at first that I had ever left it. For there was no aftermath of pain, no feeling that death had stood close by. It had not been my bitter inheritance to suffer my mother's unrelenting sleep that propelled her hour by doomed hour toward the hell of dying for no reason that made sense.

8   The hospital had gone on alert. The good doctors and the good nurses were rushing back and forth, trying everything their training had taught them to make my mother live.

9   Until the day before her operation when she was signed in at the hospital, my mother, like me, had never been an inpatient. If she thought about hospitals at all, I suspect she thought of them as way stops for the elderly on their way to heaven. And she was in no hurry. She had a love affair with life. There was nothing more beautiful to her than a child, a flower, a summer's day, a friend. On the other hand heaven was an unknown risk.

10   The change in the pattern of her days came on an innocent winter morning when she was in the backyard feeding the birds. In a moment of inattention she tripped over a stone and fell. She picked herself up, continued to scatter seed for the birds who fed on the ground, then filled the hanging feeders for those birds who preferred to feast above ground and not have to be on constant watch for the neighborhood cats.

11   When she returned to the house, wisdom told her to call her doctor. The jolt of her fall had loosened a pain inside her more intense than the soreness of her surface bruises. I think she had felt warnings of that pain before, but not to that extent of hurting, and she had pushed it out of her mind, testing the theory that mind could overcome matter.

12   The doctor came and examined her. He knew her essential strength of

mind and body. He did not mince words. He told her he was going to admit her to the hospital immediately for an operation that all signs seemed to indicate was imperative. It was all so sudden that I forgot, as did she, a tale that she had told me more than once about a frightening experience she had gone through when she was eighteen. To us both my mother in her sixties was so far distant from that girl in Springfield that she did not enter our thinking.

13   It was only when my mother was in the agony of dying and her death began to invade my own body, turning my flesh to ice, that I remembered the story.

14   When my mother was eighteen, with radiant health and a head full of dreams of a long and happy life, a tooth began to give her trouble. When home remedies were of no help and the pain persisted, she made an appointment with a dentist, who, upon examination, advised her that the tooth should be extracted.

15   She had no concern except the hope that it would cost no more than she had in her purse. When she was seated in the chair ether was administered, her eyes closed, the numbness set in, and the extraction began and ended as expected. So it appeared until the dentist began to talk to my mother and she didn't answer.

16   He raised his voice and said, "You can open your eyes now, it's all over. If you feel a bit groggy just sit awhile. It will soon pass."

17   Somewhere deep the words took root for later remembering though she could give no conscious sign of having heard. The dentist began to feel uneasy. He called her name sharply, but she did not respond. He opened a window, but the rush of air did not rouse her. He even tried lightly slapping her face, but still no reaction.

18   Time passed, and she did not stir. More time passed, and she went on sleeping. He did not want to call a colleague or a doctor and have them speculate on what he had done wrong. But he did not want to regret not having called them. It was a real dilemma.

19   Mercifully my mother waked, her strong, young body refusing to let her die with so much living undone. She snapped back into being, the pallor fading in her cheeks, the color rising, her hands no longer cold to the touch.

20   When my mother had her operation, she was, of course, put under ether, the anesthetic then in general use. Throughout her operation I sat in the waiting room with my good neighbor, Robert, whose blood was my mother's type as mine was not. In those years there was no blood bank in the hospital.

21   Robert, by nature a quiet man, a Yankee of generations of Yankees, did not expect me to make small talk. To keep a confident expression on my face, to smile in a reassuring way whenever our eyes met was the price I had to pay for being an adult. And Robert's being there when there were a dozen other things he had to do was the price he had to pay for being a caring person.

22   At last I saw my mother being wheeled out of the operating room. The surgeon came toward me smiling and was very pleased to tell me that the operation had been a complete success. In answer to my question about going to see my mother, he advised me that it was better to wait until the next day. When she waked, she would be tired and perhaps disoriented. It would be less strain for both of us if I gave her until tomorrow to get back to being herself.

23   Robert and I left the hospital; he was relieved for me and glad to have my good news to pass on to his wife, I expressing my gratitude for the comfort his presence had given me. We parted, he to go back to work, I to go home and do some walk-about chores to help me unwind.

24   But I could not erase the picture of my mother being wheeled down the corridor, her face without color, her body so still. She, who never wanted me to catch her sleeping ever since she overheard me say when I was five that mothers stayed awake all night to watch over their children, she was now rolling past me in a faraway world of her own, indifferent to my presence.

25   I went about the rest of the day trying to do some writing, but not really able to focus on anything that needed my full attention. I was really waiting for night to come and go, and morning to follow, so that my mother would be herself again in the world that she, as a child, had rushed outside to meet in the country morning, flinging her arms wide to gather every tree, every bird, every flower, every living thing around her in her fierce embrace.

26   Night came, and I was glad to go upstairs and get in bed with a book undemanding of my closest attention, and lull myself to sleep with the rhythm of its words. Just as I was beginning to drift into forgetfulness, my feet began to get cold. I rubbed them together in the hope that they would warm each other. Instead the cold began to creep up my legs.

27   I got up to check the house. Perhaps I had forgotten to lock the front door and it had blown open, or maybe a window had blown out, or the heating system had fouled itself up. But I found nothing at fault, and nothing was cold to my touch.

28   I went back to bed, and under the warm covers the cold continued to creep up my legs like no cold I had ever experienced. I had spent a winter in Moscow, where for a week the temperature was twenty-eight degrees below zero. I had cheerfully walked its streets while my American companions ran from tram to hotel with tears streaming down their cheeks.

29   This cold was beyond that. This cold now, creeping up my legs, now reaching my knees, was like death. And suddenly I knew that my mother was dying, and her dying was invading my body as a cry for help. I did not move from my bed. I did not move at all. But I never fought so hard in my life, commanding the cold to leave my body, and thus to leave hers.

30   I do not know how long it took before I began to feel it move, my knees no longer cold, my legs beginning to warm, and finally my feet free of their encasement of ice.

31   I jumped up and ran downstairs to the telephone. I called the hospital.

A young woman answered. When I told her who I was and asked how my mother was, she gasped and dropped the telephone. The waiting for her to pick it up again was one of the longest waiting periods in my life. Finally she did, then said in a painful voice, "I'll let you speak to your mother's doctor," and put down the telephone again before I could respond.

32   How long I waited for the doctor to come to the telephone I do not know. In such situations one has no conception of time. Finally he came. I heard his voice, and I will remember it as long as I live. He sounded as if he had run a long race, a long, almost unendurable race. His voice was steeped in exhaustion. But he had won. He said, "Your mother was dying. But she's all right now. Come and see for yourself tomorrow."

33   When I reached my mother's door, I could not bear to look. I did not know that until my mother told me later that I came to the door, backed away, came to the door again and again backed away, and did not make it to her bedside until the third try.

34   I suppose it was because I did not know what she was going to look like. I did not know what the toll had been in bringing her back to life. But she was sitting up in bed, her eyes bright, her cheeks like pink roses, and her voice full of animation. She was in fact herself.

35   "How do you feel?" I asked.

36   "Fine," she said. "And just look at that beautiful sun. It was snowing this morning when I had my operation. And it's already stopped."

37   I said gently, "You had your operation yesterday morning. And after it you slept a lot."

38   She said softly, "Then I lost a day. At my age I can't afford to lose a day."

39   "The whirlwind that you are, you'll make it up."

40   Now in these years I am very aware of time. Now I know, too, that a day lost is a day gone forever. When I am wasteful of time, I do not forgive myself.

DISCUSSION QUESTIONS

1. What is West's major fear?
2. How would you describe her mother?
3. The writer says: ". . . I was separated from my free will." What do you think is meant by this statement?
4. How important do you believe family is to West? Cite specific examples to support your opinion.

WRITING TOPICS

1. Reread the story; did you think the author's mother had died? In your journal, list specific, subtle clues showing that the mother did not die.
2. West writes: "Now I know, too, that a day lost is a day gone forever." Write an essay giving your interpretation of what the statement means. You may use information from your reading or personal experience.
3. Write an essay in which you describe the relationship of the author with her mother.

WOMEN

Alice Walker

Alice Walker was born in 1944 in Eatonton, Georgia. She attended Spelman College in Atlanta and graduated from Sarah Lawrence College. She published her first book, a volume of poetry entitled *Once,* in 1968 while still at Sarah Lawrence. Walker has written short stories, essays, novels, and poetry, and she has edited the works of Zora Neale Hurston and Langston Hughes. Walker's most widely acclaimed novel, *The Color Purple,* was written in 1982. The novel was awarded a Pulitzer Prize and the American Book Award; it was also made into a motion picture. Walker has also received the Rosenthal Award of the American Academy of Arts and Letters, The Lillian Smith Award of the Southern Regional Council, and a Guggenheim Fellowship. Her other works include *In Love and Trouble* (1973), *Revolutionary Petunias* (1973), *Meridian* (1976), and *Possessing the Secret of Joy* (1992).

Walker considers herself a "womanist," often writing about women who survive adversity and cruelty. She currently lives in California.

They were women then
My mama's generation
Husky of voice—stout of
Step
5 With fists as well as
Hands
How they battered down
Doors
And ironed
10 Starched white
Shirts

How they led
Armies
Headragged Generals
15 Across mined
Fields
Booby-trapped
Ditches
To discover books
20 Desks
A place for us
How they knew what we
Must know
Without knowing a page
25 Of it
Themselves.

DISCUSSION QUESTIONS

1. Walker says: "They were women then / My mama's generation." What does she mean by the statement?
2. Are today's African-American women any different from women of their mother's generation? In your small group, discuss ways they are different and similar.
3. Walker uses military metaphors to describe the women of her mother's generation. Locate them in the poem and discuss them with members of your small group.

WRITING TOPICS

1. In your journal, write a brief character sketch about a woman you feel exemplifies the qualities mentioned in the poem.
2. Write a short essay about your own mother, or female guardian, or a female friend. How has that person helped you become who you are?
3. Write a letter to the poet telling her what you like or dislike about the poem.

FROM *IN MY FATHER'S HOUSE*

Ernest J. Gaines

Ernest J. Gaines was born in 1933 on a plantation in Oscar, Louisiana, in Point Coupee Parish. The family moved to Vallejo, California, when he was fifteen years old. He first attended a community college, and then was drafted into the army. Following his army service in 1955, he resumed his studies at California State University, San Francisco. He later studied at Stanford University on a Wallace Stegner Creative Writing Fellowship. The novel *In My Father's House* was published in 1977. Gaines's other works include *A Gathering of Old Men* (1983) and his most famous novel, *The Autobiography of Miss Jane Pittman* (1971). Most of Gaines's works center around the will to survive with dignity in the face of tremendous odds. Gaines lives and writes in San Francisco, and he serves as a writer-in-residence part of the year at the University of Southwestern Louisiana in Lafayette.

1   Elijah had put away his tray of cups and glasses, and now he stood in the center of the room, clapping his hands for silence. The people were making too much noise to hear him, and he clapped again and stamped his foot. When everyone had quieted down, he told them that Reverend Martin wished to say a few words to them. The people turned to Phillip, who was already surrounded by a small crowd.

2   Phillip Martin wore a black pin-striped suit, a light gray shirt, and a red polka-dot tie. He was sixty years old, just over six feet tall, and he weighed around two hundred pounds. His thick black hair and thick well-trimmed mustache were just beginning to show some gray. Phillip was a very handsome dark-brown-skinned man, admired by women, black and white. The black women spoke openly of their admiration for him, the white women said it around people they could trust. There were rumors that he was involved with women other than his wife, but whether these rumors were true or not, he was very much respected by most of the people who knew

him. And no one ever questioned his position as leader of the civil rights movement in the parish.

3   The people had begun to applaud Phillip, and he raised his hands for silence. Shepherd, who stood next to Virginia's new tenant in the back of the room, could see the two big rings on his fingers, and the gold watchband around his wrist. The people would not stop applauding him, and Shepherd could see how the gold watchband sparkled in the light as Phillip shook his hands for silence.

4   Phillip told his audience that he didn't have a speech to give, that he only wanted to remind them about next Friday when the committee would meet with Albert Chenal.

5   "It took us years to get Mr. Chenal to hire black people in the first place," he said. "Now, after he hires them he don't want to pay them nothing. When we go up there Friday we go'n make it clear. Either he pay the black workers the same he pay the white, or we march before the door. Now, we spend more money in that store than white people do—the white people go to Baton Rouge and New Orleans—some of them even go up North and 'way to Europe. Poor black people don't have that kind of money to do all that traveling; we spend ours here in St. Adrienne. Therefore, we want our black workers to get the same pay, the same treatment, or we close down shop. We'll see how long he can last if no blacks go in his store. Mr. Chenal—"

6   Elijah, standing in the center of the room, led the applause. He clapped his hands over his head and turned completely around so others would see him and join him. Phillip waited until he had quiet again.

7   "But Mr. Chenal will challenge us," he went on. "Sure as I'm standing here talking to you, Mr. Chenal will challenge us. First, he'll offer us pennies. When we turn that down, he'll make it nickels. Turn that down, then dimes. When we turn all of this down, he go'n tell us to get out. See how long we can take the cold. You may recall he did the same thing before—not when it was cold, when it was hot. He beat us when it was hot. Yes, when it was hot. And you know how much black people love hot weather—we thrive on hot weather."

8   The people started laughing, and Phillip held up his hands.

9   "Just why d'you think so many our people leaving the North and coming back home?" he asked them. "Our good old Southern hot weather, that's why. Still, we let Mr. Chenal beat us on the hottest day. Took the crumbs he offered us and said thanks. So what will he do now, knowing how much black people hate cold weather? He go'n offer us crumbs again, and when we turn it down, he go'n tell us to get out his store. In the back his mind he go'n be thinking, They can't take cold weather. Ten minutes out there with Mr. Jack Frost, they go'n run home and drink hot toddy. He-he-he. Well, Mr. Chenal is wrong, deadly wrong, we can take cold weather." Phillip looked across the room. "What you say, Mills?"

10   Tall, gray-headed Howard Mills standing against the wall raised one big fist up in the air.

11   "Got my overcoat cleaned this week," he said. "And got me some new rubber boots to hit that rain."

12   The people laughed at Howard Mills.

13   "Jonathan, ain't you ready?" Phillip asked.

14   Jonathan, who stood next to Mills, raised both fists high up over his head.

15   "I'm ready to walk till next year this time," he said. "And I hope every last person in here is ready to do the same."

16   The people applauded Jonathan. Phillip waited for silence.

17   "Poor Albert Chenal," he said. "Poor, poor Albert Chenal. I don't hate Albert Chenal. I don't want you to hate Albert Chenal. I want you to pray for Albert Chenal. Tomorrow in church pray for Albert Chenal. Before you go to bed tonight, pray for Albert Chenal. Remember, love thy neighbor as thyself."

18   One of the two white women in the room applauded quietly. But when no one else joined her in support of praying for Albert Chenal, she brought her applause to an abrupt end.

19   Phillip went on. "Love is the only thing. Understanding, the only thing. Persistence, the only thing. Getting up tomorrow, trying again, the only thing. Keep on pushing, the only thing. You got some out there screaming Black Power. I say, what is Black Power but what we already doing and what we been trying to do all these years? Then you have that other crowd sitting in the bars—they even worse than the Black Power screamers—they saying, 'What's the use? Nothing will ever change. Hey, Mr. Wrigley, pour me another drink.' I'll call on Brother Mills again. What you say, Mills? You seen any changes around here?"

20   Mills nodded his gray head. "I'm a witness to it," he said.

21   "Jonathan?" Phillip said. "You been there, too. Well?"

22   "I've seen progress," Jonathan said. "But we have a long way to go, a long way to go."

23   "Amen," Phillip said.

24   But Jonathan was not through. He raised both fists over his head and looked around at the people in the room. "We need more people," he said. "More young people. More old people. We need the ones in the bars. We need the schoolteachers. We need them who go to work for the white people every day of their lives. We need them all. All, all, all. No reason to stay back, no reason at all. The wall is crumbling—let's finish tearing it down."

25   "Amen, amen," Phillip said, as the people applauded Jonathan.

26   Jonathan wanted to say more, but Phillip didn't give him a chance to go on.

27   "I'll call on a sister now," Phillip said. "Remember our sisters was out there first. Miss Daisy Bates, Miss Autherine Lucy, and countless more. And there's Sister Claiborne standing over there with her fine foxy self—you seen any changes, Sister Claiborne?"

28   A small gray-haired woman dressed entirely in black nodded to Phillip.

29   "Sister Jackson?" Phillip said. "Don't that bus run back of town now? And don't we even have a little bench there for you to sit on when you tired?"

30   Sister Jackson, who was about the same age as Sister Claiborne, also wearing black, and a red bouquet, nodded as Sister Claiborne had done.

31   "If you want to know about changes, talk to a couple of these sisters around here." Phillip went on. "Sister Aaron, can't you vote today for the mayor of St. Adrienne, the governor of Louisiana, the President of the United States?"

32   "Yes," Sister Aaron said. "And I'm go'n vote for the first black congressman from Louisiana, too, who will be no one other than our own Reverend Phillip J. Martin."

33   The people started to applaud, and Phillip raised his hands for silence. But the people would not be silent. Anthony McVay, the white attorney, standing on one side of Phillip, and Octave Bacheron, a white pharmacist, standing on the other side of him, each took one of his hands and held them high up in the air. And the applause was deafening.

34   After things had quieted down some, Howard Mills put on his overcoat and left the house. About a dozen other people left at the same time. But still the big living room remained noisy and crowded. Half the people were gathered around Phillip on one side of the room; the rest were in smaller groups throughout the house. Virginia's new tenant had moved. Now he was standing near the door that led out of the living room down the hall. But even when he moved, he never took his eyes off Phillip Martin. Whenever someone got between them he would move again, never getting any closer, but always keeping Phillip in sight. Yet he did it so discreetly that no one, not even Shepherd, who stood next to him most of the time, was suspicious of anything. Beverly had joined them, and both Shepherd and she moved about the room with Virginia's tenant. They were never aware that he was doing this on purpose. They felt that it was the crowd pushing them into different places.

35   For the past few minutes Joyce Anne, Phillip's ten-year-old daughter, had been playing the piano. But there was so much noise in the room that no one paid any attention to her until Crystal McVay, the wife of the attorney, moved away from the crowd around Phillip and turned to the girl at the piano. Others in the room soon joined her. Elijah, who was Joyce Anne's teacher, stood behind the crowd with his tray of cups and glasses. Each time she played a difficult piece well he would shut his eyes and shake his head from side to side. But when she came to a part that might give her some trouble, he would catch his breath and wait. Then when it was over, when she had done it in good form, he would sigh deeply (loud enough for others to hear), nod, and continue on through the crowd with his tray.

36   But not everyone near the piano was listening to the music. Phillip Martin was not. Neither to the music nor to the people around him. For the past couple of minutes he had been looking across the room where

Shepherd, Beverly, and Virginia's tenant were standing. Shepherd, who had noticed it, didn't think Phillip was looking at them in particular. They were at opposite ends of the room, there were at least three dozen people between them, so he could have been looking at anyone in that direction. Still, he looked nowhere else. And even when someone would speak to him or touch him on the arm, he would give that person his attention only a moment, then look back across the room again. He looked puzzled, confused; a deep furrow came into his forehead, and he raised his hand up to his temple as if he were in pain. Shepherd continued to watch him watching them. Suddenly he became very jealous. He knew of the minister's past reputation with women, so maybe he was eyeing Beverly now. Shepherd was angry for a moment, then he thought better of it, and he grinned at Phillip to let him know that he knew what was going on in his mind. But if Phillip saw him grin, he showed no sign that he did. Yet he looked only in that direction. When someone got between him and them, he craned his neck to see them better. Shepherd told Beverly what was going on.

37 "He's a handsome man, isn't he?" she said.

38 "Yes," Shepherd said. "And if I ever catch you anywhere near him, somebody's getting hurt."

39 "Really?" she teased him.

40 "Really," he told her.

41 Phillip was not aware that they were talking about him, he was not aware that they were even looking at him; yet he continued to stare at them, the expression on his face still showing confusion.

42 Joyce Anne was bringing her third song to an end now, and the people were applauding her performance. But Phillip Martin was not hearing a thing. He pushed his way out of the crowd and started across the room. He had taken only two or three steps when he suddenly staggered and fell heavily to the floor.

43 The pharmacist, Octave Bacheron, was the first to reach him and told everyone else to stay back. But the people did not get back, they pressed in closer. Sister Aaron, whom Phillip had called on during his short speech, cried out that he had been poisoned, and soon the word was all over the house that he had been drugged. The little wife of Octave Bacheron, who was hard of hearing, kept asking who had fallen. The other white woman, the attorney's wife, told her that it was Phillip.

44 "Phillip drunk?" Phoebe Bacheron asked. "Phillip drunk?" She was a very small woman, and she had to lean her head back to look up at the people around her. "Phillip drunk?" she asked. "Phillip drunk?"

45 No one answered her. They moved in to look at Phillip on the floor. Virginia's new tenant was there with all the others. His reddish eyes narrowed, his face trembled as he stared down at him. It seemed for a moment that he might say something, maybe even scream, but he jerked away from the crowd and went out. He was the only one who left, but there was so much confusion in the room that no one paid him any attention.

46   Alma, who had rushed to Phillip when he fell, now knelt beside him holding his head up off the floor in her lap. He had lost consciousness only a moment, as a fighter might who has been hit hard on the jaw, but now he began recognizing people around him again, and he tried quickly, desperately, to push himself up. Octave Bacheron, who knelt on the other side of him, put his small white hand on Phillip's chest and told him to lie still a moment.

47   "I'm all right," he said to Octave Bacheron. "I'm all right," he said to Alma. He looked up at all the people standing over him. "I'm all right, I'm all right," he said to them.

48   "No," Octave Bacheron said, pressing his small white hand on his chest. "Be quiet a moment. Listen to me. Can you hear me, Phillip? Be quiet. Lie still a moment."

49   "I'm all right," Phillip said. The people who stood over him canopylike could see tears in his eyes. "I'm all right. Please let me up. I have to get up. Don't let me deny him again."

50   No one knew what he was talking about. No one asked him what he was talking about.

51   "You don't feel well, Phillip," Octave Bacheron said. "Listen, you don't feel well."

52   "Alma?" Phillip said. "Alma, please," he begged her. "I'm on the floor. I'm on the floor."

53   Octave Bacheron nodded to Anthony to help him get Phillip to his feet. Jonathan, who was closer to Phillip, took his arm, but Anthony pushed him roughly aside.

54   "What do you think you doing?" Jonathan asked him.

55   "Helping your pastor," Anthony said.

56   "Ain't y'all done enough helping for one day?" Jonathan said. "That's why he's on his back now."

57   "Watch it, boy," Anthony said. "Watch your tongue there, now."

58   "Boy?" Jonathan said. "Boy?" He turned to the others in the room. "Y'all hear that, don't you? It's boy now. It's boy all over again."

59   "Please Jonathan," Alma said. "Please. Phillip's on his back. Please."

60   Jonathan and Anthony glared at each other a moment, then Anthony turned to Phillip. Phillip told them again that he was all right and he could stand on his own. But the two white men insisted on helping him to his feet, and they made him lean on them as they followed Alma down the hall to the bedroom. Elijah, Joyce Anne, and another woman followed after them.

61   Everyone had deserted the two white women now. The smaller one, Phoebe, was crying and asking why was Phillip drunk. Why did he drink? Didn't he know drinking was no good? The other white woman did not try to explain but took Phoebe in her arms and patted her shoulders. The rest of the people watched the door and waited for some kind of news from the bedroom.

62   After about ten minutes Octave Bacheron came back into the front. He told the people he believed that Phillip had fallen from exhaustion, but he

was calling the doctor to be sure. He told them that both he and Alma would appreciate it if they did not take the rumor out of here that Phillip had been poisoned. Now, he wished that they would all get their coats and leave quietly, because their pastor needed rest more than anything else.

63   The doctor, a small clean-shaven bald man wearing a trench coat over a brown tweed suit, came to the house a half hour later. He was in the bedroom only a couple of minutes, then he wrote out a prescription for two bottles of pills. Elijah followed the pharmacist uptown and brought back the medicine.

64   Now that everyone else had gone, the house was deadly quiet. The doctor, repeating exactly what the pharmacist had said earlier, told Alma that what Phillip needed most was rest—quiet and rest. Alma, Elijah, and Joyce Anne sat in the living room talking so softly among themselves that they could hardly hear each other.

65   But things were quiet and peaceful only a short while, then the telephone started ringing. Elijah, who sat nearest the telephone, would try to reach it before it rang a second time. Everyone wanted to know what the doctor had said about Phillip. "He's tired and needs rest," Elijah told them. "Other than that he's fine. Fine. Fine. He just needs his rest." Elijah would hang up the telephone, but no sooner had he sat down than it would ring again. Several people had heard that Phillip had been poisoned. "It's nothing like that," Elijah assured them. "Nothing like that. That's the kind of rumor we don't want out." Virginia Colar called from the boardinghouse. "You sure he's just tired?" she asked. "You sure he wasn't poisoned? You know how these white folks are. Remember President Kennedy, don't you? They ain't straightened that mess out yet—putting it all on poor Oswald. Remember King, don't you? Remember Long, don't you?"

66   "I remember all of them," Elijah told her. "But Reverend Martin is just tired. Everybody ate the same food. Everybody drank out the same pot of eggnog, which I made myself. Mr. Octave drank out the same cup Reverend Martin drank from. Nothing happened to him."

67   "And how you know it was the same cup?" Virginia asked. "You got to watch white folks. They sharp, them. Can switch a cup right 'fore your eyes and you'll never see it."

68   "It was the same cup," Elijah said. "Reverend Martin's little blue-and-white china cup from Maison Blanche. I know that little cup like I know my name. He drinks out the same cup every day."

69   "That's the trouble right there," Virginia said. "He drinks out the same little blue-and-white cup, and everybody knows it. Can't they go to Maison Blanche and buy another little blue-and-white cup just like his?"

70   "Listen, Virginia, now listen," Elijah said. "It was his little blue-and-white cup. His. Now, good night. I'll see you in church tomorrow."

71   Elijah sat up answering the telephone long after Alma and Joyce Anne had gone to bed. Then around midnight he went down the hall to his own room. He had been lying in bed wide-awake for about an hour when he heard Alma

and Phillip arguing out in the hall. Phillip had gotten out of bed and gone into his office, and Alma was trying to get him out of there. Elijah could hear her saying that she was going into the kitchen to warm up a glass of milk, because those pills weren't doing any good. He heard her passing by his room on her way into the kitchen, and a few minutes later he heard her going back up the hall again. It was quiet another hour, then more footsteps. Elijah listened for Alma's voice but didn't hear it. Now he called her, calling quietly: "Alma? Alma?" When she didn't answer, he got up and went to Phillip's office and knocked. It was quiet in the office, and Elijah pushed the door open and went in. Phillip sat behind his desk in the dark, facing the curtains over the window.

72   "Something the matter?" Elijah asked him.

73   "Thinking about service tomorrow," Phillip said without looking around.

74   "You ought to be in bed," Elijah said. "Let Jonathan conduct service tomorrow."

75   "I'm all right," Phillip said, still facing the curtains.

76   "The doctor want you to stay in bed," Elijah said.

77   Phillip didn't answer him.

78   "Reverend Martin, sir?"

79   "Leave me alone, will you?" Phillip said, looking back over his shoulder. "I just want to sit here and think a while."

80   Elijah went back to his room and lay on top of the covers, but a few minutes later he was knocking on the office door again.

81   "Reverend Martin? Reverend Martin, sir?"

82   "All right," Phillip said, coming out. "Good night, Elijah."

83   Phillip Martin went back to bed, but he couldn't sleep. He lay wide-awake for hours, listening to his wife snorting quietly beside him. He was trying not to think about the boy. He didn't want to think about him in here because he couldn't think clearly enough in here. The only place where he could think at all was in his office, but they came and got him out each time he went in there. He lay wide-awake, hoping for tomorrow to hurry up and get here. Alma, Elijah, and Joyce Anne would go to church, and he would have the entire house to himself.

84   Phillip lay on his side facing the wall. He wondered about the boy. But, no, how could it be? If anyone had known who the boy was, they would have brought it up yesterday.

85   Again in his mind's eye he saw the boy's thin, bearded face watching him from across the room. At first he paid it little attention, but after noticing it each time he looked in that direction, he began to ask himself why. Who was he? How did he get in here? Who invited him? He was sure he had never seen him anywhere before. He would look away a moment to answer someone's question, but when he looked back across the room he would find the boy still watching him as if no time whatever had passed. Why? he asked himself. Why? Who is he?

86   Then he remembered having heard about a stranger in St. Adrienne. The stranger had sat behind his church door the first night that he was here. Several people had seen him passing by the house. One or two had even seen him standing out in the street watching the house. Yes, and now that he remembered, Elijah had said something about inviting him to the party. But why was he standing there watching him? Why?

87   Then he knew. Even when he told himself no, it couldn't be so, he knew definitely that it was. The dream that he had a night or two before the boy got here was more than a dream; it was a vision, an omen, a warning.

88   Phillip pressed his face down against the sheet and tried not to think about it anymore. Let him think about anything else but not about this. Think about Chenal. Chenal wasn't going to be easy. Chenal knew the people needed work. Even if he paid them less than minimum they still had to work for him, because there weren't any other jobs. Phillip wondered what he would do if Chenal said no to their demands. Demonstrate against the store? Yes. What else? But suppose Chenal fired the people working for him, then what? They could eventually close down Chenal if the people demonstrated long enough against the store, but where would they work during that time?

89   Phillip started thinking about the boy again. Why? he asked himself. Why after all these years—why? And how did he know where to find me? Did she send him here? And if she did, why this game? Why sit behind the church door? Why for a week walk the street and watch the house? Come into the house, watch me, but say nothing—why? What's he want? What's he up to? He's got to be up to something. What?

90   Phillip Martin felt tired and confused. He looked at the two little bottles of pills and the glass of water on the small lamp table by the bed. He picked up one of the bottles and started to unscrew the cap, then threw it back. He wanted to knock everything on the floor, but he knew Alma would hear the noise and come into the room.

DISCUSSION QUESTIONS

1. The Rev. Martin says: ". . . black people love hot weather—we thrive on hot weather." Is he serious or is he making this statement in jest? Discuss this statement in your small group, giving specific examples to support your opinion.
2. How do you account for the apathy exhibited by some of the African Americans in St. Adrienne?
3. Who is the mysterious boy in the story? Cite specific evidence from the story to support your opinion.

WRITING TOPICS

1. In your journal, make a list of questions you think Rev. Phillip Martin should ask Albert Chenal.
2. Write a letter to the editor of the local newspaper stating your view about the low wages paid black workers by Albert Chenal and suggest some steps he should take to remedy the situation.
3. Write an imaginary dialogue between Rev. Martin and the mystery boy upon their next meeting.

MOTHER TO SON

Langston Hughes

For biographical information on Langston Hughes, see pages 91, 133, 192, and 385.

Well, son, I'll tell you:
Life for me ain't been no crystal stair.
It's had tacks in it,
And splinters,
5 And boards torn up
And places with no carpet on the floor—
Bare.
But all the time
I'se been a-climbin' on,
10 And reachin' landin's,
And turnin' corners
And sometimes goin' in the dark
Where there ain't been no light.
So boy, don't you turn back.
15 Don't you set down on the steps,
'Cause you finds it's kinder hard.
Don't you fall now—
For I'se still goin', honey,
I'se still climbin',
20 And life for me ain't been no crystal stair.

DISCUSSION QUESTIONS

1. What kind of advice is the mother giving her son?
2. The mother tells her son of some of her own experiences in life. What are they? Cite specific instances from the poem.
3. Is there any indication of a sustaining dream in "Mother to Son"? Find evidence in the poem to support your answer.
4. How would you characterize the relationship between this mother and son?

WRITING TOPICS

1. The poet uses the metaphor "crystal stair." Write an analytical essay in which you interpret this figurative language. Use examples from your reading or from your personal experience.
2. What advice do you think a daughter might have received? Would it be different from that of a son? Respond to these questions in a journal entry.

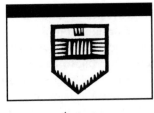

AUNT

Al Young

Al (Albert James) Young was born in Ocean Springs, Mississippi, in 1939 to Albert James Young, a musician and auto worker, and Mary Campbell Young. His family moved to Detroit in 1946, but as he grew up, Young continued to visit the South during the summers. He attended the University of Michigan at Ann Arbor between 1957 and 1961. After attending college, he worked as a professional musician, a janitor, a singer, and a disc jockey. During that time, he wrote poetry and fiction. Young received his B.A. in 1969 from the University of California at Berkeley. He is the recipient of many honors that include the National Endowment for the Arts, Fulbright, and Guggenheim fellowships. Currently, Young lectures nationally and internationally; writes poetry, fiction, and screenplays; and teaches.

Young's writing—whether poetry, fiction, or screenplays—reflects his dedication to eradicating stereotypes of African Americans. Thus, the characters in his novels and screenplays are complex. His novels include *Snakes* (1970), *Sitting Pretty* (1976), *Who is Angelina?* (1978), *Ask Me Now* (1980), and *Seduction by Light* (1988). His screenplay writing includes work on *Sparkle* (1972) and *Bustin' Loose* (1979). Young's poetry captures the joy, love, religion, family, and friendships of African Americans. His volumes of poetry include *Dancing* (1969), *Geography of the Near Past* (1976), *The Blues Don't Change* (1982), and *Heaven: Collected Poems 1956–1990* (1992).

She talks too loud, her face
a blur of wrinkles & sunshine
where her hard hair shivers
from laughter like a pine tree
5   stiff with oil & hotcombing

O & her anger realer than gasoline
slung into fire or lighted mohair
She's a clothes lover from way back
but her body's too big to be chic
10   or on cue so she wear what she want
People just gotta stand back &
take it like they do Easter Sunday when
the rainbow she travels is dry-cleaned

She laughs more than ever in spring
15   stomping the downtowns, Saturday past
work, looking into JC Penney's checking
out Sears & bragging about how when she
feel like it she gon lose weight &
give up smokin one of these sorry days

20   Her eyes are diamonds of pure dark space
& the air flying out of them as you look
close is only the essence of living
to tell, a full-length woman, an aunt
brown & red with stalking the years

DISCUSSION QUESTIONS

1. Select words, phrases, and lines from the poem that illustrate the love the speaker in the poem feels for his aunt.
2. The speaker in the poem uses some unique descriptions to portray his aunt. What do these descriptions tell you about the aunt's personality?
3. List the black dialect spellings of words and grammatical structured phrases. Discuss how the usage of these spellings and grammatical structures contributes to the emotional message in the poem.

WRITING TOPICS

1. In your journal, write a poem in which you describe a favorite family member using the names and descriptions of that person's favorite foods, stores, and activities.
2. In an essay, explain what the aunt, through her behavior, has passed down to the speaker in the poem.

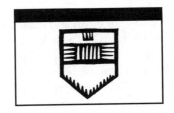

She Walked Alone

Daisy Bates

Daisy Bates was born and raised in Huttig, Arkansas. Her mother was murdered by white men and her father consequently left town, so she was raised by adoptive parents. Her adoptive parents taught her to fight against racism and injustice. Daisy and her husband, L. C. Bates, moved to Little Rock, where they founded the *Arkansas State Press*. The couple and their newspaper led the fight for integration in Little Rock. In 1952, Bates became head of the Arkansas branch of the National Association for the Advancement of Colored People (NAACP), where she served for many years.

The following selection, about the integration of Central High School in Little Rock, is from her memoir, *The Long Shadow of Little Rock*, which chronicles Bates's life and fight for civil rights. Originally published in 1962, it won the American Book Award in 1988.

1   Dr. Benjamin Fine was then education editor of *The New York Times*. He had years before won for his newspaper a Pulitzer prize. He was among the first reporters on the scene to cover the Little Rock story.

2   A few days after the National Guard blocked the Negro children's entrance to the school, Ben showed up at my house. He paced the floor nervously, rubbing his hands together as he talked.

3   "Daisy, they spat in my face. They called me a 'dirty Jew.' I've been a marked man ever since the day Elizabeth tried to enter Central. I never told you what happened that day. I tried not to think about it. Maybe I was ashamed to admit to you or to myself that white men and women could be so beastly cruel.

4   "I was standing in front of the school that day. Suddenly there was a shout!—'They're here! The niggers are coming!' I saw a sweet little girl who looked about fifteen, walking alone. She tried several times to pass through the guards. The last time she tried, they put their bayonets in front of her. When they did this, she became panicky. For a moment she just stood there

trembling. Then she seemed to calm down and started walking toward the bus stop with the mob baying at her heels like a pack of hounds. The women were shouting, 'Get her! Lynch her!' The men were yelling, 'Go home, you bastard of a black bitch!' She finally made it to the bus stop and sat down on the bench. I sat down beside her and said, 'I'm a reporter from *The New York Times,* may I have your name?' She just sat there, her head down. Tears were streaming down her checks from under her sunglasses. Daisy, I don't know what made me put my arm around her, lifting her chin, saying, 'Don't let them see you cry.' Maybe she reminded me of my fifteen-year-old daughter, Jill.

5   "There must have been five hundred around us by this time. I vaguely remember someone hollering. 'Get a rope and drag her over to this tree.' Suddenly I saw a white-haired, kind-faced woman fighting her way through the mob. She looked at Elizabeth, and then screamed at the mob, 'Leave this child alone! Why are you tormenting her? Six months from now, you will hang your heads in shame.' The mob shouted, 'Another nigger-lover. Get out of here!' The woman, who I found out later was Mrs. Grace Lorch, the wife of Dr. Lee Lorch, professor at Philander Smith College, turned to me and said, 'We have to do something. Let's try to get a cab.'

6   "We took Elizabeth across the street to the drugstore. I remained on the sidewalk with Elizabeth while Mrs. Lorch tried to enter the drugstore to call a cab. But the hoodlums slammed the door in her face and wouldn't let her in. She pleaded with them to call a cab for the child. They closed in on her saying, 'Get out of here, you bitch!' Just then the city bus came. Mrs. Lorch and Elizabeth got on. Elizabeth must have been in a state of shock. She never uttered a word. When the bus pulled away, the mob closed in around me. 'We saw you put your arm around that little bitch. Now it's your turn.' A drab, middle-aged woman said viciously, 'Grab him and kick him in the balls!' A girl I had seen hustling in one of the local bars screamed, 'A dirty New York Jew! Get him!' A man asked me, 'Are you a Jew?' I said, 'Yes.' He then said to the mob, 'Let him be! We'll take care of him later.'

7   "The irony of it all, Daisy, is that during all this time the national guardsmen made no effort to protect Elizabeth or to help me. Instead, they threatened to have me arrested—for inciting to riot."

8   Elizabeth, whose dignity and control in the face of jeering mobsters had been filmed by television cameras and recorded in pictures flashed to newspapers over the world, had overnight become a national heroine. During the next few days newspaper reporters besieged her home, wanting to talk to her. The first day that her parents agreed she might come out of seclusion, she came to my house where the reporters awaited her. Elizabeth was very quiet, speaking only when spoken to. I took her to my bedroom to talk before I let the reporters see her. I asked how she felt now. Suddenly all her pent-up emotion flared.

9   "Why am I here?" she said, turning blazing eyes on me. "Why are you

so interested in me now? You didn't care enough to notify me of the change of plans—"[1]

10   I walked over and reached out to her. Before she turned her back on me, I saw tears gathering in her eyes. My heart was breaking for this young girl who stood there trying to stifle her sobs. How could I explain that frantic early morning when at three o'clock my mind had gone on strike?

11   In the ensuing weeks Elizabeth took part in all the activities of the nine— press conferences, attendance at court, studying with professors at nearby Philander Smith College. She was present, that is, but never really a part of things. The hurt had been too deep.

12   On the two nights she stayed at my home I was awakened by the screams in her sleep, as she relived in her dreams the terrifying scenes at Central. The only times Elizabeth showed real excitement were when Thurgood Marshall met the children and explained the meaning of what had happened in court. As he talked, she would listen raptly, a faint smile on her face. It was obvious he was her hero.

13   Little by little Elizabeth came out of her shell. Up to now she had never talked about what happened to her at Central. Once when we were alone in the downstairs recreation room of my house, I asked her simply, "Elizabeth, do you think you can talk about it now?"

14   She remained quiet for a long time. Then she began to speak.

15   "You remember the day before we were to go in, we met Superintendent Blossom at the school board office. He told us what the mob might say and do but he never told us we wouldn't have any protection. He told our parents not to come because he wouldn't be able to protect the children if they did.

16   "That night I was so excited I couldn't sleep. The next morning I was about the first one up. While I was pressing my black and white dress—I had made it to wear on the first day of school—my little brother turned on the TV set. They started telling about a large crowd gathered at the school. The man on TV said he wondered if we were going to show up that morning. Mother called from the kitchen, where she was fixing breakfast, 'Turn that TV off!' She was so upset and worried. I wanted to comfort her, so I said, 'Mother, don't worry.'

17   "Dad was walking back and forth, from room to room, with a sad expression. He was chewing on his pipe and he had a cigar in his hand, but he didn't light either one. It would have been funny, only he was so nervous.

18   "Before I left home Mother called us into the livingroom. She said we should have a word of prayer. Then I caught the bus and got off a block from the school. I saw a large crowd of people standing across the street from the soldiers guarding Central. As I walked on, the crowd suddenly got very quiet. Superintendent Blossom had told us to enter by the front door.

---

1 When news reached Mrs. Bates that a mob was gathering for the opening of school, she worked throughout the night to arrange a safer meeting place for the students. The Eckfords did not have a telephone, and she did not know how to reach them. [Editors note.]

I looked at all the people and thought, 'Maybe I will be safer if I walk down the block to the front entrance behind the guards.'

19   "At the corner I tried to pass through the long line of guards around the school so as to enter the grounds behind them. One of the guards pointed across the street. So I pointed in the same direction and asked whether he meant for me to cross the street and walk down. He nodded 'yes.' So, I walked across the street conscious of the crowd that stood there, but they moved away from me.

20   "For a moment all I could hear was the shuffling of their feet. Then someone shouted, 'Here she comes, get ready!' I moved away from the crowd on the sidewalk and into the street. If the mob came at me I could then cross back over so the guards could protect me.

21   "The crowd moved in closer and then began to follow me, calling me names. I still wasn't afraid. Just a little bit nervous. Then my knees started to shake all of a sudden and I wondered whether I could make it to the center entrance a block away. It was the longest block I ever walked in my whole life.

22   "Even so, I still wasn't too scared because all the time I kept thinking that the guards would protect me.

23   "When I got right in front of the school, I went up to a guard again. But this time he just looked straight ahead and didn't move to let me pass him. I didn't know what to do. Then I looked and saw that the path leading to the front entrance was a little further ahead. So I walked until I was right in front of the path to the front door.

24   "I stood looking at the school—it looked so big! Just then the guards let some white students go through.

25   "The crowd was quiet. I guess they were waiting to see what was going to happen. When I was able to steady my knees, I walked up to the guard who had let the white students in. He too didn't move. When I tried to squeeze past him, he raised his bayonet and then the other guards closed in and they raised their bayonets.

26   "They glared at me with a mean look and I was very frightened and didn't know what to do. I turned around and the crowd came toward me.

27   "They moved closer and closer. Somebody started yelling, 'Lynch her! Lynch her!'

28   "I tried to see a friendly face somewhere in the mob—someone who maybe would help. I looked into the face of an old woman and it seemed a kind face, but when I looked at her again, she spat on me.

29   "They came closer, shouting, 'No nigger bitch is going to get in our school. Get out of here!'

30   "I turned back to the guards but their faces told me I wouldn't get help from them. Then I looked down the block and saw a bench at the bus stop. I thought, 'If I can only get there I will be safe.' I don't know why the bench seemed a safe place to me, but I started walking toward it. I tried to close my mind to what they were shouting, and kept saying to myself, 'If I can only make it to the bench I will be safe.'

31   "When I finally got there, I don't think I could have gone another step. I sat down and the mob crowded up and began shouting all over again. Someone hollered 'Drag her over to this tree! Let's take care of the nigger.' Just then a white man sat down beside me, put his arm around me and patted my shoulder. He raised my chin and said, 'Don't let them see you cry.'

32   "Then, a white lady—she was very nice—she came over to me on the bench. She spoke to me but I don't remember now what she said. She put me on the bus and sat next to me. She asked me my name and tried to talk to me but I don't think I answered. I can't remember much about the bus ride, but the next thing I remember I was standing in front of the School for the Blind, where Mother works.

33   "I thought, 'Maybe she isn't here. But she has to be here!' So I ran upstairs, and I think some teachers tried to talk to me, but I kept running until I reached Mother's classroom.

34   "Mother was standing at the window with her head bowed, but she must have sensed I was there because she turned around. She looked as if she had been crying, and I wanted to tell her I was all right. But I couldn't speak. She put her arms around me and I cried."

DISCUSSION QUESTIONS

1. Pretend that you are the student Elizabeth Eckford. With a partner, discuss how you might have acted if you had been faced with a similar situation.
2. How would you describe Mrs. Grace Lorch? What kind of person is she?
3. How do you account for Benjamin Fine's reaction to the mob's behavior? What is it in his background that makes him sympathetic toward this black child?

WRITING TOPICS

1. Pretend that you are Elizabeth and write a letter to the Commander of the Arkansas National Guard. Detail how you were treated by those very same men who were to protect all people of Arkansas, regardless of color. Be specific in expressing your personal feelings.
2. In your journal, write a short explanation of how you were helped by Mrs. Lorch, the wife of a white professor who is on the faculty at a predominantly African-American college.
3. Write a free verse poem in celebration of the kindness shown by the reporter, Benjamin Fine of *The New York Times*.

ACKNOWLEDGMENTS

I would like to thank the people who helped in the growth of this anthology: my co-author, Jesse Perry Jr.; our editor, Lisa A. De Mol; my undergraduate assistants, Antoinette Watkins, Ashley Economos, and Shelley Busby; and my graduate assistant, Torria Norman.

D. A. W.

LITERARY CREDITS

Angelou, Maya. "Willie" from *And Still I Rise* by Maya Angelou. Copyright © 1978 by Maya Angelou. Reprinted by permission of Random House, Inc.

Baldwin, James. "Sonny's Blues," was originally published in *Partisan Review*. Collected in *Going to Meet the Man* © 1965 by James Baldwin. Copyright renewed. Published by Vintage Books. Reprinted by arrangement with the James Baldwin Estate. "Stranger in the Village," by James Baldwin from *Notes of a Native Son* by James Baldwin. Copyright © 1955, renewed 1983, by James Baldwin. Reprinted by permission of Beacon Press, Boston.

Baraka, Amiri. "Preface to a Twenty Volume Suicide Note," by Amiri Baraka. Copyright © 1961.

Bates, Daisy. "She Walked Alone," by Daisy Bates from *The Long Shadow of Little Rock: A Memoir*. Reprinted by permission of the University of Arkansas Press. Copyright © 1986 by Daisy Bates.

Bontemps, Arna. "A Black Man Talks of Reaping" by Arna Bontemps. Copyright © 1963, 1973 by Arna Bontemps. Reprinted by permission of Harold Ober Associates Incorporated. "A Summer Tragedy" by Arna Bontemps. Copyright © 1963, 1973 by Arna Bontemps. Reprinted by permission of Harold Ober Associates Incorporated.

Brooks, Gwendolyn. "The Bean Eaters," from *Blacks* by Gwendolyn Brooks. Copyright © 1991.

Brown, Sterling. All lines from "Strong Men" from *The Collected Poems of Sterling A. Brown*, edited by Michael S. Harper. Copyright © 1932 Harcourt Brace & Company. Copyright renewed 1960 by Sterling Brown. Reprinted by permission of HarperCollins Publishers, Inc.

Carmer, Carl. "The Knee-High Man Tries to Get Sizable" from *Afro-American Folktales* by Roger D. Abrahams. Copyright © 1985 by Roger D. Abrahams. Reprinted by permission of Pantheon Books, a division of Random House, Inc.

Childress, Alice. "All About My Job," by Alice Childress from *Like One of the Family* by Alice Childress. Copyright © 1956 by Alice Childress. From *The African Garden*. From: *Black Scenes* by Alice Childress. Copyright © 1971 by Alice Childress.

Clifton, Lucille. "Miss Rosie" copyright © 1987 by Lucille Clifton. Reprinted from *Good Woman: Poems and a Memoir 1969–1980,* by Lucille Clifton, with permission of BOA Editions, Ltd.

Dove, Rita. "Canary," from *Grace Notes* by Rita Dove. Copyright © 1989 by Rita Dove. Reprinted by permission of the author and W.W. Norton & Company, Inc. "Magic," from *Thomas and Beulah* by Rita Dove, Carnegie-Mellon University Press, Pittsburgh 1986. Copyright 1986 by Rita Dove. Reprinted by permission of the author.

Drew, Charles R. Letters from Charles R. Drew to Lenore Robbins Drew, from The Charles Drew Papers, Box 135-1, The Moorland-Spingarn Research Center, Howard University. Reprinted by permission.

Dumas, Henry. "Valentines," by Henry Dumas appears by permission of publisher, Thunder's Mouth Press. From the book *Knees of a Natural Man,* copyright © 1989 by Loretta Dumas and Eugene B. Redmond.

Ellison, Ralph. "Epilogue" 10-page excerpt from *Invisible Man* by Ralph Ellison. Copyright © 1947, 1948, 1952 by Ralph Ellison. Reprinted by permission of Random House, Inc. "Hidden Name and Complex Fate" from *Shadow and Act* by Ralph Ellison. Copyright © 1964 by Ralph Ellison. Reprinted by permission of Random House, Inc.

Evans, Mari. "Vive Noir!" from *I Am a Black Woman* by Mari Evans, published by William Morrow, 1970. Reprinted by permission of the author.

Gaines, Ernest J. Excerpt totalling approximately 8 pages, as submitted from *In My Father's House* by Ernest Gaines. Copyright © 1977, 1978 by Ernest Gaines. Reprinted by permission of Alfred A. Knopf, Inc.

Giovanni, Nikki. "Nikki-Roasa" by Nikki Giovanni. Copyright © 1969 by Nikki Giovanni. Reprinted by permission of the author.

Goss, Linda. "The Tree of Love," by Linda Goss. Copyright © 1993 by Linda Goss.

Haley, Alex. "My Search for Roots" by Alex Haley is reprinted with permission of The Estate of Alex P. Haley. "My Search for Roots" was originally published in *Reader's Digest,* May 1974.

Hayden, Robert. "Runagate, Runagate," copyright © 1966 by Robert Hayden, from *Collected Poems of Robert Hayden* by Frederick Glaysher, editor. Reprinted by permission of Liveright Publishing Corporation.

hooks, bell. "the woman's mourning song," from *A Woman's Mourning Song* by bell hooks. Copyright © 1993. Reprinted by permission of the author.

Hughes, Langston. "The Blues I'm Playing" from *The Ways of White Folks* by Langston Hughes. Copyright © 1934 by Alfred A. Knopf, Inc. Copyright renewed 1962 by Langston Hughes. Reprinted by permission of Alfred A. Knopf, Inc. "I, Too" from *Selected Poems* by Langston Hughes. Copyright © 1926 by Alfred A. Knopf, Inc. Copyright renewed 1954 by Langston Hughes. Reprinted by permission of Alfred A. Knopf, Inc. "I've Known Rivers" from *The Big Sea* by Langston Hughes. Copyright © 1940 by Langston Hughes. Copyright © 1968 by Arna Bontemps and George Houston Bass. Reprinted by permission of Hill and Wang, a division of Farrar, Straus & Giroux, Inc. "Minstrel Man" from *The Dream Keeper and Other Poems* by Langston Hughes. Copyright © 1962 by Langston Hughes. Reprinted by permission of Alfred A. Knopf, Inc. "Mother to Son" from *Selected Poems* by Langston Hughes. Copyright © 1926 by Alfred A. Knopf, Inc. Copyright renewed 1954 by Langston Hughes. Reprinted by permission of Alfred A. Knopf, Inc. "Thank You Ma'am" from *Something in Common* by Langston Hughes. Copyright © 1963 by Langston Hughes. Copyright renewed © 1991 by Arnold Rampersad and Ramona Bass. "The Weary Blues" from *Selected Poems* by Langston

Hughes. Copyright © 1926 by Alfred A. Knopf, Inc., renewed 1954 by Langston Hughes. Reprinted by permission of Alfred A. Knopf, Inc.

Hurston, Zora Neale. From *The Eatonville Anthology.* Published by A. Philip Randolph and Chandler Owen. Reprinted by permission. "Sweat" by Zora Neale Hurston is reprinted by permission of The Estate of Zora Neale Hurston.

Johnson, Georgia Douglas. *Plumes* by Georgia Douglas Johnson. Copyright © 1927 by Georgia Douglas Johnson. Reprinted by permission of Samuel French, Inc.

Johnson, James Weldon. "The Creation," from *God's Trombones* by Weldon Johnson. Copyright 1927 The Viking Press, Inc., renewed © 1955 by Grace Nail Johnson. Used by permission of Viking Penguin, a division of Penguin Books USA, Inc. "Lift Every Voice and Sing," by James Weldon Johnson from *Saint Peter Relates an Incident* by James Weldon Johnson. Copyright © 1917, 1935, by James Weldon Johnson. Copyright renewed © 1963 by Grace Nail Johnson. Used by permission of Viking Penguin, a division of Penguin Books, USA, Inc.

Kelley, William Melvin. "The Only Man on Liberty Street," copyright 1963 by William Melvin Kelley from *Dancers on the Shore.* Reprinted by permission of Doubleday, a division of Bantam Doubleday Dell Publishing Group, Inc.

King, Martin Luther, Jr. "I Have a Dream." Reprinted by arrangement with The Heirs to the Estate of Martin Luther King Jr., c/o Writer's House, Inc. as agent for the proprietor. Copyright 1963 by Martin Luther King Jr., copyright renewed 1991 by Coretta Scott King.

Lester, Julius. "Stagolee" and "People Who Could Fly" from *Black Folktales,* by Julius Lester, published by Grove Press, copyright © 1969. Used by permission of Julius Lester.

Lorde, Audre. "Restoration: A Memorial—9/18/91," from *The Marvelous Arithmetics of Distance: Poems 1987–1992* by Audre Lorde. Copyright © 1993 by Audre Lorde. Reprinted by permission of W.W. Norton & Company, Inc.

Madhubuti, Haki R. "Assassination" from *Assassination* by Haki R. Madhubuti. Copyright © Haki R. Madhubuti, reprinted by permission of Third World Press, Chicago, Illinois. "The Union of Two" from *Killing Memory, Seeking Ancestors* by Haki Madhubuti. Copyright © 1987 by Haki Madhubuti, reprinted by permission of Third World Press, Chicago, Illinois.

Marshall, Paule. "To Da-duh, In Memoriam" by Paule Marshall. Copyright © 1967, 1983 by Paule Marshall. From the book *Reena and Other Stories.* Published by The Feminist Press at The City University of New York. All rights reserved.

McKay, Claude. "If We Must Die" by Claude McKay is used by permission of The Archives of Claude McKay, Carl Cowl, Administrator.

Morrison, Toni. "1927," by Toni Morrison from *Sula* by Toni Morrison. Reprinted by permission of International Creative Management, Inc. Copyright © 1973 by Alfred A. Knopf, Inc.

Petry, Ann. "Solo on the Drums," by Ann Petry. Copyright © 1947 by Ann Petry, renewed in 1975 by Ann Petry. The work was originally published in '47 Magazine of the Year and was reprinted in 1971 in *Miss Muriel and Other Stories.*

Randolph, A. Philip, and Chandler Owen. "The Steel Drivin' Man," originally published in *The Messenger,* ed. by A. Philip Randolph and Chandler Owen. Reprinted by permission.

Redmond, Eugene B. "Dance Bodies #1" by Eugene Redmond.

Reed, Ishmael. "Music: Black, White and Blue" by Ishmael Reed from *Shrovetide in Old New Orleans* (Atheneum). Copyright © 1978 by Ishmael Reed. Reprinted by permission.

AUTHOR-TITLE INDEX

Instructor's Manual

AFRICAN-AMERICAN LITERATURE

Second Edition

Demetrice A. Worley

Jesse Perry, Jr.

NTC Publishing Group
a division of NTC/CONTEMPORARY PUBLISHING COMPANY
Lincolnwood, Illinois USA

CONTENTS

USING THE TEXT

African-American Literature, Second Edition, is a collection of 85 selections by 70 African-American authors, with literature written from the late 1770s to 1995. The anthology contains a historical literary overview section, which students should be encouraged to read before they approach the selections in *African-American Literature*. From the days of slavery to the present, the overview outlines the historical, social, literary, and cultural factors that have influenced the many black Americans who have contributed to the African-American literary tradition. The book is flexibly designed so that it can be used as the main text in an African-American literature course or unit; as a supplemental text in an American literature, multicultural, or world literature course; or as part of an African-American studies program. Following are various options for using *African-American Literature*, Second Edition, in the English or Language Arts curriculum.

USING *AFRICAN-AMERICAN LITERATURE* IN A UNIT OR SEMESTER COURSE OF STUDY

The selections in this book can be taught in a semester course on African-American literature in one of two ways: thematically or chronologically.

Thematic Approach

The selections in the text are already organized thematically. The categories are: The Folklore Tradition; Language and Literacy; The Blues—Pain and Survival; Slavery—Time of Trial; Standing Ground; Identity; Dreamers and Revolutionaries; Women; Men; Relationships; and Family and Ancestors. You may follow this organization, or you may choose to teach the themes in another order.

Chronological Approach

To provide students with an idea of how African-American literature has developed since colonial times, you can present the selections in *African-American Literature* in chronological order, as in the following chart. The literary works are organized according to their dates of publication.

Date	Author	Title	Genre
?	Anonymous	"How Buck Won His Freedom"	Fiction
?	Anonymous	"Motherless Child"	Song
?	Anonymous	"Swing Low, Sweet Chariot"	Song
1773	Phillis Wheatley	"On Being Brought from Africa to America"	Poetry
1831	Nat Turner	"Nat Turner's Confession"	Nonfiction
1843	Henry Highland Garnet	"An Address to the Slaves of the United States of America"	Nonfiction
1848	Frederick Douglass	"Letter to His Master"	Nonfiction
1854	Frances Ellen Watkins Harper	"The Slave Mother"	Poetry
1887	Charles W. Chesnutt	"The Goophered Grapevine"	Fiction
1895	Paul Laurence Dunbar	"We Wear the Mask"	Poetry
1895	Booker T. Washington	"An Address Delivered at the Opening of the Cotton States' Exposition in Atlanta, Georgia, September, 1895"	Nonfiction
1898	Charles W. Chesnutt	"The Wife of His Youth"	Fiction
1900	James Weldon Johnson	"Lift Every Voice and Sing"	Song
1904	W. E. B. Du Bois	"Chapter 3: Of Mr. Booker T. Washington and Others"	Nonfiction
1904	W. E. B. Du Bois	"Our Spiritual Strivings"	Nonfiction
1914	W. E. B. Du Bois	"The Immediate Program of the American Negro"	Nonfiction
1919	Claude McKay	"If We Must Die"	Poetry
1920	James Weldon Johnson	"The Creation"	Poetry
1922	Langston Hughes	"Mother to Son"	Poetry
1923	Jean Toomer	"Song of the Son"	Poetry
1924	Marcus Garvey	"Speech Delivered at Madison Square Garden, March 1924"	Nonfiction
1925	A. Phillip Randolph and Chandler Owen	"The Steel Drivin' Man"	Fiction
1926	Zora Neale Hurston	from *Eatonville Anthology*	Fiction
1926	Zora Neale Hurston	"Sweat"	Fiction
1926	Langston Hughes	"I, Too"	Poetry
1926	Langston Hughes	"The Weary Blues"	Poetry
1927	Georgia Douglas Johnson	*Plumes*	Drama
1932	Sterling Brown	"Strong Men"	Poetry
1932	Langston Hughes	"Minstrel Man"	Poetry

Date	Author	Title	Genre
1933	Arna Bontemps	"A Summer Tragedy"	Fiction
1934	Carl Carmer	"The Knee-High Man Tries to Get Sizable"	Fiction
1934	Langston Hughes	"The Blues I'm Playing"	Fiction
1936	Charles R. Drew	"Letter from Charles R. Drew"	Nonfiction
1937	Margaret Walker	"For My People"	Poetry
1940	Langston Hughes	from *The Big Sea*	Nonfiction
1940	Richard Wright	"The Man Who Was Almost a Man"	Fiction
1947	Ann Petry	"Solo on the Drums"	Fiction
1951	Mary Elizabeth Vroman	"See How They Run"	Fiction
1953	Ralph Ellison	"Epilogue" from *Invisible Man*	Fiction
1953	James Baldwin	"Stranger in the Village" from *Notes of a Native Son*	Nonfiction
1956	Alice Childress	"All about My Job"	Fiction
1957	James Baldwin	"Sonny's Blues"	Fiction
1958	Langston Hughes	"Thank You, M'am"	Fiction
1959	Gwendolyn Brooks	"The Bean Eaters"	Poetry
1961	Amiri Baraka (LeRoi Jones)	"Preface to a Twenty Volume Suicide Note"	Poetry
1962	Daisy Bates	"She Walked Alone" from *The Long Shadow of Little Rock*	Nonfiction
1963	Arna Bontemps	"A Black Man Talks of Reaping"	Poetry
1963	William Melvin Kelley	"The Only Man on Liberty Street"	Fiction
1963	Martin Luther King Jr.	"I Have a Dream"	Nonfiction
1964	Ralph Ellison	"Hidden Name and Complex Fate"	Nonfiction
1964	Malcolm X with Alex Haley	from *The Autobiography of Malcolm X*	Nonfiction
1965	Lucille Clifton	"Miss Rosie"	Poetry
1965	Malcolm X	"To Mississippi Youth"	Nonfiction
1966	Robert Hayden	"Runagate Runagate"	Poetry
1966	Paule Marshall	"To Da-Duh, In Memoriam"	Fiction
1968	Nikki Giovanni	"Nikki-Roasa"	Poetry
1969	Julius Lester	"People Who Could Fly"	Fiction
1969	Julius Lester	"Stagolee"	Fiction
1970	Mari Evans	"Vive Noir!"	Poetry

Date	Author	Title	Genre
1970	Alice Walker	"Women"	Poetry
1971	Alice Childress	from *The African Garden*	Drama
1972	Haki Madhubuti (Don L. Lee)	"Assassination"	Poetry
1973	Gil Scott-Heron	"Winter in America"	Song
1973	Toni Morrison	"1927," from *Sula*	Fiction
1974	Alex Haley	from *Roots*	Fiction
1975	Maya Angelou	"Willie"	Poetry
1975	Ntozake Shange	"one thing i dont need"	Poetry
1976	Al Young	"Aunt"	Poetry
1977	Ernest Gaines	from *In My Father's House*	Fiction
1978	Eugene B. Redmond	"Dance Bodies #1"	Poetry
1978	Ishmael Reed	"Music: Black, White and Blue"	Poetry
1981	Lottie Jackson	"I Done Worked!"	Fiction
1986	Rita Dove	"Magic"	Poetry
1987	Haki Madhubuti	"The Union of Two"	Poetry
1989	Rita Dove	"Canary"	Poetry
1989	Henry Dumas	"Valentines"	Poetry
1989	Paulette Childress White	"Getting the Facts of Life"	Fiction
1989	Mariline Wilkins	"Harriet Tubman Is in My Blood"	Nonfiction
1991	Saundra Sharp	"It's the Law: a rap poem"	Poetry
1992	bell hooks	"the woman's mourning song"	Poetry
1992	Linda Goss	"The Tree of Love"	Fiction
1993	Audre Lorde	"Restoration: A Memorial— 9/18/91"	Poetry
1994	Geneva Smitherman	"Introduction" from *Black Talk*	Nonfiction
1995	Dorothy West	"A Day Lost Is a Day Gone Forever"	Nonfiction

USING *AFRICAN–AMERICAN LITERATURE* AS A SUPPLEMENT

If you are using this text as a supplement in an English or Language Arts class, in a multicultural or world literature course, or in a black studies program, the chapters can be presented in the text order. If you prefer, you could present the chapters using the following approaches:

Thematic Approach

Specific selections may also be used to cover a number of issues and topics raised in your class. Some suggestions for topics are: Cultures and/or

Multicultural Societies; Equality and Human Rights; Myths and Folktales; Men; Women; Relationships; Slavery; Struggles for Freedom; Communication; and Family.

Genres Approach

The genres in *African-American Literature*, Second Edition, can be taught separately, especially poetry, fiction, and nonfiction.

Poetry. African-American poetry has a strong tradition, from Phillis Wheatley to the Pulitzer Prize-winning Rita Dove. The following is a listing of poetry selections as they appear in this book:

Author	Title
James Weldon Johnson	"The Creation"
Saundra Sharp	"It's the Law: a rap poem"
Langston Hughes	"The Weary Blues"
Eugene B. Redmond	"Dance Bodies #1"
Rita Dove	"Canary"
Frances Ellen Watkins Harper	"The Slave Mother"
Phillis Wheatley	"On Being Brought from Africa to America"
Robert Hayden	"Runagate Runagate"
Jean Toomer	"Song of the Son"
Claude McKay	"If We Must Die"
Langston Hughes	"I, Too"
Maya Angelou	"Willie"
Lucille Clifton	"Miss Rosie"
Paul Laurence Dunbar	"We Wear the Mask"
Joyce Carol Thomas	"Where Is the Black Community?"
Mari Evans	"Vive Noir!"
Nikki Giovanni	"Nikki-Roasa"
Amiri Baraka	"Preface to a Twenty Volume Suicide Note"
Haki Madhubuti	"Assassination"
bell hooks	"the woman's mourning song"
Audre Lorde	"Restoration"
Ntozake Shange	"one thing i dont need"
Rita Dove	"Magic"
Sterling Brown	"Strong Men"
Arna Bontemps	"A Black Man Talks of Reaping"
Langston Hughes	"Minstrel Man"
Haki Madhubuti	"The Union of Two"

Author	Title
Gwendolyn Brooks	"The Bean Eaters"
Henry Dumas	"Valentines"
Margaret Walker	"For My People"
Alice Walker	"Women"
Langston Hughes	"Mother to Son"
Al Young	"Aunt"

Fiction. African-American fiction has tremendous power. In a brief amount of space, black writers are able to spin tales that capture the essence of African-American life. The following is a listing of the fiction selections (short stories, unless noted otherwise) as they appear in *African-American Literature*, Second Edition:

Author	Title
Carl Carmer	"The Knee-High Man Tries to Get Sizable"
Anonymous	"How Buck Won His Freedom"
Zora Neale Hurston	from *Eatonville Anthology*
Julius Lester	"People Who Could Fly"
A. Philip Randolph and Chandler Owen	"The Steel Drivin' Man"
Julius Lester	"Stagolee"
Charles W. Chesnutt	"The Goophered Grapevine"
Mary Elizabeth Vroman	"See How They Run"
Langston Hughes	"The Blues I'm Playing"
James Baldwin	"Sonny's Blues"
Ann Petry	"Solo on the Drums"
Arna Bontemps	"A Summer Tragedy"
Alice Childress	"All about My Job"
Ralph Ellison	"Epilogue" from *Invisible Man*
Linda Goss	"The Tree of Love"
Paulette Childress White	"Getting the Facts of Life"
Paule Marshall	"To Da-Duh, In Memoriam"
Alex Haley	from *Roots*
William Melvin Kelley	"The Only Man on Liberty Street"
Richard Wright	"The Man Who Was Almost a Man"
Charles W. Chesnutt	"The Wife of His Youth"
Zora Neale Hurston	"Sweat"
Toni Morrison	"1927" from *Sula*
Langston Hughes	"Thank You, M'am"
Ernest Gaines	from *In My Father's House*

Nonfiction.   The nonfiction selections in the book provide insight into African Americans' struggle for social, political, and economic equality. The following is a list of the nonfiction as it appears in this book:

Author	Title
Geneva Smitherman	"Introduction" from *Black Talk*
Lottie Jackson	"I Done Worked!"
Ishmael Reed	"Music: Black, White and Blue"
Frederick Douglas	"Letter to His Master"
Henry Highland Garnet	"An Address to the Slaves of the United States of America"
Nat Turner	"Nat Turner's Confession"
Mariline Wilkins	"Harriet Tubman Is in My Blood"
Booker T. Washington	"An Address Delivered at the Opening of the Cotton States' Exposition, Atlanta, Georgia, September, 1895"
W. E. B. Du Bois	"Chapter 3: Of Mr. Booker T. Washington and Others" from *The Souls of Black Folk*
Malcolm X with Alex Haley	from *The Autobiography of Malcolm X*
Ralph Ellison	"Hidden Name and Complex Fate"
W. E. B. Du Bois	"Our Spiritual Strivings" from *The Souls of Black Folk*
James Baldwin	"Stranger in the Village" from *Notes of a Native Son*
W. E. B. Du Bois	"The Immediate Program of the American Negro"
Malcolm X	"To Mississippi Youth"
Martin Luther King Jr.	"I Have a Dream"
Marcus Garvey	"Speech Delivered at Madison Square Garden, March 1924"
Langston Hughes	from *The Big Sea*
Charles R. Drew	"Letter from Charles R. Drew"
Dorothy West	"A Day Lost Is a Day Gone Forever"
Daisy Bates	"She Walked Alone" from *The Long Shadow of Little Rock*

Drama.   The three dramatic selections in this book provide a starting point for discussing the role and impact of African-American drama in our country's theatrical history:

Playwright	Title
Alice Childress	from *The African Garden*

Playwright	Title
Ntozake Shange	"one thing i dont need" from *for colored girls who have considered suicide/when the rainbow is enuf*
Georgia Douglas Johnson	*Plumes*

Songs. From field songs to spirituals to the blues to rap, music and songs have had a strong impact on African Americans as they have made a way for themselves in our country. The songs in this book provide a starting point for discussions on the role and impact of African-American music and songs:

Author	Title
Anonymous	"Motherless Child"
Anonymous	"Swing Low, Sweet Chariot"
James Weldon Johnson	"Lift Every Voice and Sing"
Gil Scott-Heron	"Winter in America"

Gender Groupings

The selections presented in *African-American Literature,* Second Edition, can be divided on gender lines in order to focus students' attention separately on the accomplishments, styles, literary techniques, and thematic concerns of African-American male and female writers. The following listings are organized according to the order of their appearance in the book.

African-American Women.

Author	Title	Genre
Anonymous	"Motherless Child"	Song
Zora Neale Hurston	from *Eatonville Anthology*	Fiction
Anonymous	"Swing Low, Sweet Chariot"	Song
Geneva Smitherman	"Introduction" from *Black Talk*	Nonfiction
Mary Elizabeth Vroman	"See How They Run"	Fiction
Lottie Jackson	"I Done Worked!"	Fiction
Alice Childress	from *The African Garden*	Drama
Saundra Sharp	"It's the Law: a rap poem"	Poetry
Ann Petry	"Solo on the Drums"	Fiction
Rita Dove	"Canary"	Poetry
Frances Ellen Watkins Harper	"The Slave Mother"	Poetry
Phillis Wheatley	"On Being Brought from Africa to America"	Poetry
Mariline Wilkins	"Harriet Tubman Is in My Blood"	Nonfiction
Maya Angelou	"Willie"	Poetry

Author	Title	Genre
Lucille Clifton	"Miss Rosie"	Poetry
Joyce Carol Thomas	"Where Is the Black Community?"	Poetry
Alice Childress	"All About My Job"	Fiction
Mari Evans	"Vive Noir!"	Poetry
Nikki Giovanni	"Nikki-Roasa"	Poetry
Linda Goss	"The Tree of Love"	Fiction
bell hooks	"the woman's mourning song"	Poetry
Paulette Childress White	"Getting the Facts of Life"	Fiction
Audre Lorde	"Restoration: A Memorial— 9/18/91"	Poetry
Paule Marshall	"To Da-Duh, in Memoriam"	Fiction
Ntozake Shange	"one thing i dont need"	Poetry
Rita Dove	"Magic"	Poetry
Georgia Douglas Johnson	*Plumes*	Drama
Gwendolyn Brooks	"The Bean Eaters"	Poetry
Zora Neale Hurston	"Sweat"	Fiction
Toni Morrison	"1927" from *Sula*	Fiction
Margaret Walker	"For My People"	Poetry
Dorothy West	"A Day Lost Is a Day Gone Forever"	Nonfiction
Alice Walker	"Women"	Poetry
Daisy Bates	"She Walked Alone" from *The Long Shadow of Little Rock*	Nonfiction

African-American Men.

Author	Title	Genre
Carl Carmer	"The Knee-High Man Tries to Get Sizable"	Fiction
Anonymous	"How Buck Won His Freedom"	Fiction
A. Phillip Randolph and Chandler Owen	"The Steel Drivin' Man"	Fiction
Julius Lester	"People Who Could Fly"	Fiction
Julius Lester	"Stagolee"	Fiction
Charles W. Chesnutt	"The Goophered Grapevine"	Fiction
James Weldon Johnson	"Lift Every Voice and Sing"	Song
James Weldon Johnson	"The Creation"	Poetry
Ishmael Reed	"Music: Black, White and Blue"	Poetry
Langston Hughes	"The Blues I'm Playing"	Fiction
James Baldwin	"Sonny's Blues"	Fiction
Langston Hughes	"The Weary Blues"	Poetry
Eugene B. Redmond	"Dance Bodies #1"	Poetry

Author	Title	Genre
Robert Hayden	"Runagate Runagate"	Poetry
Frederick Douglass	"Letter to His Master"	Nonfiction
Henry Highland Garnet	"An Address to the Slaves of the United States of America"	Nonfiction
Nat Turner	"Nat Turner's Confession"	Nonfiction
Jean Toomer	"Song of the Son"	Poetry
Claude McKay	"If We Must Die"	Poetry
Langston Hughes	"I, Too"	Poetry
Arna Bontemps	"A Summer Tragedy"	Fiction
Booker T. Washington	"An Address Delivered at the Opening of the Cotton States' Exposition in Atlanta, Georgia, September, 1895"	Nonfiction
W. E. B. Du Bois	"Chapter 3: Of Mr. Booker T. Washington and Others" from *The Souls of Black Folk*	Nonfiction
Paul Laurence Dunbar	"We Wear the Mask"	Poetry
Malcolm X with Alex Haley	from *The Autobiography of Malcolm X*	Nonfiction
Ralph Ellison	"Hidden Name and Complex Fate"	Nonfiction
W. E. B. Du Bois	"Our Spiritual Strivings"	Nonfiction
James Baldwin	"Stranger in the Village" from *Notes of a Native Son*	Nonfiction
Ralph Ellison	"Epilogue" from *Invisible Man*	Fiction
W. E. B. Du Bois	"The Immediate Program of the American Negro"	Nonfiction
Amiri Baraka	"Preface to a Twenty Volume Suicide Note"	Poetry
Haki Madhubuti	"Assassination"	Poetry
Gil Scott-Heron	"Winter in America"	Song
Malcolm X	"To Mississippi Youth"	Nonfiction
Martin Luther King Jr.	"I Have a Dream"	Nonfiction
Sterling Brown	"Strong Men"	Poetry
Alex Haley	from *Roots*	Fiction
Marcus Garvey	"Speech Delivered at Madison Square Garden, March 1924"	Nonfiction
Arna Bontemps	"A Black Man Talks of Reaping"	Poetry
Langston Hughes	from *The Big Sea*	Nonfiction
William Melvin Kelley	"The Only Man on Liberty Street"	Fiction
Langston Hughes	"Minstrel Man"	Poetry
Richard Wright	"The Man Who Was Almost a Man"	Fiction
Haki Madhubuti	"The Union of Two"	Poetry
Charles W. Chesnutt	"The Wife of His Youth"	Fiction

Author	Title	Genre
Charles R. Drew	"Letter from Charles R. Drew"	Nonfiction
Henry Dumas	"Valentines"	Poetry
Langston Hughes	"Thank You, M'am"	Fiction
Ernest Gaines	from *In My Father's House*	Fiction
Langston Hughes	"Mother to Son"	Poetry

Time Period Groupings

Two specific periods in the African-American literary tradition that make excellent supplemental units are the Harlem Renaissance and the Black Power/Black Arts Movement.

Writers of the Harlem Renaissance.

Author	Title	Genre
Claude McKay	"If We Must Die"	Poetry
James Weldon Johnson	"The Creation"	Poetry
Langston Hughes	"Mother to Son"	Poetry
Jean Toomer	"Song of the Son"	Poetry
Marcus Garvey	"Speech Delivered at Madison Square Garden, March 1924"	Nonfiction
A. Phillip Randolph and Chandler Owen	"The Steel Drivin' Man"	Fiction
Langston Hughes	"I, Too"	Poetry
Langston Hughes	"The Weary Blues"	Poetry
Zora Neale Hurston	from *Eatonville Anthology*	Fiction
Zora Neale Hurston	"Sweat"	Fiction
Georgia Douglas Johnson	*Plumes*	Drama
Sterling Brown	"Strong Men"	Poetry
Langston Hughes	"Minstrel Man"	Poetry
Arna Bontemps	"A Summer Tragedy"	Fiction
Dorothy West	"A Day Lost Is a Day Gone Forever"	Nonfiction

Writers of the Black Power/Black Arts Movement.

Author	Title	Genre
Amiri Baraka	"Preface to a Twenty Volume Suicide Note"	Poetry
Daisy Bates	"She Walked Alone" from *The Long Shadow of Little Rock*	Nonfiction
Arna Bontemps	"A Black Man Talks of Reaping"	Poetry

Author	Title	Genre
William Melvin Kelley	"The Only Man on Liberty Street"	Fiction
Martin Luther King Jr.	"I Have a Dream"	Nonfiction
Ralph Ellison	"Hidden Name and Complex Fate"	Nonfiction
Malcolm X with Alex Haley	from *The Autobiography of Malcolm X*	Nonfiction
Lucille Clifton	"Miss Rosie"	Poetry
Malcolm X	"To Mississippi Youth"	Nonfiction
Robert Hayden	"Runagate Runagate"	Poetry
Paule Marshall	"To Da-Duh, In Memoriam"	Fiction
Nikki Giovanni	"Nikki-Roasa"	Poetry
Julius Lester	"People Who Could Fly"	Fiction
Julius Lester	"Stagolee"	Fiction
Mari Evans	"Vive Noir!"	Poetry
Alice Walker	"Women"	Poetry
Alice Childress	from *The African Garden*	Drama
Haki Madhubuti	"Assassination"	Poetry
Gil Scott-Heron	"Winter in America"	Song

READING AND GROUP DISCUSSIONS

Small Group Discussion

Students should discuss the Discussion Questions and Writing Topics in small groups and with the class as a whole. The first advantage of students working in small groups is that when students work together on a task, communication abilities learned in the group transfer to the individual (O'Donnell et al.). As a result, when students receive positive and negative feedback from their peers, they can quickly reevaluate their interpretations of the text. The second advantage of group work is that group activities provide students with the opportunity to judge whether their interpretation of the reading is based on what is presented in the text or on other personal experiences (Rosenblatt, 1978). When students discuss their responses together and the interpretation or presentation of information is different among the students, a student will return to the reading to determine whether the text supports his or her interpretation or those of his or her peers (Rosenblatt, 1983).

Large Group Discussion

In addition to small group discussion, there should be whole class discussions. These classroom discussions reaffirm the students' roles as readers and their authority as readers to assert varying interpretations. Bruce Martin supports large group discussion of literature. He states, "The sharing of interpretations . . . allows us not only to engage in a similar search for meaning, but . . . to know, in fact, that several ways of making sense of the text, and especially conflicting ways, will arise and belong properly to any reading experience" (380). After class discussions, the students will either feel secure in their knowledge that the discussion supported their roles as readers, or they will realize that they need to reevaluate the role they take on while reading African-American literature. When students begin to reinterpret the way they evaluate a text, they gain knowledge of the strength or weakness of the ways that they approach literature (Rosenblatt 1983, 107). A reading journal not only facilitates students' abilities to determine character, plot, theme, and setting in African-American literature, but it also facilitates students' abilities "to 'close read' beyond the texts" (Hesse, 19–20) into the African-American literary traditions and cultures, into themselves, and into other cultures.

WRITING TOPICS
Keeping a Journal

A reading journal can enrich students' engagement with African-American literature. Writing in response to open-ended, interpretative as well as analytical questions allows students to become, as Robert Scholes defines it, "more culturally at home" in a text (27). A reading journal, usually a folder where students keep their written responses to specific questions and notes about readings, provides a space where students can record their written responses to the readings. Reader-response theory stresses that each reader interprets a given text (reading) differently because of each individual's knowledge and emotional background brought to the text when reading. A reading journal becomes a place to which students can return to reflect on their interpretations of readings, as well as reflect on what those interpretations say about them as readers.

In addition to helping students decode the texts and understand how their own knowledge shapes their understanding of the texts, a reading journal encourages development of students' reading and writing skills. Current composition theory and reading theory tell us that composing and comprehending are both part of the same cognitive process (Squire). When students read, they reconstruct the ideas expressed by another writer. To understand that writer's idea, the students must re-create that idea. Writing about texts encourages students to internalize the structure and meaning of another person's ideas. Also, when students write about what they read, they reflect on their transactions as readers. Providing students with opportunities to write about what they read allows them to draw on past reading and writing schemata to produce concrete evidence of their understanding. This moves students from relying on "you know what I mean," to providing you (as the teacher) and themselves with written responses that spell out exactly what they mean. Therefore, when students engage with a text through reading and writing, they are making connections between their personal knowledge and the text.

Writing Topics Activities

The Writing Topics activities in *African-American Literature*, Second Edition, are a combination of analytical, reader-response, and creative writing activities. This variety provides students with a selection of writing prompts to choose from, and it provides you, the instructor, with a selection of areas in which students can develop specific skills. The analytical questions are constructed to develop students' essay-writing skills: addressing a specific audience, writing for a specific purpose, developing a thesis, and developing ideas with specific evidence. The analytical writing prompts also encourage the natural use of rhetorical modes in writing: description, narration, comparison/contrast, definition, classification, argumentation, and persuasion.

The reader-response and creative writing activities in *African-American Literature*, Second Edition, allow students to respond to the literature emotionally. Reader-response theory can be seen as moving on a continuum: from subjectivism (David Bleich and William Holland) to phenomenology (Wolfgang Isher and Early Stanley Fish—affective stylistics) to structuralism (Jonathan Culler and Later Stanley Fish—authors of the theory of interpretive communities). Many of the reader-response and creative writing-based activities are based on Bleich. What is important to subjectivists, such as Bleich, is that the reader learns something about him or herself through an encounter with a text. This is especially important when students are reading the selections in *African-American Literature*. They need to understand not only the literature, but also how they view the literature. Bleich uses a four-phase approach to teaching literature:

1. thoughts and feelings (affect responses to text)
2. feelings about literature (reader subjectively re-creates the text and presents it to others)
3. literary importance (students examine their criteria for placing importance on a word, passage, or feature of a text)
4. directed responses to cultural codes.

The affect-driven questions allow the students to make connections between their own lives and the texts they are reading. The questions focusing on literary importance allow students to distinguish the impact of word choice and literary devices in a text. Finally, questions on cultural codes encourage students to examine and come to an understanding of African-American cultural codes (vocabulary and references specific to a particular culture) that the students might have ignored or not understood in their reading. The questions focusing on cultural codes allow students, as Joseph

Comprone explains, to "reconcile or work out a complex problem in defining meaning" (220).

Using the Reading Journal in the Classroom

Students should be encouraged to record their thoughts and feelings about their readings in a reading journal. They should be assured that, as the instructor, you are not looking for a specific right answer but that you expect them to thoroughly explain their responses so that you can understand what they are trying to say. You should not penalize students for spelling or grammatical errors in their reading journals. If you want to make a journal entry a class assignment, you should provide students with ample time to revise their journal entry for public examination. In addition, you should assure your students that you will respect their right to privacy if they feel that a journal response is too personal to share.

BIBLIOGRAPHY / WORKS CITED

Bleich, David. *Readings and Feelings: An Introduction to Subjective Criticism.* Urbana, IL: National Council of Teachers of English, 1975.

Comprone, Joseph. "Integrating the Acts of Reading and Writing About Literature: A Sequence of Assignments Based on James Joyce's 'Counterparts.'" *Convergences: Transactions in Reading and Writing.* ed. Bruce T. Peterson. Urbana, IL: National Council of Teachers of English, 1986: 215–30.

Hesse, Douglas. "Some Alternatives to Character, Plot, Theme, and Setting: Social Construction and Critical Thinking." *Illinois English Bulletin* 76.2: 12–21.

Martin, Bruce K. "Teaching Literature as Experience." *College English* 51.4: 377–85.

O'Donnell, Angela M., et al. "Cooperative Writing: Direct Effects and Transfer." *Written Communication* 2.3: 307–25.

Petrosky, Anthony R. "From Story to Essay: Reading and Writing." *College Composition and Communication* 33.1: 24–25.

Rosenblatt, Louise M. *Literature as Exploration.* 4th ed. New York: Modern Language Association, 1983.

—. *The Reader, the Text, the Poem: Transactional Theory of the Literary Work.* Carbondale, IL: Southern Illinois University Press, 1978.

Scholes, Robert. *Textual Power: Literary Theory & the Teaching of English.* New Haven: Yale University Press, 1985.

Squire, James R. "Composing and Comprehending: Two Sides of the Same Basic Process." *Language Arts* 60.3: 581–82.

Worley, Demetrice A. "Reading Journals: Strengthening Cultural Literacy through Reading, Writing, and Speaking Connections." *Journal of Educational Opportunity* (Summer 1990): 11–16.

THE FOLK TRADITION

MOTHERLESS CHILD

Anonymous

This particular spiritual speaks of loneliness and desire. The words might be expressing a longing for one's own mother. More likely, though, they express a feeling about the state of one's existence as a black person in an alien land.

DISCUSSION QUESTIONS

1. How might a motherless child feel?

   Some student may use adjectives such as *lonesome, dejected,* or *remorseful.* Others may respond with personal experience.

2. Do you think this song's writer actually lost his or her mother? Why?

   Students may answer either way. They should have reasons to back up their answers.

3. What kind of person might sing this song?

Again, answers will vary. Typical answers might include someone who is lonely, sad, alienated, or homesick.

THE KNEE-HIGH MAN TRIES TO GET SIZABLE

retold by Carl Carmer

Spend time discussing the role of animal characters in folktales. The knee-high man, who is small in stature, learns that it is not a person's size that makes him or her large, but what the person can do with his or her intellect.

DISCUSSION QUESTIONS

1. The knee-high man asks Mr. Horse and Brer Bull for help. When the knee-high man follows their advice, what happens to him? Why didn't Mr. Horse's and Brer Bull's suggestions work?

   The knee-high man engages in activities that are not natural for a human being, such as eating grass, running too long, and bellowing. These activities either caused him pain or made him sick.

2. What is the meaning of Mr. Hoot Owl's statement: "Well, if you don't have any cause to fight, you don't have any reason to be any bigger than you are"?

   Humans can use their intellect to reason themselves out of physical fights.

3. What type(s) of abilities does the knee-high man need in order to be "big"? Why?

   The knee-high man should use his intellect. A strong intellect would make him a "giant" among men.

HOW BUCK WON HIS FREEDOM

Anonymous

The folktale format in which a supposedly less powerful, smaller, or weaker character prevails over a stronger one was common to African and African-American folklore. Referred to as a "trickster" tale, these stories often depicted a slave outwitting a slave owner or overseer. Students should be able to discuss the reasons why slaves would find such a tale appealing.

DISCUSSION QUESTIONS

1. How does Buck outwit his slavemaster?

   He outwits his master by mimicking his master's voice when speaking to the master's wife.

2. Buck was able to sound like his master. How was he able to do that, even though he usually spoke a nonstandard dialect of English?

   One suggestion is that Buck is depicted as someone who can steal anything. Thus, he can even "steal" his master's voice. Another is the idea that Buck doesn't *have* to talk in a nonstandard dialect.

3. How would you describe Master Henry Washington?

   Descriptions will vary. Most students will think he was not too bright to entrust the care of his suit to another person—even his wife—even for a moment.

FROM *EATONVILLE ANTHOLOGY*

Zora Neale Hurston

Zora Neale Hurston wrote extensively on African-American folklore. Eatonville, Florida, was the first all-black town in the United States, and Ms. Hurston grew up there. Because the story contains some nonstandard forms of American English, you may wish to have the students read along silently as you or a student reads the selection. Many of Hurston's stories about her hometown, Eatonville, had a comic twist; however, her life at home was not very pleasant.

Notice that the animals take on human characteristics, which is called *personification*.

DISCUSSION QUESTIONS

1. How does Mr. Rabbit outwit Mr. Dog?

   He slashes Mr. Dog's tongue so that he will not be able to sing well in his pursuit of Ms. Nancy.

2. How would you describe Mr. Rabbit?

   He may be described as cunning or tricky.

3. Mr. Rabbit was able to convince Mr. Dog to meet him the next day. Why is Mr. Dog so gullible?

   Mr. Dog trusted Mr. Rabbit; he did not suspect that Mr. Rabbit was in any way deceptive.

PEOPLE WHO COULD FLY

Julius Lester

Discuss the African-American oral tradition. Focus on the importance of magic abilities. Engage students in deciding if the people literally or figuratively flew away. What type of power would the slaves have if they could "fly"?

DISCUSSION QUESTIONS

1. What identifies this as an oral story in written form, or an oral signature? How many types of oral signatures can you find? What are they?

   There is the repetition of structure from one part to the next. Key words are repeated. A moral is presented.

2. What do oral tradition signatures contribute to the oral nature of a story? What do they contribute to or detract from the written version of this oral story?

   They emphasize key words or ideas. They help us remember the story so we can pass it on to others.

3. How were the Africans looked upon by the slave traders in "People Who Could Fly"?

   The slaves were considered no more than property to be used.

4. What do you think the witch doctor whispered to the expectant mother?

   Students' responses will vary. He may have told her that when he utters a certain word, a person may return to Africa just by waving his or her arms.

5. Create a one-paragraph story and tell it to another person. Then have that person tell the story to someone else. Next, have the last person tell the story to one more person. Then have the last person tell you the story. How did the story change? Where did it stay the same? What did you learn about the oral nature of stories?

   Stories will vary. The importance of the assignment is that students will see how difficult a storyteller's job can be. They will see firsthand that it is difficult to keep a story from changing as it passes from one person to another.

THE STEEL DRIVIN' MAN

A. *Philip Randolph and Chandler Owen*

Like many popular folktales, the legend of John Henry exists in several versions. John Henry was a real person, and many versions of this legend have been spread about him. Ask students whether they know any of the versions of this tale. You may wish to have students read the selection aloud.

DISCUSSION QUESTIONS

1. John Henry was a determined man; he promised to succeed by beating the "steam-drill" to the finish line. Identify passages in the story that demonstrate this determination.

   Several passages demonstrate John Henry's determination in matters close to his heart. He was in love with Lucy, "but first he wanted her to be free, as he was." Another example is that he has been saving his money for years to buy her freedom and to pay for a house. His determination is also evident in the way he drives the steel to win the money, even though it costs him his life.

2. Name other legendary African Americans who were determined to achieve their goals. In small groups, discuss some of these goals and how they were reached.

   There are many possibilities. Harriet Tubman organized the Underground Railroad and led many slaves to freedom. Dr. Martin Luther King Jr. led nonviolent protests for civil rights.

3. How would you describe the Captain's attitude toward John Henry?

   The Captain's attitude could probably be described as condescending at best. Although he seems to treat his workers better than some, he is more concerned with winning the bet than with John Henry. He also cheats John Henry by offering him only a tenth of what he would win in the bet.

SWING LOW, SWEET CHARIOT

Anonymous

Discuss with students that the religious songs originally sung by African-American slaves are called spirituals. Many of these songs had hidden meanings. For example, this song was not only talking about going to heaven, but about a possible escape to freedom via the Underground Railroad.

DISCUSSION QUESTIONS

1. This, like many spirituals sung by the slaves, has a hidden meaning. What do you think is the hidden meaning of the first and last stanzas?

   Perhaps the slaves were signaling their desire or a possible plan to escape to freedom on the Underground Railroad. The Underground Railroad system was composed of a number of "safe houses" along a particular route that were used to hide slaves as they journeyed either to the northern United States or to Canada. Many of these homes belonged to white abolitionists; many such persons were members of the Quaker religion.

2. In the second stanza, the writer says: "I looked over Jordan and what did I see . . ." Jordan is a river in the Middle East. What do you think the metaphor "crossing over Jordan" means in the song?

   One possible answer is that slaves are crossing over a river located in the southern United States on their way North.

3. Who is the "band of angels" referred to in the song?

   Some students may think that this is a group of angels descended from heaven. It is quite possible, however, that slaves are referring to fleeing to freedom with a group of friends or relatives. To the slave, freedom from slavery would seem like heaven.

STAGOLEE

Julius Lester

"Stagolee" is a folktale interpreted by Julius Lester. You might discuss with students some of the roles folklore has served in various cultures, such as to create cultural heroes or to reinterpret events. You might wish to have students do a dramatic interpretation of this tale in class.

Stagolee is described as being a "bad" individual. Ask students to name characteristics of a "bad" individual. Does Stagolee fit these characteristics? Can students think of other examples of real or fictional individuals who fit these characteristics? One example might be Leroy Brown, from Jim Croce's song "Bad, Bad, Leroy Brown."

Discuss the role that humor and exaggeration play in the folktale. Was Stagolee really as bad as he seems? Or is his toughness exaggerated to mythical proportions?

DISCUSSION QUESTIONS

1. "Stagolee" is the story of a legendary African-American male. As with most folktales, the author uses exaggeration as a key literary device. What do you like or dislike about this tale?

   Student's answers will vary. Some students may find the sarcastic tone of the tale humorous and enjoyable. Others may find the utterly fantastic tone of the story silly or tedious. Have students discuss their perceptions.

2. What do you think makes Stagolee so tough?

   A key factor may be his resolve not to be taken advantage of or dominated in any way. Students may come up with other factors as well.

3. What can you say about the language used in this folktale? What was happening in the United States at the time this version of Stagolee's story was written?

   Students may find the language irreverent or intentionally irritating, which would fit the personality of the main character and also please a possibly downtrodden reader. This story was retold during the sixties, and references to such things as the Vietnam War and the Black Power Movement should be recognizable.

CHAPTER TWO

LANGUAGE AND LITERACY

INTRODUCTION FROM *BLACK TALK*

Geneva Smitherman

Discuss with your students that some African Americans speak a nonstandard variety of American English. Some linguists refer to such speech as Ebonics. Ebonics is the joining of the word "ebony" (black) with the word "phonics" (sound system). Others refer to this variety as African-American English (AAE). Tell students that Americans speak a variety of dialects. These dialects represent several regions of the United States, namely, southern, New England, midwestern, and western. Inform your students that slang is not a dialect of American English, and the language—nonstandard American English—spoken by some poor and isolated African Americans is not "street" language. This nonstandard variety of American English is a language system that is rooted in its West African, Caribbean, and Creole origins.

DISCUSSION QUESTIONS

1. What are some unique features of African American English (AAE)? Cite at least two examples.

Student responses will vary but should include patterns of grammar and punctuation.

2. Does the way one speaks affect communication with others? If so, how?

   Students' responses will vary. Some will believe that how one speaks does affect communication; others will believe it doesn't. Be sure they have examples to support their answers.

3. In a small group, discuss the roles of Standard English and dialects, such as AAE. Should Standard English be the official language of the United States? As you discuss this issue, consider particularly the use of language at school and in the workplace.

   Students' responses will vary. Be sure they have reasons to back up their answers.

THE GOOPHERED GRAPEVINE

Charles W. Chesnutt

Dialects capture the rhythm and emotional nature of a group's spoken language. However, dialects often give students problems because students are not familiar with them. Ask students to read a paragraph or two aloud at home before they come to class. Hearing the dialect aloud will often give students a sense of the rhythm of the dialect. (*Note:* If your students are not mature enough to read a dialect other than their own aloud, without making fun of it, you should avoid having them read a new dialect aloud in class.)

DISCUSSION QUESTIONS

1. Uncle Julius displays his shrewdness and self-interest as he attempts to outwit the white buyer and keep his own economic advantage. Select specific passages from the story which support this view of Uncle Julius's actions.

   Uncle Julius tells his story like a folktale. He attempts to scare the white landowner so he can keep harvesting the grapes from the land.

2. "The Goophered Grapevine" is a framed story, or a story within a story. How does this framing add to the development of the story?

    The framing provides a beginning and ending in Standard American Edited English, which can be seen as adding legitimacy to the story.

3. Dialect can sometimes be difficult to read. Nevertheless, it gives readers a sense of the language, style, and sounds of a particular group of people, either in a specific region of the United States or from a specific time period. Highlight some specific examples from Uncle Julius's dialect.

    Student responses will vary.

SEE HOW THEY RUN

Mary Elizabeth Vroman

This short story is about a dedicated teacher. Have students discuss what they believe are the qualities of a good teacher. Does teaching involve more than just instructing students in reading and writing?

DISCUSSION QUESTIONS

1. Many of Miss Richards's students speak a nonstandard variety of English. A new teacher, she says to herself that she must "correct" Booker's speech defects. Do you think his speech is deficient? Why? How could the teacher help him with his nonstandard dialect? Discuss these issues with your classmates.

    Students will have their own opinions about whether Booker's speech is deficient. They should know, however, that in most countries people who speak differently from the majority are considered inferior and unintelligent. There is still much discussion about whether nonstandard English "must" be discouraged at all costs.

2. How would you describe Miss Richards? What kind of person do you think she is?

Some of her primary characteristics are that she is deeply caring, emotional, and dedicated.

3. What is C. T.'s attitude about learning at the beginning of the story? At the end?

He was reluctant to learn at the beginning, because all of his previous experiences had been of failure. Miss Richards then discovers where his interests lie, and C. T. discovers his own talents. By the end of the story, his attitude has changed; he has discovered that he can succeed, and he is eager to learn more.

4. What kind of man was Dr. Sinclair? What was his attitude toward Miss Richards? Toward Tanya?

Dr. Sinclair is kind underneath his gruff exterior. He is probably worn down by numerous requests in a small, poor town and is surprised by Miss Richards's offering to cover the bill for Tanya. His attitude toward Miss Richards changes from one of kindly inattention to one of respect, after she tells him she will pay the bill and after he discovers she has correctly diagnosed Tanya's illness. His attitude toward Tanya is one of concern, but he cannot protect her against the inadequate resources of her poverty-stricken home.

LIFT EVERY VOICE AND SING

James Weldon Johnson

Give students a copy of "The Star-Spangled Banner." Discuss the origins of the song and melody. Have students think about the importance we place on our national anthem. An additional activity could have students learn more about other countries' national anthems.

Johnson wrote this poem in February of 1900. It has been called unofficially the "Negro National Anthem."

DISCUSSION QUESTIONS

1. Think about the United States of America's national anthem, "The Star-Spangled Banner." What does this song celebrate about the United

States? What does "Lift Every Voice and Sing" celebrate about African Americans? What are the similarities between the two songs? Use specific examples from both songs to support your responses.

Both songs focus on battles—"The Star-Spangled Banner" focuses on one specific battle, whereas "Lift Every Voice and Sing" focuses on the collective battles African Americans have fought. Both songs celebrate the ability to survive against horrendous odds.

2. What period of time is being discussed in the first nine lines of the second stanza? Which star does the persona refer to in the last line of this stanza? What is the connection between the first nine lines of this stanza and the reference to the "bright star"?

The first nine lines discuss slavery. The star referred to is the North Star. The North Star helped to guide African Americans to freedom.

I Done Worked!

Lottie Jackson with Sherry Thomas

Discuss with students Lottie Jackson's attitude about work and living in town. Lottie has no formal education, but she has what some would call "mother wit"; that is, she speaks both with authority and with the commoner's touch. You might wish to read this selection aloud if you think the dialect will interfere with students' reading or understanding of the selection.

DISCUSSION QUESTIONS

1. Lottie says that some of the old folks in her community look better than the young people. Do you think this is true? Why?

Some students might suggest that many older people look better than the young because they have taken better care of themselves physically and lived more moral lives.

2. What is Lottie's attitude about work? How does it differ from other people's attitudes about work? Explain.

Answers will vary. Lottie has a positive attitude about work; she gains strength through working.

3. Lottie says she earned fifty cents per day, while her husband earned sixty cents. What does she say is the reason for this disparity? Explain.

Lottie believes her husband received sixty cents mainly because he is a male.

FROM *THE AFRICAN GARDEN*

Alice Childress

Africans who were brought to the United States and slaves who were born here were denied the right to keep their names or name themselves. Therefore, naming and calling someone by his or her name have had considerable importance in African-American communities. The older man in this story, Ashley, passes this knowledge on to Simon. Ashley acts as a historian, passing on knowledge that cannot be found in a book.

DISCUSSION QUESTIONS

1. Ashley gives Simon a lesson on the history of some African-American names. Why is this lesson an important one for Simon to learn?

Naming is an important part of African-American culture. Simon needs to learn that his name is important and that African Americans have not always had the right to name themselves any name they wanted.

2. Old Soldier says he is an "old soldier." Is he referring to his age or to something else? Why does Old Soldier steal meat and sell it for a low price to people in the neighborhood?

The man is an "old soldier" in the art of surviving as a poor black person. He sells the meat at a low price so people who could not afford to buy the meat at the store have a chance to buy and eat meat.

3. What type of relationship do Simon and Ashley have? Why is this relationship important not only for Simon, but also for Ashley?

Ashley takes on the role of a grandfather or older uncle who can help Simon understand what it means to be black and an American.

4. Ashley tells Simon, "we are in some terrible deep trouble . . . and we in it together." Who are the "we"? What is the "deep trouble"? Why are the "we" in this trouble together?

The "we" is all black people. The trouble is the fighting between blacks. "We" have to stop both hating ourselves and defining "being black" as being one certain type of behavior or characteristic.

THE CREATION

James Weldon Johnson

James Weldon Johnson is noted for what have been called "sermons in verse." Johnson recorded these verse sermons while listening to poor African Americans as he traveled in rural areas of the South. As you or one of the students read the selection aloud, have everyone pay attention to the descriptive words and the musical quality of the poem.

DISCUSSION QUESTIONS

1. "The Creation" is taken from a collection of Johnson's poems entitled *God's Trombones*. His technique in writing this poem is similar to a sermon preached by an African-American minister. In a small group, discuss this technique.

One possible technique students may explore is that of "call and response." This technique has been used by slaves in the field as well as by African-American preachers. Another technique is the poetic way sermons are rendered by African-American preachers.

2. What do you notice about Johnson's use of the English language? How would you classify this language?

Johnson uses standard American English rather than a dialect of English.

CHAPTER THREE

THE BLUES–PAIN AND SURVIVAL

MUSIC: BLACK, WHITE AND BLUE

Ishmael Reed

Discuss with students that they will read a critical review written by Ishmael Reed, a well-known writer and professor at the University of California, Berkeley. Reed is reviewing the book *Music: Black, White and Blue* by Ortiz Walton. You may wish to tell the students that such reviews appear frequently in newspapers, in magazines such as *Newsweek, Time,* and *The New Yorker,* or in scholarly professional journals. Reviewers give their personal opinions regarding the content of the item being reviewed. Other reviewers may present a different point of view.

DISCUSSION QUESTIONS

1. According to the book, Walton writes that there are "too many symphonies." What do you think this statement means? Do you agree or disagree with it? Why?

Walton thinks that too many acclaimed musical compositions are centered around the European experience, and that music from other venues is dismissed.

2. Reed suggests: "The trouble with much criticism of Afro-African American art (music, dance, painting, literature) is that politicians control it . . . with their minds already made up." In a small group, discuss what you think the writer means by this statement.

Some students might suggest that much of the criticism of the arts as performed by African Americans is controlled by a power structure of which blacks are not a part.

3. Remembering that this review was written in 1972, whom do you think Walton is referring to when he talks about the "Public-Enemy-Number-One" cast of characters?

Students may suggest that the "enemies" refers to control of the music industry by possible crime bosses.

THE BLUES I'M PLAYING

Langston Hughes

Discuss the blues structure with your students. Make sure they understand how the first line is changed slightly in the second line. Emphasize that the blues are not about sorrow, but are about celebrating survival in the face of adversity. Highlight the connections between the oral tradition and the blues—a story being told to provide a lesson, the use of call (the first two lines) and response (the last line), the use of pattern, and the use of words that are easy to remember (rhyming words).

DISCUSSION QUESTIONS

1. In part IV of the story, Dora Ellsworth holds a particular position concerning art. In this same section of the story, Oceola holds another position. What are these two positions? Use specific examples from the story to support your responses.

Dora Ellsworth "believed in art of the old school, portraits that really and truly looked like people, poems about nature, music that had soul in it, not syncopation." Oceola believed music "demanded movement and expression, dancing and living to go with it."

2. Discuss Hughes's use of irony when the narrator discusses Mrs. Ellsworth. Why is this tone effective for the story?

   Irony is an appropriate tone to use when discussing Mrs. Ellsworth because she believes that her definition of art is the only definition of art. She also believes she is helping Oceola, when actually she takes Oceola away from the environment Oceola loves and thrives in.

3. Describe Mrs. Ellsworth's characteristics at the beginning of the story and at the end of the story. Does she change? Why or why not?

   Mrs. Ellsworth's character stays the same.

4. What happens to Oceola when she plays jazz and blues music? Explain why she feels the way she does.

   Oceola loses herself in the music when she plays. She feels connected to the music and the black people who enjoy her music.

5. How does Oceola resolve the conflict between her beliefs and Mrs. Ellsworth's beliefs? Has she grown from resolving this conflict? Why or why not?

   Oceola chooses marrying Pete and playing the type of music she wants to play. She grows because she recognizes the value of European-based music *and* the value of the blues and jazz.

IT'S THE LAW: A RAP POEM

Saundra Sharp

With your students, discuss the functions of laws. Why do we need them? How does obeying laws differ from treating oneself and others well out of respect? Note that politicians usually respond to situations by coming up with new laws. Is this a good strategy? Does having more laws make people more responsible for their own actions?

DISCUSSION QUESTIONS

1. In stanzas six through nine, the speaker in the poem makes reference to "rules" we need to respect ourselves. To whom is the speaker addressing these rules? Why is the speaker addressing this particular audience? How are these rules different from the laws to which the speaker refers in stanzas one through four?

   The speaker is addressing these rules to young people—she makes reference to staying in school. Young people need to have control over themselves instead of letting outside forces control them. The laws in stanzas one through four keep us from hurting other people. The rules in stanzas six through nine will help keep us from hurting ourselves.

2. Analyze the difference between laws that the government enforces and the "laws" we impose on ourselves. Use specific laws from the poem to support your answer.

   The government imposes laws to protect us from being physically hurt and to protect our civil rights. Laws we impose on ourselves have more to do with our emotional states.

3. Which elements in this poem make it "a rap poem"? In what ways are these rap elements similar to blues elements? In what ways are they dissimilar?

   The topic of the poem—laws in America—and the rhyme scheme help make the poem sound like a rap. The repetition of basic line structures is similar to the blues. The "take action" nature of the poem makes it dissimilar to the blues.

SONNY'S BLUES

James Baldwin

Baldwin's "Sonny's Blues" is a story about two brothers, one who adhered to the philosophy of mainstream society, the other who followed his own path of nonconformity. Sonny's use of drugs resulted in alienation from his family for a period of time. You may either begin reading the story aloud while students follow along, or you may have the students read the story in small groups. There may be particular passages that students want to discuss with the entire class. You may also wish to discuss the conclusion; the "cup of trembling" mentioned in the last sentence is a biblical allusion (Isaiah 51: 17–22).

DISCUSSION QUESTIONS

1. What was Sonny's relationship with his father?

   One possible answer is that Sonny's relationship was weak, yet it consisted of love and respect.

2. Sonny maintains that there is no one to talk to when one wishes to let go of the "storm inside." What do you think the "storm inside" is? Do you agree with the statement? Why?

   The storm inside might refer to pain or trouble one is experiencing at a given point in time.

3. What do you think the writer means when he says: ". . . how the stones of the road she had walked on must have bruised her feet"?

   Some students may suggest that, as she traveled through life, she experienced difficult circumstances.

THE WEARY BLUES

Langston Hughes

This poem by Hughes is the first to make use of the blues form. "The Weary Blues" is said to have launched Hughes's career as a writer. The poem took first place in a poetry contest in 1925 sponsored by *Opportunity* magazine.

DISCUSSION QUESTIONS

1. What do you think Hughes means when he uses the term "weary blues"?

   One possible answer is "tiresome" or "exhausted."

2. Are African Americans the only persons who can "have the blues"?

   No, there is no scientific evidence to support this idea.

3. The author says the musician was "droning a drowsy syncopated tune." What do you think he means by this metaphor? Discuss with your small group.

   The musician was humming a sleepy rhythm.

DANCE BODIES #1

Eugene B. Redmond

Discuss with students how dances, such as the waltz and the Charleston, represent the emotions of a specific time. Have students discuss how their dances represent their emotional states.

DISCUSSION QUESTIONS

1. In this poem Redmond uses italic type and regular type to convey the poem's message. What topic is covered in the italic print? What role does the italic print play within the poem?

   Dance steps are presented in italics. The italic print seems to have movement, just as dance steps do.

2. The persona in the poem states *"Breakdown the walls, brother!"* What types of walls are being referred to in this line? Why is it important to break down these walls?

   Students' responses will vary. The walls could be the restraints we place on ourselves.

3. Which lines in the poem are similar to the blues song pattern? Which other blues elements does this poem contain? Theme? Language?

The lines in italics, the dance steps, repeat like a blues song. The poem contains a theme of survival, which is a blues theme.

SOLO ON THE DRUMS

Ann Petry

Many musicians use music as a way to work through their pain. The day Kid Jones's wife leaves him for the piano player in the band, Kid Jones performs his best drum solo ever as he works through his own grief and the grief of all African-American men who have lost a woman they loved to death or to another man. Discuss with your students how working through pain does not always provide a happy ending. At the end of the story, Kid Jones is no longer angry, but neither is he happy.

DISCUSSION QUESTIONS

1. Describe Kid Jones's state of mind when he begins to play the drums. How does this description compare to his feelings when he finally stops playing the drums?

Kid Jones is despondent about his wife leaving him for the piano player. He has put his entire being into playing the drums and has spent his anger.

2. What does Kid Jones work out about his life while playing the drums?

Kid Jones is empty. He has given everything to playing the drums.

3. Using specific evidence from the story explain the audience's reaction to Kid Jones's first drum solo.

The band members look at him in astonishment. A young man's face is filled with awe as he listens.

4. At the end of the story, why does Kid Jones compare himself to a puppet on a string? Is Kid Jones's view of himself distorted? If so, how?

Life manipulates Kid Jones instead of his manipulating life. He can learn to control how he reacts to life.

CANARY

Rita Dove

Bring in some photographs of Billie Holiday and share them with your students. Point out her signature flower, a gardenia in her hair. Bring in a recording of some of Holiday's music. Discuss Holiday's life and voice with your students.

DISCUSSION QUESTIONS

1. The poem's persona describes Billie Holiday using such phrases as "burned voice" and "ruined face." What led to Billie Holiday having a "burned voice" and "ruined face"?

   Holiday's life was full of sorrow. She also abused drugs.

2. The second stanza is enclosed in parentheses. How would the poem change if the parentheses were removed?

   The stanza in parentheses emphasizes how Holiday's music moves us listeners. Holiday used drugs to stimulate her own emotional experiences.

3. Select words or phrases from the poem which support the idea that this poem has blueslike qualities.

   This is a blues poem in that it is a poem about how the music and memory of Holiday survive, though her drug-induced decline was sorrowful.

4. The last line of the poem reads, "If you can't be free, be a mystery." What does the word "free" mean? How could being a mystery compensate for not being free?

   The word "free" could refer to being free of the restraints of society or the restraints we place on ourselves. We create mystery in our lives to hide our insecurities.

CHAPTER FOUR

SLAVERY—TIME OF TRIAL

THE SLAVE MOTHER

Frances Ellen Watkins Harper

Spend time discussing the impact slavery had on the African-American family. As a lecturer at abolitionist meetings, Harper spoke against slavery and read her poetry mainly to audiences composed of white women. Discuss with students what Harper is trying to express about the slave family in this poem and the connection she wanted to make between how both white mothers and black mothers feel a horrible sense of loss when a child is taken from them.

DISCUSSION QUESTIONS

1. Select words from the poem that evoke emotion. Discuss how Harper used these words in her writing on the antislavery movement.

   Answers will vary. Have students focus on why these words evoke an emotion that could be used to fight slavery.

2. This poem is written in four-line stanzas with each quatrain expressing a complete idea. How do the quatrains work together to create a vivid description of this aspect of slavery?

Each quatrain adds an element of explanation to the opening shriek, building to the final heartbreaking metaphor.

3. Why was it an advantage for slave owners to separate mothers from their children?

Students will probably speculate that mothers and children were separated in situations where the slave owner stood to make money by selling a young slave to someone else who wanted the child. In addition, they may suggest that the owner thought the mother would be more industrious in her work without a child around.

4. In the last stanza, the persona states "The only wreath of household love." What is this figurative wreath? Why would a slave mother's home have a limited number of symbols of "household love"?

The son is the figurative wreath of household love. Slaves were not allowed to have possessions that would "adorn" a home.

ON BEING BROUGHT FROM AFRICA TO AMERICA

Phillis Wheatley

Phillis Wheatley was well treated as a slave. Some people believe that since she did not suffer under the harsh conditions that most slaves lived under, her poetry does not present an accurate view of a slave's life. Others have pointed out that Wheatley's education and religious background may be merely disguising an ironic or sarcastic tone. These two views of Wheatley's work should lead to a lively discussion of the tone of this poem.

DISCUSSION QUESTIONS

1. In lines 7 and 8, to what does the word "refined" refer? Why would this type of action be important during the religious time in which Wheatley lived?

The word "refined" refers to blacks being converted to Christianity. A person would not be able to enjoy the afterlife unless he or she was a Christian.

2. Is the speaker in the poem sincere when he or she says, "'Twas mercy brought me from my pagan land"? Why is mercy important to the speaker?

The speaker can be seen as sincere. The speaker did not know about Christianity when she was in Africa.

3. In line 7 the speaker uses the phrase "Negroes black as Cain." Is the speaker referring to the color of Negroes or to something else? Explain your response.

The speaker is referring to the blackness of Cain's sin.

RUNAGATE, RUNAGATE

Robert Hayden

You may wish to discuss with the class several terms from the poem that may be unfamiliar to them. On the other hand, you may wish to have students in small groups research terms such as *mulatto, patterollers,* and *hants* (ghosts). The poet lists names of several persons who fought against slavery; have students research each one and be prepared to share their findings with the class.

DISCUSSION QUESTIONS

1. Discuss lines 15 to 17 in your small group. What do you think the poet means here?

Students may suggest that many slaves will attempt to escape with tears or with happiness, and some through death. Some may escape dressed in their finest clothes, yet still in chains.

2. Part I of the poem is written in free verse: the slaves' flight for freedom is shown by placing certain words in a specific arrangement on the page. Locate these words and discuss how they are visually displayed.

   They are displayed in a staggered manner as if one were running to avoid capture or detection; breathlessness is suggested. The spare use of punctuation keeps the action moving.

3. What role did Harriet Tubman play in the slaves' search for freedom?

   Tubman helped more than 300 slaves escape to freedom. She has been called the Moses of her people.

4. Who is the person who is armed and known to be dangerous?

   Harriet Tubman; she traveled carrying one or more pistols.

Letter to His Master

Frederick Douglass

Frederick Douglass, upon gaining his freedom from slavery, became a tireless fighter for the eradication of slavery. Although he had little or no formal education, he spoke with eloquence about the abolition of slavery. You may also wish to discuss other African Americans who were eloquent spokespersons against slavery and segregation, such as Harriet Tubman and Martin Luther King Jr.

Discussion Questions

1. What do you think Douglass means by the statement at the end of paragraph 6: ". . . You must give account at the bar of our common Father and Creator . . ."?

   The slaveholders will have to confess before God about the inhuman treatment of their fellow human beings.

2. What is the tone of Douglass's letter to his former slaveholder?

   The tone is courageous and firm, yet conciliatory.

3. In paragraph 7 Douglass says: "I shall make use of you as a weapon with which to assail the system of slavery. . . ." What does he mean by the statement?

Douglass would use his experience under this particular slaveholder to speak out on the evils of slavery.

AN ADDRESS TO THE SLAVES OF THE UNITED STATES

Henry Highland Garnet

Henry Garnet escaped from slavery when he was nine years old; he, unlike most slaves, lived with both his mother and father in New York. Even as a runaway slave, he was able to enroll in an educational academy in New Hampshire. He later became a minister in the Presbyterian church.

You may wish to discuss the role religious leaders have played in the freedom struggles of African Americans. (Martin Luther King Jr. is one example.) Garnet addresses the slaves as a free man.

DISCUSSION QUESTIONS

1. Henry Highland Garnet is a minister of the gospel when he delivers this speech. How else would you describe him?

He is most probably an abolitionist, a militant fighter against slavery.

2. Garnet escapes from slavery in 1842 and finds his way to New York City and freedom. In paragraph 9 he says: "Your condition does not absolve you from your moral obligation." What does he believe is the moral obligation of the slaves?

He suggests that the slaves have an obligation to live as free persons and to secure that freedom by any means.

3. Garnet lists several Africans and African Americans who have fought for the freedom of black people. In your small group, make a list of such

people, either women or men. Be prepared to discuss their contributions with the class.

Students might list people such as Denmark Veazie, Toussaint L'Ouverture, Joseph Cinque, and Nat Turner.

NAT TURNER'S CONFESSION

Nat Turner

Nat Turner is the well-known slave who organized a revolt against his master and other slave owners. His was not the only revolt by slaves. Many went unreported and did not gain the notoriety as did the one by Turner and his followers. Not all slaves were passive in their slavery; you may wish to explore further with your class the idea of passivity by slaves. You may wish to appoint research teams or ask for volunteers to research the idea of passivity.

DISCUSSION QUESTIONS

1. It is said that slaveholders used verses from the Bible to justify slavery. Did Nat Turner do the same thing to justify his fight for freedom? Discuss this question by giving specific examples taken from the selection.

   Yes, he did. One example he used is: "Seek ye the Kingdom of Heaven and all things shall be added unto you."

2. How did Turner describe Joseph Travis, one of his slavemasters?

   Joseph Travis was kind, according to Turner, and trusted him.

3. If all human life is sacred, was Nat Turner justified in doing what he did? Why or why not?

   Students may or may not believe that Turner was justified. They should have reasons for thinking as they do.

HARRIET TUBMAN IS IN MY BLOOD

Mariline J. Wilkins

Discuss with your students how historical "fact" is not always true. As students read the story, ask them to pay attention to the places where Wilkins points out how the legends about Harriet Tubman are different from the reality. Are people more interested in a flamboyant person than an "ordinary" one? Why would Wilkins be concerned about setting the story straight?

DISCUSSION QUESTIONS

1. Chart the progress of Wilkins's story. Does it seem more like an essay or an oral folktale? Use specific examples from the text to support your response.

   It shares more characteristics with an oral folktale than an essay. The story jumps around and covers a large variety of information about Tubman and Wilkins's family members.

2. Which historical "legends" about Harriet Tubman does Wilkins clarify?

   Wilkins clarifies the historical legends of where Tubman was hit on the head, how Tubman did not wear a man's hat or clothing while rescuing slaves, how Tubman's name was actually Harriet Tubman Davis, and how Tubman engineered the Combahee River Battle.

3. Why is Wilkins concerned about presenting the "true" picture of Harriet Tubman?

   Wilkins believes that historians and the movie producers have presented a distorted view of Tubman.

4. Should readers accept the credibility of Wilkins's remembrances of Tubman? Why or why not?

   Wilkins's story should not be discounted. It should be believed in that she is passing down family history. We know that historians are not infallible and that they have been known to record historical "facts" in the way that they feel is most appropriate.

SONG OF THE SON

Jean Toomer

Discuss with your students the connections they have with the cities and towns in which they were born. Why are these places special to them? Jean Toomer felt connected to the land when he visited the South. Discuss with your students the possibilities of being connected to a land or era in which they were not born.

DISCUSSION QUESTIONS

1. The speaker in the poem refers to a "parting soul in song." What souls are parting from where in this poem?

   The connection African Americans had with the land is the soul that is parting. African Americans were moving from the agrarian South to the urban North.

2. In the second stanza, why does the speaker in the poem refer to himself as "Thy son"?

   The persona recognizes that he is a part of the land even though he does not live there.

3. How does the speaker in the poem propose to save what is being lost? Why is this method an effective one?

   The persona proposes to celebrate the land in poetry.

CHAPTER FIVE

STANDING GROUND

IF WE MUST DIE

Claude McKay

Claude McKay wrote this poem in response to race riots between African Americans and whites in various cities in the United States in 1919. Metaphor plays an important role in McKay's poem. The images of animals and blood help to make his poem more aggressive. Discuss with your students the use of active and passive resistance by people of color in the fight for political, economic, and social equality.

DISCUSSION QUESTIONS

1. McKay wrote this poem in the form of a Shakespearean sonnet. What problem or situation is presented in the three quatrains? What solution or resolution is presented in the couplet?

   In the three quatrains, McKay describes how African Americans must not feel as though their deaths are without valor. His resolution is that African Americans must fight back against the racists and die with dignity for the causes they believe in.

2. McKay uses similes and metaphors throughout the poem to describe the treatment of African Americans. What do you think the speaker means in lines 1 through 4?

McKay is stating that if African Americans must die, at least it should not be without distinction and honor, as is the death of unknowing farm animals herded to their slaughter.

3. What is the "one deathblow" discussed in line 11? How will it stop the "thousand blows"?

Opinions will vary, but most students should feel that the single deathblow refers to that small, yet surprising injury often inflicted by a far weaker opponent engaging a superior force. Many students will argue that one deathblow does not so much stop the thousand blows as it does make a point of gallant defiance in the face of certain defeat.

4. The speaker in the poem says "If we must die, O let us nobly die, . . ." Who would consider their death noble? Why? What are the advantages of a noble death over a less than noble death?

Other African Americans would consider those who gave their lives as having died nobly because the odds were stacked against them. The advantage of a noble death is that it can provide inspiration for others to continue to resist oppression.

I, Too

Langston Hughes

One way to introduce Langston Hughes's poem is to have a student read the poem aloud and then divide the class into groups and have each group discuss the social and financial situation of African Americans after World War I. In addition, the groups should discuss why all blacks would not have felt like they were being treated like "Americans" in light of what was going on in the United States during the "Roaring Twenties." The groups can then share their responses with the whole class.

DISCUSSION QUESTIONS

1. The poem begins with the line "I, too, sing America." It ends with the line "I, too, am America." What are the similarities and differences between these two statements?

   These statements have similar words and identical form; they both indicate a pride in America. These statements differ by virtue of their relationship: the last sentence gives a reason for the first.

2. The first line of the second stanza reads: "I am the darker brother." Whose "darker brother" is the speaker in the poem? Discuss the multiple meanings of the word "darker" and how those definitions affect the meaning of the line and the meaning of the poem.

   Dark can refer to more than color, such as skin tone. Dark can also mean secretive or hidden away. Many whites have not treated blacks as their equals—they have kept African Americans in the shadows, hidden.

3. Who or what are the "They" referred to in the second stanza? What role or roles do you think "They" have played in the poem's speaker's life?

   "They" could be white employers or white society in general. "They" have played a role of domination in the speaker's life, having not treated the speaker as an equal.

4. In the third stanza, the speaker says: "Nobody'll dare / Say to me, / 'Eat in the kitchen,' / Then." What is the tone of these lines? How is this tone different from the tone in the first and second stanzas?

   There is a forceful tone in these lines, and it differs from the more relaxed, matter-of-fact tone in the first and second stanzas. The speaker is stating that at that time he or she will not be moved from the table where he or she has a rightful place.

A SUMMER TRAGEDY

Arna Bontemps

In this story Arna Bontemps's characters, Jeff and Jennie Patton, make a decision to end their lives. This decision is not made lightly and is made only after the couple believe that they no longer can give each other the care that they require and that Jeff cannot farm his land. Discuss with your students the hardships of aging and financial stress. The focus of this story is not so much the death of this older couple but on their decision, for once in their lives, to act independently on what they consider to be their best interests. Suggest to your students that they research the role of the sharecropper during the Depression.

DISCUSSION QUESTIONS

1. How do the time and place in which the story is set help shape the story?

   The rual setting and the Depression-era poverty of the times—the early 1930s—help to make the action of the story believable.

2. What types of crops did Jeff and Jennie grow on their farm? Were they successful farmers? Why or why not?

   Jeff and Jennie grew cotton on the land they worked for forty-five years. They were not successful farmers in that they did not own their land, they were in debt, and the nutrients in the soil had been used up from continually growing cotton.

3. How have the hardships that Jeff and Jennie have endured and shaped them as individuals? As a married couple?

   Students' responses will vary. One possible answer is that each hardship they have endured—the death of their children, the loss of crops and income—has hurt them as individuals but, more importantly, has caused them to be critically dependent on each other.

4. At the end of the story, as Jeff and Jennie's car goes in the stream, what was your reaction? What do you assume happened? Support your responses with specific information from the story.

   Students' responses will vary, depending on how well they have surmised the story's ending. (The title is a big clue that many may have picked up on.) They should find plenty of evidence in the story to support a conclusion that the couple felt they had no alternative to suicide. (*Note*: Discussions of suicide—both regarding this story and in real life—should be handled in a sensitive manner.)

5. Against whom or what do you think Jeff and Jennie take a stand? Do you think their choice of action was the best one? Why or why not?

Jeff and Jennie take a stand against a society or life in general that did not allow them to have any control over their destinies. Whether or not their choice was "the best one" is debatable. They could have taken a stand by living—fighting the odds against them. However, their choice of dying can be seen as allowing them to have power against a system (the share-cropping system or even the aging process) they could never overcome.

WILLIE

Maya Angelou

Maya Angelou illustrates the determination of the human spirit in this poem. Discuss with your students how physical handicaps and aging can limit how we move our body parts *without* limiting us mentally or spiritually. Have students discuss how Willie embodies the spirit of African Americans as they have struggled to survive in the United States.

DISCUSSION QUESTIONS

1. The poem begins by the speaker saying, "Willie was a man without fame" and ends with a quotation from Willie, "I am the Rhyme." How does the first line prepare you for the rest of the poem? When you reach the last line of the poem, do you still feel the same way about the poem? How did your thoughts change or stay the same?

   Students should feel that the "Willie without fame" is shown to be the "every person" that embodies the unconquerable spirit of African Americans. Their thoughts about Willie should have changed as they move from concerns about an individual to appreciation of Willie as a symbol of a race of people.

2. Why do you think Willie describes himself using metaphors that refer to nature and children?

   The future of the world lies in the hands of the world's children. Willie is a part of the natural beauty of the world and his soul possesses qualities that are childlike in their simplicity and innocence.

3. How does Willie stand his ground? What belief has he refused to give up? How is this belief supported by the last stanza of the poem?

Willie stands his ground by refusing to be limited and defined by physical capabilities or the opinions and actions of others. He recognizes his
inner beauty and his interconnectedness to nature and the spirit of hope.

AN ADDRESS DELIVERED AT THE OPENING OF THE COTTON STATES' EXPOSITION IN ATLANTA, GEORGIA, SEPTEMBER, 1895

Booker T. Washington

Booker T. Washington is well known for cofounding Tuskegee Institute
(now Tuskegee University) and for his autobiography *Up from Slavery*. Some
of your students might know that Washington is also known for his belief in
vocational education for African Americans. Discuss with your students the
pressure Washington was under when he made his address; Washington was
the first black person to speak before an Exposition audience composed of
southern and northern industrialists. In this speech Washington attempts not
to insult his white audience while making a plea to them to hire African
Americans instead of immigrants to work in their factories. On the other
hand, it is important to point out to students that Washington advocated that
blacks give up their right to vote, focus on vocational training, and interact
with whites only in a work situation. Also, discuss with students how whites,
and not blacks, labeled Washington as the leader of African Americans.

DISCUSSION QUESTIONS

1. Using specific evidence from the speech, explain the similarities and differences between the two ways (first, concerning black people; second,
   concerning white people) Washington uses his analogy of "Cast down
   your buckets where you are."

   Washington wanted blacks to focus on working in their local communities. Washington wanted the white industrialists to hire black workers
   instead of immigrants.

2. Washington states: "It is at the bottom of life we must begin, and not at
   the top. Nor should we permit our grievances to overshadow our opportunities." Do you agree or disagree with this statement? Why?

Student responses will vary. Washington believed if blacks started in the most humble position, then eventually blacks would show whites that they could make a positive contribution to society.

3. One of the most often quoted lines from this speech is: "In all things that are purely social we can be as separate as the fingers, yet one as the hand in all things essential to mutual progress." Why would Washington want to assure southern and northern industrialists that blacks and whites do not have to socialize together, but that they could work in businesses together?

Washington did not want to offend his audience by suggesting that blacks and whites should socialize together, but he did want to emphasize that blacks and whites could work together so whites would hire blacks instead of immigrants to work in their factories.

4. Washington's critics often accused him of not being an aggressive fighter for the advancement of African Americans. Using specific examples from this speech, illustrate how Washington is working for the advancement of African Americans.

Washington, through advocating the hard-working, loyal, and humble nature of African Americans, was trying to convince the industrialists that the black people, with whom the industrialists were familiar, would make better employees than foreigners, with whom the industrialists were not familiar.

CHAPTER 3: OF MR. BOOKER T. WASHINGTON AND OTHERS

W. E. B. Du Bois

W. E. B. Du Bois was an intellectual who opposed Booker T. Washington's advocating that blacks give up their right to vote, focus on vocational training, and interact with whites only in a work situation. In this chapter from *The Souls of Black Folk*, Du Bois presents his counterargument to Washington's position. In addition, Du Bois argues that African Americans should select their own leaders instead of whites dictating who their leader is (as in the case of Washington).

DISCUSSION QUESTIONS

1. What does Du Bois identify as Booker T. Washington's "Atlanta Compromise"? Why does Du Bois consider it a compromise?

   Du Bois identifies Washington's willingness to divert the energy that was driving blacks to their rightful place as American citizens for ideals of material prosperity as Washington's compromise.

2. Why does Du Bois critique the identification of Negro leaders by groups outside of the black community?

   Du Bois felt that only a specific group of people can identify the qualities they want their leader to have.

3. According to Du Bois, Booker T. Washington asked black people to give up three things. What are these three things, and why does Du Bois consider the loss of them detrimental to black people as American citizens?

   The three things are political power, civil rights, and higher education. Without these three things, African Americans cannot be full American citizens.

MISS ROSIE

Lucille Clifton

Many of us are aware of the situation of homeless people in the United States. We do not, however, know many of the homeless on a personal level. In this poem, Lucille Clifton creates a speaker who not only personally knows an African-American homeless woman, but who also knows that woman's history. The knowledge the speaker has of where the woman has been in life and who she is now gives the speaker strength to survive. Discuss with your students the importance of seeing each person as an individual who has worth, even if that person has had misfortune change his or her life.

DISCUSSION QUESTIONS

1. The poem names the homeless woman as Miss Rosie. What is the significance of the speaker's knowing Miss Rosie's name? Of the speaker knowing that the homeless woman was once called the "Georgia Rose"?

The significance of the speaker knowing Miss Rosie's name—knowing she was once called the "Georgia Rose"—is that the speaker knows of the glory of Miss Rosie's life before she became a street person.

2. This poem does not have any punctuation except for one comma. How do the line breaks (where each line ends) help control the feeling of the poem?

   The line breaks serve as punctuation, controlling the feel of the poem by making the reader pause at the line breaks.

3. The speaker watches Miss Rosie and sees the conditions in which Miss Rosie is living. These conditions, however, do not make the speaker lose respect for Miss Rosie. Why not?

   The speaker does not lose respect for Miss Rosie because she knows that a person is more than just his or her outward appearance. She knows Miss Rosie's history. She knows a part of Miss Rosie's life.

4. The poem ends with the speaker saying "I stand up / through your destruction / I stand up." What do you think these statements mean? Why do you think the speaker feels this way about Miss Rosie's situation?

   The speaker gains strength to keep surviving by seeing Miss Rosie in her present condition. She shows respect for Miss Rosie.

CHAPTER SIX

IDENTITY

WE WEAR THE MASK

Paul Laurence Dunbar

People wear masks for varied reasons at different times. Have students read the poem silently and discuss the types of masks they believe are worn in this poem. The mask wearer in this poem confirms to a degree the stereotype that was often assigned to African Americans in comedy sketches as well as in other walks of life.

DISCUSSION QUESTIONS

1. For whom is the poet speaking in "We Wear the Mask"?

   The poet is speaking for African Americans.

2. How important is it for wearers of masks to "let the world dream otherwise" about their true feelings?

   Students should be able to think of a time when they or one of their friends or relatives pretended to have a type of mood opposite from the one they actually displayed.

3. Do you know people who wear masks? What do those masks usually hide?

Students should be able to think of instances when either they or others whom they know have disguised their true feelings or motives.

FROM *THE AUTOBIOGRAPHY OF MALCOLM X*

Malcolm X with Alex Haley

Alex Haley, the author of *Roots*, collaborated with Malcolm X on his autobiography. Malcolm X was known for his ability to speak and hold audiences spellbound. His autobiography demystifies him and makes him a real human being. You may wish to discuss his strong relationship with his mother, especially during the time he was known by his original name of Malcolm Little. He joined the Black Muslim movement while in prison and changed his named to Malcolm X.

DISCUSSION QUESTIONS

1. How would you describe Malcolm's father? Why do you think he was the kind of person he was?

Some students might suggest that Malcolm's father is a strong African-American man; he was self-reliant.

2. After his father's death, Malcolm says of his mother, "We couldn't see, as clearly as she did, the trials that lay ahead." What do you think he meant by this statement? Cite some examples from the selection.

Malcolm's mother knew she had responsibilities that were solely hers when her husband was killed. She had to take care of eight children, and she had to fight with an insurance company about her husband's death benefits.

3. Malcolm X sensed that he would someday die a violent death, as his father did. Cite some specific examples from the reading that support his prognostication.

Malcolm speaks at the outset of his story about dying a violent death.

HIDDEN NAME AND COMPLEX FATE

Ralph Ellison

Ellison suggests that the personal experience of a writer must become secondary to one's craft as a writer. He maintains that the particular facts of injustice are beside the point. Ellison differentiates between being Black and being a writer. You may wish to have students discuss the two points of view in their small groups after they have read the selection. You may wish to begin reading the selection in class and have students continue reading the selection at home or silently in class. Ellison also talks about the functions of a name; you may wish to discuss these functions as ways for persons to create an identity.

DISCUSSION QUESTIONS

1. What, according to Ellison, are the functions of a name?

Names contain all of the values and traditions of our familial past.

2. How does Ellison view the personal experience of the writer in relationship to his art?

There is a close relationship between the writer's experience and his art.

3. Does Ellison differentiate between his identity as an African-American male and his identity as a writer?

No, he does not.

4. What is the main concern of the American novel, and what does a multicultural society contribute or require?

Students might discuss the fact that the novel in America concerns itself with the idea of one-and-the-many, the mosaic, and the diversity within the idealized character called "the American."

WHERE IS THE BLACK COMMUNITY?

Joyce Carol Thomas

Discuss with students what it means to stereotype people. Have your students discuss how one group of people or one type of situation cannot represent everybody who is a member of a certain group of people.

DISCUSSION QUESTIONS

1. Many people seem to think African Americans live in one specific black community. Using specific information from the poem, explain why the black community cannot be in one place.

   All black people are not the same. They have different incomes, levels of education, and religions. They have different dreams and visions.

2. What types of images does each stanza evoke about African Americans? Choose two adjectives that summarize all of the images and explain why these two adjectives best describe them.

   Students' responses will vary. Students should realize that the images contained in the poem are varied and that the people they describe are equally varied.

3. The speaker describes images of African Americans that are not the ones often highlighted on the evening news. Identify these images and explain why they aren't the ones we see in the news.

   All of the images are of black people in a specific place. These are considered "ordinary" people in "ordinary" places. The "ordinary" is rarely considered newsworthy.

OUR SPIRITUAL STRIVINGS

W. E. B. Du Bois

W. E. B. Du Bois, the recognized intellectual thinker and leader of modern African Americans, discusses in this essay the struggle that blacks endure in order to attain what some have called a "self-conscious personhood." You may wish to discuss with students a term used by Du Bois—"the problem" as it pertains to African Americans.

DISCUSSION QUESTIONS

1. Du Bois published *The Souls of Black Folk* in 1903. He speaks to what many called the "Negro Problem." Is there still such a problem today? If not, why not?

   Student responses will vary.

2. At the end of paragraph 2, Du Bois says: ". . . walls strait [straight] and stubborn to the whitest but . . . unscalable to the sons of night." Who, in your opinion, are the sons of night?

   More than likely, he refers to African Americans as the sons of night.

3. In your small group, discuss what you believe to be the status of black people at the time Du Bois wrote this essay in 1903. Remember that only forty years had passed since the signing of the Emancipation Proclamation in 1863.

   The state of the African American at this time centers on uncertainty and weariness. However, African Americans were still hopeful at the prospect of gaining complete freedom.

ALL ABOUT MY JOB

Alice Childress

Discuss with your students the impact that our jobs should have on our lives and on our identities. Does our education or social position determine what type of person we are as well?

DISCUSSION QUESTIONS

1. What characteristics does the woman narrator display in this story? Use specific information to support your general statements. Are these characteristics connected to the type of work she does?

   The narrator is straightforward and honest. These characteristics are not connected to the type of work she does.

2. The protagonist states ". . . the idea of the pictures was to show how we are improvin' ourselves by leaps and bounds through the kinda work that we're doin'." What types of "improvements" have the black people attending the bazaar made in their lives? Have these improvements had an impact on how they treat people they consider beneath them in social standing? Why or why not?

   The blacks attending the bazaar have made advancements in education and economic levels. These improvements have not improved how they treat people they consider below them in social standing. Education and money do not make people "wise."

3. The narrator in the story first tells her friend, Marge, that she is not proud of working as a domestic, but by the end of the story she tells Marge she is proud. Why does the protagonist change her mind?

   The narrator begins to recognize the value of hard, honest work.

4. What is the significance of the protagonist not having a name?

   The narrator could be any African-American person.

STRANGER IN THE VILLAGE

James Baldwin

Baldwin tells about his experiences as a lone black man in a small Swiss village where he had gone to write. It is believed that no African Americans had ever lived in this village. However, it was a custom of the villagers to purchase Africans in order to convert them to Christianity, though it is unlikely that there was ever any contact between the purchasers and the Africans whom they bought.

DISCUSSION QUESTIONS

1. What did the village people think about Baldwin and how did they react to him?

   The people viewed him with curiosity. Some thought he was an oddity, some mistrusted him, and others wanted to be considered his friend because he was "different."

2. Baldwin says being called *Neger! Neger!* by the children caused him to react by trying to be pleasant. What experience did he have in America that caused him to react this way?

   As an African American his experience had always been that he had to make people, especially white people, like him.

3. What do you think Baldwin means when he says that the most illiterate villagers, in a way, are related to Dante, Shakespeare, Michelangelo, and others and that he is not?

   The persons whom Baldwin names are Caucasian, and he is not.

EPILOGUE FROM *INVISIBLE MAN*

Ralph Ellison

At the end of Ralph Ellison's *Invisible Man,* the unnamed protagonist, the invisible man, has retreated to an underground hole where he attempts to analyze his feelings of invisibility. Feeling "invisible" among others is a universal feeling. However, when this feeling is coupled with personal knowledge of racism and discrimination, it can paralyze a person. Discuss these issues with your students.

DISCUSSION QUESTIONS

1. Is the unnamed protagonist figuratively or literally "invisible"? Use specific information from the reading to support your response.

   The protagonist is figuratively invisible.

2. Whom does the invisible man blame for his invisibility? Others? Himself? Both? Why?

   He blames himself and others. Others have been trained not to see him and he has let their treatment influence how he sees himself.

3. By the end of the reading, does the protagonist come to a sense of self? Support your response with specific information from the reading.

   The protagonist comes to a limited sense of self and knows that knowing one's self is a lifelong process.

CHAPTER SEVEN

DREAMERS AND REVOLUTIONARIES

VIVE NOIR!

Mari Evans

In Mari Evans's poem, the speaker challenges whites to imagine what life would be like if everything important in life were black, and whites were in the minority. Discuss with students how it is a part of human nature to resist change, and why, sometimes before we can envision change, we have to see the new point of view radically.

DISCUSSION QUESTIONS

1. Evans uses limited punctuation in this poem. There are no commas or periods and sentences start with lowercase letters. She uses ellipses three times and a question mark once. How does the placement of the words on the lines and the limited use of punctuation affect the overall feeling of the poem?

   This poem reads like stream of consciousness. It is as though we hear the thoughts as they are going through the speaker's mind. The lack of formal punctuation makes us read the poem quickly. The placement of the words and lines, however, makes us slow down in our reading of the poem.

2. The speaker in the poem refers to himself or herself with a lowercase *i*. Who do you think the speaker is? How would you describe the speaker based on the description or images he or she presents in this poem?

The speaker is a person who has decided she or he is tired of the way life has been for many African Americans. From the speaker's descriptions, we can say that the speaker wants radical change to occur.

3. Throughout the poem the speaker is talking to someone whom he or she calls "baby" and "you." To whom is the speaker addressing the poem? What is the speaker's attitude toward this person or group?

The speaker is addressing the poem to the collective "you" that persists in oppressing African Americans in the United States. The speaker has a negative attitude toward this "you."

4. Is the speaker in the poem a dreamer or a revolutionary? Why? Use specific information from the poem to support your response.

Students' responses will vary. Be sure they cite specific instances in the poem to back up their responses.

NIKKI-ROASA

Nikki Giovanni

As has been expressed in Dunbar's "We Wear the Mask" and Thomas's "Where Is the Black Community?" the view that some whites have of African Americans' lives often does not match reality. This contradiction can lead some whites to make assumptions about black people's happiness and unhappiness. Nikki Giovanni's poem forces us to examine stereotypes and our assumptions about other people's lives.

DISCUSSION QUESTIONS

1. In lines 24 through 26, the speaker says that a "white person" would not understand that "Black love is black wealth." Why or why not? Do you agree?

Responses will vary. Many students will agree that white society has a poor idea of what matters to African Americans.

2. In lines 18 and 19, the speaker says "and though you're poor it isn't poverty that / concerns you." What things are important to the speaker? Why would these things be more important than poverty?

The speaker in the poem is concerned about her family and feeling loved within her family. With a family's love, poverty can be survived.

3. Examine the occasions the speaker describes. What conclusions can you draw about these occasions? Is there something special about the locations or the people who are involved?

Some occasions the speaker describes are "happy birthdays" and "very good christmases." The occasions and even the people are not necessarily "special"; the important thing is that the family, a group of loved ones, is together.

4. The poem begins with the line "childhood remembrances are always a drag" and ends with ". . . all the while I was / quite happy." Are these two thoughts contradictory? Use words and phrases from the poem to support your answer.

The poem illustrates the contradiction that can exist if people look only at external issues. Even though the speaker's family lived in poverty, they were not poor because they had a wealth of family love.

THE IMMEDIATE PROGRAM OF THE AMERICAN NEGRO

W. E. B. Du Bois

W. E. B. Du Bois's call for political, industrial, and social equality for African Americans in 1914 is a call that is still being made by today's African-American leaders. Students should be encouraged to discuss the necessity of all three aspects over the necessity of only one or two.

Discussion Questions

1. Du Bois opens his essay by stating that "The American Negro demands equality—political equality, industrial equality, and social equality." The essay was written in 1914. Why was it necessary for African Americans to insist on equality in each of these areas then?

   Without political equality, African Americans have no power to elect officials to represent them or to determine the laws of the country. Without industrial equality, African Americans cannot earn enough money to support themselves. Without social equality, African Americans cannot experience the rights and privileges of U.S. citizens.

2. Du Bois presents four practical stages to accomplish the goal of equality. Identify these steps and establish the connections between them and Du Bois's three aspects of equality.

   The four steps include the following: 1. The American courts must protect the legal rights of all American citizens; 2. All legal discriminations based on race and color must be eliminated; 3. All American citizens must interact with each other; and 4. The press must publish the truth about conditions for blacks in America. The four steps are directly related to Du Bois's aspects of equality.

3. Du Bois argues against giving African-American children only vocational training. He says that African Americans will not have "decency and honour until the house servant becomes the Servant in the House." What does Du Bois mean by this statement?

   Du Bois means that African Americans cannot have "decency and honour" in the United States until they are in positions of power: political, economic, and social power. "The Servant in the House" means serving as an elected official in the House of Representatives.

PREFACE TO A TWENTY VOLUME SUICIDE NOTE

Amiri Baraka (LeRoi Jones)

Written for his daughter, Kellie Jones, this poem is said to present a great technical rendering. Discuss the imagery found in the poem and how it reflects the emotions expressed.

DISCUSSION QUESTIONS

1. What is the poet's attitude about life as expressed in lines 1 and 2 of the first stanza?

   Students might find different emotions expressed, such as resignation, isolation, or depression.

2. What do you find ironic about the poem's title?

   Through discussion, students should see the irony, as well as the hyperbole, in the idea that a suicide note would consist of twenty volumes. Students should recognize that the poem begins in despair and ends with hope.

3. After having read the last stanza of the poem, what do you think the poet's attitude is about suicide?

   Students' answers will vary. They should realize that the poem ends with hope; therefore, the poet's attitude about suicide has changed.

ASSASSINATION

Haki Madhubuti (Don L. Lee)

This poem was written in memory of Martin Luther King Jr. While students may be familiar with the events surrounding the assassination of Dr. King, you may wish to remind them that Dr. King was visiting in Memphis,

Tennessee, to support the garbage collectors who were on strike. While standing on the balcony of the Lorraine Motel, along with other civil rights workers, he was shot and killed by a sniper reportedly located in a building directly across from his motel.

DISCUSSION QUESTIONS

1. Who is the "they" the speaker is referring to in the poem?

   Students will probably think "they" are the police or the FBI.

2. Lines 21 to 25 say: "they came running in the wrong direction." Discuss the irony of this statement.

   The policemen should have been running toward the direction of the gunshots in order to apprehend the person rather than toward where King lay dying.

3. What, in your opinion, is the right direction?

   Students may suggest that running toward the area from which the gunshots were fired is the right direction.

4. How does calling the victim "the King" make the poem more powerful than if the poet referred to Dr. King by name?

   One possibility is that by calling him "the King," the speaker gives the victim a more important title and status than an ordinary person. Another possibility is that if Dr. King had been a real king, the policemen and security officers would have reacted more quickly to apprehend the assassin.

WINTER IN AMERICA

Gil Scott-Heron

In 1973 when Gil Scott-Heron first published this song, America was still involved in the Vietnam War, protests were going on across America's university campuses, and the women's rights movement was gaining power.

However, the strong push for civil rights that America witnessed in the 1960s had waned. Discuss with your students how other national concerns shifted America's attention from the civil rights movement.

DISCUSSION QUESTIONS

1. Scott-Heron uses the phrase "winter in america" as a metaphor through-out the song. What does this metaphor represent? Why is it an effective metaphor? Use specific information from the song to support your responses.

   It represents the death of the civil rights movement. It is an effective metaphor because in the winter plants die and are covered with ice and snow.

2. The speaker says, "All of the healers done been killed or put in jail." Which African-American healers and leaders were killed or jailed? How did their deaths or imprisonment affect African-American communities?

   Malcolm X and Martin Luther King Jr. were killed. Leaders of the Black Panther party were jailed. The "leaders" who had encouraged African Americans to change American society and laws were not there to moti-vate blacks to action.

3. The song ends with the speaker saying "ain't nobody fighting 'cause nobody knows what to save." Is the speaker giving up the hope that conditions in American can change? Why or why not?

   The speaker is saying that Americans are divided over which issues are of importance. Thus, no issues receive the support that they should.

TO MISSISSIPPI YOUTH

Malcolm X

Before students read the selection, you may wish to have several of them do some research on the life of Malcolm X and be prepared to share their findings with the class. Malcolm X was called upon many times to give inspirational talks to various groups of African Americans. The audience for this particular speech is a group of young African Americans from Mississippi.

DISCUSSION QUESTIONS

1. Malcolm X says that young people should look, listen, and make their own decisions before taking any action. Do you agree with this advice? Why or why not?

   Students' answers will vary. They should be able to discuss this question by relating it to a personal experience.

2. At the time he made this speech, Malcolm X was opposed to nonviolence unless everyone was forced to behave nonviolently. How do you think he would react if he were alive today? Do you think his opinions might have changed?

   Students' answers will vary. Some may believe he would still oppose nonviolence; others may believe that he would have changed his mind. His visit to Mecca brought a change in his attitudes toward whites and violence; he would probably speak out against it.

3. Malcolm X maintains that he does not criticize those persons who advocate nonviolence in gaining freedom for African Americans. Name one or two people to whom he might be referring.

   He was speaking here about Martin Luther King Jr.

I HAVE A DREAM

Martin Luther King Jr.

This speech was given at a mass civil rights rally in Washington, D.C., in 1963. Have students read the speech aloud or play a recording of the speech by Dr. King. Have students discuss memorable or favorite lines.

DISCUSSION QUESTIONS

1. King says: "We must forever conduct our struggle on the high plane of dignity and discipline." Discuss in your small group what you think he means.

   He believed that African Americans should always act in a civil and well-controlled manner.

2. What is this "check" King mentions in his speech?

   A "check" of justice in all aspects of one's being.

3. When King made this speech, there was blatant segregation and discrimination against African Americans. If he were alive today, what kind of speech would he make, and what are some of the things he might say?

   Students' answers will vary. One possibility is that King would make the same speech, while addressing himself more to the dire economic situation in which many African Americans find themselves today.

CHAPTER EIGHT

WOMEN

THE TREE OF LOVE

Linda Goss

Discuss with your students the strength and beauty of trees. Point out how trees can withstand the elements of nature but also how they are susceptible to disease and the elements.

DISCUSSION QUESTIONS

1. What does the protagonist's grandmother mean when she says "Old Willa was a love tree and the Tree of Love gives shade to all"? Is her comment a metaphor? Explain your response.

   The grandmother's comment is a metaphor for the love and strength that is passed from one generation to the next in African-American families.

2. In your small group, find and discuss some of the folkloric events in this story. How do these details add to the story's plot and theme?

Student responses will vary. Some folkloric elements are the supposed mystical powers of Old Willa and Old Willa hiding Uncle Love Joy from the slave catchers. These events make us believe that Old Willa is almost a person rather than "just" a tree. Another folkloric element is that the story is retold by the author's mother, thus verbally passing on the story of Old Willa.

3. What type of strength does the protagonist get from her mother's story? Why would the protagonist need this strength as an administrator working in a company in New York?

From her mother's story, the protagonist gets a sense that she is loved and is a part of the universe. A place of business is often impersonal, and its atmosphere is such that it tends to take away our sense of belonging to a group that loves us.

THE WOMAN'S MOURNING SONG

bell hooks

Discuss the nature of a "mourning song" with your students. Bring an example of a mourning song to class. Discuss with students the similarities and differences between the song you bring into class and bell hooks's poem. Have a student do an interpretive reading of hooks's poem. Discuss with students the process of bread making and how this process could be used as a metaphor.

DISCUSSION QUESTIONS

1. What is the woman mourning in this poem? Use specific lines and phrases from the poem to support your response.

The woman is mourning the death of a loved one, probably a husband. One phrase from the poem to support this is "go away death / go from love's house / go make your empty bed."

2. Identify the blues qualities and/or structures in this poem. How do these elements contribute to the meaning of the poem?

Blues qualities and structures include the repetition of lines and images of sorrow and survival.

3. In line 10, who are the singers to whom the speaker refers? What does the speaker mean when she says "the warmth of many ovens / comforts"? What are the connections between lines 8 through 10 and lines 11 through 13?

The singers are other women. The speaker is saying that knowing there are women across the world doing the same thing that she is doing gives her comfort even though she is alone in her kitchen. The connection is that the woman is not alone in the world.

GETTING THE FACTS OF LIFE

Paulette Childress White

Sometimes stories about life are not enough to prepare us to live our lives. Instead, it is necessary that we experience life in order to understand it. Paulette Childress White's character Minerva learns, as she begins her journey from being a girl to being a woman, that "life" is a complicated thing. As Minerva observes how some men and a white social worker treat her mother and herself, she realizes that being an African-American woman "sometimes must be hard."

DISCUSSION QUESTIONS

1. Why hasn't Minerva thought about her family being on welfare even though the family has been on welfare for a year?

At twelve, Minerva still retains most of the innocence and detachment typical of children her age. Her sudden awareness of her family's financial state is a sign of her moving from the "carefree" world of a child to the serious world of an adult.

2. How do Minerva and her mother interact with each other when they are alone? When they are with others? Why are the two types of behavior important?

Minerva and her mother have a close relationship. In private, Minerva and her mother laugh and talk with each other. In public, they both are quiet and Minerva knows how to "read" her mother's looks in order to know what she should and should not do. These behaviors protect them from the harshness of the world outside of their family.

3. Minerva says she is: "chief baby-sitter, biscuit-maker and broom-wielder." Does being one of two sisters in a family of eight children have an influence on these descriptions?

Minerva plays a "traditional" female role in her family as an older daughter, that of caregiver. She defines herself realistically and somewhat proudly.

4. At the beginning of the story, how does Minerva feel about moving from childhood into womanhood? How does she feel at the end of the story? Use specific evidence from the story to support your responses.

Minerva is pleased with her life the way it is. She does not believe that she can be a "good" woman (i.e., play the roles traditionally assigned to women). Encourage students to see how society tends to limit women's roles.

5. Discuss the "facts of life" that Minerva gets from being a sister and daughter, from the African-American community she lives in, and from the white case worker. How do they prepare her for life as a black woman?

Students responses will vary. One of the "facts" she learns is her mother's dignity and strength in the face of difficulty. Another "fact" is the patronizing way her mother is treated by the white case worker. Yet another is that it is hard to be a woman.

RESTORATION: A MEMORIAL— 9/18/91

Audre Lorde

In 1992 Audre Lorde died of breast cancer. She spent her writing career trying to illuminate readers to racial and social liberation issues. As this poem clearly illustrates, Lorde did not give in easily to death. Discuss with your students Lorde's use of the aftermath of a natural disaster, hurricane Hugo, to talk about how a woman recovering from chemotherapy looks to rebuilding her life after experiencing the loss of a loved one.

DISCUSSION QUESTIONS

1. Mark the metaphors and similes in this poem. What makes each unique or stand out from the other words and descriptions in the poem?

   Student responses will vary. The metaphors and similes all contain vividly described objects. Even in death and destruction there is a beauty that reminds us that we are alive.

2. The first two lines in the second stanza read: "Somewhere it is Tuesday / in the ordinary world." Why does the speaker make reference to "the ordinary world" as if she were not a part of it?

   The speaker's life is filled with her cancer and the loss of a loved one. She does not feel connected to what is going on around her.

3. In the last line of the poem, the speaker says "Learning to laugh again." Is the speaker's ability to laugh again a sign of weakness or strength? Support your response with words, phrases, or lines from the poem.

   The speaker's ability to laugh again is a sign of strength. She appreciates the beauty of what she has, even her cancer, as a sign of being alive.

TO DA-DUH, IN MEMORIAM

Paule Marshall

In many communities, knowledge about life and different cultures is passed from older relatives to younger ones. However, as Paule Marshall illustrates in her story, the messages behind the stories are not always clear to the storyteller or listener, especially as a child. Discuss with your students the importance of listening closely to older relatives and "reading between the lines."

DISCUSSION QUESTIONS

1. Compare and contrast the personalities of Da-Duh and the granddaughter. In what ways are they similar and dissimilar? What do these similarities and differences say about them?

   The grandmother and granddaughter are proud; they do not think about how their words affect others; they are stubborn; and they even share some similar physical qualities. They resist each other because they are so much alike.

2. Da-Duh becomes ill after hearing that the Empire State Building is taller than the tallest hill on the island. Why does this information disturb the grandmother?

   To the grandmother the island is the only real world that exists. Once she acknowledges that another world exists, and that it has used technology to build something bigger than the largest natural thing she knows, she feels insignificant and seems to lose her will to live.

3. Is the granddaughter responsible for Da-Duh's death? Why does she consider her painting tropical landscapes penance, or atonement for a sin?

   The grandmother seemed to make the decision to die. However, the granddaughter was not directly responsible for her death—only insensitive to how her grandmother viewed life. By painting the tropical landscapes in a room above a factory, the granddaughter is trying to unite the best of the natural world that her grandmother offered her with the technological world that the granddaughter lives in.

ONE THING I DONT NEED

Ntozake Shange

Since this poem was originally written for performance (as part of Shange's choreopoem *for colored girls*—a work combining dance, music, drama, and poetry), you may have a student prepare to do an oral interpretation or dramatic reading for the class. You may check with your media resource department or the library for the recording of the performance of *for colored girls*. As students read the poem, have them think about the word "sorry."

DISCUSSION QUESTIONS

1. Using specific examples from the poem, show how "sorry" has filled the speaker's life.

   Among examples of all-consuming "sorrys" are lines 3 through 11, 17 and 18, and 26 and 27.

2. Who is speaking in lines 14 and 15 and lines 21 through 25? Why are these lines indented?

   In lines 14 and 15 we hear the collective voice of the people who have filled the speaker's life with "sorry." In lines 21 through 25 we hear the narrator's voice as she leaves a message announcing a refusal to accept "sorry" any longer. The lines are indented to indicate a different voice speaking in the poem.

3. Reread the third stanza. How did the speaker in the poem modify her life to have a relationship with the other person? What impact did this modification have on her personality?

   The speaker will no longer play a passive role in the relationship. This change in her behavior allows her to express a full range of emotions — to be herself.

4. Compare the speaker's tone at the beginning of the poem and at the end of the poem. Are there similarities? Differences? What do these tones tell you about the speaker's attitude change?

   At the beginning the speaker sounds as though she wants something to change her life but she does not know how to go about making that change occur. As the poem progresses, the speaker gains strength and makes a decision about what she wants her life to be like. By the end of the poem the speaker has a strong sense of herself and of what types of behavior she will and will not tolerate from others.

MAGIC

Rita Dove

Deception, like magic, can make things appear out of nowhere and make other things disappear from sight. Rita Dove shows how as children we attempt to make our worlds better by detaching ourselves emotionally from the world around us. The questions you should ask your students are how long can emotional detachment protect us and what price do we have to pay in the long run for that emotional detachment. (Students may need to be told that in lines 8 through 11, the girl is sharpening household knives the old-fashioned way—on a spinning grinding stone or wheel.)

DISCUSSION QUESTIONS

1. What is the emotional connection between the girl and the world in which she lives? How does the girl in the poem feel about her life? Support your description with words and phrases from the poem.

   Responses will vary. The girl in the poem feels detached from the world in which she lives.

2. The poem states "So she rehearsed deception . . . ." Why is magic an important part of the girl's life?

   Responses will vary. The girl performs a life; she does not live a life. Through deception she can protect herself from being hurt by the world in which she lives.

3. Why is the picture of the Eiffel Tower in the Sunday paper a sign? Why is it important for her to "make it to Paris one day"?

   The girl is looking to escape her "normal" world. She wants the adventure that she believes Paris, a bright and exotic place, will offer her.

4. Is the young girl's dream of going to Paris realistic? What might keep her from obtaining her dream?

   By continuing to exist in a world of dreams and deception, she might lack the ability to take the concrete steps necessary to make her dream come true.

PLUMES

Georgia Douglas Johnson

In this play Georgia Douglas Johnson illustrates the agony a poor, rural African-American mother goes through as she tries to give her daughter's death a sense of dignity. Discuss with your students how drama allows us to understand the characteristics of a person through the use of dialogue and stage directions.

▣

DISCUSSION QUESTIONS

1. The play *Plumes* occurs in "a poor cottage in the South" in the 1920s. Explain how the setting of the play influences the action in the play. Use specific examples from the play to support your response.

   Since the play is set in a poor, rural community, and at a time in the distant past, it is not surprising that Charity does not have enough money to pay both for a doctor for her daughter and to bury her. Because the play is set in the rural South, we understand why Charity, as a poor African-American woman, does not completely trust a white doctor. We are not surprised that she values superstition and home remedies over the advice and treatments of the white doctor. The setting of the play makes its action believable.

2. In a play the character's name and the actor's facial expressions and body language convey as much information to the audience as the lines the actor speaks. Look up the definition of "charity" in a dictionary. Examine the stage directions for Charity. Describe Charity's characteristics using the definition of her name and specific examples from the stage directions to support your response.

   The word *charity* means an act or feeling of generosity. Charity's act of generosity is the desire to give her daughter a burial that reflects the importance of her life.

3. Why is it so important to Charity that her daughter, Emmerline, have a nice "putting away"? What do the "plumes" represent to Charity?

   It is only after Emmerline's death that Charity will be able to do something for her daughter that shows how important her daughter was. The "plumes" represent a richness that Charity could never give her daughter during her life. They also represent the importance of Emmerline's life.

4. Charity states that she loves Emmerline, but when the doctor offers to operate on Emmerline for fifty dollars, Charity hesitates because of what Tildy read in the coffee grounds. Why do you think Charity, as an African-American woman living in the South, would place more trust in the coffee grounds than in the white doctor saving her daughter's life?

Sadly, it is more than likely that in Charity's life the "wisdom" of coffee grounds is more attractive and acceptable than that of white doctors.

5. Emmerline dies before her mother makes a decision about the operation. Is Charity responsible for her daughter's death? Why or why not?

Charity is not responsible for Emmerline's death. Medicine or operations do not always cure a patient. Sometimes patients still die after receiving medication or having an operation.

CHAPTER NINE

MEN

STRONG MEN

Sterling Brown

You may wish to have students read the poem silently or to each other in their small groups before discussing the poem with the class.

DISCUSSION QUESTIONS

1. What does the poet mean when he says: "They taught you the religion they disgraced"?

   Students' responses may vary. One possibility is that religion teaches that each person is responsible for other people; that is, "I am my brother's keeper." The slaveholders and their overseers did not practice this admonition.

2. Who are the "they" in the poem? Why do you think the poet used this pronoun rather than a noun that is more specific?

   The "they" are the slaveholders. Students' answers may vary on the second part of the question. For example, using "they" makes the actions of the slaveholders and oppressors more universal. It's not just a particular person being blamed, it's a whole group of people.

3. Discuss the effect of dialect interspersed with standard English. What was the poet trying to convey? Do you think it was successful?

A possible answer is that the mixing of dialect and standard English underscores the differences between the oppressors and the slaves. The slaveholders speak well but do horrible things. The slaves, who speak in dialect, struggle to keep their spirits up and to keep getting stronger. Another possible answer is that the dialect functions like the refrain of a song, gathering meaning as the song progresses.

MY SEARCH FOR ROOTS

Alex Haley

Students may know about the story *Roots* and how it came to be. However, you may wish to inform students about the long search Haley conducted in order to discover his ancestral home. Haley remembered stories told by his female relatives concerning an African by the name of Kunta Kinte. These stories motivated Haley to begin the search for his roots.

Roots was a very successful television miniseries in the 1980s. You may wish to show portions of the miniseries when you study this selection.

DISCUSSION QUESTIONS

1. Who told the writer about his ancestor?

His grandmother and other older relatives.

2. How does the *Lord Ligonier* figure in Haley's story?

This is the ship on which Haley's great-great-great-grandfather had been brought from Africa as a slave.

3. Who is Kinte and how was he captured?

Kinte is Haley's great-great-great-grandfather, who was captured near his village while he was chopping wood to make a drum.

4. Would Alex Haley have been able to research his family tree without being told the story by his grandmother? Why or why not?

   If he had not heard the story from his grandmother, he would not have had a beginning source of information with which to connect.

SPEECH DELIVERED AT MADISON SQUARE GARDEN, MARCH 1924

Marcus Garvey

Discuss with students the life of Marcus Garvey. Garvey was the first to start an organized effort designed to foster a back-to-Africa movement for African Americans. Former American slaves were the founders of what is known today as Liberia, a West African country.

You might ask your students what would happen if all immigrant Americans were to return to the land of their ancestors.

DISCUSSION QUESTIONS

1. Garvey suggested that Africa should be the homeland for American blacks as well as for all blacks who were held as slaves by other countries. He thought all blacks should return to Africa. Keeping in mind when this speech was delivered (1924), what do you think of Garvey's proposal?

   Students' answers will vary. During this time there was great interest on the part of many blacks to return to Africa; however, most did not know the country from which they came.

2. Do you think Garvey was practicing racism when he made his proposal? Why or why not?

   Some students may feel that Garvey was advocating separatism, a form of racism.

3. In your small group, discuss Garvey's statement: "We are strangers in a strange land." What does he mean, and who are the strangers?

It is quite possible that Garvey expressed the sentiments of many blacks at the time. This country was different from their own and certainly they were treated as strangers rather than as persons who helped build the country with their labor over many years.

4. What do you think America would be like if every African American had returned to Africa?

African Americans have contributed greatly to our culture and the United States would have a different culture without their presence. Booker T. Washington created peanut butter. African Americans have contributed greatly to music—jazz, the blues, rock-and-roll—as well as literature (as evidenced by the selections in this book). Numerous other examples can be raised.

A BLACK MAN TALKS OF REAPING

Arna Bontemps

In introducing the poem, read it aloud to the class. Before students begin a general discussion of the poem, you may wish to have them list several questions they have about the poem in their writing journals. They may also do this in their small groups and then select a spokesperson to ask the questions of the whole class.

DISCUSSION QUESTIONS

1. What does Bontemps mean when he says "feed on bitter fruit"?

The metaphor might mean that African Americans continue to experience many demoralizing aspects of life ever since slavery.

2. What does it mean *to glean,* and what type of person would more than likely engage in the act of gleaning?

Gleaning is the act of collecting, bit by bit, grain that has been left behind by reapers. A poor person might be someone who would glean in order to get food.

3. The poet says: "I planted safe against this stark, lean year." What do you
   think he means by the statement?

   Students' answers will vary. Bontemps might be speaking of those free-
   doms won by a person who had been so dehumanized, yet found the
   courage to build a strong foundation of individual worth.

FROM *THE BIG SEA*

Langston Hughes

In this selection, Hughes tells how he came to write the well-received
and enduring poem, *The Negro Speaks of Rivers*. You might ask a student to
read the poem aloud to the class.

DISCUSSION QUESTIONS

1. *The Big Sea* was Hughes's first autobiography. How did he come to write
   the poem "The Negro Speaks of Rivers"?

   Hughes wrote the poem on his way to Mexico to visit his father; he completed it on the train just outside of St. Louis and published it in 1920.
   He was thinking about what the Mississippi River meant to African-
   American slaves, and the rivers from their homelands, and the poem
   developed from those thoughts.

2. What was Hughes's relationship with his father? With his mother?

   His relationship with his father is tenuous at best; his father was not
   impressed with Hughes's interest in literature. He hoped that his son
   would become a businessman such as he was. His relationship with his
   mother is about the same; she wants her son to go to work to support
   her instead of going to college.

3. What is your opinion about Hughes's statement: ". . . the old story of
   divorced parents who don't like each other, and take their grievances out
   on the offspring"?

While it is not always the case, divorced parents can sometimes use their children as a weapon to cause either grief or retribution.

4. Who is the *I* in the poem "The Negro Speaks of Rivers"?

Many students may recognize the *I* as Africans living on the continent as well as their brothers and sisters who are a part of the diaspora.

THE ONLY MAN ON LIBERTY STREET

William Melvin Kelley

This story takes place in a small, Southern town, where horse and buggy are the popular mode of transportation for the well-to-do and relations still seem to be very segregated. How does the setting affect the reading of the story?

Also discuss the narrator. The story is told from the point of view of the daughter of an interracial couple. How do you think it affects her?

DISCUSSION QUESTIONS

1. Mister Herder says: "Why should I live in that house when I must come here to know what a home is?" What do you think he means by this statement?

   The house on Liberty Street contains those human components, such as friendliness and companionship, of which a "home" consists.

2. How would you characterize Maynard Herder?

   Herder is a man of conviction, yet shows some signs of weakness. He is also kind and means well, as he wants to do right by Jennie and her mother.

3. What irony, if any, do you see in the title "The Only Man on Liberty Street"?

There is irony in the street's name; although Herder elects to live with Josie and Jennie, he is eventually deprived of the liberty to stay there by the demands of his white wife and others in the community.

MINSTREL MAN

Langston Hughes

This is a good poem to begin a discussion of perception versus reality. A minstrel is supposed to be a happy creature, but the man presented in the poem is feeling much differently.

DISCUSSION QUESTIONS

1. Historically, the minstrel has been a happy-go-lucky stereotype of African-American men. Langston Hughes offers a different perspective on how the minstrel acts. In your small group, discuss what you think this new perspective is.

   Some students may suggest that the new perspective shows the minstrel's questioning the stereotypical rendering of his being.

2. Is the person in this poem wearing a mask? If so, how can you tell?

   Yes, the person is "wearing" a mask; one example is found in the second stanza, lines 9 to 12.

3. What do you think the person is hiding behind his mask?

   It may be that the person is hiding his or her true feelings of pain and sorrow, while at the same time displaying a carefree spirit.

4. Compare this poem with "We Wear the Mask" by Paul Laurence Dunbar. How do these poems differ in their support of mask wearing?

   Answers will vary. "We Wear the Mask" takes a more vocal stance in support of wearing masks. "Minstrel Man" takes a more subdued, but stinging, position.

THE MAN WHO WAS ALMOST A MAN

Richard Wright

Have students discuss their definition of a *man* in a small group. What kinds of adjectives do they use to describe a man? Does Dave exhibit any of these characteristics?

This story is written in nonstandard American English. Does the dialect used affect students' reading of the story?

You may wish to show the videotape of this story—*Almos a Man*, starring La Var Burton. The tape is available through Fearson/Janus/Quercus, 500 Harbor Boulevard, Belmont, CA 94002.

DISCUSSION QUESTIONS

1. How did the accidental shooting of the mule change Dave's life?

   Dave left home to avoid further humiliation and to prove that he really was a man.

2. Why did Dave's mother give him the money for the gun?

   Dave pesters his mother and wears her down with his arguments. Finally, she relents and agrees to give him the money, but the gun is to be for Pa, not for Dave.

3. What is the relationship between Dave and his mother? Between Dave and his father? In your small group, discuss how his parents' actions did not teach him the maturity he so desperately wanted.

   The relationship between Dave and his mother seems to be a fairly typical relationship between mother and son. She is strict with him, but also allows him a bit of freedom and independence. The relationship between Dave and his father is more distant. His father orders Dave to do things, but doesn't pay much attention to him. Answers will vary as to how their actions did not teach him maturity. One possibility is that they both order him around, without letting him develop responsibility for his own actions.

CHAPTER TEN

THE UNION OF TWO

Haki R. Madhubuti

As an educator, writer, and publisher, Haki Madhubuti has made a commitment to strengthen the African-American community. Discuss with your students how we seek out wise individuals to provide us directions on how to live better lives. Sometimes these sages respond with riddles or send us on quests. Sometimes these wise ones tell us in plain language what we must do in order to grow, to love, and to pass our knowledge to future generations.

DISCUSSION QUESTIONS

1. The speaker in the poem says "those who grow into love / remain anchored / like egyptian architecture and seasonal flowers." With a partner, analyze this simile and provide an interpretation of it.

Both "Egyptian architecture" (sturdy) and "seasonal flowers" (delicate) have withstood the passage of time. Those people whose love is sturdy and delicate will remain in love with each other.

2. To what other idea does the speaker in the poem connect the institution of marriage? Why is this connection important to African Americans?

The speaker says "that the nations start in the family." If African Americans are to continue to grow as a people, they must have strong families. Strong families come from strong marriages.

3. What characteristics of this poem are similar to those found in folktales or stories from the oral tradition? What impact do these characteristics have on the message in the poem?

The poem is the answer to a question. It has a moral. Repetitious sentence structures aid in memorizing it.

THE WIFE OF HIS YOUTH

Charles W. Chesnutt

Intraracial prejudice—prejudice within a race due to social, economic, or physical differences of its members—is not discussed as much as interracial prejudice between different races. In this story, Mr. Ryder must balance the importance of his position within the Blue Vein Society—an organization of African Americans who are proud of their light skin—and his love of and loyalty to the dark-skinned wife from his youth. Discuss with students how discrimination within a race is just as hurtful as discrimination between races.

DISCUSSION QUESTIONS

1. By the narrator's description, Mr. Ryder would not seem to fit exactly into the Blue Vein Society. Why has he been allowed to stay? What role does he play for the society?

Mr. Ryder is the "token" dark-skinned African American that the Blue Vein Society allows to be a member so that they can feel as though they are not prejudiced against those with darker skins.

2. 'Liza Jane tells Mr. Ryder that she has been searching for her husband, Sam, for more than twenty-five years. In your small group, discuss why

you think 'Liza Jane has continued to search for Sam after all that time. Use specific information from the story to support your conclusions.

'Liza Jane loved her husband. Even though there was no legal tie between them (slaves were not permitted to legally marry), when she made her marriage vows with Sam, she made them for life. The story she tells contains the evidence of her love and dedication toward her husband.

3. After talking with 'Liza Jane, Mr. Ryder went into his house: ". . . he went upstairs to his bedroom, and stood for a long time before the mirror of his dressing-case, gazing thoughtfully at the reflection of his own face." What were some of his thoughts as he stood in front of the mirror?

Responses will vary. Some will say that he finally recognized the Blue Vein Society for what it was—a bigoted group. Others may say he was pondering his fate—should he do the honorable thing, though it may cost him status and possibly happiness?

4. When Mr. Ryder introduces 'Liza Jane to the Blue Vein Society as "the wife of [his] youth," what does he lose? What does he gain?

Mr. Ryder gains the love and respect of the Blue Vein Society. However, unless the society changes its whole reason for existence, it is more than possible that Mr. Ryder will lose his place within the organization. His choice of 'Liza Jane could be taken as a threat to the sensibilities of the members.

THE BEAN EATERS

Gwendolyn Brooks

In this poem Gwendolyn Brooks presents an image of a couple that have suffered many hardships but are still able to reflect back on their lives with "twinkling and twinges." Discuss with students how large amounts of money and expensive material goods are not necessary items for a good relationship. If two people love and are committed to each other, it is possible for that relationship to survive when there is no money.

DISCUSSION QUESTIONS

1. What type of relationship does the couple have? Use specific information from the poem to support your opinion.

   The couple has a loving relationship that has survived many hardships. They remember their life with "twinklings and twinges."

2. In your small group, discuss the economic situation of this couple. Refer to words and phrases from the poem.

   The old couple is living in poverty. They eat mostly beans, off cheap plates and silverware.

3. What is unique about this couple? The couple's names are never given. How does this namelessness add to their uniqueness?

   The couple's uniqueness is their love for each other even though they do not have expensive material goods. Their namelessness means they could be any African-American couple.

4. The couple's room is described as being ". . . full of beads and receipts and dolls and clothes, / tobacco crumbs, vases and fringes." What do these items tell you about the life that the couple has had together?

   These items tell us that it has been small things in life that have made this couple happy.

SWEAT

Zora Neale Hurston

In Zora Neale Hurston's story, a snake (which caused Eve so many problems in Eden) balances the odds against a mentally and physically abused wife. Because of the heavy use of dialect, you may wish to have a part of "Sweat" read aloud after students have read it on their own silently. Discuss the concepts of fate and poetic justice with students.

DISCUSSION QUESTIONS

1. Delia sweats while she earns a living washing clothes in hot water. Some townspeople say that they would not want to eat at Delia's house because the food would taste like sweat. How much "sweat" has Delia contributed to saving her marriage? What toll has this "sweat" taken on Delia's physical and mental health?

   Student responses will vary. The toll that "sweat" has taken on Delia's physical and mental state is that she has changed from a pretty, fun-loving woman to a thin, uptight, older woman.

2. Delia often expresses herself through African-American folk proverbs or religious statements. Choose two of these expressions and explain how they foreshadow events in the story.

   Some of the African-American folk proverbs include "whatever goes over the Devil's back, is got to come under his belly"; "Ah done took an' took till mah belly is full up tuh mah neck"; and "Ah hates you lak uh suck-egg dog." Some of the religious statements include "AMEN"; "Jesus, have mussy"; "Mah cup is done run ovah"; and the gospel songs she sings.

3. The townspeople all know that Sykes mistreats Delia. What unified action do they take to express their displeasure? Is this an effective action? Why or why not? What else could the townspeople have done?

   When Sykes and Bertha arrive at the store, the men talking on the store's porch stop talking and leave. They do not return until Sykes and Bertha leave the store. This is not an effective action. Sykes does not care what the people in the town think about him. Some of the townspeople could have talked to Sykes about his behavior.

4. After Sykes has been bitten by the snake, Delia hears him call her name. Why doesn't she respond to his calls for help? Since she does not respond, is Delia partly responsible for Sykes's death? Why or why not?

   Delia has turned Sykes's fate over to a power other than herself. Student responses will vary as to whether or not Delia is responsible for Sykes's death. Whichever position they take, students should be able to support their positions with information from the story.

LETTER FROM CHARLES R. DREW

Charles R. Drew

Discuss the importance of letter writing in the 1930s (and through the 1950s) between young men and women who were in love. Love letters played an important part in the lives of many African-American military people during World War II. Many letters such as this one were kept for many years afterward.

Charles Drew, a medical student, wrote many love letters to Lenore, who later did become his wife.

DISCUSSION QUESTIONS

1. How would you characterize Charles Drew's feelings toward Lenore?

   Answers may vary. He is deeply in love with Lenore and wants to marry her.

2. What does Drew mean when he says, ". . . when I would much rather be weak"?

   He is not talking about physical weakness; he wants to show the soft side of himself, especially in his relationship with Lenore.

3. In your small group, discuss what you think Lenore's next letter might contain. What might she say about the type of prospective husband she would like?

   She might confess her love for Drew, or she might tell him he's being too pushy. Students may come up with a variety of characteristics that she would want in a husband.

1927 FROM *SULA*

Toni Morrison

This selection is an excerpt from Toni Morrison's novel *Sula*. Discuss how society defines roles for marriage. Ask your students to list what they think a husband and a wife should do or be in a marriage. In small groups, have the students compare their responses. How many of their responses are based on reality (the roles they see their parents(s) playing)? How many are based on what they "think" husbands and wives should do or be?

DISCUSSION QUESTIONS

1. Describe Nel and Sula's relationship. Use specific examples from the chapter to support your responses.

   Nel and Sula have a close friendship. They complete each other's thoughts. Sula cares about Nel and openly shares her feelings with Nel. They do not fight with each other.

2. Why was it important for Jude to marry? What would marriage give him?

   Jude cannot find a job that he believes is appropriate for a "man." Marrying Nel will make it acceptable for him to work at the hotel instead of at a "manly" job because he will have a family for which he is responsible.

3. Was Jude in love with Nel? What does this statement say about Jude's view of his relationship with Nel: "Whatever his fortune, whatever the cut of his garment, there would always be the hem—the tuck and fold that hid his raveling edges; a someone sweet, industrious and loyal to shore him up"?

   Nel was in love with Jude, whereas Jude found Nel acceptable. He believed their marriage would make him stronger.

4. What is the community's reaction to the marriage of Nel and Jude? By marrying, how have Nel and Jude fit the roles the community has established for men and women?

The community is happy that a real wedding is occurring. The community expects young men and women to marry after graduating from high school.

VALENTINES

Henry Dumas

Discuss with students how a simple declaration of love is often more powerful than an elaborate one. Also, you could discuss how the media provide limited visual images of African Americans in love. One example the students may bring up is the relationship of Dr. and Mrs. Huxtable from the television program *The Cosby Show*.

DISCUSSION QUESTIONS

1. Select two lines from the poem that could be interpreted as an apology. Discuss how these two lines are an effective way to apologize without using the word "sorry."

   The first and second lines and the fifth through seventh lines could be an apology. This apology sounds sincere.

2. Discuss the words, phrases, and lines that make this a love poem.

   Student responses will vary. Be sure they use specific lines from the poem, such as "you already have my heart."

THANK YOU, M'AM

Langston Hughes

You may wish to begin by discussing with students how it feels to get caught doing something wrong. Clearly this story focuses on this moral issue. Students may or may not identify with the boy in the story. In their small groups ask them to discuss whether they can sympathize with Mrs. Washington Jones after they have read the story.

DISCUSSION QUESTIONS

1. What kind of person was Mrs. Washington Jones? In your small group, describe her personality and her physical presence.

   Answers will vary. Some possible characteristics are: firm, motherly, slow-moving, sure of herself, strong.

2. Mrs. Washington Jones said she had done things that she would not tell anyone else. Do you think some of the things she would not tell helped her relate to Roger? Why or why not?

   She came from circumstances similar to his; she had been poor and had wanted wonderful things that her parents weren't able to give her.

3. Roger wanted to say something other than, "Thank you, m'am." What else do you think he might have said to Mrs. Washington Jones?

   Answers will vary. He might even have said "I love you."

CHAPTER ELEVEN

FAMILY AND ANCESTORS

FOR MY PEOPLE

Margaret Walker

You may wish to do a choral reading with this poem, or you may wish to assign two students to read alternating stanzas. The poem is written in free verse and divided into ten stanzas. You may wish to divide discussion of this poem over more than one class period.

DISCUSSION QUESTIONS

1. In the sixth stanza, Walker talks about the dispossessed, lost, and disinherited. About whom is she speaking? Do you agree with her description of these people?

   Students' answers may vary. Some students may refer to the many poor African Americans with whom she was familiar while growing up in Birmingham, Alabama.

2. How would you describe stanza nine? What is the poet's attitude toward her people?

Students' answers may vary. Stanza nine focuses on inclusion rather than on exclusion. She sees her people somewhat stymied by the system, yet trying to create a better life for themselves in a world that can accommodate all people.

3. In your small group, discuss what you think this poem means.

Students' answers will vary. Some may see the poem describing the lives of people who are fighting against circumstances and trying to make better lives for themselves. Walker's poem seems to be a rallying cry to these people that they can make the world and their lives better.

A Day Lost Is a Day Gone Forever

Dorothy West

This selection is a personal essay, in which a writer reflects on something from his or her life that contains a greater significance. In this instance, West reflects on the significance of each day of being alive.

West also discusses her relationship with her mother. You might discuss with the class how West views her relationship with her mother, and how that relationship affects her life.

DISCUSSION QUESTIONS

1. What is West's major fear?

Her fear is centered around her surgery, specifically the anesthesia. She is not sure she would awaken again.

2. How would you describe her mother?

Her mother is a strong woman who exhibits a great determination to survive her surgery.

3. The writer says: ". . . I was separated from my free will." What do you think is meant by this statement?

The writer no longer had control of her very being; she was now in the complete control of the medical personnel.

4. How important do you believe family is to West? Cite specific examples to support your opinion.

West and her mother seem to have a strong bond between them. For example, when her mother almost dies in the hospital, West can feel her death invade her own body. Also, while her mother is still unconscious from the anesthesia, West cannot concentrate on anything else.

WOMEN

Alice Walker

This poem is dedicated to African-American grandmothers, but it also may pertain to grandmothers of other ethnic groups.

This poem has proven accessible to most students. You may wish to read the poem aloud to the class, then have students read it silently. You may also want to discuss the literary term *metaphor* before discussing the poem.

DISCUSSION QUESTIONS

1. Walker says: "They were women then / My mama's generation." What does she mean by the statement?

Walker may mean that her mother's generation was able to withstand more hardships than she. They were uneducated but were strong in their determination to secure some success for their children.

2. Are today's African-American women any different from women of their mother's generation? In your small group, discuss ways they are different and similar.

Students' answers will vary.

3. Walker uses military metaphors to describe the women of her mother's generation. Locate them in the poem and discuss them with members of your small group.

Walker writes of "Headragged Generals" who led armies across mined fields and booby-trapped ditches, metaphors for obstacles to education for their offspring.

FROM *IN MY FATHER'S HOUSE*

Ernest J. Gaines

This story, like other stories by Gaines, consists of interesting character sketches of ordinary people. Discuss some of the descriptions and actions of various people in this story, and what the descriptions tell you about their characters.

DISCUSSION QUESTIONS

1. The Rev. Martin says: "black people love hot weather—we thrive on hot weather." Is he serious or is he making this statement in jest? Discuss this statement in your small group, giving specific examples to support your opinion.

   Some students will agree with the quote; others will see that he's making this statement in jest.

2. How do you account for the apathy exhibited by some of the African Americans in St. Adrienne?

   It might be that the African Americans have lost faith in a city government that has very seldom responded to their needs.

3. Who is the mysterious boy in the story? Cite specific evidence from the story to support your opinion.

   The boy is probably Rev. Martin's son, who he once denied. More evidence of the boy's identity is obtained from what the characters do than what they say. For example, Shepard becomes jealous because he knows of Rev. Martin's "past reputation with women." The Rev. Martin, after he faints, says, "Don't let me deny him again."

MOTHER TO SON

Langston Hughes

This poem is written in nonstandard American English. Hughes wrote in both standard and nonstandard English; you may wish to find a poem by Hughes in standard English to demonstrate his ability to code-switch.

Before beginning the discussion, you may wish to read this poem aloud to the class. You may also want to review the idea of *metaphor*.

DISCUSSION QUESTIONS

1. What kind of advice is the mother giving her son?

   She recognizes the hardships her son may face, yet she encourages him not to give up and to continue seeking his goals.

2. The mother tells her son of some of her own experiences in life. What are they? Cite specific instances from the poem.

   She tells him of the many hardships, disappointments, and derailments she has had, yet she continued striving. For example, she has lived in broken-down, beat-up places, "with no carpet on the floor." She has also kept going through disappointment and heartache, "Where there ain't been no light."

3. Is there any indication of a sustaining dream in "Mother to Son"? Find evidence in the poem to support your answer.

   The mother's admonition to her son is evidence enough to support the idea of a sustaining dream. In addition, she speaks of her continued climbing to reach her goal, even though life has dealt her an unfortunate hand.

4. How would you characterize the relationship between this mother and son?

   Students should figure out that the mother dearly loves her son and can surmise that the son accepts his mother's advice without resentment.

AUNT

Al Young

Discuss with your students how family members other than our parents have influential roles in our lives. Often when we think of an influential person, we do not think about a flamboyant person. Discuss how a flamboyant person can have a positive impact on our lives.

DISCUSSION QUESTIONS

1. Select words, phrases, and lines from the poem that illustrate the love the speaker in the poem feels for his aunt.

   Student responses will vary. Some possibilities are "Her eyes are diamonds of pure dark space" and "a full-length woman."

2. The speaker in the poem uses some unique descriptions to portray his aunt. What do these descriptions tell you about the aunt's personality?

   The aunt is a person who does not care what other people think about her. She has a strong sense of self.

3. List the black dialect spellings of words and grammatical structured phrases. Discuss how the usage of these spellings and grammatical structures contributes to the emotional message in the poem.

   The use of AAE grammatical structures and spellings helps convey the rhythm of the aunt's life.

SHE WALKED ALONE

Daisy Bates

This story took place in the 1950s, when schools in the South were separate and unequal. The Supreme Court ordered the schools to desegregate, to allow students of any ethnicity to enroll. Daisy Bates, who tells this story, was a leader in the National Association for the Advancement of Colored People (NAACP) at the time and supported the integration of schools.

DISCUSSION QUESTIONS

1. Pretend you are the student Elizabeth Eckford. With a partner, discuss how you might have acted if you had been faced with a similar situation.

   Students' answers will vary. Some may be frightened under the same circumstances; some might be bold.

2. How would you describe Mrs. Grace Lorch? What kind of person is she?

   Students may see her as a good-hearted person who believed in freedom and justice for all people.

3. How do you account for Benjamin Fine's reaction to the mob's behavior? What is it in his background that makes him sympathetic toward this black child?

   Benjamin Fine is Jewish and may have experienced prejudice and discrimination that make him sensitive to Elizabeth's pain.

FOR FURTHER READING

This special bibliography has been prepared to assist you in recommending or assigning additional readings by the authors whose works are included in *African-American Literature*, Second Edition. Significant books that are presently out-of-print (OP) are identified as such; this should not preclude you from consulting a library for a copy. Only books of authors' original writings are listed here; books for which they were merely an editor or compiler are not included.

Note: Not all of the books listed below are appropriate for all students.

Angelou, Maya
Autobiographies
  All God's Children Need Traveling Shoes (Random, 1991)
  Gather Together in My Name (Bantam, 1985)
  Heart of a Woman (Bantam, 1984)
  I Know Why the Caged Bird Sings (Bantam, 1983)
  Singin' and Swingin' and Gettin' Merry Like Christmas (Bantam, 1985)

Nonfiction
  Won't Take Nothing for My Journey Now (Bantam, 1994)

Poetry
  And Still I Rise (OP)
  The Complete Collected Poems of Maya Angelou (OP)
  I Shall Not Be Moved (Bantam, 1990)
  Just Give Me a Cool Drink of Water 'Fore I Die (OP)
  Life Doesn't Frighten Me (OP)
  Oh Pray My Wings Are Gonna Fit Me Well (OP)
  On the Pulse of Morning (Random, 1993)
  Poems: Maya Angelou (Bantam, 1986)
  Shaker, Why Don't You Sing? (OP)

Bates, Daisy
  The Long Shadow of Little Rock (U of Arkansas P, 1987)

Baldwin, James
Nonfiction
  The Devil Finds Work (Dell, 1990)
  The Evidence of Things Not Seen (Holt, 1995)

The Fire Next Time (Random, 1992)
No Name in the Street (Dell, 1986)
Nobody Knows My Name (Random, 1992)
Notes of a Native Son (Beacon Press, 1990)
The Price of the Ticket: Collected Nonfiction 1948–1985 (St. Martins, 1985)

Novels
Another Country (Vintage, 1993)
Giovanni's Room (Dell, 1985)
Go Tell It on the Mountain (Dell, 1985)
If Beale Street Could Talk (Dell, 1986)
Just Above My Head (Dell, 1980)
Tell Me How Long the Train's Been Gone (Dell, 1986)

Plays
The Amen Corner (Dell, 1990)
Blues for Mister Charlie: A Play (Random, 1995)

Poetry
Jimmy's Blues: Selected Poems (St. Martin, 1990)

Short Stories
Going to Meet the Man (Random, 1995)

Baraka, Amiri (LeRoi Jones prior to 1968)
Autobiography
The Autobiography of LeRoi Jones–Amiri Baraka (Lawrence Hill Books, 1997)

Nonfiction
Blues People: Negro Music in White America (Morrow, 1971)
Eulogies (Marsilio, 1996)
The Music: Reflection on Jazz and Blues (Morrow, 1987)

Novel
The System of Dante's Hell (OP)

Plays
Dutchman and The Slave: Two Plays (Morrow, 1971)

Poetry
Black Magic: Collected Poetry 1961–1967 (OP)
LeRoi Jones/Amiri Baraka Reader (Thunder Mouth, 1991)
Preface to a Twenty Volume Suicide Note: Collected Poetry (OP)
Transbluesency (Marsilio Press, 1995)

Bontemps, Arna
Biography
  George Washington Carver (OP)

Novels
  Black Thunder (Beacon Press, 1992)
  God Sends Sunday (OP)

Poetry
  Personals (OP)

Short Stories
  The Old South: "A Summer Tragedy" and Other Stories (OP)

Brooks, Gwendolyn
Autobiography
  Report from Part One: An Autobiography (OP)
  Report from Part Two: An Autobiography (Third World Press, 1996)

Collected Works
  The Gwendolyn Brooks Library (6 vols.) (Moonbeam, 1991)
  Blacks (Third World Press, 1991)

Novel
  Maud Martha (Third World Press, 1993)

Poetry
  Annie Allen (OP)
  The Bean Eaters: Poems (OP)
  Beckonings (Broadside Press, 1975)
  Blacks (Third World Press, 1991)
  Family Pictures (OP)
  In the Mecca (OP)
  The Near-Johannesburg Boy and Other Poems (Third World Press, 1991)
  Riot (OP)
  Selected Poems (Harper and Row, 1982)
  To Disembark (Third World, 1992)

Brown, Sterling
  The Collected Poems of Sterling A. Brown (Another Chicago Press, 1990)
  The Last Ride of Wild Bill & Eleven Narrative Poems (Broadside Press, 1975)

Carmer, Carl
  Stars Fell on Alabama (University of Alabama Press, 1985)

Chesnutt, Charles W.
Novels
- *The Colonel's Dream* (OP)
- *The House Behind the Cedars* (University of Georgia Press, 1995)
- *Mandy Oxendine: A Novel* (University of Illinois Press, 1994)
- *The Marrow of Tradition* (University of Michigan Press, 1969)

Short Stories
- *Conjure Woman* (University of Michigan Press, 1969)
- *The Conjure Woman & Other Conjure Tales* (Duke, 1993)
- *The Short Fiction of Charles W. Chesnutt* (OP)
- *The Wife of His Youth, and Other Stories* (University of Michigan Press, 1968)

Childress, Alice
Novels
- *A Hero Ain't Nottin but a Sandwich* (Avon, 1977)
- *Like One of the Family: Conversations from a Domestic's Life* (Beacon, 1986)
- *Rainbow Jordan* (Avon, 1982)

Plays
- *Mojo & String* (Dramatists Play, 1971)
- *Wine in the Wilderness* (Dramatists Play, 1969)

Clifton, Lucille
- *Good News about the Earth: New Poems* (OP)
- *Good Times: Poems* (OP)
- *Good Woman: Poems and a Memoir, 1969–1980* (BOA Editions, 1987)
- *Next, New Poems* (BOA Editions, 1987)
- *An Ordinary Woman* (OP)
- *Quilting: Poems 1987–1990* (BOA Editions, 1991)
- *Two-Headed Woman* (OP)
- *The Terrible Stories* (BOA Editions, 1996)

Douglass, Frederick
Autobiography
- *Life and Times of Frederick Douglass* (Citadel Press, 1983)
- *My Bondage and My Freedom* (U of Illinos P, 1987)
- *Narrative of the Life of Frederick Douglass* (Dover, 1995)

Collected Works
- *Speeches, Debates, and Interviews 1881–1895* (Yale University Press, 1992)

Dove, Rita
Novel
   Through the Ivory Gate: A Novel (Random, 1993)

Play
   The Darker Face of Earth (1993)

Poetry
   Grace Notes: Poems (Norton, 1991)
   Museum (Carnegie-Mellon, 1983)
   Thomas and Beulah (Carnegie-Mellon, 1985)
   The Yellow House on the Corner (Carnegie-Mellon, 1989)
   Mother Love (Norton, 1996)
   Selected Poems of Rita Dove (Random, 1993)
   The Poet's World (OP)
   Ten Poems (OP)

Du Bois, W. E. B.
Autobiography
   The Autobiography of W. E. B. Du Bois: A Soliloquy (International, 1968)
   Dusk of Dawn: An Essay toward an Autobiography of a Race Concept (Transaction, 1991)
   In Battle for Peace: The Story of My 83rd Birthday (Kraus-Thomson Organization, 1976)

Nonfiction
   The Education of Black People: Ten Critiques (Monthly Review Press, 1975)
   The Gift of Black Folk: The Negroes in the Making of America (Kraus-Thomson Organization, 1975)
   The Souls of Black Folks: Essays and Sketches (Modern Library, 1996)
   W. E. B. Du Bois Speaks: Speeches and Addresses (Pathfinder, 1991)

Dumas, Henry
   Ark of Bones & Other Stories (OP)
   Goodbye, Sweetwater: New & Selected Stories (Thunder Mouth, 1988)
   Jonah and the Green Stone (OP)
   Knees of a Natural Man (OP)
   Play Ebony (OP)
   Poetry for My People (OP)
   Rope of Wind and Other Stories (OP)

Dunbar, Paul Laurence
Collected Works
   The Collected Works of Paul Laurence Dunbar (Reprint Services, 1990)

Life and Works of Paul Laurence Dunbar (Winston-Derek, 1992)
The Paul Laurence Dunbar Reader (OP)

Poetry
  The Complete Poems of Paul Laurence Dunbar (Hakim, 1993)
  The Collected Poetry of Paul Laurence Dunbar (University Press of
    Virginia, 1993)
  Lyrics of Lonely Life (Ayer, 1992)
  Majors & Minors (OP)
  Oak and Ivy (OP)

Short Stories
  The Best Stories of Paul Laurence Dunbar (Reprint Service, 1992)

Ellison, Ralph
  Going to the Territory (Random, 1995)
  Invisible Man (Random, 1995)
  Shadow & Act (Random, 1995)

Evans, Mari
Plays
  Eyes (OP)
  River of My Song (OP; adaptation of Hurston's *Their Eyes Were Watching
    God*)

Poetry
  A Dark & Splendid Mass (Writers & Readers, 1992)
  I Am a Black Woman (Writers & Readers, 1992)
  Nightstar: 1973–1978 (UCLA CAAS, 1981)
  Where Is All the Music? (OP)

Gaines, Ernest J.
  The Autobiography of Miss Jane Pittman (Bantam, 1982)
  Catherine Carmier (Random, 1993)
  A Gathering of Old Men (Random, 1992)
  In My Father's House (Random, 1992)
  A Lesson before Dying (Random, 1993)
  Of Love and Dust (Random, 1994)

Garnet, Henry Highland
  A Memorial Discourse (OP)
  The Past and the Present Condition and the Destiny of the Colored Race
    (OP)
  *Walker's Appeal & Garnet's Address: To the Slaves of the United States of
    America* (Winston-Derek, 1994)

Garvey, Marcus
Message to the People: The Course of African Philosophy (Majority Press, 1986)
Philosopy & Opinion of Marcus Garvey (OP)
The Political Works of Marcus Garvey (OP)
The Tragedy of White Injustice (Basic Choice, 1978)
The United States of America vs. Marcus Garvey (OP)

Giovanni, Nikki
Autobiography
Gemini: An Extended Autobiographical Statement on My First Twenty-Five Years of Being a Black Poet (Penguin, 1985)

Nonfiction
Sacred Cows . . . & Other Edibles (Morrow, 1989)
Racism 101 (Morrow, 1994)

Poetry
Black Feeling, Black Talk, Black Judgment (Morrow, 1971)
Cotton Candy on a Rainy Day (Morrow, 1980)
Ego Tripping and Other Poems for Young Readers (Hill, 1993)
Selected Poems of Nikki Giovanni (Morrow, 1996)
Those Who Ride the Night Winds (Morrow, 1984)
Vacation Time: Poems for Children (Morrow, 1981)
The Women & the Men (Morrow, 1979)

Goss, Linda
Jump Up and Say!: A Collection of African-American Storytelling (with Clay Goss; Schuster, 1995)
Talk That Talk: An Anthology of African-American Storytelling (with Marian E. Barnes; Schuster, 1989)

Haley, Alex
Alex Haley's Queen: The Story of an American Family (Avon, 1994)
The Playboy Interviews (Ballantine, 1993)
Roots (Dell, 1980)

Harper, Frances Ellen Watkins
Novel
Iola Leroy: or, Shadows Uplifted (Oxford University Press, 1990)

Poetry
Atlanta Offering: Poems (OP)
Complete Poems of Frances Harper (Oxford University Press, 1988)
Moses: A Story of the Nile (OP)

Minnie's Sacrifice, Sowing & Reaping, Trial & Triumph (Beacon Press, 1995)
Poems (OP)
Poems of Frances Harper (OP)
Poems on Miscellaneous Subjects (Kraus, second edition)
Sketches of Southern Life (OP)

Hayden, Robert
American Journal (Liveright, 1982)
Angle of Ascent: New and Selected Poems (OP)
Collected Poems (Liveright, 1996)
The Collected Prose (University of Michigan Press, 1984)
Heart-Shape in the Dust (OP)
Selected Poems (originally titled *A Ballad of Remembrance*; OP)
Words in the Mourning Time (OP)

hooks, bell
Ain't I a Woman? Black Women & Feminism (South End Press, 1981)
Black Looks: Race & Representation (South End Press, 1992)
Feminist Theory: From Major to Center (South End Press, 1984)
Sisters of the Yam: Black Women & Self-Recovery (South End Press, 1993)
Talking Back: Thinking Feminist, Thinking Black (South End Press, 1989)
Teaching to Transgress: Education As the Practice of Freedom (Rutledge, 1994)
A Woman's Mourning Song (Writers & Readers, 1992)
Yearning: Race, Gender, & Cultural Politics (South End Press, 1990)

Hughes, Langston
Autobiography
The Big Sea: An Autobiography (Hill & Wang, 1993)
I Wonder as I Wander (Hill & Wang, 1993)

Novels
Not Without Laughter (Scribner, 1995)

Plays
Black Nativity (Dramatic Publications, 1992)
Mule Bone (HarperPerennial, 1991)

Poetry
Ask Your Mama: Twelve Moods for Jazz (OP)
Collected Poems of Langston Hughes (Random, 1995)
The Dream Keeper and Other Poems (OP)
Montage of a Dream Deferred (OP)
The Negro Mother and Other Dramatic Recitations (OP)
The Panther and the Lash: Poems of Our Times (Knopf, 1993)

Selected Poems of Langton Hughes (Knopf, 1993))
The Weary Blues (OP)

Short Stories
  The Best of Simple (Farr, 1990)
  Laughing to Keep from Crying (OP)
  The Return of Simple (Farr, 1995)
  Short Stories of Langston Hughes (Hill & Wang, 1996)
  Something in Common and Other Stories (OP)
  Ways of White Folks (Random, 1990)

Hurston, Zora Neale

Autobiography
  Dust Tracks on a Road (HarperPerennial, 1996)

Collected Works
  *I Love Myself When I Am Laughing...and Then Again When I Am
  Looking Mean and Impressive: A Zora Neale Hurston Reader* (Women's
  Press, 1985)

Nonfiction
  Folklore, Memories, and Other Writings (Library of America, 1995)
  The Sanctified Church (Turtle Island Foundation, 1983)
  Tell My Horse (HarperCollins, 1990)

Novels
  Jonah's Gourd Vine (HarperCollins, 1990)
  Moses, Man of the Mountain (HarperPerennial, 1991)
  Seraph on the Suwanee (HarperCollins, 1991)
  Their Eyes Were Watching God (HarperCollins, 1995)

Short Stories
  The Complete Short Stories of Zora Neale Hurston (HarperCollins, 1995)
  Mules and Men (HarperCollins, 1990)
  Spunk: The Selected Stories of Zora Neale Hurston (Turtle Island
  Foundation, 1985)

Johnson, Georgia Douglas

Poetry
  Bronze: A Book of Verse (OP)
  The Heart of a Woman and Other Poems (OP)
  The Selected Works of Georgia Douglas Johnson (Hall, 1997)
  Share My World (OP)

Plays
  The Baby Who Knew Too Much (GA Johnson Publishing, 1993)
  Plumes (OP)
  Townpath to Freedom (GA Johnson Publishing, 1988)
  Webster's Gold (GA Johnson Publishing, 1990)

Johnson, James Weldon
Autobiography
  Along This Way: The Autobiography of James Weldon Johnson (Penguin, 1990)

Nonfiction
  Black Manhattan (Da Capo, 1991)

Novel
  Autobiography of an Ex-Coloured Man (Dover, 1995)

Poetry
  Fifty Years and Other Poems (OP)
  The Book of American Negro Poetry (OP)
  The Books of American Negro Spirituals (OP)
  God's Trombones: Seven Negro Sermons in Verse (Viking Penguin, 1990)
  Saint Peter Relates an Incident: Selected Poems (Penguin, 1993)

Kelley, William Melvin
Novel
  Dem (OP)
  Different Drummer (Doubleday, 1990)
  A Drop of Patience (Ecco Press, 1996)
  Dunfords Travels Everywheres (OP)

Short Stories
  Dancers on the Shore (Howard University Press, 1984)

King, Martin Luther
Nonfiction (including sermons)
  I Have a Dream: Twenty-Four Writings & Speeches that Changed the World (Harper, 1992)
  Stride Toward Freedom: The Montgomery Story (Harper SF, 1987)
  Testament of Hope: The Essential Speeches & Writings of Martin Luther King, Jr. (Harper, 1990)
  Where Do We Go from Here? Chaos or Community? (Beacon Press, 1989)
  Why We Can't Wait (NAL-Dutton, 1988)

Lee, Don L. (See Madhubuti, Haki)

Lester, Julius
Autobiography
  Lovesong: Becoming a Jew (Arcade Publishing Inc., 1995)

Novels
  And All Our Wounds Forgiven (Harcourt, 1996)
  Do Lord Remember Me (Arcade Publishing Inc., 1995)
  Othello (Scholastic, 1995)

Retellings
  Black Folktales (OP)
  How Many Spots Does a Leopard Have? (Scholastic Inc., 1994)
  The Knee-High Man & Other Tales (NAL-Dutton, 1992)
  The Tales of Uncle Remus (OP)

Short Stories
  Long Journey Home (Scholastic Inc., 1988)
  This Strange New Feeling (Scholastic, 1985)

Lourde, Audre
  The Black Unicorn: Poems (Norton, 1995)
  A Burst of Light (Firebrand Books, 1988)
  Marvelous Arithmetics of Distance (Norton, 1994)
  Our Dead Behind Us: Poems (Norton, 1994)
  Zami: A New Spelling of My Name (Crossing Press, 1983)

Madhubuti, Haki R.
Nonfiction
  Black Men: Obsolete, Single, Dangerous?—The Afrikan American Family in Transition (Third World Press, 1990)
  Dynamite Voices: Black Poets of the 1960s (OP)
  Million Man March/Day of Absence: A Commemorative Anthology (Third World Press, 1996)

Poetry
  Black Pride (OP)
  Book of Life (Third World Press, 1992)
  Don't Cry, Scream (Third World Press, 1992)
  Groundwork: New and Selected Poems of Don L. Lee/Haki Madhubuti, from 1966–1996 (Third World Press, 1996)
  Killing Memory, Seeking Ancestors (Lotus Press, 1987)
  Think Black (OP)

Malcolm X
Autobiography
  The Autobiography of Malcolm X (with Alex Haley; Balatine, 1992)

Speeches
  By Any Means Necessary: Speeches, Interviews, and a Letter by Malcolm X
    (Pathfinder, 1992)
  The End of White World Supremacy (Arcade By Publishing, 1994)
  February, 1965: The Final Speeches (Pathfinder NY, 1992)
  Malcolm X Speaks Out (Andrews & McMeel, 1992)
  Malcolm X Speeches: January 1965 (Pathfinder NY, 1994)
  Malcolm X Talks to Young People (Pathfinder, 1991)
  Two Speeches by Malcolm X (Pathfinder, 1990)

Marshall, Paule
Novels
  Brown Girl, Brownstones (OP)
  Chosen Place, The Timeless People (Random, 1992)
  Daughters (NAL-Dutton, 1992)
  Praisesong for the Widow (NAL-Dutton, 1984)

Short Stories
  Reena and Other Stories (Feminist Press, 1983)
  Soul Clap Hands & Sing (Howard University Press, 1988)

McKay, Claude
Autobiography
  A Long Way From Home (Pluto, 1985)

Collections
  My Green Hills of Jamaica: and Two Jamaican Short Stories (OP)
  The Passion of Claude McKay: Selected Poety and Prose 1912–1948 (OP)

Novels
  Banana Bottom (OP)
  Banjo (OP)
  Home to Harlem (Nebraska UP, 1987)

Poetry
  Constab Ballads (OP)
  Harlem Shadows (OP)
  Selected Poems of Claude McKay (Harcourt, 1981)
  Songs of Jamaica (OP)
  Spring in New Hampshire and Other Poems (OP)

Morrison, Toni
Nonfiction
  Playing in the Dark: Whiteness & the Literary Imagination (Random, 1993)

Novels
  Beloved (NAL-Dutton, 1991)
  The Bluest Eye (NAL-Dutton, 1994)
  Jazz (NAL-Dutton, 1993)
  Song of Solomon (NAL-Dutton, 1993)
  Sula (NAL-Dutton, 1993)
  Tar Baby (NAL-Dutton, 1993)

Petry, Ann
Novels
  Country Place (OP)
  The Narrows (Beacon, 1988)
  The Street (Houghton, 1992)

Short Stories
  Miss Muriel and Other Stories (Beacon, 1989)

Redmond, Eugene B.
  Drumvoices: The Mission of Afro-American Poetry (OP)
  The Eye in the Ceiling: Selected Poems (Writers & Readers, 1991)
  In a Time of Rain & Desire: New Love Poems (OP)
  River of Bones and Flesh and Blood (OP)
  Rope of Wind and Other Stories (OP)

Reed, Ishmael
  Airing Dirty Laundry (Addison-Wesley, 1995)
  Conjure: Selected Poems (OP)
  Flight to Canada (Macmillan, 1989)
  Japanese by Spring (Viking Penguin, 1996)
  Mumbo Jumbo: A Novel (Schuster, 1989)
  New & Collected Poems (Schuster, 1989)
  The Terrible Threes (OP)
  The Terrible Twos (Macmillan, 1988)
  Writing Is Fighting: Forty-three Years of Boxing on Paper (Addison-Wesley, 1996)
  Yellow Back Radio Brake-Down (OP)

Scott-Heron, Gil
Novel
  The Negro Factory: A Novel (OP)

Poetry
   Small Talk at 125th and Lenox: A Collection of Black Poems (OP)

Recordings
   Don't Give Up (Mother Records, 1994)
   Free Will (BMG Music, 1993)
   Spirits (TVT Records, 1994)

Shange, Ntozake
Novels
   Betsey Brown: A Novel (OP)
   Liliane: Resurrection of the Daughter (St. Martin's Press, 1995)
   Sassafras: A Novella (OP)
   Sassafras, Cypress and Indigo (St. Martin's Press, 1983)

Plays (some with poetry and dance)
   *for colored girls who have considered suicide/when the rainbos is enuf: a
      choreopoem* (Macmillan, 1989)
   From Okra to Greens: A Different Kinda Love Story (OP)
   A Photograph: Lovers in Motion (OP)
   Three Pieces (St. Martin's Press, 1992)

Poetry
   A Daughter's Geography (St. Martin's Press, 1991)
   From Okra to Greens: Poems (OP)
   The Love Space Demands: A Continuing Saga (St. Martin's Press, 1992)
   Ridin' the Moon in Texas: Word Paintings (St. Martin's Press, 1988)

Sharp, Saundra
   Black Women for Beginners (Writers & Readers, 1993)
   Typing in the Dark (Writers & Readers, 1991)
   From the Windows of My Mind (OP)
   In the Midst of Change (OP)
   Soft Song (OP)

Smitherman, Geneva
   Talkin & Testifyin: The Language of Black America (Wayne State Univer-
      sity Press, 1986)
   Black Talk: Words & Phrases from the Hood to the Amen Corner (Houghton,
      1994)

Turner, Nat
   The Campaign of Nat Turner (OP)
   The Confession, Trial and Execution of Nat Turner, the Negro Insurrectionist
      (OP)

The Confessions of Nat Turner: Leader of the Late Insurrection in Southampton, VA (OP)

Thomas, Joyce Carol
Black Child (OP)
Bright Shadow (Avon, 1983)
Brown Honey in Broomwheat Tea (HarperCollins, 1996)
A Gathering of Flowers (HarperCollins, 1992)
Gingerbread Days (HarperCollins, 1995)
Marked by Fire (Avon, 1982)
Water Girl (Avon, 1986)
When the Nightingale Sings (HarperTrophy, 1994)

Toomer, Jean
Cane (Liveright, 1993)
The Collected Poems of Jean Toomer (University of North Carolina Press, 1988)

Vroman, Mary Elizabeth
Ester: A Novel (OP)
Harlem Summer (young adult novel; OP)

Walker, Alice
Nonfiction
Belief in the Love of the World: A Writer's Activism (Random, 1997)
In Search of Our Mothers' Gardens: Womanist Prose (Harcourt, 1983)
Living by the Word: Selected Writings (Harcourt, 1989)
The Same River Twice: Honoring the Difficult (Wheeler, 1996)
To Hell with Dying (Harcourt, 1993)

Novels
The Color Purple (Harcourt, 1982)
Meridian (Harcourt, 1990)
Possessing the Secret of Joy (Schuster, 1992)
The Temple of My Familiar (Pocket Books, 1990)
The Third Life of Grange (Pocket Books, 1991)

Poetry
Goodnight, Willie Lee, I'll See You in the Morning: Poems (Harcourt, 1984)
Her Blue Body Everything We Know: Earthly Poems (1965–1990) Complete (Harcourt, 1993)
Horses Make a Landscape Look More Beautiful: Poems (Harcourt, 1986)
Once: Poems (OP)
Revolutionary Petunias and Other Poems (OP)

Short Stories
  The Complete Stories/Alice Walker (The Women's Press, 1994)

Walker, Margaret
Nonfiction
  How I Wrote "Jubilee" (Third World, 1977)
  How I Wrote "Jubilee" and Other Essays on Life and Literature (Feminist
    Press, 1990)
  *Richard Wright, Daemonic Genius: A Portrait of the Man, A Critial Look
    at His Work* (OP)

Novel
  Jubilee (Bantam, 1984)

Poetry
  For My People (OP)
  October Journey (Broadside Press, 1973)
  Prophets for a New Day (Broadside Press, 1970)
  This Is My Century: New and Collected Poems (University of Georgia Press,
    1989)

Washington, Booker T.
  Up from Slavery (GUP, 1995)
  Negro in the South (Carol Publishing Group, 1989)

West, Dorothy
  Children's Catalog (OP)
  Living Is Easy (Feminist Press, 1995)
  The Richer, The Poorer: Stories, Sketches, & Reminiscences (Doubleday,
    1996)
  The Wedding (Doubleday, 1996)

Wheatley, Phillis
Collections
  Collected Works of Phillis Wheatley (Ohio U P, 1989)
Poetry
  Poems of Phillis Wheatley (Applewood, 1995)
  Poems on Various Subjects, Religious and Moral (OP)

White, Paulette Childress
  Love Poem to a Black Junkie (Lotus, 1975)
  The Watermelon Dress: Portrait of a Woman (Lotus, 1984)

Wright, Richard
Autobiography
   American Hunger (HarperCollins, 1983)
   Black Boy: A Record of Childhood and Youth (HarperCollins, 1993)

Collections
   The Richard Wright Reader (OP)
   Richard Wright: Works (2 vols.) (Library of America, 1991)

Nonfiction
   Black Power (HarperCollins, 1995)
   White Man, Listen! (HarperCollins, 1995)

Novels
   Lawd Today (Nebraska U P, 1993)
   The Long Dream (OP)
   Native Son (HarperCollins, 1995)
   The Outsider (HarperCollins, 1995)
   Savage Holiday (OP)

Short Stories
   Eight Men (Thunders Mouth, 1987)
   Uncle Tom's Children: Four Novellas (OP)
   The Color Curtain (University Press of Mississippi, 1995)
   Pagan Spain (HarperCollins, 1995)
   Rite of Passage (HarperCollins Children's Books, 1996)

Young, Al
   Bodies & Soul (Creative Arts Books, 1981)
   Drowning in the Sea of Love: Musical Memoirs (OP)
   Heaven: Collected Poems 1958–1988 (Great Arts Books, 1988)
   Kinds of Blue: Musical Memoirs (Great Arts Books, 1984)
   Sitting Pretty: A Novel (Creative Arts Books, 1986)
   Straight No Chaser (Great Arts Books, 1994)
   Things Ain't What They Used to Be (Great Arts Books, 1987)